Hebrew Union College-Jewish Institute of Religion At One Hundred Years

Hebrew Union College-
Jewish Institute of Religion
At One Hundred Years

Edited by SAMUEL E. KARFF

Hebrew Union College Press

1976

*Published
with the assistance of the*
HENRY ENGLANDER–ELI MAYER PUBLICATION FUND,
established in their honor by
Esther Straus Englander and Jessie Straus Mayer

LIBRARY OF CONGRESS CATALOGING IN PUBLICATION DATA

SAMUEL E. KARFF

HEBREW UNION COLLEGE-JEWISH INSTITUTE
OF RELIGION AT ONE HUNDRED YEARS

Including History and Essays

RS1235.3055   1975   222′77′07   75-17290

Designed by Ralph Davis

PRODUCED IN THE UNITED STATES OF AMERICA

To the HUC-JIR communities
of the next one hundred years
צלח רחב על־דבר־אמת

Contents

RABBI SAMUEL E. KARFF

Introduction

THE CELEBRATION OF ONE HUNDRED YEARS OF EXISTENCE IS, FOR AN institution no less than for mortal man, a notable event. History is strewn with the remains of human enterprises which, far earlier in their development, have either failed to meet the creative requirements of survival or fallen prey to man's periodic bursts of destructive fury.

Rabbinic seminaries are amply represented on the list of once proud academies from whom the breath of life has departed. Our century has taken an especially awesome toll. Hence there is all the more reason for jubilant gratitude and reconsecration as we mark the Centennial of the College-Institute.

In anticipation of this festive occasion, the late president of the College-Institute, Dr. Nelson Glueck, and the then chairman of the Board of Governors, S. L. Kopald, Jr. established a Centennial Committee to determine and implement a meaningful observance. Dr. Fritz Bamberger, assistant to the president, was mandated to draw up an overall plan, which included the publication of the history of the College-Institute with special emphasis on the scholarly contributions of its faculty. A Faculty Advisory Committee met with the editor to help shape the project. Its members included Professors Martin Cohen, Michael Meyer, Jacob R. Marcus, and Ellis Rivkin. Dr.

Bamberger, also a member of the committee, has been singularly helpful in every phase of this publication project.

Professor Michael Meyer was invited to write the overall institutional history. The proposed length of this essay was initially far more restricting. In time, as the research was conducted and the first draft evolved, it became apparent that the material was too rich and plentiful for its procrustean bed. What emerged was a multidimensional account of the development of a Jewish institution against the backdrop of an expanding American Jewish community and a turbulent world. The author suggested that excessive condensation would severely impair the comprehensiveness of the work. The editor concurred.

The second part of the volume consists of five essays which focus on the Hebrew Union College–Jewish Institute of Religion's contribution to the disciplines comprising the world of Jewish study. Sheldon Blank surveys research and teaching in the field of Bible; Lewis Barth, rabbinics; Lou Silberman, theology and philosophy; Martin Cohen, Jewish history; and Ezra Spicehandler, Hebrew literature.

All the contributors are themselves alumni of the College-Institute, and all but one are presently members of its faculty. This consideration may have led some to underplay their own significant contributions.

In an enterprise of this sort, occasional overlapping is unavoidable. Some members of the faculty actively contributed to more than one discipline. Thus Kaufmann Kohler, in addition to dominating a major section of the Meyer history, is also represented in the chapters devoted to Bible, rabbinics, and theology. Understandably, these essays reflect the temperament and biases of the contributors. Some are more comprehensively expository, others more boldly evaluative. Patterns of organization also vary. Hopefully this diversity will enliven rather than encumber the reader's task.

One of the cherished jewels of the College-Institute, especially during the latter half of its history, has been a rigorous commitment to academic freedom. How natural the resolve that such freedom must crown the efforts to chronicle and assess the College-Institute itself. This was to be no carefully orchestrated symphony of self-congratulation. Discordant themes were not to be silenced. Respect for truth would not be drowned out amid a hallelujah chorus of institutional pride. Avoiding the apologetic pitfall of most anniversary volumes would itself lend distinction to our effort. Moreover, a volume which forthrightly chronicles the triumphs and fumblings, the lofty idealism, and the less noble impulses of Jewish institutional life would be more interesting to read and infinitely more credible.

This ground rule was made possible by a dual faith: a confidence in the sophistication of the potential reader, and a trust in the overriding merit of the institution to which the volume is dedicated. That confidence has not been misplaced, for these pages provide ample reason to celebrate the vitality of the academy which has diligently nurtured the garden of Torah and creatively enlarged the opportunities for a meaningful Jewish vocation. During the past century, the College-Institute has trained legions of academicians, congregational rabbis, cantors, religious-school administrators and teachers, and more recently, it has pioneered a new concept of professionalism in the field of Jewish communal service.

By self-definition, however, the College-Institute has always been primarily devoted to the training of rabbis. From its very inception the school groped for the ideal profile of the American rabbi, clearly understanding that the traditional halakhic role of legal scholar and decisor would be overshadowed by the agadic role of preacher, conductor of worship, inspired mentor, and apologist for faith.

The tension between dedication to a dispassionate scholarship *(Wissenschaft)* and the grooming of able defenders of the faith is tangibly present in the annals of the institution. The discipline of mastering a Talmud folio or a Maimonidean treatise has not always appeared congruent with the Jewish community's demand for captivating preachers and empathic counselors. Some faculty members held the role of congregational rabbi in ill-concealed contempt. Others took pride in cultivating leaders who could meet both the standards of the academy and the expectations of a congregation.

What does emerge rather consistently, through all the presidential administrations of the College-Institute, is a commitment to the rabbinate as a learned profession. The rabbi trained by the College was not only expected to be a presentable, effective communicator, but a mentor rooted in the classic sources of his people and its faith. At times that expectation loomed more as pious hope than radiant reality.

But its very presence placed the burden of argument upon those who would diminish the academy's high standards of Jewish learning. Whatever else the term *reform* conveyed, it was self-consciously defended against the connotation of Jewish illiteracy.

The College-Institute's identification as a citadel of Reform Judaism is central to the expressed concerns of all its presidents, at least after Wise. The articulation of a distinctive Reform attitude seems to have been accented in part by mundane institutional requirements: how justify the claim to support of the College-Institute vis-à-vis the Jewish Theological Seminary, or the Rabbi Isaac Elchanan Theological Seminary. Beyond such considerations, however, was the vision of a liberal movement which without undue sectarianism could chart the most fruitful course for American Jewry. For its presidents, if less clearly at times for some members of the faculty and students, Reform was a badge of honor, a rallying cry.

Isaac Mayer Wise believed that the College's brand of modernity was most congenial to the openness of an expanding America. In the Kohler and Morgenstern eras, Reform's commitment to critical scholarship provided the tools to identify the essence of Judaism, purify the faith of it's medieval dross, and distinguish between the higher and lower reaches of the Jewish spirit. Nelson Glueck served at a time when German and East European Jewry closed ranks in America; when, thanks to Hitler, the Zionist controversy had become an anachronism. Nevertheless he too insisted that the Reform movement remained preeminently suited as the model for Jewish life in an increasingly open society.

At various times Reform served as code word for a non-Zionist or anti-Zionist orientation, an unequivocal commitment to the Diaspora, an invitation to fuller Jewish participation in the mainstream of American life, a deemphasis of the ritual trappings of the faith, and a renaissance of the prophetic commitment to social justice. In each era scholarship and teaching at the College reflected some consciousness of bearing the Reform banner. In history and theology classes an evolutionary perspective legitimated Reform as the latest unfolding of the Jewish spirit. In Bible classes one became much aware of the human role in creating and editing the text and of the prophetic rejection of a ritualistic fetishism. The teaching of Talmud and Codes accented the dynamic trends within the halakhic system itself, or alternately, those rigidities which necessitated the birth of a Reform movement.

In the present generation, the College-Institute faculty has continued to project a Reform self-consciousness. Historian Ellis Rivkin contends that Jewish survival is very much the fruit of bold Jewish creativity, which in each age facilitated radical change in response to novel conditions. Although this finely honed adaptability was present in every epoch of the Jewish past, the Reform movement, he claims, has dared to acknowledge its reality and grant it normative value. Philosopher Alvin Reines has identified radical freedom (polydoxy) as the most appropriate hallmark of Reform Judaism. He has taught his students that no canons of belief or practice can be employed as the touchstone of Jewish authenticity. What distinguished the Reform Jew is a commitment to radical freedom itself. Theologian Eugene Borowitz, though far more concerned about the limits of freedom and more persuaded of basic continuities in Jewish belief and practice, has always spoken and written from the perspective of a liberal theologian who is unprepared to surrender the autonomy of his Torah-cultivated and people-centered conscience. Of those faculty members evincing an interest in a current *halakha,* Eugene Mihaly has been most unequivocal in identifying Reform Judaism with the creative trends in classical rabbinic Judaism.

This volume also reveals the College-Institute to have been at the very center of the Reform movement's continuing quest for self-definition. Changes in the American Reform movement's self-understanding are amply reflected within its gates, most dramatically perhaps in the reassessment of Zionism and the changing *minhag* of chapel worship, where the wearing of *tallit* and *kipa,* unthinkable in the Kohler era, became initially a focus of controversy and ultimately an acceptable option in the latter days of Nelson Glueck.

As noted earlier, for much of the College-Institute's existence academic freedom was a central value. This did not prevent the issue of limiting freedom from arising periodically, and at certain moments those limits became abrasively evident. Wise's prohibition of a critical view of the Torah and Kohler's attitude toward Zionist and humanistic professors are cases in point.

Even in a secular university academic freedom is not unproblematical. There are occasions when those in authority must determine whether a certain thesis can be advocated publicly without debasing the university's commitment to civil discourse or the credo of Western humanism. If the value of academic freedom is in competition with other values in a secular institution, how much the more so in a seminary committed to the education of Jewish leaders and the transmission of a particular heritage. It is instructive to follow this problematic of academic freedom through the various administrations of the College-Institute. The presidents and Boards of Governors seemed progressively disinclined to violate the conscience of student or faculty. The contributors to this volume are themselves unequivocally committed to that freedom and note its presence with enthusiastic pride.

At the same time, the presidents of the College-Institute each nourished some vision, clearly or unclearly defined, of a cherishable Jewish truth and a significant Jewish vocation. Each, committed though he was to high levels of academic proficiency, saw scholarship as a tool with which to understand, appreciate, and transmit a Jewish faith. However radical their departure from orthodoxy, each President championed a religious as contrasted with a purely cultural-humanistic view of Jewish life. Though not all faculty or students formally professed a three-dimensional covenant (God, Torah, and Israel), the chapel service and the ordination ceremony were conspicuous symbolic reminders of the College-Institute's commitment.

The interplay between a search for truth grounded in the prevailing codes of the academic fraternity and the search for a transmissable heritage is aptly articulated by biblical scholar and veteran faculty member Sheldon Blank. In his essay on the teaching of Bible at the College-Institute, Blank distinguishes three approaches to texts: (1) the quest for the author's original intent; (2) the meaning attributed to this text during centuries of commentary and interpretation; (3) the pursuit of a truth and a value appropriable by contemporary man. While some members of the faculty stressed one or another, others could claim to have been concerned with all three dimensions. Blank adds significantly that "the trend in the shifting scene has been toward the study of the Bible as a search for roots and nurture requisite for growth and stability."

Student-faculty relations is a recurring theme in the history of our academy. If student expectations were not always fulfilled, members of the faculty also nursed their disappointments. In the eyes of the student, some faculty members lacked erudition or Jewish commitment or pedagogic finesse. In faculty perspective, some students were sorely wanting in intellectual vigor or seemed excessively preoccupied with the "practical" dimensions of their future rabbinic calling.

The relationship between teacher and student, like that of father and son, or rabbi and congregant, is riddled with emotional complexity. We may challenge and contend as part of the struggle to affirm. The debt the student owes his mentor may not always be consciously acknowledged in the latter's lifetime. Many a student rebel emerged from the College-Institute as Judaism's impassioned champion and was destined to reenact from the other side of the table the lively dialogues of his student past. On those occasions when discipleship was real and acknowledged, the relationship between teacher and student became a sustaining bond of abiding significance.

For both faculty and student the question arose periodically: is the seminary only an academy to master texts and skills, or also a *Kehilla kadosha,* a miniature Jewish congregation? The first conception provided a less demanding standard of judgment than the second. If a rabbinic seminary may be expected to nurture worthy models of Jewish life, the historian will hold it accountable for the level of mutual respect among faculty, students, and administration, the degree to which it enkindles and satisfies hungers of the spirit, and its responsiveness to crises in the larger Jewish community and the world. Meyer's essay does not hesitate to apply such a standard of judgment. He records both the successes and the failures.

Each alumnus who reads this work must inevitably view it from the perspective of his own student days and the perception of his calling today. The editor now asks the same privilege. At the outset we must concede that the image of the rabbinic calling as a last chance for impecunious lads (an understanding widely held in the Wise era) is no longer applicable. Nor need the rabbinate serve as surrogate for men and women whose first love is a secular academic career, or some form of social work. There are ample patterns of social mobility available to the bright Jewish lad in America today. Indeed, the rabbinate as profession has found it necessary to compete with a wide range of attractive vocational options. In partial recognition thereof, the Jewish community has generously offered its rabbinic leaders a level of compensation which does not require a substantial measure of financial sacrifice.

The role expectations of the rabbinate have also changed markedly. Not so many years ago, the well-spoken Reform rabbi was the chief advocate of American Jewry's claim to full equality in this land. In pressing that claim the rabbi was expected to refute the canards of benighted Christian clerics. How many sermons were delivered over the years on the theme "Who Crucified Jesus?" How many reassurances were given that we Jews did not do it? A rabbi's stature was often measured by the skill with which he cultivated the goodwill of the Gentile community. By now this role of rabbinic apologist has diminished considerably. The American Jewish community has come of age and feels less obliged to submit to such demeaning tests of virtue. Moreover, the level of overt antisemitism has considerably ebbed.

Neither is the liberal American rabbi still cast as the broker of the best in American culture to a constituency deprived of a college education. The overwhelming majority of his congregants are college-educated men and women who most appreciate his demonstrated mastery of *Judaism* and his capacity to transmit it effectively. That very combination of intellectual integrity, faith, and communicative skills for which the rabbi yearned in his student days, his more sophisticated congregants now seek from him. They are not in need of the rabbi to further their acceptance in the larger society, but to offer them, within the life of the synagogue, that nurture of the mind and spirit not readily available in the mass media or the marketplace. Less than ever can the American Jewish community afford mediocrity in its rabbinic leadership. More discerning than ever before is the constituency whose respect and responsiveness the rabbi covets.

Religion, says Robert Bellah, is "an imaginative statement about the truth (the worthwhileness) of the totality of human experience." In a culture with increasingly specialized roles, great physical mobility, and intense fragmentation, the rabbi is commissioned to foster a sense of the whole. He is enlisted to help Jews find in the wisdom and symbols of their heritage the power to perceive their lives as part of a significant story.

More than ever will the conscientious rabbi feel the need to draw upon the classical texts. More than ever will he need to wrestle with the possibilities and limits of halakhic and aggadic change. He must grope for that balance between revision and reappropriation which alone can grant him the grace of authenticity. That task must surely be initiated within the walls of the College-Institute. The tone and temper it assumes will provide an operational definition of the word *reform.*

The agenda of the American rabbinate today, as in the past, will be shaped not only by the inner dynamic of the faith, but by the cues of the larger culture. Curriculum planners cannot ignore the revolutionary developments in genetics, or the new attentiveness to the deeper, nonrational levels of man's being, or the women's liberation movement. The College-Institute must help the future Jewish leader relate the sensibilities of the larger culture to the time-hallowed experiences and values of a millennial people.

If the rabbi is to maintain a leadership role in the larger Jewish community, either directly or through his influence upon the "influentials," he cannot do so by invoking a title. His leverage will depend on his understanding of the Jewish past and present, his grasp of the general human condition, and his capacity to earn a respectful hearing for his views. The College-Institute must help arm him with the intellectual and pragmatic skills for such a role.

Apart from any personality traits which enhance his claim, the rabbi's leadership role is ultimately grounded in his vision of the goals of a covenant community. It remains his task to teach by precept and example what it means to be a son or daughter of a covenant which binds a people, Israel, to a living God and summons this people to be a blessing. Through its century of existence the College-Institute has affirmed fidelity to this covenant. As we enter the next century, may that devotion be renewed among its lay leadership, its administration, its faculty, students, and alumni.

The future of the college has been placed in very able hands. How fitting that this volume concludes with an essay from the president of the College-Institute, our gifted and cherished colleague, Alfred Gottschalk. He has donned the mantle at a potentially critical and challenging time. May God strengthen his hand and heart and quicken our response to his vision.

PART ONE
A Centennial History

By

Michael A. Meyer

Preface

PREVIOUS MILESTONES IN THE LIFE OF THE HEBREW UNION
College have occasioned efforts to write its history.[1] In each instance,
the records were examined and a chronological account presented to
the world. These superficial narratives dutifully mentioned the names
of all faculty, prominent lay leaders, and alumni, and they invariably
described the school as going from strength to strength. There was
little attempt at critical analysis. Although a quarter of a century
has passed since the last account was written, it was at no time my
intention merely to carry such a tale on to the centennial year, while
relying on earlier studies for the preceding periods. Instead, it has
been my consistent purpose to write a complete history of the HUC-
JIR which would be unlikely to resemble those of my predecessors.

As a member of the College-Institute faculty, I am of course in
accord with the school's stated goals, and consequently this account
has been written out of a sincere endeavor at sympathetic understanding. But I have also remained aware of my responsibility as a
Jewish historian, dedicated to the tradition of *Wissenschaft des Judentums*—the impartial, scientific study of the Jewish past. Consequently,
I have made every effort to tell the story of the HUC-JIR with utmost
honesty, including the failures and the unpleasant wrangles no less
than the accomplishments and expressions of unity, the struggles for
power no less than the lofty idealism.

[3]

An institution is composed of men whose actions affect its destinies. The historian cannot escape the onerous task of passing judgment on those who have played the most prominent roles. I have not shirked this duty, though I am well aware that, especially for the recent period, my conclusions will be disputed by many. Throughout I have been guided by the classical motto: *amicus Plato, sed magis amica veritas.* An institution which has reached the age of one hundred years has acquired a maturity and standing which enable—indeed require—it to present its past unvarnished, both for the sake of its own self-understanding and for the benefit of the public at large. It is a tribute to the College-Institute that when I first undertook to write this history I was given access to all records and complete freedom to reach my own conclusions. At no point was any effort made to force me to alter them.

My goal has been what the German historian Wilhelm Dilthey called *Verstehen:* the kind of probing understanding which sets off historical knowledge from the natural sciences on the one hand and from belles-lettres on the other. I have sought to comprehend the problems and tensions which recur in every phase of HUC-JIR history and seem endemic to the character of any modern rabbinic seminary. I have tried, as well, to isolate the novel elements and to relate them to the period of their appearance. Moreover, I could not omit dwelling on some of the circumstances of student life and trying to discover how its texture changed over the course of almost a century. I have consistently endeavored to see the history of the College-Institute in the context of American history in general and American Jewish history in particular. The periodization I have chosen follows the tenure of presidents. Not only did such a division prove to be convenient, but I became increasingly convinced that it reflected genuine transformations in the character of the institution.

The written sources utilized include both printed and archival materials. They have been supplemented for the more recent epochs by dozens of interviews conducted over a period of more than three years. My respondents included all living one-time chairmen of the Board of Governors and some of its other members, faculty of the older generation, administrators, students from various periods, and others associated in some significant way with the school. My thanks are due to all who kindly gave of their time and consented to answer my questions. Tape recordings were made of interviews with the following: Gertrude Adelstein, Robert S. Adler, Rissa Alex, Alice Bachrach, Bernard Bamberger, Fritz Bamberger, Leonard Beerman, Sheldon Blank, Richard Bluestein, William Dever, Leon Feuer, Abraham Franzblau, Solomon Freehof, Helen Glueck, Albert Goldman, Robert P. Goldman, Alfred Gottschalk, Harold Hahn, Henry Hofheimer, David Jacobson, Robert Katz, I. Edward Kiev, Edward Klein, S. L. Kopald, Jr., Samson Levey, Ernst Lorge, Jacob R. Marcus, Sidney Meyers, Sanford Ragins, Victor Reichert, Kenneth Roseman, Morton Rosenthal, Jacob Rudin, Joe D. Seger, Ezra Spicehandler, Samuel Sandmel, Jack Skirball, Donald Splansky, Paul Steinberg, John Tepfer, Moses Weiler, Herbert Weiner, Hiram Weiss, and Isaiah Zeldin. Other individuals were kind enough to answer specific written or oral inquiries. Although these interviews and inquiries have been of immense value, I have not quoted from them directly or referred to them in the notes. I did not want to hold my informants responsible for any statement they might have made without sufficient reflection nor to give the impression that the conclusions drawn are anything other than my own.[2] The recordings and correspondence have been deposited in the American Jewish Archives and are available to scholars on a restricted basis.

Various friends and colleagues have read one or more of the sections or chapters, contributing valuable suggestions regarding style and substance and saving me from unperceived errors. I am grateful to all of them and especially to those who read the entire work or more than a single chapter: Fritz Bamberger, Stanley Chyet, Alfred Gottschalk, Jacob R. Marcus, Carl Hermann Voss, and the editor, Samuel Karff. Of course they bear no responsibility for the final version; that burden is mine alone. Manuscript typing was devotedly performed by Marsha Bernstein; Steven Bob served as my research assistant for the final chapter. Particular thanks are due to the staff of the American Jewish Archives and especially to its archivist, Fannie Zelcer, for consistently friendly and generous help.

This account ends with the death of Nelson Glueck in the year 1971. With the presidency of Alfred Gottschalk, a new epoch begins in the history of the College-Institute. Its contours are still being shaped; its evaluation would surely be premature. I therefore leave untouched the final four years of the school's first century. Other historians, with fresh insights, will at some time in the future once again take up the theme.

MICHAEL A. MEYER

Cincinnati, Ohio
Erev Rosh Hashana 5735

IN THE DAYS OF
ISAAC MAYER WISE

> The world belongs to him who
> dares—I. M. WISE, *Reminiscences*

I T WAS A SOLEMN, EVEN
an historic occasion. Long before the appointed hour, the spacious
Bene Yeshurun Temple was crowded with ladies and gentlemen, both
Jews and gentiles, drawn from Cincinnati's economic and cultural
élite. Precisely at half past seven in the evening a sonorous organ
preludium opened the festive program. In dignified procession the
participants ascended the platform. An augmented choir, accompanied
by a complete orchestra, sang a stirring hymn, electrifying the audience
of two thousand. Carried away with admiration, the reporter for the
American Israelite later wrote: "The grand and palatial building,
with its oriental fresco lit by hundreds of gas flames, filled to its utmost
capacity by the highest intelligence of the city, now fairly ablaze with
that higher inspiration which classical music arouses in appreciative
souls, presented a panorama to the quiet observer, which no pen can
describe, no artist paint, and no eloquence reproduce." [1]

That evening, Sunday, October 3, 1875, marked the Opening
Exercises of the Hebrew Union College, the first permanent modern
rabbinical seminary in America and today the oldest and largest

anywhere in the world. Yet the throng gathered for music and formal addresses in the Plum Street Temple a hundred years ago had little reason to hope for so bright and promising a future. For behind the impressive pomp and ceremony lay an institution of only the most modest circumstances and of questionable capacity for endurance.

A more realistic picture of the Hebrew Union College at its inception could be gained only the next day when a total of nine students aged thirteen to seventeen, most of them from poor families, gathered for registration in the basement vestry rooms of Bene Israel's Mound Street Temple. Most of them were not serious about their studies, and even those who were hardly looked like future rabbis. It was a very humble beginning, quite out of proportion with the previous day's celebration. And yet it was also a culmination, the result of historical developments, combined with individual initiative and persistence, which had made even this modest start possible. The history of the Hebrew Union College in its full scope commences neither with the Opening Exercises nor with the first class lesson. The College's beginnings must be traced back to the earliest proposals for a modern rabbinate in Europe and the United States, and even beyond them to the development of a modern Jewish consciousness in the West. Nor can the tale be told without due regard for the earlier career and personality of its founder and first president, Isaac Mayer Wise.

The progressive acculturation and social integration of the Jews, which proceeded with increasing rapidity in Central and Western Europe during the late eighteenth and early nineteenth centuries, eroded the authority of the traditional rabbinate. As ever larger numbers of Jews, especially of the upper class, adopted a way of life at variance with the accepted pattern, the established religious leadership, which for the most part remained unchanged in its outlook, came increasingly to appear as an anachronism which had survived irrelevantly from an earlier period of Jewish isolation. In addition, modern states began to regard the legal prerogatives of Jewish communities as incompatible with the tight political structure required for efficient government, reducing or eliminating the wide-ranging autonomy which they enjoyed in the past. For the rabbis this meant a distinct curtailment of their powers. If the Jews were to live under the civil laws of France or Prussia rather than those of the Bible and the Talmud as interpreted by Jewish tradition, then, it became clear, the rabbinate as an institution would either have to restrict its authority to the highly limited legal sphere still allowed it, or reconstitute itself in terms of the new opportunities which were becoming available even as old prerogatives were melting away.

The type of rabbi called for by the new situation was not the legal scholar and decisor. As Jews in the West came under the influence of Christian society, they refashioned their image of the rabbi according to that of the Christian minister, regarding the latter as exemplary of the proper role for a clergyman in the modern world.[2] The rabbi was to preach, to conduct services, to teach children, to be a pastor to his flock. He was also to be a scholar, but his scholarship was expected to extend to secular learning as well as to Jewish studies.

The process of Jewish acculturation and even of rabbinic role transformation was well advanced before any institution was created to train the kind of rabbi required by the new circumstances of Jewish life. The principal religious leaders of modern Judaism in Germany during the nineteenth century all received their rabbinical training privately or in orthodox yeshivot. From radical to neo-orthodox, from Samuel Holdheim and Abraham Geiger to Zacharias Frankel and Samson Raphael Hirsch, they all combined a wholly traditional Jewish education with advanced secular studies at a university; none of them was the product of a seminary which had itself embodied the intellectual values of modern culture. Until mid-century, no such institution had come into existence.

It is true that as early as 1829 the Italian Instituto Rabbinico Lombardo-Veneto was opened in Padua and that same year the old yeshiva in Metz was transformed into the École Centrale Rabbinique. But these two institutions for the most part simply perpetuated the traditional curriculum both in content and in approach. Moreover, they remained weak and fragile, serving relatively small Jewish communities and exercising only the most limited influence.

In Germany, both Abraham Geiger and Ludwig Philippson urged the creation of a Jewish theological faculty as part of a major university as early as the mid-1830s. But their pleas found no response. There was neither a German university willing to lend the dignity of its name to Jewish studies nor funds available within the Jewish community for its support. It was only at mid-century, when a large legacy was specifically designated for a rabbinical and teachers' seminary, that an institution for the training of rabbis could at length be established in Germany. The *Jüdisch-theologisches Seminar,* which opened in Breslau in 1854, was not the Jewish theological faculty of a university, as Geiger, who championed the integration of Jewish with secular learning, had hoped, but a separate institution of distinctly conservative bent. Zacharias Frankel, an advocate of only the most moderate reform in conformity with what he called "positive-historical Judaism," became its president. The tone he set for the institution combined great reverence for tradition with a commitment to scientific investigation of Jewish sources up to, but not including, the Pentateuch.

Geiger, who had hoped to gain the presidency for himself, was forced to wait nearly twenty years longer until it became possible to found the *Hochschule für die Wissenschaft des Judentums* in Berlin in 1872. Unlike the Breslau Seminary, the *Hochschule* was dedicated to presenting various points of view, from the traditional to the most radical. At this institution Geiger was finally able to play a leading role during the last period of his life. Only a year later, the third modern rabbinical seminary was founded—again in Berlin. This was the *Rabbinerseminar* of German othodoxy. Thus, by the time Isaac Mayer Wise founded the Hebrew Union College in 1875, German Jewry—to which most of the Jews in America traced their origins—had provided for the training of modern rabbis of all shades of opinion.[3] But American Jewry still remained bereft.

As the father of organized Reform Judaism in the United States, Isaac M. Wise has been revered as hero and exemplar. A great deal has been written about him, most of it pietistic and reverential.[4] Yet Wise was both a less saintly and a more interesting figure than the portrait his admirers have usually drawn. Indeed, one may argue that had he not possessed less attractive, aggressive qualities of character along with indubitable virtues, he would scarcely have been able to succeed where modesty and humility could only have brought hesitation and ultimate failure.

Contemporaries noted that Wise rarely referred to the early years of his life in Europe.[5] He preferred to draw a curtain over them, leaving the motives for his silence a riddle to which one can only guess at the answer. Perhaps it was because of personal pains and disappointments which he had suffered, perhaps because the education he had received, the position he had held, were not what he would later have liked them to have been. Or perhaps he really felt that in coming to America he had taken on a new identity, sloughing off the old one as a worn-out or ill-fitting garment. In any event, we know that he remained ambivalent about all things German: he wrote novels in his mother tongue and confided more intimately in the readers of the German-language *Deborah* than in the larger circle which received his English newspaper, the *American Israelite*.[6] But basically he was an Americanizer who saw it as his task to establish a distinctly American Judaism unrestrained by its roots in Europe.

Wise was born in Steingrub, a small village in Bohemia, on March 20, 1819. The son of a poor Jewish schoolmaster, he received Jewish and secular educations which later proved less than adequate to the tasks he would undertake in America. At the age of twelve he set out for Prague, where he studied in the yeshiva and gained a high school education in secular studies. Later he may have attended classes at the Prague University and possibly at the University of Vienna for a brief time as well; but he seems not to have been a registered student and he received no academic degree. His Jewish studies apparently resulted in the receipt of some manner of diploma from Rabbis Rappaport, Freund, and Teweles in Prague in 1842, but since Wise never displayed the document, the question of the degree of authority it gave him must remain uncertain. In any case, it was sufficient for the young man to gain the position of preacher and schoolmaster in the Bohemian village of Radnitz, where he served for three years from 1843 to 1846 before making the decision to come to America.

Contemporary evidence for Wise's motives in leaving the Habsburg

Empire is lacking. In later years he liked to attribute his emigration with a wife and infant child to the political disabilities Jews suffered there and to his ingrained love of freedom. But it seems probable that there were personal reasons as well: dissatisfaction with what the future held for him in Radnitz and a vision of the unlimited possibilities that beckoned in the United States. That Wise was able to uproot himself from his familiar surroundings and face so uncertain a future bears early testimony to the daring and self-confidence which prompted so many of his actions in later years.[7]

Wise possessed a personality capable of producing enormous gyrations of depression and self-doubt alternating with virtually messianic pretensions and incredible sustained energy. The inner anxiety which must have beset him as he approached the new land resolved itself for him in a most remarkable dream as his ship was nearing the coast of North America. He later recalled the dream often; indeed it became the paradigm and lodestar of his life. Wise dreamed that a storm arose, driving the ship upon the rocks. But at the last moment, with wife and child, he leaped to the shore and with the break of dawn marched forward to ascend the mountain that loomed before them. The dream continues:

Then as though the measure of woes was not yet full, hollow-eyed, ghostly, grinning dwarfs, lascivious, ragged goblins, and tiny poodles, with large, hollow, puffed-out heads, came towards us on the narrow path, opposed our further progress, and mocked me mercilessly. I brushed them aside; but for every ten that I pushed away a hundred arose from out the bare rock. They came in the shape of night-owls, and deafened me with their cries; they sizzed about me like angry wasps, and stung me; they placed themselves, like stupid blocks, in my path; in short, they did everything to harass me and prevent my further progress. My wife at my side wept bitterly, the child in my arms cried for fright, but my courage, strength, and confidence grew. I begged, implored, avoided, circumvented them, all to no avail. Then I marched straight through the crowd of dwarfs, paid no attention to their ravings, dashed them aside to the right and the left, until finally, weary and perspiring, we reached the summit of the mountain. Arriving there, I saw the most beautiful and glorious landscape, the richest, most fertile meadows, but I sank fainting; thereupon I awoke, and found that it was all a dream. . . .[8]

In the years which followed, as Wise became embroiled in one controversy after another, as he struggled to become the leader of a united American Jewry, he was at times stricken by self-doubt, hypochondria, presentiments of death, and even wishes for his own destruction. At one point he seriously considered leaving the rabbinate to take up a career in law. But the source of strength which had prompted the supreme confidence of that well-remembered (and doubtless embellished) dream was in the course of time increasingly to banish all countervailing forces of despair. Wise became convinced that "the world belongs to him who dares," and came to see himself as the humble servant of an optimistic idealism which must always ultimately succeed. He learned never to hesitate once he had embarked upon a course of action: "I rarely asked myself whether I was competent to do this or that after I had determined upon it. I said to myself continually: 'A person can learn whatever he does not know, and whatever he can not accomplish in one year can be achieved in five or ten years. Patience, industry, perseverance, and a little ability will overcome all obstacles.' " Where others were held back by qualms and misgivings, or where their fortitude crumbled in the face of opposition, Wise marched right on, always certain in the depths of his soul that those who stood in his path were only pygmies whom he would sooner or later dash against the rocks to the left and the right. Wise came to see himself as a "child of destiny," an apposite designation in a nation then bent upon achieving its "manifest destiny." His brash audacity, his firm belief that he "had talent for all things," created an aura of strength which enabled him to exercise influence over those who came into contact with him. Combined with a quick mind and an agile pen, it made the ill-trained country preacher into the foremost religious leader of American Jewry in the nineteenth century, and it enabled him to become the prime creator of its first national religious institutions.[9]

Wise's earliest years in the United States were spent as a rabbi in Albany, New York. It was here that he became Americanized, and here he proceeded autodidactically, as best he could, to fill in the gaps in his education. Here, too, he began to propagate religious reform, introducing a mixed choir and confirmation, publicly stating that he believed neither in bodily resurrection nor in a personal messiah. But he also showed that he was not a radical: he insisted his congregants observe the Sabbath by closing their businesses; he advocated only moderate reform of the ritual. When Wise left Albany for Cincinnati in the spring of 1854, it was not so much because of the difficulties which had been put in his way as a reformer (though there had been some problems) as because the landscape of the West seemed to offer—in the imagery of the dream—"the richest, most fertile meadows."

At mid-century, Cincinnati was truly the Queen City of the West, the largest metropolis west of the Allegheny Mountains and in 1860 the sixth-largest city in the country: a bustling commercial entrepôt on the busy Ohio River. It was also the center of learning for the West. Cincinnati College had been chartered as early as 1819, and since 1831 the city had boasted a public high school as well. Jews had lived in Cincinnati since at least 1817. Attracted by the abundance of business opportunities, their numbers swelled to about ten thousand by the Civil War. Most of them came from the small towns of southern Germany, some from Poland and England. By the time Wise arrived, there were four congregations, two quite large: Bene Israel (founded in 1824) and Bene Yeshurun, the congregation to which Wise was called (founded in 1839). Though well established, the Jewish community was not yet affluent; that would come only after the war. But Cincinnati seemed clearly to be a city with a promising future and its Jewish community appeared certain to increase in size. Here Wise could flourish in an atmosphere still redolent with the pioneering spirit that so well fit his own view of life. Here, where traditional ways of doing things were ever being challenged by new prospects, where a man was more admired for his achievements than for the profundity of his thought—here Wise could unleash the full energy of his spirit and hope to find a sympathetic, even enthusiastic response.[10]

He lost no time. In speedy succession Wise established himself securely not only as rabbi of his own congregation but for a time of Bene Israel as well. He founded and almost single-handedly edited two weekly newspapers, one in English and one in German, which spread his influence across the country. In October of 1855 he organized a conference of rabbis in Cleveland which adopted a very conservative platform intended to lay the groundwork for further efforts at unity within "American Israel." Two years later he published his prayerbook, *Minhag America*. One marvels at this amazing record of frenetic, productive activity! But despite Wise's best efforts, the first two decades in Cincinnati did not yet bring about the unification under his own aegis that he was seeking so persistently. Nor did they bring to fruition his dream of founding a school for higher Jewish learning in the United States—though he had harbored that desire almost from the moment he first stepped upon these shores.

As early as 1848, Wise had called for a congregational union in the pages of Isaac Leeser's *Occident*, deploring the lack of Jewish education and mentioning specifically the need for "better educated men to fill the pulpit." [11] But in this early period Wise was thinking rather of a general college under Jewish auspices, one which would teach secular as well as Jewish subjects and train young men for a variety of professions rather than for the rabbinate alone. As this was a time when large numbers of such denominational schools were being founded throughout the United States, but especially in the West, it is not surprising that the energetic and ambitious Wise should try his hand at establishing such an institution for the Jews very shortly after his arrival in Cincinnati. Using the day school of Bene Yeshurun as the basis, he hoped to create a "Hebrew College." But when his Zion College, as the school was named, opened in the fall of 1855, it could boast only a handful of students and the most limited financial support. Jewish businessmen were not at all convinced that their children needed a college education to succeed, nor were supporters outside Cincinnati easily persuaded to contribute to Wise's venture, especially as he acted without consulting them. When a financial panic struck in 1857, the sources of the college's income dried up and the school ceased to exist. Thus Wise's first effort to found an institution of higher learning failed totally. But the venture did teach him a twofold lesson: that a rabbinical seminary was the more necessary and feasible project, and that such a seminary could only be supported by a preexisting union of congregations brought into being specifically for that purpose.[12]

For the next two decades conditions remained unpropitious. In the years immediately before and during the Civil War few new colleges were established anywhere in America, and even in the period directly following that upheaval, circumstances were not yet favorable. Once funds became available in Cincinnati, the building of magnificent synagogues took precedence. These structures seem to have been more important for the Jewish self-image in America than were cultural institutions.

Efforts by others to establish a school of higher Jewish learning during this period all failed. In 1865 the radical reformers in New York City created the Emanu-El Theological Seminary Association, but they were unable to establish an actual seminary. In Philadelphia, Wise's sometime ally sometime opponent, the conservative Isaac Leeser, brought about the creation of Maimonides College in 1867. It admitted eleven students, but only five completed the first year, three went on to the second, and only one—without benefit of diploma —became a practicing rabbi. Leeser's death, shortly after the school opened, dealt it a crippling blow; after six years the seminary ceased to exist.[13]

As these other attempts proved unsuccessful, the initiative passed once again into the hands of Wise. To succeed he needed a respectable number of students willing to study for the rabbinate and he needed a steady source of funds. The former he could recruit through the personal contacts he had established, his own reputation, and the lure to poor, immigrant parents of a respected professional standing for their sons. The funds would be forthcoming through the establishment of a congregational union. In the pages of the *Israelite* he now began to agitate in earnest for such a union and a seminary. Yet it was a quite fortuitous event that provided the final impetus: a donation in the considerable amount of $10,000, which was given with a very clear stipulation.

Henry Adler of Lawrenceberg, Indiana, was a Jew of substantial means, though not among the truly wealthy. Toward the end of 1870 he proposed for the first time to give $10,000 in trust to Wise's congregation for the establishment and support of a rabbinical college. It was his offer which set the organizational process actively in motion. Although a rabbinical conference which Wise convened in Cincinnati in 1871 expressed approval of a union of congregations, a sense of urgency was not created until Adler spelled out his terms in February of 1873, including the proviso that if the seminary (he preferred to call it "Jewish theological faculty") should not be established within three years, then the gift would revert to the donor. In later years the Adler donation was referred to repeatedly on ceremonial occasions as giving the College its start. But its significance seems to have lain less in the immediate income which it provided—since most of the interest from the $10,000 was paid out to Adler during his lifetime—than in the impetus it gave to act quickly lest this sizable sum be lost.[14]

The first tangible step had already been taken on October 10, 1872, when Moritz Loth, the president of Wise's congregation, recommended in his annual report that Bene Yeshurun assume the initiative in establishing a congregational union. Together with four other Cincinnati synagogues, it then issued a joint call for a general convention to take place in Cincinnati the following summer. Twenty-eight congregations from the Midwest and South sent representatives. A constitution was adopted stating that the Union's "primary object" was to establish a "Hebrew Theological Institute," its operation to be supported by dues of one dollar per member from each of the constituent congregations. A sinking fund, to be obtained from gifts and bequests, would be invested to provide additional income and security. It was decided that the Institute would open only after $60,000 had been collected; a building would be built once assets reached $160,000.[15]

When the first regular council of the newly formed Union of American Hebrew Congregations met the following year in Cleveland, the amount which had been raised was a pitiful percentage of the goal laid down. The year 1873 had witnessed a financial panic of extraordinary severity and persistence which had affected the business interests of the wealthier Jews. Though fifty-five congregations had now joined the Union, the prospects of gathering sufficient funds to open the College looked bleak indeed. The situation appeared no more promising at the second council, held in Buffalo in 1875. By now there were seventy-two congregations, but the total assets as of June 30, 1875, not including the Adler gift, barely exceeded $5,000. By any strict construction of the constitution, the College should never have been opened that fall as planned. It was decided, however, to proceed nonetheless; the opening of the Preparatory Department was deemed not yet to be the "permanent establishment of the College." [16] Thus the impressive exercises in the Plum Street Temple that fall diverted attention from the shaky financial condition of the incipient institution even while the festive oratory sought to inspire confidence in its success. The effect was apparently as desired, for in the following months generous contributions were made, especially by the Jews of Cincinnati. By December there was already a total accumulation of $64,000, though most of it was in as yet uncollected pledges.[17] Within a few months after it had opened, the school could be considered "permanently established."

Wise had decided to begin the College with a single class, adding another one each successive year. The total program was to consist of eight years. Students were to spend the first four years in a Preparatory Department while taking classes concurrently at one of the public high schools, the second four in the Collegiate Department while studying at the recently municipalized University of Cincinnati. Thus the fall of 1875 found Wise, the unpaid president, along with an assistant, Solomon Eppinger, instructing a small class from four until six on weekday afternoons. Though Wise put the best face he could on the school's circumstances whenever he wrote of the College in the *American Israelite* or reported to the newly constituted Board of Governors,[18] it really amounted to little more than an intensive religious school. Recalling those first days two decades later, the founder wrote: "There sat the wise men of Israel, namely the good old teacher Solomon Eppinger and fourteen noisy boys, most of whom had come only to kill time and at the command of their parents. Four of them wanted to study; ten wanted to make noise. . . . No one who failed to see the embryonic college can imagine how ridiculous was this little hole-in-the-wall of a school in its not-too-bright cellar, carrying the pompous name of college. Fortunately we did not have to be ashamed in front of visitors, for none came." [19]

But with persistent effort the school slowly grew and, as a result, the need for some permanent quarters became apparent. After two years the classes were moved from the basement of the Mound Street Synagogue to that of the Plum Street Temple, but these quarters, too, were deemed only temporary. When an attractive private mansion at a bargain price became available in 1880, the Union leaders decided to use their limited funds to purchase it for $25,250 and renovate it for instructional purposes. The building was located on West Sixth Street, at that time a most fashionable section of the city and in close proximity to the large Reform temples. Its design served the purposes of the College very well. Three stories in height, with an elegant free-stone front, the structure presented an impressive appearance, and once the name of the College was hewn above the entry in large gold letters, it gave the school an identity of its own and an aura of permanence which it had not previously enjoyed. On the first floor there was space for the rapidly expanding library as well as for a richly furnished president's office; on the second floor, bedrooms were turned into an adequate number of classrooms; and on the third floor a large hall was soon converted into a chapel. The building, which was dedicated on April 24, 1881, served HUC for thirty years until at length it was deemed no longer of sufficient size and its location no longer desirable.[20]

The students who entered the College were required to pass an examination in Hebrew reading and conjugation of the regular verb. They had to be able to translate at sight any passage from the Book of Genesis and were to be familiar with the history of Israel from Abraham to Zerubbabel. They also had to possess the qualifications

for admission to a public high school. Considering the students'
limited preparation upon entry, the small number of class hours per
week available, and the fatigue of the students in the late afternoon
after a full schedule at the high school, the curriculum devised for
the Preparatory Department was remarkably, even absurdly, ambitious. At the end of four years—and before beginning the Collegiate
Department—a student was to have mastered Hebrew and Aramaic
grammar, read in the original most of the Bible and large selections
from rabbinic literature, including portions from both the Babylonian
and the Palestinian Talmuds, and familiarized himself with the
entire span of Jewish history.[21]

Wise made every effort to fulfill the prescriptions of the curriculum.
It was of great importance for the future of the school that scoffers,
who had argued the impossibility of teaching classical Jewish texts
to American youngsters, be proven wrong, and that traditionally
inclined opponents find that the College's students were learning
what had always been required of a rabbi. Thus in his regular reports
to the Board of Governors, later printed in the *American Israelite,*
Wise was ever at pains to indicate precisely how many chapters of
Psalms had been covered in the preceding month, how many pages
of *Mekhilta,* and the like. In order that the achievements of the
College's instruction be presented to the Jewish world at large, it
was decided to employ a then common practice in American education: the public examination conducted by outside examiners. From
1877 until 1889 (when the task was given to the president and faculty), groups of three examiners were regularly appointed by the
Union at its councils. These panels, which included rabbis and laymen
of varying points of view, repeatedly expressed appreciation of the
school's accomplishments. Their only evident criticism was directed
at Wise's over-ambition, which allowed students to begin study of
talmudic writings when they had as yet insufficiently mastered the
Pentateuch.[22]

The nature of the curriculum for the Collegiate Department remained undetermined until a commission of nine was selected to
formulate a complete plan of studies at the Union council in 1878.
Composed of both rabbis and educated laymen, reformers and con-

servatives, it of course counted Isaac Mayer Wise among its members. Yet before the commission could meet, Wise decided to formulate his own program and to submit it to the other members in advance of their deliberations. His hope was that they would either allow it to stand intact or make only minor alterations. But to his dismay, the commission refused to accept Wise's proposal and insisted on formulating its own, which was adopted by the Union the following summer. As a result, Wise was constrained to write a dissent, though he did not present it officially. The differences between Wise's two documents and the official commission report shed some interesting light on the president's priorities for the curriculum.[23] Unlike his colleagues, he was certain of the necessity for each rabbinical student to be familiar with a number of Semitic languages. However, he was less convinced than they of the importance of stressing the German language in the HUC curriculum, since Wise was not committed to its preservation as the language of the sermon and prayerbook in America.[24] He further criticized the majority for failing to note the necessity of determining a new method for the study of *halakha* based on the comprehension of its guiding principles. Finally, he questioned their desire to institute an additional ninth year of exclusive study at the College after the student's completion of his university program;[25] Wise was not in favor of protracting rabbinic studies and apparently wanted to produce the first graduates as quickly as possible. Considering the president's character, it is not surprising that, although the majority report was adopted by the Union and even signed by Wise himself, the actual curriculum instituted was in every respect in line with Wise's personal opinions.

The curriculum as it finally evolved in practice consisted basically of four subjects: biblical exegesis utilizing both traditional and modern commentaries, Talmud (including Codes), philosophy of Judaism (restricted to medieval texts), and history of Judaism. In addition, there were language courses in Syriac, Arabic, and "Assyrian" (Hebrew and Aramaic having been mastered in the Preparatory Department). There was also some "New Hebrew" (medieval) poetry, theology (taught by Wise), and in the senior year two hours of homiletics. About two-thirds of a student's time in the Collegiate Department, and an even larger percentage in the Preparatory Department, was taken up with translating texts and learning grammar.[26] No alternatives were available at any level.

In accordance with then current American educational practice, little time was apportioned for modern writings, for lecture, or for discussion. Wise explained this emphasis pedagogically: Bible and Talmud had to be mastered first before recent synthetic works would be of any value; Jewish theology could not be fruitfully studied until the texts upon which it rested were well known. "It is illegitimate," he wrote in one of his reports, "to speculate and theorize without the proper basis. Hence, the inevitable conclusion that those only who have a respectable knowledge of Jewish literature must be admitted to the study of Jewish theology, in order not to educate sophists." [27] Only upon reaching their junior and senior years in the Collegiate Department did students orally present and then debate papers on theological subjects. But pedagogic considerations were not the only ones which played a role in the emphasis given to sources in this curriculum. Concentration upon the texts enabled Wise to elude the often posed question whether the Hebrew Union College was orthodox or reformist in approach by replying simply that there was little in the curriculum to make it the one or the other: the classical sources of Judaism were the common possession of all Jews.

Though it is not possible to measure the quality of the students' learning in those early days, the quantity of material which in some fashion at least they managed to absorb is astounding when one considers the concurrent obligations (including classical and modern languages) at the high school and university. During the year 1883–84, for example, the senior class actually read forty-nine full folio pages of Talmud, forty chapters of Codes, and twenty chapters of Midrash Rabba; they also heard lectures on talmudic literature, methodology, and terminology. In Bible they read forty chapters of Ezekiel plus Ecclesiastes, Song of Songs, and a number of Minor Prophets; and in philosophy they studied Joseph Albo's *Sefer ha-Ikarim* and Saadia's *Emunot ve-Deot*. In addition, they wrote Hebrew compositions and heard regular lectures on Jewish history and theology.[28] Finally, the senior year was also the time when students were required to write a rabbinical thesis and (though this requirement was eventually dropped) "stand final examination in all subjects of the collegiate course, read *prima vista* (or after a short preparation) any part of the Hebrew Bible, the ancient Targumim and commentaries, Talmud, Midrash, Code, the philosophical and poetical literatures of the Hebrews. . . ." [29] The quantitative achievements of the lower classes (at least on paper) were hardly less remarkable.

The faculty which taught according to this curriculum grew slowly as year after year was added on to the school and as funds became available. At the very beginning there was only Wise himself along with Solomon Eppinger, an elderly teacher in Wise's religious school who was the only one to receive a regular salary. Max Lilienthal, the rabbi of Bene Israel, who joined the staff the second year to teach history, like Wise taught without compensation. During the initial period there was no figure of scholarly stature who was a regular member of the faculty; indeed none such was required to teach basic texts to the high school students who at first made up the entire student body. But with the opening of the Collegiate Department in 1879, the need for a full-time teacher of recognized credentials became imperative. Fortunately, Wise was able that year to persuade the capable Moses Mielziner to join the faculty as professor of Talmud. Mielziner, who would teach at the Hebrew Union College for more than two decades, had studied in Germany with the radical reformer Samuel Holdheim and received his rabbinical diploma from the Hungarian rabbi Leopold Loew; he also possessed a Ph.D. from the University of Giessen. Before coming to Cincinnati, he had been a rabbi and teacher in New York City. When he moved to Hebrew Union College, he was undoubtedly the ablest modern talmudic scholar in the United States. Of even greater immediate significance, he possessed the ability to teach rabbinic sources in a fashion which made them meaningful to his students. Expounding the Talmud in English from the original Hebrew and Aramaic text, as was done at the College, was a pioneering task which required the development of a hitherto nonexistent technical terminology. In this effort he was eminently

successful. Mielziner also created a "scientific" method of presenting the Talmud which the examiners in 1884 praised for enabling
students to read and explain some of the most difficult passages after
an hour's preparation. In his teaching he would also draw comparisons
with Roman and modern law and would concentrate on subjects,
such as the marital laws, which seemed to be of particular contemporary relevance.[30]

Until the 1890s, the other regular members of the faculty were of
distinctly lesser stature. They consisted of whomever Wise could
persuade to accept a teaching position at the meager salary offered
by the Board of Governors.[31] Some gained the respect of their students, others did not; one, Heinrich Zirndorf, who was the first
regular professor of Jewish history, failed so egregiously in his teaching that students openly reviled him, and the board, after much
acrimony, was eventually forced to dismiss him.[32] Those faculty
members who came toward the end of Wise's presidency—Gotthard
Deutsch in history, Max Margolis in Hebrew, Moses Buttenwieser
in Bible—elevated the level of the College considerably, but Mielziner
remained the senior scholar and the most important of the regular
teachers during Wise's presidency.

The faculty member's lot in the early days of the College was not
an enviable one. Compensated at from about half to only slightly
more than the salaries earned by the first graduates,[33] he was forced
to accept other employment—preaching, editing, teaching religious
school—in addition to the thirteen to sixteen hours per week spent in
his classroom at the College. He possessed no tenure; each faculty
member stood for yearly reelection by the Board of Governors. He
enjoyed no pension or security other than what he could set aside on
his own. Monthly, he was required to submit to the president a report
on the material covered in his classes. By explicit ruling of the Board
of Governors he was prohibited from spending any portion of class
time on "matters foreign to the instruction set for the respective
hour" or to dismiss his classes before the bell.[34] Lack of funds during
the early years meant that the faculty was usually understaffed. Classes
were combined and advanced students were employed to do some
of the more elementary teaching. In 1882–83, when the final eighth

year of the school was added, the total faculty—diminished by a number of deaths—consisted of Mielziner, Eppinger, and Wise. In 1887,
when the size of the student body for the first time demanded eight
separately taught classes, there were still only five faculty members
to teach them. In later years, one professor served as the "ordinarius"
for each class, individual faculty members thus bearing responsibility
for the welfare of a particular segment of the student body.

No less meager than the faculty were the size and quality of the
Hebrew Union College library in the first years. Nearly all of the
early books were gifts donated by friends around the country. Aside
from an abundance of worn-out prayerbooks, these contributions consisted mostly of Bibles, Mishnas, Hebrew grammars, and dictionaries.
By the end of the first year there was a total of 103 usable volumes,
all dutifully enumerated by Wise in his report to the Board of Governors.[35] In the beginning, the books received little care. When the
first catalogue was undertaken in 1878,[36] it was discovered that seventy-
two volumes had been lost or destroyed, constituting at that time a
considerable portion of the library's total holdings. Each student,
we learn from a report, considered himself the librarian.[37] At length, a
faculty member was persuaded to take on the additional duties of
supervising the library—for which he was paid the munificent salary
of $50 per year. Not until 1878 did the council of the Union authorize
an appropriation specifically for the purchase of books. These funds,
plus an increasing number of donations, thereupon enabled the library
to grow very rapidly so that by 1881 it possessed 7,800 volumes,
making it the largest Jewish library in the country. Its preeminence
was permanently assured when Rabbi Samuel Adler, upon his death
in 1891, willed his private collection to the College. His rich assemblage
of some 1,600 bound volumes and 300 pamphlets of Hebraica and
Judaica was the first major acquisition to come into the College's
possession, though smaller collections of some importance had been
received earlier. By the end of the century, the Hebrew Union College
library possessed more than 14,000 volumes, including a number of
rare and precious works.[38]

Of the students who attended Hebrew Union College during its first quarter century, the majority by far were born in the United States. They came from poor families of German origin in the Midwest and South or were the wards of Jewish orphanages. Well-to-do Jewish parents would not hear of their sons entering a profession which was for the most part poorly paid and lacking in prestige. Becoming a rabbi was widely considered the last resort for a young man, appropriate only for someone who, as an Alabama congregation candidly wrote to the Board of Governors, "is not fit for anything else." Two of the Union's leaders in Cincinnati did in fact send their sons to the Preparatory Department for a time, but their intent seems to have been nothing more than to supply their progeny with a somewhat more intensive Jewish education and to bolster the number of pupils. For serious students Wise was forced to turn to those families for whom the tuition-free education offered by the Hebrew Union College in conjunction with high school and university studies provided an opportunity they could not otherwise afford. In some cases Wise himself knew the parents from his wide-ranging and frequent trips to preach and to dedicate synagogues in the small towns of the Midwest; in other instances word of the new school had come through his two newspapers. Contact was also maintained with the Jewish orphan asylums and a scholarship was offered to one student from each of them. As Wise's colleague, Max Lilienthal, had noted at the Opening Exercises, the composition of the student body was really quite in keeping with traditional precedent: "Our old rabbis have already said, thousands of years ago, 'Take care of the poor, they will be your scholars and your teachers.' " [39]

Since the students were without means, they were supported financially by the Board of Governors, which provided them with all necessities from books to clothing, food, and lodging. In fact, for the first four years of the College's existence the majority of its total budget was expended to care for these "indigent students," as they were called. In the course of their stay at the College, some of them tried to outgrow or forget their humble origins. A few anglicized their names; one amused a professor when in his presence he tried to prevent his father from gesticulating with his hands. [40]

The age range of the students was such as to place the immature

teenager at the same class table with the more grown-up, but Jewishly
ignorant, older pupil. In the year 1876–77, the lowest grade had nine
students ranging in age from thirteen to twenty-eight. Although in
1888 the Board of Governors passed a resolution to make fifteen the
minimum age of admission, it was not consistently observed and an
age range from fourteen to twenty in a single grade still obtained
as late as 1896. Finally, in 1898, the age for admission was raised
to sixteen years.[41]

Most of the students were quartered in a boarding house or else
lived with Cincinnati families whose children they sometimes tutored;
their lodgings were closely supervised by a committee of the Board
of Governors. Life in such a boarding house, as one occupant later
recalled it, was hardly luxurious. Students lived four in a room on the
third floor, slept together in trundle beds, and sometimes had to study
in overcoats for want of proper heating. Aside from the beds, their
furniture consisted of four kitchen chairs, one table, and a single
study lamp. In the morning the students were roused by a bell and
assembled downstairs while one of their number rushed through
the Hebrew prayers as speedily as possible. The food was cheap and
poorly cooked, so that whatever spending money students had went
for eating in restaurants. When one of them needed clothing, he
went to a particular member of the Board of Governors who owned
a wholesale clothing business. Upon seeing a student with such a
request, the clothier would bluster loudly: "What, again?"[42]

Explicit rules and regulations closely governed the life of the student in his boarding house. He was required to rise daily at 6:15 during
the winter months and at 5:45 during the summer (though he might
rise as early as four if he desired to study). Ten o'clock was mandatory
bedtime for those in the Preparatory Department, eleven for those
in the College. Students were cautioned against boisterous talk-
ing and laughing at meals and to avoid physical quarrels. The superintendent of the house reported monthly to the Board of Governors
on the deportment of the young men under his charge. The College
building, too, had its rules: students were allowed to enter only by
the side entrance; they were cautioned not to deface the property,
open mail addressed to the College, or visit the president's room in

his absence. Only one book at a time might be taken out of the library except by permission of the president of the Board of Governors. Teachers in all classes reported regularly not only on student progress but also on attendance and behavior in the classroom.[43]

Such rules, however, were often broken. This was an age in which the authorities of every school tried to exercise strict control over their charges and in which students frequently engaged in rebellion, malicious pranks, and even violence against instructors and college presidents.[44] Hebrew Union College students were no different from their compeers in other institutions. Wise and Mielziner seem to have suffered little from their diabolical imaginations but others were not so fortunate, especially those whose fiery tempers presented a particular challenge to student incitement or whose accents called forth a talented mimicry.[45]

In those days the Hebrew Union College was a family in a very real sense, not merely in the metaphoric one in which the term was often later used. Each student from outside the city had one member of the board who was declared his legal guardian during his stay at the College.[46] The faculty, the president, and to the largest extent the board exercised a parental role toward the students, and they, in turn, replied with all the ambivalences of love and rebellion that characterize such a relationship. Wise, as a rule, was gentle and understanding in his treatment of students, thus earning their love and respect. But his posture was possible only because the Board of Governors chose to exercise discipline directly. Students delinquent in their studies or guilty of misconduct were frequently summoned before the board and given a reprimand by its president or occasionally even expelled. In 1892 a particularly severe breach of discipline produced a memorable scene. Saturday afternoon, April 9th, all the local members of the Board of Governors, faculty (except for Wise), and student body gathered in the College chapel after the service to hear the president of the board solemnly exhort the students to perform the duties expected of them in the College vis-à-vis their teachers and the Board of Governors, all of whom were ever ready to aid them. He then publicly reprimanded two students for being involved in a brawl and reduced one of them to a lower grade for a year as punishment.

Another student, he announced, had failed to pass his examinations satisfactorily and consequently had been stricken from the roll.[47]

The pressure under which students labored, and their sometimes difficult personal adjustments to the life of the College, produced one notable tragedy in those early years. A deeply disturbed student, who had left the school in 1889 after apparent misconduct, was allowed to reenter a year later. He and a younger pupil who came under his influence entered into a suicide pact and together one day each of them shot himself. Although a note signed by both students explained that they had been treated kindly by everyone at the College and did not hold the institution responsible for their act, hostile Jewish newspapers chose to blame the College. At a funeral service held in the HUC library, the president of the Board of Governors eulogized them moralistically, saying "they were wrong, . . . these poor, misguided friends." [48]

Yet if life at the College had its rigors and even its tragedies, if the students were often more children than prospective religious leaders, the Board of Governors more stern disciplinarians than enlightened educators, there was much that characterized the College in those days which inspires admiration. Academically, every effort was made to maintain a demanding curriculum. Socially, a spirit of close unity prevailed, perhaps especially because the school was a pioneering venture whose value outsiders so often called into question. The students took pride in the accomplishments of their alumni and a deep feeling of fellowship existed among them; there were "close companionships and devoted friendships." [49]

At the very beginning, Wise created a literary society for the students which he called *Atzile Bene Yisrael* ("Noble Sons of Israel") and which was later divided into two sections for students of the Preparatory and Collegiate Departments. These societies met weekly for debates, declamations, music, and drama. Though the students seem to have enjoyed this activity, participation in the societies was mandatory, and their secretaries were even required to hand in monthly reports to the secretary of the faculty.[50] Not until the last decade of Wise's presidency did students become more independent and desirous of taking their own initiatives. In 1896—on their own responsibility and without financial assistance from the Board of Governors—they founded the first College periodical: the *HUC Journal,* published monthly during the school year until 1903. Students, faculty, alumni, and friends of the College contributed to this new venture. In a most lively fashion its pages reflected the major issues of the day. The Dreyfus case, Zionism, and Sunday Sabbath observance were discussed there along with American phenomena bearing on Judaism, such as the number of Jews attracted to the appearances of the agnostic orator Robert Ingersoll or the controversy over the teaching of Bible in the public schools. There were also précis of sermons given in chapel, book reviews, and scholarly papers. The students' level of thought and expression, as evidenced by the *Journal,* was remarkably high; their tone was serious and thoughtful, neither flippant nor sophomoric.[51]

In those same years the students were also exposed to occasional lectures delivered by prominent Jews not associated with the Reform movement: the novelist Israel Zangwill suggested to them that on account of its poetic beauty the ancient liturgy should remain unchanged, and Zvi Hirsch Masliansky, the famous Jewish nationalist preacher, on two occasions addressed the students in Hebrew. In this period, too, we find the first evidence of student social concern when one student urged his fellows to form a "College Settlement" on the model of the one run by the University of Cincinnati and to spend their spare time leading societies, clubs, and classes among the Jewish poor of the city.[52]

Religious services took a large share of the time that students had left over from their studies—and of course attendance was required. It was assumed that a prospective rabbi would want to devote himself regularly to prayer. Moreover, once he reached the Collegiate Department, a student would officiate at High Holy Day services in a small congregation, and it was important that the young College not be embarrassed. Aside from the daily services held in the boarding house, the student was expected to participate in worship each Saturday morning at one of the local synagogues. At the College an attempt was made to perpetuate the traditional Jewish association of study with prayer by the regulation that every class be opened and closed with the *birkhot ha-tora* or an extempore prayer by one of the students.[53]

The regular weekly Hebrew Union College service took place on Saturday afternoons following an hour of classes. It was held in the chapel on the third floor and attended by all students and faculty; often, as well, by members of the Board of Governors. Students of the junior year conducted the service while seniors gave the sermon. The speakers were required to submit their speeches in advance to the professor of homiletics for corrections, while readers had to hold a rehearsal before the professor of liturgy on the preceding day. During the services *kaddish* was read at the *yahrzeit* of College benefactors, some of whom had made the reading a stipulation in presenting their gifts.[54]

The student sermon and reading were frankly regarded by Wise as "examinations in homilectics," [55] and as such they served a valuable pedagogic function for the preacher and the reader. But it is interesting to note that the the question of the role of the chapel service in the life of the College—so much agitated in later years—had become an issue in some minds even before the turn of the century. In April 1899, Wise's assistant at Bene Yeshurun, Louis Grossmann, a graduate of the College and later its professor of ethics, suggested in the *HUC Journal* that it was "not quite congruous with a high sense of religiousness to turn worship into an academic exercise" and he expressed doubt as to whether the weekly services "contribute much toward the development and intensification of the Jewish spirit in the students. . . ." The student service, he added, should be "a religious experience that goes deep down into the heart of each one of those who attend it, as much as of those who officiate in it." If there was a desire for religious ecstasy and spiritual strengthening, he concluded, then the service would have to be a "communion" shared in by all, professors as well as students.[56]

During the early period of its history, the College, which had been created by the Union of American Hebrew Congregations, remained under the close supervision of its parent organization; it was not even incorporated as a separate institution. For its part, the UAHC, though increasingly devoting itself to other enterprises, as late as 1900 still appropriated nearly all of its budget directly or indirectly for the support of the College. The councils of the Union elected the entire Board of Governors, which was obliged to present reports and proposed budgets to the Union for approval. Fund-raising and the investment of assets were entirely the function of the Union, which was also the owner of the College property.

In raising funds the Union relied on a number of sources: congregational dues, fixed yearly contributions, and one-time donations and bequests. A special fund was also created for indigent students (later called "stipendiary fund"), which received contributions largely from ladies' auxiliaries organized for this purpose in various communities. The amount realized yearly in congregational dues depended, of course, upon the size of the Union, which, for economic and ideological reasons, did not grow steadily during this quarter century. The number of congregations increased from fifty-five in 1874 to a high of 104 in 1879, remained at about that level for a short time, then fell off, rising again to stand at ninety-nine in 1900. Total individual membership described a somewhat more steady upward curve as member congregations increased in size and larger ones joined the fold. Beginning with 1,966 dues-paying members in 1874, it reached 9,845 in 1900.

Compared with dues, the amounts raised from donations gyrated far more wildly, depending apparently on the degree of effort put into fund-raising in any particular year. Not infrequently, the amount collected one year would be halved the next and then rise again to the original height or higher the third year. Nearly half of the total donations usually came from Cincinnati. Throughout the entire period there were extraordinarily large contributions only in the year 1894, when two estates, one in Cincinnati and one in Pittsburgh, brought in a total of approximately $25,000, constituting about half of the total receipts for that year.[57]

The financial situation of the Union was throughout this period a precarious one. Beginning its existence during the drawn-out financial crisis of 1873, the Union suffered again during the panic of 1893–97.[58]

At various times it was beset by ideological opponents from the left and from the right. Yet even in more prosperous and less troubled periods, there seem never to have been sufficient funds to finance its program properly. In 1883 an attempt was made to call upon B'nai B'rith and other lodges to support the indigent students' fund but, though some individual lodges did respond, it met strong opposition on the part of B'nai B'rith's Executive Committee, which regarded all specifically religious institutions as beyond its proper sphere of activity.[59]

Union assets were divided between a general fund, used for operational expenses, and a sinking fund (later called "Endowment Fund") from which only the interest could be used. Congregational dues went into the general fund; all other donations accrued to the sinking fund.[60] Originally, the latter was invested exclusively in United States government bonds; only in 1884 was authorization given to invest it in first mortgages, which at 6 percent yielded twice the income of the bonds.[61]

Until the purchase of the College building in 1881, the income of the Union consistently exceeded its expenditures. But once the structure was opened, fund-raising enthusiasm waned and subscriptions to the sinking fund remained unpaid even as ongoing expenditures increased.[62] The result was a continuous borrowing from the sinking fund for the operational fund (begun with the purchase of the building)[63] and the reduction of liquid assets from over $50,000 in 1880 to a level of from about $20,000 to $28,500 until the fortuitous bequests of 1894 again brought assets up to the point they had reached fourteen years earlier.

For the Hebrew Union College, the financial situation of the Union meant persistent pressure to cut corners: to make do with senior students as teachers since new regular faculty could not be appointed, to turn down students who would otherwise have been admitted to the school because no stipendiary aid was available. During the first decade, as the school grew from a single class to a full eight-year institution, the College's budget increased rapidly. Beginning with an allocation of about $3,000 in 1875–76, it advanced to about $16,000 in 1885–86. But from there it proceeded to fluctuate according to the funds the Union could provide at any particular time. A sizable portion, an average of about $5,000 per annum, was always devoted to student support.[64] In Wise's final year, 1899–1900, the budget stood at $22,000.

Immediate control over the affairs of the College rested in the hands of the Board of Governors chosen by the Union. It was this body which elected Wise and was further charged with yearly reelecting or dismissing him, along with the rest of the faculty. Through its committees and as a whole it admitted (and at times examined) entering students, provided for their material needs, disciplined them, and if necessary suspended or dismissed them. Although the board was to be broadly representative, at the beginning eight of its twelve members were from Cincinnati, and even after the total membership was raised to twenty-four in 1878, at first nine, and later twelve, members continued to be from the home city. Moreover, it was the Cincinnati members of the board, meeting monthly throughout the year, who made all the significant decisions for the school. Members from other cities were rarely present at the sessions; all committee chairmen were from Cincinnati as, of course, were the officers. The men who ran the College—and the Union—were the same men who played leading roles in congregations Bene Yeshurun and Bene Israel. As one of the first students recalled, in those years "the H.U.C. was to all intents and purposes the ward of the two large Cincinnati Reform Congregations. . . ."[65]

A word must be said here on what the College meant to these immensely dedicated Cincinnati Jewish businessmen who so directly ran the institution. Like Wise, they were of course concerned with providing a native American Jewish religious leadership. But to their minds, they were doing more than that: they were also taking underprivileged boys and providing them with a secure future to which they could not otherwise aspire. In 1881, the president of the Board of Governors described the indigent students' fund as "that grand charity . . . , which in the past years has enabled us to take from the orphan asylums some of their brightest inmates and give them and other deserving young men of our faith, that great boon—a first-class religious and secular education." [66] Because they devoted both their time and substance to the cause, they thought it only proper that they should receive a measure of gratitude and deference on the part of the students. If students did not respond in the proper spirit, as sometimes happened, they were considered unworthy of receiving the institution's benefits.[67] When on one occasion a young man dared in chapel to interpret the text *he-ashir lo yarbe* ("The rich shall not give more": Exod. 30:15) to mean that the rich were too exclusively favored with prerogatives, the vice-president of the board, who was present, took offense and created such a stir that an article on the altercation—apparently supplied by a student informant—appeared in a Cincinnati newspaper two days later.[68]

Until Wise's death and for a decade thereafter, the president of the Board of Governors was Bernhard Bettmann, a prominent Cincinnati clothier. Born in a small town in Bavaria, he settled in Cincinnati in 1850, joined Congregation Bene Yeshurun, and had already played an active role in Wise's Zion College of 1855. A life-long Republican, he was active in both local and national politics and served for a time on the Cincinnati School Board and as collector of Internal Revenue for the First District of Ohio. He was also the first president of the United Jewish Charities of Cincinnati, a pioneer of such organizations in the United States. To his work for the College Bettmann brought vigor, executive ability, a modicum of Jewish knowledge, and some literary talent.[69] Serving for thirty-five years in his position, it is understandable that, once accustomed to a particular manner of doing things, he was resistant to the introduction of changes and may have resented any challenges to his authority.[70] But he was very much devoted to Wise and liked to think of himself simply as "the Hur who upholds the hands of Moses."

The vice-president of the Board of Governors from 1875 until his death in 1905 was Julius Freiberg, an immigrant from the Rhineland who arrived in Cincinnati in 1847. His flourishing distilling business soon made him one of the wealthiest Jews in the city. Unlike Bettmann, he was a member of the Bene Israel congregation, which he served as president at various times. He, too, was active in a variety of other Jewish and nonsectarian causes.[71] Freiberg took his religion quite seriously, so much so that even skeptics were convinced of his earnestness.[72] In his later years he seems to have attended the HUC chapel with great regularity. A religious conservative, he resisted liturgical changes, especially any reduction in the amount of Hebrew used in the worship service.[73]

Wise's position vis-à-vis the Board of Governors was considerably weaker than that of some of his successors. Though corresponding to the fashion of the day, the formula Wise used in signing his reports—"your most obedient servant"—was not entirely meaningless. Officially, Wise was merely president of the faculty, and as such he was directly responsible in all matters to the Board of Governors and to its president. As he was not paid for his duties (although the Union bought him a house in honor of his seventieth birthday), he could feel less beholden to the board than would otherwise have been the case. But when it came to disagreements, it was Wise who was forced to back down (or at least to beat a strategic retreat).

The differences of opinion which arose from time to time almost always had to do with finances. Wise wanted to build the school as rapidly as possible. He was eager to hire faculty and sarcastically reproached the board when it was unable to provide the funds. Desirous of building as large a student body as possible, he was both far more ready than the Board of Governors to admit questionable students and far more reluctant to expel academic and disciplinary offenders. When insufficient funds were available for all the indigent students who wanted to enter, Wise would sometimes support them himself out of his $50-per-month presidential allowance. But ultimately the board insisted upon its right to accept or reject indigent students according to its own judgment, and Wise had no choice but to submit.[74]

The general picture one derives with regard to the administration of the College in its first quarter century is that of a small group of Cincinnati laymen running its affairs in all matters except those specifically academic, and of a College president, himself a teacher, carrying on the day-to-day functions and presiding over the faculty. Of subordinate administrators or even regular secretarial assistance there is no evidence. Wise handled the College correspondence alone. Only later was he assisted by two other members of the faculty who, in addition to their regular duties, served as secretary and registrar respectively.

In view of the rigors of the curriculum, it is not surprising that a great many of the early students did not complete the course of studies. Some were eliminated when they failed to pass their examinations in the high school or university, others were dismissed for academic weakness at the College or for breach of College discipline. Still others left of their own free will to seek careers in more lucrative occupations; according to Julius Freiberg's pun, they preferred "the study of *Mono Revokhim* (a share of profits) to *More Nevokhim* [sic] (of Maimonides)."[75] Of the dozen or so regular students in the first class of the school, seven made it to graduation from the Preparatory Department, celebrated for the first time in 1879. They received the degree of Bachelor of Hebrew Literature (later: Letters) with the Hebrew title: *ḥaver le-atzile bene yisrael.*[76]

Fewer students persevered all the way to ordination. Of the original class, only four were ordained at the first such exercises, held on July 11, 1883. Yet though the number of graduates was small, their ordination—far more than the opening ceremonies eight years earlier—was an occasion for genuine rejoicing. It was the first time in the history of American Jewry that such an event had taken place. Once again the Plum Street Temple was filled to capacity and ablaze with lights; once again there was resounding music and festive oratory. Among the guests gathered within the richly ornamented shrine were representatives from seventy-six congregations, concurrently celebrating the tenth anniversary of the Union. Wise, who had taught the graduates personally for eight years and knew each of them intimately, pressed the "kiss of ordination" upon every forehead, gave each one his blessing, and proclaimed: "In the name of God and by the authority of the Governors and of the Union of American Hebrew Congregations, and in the name of all good men, I declare you to be rabbis of the Jewish faith, that you may preach the Word of God to the people, that you may be patriots in America and standard-bearers of the people." Each graduate received a *semikhat hora'a* in Hebrew and English bestowing upon him the privileges of rabbi and teacher. According to one observer, many were the tears of joy that were shed and more than one of the rabbis present was heard to exclaim: *ashre ayin ra'ata kol ele*—"Happy the eye that saw all these things!" [77]

Yet this splendid occasion, like the earlier Opening Exercises, screened a problematic situation which could not long remain unnoticed. In 1875 the festive exercises of inauguration had veiled the humble circumstances—so clearly apparent the next day—under which the school began; in 1883 the even more joyous and solemn ceremony of the first ordination—in which the conservative Rabbi Benjamin Szold of Baltimore gave the opening address and in which the New York Reform rabbis Gustav Gottheil and Kaufmann Kohler both gave speeches—concealed the opposition to the College which had manifested itself not long before and which was about to emerge decisively once again. If the counterpart to the Opening Exercises was the next day's scene in the basement of the Mound Street Temple, the complement to the first ordination was the spectacle that met the eye within three hours after the final benediction— at a grand dinner to celebrate the occasion, the so-called Trefa Banquet.

Wise had tried to make his school a rabbinical seminary for all of American Jewry. The achievement of this goal required that he win over to the Union and College both the conservative and the radical religious leadership despite the profound differences which separated them. Although the unity displayed by the program of that first ordination ceremony must have made it seem to him that he had attained his aim, the process had been a difficult one and the success proved only momentary.

From the time that Wise came to America, he had cultivated relations with Isaac Leeser, the Philadelphia Jewish leader of conservative bent in whose *Occident* he had published most of his first essays. Leeser participated in the Cleveland Conference which Wise called in 1855 and was impressed by Wise's willingness to uphold the authority of the Rabbinic tradition. Though in his prayerbook, *Minhag America,* Wise displayed his opposition to the traditional hopes for rebuilding the Temple, reinstituting the animal sacrifices, and restoring the Davidic dynasty, his relations with the moderate elements in the conservative "Historical School" remained sufficiently cordial for him to enlist their support for the Union and the College. Thus Rabbis Sabato Morais of Philadelphia, Frederick de Sola Mendes of New York, and Benjamin Szold of Baltimore participated in Union councils and served as examiners for the College, as did the conservative layman Lewis Dembitz of Louisville, Kentucky, who was also a member of the Union's Executive Board. Mendes for a time even served on the College's Board of Governors.[78] By the year of the first ordination, the UAHC had on its rolls a number of major congregations which were quite traditional in character, including those led by Szold in Baltimore, Marcus Jastrow in Philadelphia, and by Mendes and Aaron Wise in New York. Morais' congregation in Philadelphia had not joined on constitutional grounds, but it was in sympathy with the Union's objectives.

Though not consistent in the matter, Wise had on occasion tried to avoid the label "reform," once preferring to call himself "a historical Jew" and another time assuring a questioner that he considered himself orthodox.[79] He was certain at first that he needed the support of the moderates in order for the Union and College to succeed, and he acted accordingly. But he was convinced as well of the importance of enlisting the active cooperation of those who stood to his left on the religious spectrum—the radical reformers of the East.

Wise's dispute with Rabbis David Einhorn, Samuel Hirsch, Samuel Adler, and the others who shared their inclination to uncompromising religious change and adaptation was of long standing by the time the College was opened. His feud with Einhorn went back to the Cleveland Conference of 1855, which this staunch radical had mercilessly attacked for its failure to abrogate the authority of the Talmud. To give form to their own conception of Judaism, Einhorn and Adler called a rabbinical conference to Philadelphia in 1869, where a set of principles was adopted declaring the universal mission of Judaism and rejecting what were regarded as archaic or needlessly particularistic elements. Though Wise, who was also present, expressed agreement with the spirit of the declaration, it was basically Einhorn's creation and Wise afterwards began to take issue with some of the formulations in his newspaper. The Philadelphia

Conference did not offer a milieu in which Wise could easily assert himself. The eastern reformers possessed the formal training in classics and European philosophy which Wise lacked; they also shared a devotion to German culture which made them question Wise's program of rapid and complete Americanization of Jewish religious life. Wise, in turn, claimed that they remained foreigners to the American scene and hence could not serve as leaders for American Jewry—certainly not for the next generation. "These gentlemen," he wrote of them, are "unfit for the American pulpit." [80]

If one also considers the sectional rivalry that had emerged between East and West, apparently among laity no less than among rabbis, it is easy to understand why the original call to form the UAHC did not go out to congregations in the East. Initially it was thought that a college in Cincinnati, presided over by Wise, could attract support only from the surrounding region. But once the Union was established, the desire arose to stretch its influence as far as the Atlantic, and overtures were made to congregations east of the Alleghenies. The Western leaders even expressed their willingness to make certain concessions in the constitutional structure of the Union in order to give the Eastern congregations a share in making decisions. The ingathering of the Easterners occurred in 1878 at the Fifth Union Council, held in Milwaukee, and in the period immediately thereafter. Nineteen representatives from Temple Emanu-El of New York were present on that occasion along with their rabbi, Gustav Gottheil; Einhorn's congregation, Beth El of New York, was also represented.

Little more than a year earlier, in February 1877, the Eastern reformers had begun their own rabbinical school in New York City with some thirty pupils at various levels. Gustav Gottheil was its superintendent; the expenses were paid by the already existing Emanu-El Theological Association and by Temple Emanu-El itself. The Union leadership initially looked askance at this rival school and refused even to wish it well.[81] But the sentiment in favor of unity emerging on both sides during the following months led to a decision at the Milwaukee Conference to adopt the New York institution as a preparatory school for the HUC. The Union paid about half of its budget. It existed for a number of years until a decrease in the size of the student body and lack of local support led to the school's termination in 1885. Only a handful of its very few graduates went on to the College in Cincinnati.

Thus by 1883 the major radical reform congregations had joined the Union and the drive for a separate rabbinical institution in the East had been successfully neutralized. Moreover, the presence of the radicals had not yet driven out conservative congregations which were already members of the Union or deterred new ones from joining thereafter. With the exception of the rigidly orthodox, all major Jewish congregations stood in support of the College at the time of its first ordination.

At half past seven in the evening of that same day of ordination, some two hundred of the distinguished guests gathered in Cincinnati's famed Highland House for a lavish banquet to celebrate the occasion. But no sooner had the invocation been spoken and the waiters begun to serve the food, when a commotion stirred the banquet hall. Two rabbis arose from their seats and left the room; three other guests indignantly refused to partake in the meal. Littleneck clams on the half shell had been placed before them as the first course of the elaborate menu; crabs, shrimp, and frogs were to follow. The arrangements had been handled by a committee of Cincinnati laymen who hired a caterer and also paid the entire cost of the dinner. Wise himself had not been party to this breach of *kashrut*. Indeed, it was politically so preposterous a faux pas that he would never have allowed it to happen. But that it could have occurred at all simply brought into focus what the afternoon's ceremonies had so deftly obscured: the supporters of the College represented such a wide spectrum of attitudes to Jewish tradition that the alliance forged over the previous few years was unlikely to remain long intact.

The influence of the Trefa Banquet upon the events which followed must not be exaggerated.[82] Had the food served that evening been in strict accordance with Jewish dietary regulations, the forces already at work to bring about a split would not have been halted in their course. The Russian pogroms of 1881 had unleashed a flood of

Jewish immigration to the United States from Eastern Europe. These newcomers, whose numbers were to swell vastly in succeeding decades, did not share in the heritage of German Reform nor did they define Judaism in universalistic religious terms. The conservatives thus found themselves with a new constituency which, except for its politically radical elements, espoused a more traditional Judaism than that of most of the Union's congregations. At the same time, the presence of the immigrants drove the reformers to define their own position even more sharply.[83] In 1885 Kaufmann Kohler of New York convened a rabbinical conference at Pittsburgh which adopted a truly radical platform: a "declaration of independence" from traditional concepts and practices. Wise was put into a position where he had to cast his lot either with the reformers or with the conservatives. By participating in the Pittsburgh Conference, presiding over its deliberations, and enthusiastically approving its platform he signaled clearly that he had chosen sides.

Even before the Pittsburgh Conference, Wise's direction had become apparent. In the wake of the Trefa Banquet he had allowed himself to be drawn into a discussion of *kashrut* wherein he abused those who disagreed with him and left no doubt that he regarded the dietary laws as of little spiritual significance. Personally, he refrained from pork, apparently on sanitary grounds, and in his home he excluded all seafood except oysters—which he thought Moses had not prohibited. But as the dietary regulations were not part of the Law of the Covenant he did not consider them obligatory; they were only "purely national laws for Israel, local and temporary. . . ." Moreover, adherence to them in the present often produced a fanaticism which he regarded as destructive of genuine religion.[84]

As it thus became apparent following the first ordination that both in practice and in theology Wise had cast his lot with the reformers, the conservative elements in the Union began to withdraw their support. One after another the more traditional congregations left the UAHC and their leaders turned their efforts to the establishment of a new seminary, more in line with their own interpretation of Judaism. In 1887, some of the same men who had been active in support of the Hebrew Union College were among the founders of the Jewish Theological Seminary in New York. They now argued that the College could not expect conservative Jewish congregations to support an institution headed by a man who had shown himself to be a radical. They would scarcely any longer accept the response that the president and faculty taught only from the sources and expounded only the views of the ancient rabbis, "reserving their own opinions and keeping the minds of the students free from bias and untrammeled from the various dogmas now extant."[85] Wise had shown his colors; there could be no turning back the course of events which followed. The College, originally intended as a seminary for the entire American rabbinate, became an institution for the Reform movement alone.

The departure of the conservatives did not, however, prevent the progress and development of the College. In the late eighties and in the nineties the faculty was expanded and improved, enrollment grew, and increasingly graduates of the College came to occupy important pulpits around the land. By 1889, Wise and his disciples were able to organize the College alumni, along with similarly minded colleagues, into the Central Conference of American Rabbis, thus completing the triad of organizations Wise had called into being.

Some of the graduates, who continued with their studies while in the field, earned Doctor of Divinity degrees from the College.[86] Their achievement entitled them to a listing in the catalogue as corresponding members of the faculty. The same degree was also bestowed *honoris causa* on leading Jewish scholars in Europe, such as Moritz Lazarus, David Woolf Marks, and Moritz Steinschneider, as well as on a few American Jewish leaders, including Benjamin Szold.[87]

It was during these latter years of the College's first quarter century that two issues came to the fore which split president, faculty, and student body. The first was theological, the second a question of the Jewish people.

Though in some respects Wise was a theological radical, in others he was adamantly conservative. He was a thoroughgoing rationalist and universalist in religion who rejected whatever elements of "tribal religion" he found in Judaism; he disbelieved in such doctrines as the resurrection of the body, and in his theological writings even cast doubt on whether God could properly be called personal.[88] But he possessed an unshakable faith in biblical revelation as the message of God by the hand of Moses. "Judaism is inviolable as a revelation," he wrote; "it is Mosaic and Sinaitic, or it is nothing."[89] Therefore Wise rejected the Higher Criticism of the Bible, which sought to show that the Pentateuch was made up of various independent sources and was not the work of Moses. When the curriculum for the Collegiate Department was first formulated in 1878, Wise had opposed the wish of other commission members to include critical study of the biblical text as one of the subjects to be taught, and as a later report of outside examiners shows, Wise got his way.[90] No textual emendations of the Torah were permitted at the College during his lifetime. When, on one occasion, he visited a classroom where the professor was expounding Wellhausenian biblical criticism, he was so overcome with anger that he pounded the table with his fist and exclaimed: "I will not have this taught in this college. Moses was the author of the Torah. That is one of the fundamentals on which we build."[91] For Wise all of Judaism depended on the authenticity of the Torah. If the Pentateuch were a late creation, "a patchwork stitched together by deceitful priests," then, in Wise's view, there would be no basis to believe in a God who was merciful, just, loving, and true.[92] In 1891, he published his *Pronaos to Holy Writ* in order to establish the authenticity of the Pentateuch, and he thereafter used it as a textbook in one of his courses. But though Wise tried to exclude from the halls of HUC what he regarded as the "excrescences of the age," increasing numbers of both faculty and students found themselves unable to share his view.[93] The resulting conflict was the cause of much bitterness during Wise's last years.[94]

The second major issue to occupy the College community toward the end of Wise's administration was the question of Zionism. The First Zionist Congress, held in Basle in 1897, had forced the American Reform movement to take a stand on Jewish nationalism without delay. At the CCAR meeting that same summer, the assembled rabbis unanimously declared that the establishment of a Jewish state represented a misunderstanding of Israel's mission; a year later the UAHC added its voice by announcing that "America is our Zion."[95] For a time it was Wise's own opinion that the Holy Land could perhaps play a significant role as a refuge for the persecuted Jews of Eastern Europe. But he argued as well that no one could believe Jews would leave "the great nations of culture, power and abundant prosperity . . . to form a ridiculous miniature state in dried up Palestine."[96] It was impossible for him to declare that America was Exile and thus he could never be a Political Zionist. He even made some effort to exclude Zionism from the College: shortly before his death he refused use of the chapel to an outside speaker who desired to discourse on the subject, an action readily concurred in by the Board of Governors.[97]

Unlike biblical criticism, Zionism was an issue on which most faculty and students agreed with Wise. Only one member of the teaching staff, Caspar Levias, publicly defended it, and his essay was more a refutation of anti-Zionism than a fervent advocacy.[98] Gotthard Deutsch (history), Louis Grossmann (ethics), and David Philipson (homiletics) actively gave vent to their opposition. As the students themselves admitted: "The entire trend of our work at College is such as to lead us away from [Zionism]."[99]

Nevertheless, there was a considerable minority among the students who were actively pro-Zionist, and in the last two years of the century some of their number gained sufficient influence on the editorial board of the *HUC Journal* to express their point of view forcefully in the magazine's pages. The first such statement came from the pen of a man who was later to be known as one of the severest critics of Political Zionism: William H. Fineshriber. In the December 1898 issue he wrote: "We do not regard Washington with the same emotions with which we think of Jerusalem; the historical associations are lacking; the much-despised but necessary poetry is not there." After commenting on the prevalence of racial antisemitism in the United States, he concluded: "Germany is for and of the Germans; France is for and of the French; why not a Judea for and of the Jews?"[100] The following year the *Journal* published synopses of articles by the Zionist leaders Max Nordau and Israel Zangwill; it devoted an entire issue to a symposium on Zionism, including contributions from both sides, but featuring a student editorial distinctly favorable to the movement. At Wise's death, Zionism was assuredly not the philosophy of the College, but it had won over a portion of the student body which—at least in the pages of its *Journal*—was freely advocating the Zionist cause.

As the College completed the first quarter century of its existence, its financial condition was not yet secure. In the last years of Wise's administration, a persistent demand by the University of Cincinnati that HUC students pay tuition precipitated a protracted, acrimonious dispute and threatened to ruin the College.[101] The UAHC, which had scarcely grown in total individual membership over the last few years, still had fewer congregations than in 1879, and the College budget had to be kept at the lowest possible level. Wise could not be replaced even had he desired it, as there were no funds to engage a salaried president.

Still, there was also a mood of deep satisfaction pervading the College, a result of the genuine accomplishments of twenty-five years. Altogether nearly half a million dollars had been raised by the Union, seventy-five rabbis had been ordained, and two young women had received Bachelor of Hebrew Letters degrees. A much larger number of students had received some amount of Jewish education at the school, and the student body had reached the respectable size of seventy-three. The faculty of ten and the rich library were second to none; the alumni of the College had easily been placed in congregations, and a number of them had attained prominent positions.

In great measure this success had been due to the amazing persistence, dogged determination, and self-assured vision of Isaac Mayer Wise. In the years that he served as president, his character had not changed. There was definitely an unpleasant side to his personality, which even his disciple and admirer David Philipson privately called "envious and jealous," adding: "He can not endure that any one shall stand near him; independent in thought and action, he must rule. . . ."[102] In his old age Wise was still pushing aside those who stood in his way, the dwarfs of the shipboard dream. But he was also approaching the "beautiful and glorious landscape"—which, had he been a different kind of man, might never have come into view.

Certainly his dedication to the vision and to its realization was almost inhumanly total.[103] Moreover, to those who shared his opinions, to his disciples who had graduated from the College and to those still within it, Wise was beloved as their teacher and guide.[104] They owed him very much.

On Saturday, March 24, 1900, Wise was lecturing as usual to his afternoon class at the College; even at the age of eighty, he had not relinquished his duties. At the end of the hour the aged leader collapsed from a severe stroke and died two days later. His death, coming, as Wise had hoped, while "in harness," threw the College into a situation of vacillation and decline from which it did not speedily recover.

A THEOLOGICAL SCHOOL FOR REFORM JUDAISM

Research and reverence must ever
go hand in hand—KAUFMANN
KOHLER in the *HUC Monthly*

T HE FOUNDER OF THE
Hebrew Union College had scarcely been laid to his eternal rest when
the future of his institution became a subject of general debate.
Various possibilities were proposed, not alone within the circles of the
College but by members of the American Jewish community at large.
Three basic questions needed decision: Should the College remain in
Cincinnati? Should it be merged with a university or possibly combined
with the Jewish Theological Seminary? And finally, who should suc-
ceed Isaac Mayer Wise? [1]

In 1900 there was by no means general agreement that the Queen
City was still the best site for a rabbinical seminary. There was now
considerable sentiment that the time had come to establish more direct
contact with the most advanced thinking in the humanities by bringing the College into relationship with one of America's leading uni-

versities. The chief proponent of this viewpoint was Rabbi Emil G. Hirsch of Chicago, one of the dominant figures in the American Reform movement after the death of Wise. Hirsch had been trained at the *Hochschule* in Berlin, an institution as intensely devoted to *Wissenschaft des Judentums* and the education of scholars as to the practical training of rabbis. Like the other German seminaries, the *Hochschule* expected its graduates to earn a university Ph.D. in addition to their ordination. In the pages of his influential *Reform Advocate*,[2] Hirsch argued that the interests of Jewish scholarship, more than those of the pulpit, had to predominate in the reorganization of the College. Following his own teacher, Abraham Geiger,[3] Hirsch therefore drew the conclusion that the HUC could hope to do its proper work only in conjunction with a "genuine university"—and to his mind, the University of Cincinnati ranked hardly above a European high school. Because the graduates of the College had not had the opportunity to avail themselves of advanced training in philosophy and other secular disciplines, they were incapable of dealing with the major intellectual challenges of the age. Hirsch also noted that a number of Christian seminaries had recently sought to achieve closer relations with the larger universities and had made the bachelor's degree a prerequisite for admission to theological studies.

Hirsch was not alone in this point of view. It was actively propagated as well by Rabbi Jacob Voorsanger of San Francisco and concurred in by a number of Jewish journals.[4] Yet it does not seem to have been the sentiment of most alumni, and certainly not of the Cincinnati members of the Board of Governors. As against Hirsch's conception of the rabbi as scholar and intellectual, there were others who held the conviction that what Wise had wanted, and what the school should continue to produce, was not a ministry of scholars but—in the words of Rabbi Max Heller, a leading alumnus—"first of all, sensible, practical, American men, who would understand the people. . . ."[5] Admitting his prejudice in favor of Cincinnati, Heller defended its university as possessing a number of highly capable scholars and concluded that the College should be left in the hands of the Jews of Cincinnati for whom it "has always been a source of noble pride. . . ."

The second serious proposal set forth in the spring of 1900 was for a merger of the Hebrew Union College with the Jewish Theological Seminary. In May and June of 1900, the *American Hebrew* of New York City featured a symposium on the question of whether such a union would be desirable and feasible. The letter which the paper circulated to invited participants stressed the financial plight of both institutions and urged that the possibility of their union receive serious consideration. The fifteen replies received from individuals associated with both schools as well as from other community leaders ranged from enthusiastic affirmation to out-of-hand rejection. The most weighty opinions on the affirmative side came from two leading Reform Jews of New York who had taken an interest in the Jewish Theological Seminary while supporting Reform institutions as well: the financier Jacob H. Schiff and the lawyer Louis Marshall. Schiff wanted HUC moved to New York because the metropolis possessed an academic atmosphere lacking in Cincinnati and in addition could more easily provide the financial resources necessary for its support. Of men directly associated with the College, only one expressed a similarly affirmative position, Professor Gotthard Deutsch. Startlingly he argued that "there are no fundamental differences between the various sections of Judaism in this country." No one directly associated with the Seminary considered the hiatus so narrow.

Opposition to the suggestion came from both sides. Bernard Drachman of the JTS faculty stressed the lack of unity regarding even essentials, while Henry Morais, the son of one of the Seminary's founders, in an unsolicited response,[6] expressed his opinion that such a union "would be destructive of the very purposes for which the Jewish Theological Seminary was planted." Julius Freiberg, president of the UAHC, was no less derisive of the proposal: yes, a merger could be considered, he responded icily, if the proposal were made by a properly accredited delegate to a biennial council of the Union.

All suggestions for removing the College from Cincinnati were summarily rejected by its local lay leadership. In fact, the recorded minutes of the HUC Board of Governors and the *UAHC Proceedings* make no reference to these matters whatever. Both College and Union were firmly in the hands of Cincinnati Jews determined to maintain

Wise's seminary in their own city and to perpetuate it as a distinctly Reform institution. The only question they thought necessary to consider seriously was finding a qualified successor to its founder.

The urgent need of filling Wise's position was solved temporarily by the appointment of Moses Mielziner, the professor of Talmud, as president pro tem. Mielziner, then over seventy years of age and the senior member of the faculty, was an obvious choice in view of the intent to keep the College running on its old tracks until the decision on a permanent successor could be reached. For nearly three years this universally beloved, meek, and modest man tried to keep the school going as best he could. But it was not within his powers to overcome the prevalent atmosphere of uncertainty and interregnum. The number of students decreased steadily each year; by 1903 there were only thirty-six, less than half as many as five years earlier. Moreover, Mielziner was not a well man. Already in the fall of 1901 he became ill and was able to attend to his duties only three days out of the week; soon his condition worsened, and on February 18, 1903, he died. Gotthard Deutsch was immediately selected to take his place until the end of the academic year, and the following day a permanent successor was finally chosen to take office in the fall.

Before the Board of Governors reached the stage of selecting any specific candidate, it had thought it necessary first to consider a question of principle: Should the new president be primarily a scholar whose prestige would gain respect for the College, or should he rather be a practical man who could assure its financial support? After finding that the English scholar Israel Abrahams was not interested in the position,[7] the board's selection committee determined to pick a man of the second type. Late in 1902, it turned to J. Leonard Levy[8] of Pittsburgh, a most successful rabbi, a powerful orator, and an efficient man of affairs. Only when Levy proved unwilling to give up his new position at Rodef Shalom Congregation[9] did the committee turn to Kaufmann Kohler of New York. They offered him a salary of $6,000 and in February 1903 brought the rabbi of Temple Beth El to Cincinnati for an interview with the local members of the board. While he waited outside, they voted unanimously for his appointment.

Kohler was in various respects a highly desirable candidate. Most significantly, he was a man who had an outstanding reputation as a theologian, a preacher, and a scholar—each deemed important in the head of a seminary. While Wise had not himself been a systematic Jewish thinker, he had given theological direction to the school and had personally taught the courses in theology. Kohler, then editor of the department of philosophy and theology of the *Jewish Encyclopedia,* was the foremost expositor of Jewish thought in the ranks of American Reform. More than anyone else, he would be able to set a definite theological course for the College. Moreover, as an accomplished preacher (despite his heavy German accent), he could provide a model of pulpit style for the students. Finally, being a scholar of considerable note in the Bible and Apocrypha, Kohler could bring the scientific study of Judaism to Cincinnati, thus to some extent at least satisfying rabbis like Emil G. Hirsch—his brother-in-law—who desired HUC to become a more scholarly institution.

There were, however, other reasons as well for the choice of Kohler. Already before Wise's death the UAHC had embarked on a campaign to raise $500,000 as an endowment for the College. In the spring of 1900 this effort became associated with perpetuating the memory of the founder, and the "Isaac Mayer Wise Memorial Fund" came into being. It was hoped that the great tide of appreciation for Wise's accomplishments that swept the country after his death could be utilized to bring in the half million dollars quickly. But by 1903 no more than $150,000 had been gathered.[10] In selecting Kohler, the board hoped that through his connections with wealthy Jews in New York the new president would be able to raise a large portion of the amount still unattained. In fact, there was even some thought given to linking his salary to the success he achieved as a fund-raiser.[11]

Finally, the selection of Kohler was also influenced by the course of events at the Jewish Theological Seminary. In 1902 the Seminary had been reorganized with a Board of Directors that included leading members of the Reform community, notably Jacob H. Schiff[12] and Louis Marshall. By the end of that year, its leaders had secured an endowment fund in the amount of half a million dollars and had called the outstanding scholar Solomon Schechter from England to be its new president. Unable to bring HUC into merger with JTS in

New York, Schiff and Marshall had made the decision to devote their efforts primarily to the Conservative seminary. The Cincinnati leadership found itself in an unprecedentedly competitive situation, and in choosing Kohler had its revived rival very much in mind.[13] Not only did the new state of affairs make imperative the selection of a leading scholar—to match Schechter—it also lent weight to the choice of someone from New York, who was known in that community, but whose progressive outlook would clearly differentiate the College from the Seminary. Kohler, as a radical reformer, was ideally suited to stress the distinction.

Kaufmann Kohler had spent his childhood in an atmosphere of orthodoxy. Born in the Bavarian town of Fürth in 1843, he grew up in a circle of family and friends committed to strict observance of Jewish law and fearful of the consequences of advanced secular education. As a young man he went to study Talmud with the better-known traditional scholars of Germany: in Altona with Jacob Ettlinger at his well-known yeshiva and in Frankfurt with Samson Raphael Hirsch, the leading figure of Jewish Neo-Orthodoxy. But he also made the fateful decision to study at German universities, and there his orthodoxy was speedily shattered. As he recalled it much later, the inner conflict was nothing less than traumatic: "I passed days and weeks of indescribable woe and despondency; the heavens seemed to fall down upon me and crush me. . . ."[14] But painful as it was, there could be no turning back. The exposure to scientific method had cut away the roots of his faith in traditional Judaism; the doctoral dissertation he wrote on "The Blessing of Jacob" embodied biblical criticism's most novel principles. He came under the influence of Abraham Geiger, whom he had studiously avoided while still a pupil of Hirsch. By adopting Geiger's historical, evolutionary understanding of Jewish tradition he was able to salvage his faith. But the sudden disillusion with orthodoxy left a deep and permanent imprint on Kohler's personality, and even in the later years of his life, when he assumed the presidency of the College, it was still in evidence. Because his break with the ambience of his childhood had been purchased at so great a psychological price, he could not help but stress the specific differentiae of Reform and resist vigorously any backsliding in the direction of tradition by either faculty or students.

Highly recommended by Geiger, Kohler began a successful rabbinical career in the United States, first in Detroit from 1869 to 1871, then at Temple Sinai in Chicago, and finally for twenty-four years at Temple Beth El in New York City. Married to a daughter of David Einhorn, he carried on the rationalist Reform tradition of his father-in-law. By the time he was invited to assume the presidency of the College, Kohler was already sixty years old. His very age, however, made him more generally acceptable than a younger man of more questionable status.[15]

Though he was a scholar of considerable scope, during the years of his presidency at the College Kohler devoted himself especially to the area of Jewish thought, publishing, first in German and then in English, his best-known work: *Jewish Theology Systematically and Historically Considered.* His thought was not very original. In every major respect it was a continuation of the concepts first formulated by Abraham Geiger, Samuel Holdheim, and others in Germany and brought to these shores by David Einhorn. Its foundation was faith in the universal God of prophetic Judaism, who is known through a progressive process of revelation directed at the mental and moral faculties of men. By His providence, God guides all human destiny and gives assurance of ultimate redemption. But to Israel God assigned a special task: He chose it as His people and imposed upon it the historic mission to bear the lofty truths of religion to mankind. Its customs and practices are not properly to be regarded as commandments of God, but rather purely as means to the end of religious exaltation and the investment of life with holiness. Unless they serve a moral and religious purpose they are best discarded and supplanted by new forms of practice and observance. Only a Judaism which is flexible in its structure of beliefs and practices and open to the influences of the modern world will, according to Kohler, be able to persevere and thus bring its message to mankind. His writings and sermons consistently exuded confidence in the pace of moral progress, in the continuing achievements of the human mind, and in the ability of Reform Judaism—for him the only true Judaism—to draw closer the messianic future.

Kohler had little patience with contradictory ideas of Judaism, and when he became president of the College he set out to exclude their advocacy from its halls. The symbols of traditionalism—head covering and prayer shawl at worship services, for example—were strictly forbidden in the chapel; the understanding of Judaism as involving observance of ritual commandments was banished from the classrooms. "Not by Romanticism and Ritualism or Legalism," he declared in his address to the rabbinic graduates of 1914, "but by the accentuation of the eternal principles of our prophetic truths can our faith be revitalized." [16] No less forbidden was any form of Jewish nationalism which challenged the notion that Israel's future lay in its religious mission as a people scattered among the nations, especially when—as in the case of certain Zionist leaders—nationalism was combined with atheism. In fact, Kohler felt a great deal more honor and respect for a traditional Jew like Solomon Schechter whose Zionism, Kohler argued, was aimed at unfolding the religious soul of the Jew,[17] than for secularists who regarded the Jewish religion as an inessential and outmoded expression of cultural nationality.

Kohler did not believe that the Hebrew Union College was like a university which must allow every point of view a fair hearing. He did grant in principle that freedom of thought and independence of research were important, but scholarship, to his mind, was not the college's primary aim. Rather, the goal was indoctrination in Reform Judaism. He inserted the following paragraph into the catalogue for 1906:

> A rabbinical school, however progressive its tendency, must necessarily have a positive Jewish character. It fails of its purpose if it treats Judaism, with all of its treasures of literature and history, as a matter of the past only, and not as an ever-living and ever-progressive truth to guide and to inspire generations to come. There must be unity and harmony in the system of instruction, and the various branches of study must be so interrelated as to lead to, and culminate in, the inculcation of the doc-

trines of Judaism as a living faith and as the life-mission of the Jew.

He saw it as the duty of president and faculty to mold the character and outlook of the rabbinical students who came to the College, preferring young men who were "pliable" [18] to those with views already formed. Above all, he was concerned to create a religious atmosphere at the College, for Kohler in his later years, despite his disregard of ceremony, his affirmation of radical criticism, and his rationalist theology, was basically a deeply religious man of untroubled faith, and he desired that every aspect of College life reflect a similar commitment.

Immediately upon taking over his duties in the fall of 1903, the new president proclaimed his wish that "the attitude of professors and the conduct of the students should be thoroughly religious, manifested by regular attendance at divine service as well as in the religious spirit which is to prevail in the studies and the teaching. The whole atmosphere should be a religious one and the daily lessons begun with religious exercises." [19]

During the first months of his administration, Kohler instituted a daily worship service in the College chapel and somewhat later a Friday evening *Kabbalat Shabbat* in addition to the existing service on Saturday afternoon. A resolution of the Board of Governors, later incorporated into the catalogue, made it explicit that both faculty and students were required regularly to attend all services. When most of the professors protested the board's decision as interference in their private religious lives, they were informed that their presence was required in order thereby to "set a proper example to the students." [20] Kohler also introduced the consecration service on the day preceding ordination. When this ceremony was first held, in 1904, each graduate gave a five-minute address of personal consecration to his life's task, speaking in the College chapel to relatives, close friends, faculty, and members of the College board.[21]

Even more than in Wise's time, the College chapel now came to be the focus of the institution. Here the president would frequently comment to faculty and student body on particular issues of general Jewish concern or of consequence to the life of the College. More than the classrooms, the chapel represented a direct expression of Reform Judaism, appearing in its two most prominent forms: prayer and the sermon. Both had to be so regulated as to present a model of Reform Judaism in its single legitimate variety. Kohler believed, for example, that it was proper to bow physically while reciting the Adoration, and one Saturday afternoon, following the service, he made an address to the students urging them to do so.[22] So, too, Kohler would allow only those student sermons which he had previously seen and approved in advance to be given in the chapel.[23] His criteria for rejection were by no means limited to homiletical quality, but included as well the degree of adherence to his own version of Reform.

Throughout the eighteen years of his administration, Kohler maintained his perception of the Hebrew Union College as a religious institution devoted to a clearly defined Reform understanding of Judaism. His innovations, his accomplishments, frustrations, and failures, and most of the major controversies that afflicted the school during those years, are explicable in terms of this fervent and sincere, but necessarily intolerant commitment to shaping the College community according to his own ideal of Reform Judaism.

Even before he took office as president, Kohler indicated to the Board of Governors that the existing rabbinical curriculum was not acceptable to him. He would not allow a new catalogue to go out bearing his name as responsible for the College until certain "essential changes" had been made.[24] As faculty minutes for the early years of the Kohler administration are not extant, there is no record of the prolonged, and no doubt vehement, discussions that preceded the issuance of the first revised catalogue in January 1905, nearly a year and a half after Kohler took office. It is a pity, for the changes that appear here officially for the first time are striking.

The rabbinical program was now extended from eight to nine years, the final year to be devoted exclusively to studies at the College after completion of the secular bachelor's degree. Although this additional year had already been proposed by Wise and had even appeared tentatively in earlier catalogues, it was now carried through for the first time. Kohler thought that he could raise the academic level of the College by converting it gradually into a postgraduate institution. He would have liked the curriculum to include three years after university graduation,[25] but this was apparently not yet feasible. Sporadic attempts to raise the minimum level of secular knowledge at admission from the lowest grade of high school to its junior year proved to be failures. Yet the tendency to increase the degree of student maturity was at least apparent at this stage and continued to manifest itself during succeeding administrations.

With regard to its content, the new curriculum of 1905 varies markedly from its predecessor. The most obvious change is the total elimination of any instruction in modern Hebrew. During the last year of Wise's presidency, and especially during the interim leadership of Moses Mielziner, Caspar Levias had taught selections from modern Hebrew writers including the Cultural Zionist Ahad Ha-'Am. In the catalogue of 1903, modern Hebrew appeared for the first and only time in this period as a regular subject. That same spring Gotthard Deutsch, on the single occasion when he ordained the graduates, composed and read his charge to them in rhymed Hebrew.[26] Kohler, however, did not share this enthusiasm for modern Hebrew, and in his very first speech to the students, at the opening of the Preparatory Department in 1903, he expressed his attitude and intentions in the most forceful terms:

> The College should have a thoroughly American character. The students should endeavor to be imbued with the American spirit, and this includes the mastery of English diction. Neo-Hebraic Literature may be a necessity for Russian Jews who have no genuine national literature from which to derive culture and idealism. For us the English literature is a source of culture and enlightenment; wherefore Neo-Hebraic Literature will be abolished here.[27]

And abolished it was, not to be taught again until after Kohler's retirement.

For modern Hebrew the new president substituted Midrash, especially that portion of this exegetical literature which would be homiletically useful to the modern rabbi. Although previous curricula did include some attention to Midrash, in Kohler's time it became one of the primary fields of study. Talmud receded relatively in significance. Unlike Wise, Kohler no longer felt the need to justify his curriculum to the Orthodox. After all, HUC was now clearly a Reform institution and *halakha* was of little consequence to Reform Judaism. Study of Talmud possessed value only insofar as it was conducted from a historical perspective, "as the most potent factor of Judaism of the past" [28] and as a source for moral maxims. According to Kohler, the student must be enabled "to discern the living ethical and spiritual truth beneath the stagnant form of the Halakah and the inane discussions that fill so many pages of the Babylonian Gemarah." [29]

The apparent criterion of usefulness to the rabbi also made for the elimination of the Semitic languages with which students had been required to gain at least a passing acquaintance in Wise's time. Syriac and Arabic were at first made optional, then dropped altogether. Subjects more appropriate to a training school for pulpit rabbis now took their place. Regular courses in liturgy appear for the first time in the catalogue of 1905. A year later there is a course in sociology (Jewish philanthropic organizations) taught by Boris D. Bogen, superintendent of the Cincinnati United Jewish Charities. Training in elocution, first requested by the students as early as 1885 and instituted outside the regular curriculum, now becomes an integral part of the program, and its teacher is listed as one of the "special instructors" in the catalogue. Similarly, pedagogics, taught for many years by Louis Grossmann, the rabbi of Bene Yeshurun and from 1909 to 1922 the principal of a Teachers' Institute run by the College,[30] comes to assume a more prominent role in the curriculum.[31]

While during the first quarter century, the function of the Preparatory Department had been basically to provide linguistic skills, in Kohler's time these first years of a student's attendance at the College were—in addition—utilized for initial ideological indoctrination. All four preparatory grades now received regular instruction in "catechism" from the president himself. Admission to the Collegiate Department required familiarity with "the essential doctrines of the Jewish religion."

Another subject that was added, in this instance not for practical or ideological reasons but because it was one of Kohler's specialties, was apocryphal and Hellenistic literature. Later the president also gave a course of readings in the New Testament, likewise one of his scholarly interests.

In sum, the new curriculum clearly reflected the commitments and predilections of the new president. It expressed his conception that the College was not the equivalent of the Semitics faculty of a university and likewise not a modern yeshiva. It was a theological institution for training future Reform rabbis in the principles of their faith and the techniques of their profession. Unfortunately for Kohler, not all of his colleagues on the faculty shared that view.

In 1903 the College faculty consisted of nine members. Two, David Philipson (homiletics) and Louis Grossmann (ethics and pedagogics), were the rabbis of the two large Cincinnati Reform congregations and taught only a few hours per week. Of the full-time members, the oldest was Sigmund Mannheimer, a simple pedagogue nearly seventy years of age, who had taught Hebrew and been librarian for nearly twenty years. With the exception of Judah Leon Magnes, a recent graduate of HUC who left the faculty for a pulpit in New York City after a year and a half,[32] the remaining full-time members were all slightly under or over the age of forty. Of these, Ephraim Feldman, a gifted teacher of philosophy, had been on the faculty the longest, ever since he received an appointment during his student days at the College in 1883. Gotthard Deutsch, the historian, had come in 1891; Caspar Levias, who principally taught Bible and Aramaic, received his appointment in 1895; Moses Buttenwieser, whose field was Bible, had joined the faculty in 1897; and finally, Henry Malter, who specialized in medieval Jewish philosophy and rabbinics, had been the last of Isaac Mayer Wise's appointments, arriving from Europe in 1900.

Status on the faculty was not, however, strictly a matter of seniority. An important distinction was possession of the European Ph.D. The four members of the faculty who had gained this degree—Deutsch, Buttenwieser, Malter, and Magnes—enjoyed a measure of prestige and security not shared by their colleagues. Philipson and Grossmann both had the D.D. degree from HUC and, since they served on the faculty without compensation, were honored with the title of professor; so, too, was Feldman after serving for sixteen years, though, like Mannheimer, he possessed only a bachelor's degree. Levias, with a master's degree, remained an instructor, as did all those appointed more recently. The dean of the faculty after Mielziner's death—and addressed as such [33]—was therefore Professor Gotthard Deutsch; it was he who received by far the highest remuneration, $3,250 in 1902–3.

As was to be expected, the appointment of a new president from outside the College produced a measure of resentment on the part of at least a portion of the faculty. Deutsch, in particular, at first fought against Kohler, principally, it seems, because Deutsch had himself actively sought the presidency and had even been given some reason to expect he might be chosen.[34] But as Kohler treated him with respect and kindness, Deutsch soon reconciled himself to the new president and cooperated with him. Certainly he had no cause to fear for his position. Other faculty members, however, were not so fortunate. For not only did the new president press for curricular revision, he also intended to reconstitute the faculty. He wanted to replace those individuals who either lacked proper scholarly qualifications or were out of sympathy with his view of Reform Judaism—or both. Deutsch and Buttenwieser were vulnerable on neither score; Magnes left before Kohler decided to take action; Malter, though not of Kohler's views, possessed excellent scholarly potential; Mannheimer might be expected to retire shortly. That left Caspar Levias and Ephraim Feldman. The former was the earliest member of the faculty openly to express his sympathy for Zionism, the latter was an autodidact of mildly cynical tendencies who could not bear Kohler's rhetoric. Neither man possessed a doctorate or had the reputation of a productive scholar; both were born in Eastern Europe.

On May 3, 1905, Kohler proposed to an executive session of the board that it dismiss Levias and Feldman as soon as feasible. His grounds were their failure to inspire the students properly: they lacked religiosity and provided no example of creative scholarship.

Specifically, Kohler held that Levias was no more than a grammarian while Feldman "cannot inspire the students with love for the sacred cause, because he has not a spark of religion in his soul." As a substitute for these two men, Kohler proposed an individual in whom he possessed the utmost confidence: "a scholar of note, a man of high aims and ideals, thoroughly imbued with the spirit of Reform Judaism, no Zionist, not a one-sided man, and his coming here will be hailed with joy by every student and alumnus of the College." Yet, ironically, this man on whom Kohler placed such high hopes was to prove his most bitter opponent. It was Max Margolis.

In 1905 Kohler had every reason to expect that Margolis would stand by his side in revamping the College. From 1893 to 1897 Margolis had taught at HUC before leaving for a position at the University of California. Repeatedly he had expressed his sympathy with the Reform movement, and as a member of the CCAR he had in 1903 proposed the adoption of a creed for Reform Judaism which was based on conceptions no less radical and critical than those of Kohler. Though a Lithuanian Jew by birth, Margolis had clearly indicated his commitment to Israel's vocation as the "teacher of mankind" and in the summer of 1905 (after he had been appointed to the faculty) stated very explicitly: "We are neither Zionists nor Paulinists. . . . To us the Jewish body is not an *ethnos,* but an *ecclesia.* . . . We look upon the dispersion as final." [35]

But by the time Margolis came to the Hebrew Union College in the fall of 1905, he was no longer certain about the views he had expressed earlier that year. A process of inner reorientation, which he later claimed had been initiated with his introduction to Ahad Ha-'Am's essays in 1903, was gradually transforming him from a radical universalist into a Zionist. [36] When he arrived at the College he found two members of the faculty who were able to encourage him in hastening the process. Although Levias, unlike the non-Zionist Feldman, [37] had indeed been dismissed, there remained two instructors who were outspoken Jewish nationalists: Henry Malter and Max Schloessinger. The three men became closely associated and set themselves against those members of the faculty not sharing their views. [38] In a single academic year, 1906–7, all of them were to express their disaffection with the College and its president and ultimately to tender their resignations to the board.[39]

Henry Malter had been unhappy at the College and eager to leave even before the appointment of Kohler. He longed to receive a position at the newly reorganized Jewish Theological Seminary, which was located in the heart of Jewish intellectual life, enjoyed a more secure financial foundation, and would, he thought, be paying higher salaries. He was not at all devoted to Reform, which he thought had destroyed historical Judaism, holding on to no more than the vapid sermon. When Kohler came, Malter found to his regret that the new president was "totally a rabbi" and demanded of him, against his will, that instead of teaching talmudic dialectics he concentrate on the faith, ethics, and sanctity the Talmud contains. Of course Kohler was out of sympathy with the Zionism Malter had freely expressed in an extended article in the *HUC Journal,* the last installment of which, Malter claimed, Kohler had prevented from appearing. He had felt very lonely at the school until the arrival of Schloessinger and Margolis.[40]

Unlike Malter, Max Schloessinger had been appointed by Kaufmann Kohler himself. He came in 1904 to replace Magnes, who had been instructor in Bible and rabbinic literature as well as librarian. He was a German Jew who had received his Ph.D. at the University of Berlin and was a promising scholar. Though sympathetic to Zionism, he seems not to have expressed himself on the subject in print before his appointment to the faculty.

It was not long before these three men began openly to challenge Kaufmann Kohler's leadership, in the first instance bringing a student complaint about the content and quality of the teaching over the president's head to the Board of Governors. The tactic, which was manifestly intended to embarrass Kohler, resulted in the president's charging the trio with showing "a spirit of rancor and insubordination." He further told the board that "some" of them had demonstratively shown their lack of sympathy for Reform Judaism by not attending the school's religious exercises and that they desired to crowd weaker men, such as Buttenwieser and Mannheimer, out of the College altogether. Though not including the matter in his accusation, he also reiterated his intention "to make the College stand for the principles of Reform Judaism and not for unreligious Zionism or nationalism. . . ." [41]

The following academic year brought to a head the ill feeling the three men harbored toward the College in general, toward Kohler in particular, and toward most of their other colleagues. Their resignations cannot be explained by reference to any single cause. At least three factors played a role in the dispute: money, personalities, and Zionism.

It seems likely that Malter did not intend for the Board of Governors to accept the resignation he submitted to it in December of 1906. Throughout his lengthy letter he deals only with grievances regarding the conditions of his employment and especially the failure of the board sufficiently to increase his salary vis-à-vis those received by his colleagues. He points out his contributions as a teacher, makes no complaint against Kohler, and says nothing of any ideological disaffection. The board was apparently expected to raise his salary appropriately and thus bring about withdrawal of the resignation. But despite some negotiation, no agreement was reached. As student enrollment was lower than it had been in years, there was little need to retain him, and Malter's resignation was thus accepted.[42]

Although Malter's letter did not even hint at the Zionist issue, it may well be, nonetheless, that the board refused to raise his salary for reasons other than financial stringency alone. For as a scholar of American Zionism has recently pointed out,[43] it is quite likely that Solomon Schechter's public declaration of his adherence to the Zionist cause in December 1906 had its effect on the leadership of the Hebrew Union College. Shortly after that well-publicized statement, a member of the board felt it necessary to introduce a resolution specifically reaffirming that the Hebrew Union College remains dedicated to the motto: "America is our Zion." [44] This attitude must have affected Malter's case even as it surely affected the two which followed.

After Malter's resignation, Schloessinger publicly committed himself to Zionism. In an extended article in the Baltimore *Jewish Comment,* beginning January 4, 1907, he argued against David Philipson that Reform Judaism and Zionism were reconcilable. The following month Kohler refused to give Schloessinger permission to attend a banquet in New York honoring Shmarya Levin, "the Zionist agitator of Warsaw." [45] When Schloessinger went nevertheless and even offered a toast entitled "Zionism in the West," Kohler preferred charges of insubordination against him before the board. Committed to anti-Zionism and given the choice between the president and a member of the faculty, the board, after examining both men, of course sustained Kohler, with only Maurice J. Freiberg and Jacob Ottenheimer voting in the negative.[46] Schloessinger's resignation followed in March.

The case of Margolis was the most complex of the three. Like that of Malter, it too involved compensation, although in 1906 Margolis was receiving $3,600, the same amount as Deutsch, and more than any other member of the faculty.[47] Even before the Zionist issue came to a head, he had made several applications for positions elsewhere. After his years at Berkeley, Margolis did not find it easy to adjust to the atmosphere and conditions of a theological school; the chapel exercises he regarded as "unacademic." A powerful personality—according to Kohler, "domineering"—he was unable to tolerate the strict control which the president maintained over the faculty in the early years of his administration. Even had there been no ideological disagreement between the two men, it is unlikely that they could have remained together for long in the same institution.[48] An oral tradition goes so far as to suggest that Margolis at one point harbored the ambition of displacing Kohler as president.[49] Be that as it may, it was the issue of Zionism, in this instance appearing in academic garb, into which their personal conflict was channeled.

As a letter from the students supporting him attests, Margolis did not blatantly preach Zionism in the classroom, though, like Schloessinger, he confessed his adherence to the movement in the *Jewish Comment,*[50] and in one instance he gave voice to it from the pulpit of the chapel.[51] Instead, he did something which to Kohler's mind was far more damaging: he read Zionism into the Prophets without mentioning it by name. In this way Margolis was able to bring his advocacy of the Zionist cause under the umbrella of *Lehrfreiheit*. After all, was he not entitled to teach the subject matter of his courses as he saw fit, free of any external pressures? For Kohler, however, placing a nationalistic interpretation on Isaiah and Micah, the great fountainheads of Reform's universal mission to the nations, was nothing short of treason to the cause of the College. Obviously, he could not tolerate it. This is what he told the board about Margolis:

> He infuses ideas subversive of the very fundamental principles of American Reform Judaism in his teachings of the Prophets and of the Pentateuch without characterizing them as Zionistic and this is by far more pernicious than if he would openly speak as a Zionist. It is the poison instilled in sugar-coated pills that is much more harmful than the one labelled as such. Against the latter we can be cautioned. We learn how to deal with Zionism by hearing all its arguments and then refuting its premises by pointing out that it is un-Jewish, irreligious and un-American. But if it is taught under the guise of exegetical science, then it works insidiously, *undermining* the very foundations of Reform Judaism. . . . The whole teaching of Prof. Margolis is nothing less than playing into the hands of the Anti-Semitic Professors of Biblical Exegesis in Germany and elsewhere. *It is Un-Jewish.*[52]

In response to Margolis's biblical interpretations, Kohler took two steps: first he relieved Margolis of responsibility for teaching the prophetic literature, turning his courses in this field over to Buttenwieser; second, he justified his policy publicly in articles he wrote for the Jewish press stressing that in a rabbinical school academic freedom must have its limits. Even as the Jewish Theological Seminary could not allow critical dissection of the Pentateuch, so too, he argued, the Hebrew Union College could not permit "twisting and distorting of the grand universal teachings of the prophets."[53] When Margolis reacted to the president's rejection of his mode of teaching by submitting a letter of resignation, the board, after some hesitation, accepted it. One-third of the faculty thus departed in a single academic year and Kohler was forced to rebuild his staff anew. Yet amazingly, even after the experience of 1906–7, he did not reconstruct it entirely in his own image.

In the summer of 1907, following the resignations, the faculty was reduced to only the president and four full-time teachers. Of these, two were shortly to die: Mannheimer in 1909 at the age of seventy-four and Ephraim Feldman a year later on the day he was to receive an honorary doctorate on the occasion of his silver anniversary on the faculty. Only Gotthard Deutsch and Moses Buttenwieser would continue at the College for any length of time, the one until his death the year of Kohler's retirement, the other until well beyond it. Even David Philipson was no longer a part-time regular member of the faculty. When the Union council had given him the choice of serving either on the Board of Governors or on the faculty but not both, he had chosen the former as the position of greater influence and prestige.

To replace his losses, Kohler turned first to Julian Morgenstern, a graduate of the College who after his ordination in 1902 had gone to Germany and earned a Ph.D. in Semitics at Heidelberg. Both a young man and clearly a Reform Jew, Morgenstern was most unlikely to present either personal or ideological opposition to the president. He was obviously a safe choice. Kohler's second selection, however, was more daring. For the chair of philosophy he proposed the name of David Neumark, an older man of orthodox upbringing, an enthusiastic Hebraist, and a Cultural Zionist. Such an individual could be chosen only because he possessed certain characteristics that offset those considered less acceptable: specifically his Galician (not Russian) birth, his Berlin Ph.D., and his ordination from the *Hochschule*. For his part, Neumark somehow managed to feel at home on the faculty of the Hebrew Union College. Though traditional in practice and continually at odds with his universalist and intermarried[54] colleague Moses Buttenwieser, Neumark was able to get along with Kohler while yet maintaining his own views. What made Neumark fit into the atmosphere of HUC was his commitment to a liberal interpretation of Judaism and his opposition to strictly secular forms of Jewish nationalism—though he insisted that Cultural Zionism was perfectly compatible with Reform. In fact, to his mind the entire spectrum of the Zionist movement—from Herzl to Sokolow to Aḥad Ha-'Am—

consisted of Reform Jews, even if they were unwilling to admit that fact to themselves.[55]

Kohler made two additional appointments after the deaths of Mannheimer and Feldman. In place of the former he appointed Henry Englander, another graduate of the College, who had received a doctorate from Brown University and for a time taught Hebrew and Bible there. Though not an important scholar, Englander was mild-mannered and universally beloved; serving as registrar in addition to his teaching duties, he bore much of the weight of day-to-day administration in the last decade of Kohler's presidency. To replace Feldman, Kohler appointed Jacob Z. Lauterbach, like Neumark a Galician by birth and a relatively more traditional Jew though, unlike his colleague, not explicitly a Zionist. Lauterbach had been ordained at the Orthodox *Rabbinerseminar* in Berlin and possessed a Ph.D. from the University of Göttingen. He had come to the United States to work on the *Jewish Encyclopedia* and after its completion had held a number of pulpits. On the faculty, Lauterbach, though himself clearly committed to Reform Judaism, came to represent the claims of tradition and the continuing value of the *halakha,* if not as norm then at least as a significant precedent in determing Reform Jewish practice. In 1915, his foremost disciple, Solomon Freehof, joined the faculty upon graduation. A man of both scholarly and homiletic talents, Freehof taught at the College for nine years before leaving for the pulpit rabbinate. Kohler made only one additional faculty appointment during his term of office: a year before his retirement he selected the promising young scholar Jacob R. Marcus to be an instructor in Bible and rabbinics.

Aside from the appointments of Freehof and Marcus, the faculty did not change at all from 1911 to 1921. Except that it contained no Russian Jews, it was a well-balanced group, including older and younger men, some favorably disposed to Zionism and some who opposed it vociferously, some who were better at scholarship, others who were more successful as teachers. The men who had grown up in Europe tended to be poor pedagogues from whom students gained some inspiration but little substance. The more systematic instructors were the younger men: Englander, Morgenstern, Freehof, and Marcus.

By today's standards, the salaries received by the faculty were meager indeed, and the teaching obligations onerous. Professors still received far less compensation than even recent graduates active in the pulpit.[56] They still taught thirteen to fourteen hours per week, more than was customary at other academic institutions.[57] But faculty security and benefits underwent a slight amelioration: in 1907 the Board of Governors instituted the granting of tenure at the end of six years, requiring reelection only for the more recent appointees; and in 1914 it approved a faculty retirement plan at 40 percent of salary, though the benefit applied only to men who had taught at the College for at least twenty-five years.

In the last decade of the Kohler administration the faculty began for the first time to assert itself vis-à-vis the president and the Board of Governors. While Kohler had begun as a strong executive, intent on imposing his will on his colleagues, in his final years he seems to have lost some of his authority. His relationship to the faculty became more democratic, more like a chairman to a group of peers.[58] The faculty also successfully demanded from the Board of Governors that it relinquish prerogatives which it had previously kept for itself. During this period it was able to increase its role in such areas as admissions, scholarships, discipline, and the assignment of advanced students to temporary congregational positions. The faculty further insisted that it be consulted on the invitation of outside speakers and that the catalogue list its various committees.[59]

At the same time that the faculty was being rebuilt, the College was also engaged in the relocation and expansion of its physical facilities. Already when Kohler took office, it was apparent that the old building on West Sixth Street could no longer satisfactorily meet the needs of the College. Not only was it now too small to house adequately the rapidly expanding library, but its location in a number of respects had become distinctly undesirable. As early as the 1890s, residential land values had dropped in the Cincinnati basin area and wealthier citizens—among them the German Jews—had begun fleeing to the "hilltop" suburbs to the north.[60] Their places were taken by poorer people, in part blacks and also in part Jews from Eastern Europe. The old building found itself in the vicinity of cabbage markets, stockyards, and population elements unrelated or unfavorable to Reform Judaism. Most of the board and faculty no longer lived downtown, and by 1897 at least twenty-five students were living in Walnut Hills or another suburb.[61] Much time was lost in getting to and from the school, especially since during the 1890s the University of Cincinnati, where most of the students continued to do their undergraduate work, had moved from the basin up to Burnet Woods Park in Clifton.

In March 1903, the Union of American Hebrew Congregations decided to appoint a committee to consider the feasibility of transferring the College to a more desirable location in the city. After some years, suitable land was purchased, ideally located opposite Burnet Woods, in close proximity to the University and to a high school then about to be constructed. The parcel, comprising some eighteen acres and possessing a 666-foot frontage on Clifton Avenue, was acquired for $31,000—more than the total cost of the old property, which was later sold for a pittance to the Colored Industrial School of Cincinnati.[62]

Raising sufficient funds to build on the newly acquired site turned out to be no easy task. The Union was increasingly concentrating its efforts on other projects: especially on the activities of the long-established Board of Delegates, devoted to the protection of Jewish rights, and on the effort to expand the influence of the Reform movement through a program of synagogue and religious-school extension. The College received a proportionately declining share of the Union's revenues. At the same time the Jewish Theological Seminary was competing for funds from Reform philanthropists in the East. Finally, there was the embarrassing fact that the size of the student body did not exceed forty-two during the first eight years of Kohler's administration. The old building may have been bursting at the seams with books, but certainly not with students. What saved the campaign was the munificence of three individual contributors, none of them from Cincinnati. Julius Rosenwald, the philanthropic president of Sears, Roebuck and Company donated $50,000 while Jacob H. Schiff gave the building fund half that amount. These two contributions together covered nearly half the cost of the administration and classroom building. Earlier in the campaign, Isaac W. Bernheim of Louisville, an ideologically assimilationist Jew who had made his fortune in the Kentucky distilling business, volunteered to pay the entire construction cost for a separate library building, a sum which ultimately totaled about $50,000.

Cornerstones for both structures were laid on April 25, 1911, and in the fall of 1912, the College could at last move up to the rarified atmosphere of Clifton. That winter it held appropriate ceremonies of dedication in the presence of about 450 delegates gathered for the Twenty-third Biennial Council of the Union. Orations were delivered by the president and by Rabbi Jonah B. Wise, a son of the founder. But the dignitary who stirred the most interest was Solomon Schechter, president of the Jewish Theological Seminary. In greetings from "His Majesty's Opposition," Schechter testified to his lack of sympathy for Reform, but at the same time stressed that Reform and Conservative Judaism shared a common concern for Jewish learning and the common need to undertake something approaching Kohler's favorite notion of the mission of Israel: to proclaim the great truths of Judaism to the world.[63] His presence was indicative of the cordial relations that existed during this period between Schechter and Kohler, as also between the two institutions.[64]

The new structures were executed in a variation of the English Tudor style then popular in Cincinnati. A large facsimile of the Tablets of the Covenant, engraved in stone, was placed between decorative towers above the main entry to the administration building. Inside, there were twelve classrooms, offices, meeting rooms, and a chapel complete with pipe organ seating about 350 in individual wooden chairs. The library contained a large reading room boasting a ceiling of wooden beams and stacks to accommodate 50,000 volumes. The facilities, according to Deutsch, were lavish.[65]

The collection of books to be housed in the new library had been greatly improved in the five years preceding the move to Clifton. When Kohler became president in 1903, he complained that it was "a haphazard collection without real benefit to any."[66] His first step to remedy the situation was to relieve the aging Mannheimer of his duties as librarian in favor of Magnes and then Schloessinger. To assist him, the latter in 1906 secured the services of Adolph S. Oko, who had worked in the cataloguing department of the New York Public Library. When Schloessinger left a year later, Oko took over and became the first professional librarian in the history of the school. Only twenty-four years of age when he assumed full responsibility for the library, he remained in his position for more than a quarter of a century and during that period built a first-rate collection.

Oko was a Russian Jew of unusual intelligence, executive ability, and assertiveness. He was an atheist, possessed a highly abrasive personality, and despised faculty and students. Yet he succeeded in developing a quite cordial relationship with the president, who prized his librarian's talents. Once in office, Oko immediately set out to rationalize the library. The catalogue, which he claimed "belonged in method and form to the dark ages of cataloguing," was revised; every effort was made to give the library balance and coherence. Irrelevant volumes that had accumulated from donations over the years were eliminated.

Oko's foremost objective, however, was expansion. Within the scope of Judaica, he intended to purchase simply "everything." [67] His most valuable acquisitions were made shortly after World War I when, on a trip to Europe, he was able to obtain some 18,000 items. They included the very valuable A. Freimann Collection, containing thirty-three Hebrew incunabula, and the Eduard Birnbaum Collection of Jewish music, the most important and largest of its kind. Being an ardent devotee of Spinoza, Oko began a collection of Spinozana which is still one of the finest in the world. He would have liked to make the Hebrew Union College Library also a major depository of manuscripts, but in this one area he had to admit failure. When the Elkan N. Adler manuscript collection became available in 1922, Oko did his best to cajole and shame the Board of Governors into raising the $120,000 to purchase it.[68] The board, however, was concerned at the time with the need for a dormitory; it did not share the librarian's enthusiasm for the acquisition, and the manuscripts ultimately went to the JTS.

In Oko's time the library also became the custodian of the Hebrew

Union College Museum. Begun in 1913 as a project of the National Federation of Temple Sisterhoods, which called upon its members to send ceremonial objects, the museum was originally in the charge of Professors Lauterbach and Englander. As the collection grew, however, it was decided to turn it over to Oko. His enterprise raised the museum, likewise, to the first rank when in 1925 it acquired the large and magnificent Salli Kirschstein Collection consisting not only of ceremonial objects, but also of graphic art, tapestries, ceramics, carvings, and illuminated scrolls.[69]

With the reconstitution of the faculty and the construction of the new buildings, morale at the College, severely shaken by the 1907 dispute, began to improve markedly. The new facilities, the prominence of the instructors, and the greater availability of financial aid now drew more—and apparently better—students to Cincinnati. The size of the student body, which reached a nadir of twenty-eight in 1906–7, grew rapidly beginning in 1911–12, ascending to a peak of ninety-three in 1915–16. There was also a more studious attitude. Kohler was pleasantly surprised to find a spirit of earnestness and diligence he had seldom encountered at the College before.[70]

As it expanded, the student body began to show signs of independent enterprise. In 1914, after the lapse of a decade, the students once again undertook the publication of their own magazine. Named the *Hebrew Union College Monthly,* it was to be the longest-lived of all the student publications, running for thirty-four volumes until 1949. Its first editor, Abba Hillel Silver, was typical of a number of gifted young men who were to graduate from HUC in the final Kohler years. Some of them published serious pieces of Jewish scholarship in the *Monthly.* In 1911, a student, Morris Lazaron, formed a Literary Society which invited prominent speakers and arranged student debates on the issues of the day. In 1920, it held sessions during the summer in New York City, arranging interviews with such diverse figures as the liberal journalist Walter Lippmann, Rabbi Judah Leon Magnes, the black intellectual W. E. B. Du Bois, and the founder of Ethical Culture, Felix Adler.[71] Student-body activities opened each year with a student banquet featuring oratory and

music by the HUC choir and orchestra. In the winter there was a
Hanukkah party sponsored by the Literary Society as well as an
occasional special event, such as a dinner for a professor who had
recently published a book. The HUC basketball team, while not outstanding, served as a focus for student spirit; there were even school
songs and cheers, and by 1922 HUC had its own athletic coach.

Although there was still no dormitory and students continued to
live in private homes or boarding houses, a student room in the new
administration building served as the focus for activities. During these
years a number of musical satires on life at the College were produced,
the most noted of which seems to have been "The Quest of the Holy
Dagesh," describing a journey of HUC faculty members to Palestine
in search of that highly significant, if tiny, characteristic of Hebrew
grammar. A few students formed a secret Hebrew-letter fraternity,
Yod-Kaf-Tav, whose members pledged themselves to abstain from
eating pork and shellfish, to marry within the faith, and carefully to
observe Sabbaths and Jewish holidays. The society was also Zionistic,
though some Zionist students chose to associate themselves with an opposing faction.[72] In imitation of the custom of secular schools, fresh-
men at the College were regularly subjected to hazing.

A statistical study made for the period 1904 to 1929 [73] permits
certain generalizations about the HUC students of that period. The
majority were native-born Americans and came from the northern and
eastern sections of the United States. More than 70 percent had
parents who had immigrated from Eastern Europe, and 28 percent
had themselves been born there. The average incoming student was
about nineteen years old, came ready to enter the sophomore class
at the University, and (if he completed the course) attended the
College for six and one-half years. About a quarter of the students
were still in high school at their admission, while somewhat more
than 15 percent had already received a bachelor's degree. More than
half of the entering students began at the bottom, in the "D" grade
of the Preparatory Department, but a number of these, especially the
ones who were advanced in their secular education, were able to complete the course in less than the full span of nine years. Slightly more
than half of those who entered made it to ordination; about 30 per-

cent withdrew voluntarily, while about 15 percent were dismissed for a variety of reasons. Of 347 students, only three were married when they entered the school; less than 10 percent were married before graduation.

The period of the survey is marked by a number of significant trends. Age at admission rose steadily during these twenty-five years as did academic status. While in the period 1904 to 1909 only 64 percent of the entering students were rated by their schools as above average scholastically, 95 percent of the students entering from 1915 to 1919 were above the average. At the same time an increasing proportion of students were coming to the College with virtually no Hebrew preparation at all, as indicated by the rising percentage of those admitted to the lowest grade of the College.

Many of the entrants were young men of ambition and ability from poor families who lacked the means to provide them with an advanced education. At the College they could without expense prepare for a well-paying career of some prestige—for many the only such career that was open to them. This situation was not materially different from what it had been in Wise's time, the only change being that now the students were mostly from poor East European families instead of poor German ones. In order to put the best face on obvious realities, Kohler changed the catalogue to read "scholarships" instead of "stipends," and "deserving" students in place of "indigent" ones.[74] Scholarships were made available only to students who had achieved a level of academic excellence at the College; others received loans. In 1912 over 75 percent of the students were receiving some form of aid, generally totaling $30 per month.[75] Technically the loans were to be repaid to the College after ordination, but few in fact were.[76]

As future rabbis, students were expected to refrain from the vices in which their fellows in other disciplines indulged. Gambling and smoking were strictly forbidden to students on the College grounds. In accordance with the morals of the day, board and faculty insisted that students remain virgins until their marriage. Despite the lure of easily accessible bordellos in the Cincinnati area, premarital sexual activity was considered grounds for expulsion.[77]

Even as the private lives of students continued to be subject to scrutiny by the authorities of the College, so, too, their freedom of political expression was limited. When a student, Sidney Goldstein, in 1904 gave a sermon propagating socialism, Kohler publicly rebuked him for treating the subject of justice from a socialist point of view.[78] At least one student seems to have been dismissed from the College on account of his propagation of socialism.[79] On the other hand, theological doubts were, as a rule, tolerated so long as they did not result in outright atheism. In general, the faculty seems to have been considerably more tolerant of student deviation from the norms of Reform Judaism than was the Board of Governors.[80]

Kohler himself, however, did not swerve from his conviction that the Hebrew Union College could not tolerate the public expression of views contradictory to what he considered the principles of Reform Judaism. While he welcomed students who were Zionists and allowed the Zionist leader Stephen S. Wise to speak (on a non-Zionist topic) in the chapel, he was still unwilling to permit the College to become a forum for views antithetical to his notion of Reform. In the fall of 1914, the student Literary Society produced a situation which made that quite clear. As one of their speakers they invited Horace M. Kallen, a professor of philosophy at the University of Wisconsin, who was an outspoken secularist and Zionist. When Kohler learned of the invitation, he wrote to Kallen rescinding it, thereby releasing a furor not only in the student body but within the Jewish community at large. Kohler's opposition was based on two remarks Kallen had made in a speech he delivered at a dinner of the Intercollegiate Menorah Association a year earlier. There Kallen had branded the Jewish mission idea "a barbarous and egotistical doctrine, certainly unfit for citizens of a democratic country." He had further declared himself "an adherent of no religion," implying that it was not necessary to believe in God in order to be a good Jew.[81] When four members of the board of the Literary Society, on their own initiative and apparently without the support of the students as a whole, then wrote to Kallen apologizing for their president and hoping thereby to mitigate Kallen's resentment towards the College,[82] their action was taken as a breach of discipline and they were punished by a decision to deny them special distinctions.[83]

The Kallen affair prompted a number of Reform rabbis, who were themselves unhappy with Kohler's policies, to force him to yield ground. At the Union Biennial in January 1915, Rabbi Max Heller, the father of one of the students who had written the letter, along with several other delegates, prevailed upon the Board of Governors to call an "Executive Conference" where they might express their grievances. At the meeting, held on February 15, 1915, Heller, along with Stephen S. Wise, achieved a resolution, later endorsed by the Board of Governors, which stated that while, as in the past, Kohler alone would prescribe who might speak in the chapel, he would not object to Zionist addresses being delivered elsewhere in the building nor would he reject student sermons dealing with Zionism provided they were religious in tone and otherwise unobjectionable to him.[84] Thereafter students were indeed allowed to advocate Zionism from the chapel pulpit,[85] though a sermon denying revelation was rejected by Kohler as late as 1921.[86]

One other major affair was to shake the College during the Kohler administration. Like the earlier dispute concerning the Zionism of Malter, Schloessinger, and Margolis, it too aroused violent emotions. Once again the issue was conceived as involving the good name of Judaism—and of the College in particular—in the gentile community. In this latter instance, however, it was not a matter of Jewish versus American nationalism; it involved loyalty to the United States in its war against Germany. In 1917, in a highly charged atmosphere of intense patriotism which allowed for little tolerance of divergent opinion, a professor at the College gave reason to believe he did not share that loyalty. Though he was the most senior and venerated member of the faculty, the board quickly came to the brink of dismissing him from his position.[87]

Gotthard Deutsch[88] combined a prodigious memory with an incapacity to integrate the vast array of data he had at his command. Unable to write synthetic history, he occupied himself with writing encyclopedia and newspaper articles on various Jewish subjects and

compiling a vast card catalogue of historical "facts." Deutsch unquestionably possessed a political attachment to the United States,
his adopted country, and he was sufficiently interested in Cincinnati
affairs to gain election to the Board of Education. A Cultural Zionist
in his later years, who enjoyed lecturing [89] and writing in modern
Hebrew and Yiddish, Deutsch eschewed its political variety. Though
he would raise funds to buy trees in Palestine, the United States was
definitely his country.

America was not, however, his cultural homeland. Like many of
the German Jews who had received their education in Germany,
Deutsch remained culturally a German. His children were taught
German before they learned English, his diary until the final years was
conducted in German (then in Hebrew!), and he was an active member of the local German Literary Club. When, on the eve of Passover
in 1917, the United States declared war, he was so shaken that he
was unable to conduct the *seder;* for six months thereafter he could
not bring himself to attend services in the College chapel. Though
his sons joined the American armed forces, he gave vent to his own
feelings by joining and playing an active role in a left-wing pacifist
group called the People's Council for Democracy and Peace. The
United States government soon declared this organization inimical
to the welfare of the country, and on October 5, 1917, its meeting
was broken up by U. S. Secret Service men and local detectives.
Deutsch had left ten minutes before the raid so his name was not
recorded, but the following day his picture was spread on the front
page of the *Cincinnati Post* as one of the leaders of the organization.
He was specifically listed as "dean of the Hebrew Union College." The
Board of Governors, whose chairman had been receiving police reports
on Deutsch's activities, could no longer ignore the political affiliations
of the College's professor of history; his activities reflected on the
school as a whole and they were a distinct embarrassment to it.

Already shortly after the United States entered the war, the
president of the Board of Governors, Edward Heinsheimer, had addressed the students in chapel warning that anyone who openly expressed disloyalty would be subject to expulsion.[90] When Deutsch
continued to be active in the People's Council, he was first informally

warned that it might cost him his job. Then, after the incident of October 5th, he was summoned before the Board of Governors and required to disavow and sever his relationship with the organization. When he agreed, all concerned were relieved and hoped that the matter was closed.

But then Deutsch made a foolish error. Called to Federal Court as a character witness for a friend applying for naturalization, he was asked by the judge: "Who do you want to win in this war?" Considering the question inappropriate as addressed to a witness, Deutsch refused to reply. The next day the incident appeared under a large headline in the *Cincinnati Enquirer,* and within a week Deutsch again stood before the Board of Governors. Unable to resolve the matter immediately, the board agreed unanimously at least to express its own sentiments by displaying prominently on all the bulletin boards of the College the following notice:

> The Hebrew Union College was founded to have the young men whom it educates for the ministry preach and teach Reform Judaism and promulgate American ideas and ideals. Loyalty and patriotism have characterized the institution since its establishment.
>
> THIS IS OUR COUNTRY. We know no other fatherland than the land in which we live and no other flag than the flag which floats over it. Our country is at war and all of its citizens must be not passively, but actively loyal and patriotic. No one who does not subscribe to these sentiments is welcome within the walls of the College.[91]

In fact, 30 percent of the students eventually volunteered for active service or welfare work.

The agitating case of Gotthard Deutsch was postponed until a special meeting on December 11th. But that meeting had scarcely begun when, as the minutes tell us, "the members were shocked by the sudden collapse of President Heinsheimer who breathed his last without ever regaining consciousness. The members dispersed without formal adjournment."

The matter was not settled until two weeks later when the board voted ten to nine to censure Deutsch, those in the negative favoring outright dismissal. The board had received letters in support of Deutsch written, mostly upon his own request, from major contributors to the College (including Marshall and Schiff) as well as from alumni, the faculty, and the student body. Even more, his cause had been advanced by the willingness of five out-of-town members of the board—all graduates of the College—to attend the meeting and vote for the less drastic course of action. Of those favoring dismissal, all were Cincinnatians; only five local members—Oscar Berman, Felix Kahn, Alfred Mack, Murray Seasongood, and the new president, Alfred M. Cohen—were willing to buck public opinion to retain Deutsch. Even after the vote, a sizable minority of the board continued to fight for the errant professor's elimination from the faculty, dredging up new and damaging evidence regarding the extent of his pro-Germanism. One member of the board, Samuel Ach, preferred to resign rather than continue to be associated with the College.

During the Kohler administration the composition of the Board of Governors was little different from Wise's day. Although in 1917 it was expanded to thirty members, one-half still were Cincinnatians, while the rest were mostly prominent rabbis, especially graduates of the College. Except in so extraordinary a situation as the Deutsch case, the local members ran the affairs of the school.[92] They continued to be conservative businessmen and professionals, nearly all of German-Jewish extraction, and drawn from the prominent Reform Jewish families of the city: two Freibergs and two Macks served concurrently; leading attorneys and local politicians, such as Harry M. Hoffheimer and Murray Seasongood, joined its ranks. There seems to have been only one individual who was an active Zionist: Oscar Berman, a Lithuanian Jew of great wealth active nationally in the Keren Hayesod of America; he was briefly even vice-president of the board.

After the retirement of Bernhard Bettmann in 1910, the presidency of the board came into the hands of Edward L. Heinsheimer, a member of Bene Yeshurun associated with the College from the time he had briefly been a student there during its very first years. A charter member and later president of the Cincinnati Stock Exchange,

Heinsheimer was a man of considerable substance and active in a number of local Jewish charities aside from his participation on the board of the College. Like his predecessor, Heinsheimer would come regularly to Sabbath afternoon services and—though keeping his social distance—he took an interest in the welfare of the students.[93] After his sudden death while conducting the board meeting, Heinsheimer was replaced by Alfred M. Cohen, who retained the position for twenty years until 1937. Cohen, too, had once been a pupil of Isaac Mayer Wise, who had hoped to make a rabbi of him. But Cohen chose a law career instead, which he combined with the presidency of a local bank and a political career on the Cincinnati City Council and in the Ohio State Senate. He was associated with the Bene Israel congregation, which he served for many years as secretary and for a time as president. Later he became best known as the international president of B'nai B'rith from 1925 to 1938. Cohen was a man of stature both within and outside the Jewish community whose prestige and numerous personal contacts worked to the benefit of the College.

However, the most powerful influence on the Board of Governors seems to have been the rabbi of Bene Israel (since its move "uptown" known as the Rockdale Avenue Temple), David Philipson. As the only rabbi among the local members of the board, as a graduate of the College, and from 1888 to 1906 a regular member of the faculty, Philipson possessed a specialized knowledge of the school's affairs to a degree that the other members did not. Especially in matters affecting faculty and students, Philipson's voice was crucial. He was the force behind Kohler, and according to one recollection, "the uncrowned king of the College." [94]

During the Kohler years, the school continued to depend entirely on the UAHC for its financial support; it engaged in no fund-raising of its own. Although the number of congregations in the Union did not grow appreciably in the decade preceding the conclusion of World War I, generally remaining slightly below two hundred, individual membership rose by better than 50 percent to over twenty-five thousand in 1919. Financially, it became much stronger. The Wise Memorial Fund had brought in nearly $400,000 by the time it was terminated in 1911, giving way to the College Building Fund. That campaign was in turn succeeded, after the lapse of a few years, by the Wise Centenary Fund, which in 1919 collected better than $300,000. By the end of 1922, the College could boast a yearly budget of $141,000 and an Endowment Fund in excess of half a million dollars. The Union's total assets, including $700,000 for the library building and its contents, came to $1,744,483.[95]

During the last years of his presidency, Kohler had become increasingly weaker and less able to exercise his office. Already an old man when he became president, he gradually began to show distinct signs of advancing senility.[96] At length it was decided that, despite his initial reluctance, Kohler, would have to retire in order to make room for a younger and more energetic man. On February 23, 1921, he tendered his resignation, "being thus advised by his physician." After eighteen years it was again time to choose a new president; and again the outcome was by no means obvious from the start.

AMERICAN RABBIS FOR AMERICAN ISRAEL

> The period of dominant foreign ideas and principles in the Judaism of America is passing. . . . The new day of one, united, common American Judaism is dawning for us and our children—JULIAN MORGENSTERN in the *CCAR Yearbook,* 1919

ISAAC MAYER WISE HAD once believed in the possibility of a united American Jewry. But the sharp social and religious cleavages between the earlier German-Jewish immigrants and the later East European ones had destroyed that possibility. In the years that Kaufmann Kohler served as president of the College, Jews of German origin often chose to isolate themselves in their own circles, many expounding Reform Judaism as the particular faith of their social class. But by the time Kohler retired, the first legal restriction on immigration to the United States, the Immigration Quota Act of 1921, had been written into law. The second and even more severe limit was to be set shortly thereafter in 1924. The heretofore fluid substance of American Jewry thus seemed at last to be settling into a fixed mold. It became possible to assert that the sons and daughters of the German and East European Jewish immigrants would remove the social barriers and that Wise's hope for a single American Judaism would again have a basis in reality. Julian Morgenstern, the first American-born president of the College, undertook to revive Wise's dream.

Yet despite his hopes, neither he nor most of the Reform movement were quite ready to break out of isolation; Morgenstern himself questioned the wisdom of too precipitous an integration. The next quarter century in the history of the Hebrew Union College was therefore a period in which the school remained fundamentally entrenched in the mid-American environment of Cincinnati, still somewhat disdainful of the mighty and diverse Jewish community east of the Alleghenies. But at the same time it was a period of greater theological and ideological freedom, of increasing scholarly achievement, and—with the approach of the Holocaust—of notable acceptance of moral responsibility.

With the retirement of Kaufmann Kohler, two prominent Reform rabbis seemed the most likely candidates to succeed him as president of the College. Though there was some mention as well of Rabbis Samuel Schulman of New York, Henry Cohen of Galveston, Martin Meyer of San Francisco, and Julian Morgenstern of the College faculty,[1] the principal contenders were William Rosenau of Baltimore and David Philipson of Cincinnati. Each of the two was a graduate of the College, each had been president of the CCAR and was an active member of the Board of Governors. Each possessed an earned doctorate and had published scholarly books and articles. Philipson had also served on the faculty of the College. Although at its meeting of January 29, 1921, the Board of Governors received the report of its selection committee recommending William Rosenau for the position, a minority of the committee felt strongly that more time was needed to make a final decision. The minority therefore recommended that in the interim a member of the faculty, Julian Morgenstern, should serve as "acting president." That fall the board decided to accept the minority report and by a vote of nine to six selected the forty-year-old Morgenstern over his older colleague Henry Englander for the interim position.[2] In the months that followed, Philipson and Rosenau effectively canceled each other out. Both anti-Zionists, the two men were good friends and were reluctant to engage each other in a popularity contest. Philipson, moreover, wanted both to be president of the College and to retain his position at the Rockdale Temple, an arrangement unpalatable to most members of the board.[3] The situation that emerged was ideal for the success of a "dark horse" candidate.

Julian Morgenstern had long desired the presidency. As early as 1917, after he had been teaching at the College for ten years, the thought suggested itself to him, as he wrote in his autobiography, "that I might aspire to an even larger and higher service." He was encouraged in this ambition by a member of the faculty to whom he was particularly close.[4] To strengthen his position, Morgenstern, in 1917, as chairman of the CCAR Nominations Committee, selected himself for the Executive Committee, removing among others the name of David Philipson.[5] That same year he also became president of the HUC Alumni Association and began to build up a following among members of the Board of Governors. In 1919, Rabbi Henry Berkowitz of Philadelphia, a member of the Board of Governors, told Morgenstern he believed him qualified for the College presidency. Two years later, in the midst of his active campaign, Morgenstern used the occasion of congratulating Berkowitz on his birthday to remind him of his earlier positive evaluation. The letter to Berkowitz reveals Morgenstern's remarkable confidence in his own fitness for the job and in his chance of attaining it. He wrote:

> I firmly believe that I am in every way absolutely the best man for the position, high and honored though it may be. . . . Even though the Cincinnati members of the Board, who see me close at home, as a prophet in his own land as it were, do not seem, at least not the majority of them, to share my own good opinion of myself, none the less when the final election does come, if only my name is properly presented, my chances of being elected are rosy indeed.[6]

Having gained the position pro tem, Morgenstern left no stone un-
turned to prove himself capable of the task, in this way assuring
his final election. During 1921–22 he traveled from one major Jewish
community to another speaking on the College, raising money, and
recruiting students. At the same time he appointed new members of
the faculty and oversaw the formulation of a revised curriculum. By
May of 1922 he had sufficiently demonstrated his capacities for William Rosenau to urge the Board of Governors that Morgenstern be
made permanent successor to Kaufmann Kohler. That fall Morgenstern was duly elected to a two-year term, though not by a unanimous
vote.[7]

The new president, who was to determine the destiny of the College
for more than a quarter of a century, had entered HUC with little
enthusiasm and had passed through its curriculum without distinction.
He had been born in 1881 in St. Francisville, Illinois, the son of a
poor family of German-Jewish origin. His father had tried his hand
with limited success at various occupations in a number of small
midwestern towns before settling down in Cincinnati as a bookkeeper.
There his parents joined the Bene Israel congregation and sent their
son to Philipson's religious school. Their home was nearly barren
of Jewish ritual and observance. Not until he was a senior at HUC did
Morgenstern attend a traditional Passover *seder,* and at no time did
he regard ritual observance as of primary significance in Judaism.
Even after his retirement from the presidency, Morgenstern still felt
"distinctly ill at ease in an intensely ceremonial environment, and
still to a considerable extent playing the role of spectator rather than
of participant."

In 1894 he was confirmed at the age of thirteen, and he entered
Hebrew Union College that same fall. Since he had no ability for
business, no interest in law or medicine, it was decided by his father
along with Rabbi Philipson that he should become a rabbi. Once
at HUC, he studied little but managed to be ordained by "stumbling
through the eight years' curriculum of the College as little affected by
it as a student (?) could possibly be." He became a rabbi, he later
wrote, "more by inertia than anything else." Upon his ordination

in 1902, the still very young man went to Germany, less out of any
fervent desire to continue his studies than because his parents wanted
him to meet members of the family who had remained in Europe.
Once in Germany, however, his attitude to his studies finally changed.
Judah Magnes, then a student at Heidelberg, persuaded him to take
up Semitic languages and within two years he had completed his
doctorate *summa cum laude*. He returned to the United States, and
after three years as rabbi in Lafayette, Indiana, proposed himself
to Kohler for a vacancy on the faculty. Thanks to a good word from
Philipson, he was immediately appointed instructor in Bible and
Semitic languages.[8]

During the fifteen years that he served on the faculty before becoming president, Morgenstern developed both a distinctive method
in biblical studies and a vague philosophy of Judaism. Beginning with
the philological approach of the Wellhausen School, he gradually
came to place greater stress on sociological and historical factors in
textual analysis. From the first, he was interested in the connection between forms of observance and the development of religious ideas,
and in tracing the evolution of biblical faith from primitive to more
exalted expressions. In his dissertation he focused on the doctrine
of sin in the Babylonian religion, declaring that it bore startling re-
semblances to equivalents found in both Judaism and Christianity.
He saw Judaism as gradually extricating itself from the primitive
notions and superstitions to which it had been exposed in the Ancient
Near East. As a scholar, he was basically interested in understanding
how that emergence came about. To support his sometimes highly
imaginative theories, he freely emended the biblical text. Both in
his earlier work on Genesis and his later writing on Amos, Psalms,
and the ancient calendar, he applied biblical criticism without com-
punction.[9] When he was chosen president, scientific, analytic study
of the Bible—his special field of competence—became a central
pillar of rabbinic education.

Morgenstern's philosophy of Judaism was based on the same con-
ception of religious evolution that he employed in his scholarly work.
He believed in God's revelation to mankind through Israel and in
Israel's historical role as the bearer of a progressively better understood

religious and moral message.[10] But he was not primarily a theologian and he felt no need to indoctrinate students at the College with a definite theological position. Himself a theist, he tolerated religious humanism among both faculty and students. While he wavered considerably over the years on Zionism, he always managed publicly to remain between its outright proponents and its most vociferous critics. Usually he preferred to call himself neither Zionist nor anti-Zionist, but "non-Zionist." Both theologically and ideologically, his position was well suited to maintaining the support of the widest spectrum of the Reform movement.

Unlike Kohler, Morgenstern therefore did not come into office as president of the College with any desire to impose specific beliefs and convictions. He was more determined to bring about certain changes in the structure and character of the institution following the administrative lassitude of the final Kohler years. When Morgenstern took office, the presidency was weak, the faculty needed new blood, the virtually unaltered curriculum of twenty years lacked flexibility. There were far more positions available for young rabbis than could possibly be filled by each year's graduating class and there were insufficient qualified candidates for admission. In New York, Stephen S. Wise was creating a rival rabbinical school[11] whose graduates would be candidates for the open pulpits. Morgenstern lost no time in responding to his situation. Scarcely elected as acting president, he began immediately to reshape the school, giving the task all of his eager ambition and energy. Favored by auspicious economic conditions, he was able to make the first decade of his presidency—up to the Great Depression —a period of considerable expansion.

With the retirement of Kaufmann Kohler and the death of Gotthard Deutsch, both occurring in 1921, and the retirement of Louis Grossmann early in 1922, major subject areas at the College were left without instructors. Though not yet permanently in office, Morgenstern immediately set out to fill the void—and even to enlarge the faculty beyond its former size. Within a year he had gained board approval for five new appointments. Two of the men remained at the College for only a brief time. The one, Louis B. Wolfenson, possessed a doctorate from Johns Hopkins in Semitics and had taught for fourteen years at the University of Wisconsin before coming to HUC to teach Hebrew language. But unfortunately his knowledge of Hebrew proved to be considerably less than anticipated, and after two years he was not reappointed. The other, Henry Slonimsky, who had been associated with the Jewish Settlement in Cincinnati, was asked to teach pedagogy and ethics in place of Grossmann, but Slonimsky was not happy at the College and very shortly after his appointment accepted Stephen S. Wise's invitation to join the faculty of the Jewish Institute of Religion.

The three other new professors all remained on the faculty until their death or retirement. Of these, one, Jacob Mann, achieved fame principally as a scholar. When he came to the College to replace Deutsch in Jewish history, Mann had already published the first part of his work on Egyptian and Palestinian Jewry under the Fatimid caliphs. He was a Galician Jew who had gone to England and there earned both a doctorate and ordination as an Orthodox rabbi before coming to Cincinnati. During the eighteen years that he remained on the College's faculty, until his death in 1940, Mann's reputation as a scholar—especially deriving from his work on the documents of the Cairo *Genizah*—greatly heightened the standing of the College as a scholarly institution. In 1927–28 he was invited to serve as visiting professor at the fledgling Hebrew University in Jerusalem. Mann's classes at the College, however, did not have wide appeal. Mann was a representative of *Wissenschaft des Judentums* in its most minute and exacting form. He was a careful, erudite scholar who purposely abstained from broad generalizations and fanciful theories in the classroom no less than in his writings; he read his fact-packed lectures from note cards, scrupulously avoiding subjective comment. Though they admired his great learning and personal modesty, few students desired such a diet. With the exception of an occasional disciple, they often spent their time in his courses writing letters or preparing for other classes. No doubt Mann would have been more appreciated in a university, teaching men who themselves wanted to be scholars.[12]

Very different were the courses offered by Morgenstern's new appointment in Midrash and homiletics, Israel Bettan. Bettan's approach to his subjects was above all to stress their practical value to the future Reform rabbi. Born in Kovno, Lithuania, Bettan had attended the famous Slobodka Yeshiva before making his way via the Isaac Elchanan Yeshiva in New York to the rabbinical course at HUC. Upon graduation, he spent ten successful years in a pulpit in Charleston, West Virginia, receiving an earned D.D. degree from the College before accepting Morgenstern's invitation to join its faculty. Bettan proved to be an ideal counterweight to Mann. He was little interested in scholarship, more concerned with developing his students' ability to think creatively than with plunging them into the factual data of the past. His classes in Midrash consisted less of critical textual study than of inquiring into the spirit of the writers and applying their insights to contemporary reality. Indeed, Bettan frequently preferred to speak of politics, international relations, and his beloved Cincinnati Reds rather than the subject at hand—to the dismay of some students. He conducted his homiletics courses as give-and-take discussions, lecturing for only a small portion of the hour. He felt most at home when he was engaged in lively debate. In class, as on the pulpit, Bettan would often enthrall his listeners with his well-selected quotations from English literature, his skill as a raconteur, and his satiric wit. He possessed particular ingenuity in using biblical texts and midrashim to make a point, without thereby allowing the text to be a mere pretext. During his entire life, Bettan was a universalist, consistently negative on Zionism, unfriendly to ceremonialism and to the increased use of Hebrew in the prayerbook. Perhaps he did not want Slobodka to pursue him to HUC. Though he retained some traces of an accent and Yiddish intonations were sometimes heard in his voice, his mastery of English language and style was impeccable. For thirty-five years, until his retirement and death in 1957, this immigrant Jew from Eastern Europe was able to serve as an example of the specifically American Judaism which Morgenstern was seeking to create.[13]

There was one further appointment made that first year. It came in a field not previously represented at the College: Jewish social studies. Social justice had been a recognized part of Reform Judaism in America at least since the time Emil G. Hirsch insisted that a plank on the subject be inserted into the Pittsburgh Platform of 1885. But there had not been a full-time teacher at the College to deal specifically with the social doctrines of Judaism, relating them to American society and to the welfare agencies of the Jewish community. Morgenstern decided to fill that void by appointing Abraham Cronbach, a most unusual man, who over a period of twenty-eight years at the College presented a remarkable personal example of applied ethics. For many students during that time he provided a source of inspiration; from others he evoked anger or ridicule; but few could ignore him.

Like Bettan, Cronbach was a graduate of the College and had received its earned D.D. But unlike his colleague, he was a native-born American and possessed virtually no childhood Hebrew education. When he joined the HUC faculty after a not very successful pulpit rabbinate and a brief period of institutional chaplaincy, Cronbach was already a man of forty with well-developed ideas in the two areas where he would possess greatest influence: theology and applied social ethics. In New York, Cronbach had come under the influence of Felix Adler, the founder of the Ethical Culture movement. From Adler he adopted the notion that religion was essentially reverence for the human personality, that it was concerned more with high aims and noble purposes than with dogma or ritual. Like Adler, Cronbach considered himself a humanist and a universalist. He became the only member of the faculty who would perform mixed marriages. Cronbach's religious humanism won him numerous disciples, especially during the earlier period of his teaching at the College, when many students were searching for a nontheistic expression of Judaism.

But much more than for his theological position, Cronbach was known for his moral qualities of character and his endeavors to apply religious ethics to contemporary society. World War I had made him into a lifelong pacifist; it had become his firm conviction that it was better to suffer injury than to inflict it. Shortly after his appointment, Cronbach decided to circulate a "Pledge for Jewish Pacifists" among the students only to have the Board of Governors make him desist.[14] Finding it unjust that only those who died in war should be remembered on national holidays, Cronbach instituted the custom of going yearly on Decoration Day with a few students and others from the community to a local cemetery to lay flowers on the graves of "heroes of peace." They might include a railroader, a factory worker, a fireman who had perished in the line of duty, or a woman who had died in childbirth. Cronbach counseled his students to protest injustices loudly but always insisted that the protest be nonviolent, within the law, and supported by personal example. He demanded absolute honesty. Not all students at any period of his tenure at the College reacted favorably to Cronbach. For some he was simply too "saintly," an incongruous Christ-like figure in a Jewish seminary. His personal eccentricities, his severe austerity, the high-pitched, quavering voice, and the meticulous manner in class—these kept some students at a distance even from the first. But until the mid-thirties Cronbach was doubtless one of the primary influences on the student body. His unquestioned spirituality and commitment to social justice counterbalanced the tendency of others to make the College into an ivory tower.

Yet in the late thirties Cronbach's popularity definitely waned, not because he himself had changed, but precisely because he remained so unswervingly true to his original convictions. Cronbach was simply unable to believe that evil could not be won over by good. As the Nazi menace began to loom large in Europe, he wrote a letter to Hitler seeking to elicit a friendlier attitude toward the Jews and declaring that the German dictator, too, belonged to the Kingdom of Heaven. Shortly thereafter, he naively favored an "act of magnanimity" whereby funds would be raised by Jews in the United States for a relief program in Austria, in this way hopefully moderating Nazi hostility.[15] By the time of the Holocaust, Cronbach no longer enjoyed a great following among the students. Most had turned their backs on the pacifism, the anti-Zionism, anti-ceremonialism, and even the humanism which Cronbach continued to espouse. Yet some at least could not hide their admiration when a decade later, in 1953, three years after his retirement, Cronbach almost alone among Jewish leaders sought clemency for condemned spies Julius and Ethel Rosenberg, even daring to speak at their funeral. To the very end of his life he maintained the courage of his convictions.[16]

The initial five appointments still left one significant gap: there was no one to replace Kohler as professor of theology. Morgenstern had hoped to make an immediate appointment in this area as well, but controversy over the most suitable candidate delayed the decision for a year. Two names were considered: Hyman Enelow of Temple Emanu-El in New York City and Samuel S. Cohon of Chicago. By 1922, Enelow had published a number of volumes and established his reputation as a theologian and scholar. Morgenstern, however, favored the younger and less-known Cohon, believing that he would be a more effective teacher.[17] In this regard Morgenstern erred, however, for Cohon did not in fact inspire his students in the classroom; his presentations lacked fire, originality, depth of insight. Although students agreed that he possessed tremendous knowledge and though they respected him as a person, only very few felt that Cohon's eclectic theology directly influenced their own convictions.

Cohon's basic significance for Reform Judaism, however, did not lie in his teaching. In the thirties he achieved extraordinary influence through the practical work he did for the Central Conference of American Rabbis, formulating its new platform and editing the revision of its prayerbook. A Russian Jew not seeking to escape Jewish particularity, Cohon brought to Reform—including the College— an appreciation of tradition, a love of modern Hebrew, and a conception of religious peoplehood that ultimately made him—despite his shortcomings in the classroom—a crucial figure in the transition from classical to present-day Reform Judaism.[18]

The selection of Cohon in 1923 was followed a year later by the appointment of Abraham Z. Idelsohn to teach Jewish music, a discipline not previously represented at the College. A pioneer of Jewish musicology, Idelsohn had been a cantor in Europe and taught for a number of years in Jerusalem, where he collected and published the music of Oriental Jewish communities. His career at the College was cut tragically short by failing health that began in 1930 and forced his retirement four years later. A similar fate befell Sol Finesinger, who was appointed in 1925 to teach Hebrew and later Talmud. After a dozen years of very devoted teaching, Finesinger began to suffer nervous breakdowns in 1937 and had to be relieved of his duties shortly thereafter.

The last stage in Morgenstern's expansion of the faculty was his appointment of three recent graduates of the College returning to the United States after doctoral studies in Europe. In 1926 Sheldon Blank, who had received his doctorate in Jena, was made instructor in Hebrew (later also Bible), and Jacob R. Marcus, who had earlier been an instructor, returned from a leave of absence with a Berlin doctorate to become assistant professor of Jewish history. Shortly thereafter, in 1928, a third graduate who had gone to Europe for advanced study, Nelson Glueck, received a position as instructor in Hebrew language and Bible. Six years after Morgenstern's initial election the faculty had thus been increased to twelve regular full-time members, not including the president. Most of them were younger men.

The expansion of the faculty was justified by a continuous increase in enrollment. From World War I to the beginnings of the depression the size of the student body doubled, reaching 120 in 1929. During the early twenties, there were not enough graduates to meet the demand for newly ordained rabbis; thirty-nine positions remained unfilled in 1920, thirty-seven in 1923. The Board of Governors found it necessary to urge members of the CCAR to provide suitable candidates for the rabbinate.[19] In order to encourage students to come to the College, scholarships and loans were freely offered and special tutorial assistance was given to those with little preparation. As long as there was an obvious need for rabbis, the admissions policy of the College remained highly unselective. Even students with virtually no Hebrew knowledge whatsoever were at least accepted on probation or given "pre-preparatory" instruction. In 1925, among all applicants, only one was refused admission, and the situation was similar in the years immediately following.[20]

It was hoped, too, that a more flexible curriculum would attract more and better students. Ever since Kohler had first tried it—unsuccessfully—in 1906,[21] the introduction of a limited elective system to supplant the rigid division of the curriculum according to years had remained under discussion. But the small size of the faculty and the large number of required courses to be taught students during a nine-year stay precluded the possibility of allowing for flexibility and choice. By the time Morgenstern took office, most institutions of higher learning had replaced the class system with one based on credits,[22] and in the fall of 1922 the credit system was finally introduced permanently in the Collegiate Department of HUC as well. A minimum of seventy-nine credits was initially required for ordination. These were divided between required courses and electives, and for a time according to a system of one major and two minors. Some selection and specialization thus became possible, though the proportion of electives was always less than one-fourth of the total number of courses taken.

The minimal secular educational level of entering students was gradually raised, first to the third year of high school, and in 1924 to high school graduation. By 1926, a student had to receive his bachelor's degree at least three years before ordination, making possible a reduction in the total College curriculum from nine to eight years. Finally, beginning in 1930, only college sophomores were admitted to the Preparatory Department and a B.A. was required for admission to the Collegiate Department. Morning classes were offered for those who had finished their university work so that the increasing number of students now entering the school with B.A. in hand could complete their rabbinical studies in as little as five years or, with advanced standing, even in three.

In accordance with the common practice of universities and seminaries at the time, students during the early years of the Morgenstern administration were required to attend classes regularly. A comprehensive examination was introduced at the end of the Preparatory Department and, for a time, also a general examination, oral or written, upon completion of the Collegiate curriculum. All classes were supposed to include monthly or bi-monthly reviews and quizzes.[23] Generally twice each year the faculty would review the entire student roster at its meetings, allowing each professor to comment on problematic individuals.[24] Those found inadequate, either in scholarship or in character, were dismissed from the school.

In his senior year, as heretofore, each student wrote a thesis in the area of his choice. From time to time individual members of the faculty urged that every thesis should involve the use of Hebrew sources, but although for a period during the thirties that became the official policy, exceptions seem to have been made even then.[25] Upon completion of his rabbinical studies, the student was graduated in a ceremony held on the campus. Formally attired in striped pants and cutaway, he marched with the faculty from the library to the chapel, there to receive a personal, and in each case a different, biblical charge from the president as part of his ordination.

For a time it appeared that one of Morgenstern's earliest ordinees would be a woman. David Neumark's daughter, Martha, had been a student at the College since 1919, when she entered the "C" grade. Unlike the two young women who had received a Bachelor of Hebrew Letters degree already in Wise's time, Martha was determined to seek nothing less than ordination. In the spring of 1921, at the age of seventeen, she petitioned the faculty for permission to officiate at High Holy Day services that fall in the event that a pulpit was available. After lengthy discussion, a faculty vote resulted in a tie. Kohler broke the impasse by voting to approve the petition provided that the congregation in question would have no objection.[26] Kohler also realized that in view of Martha's request the general issue of whether to ordain women could now no longer be ignored, and he suggested to the Board of Governors that a joint board-faculty committee be appointed to present a recommendation.

The majority of the committee, including its chairman, David Philipson, reported that it saw "no logical reason" why women should not be entitled to receive a rabbinical degree, but "because of practical considerations" it suggested that their admission to the College with the aim of becoming rabbis be discouraged. Only Henry Englander was entirely favorable to women becoming rabbis, while Jacob Z. Lauterbach and board member Oscar Berman were opposed to the ordination of women under any circumstances. In their minority report, Lauterbach and Berman gave ten reasons for their objection, ranging from respect for religious tradition to fears that the Reform synagogue would become even more "an affair of the women" than it already was and that the presence of women in the small classrooms of the College might "have a tendency to distract some of the students from their work." The Board of Governors could not make up its mind what to do with the committee report and so referred the issue to the faculty for a decision on the attitude of Jewish law.[27] That winter the faculty obediently performed its assigned task, Lauterbach easily showing that the rabbinic view was against ordaining women while Buttenwieser pointed to Deborah, Hulda, and Miriam to prove that the spirit of the Bible was favorable. In the end, after much learned and protracted debate, Lauterbach himself reluctantly proposed, and the faculty unanimously adopted, a resolution that, the *halakha* notwithstanding, "in view of the fact that Reform Judaism has in many other instances departed from traditional practice, it cannot logically and consistently refuse the ordination of women." [28] The following summer the Central Conference of American Rabbis also discussed the issue and by a vote of fifty-six to eleven declared, likewise in a negative affirmation, that women "cannot justly be denied the privilege of ordination." [29] Finally, on February 27, 1923, the matter came back to the Board of Governors for final disposition. Despite the views of faculty and CCAR, the board voted "that no change should be made in the present practice of limiting to males the right to matriculate for the purpose of entering the rabbinate." Board members David Philipson and Carl Pritz asked that their votes be recorded in the negative.[30] Though she had thus lost her case, Martha Neumark nonetheless remained a student at the College until shortly after her father's death in December of 1924. In succeeding years, women from time to time participated in classes at the College, but none would be ordained until nearly fifty years later, in 1972.

The manner of Morgenstern's election and his immediate, firm grasp of the presidency did not endear him to his one-time mentor David Philipson. The Rockdale Ave. Temple rabbi, who during the twenties remained one of the most influential members of the Board of Governors, could not forgive Morgenstern for outmaneuvering him in the election. When the new president even refused to appoint the older man as professor of homiletics, he grievously compounded the injury. The result was that Philipson used every possible opportunity to place obstacles in Morgenstern's path—whether the issue was curriculum, a new appointment, or any other matter in which the authority of both president and Board of Governors was involved. Continual friction between the two men seemed inevitable. To Philipson, who had no children of his own, Morgenstern was an ungrateful son, while Morgenstern, for his part, seems to have labored under a compulsive need to destroy the older rabbi, even using the occasion of a faculty luncheon in honor of Philipson's seventieth birthday to offer him a public rebuke. Their strained relationship was never fully resolved and it hung as a cloud over Morgenstern's administration of the school.[31]

Fortunately, the president's relationship with other members of the Board of Governors was quite cordial. After some initial resistance, its genial chairman, Alfred M. Cohen, was perfectly willing to allow the new president to relieve the board of responsibility for most of the internal government of the school. When he came into office, Morgenstern had immediately set about to correct what he regarded as the board's encroachments on the duties and tasks of the president. He intended "to educate it to a new method," and he rapidly succeeded in doing so.[32] Only when insurance man Ralph Mack replaced Cohen in 1937 did the new chairman briefly attempt to exercise independent criticism of the Morgenstern administration and to reassert the earlier prerogatives of the board.[33] But his effort did not last. By the time busy physician Hiram B. Weiss took over six years later, Morgenstern's authority to run the school as he saw fit was again unquestioned.

And he did run the school. Every administrative matter came under his direct control; no issue was too insignificant for his attention. The president personally conducted correspondence with prospective students, arranged the faculty teaching schedule, handled matters of student discipline and placement, prepared the budget and the catalogue, and taught his courses in Bible as well. Nothing that occurred at the College was unknown to him.

As Morgenstern succeeded in impressing the Board of Governors with the prerogatives of his office, so did he quickly make his authority clear to faculty and students. Faculty meetings lasted long into the night and the most minute matters were discussed in great detail; but, except when a crisis arose, major decisions, were made by the president. In general, Morgenstern remained distant from his colleagues, not wholly one of their number.

For the students, the change in administration was initially most welcome. Morgenstern had always been appreciated as a fine teacher. Now, as president, he was engaged in augmenting the faculty and introducing a new elective system. The air seemed freer, interest in studies more genuine: "There is a new atmosphere at college," one student wrote.[34] Yet the enthusiasm was remarkably short-lived, in some instances turning even to fear or outright hatred of the president.[35] Why this shift should have occurred is a question which allows of no easy single answer. In part the resentment that a portion of the students harbored toward Morgenstern over the years was due to the power he exercised over their lives. How well a student did in the president's Deuteronomy course had a great deal to do with his tenure at the College; as Morgenstern enjoyed the sole prerogative of securing pulpits for graduating seniors, his evaluation was also crucial in determining a student's long-term future. The president's manner was likewise a factor. Though he felt himself a father to his rabbinical students and knew their hearts from his own experience, Morgenstern maintained a distance from the students that some interpreted as coldness or lack of human concern. He seemed to some to have transferred the great analytic ability and calm scientific detachment he exercised on texts in the classroom to his relations with people.

Yet, though basically the austere scholar, Morgenstern could at times display a warm sense of humor, and he nearly always manifested an unlimited zeal for the cause of the College and for Judaism as he perceived it. Certainly at least a portion of the ill will some students expressed toward Morgenstern would have emerged no matter who was president. Hostilities engendered by their own ambivalence about the rabbinate, their guilt about accepting scholarships and loans, and their need for self-assertion were bound to focus on the pervasive source of authority. As Morgenstern delegated none of his powers, all discontent necessarily was directed at him. If, despite the fact that the president imposed no ideological conformity on the students, some nonetheless claimed they felt repressed, it was no doubt due in large measure to an inner need to be rebels and not alone to the objective nature of Morgenstern's administration.

Early in 1925 the tensions created mainly by the contradictory policy of attempting to raise academic standards while exercising little discrimination in admission led to a severe crisis. The appeal for more students had produced unprecedentedly large numbers in the entering classes beginning with 1921. Some of the students soon proved to be either intellectually or emotionally incapable of managing their studies. Cheating on examinations, both in courses taken at the University of Cincinnati and in those taken at HUC, became so severe a problem that Morgenstern saw fit to convoke a special assembly in order to lecture students on the subject.[36] Within a brief period, in February 1925, one student committed suicide in the classroom building while another, a student in the "D" grade, eloped with a married woman, the mother of three children. The morale of all concerned dipped exceedingly low. Some students withdrew from the school, others were suspended or dismissed. By the end of March enrollment had dropped from 108 at the beginning of the school year to ninety-one. With this reduction in the student body, however, the crisis finally passed and things began to run more smoothly once again. The following year Morgenstern could believe the school had safely traversed the "turmoil and trial," the "restlessness and friction" of those first years.[37]

Despite their problems, the students in the bleak winter of 1925 had at least one cause for great content: the dedication—at long last—of the Hebrew Union College dormitory. As much as a decade earlier students had expressed their desire for a residence on campus to replace their dingy and inconvenient accommodations in boarding houses and private homes.[38] Most were living in Avondale, now rapidly becoming the Jewish neighborhood of Cincinnati, a mile or two distant from the school. They were forced to spend considerable time each day on the trolley or in some instances—for want of the fare—making their way to- and from the College on foot. The students' desire for a dormitory was given a large boost by J. Victor Greenebaum, a young Cincinnati physician, who in 1916 established a Department of Hygiene at the College to provide medical services for the students. Together with a committee, he made a survey of the students' living quarters which resulted in the recommendation of a dormitory—for the sake of student health. The proposal found favor in the eyes of the board, which at the time was concerned not only with improving the students' physical welfare and living conditions but with their qualities of character as well. As Alfred M. Cohen put it in his address at the graduation exercises in 1921: "If occasionally we detect in the manners of our students and graduates some things that do not square with what we deem becoming, we ought not be surprised if we will but remember that, though needing in greatest measure the refining restraint of proper Jewish environment, that privilege has not been theirs in the years when life habits are formed." At the same time the dormitory proposal was brought before the Council of the UAHC and the sisterhoods officially took it over as their special project. During the following four years they managed to raise about $250,000 to pay for the building.[39]

While the dormitory was going up in one part of the campus, a gymnasium, complete with swimming pool, basketball court, and a boxing and wrestling room was being raised behind the chapel. The gymnasium was the gift of a single donor, Mrs. J. Walter Freiberg, who offered to erect and equip it in memory of her recently deceased husband, a member of the College board and for ten years president of the UAHC. Like the dormitory, the gymnasium, too, was expected to have a beneficial effect on student health and morale, Morgenstern, for one, being convinced that lassitude in studies was related to insufficient exercise. Once the gymnasium was completed, all students were required to participate in the athletic program of the College. Cups and medals were awarded for superior achievement in various sports—"muscular Judaism," some called it with mild satire.[40]

Students began to move into the dormitory in the fall of 1924. About a hundred, virtually everyone not a Cincinnatian, came to live in the large brick structure planned to accommodate 119. Their life in the dormitory was at the very least comfortable, and certainly a marked improvement over previous conditions. For some students coming from poor families it represented a style of life not enjoyed in their own homes. With few exceptions, everyone had his own private room with bed, desk, bookcase, and easy chair. His bed was made daily by a member of the staff, his clothes cleaned for him in the basement laundry room. The food, by common dormitory standards, was excellent, and it was served to the students on white tablecloths by uniformed waiters. Everyone even had his own personal napkin ring. Though the meals were not kosher, pork and shellfish were excluded from the menu (as were the typically Jewish foods many of the young men had been used to eating at home). On the first floor there was a large living room with piano, lounging chairs, and a red brick fireplace. All was in the style of college houses in leading private universities.[41]

The vast majority of the students in this period continued to be American-born sons of poor East European immigrants. They came, of course, for a variety of reasons, from the most lofty to the most banal. But there were few instances in which a career in the rabbinate would not represent a social advance. The majority were from the Midwest and South with extraordinarily large contingents usually present from Cleveland and Cincinnati. Relatively few were from New York and New England.[42] Since many of the students, coming from Orthodox and Conservative homes, had had little contact with the Reform movement before coming to HUC, an uneasy relationship was sometimes created between themselves and the culturally very dissimilar German-Jewish Reform congregants whom they served in bi-weekly or Holy Day pulpits.[43]

During the Morgenstern administration students enjoyed virtually complete freedom of expression. They were at liberty to be Zionists or non-Zionists, theists or humanists, conservatives or socialists, pacifists or nonpacifists. They could and did invite controversial agnostic lawyer Clarence Darrow to speak to them in 1930, though they thereby provoked board member William Rosenau's anger at the president for not rescinding the invitation.[44] Student sermons were no longer censored; in the pages of the *HUC Monthly* students could openly criticize the College without provoking any disciplinary action. It was Morgenstern's view, privately expressed, that such critiques furnished "a very good outlet and safety valve for surplus steam" and thus prevented explosions of discontent. Moreover, any attempt to muzzle student opinion could only lead to radicalization. "It is best, therefore," he concluded, "to let these boys speak their pieces and pay as little attention to them as possible."[45]

Intellectual freedom, however, was accompanied by an expectation of conformity in conduct. In his classes Morgenstern insisted that students always appear in necktie and jacket. When he would invite a group to his home for a meal, it was often an ordeal for the ungainly young men to display proper grace at the table.[46] Cora Kahn, for many years instructor in elocution, took particular pains to impress the importance of proper manners and appearance. The cloistered atmosphere of the dormitory was intended to have a beneficial effect on the development of character. As in Kohler's time, students were expected to remain bachelors; they were explicitly advised to restrain their sexual impulses, sublimating them through hard physical and intellectual labor.

At the beginning of the Morgenstern administration there were virtually no married students. In 1925, one man received special permission from the faculty to marry, but it was specifically noted that the instance should not be allowed to become a precedent. Later, during the depression, students who married were deprived of financial support from the College. Only in the last years of Morgenstern's administration did the number of married students rise appreciably, reaching a total of seventeen out of a student body of about seventy.[47]

Within the walls of the dormitory there was rarely a single student community. Of course there was always some system of student government, but close relationships seem rather to have been formed within smaller groups: factions, "cliques," or subcommunities. Men who shared a common outlook, based on similar intellectual interests, religious concerns, or political ideology, tended to cluster together, often eating regularly at the same table, sometimes sharing contempt for fellow students not of their group. With their friends, students gathered in the living room (called "bumming room") to talk theology, Zionism, social justice, and to keep abreast of what was going on in the larger world outside. They measured the virtures and foibles of the professors, referring to them—whether out of affection or a desire slightly to demean—invariably by diminutives: Buttsy, Lauty, Morgy, Izzy, Crony, and the like. Students usually entered the College with a measure of naive idealism which was quickly shattered by the cynicism of upperclassmen and by the disillusion engendered by the realities of College life. But by the time they were ordained, most of them seem to have emerged with a no less deep, if somewhat more sober, commitment to their vocation in life.

The dormitory offered students a great deal: comfort, protection from loneliness, lively intercourse with fellow students. But living there for a long time—in some instances for as long as eight years—tended ultimately to narrow a man's outlook and limit his social concern. As one perceptive student wrote in his diary:

> The pressure of the herd dulls the fine edge of individuality. The constant contact of like-minded, like-purposed students becomes wearing in the extreme. We not only eat the same food but we digest the same ideas. We live in a common thought milieu and since the daily schedule of our lives is so much alike we bring the same apperceptive mass to the ideas of our classroom. . . .
>
> How can one gain sympathy for the disinherited when for six to eight years he is supported in comfort by contributions from those who own the fat places of the earth? [48]

There were in fact various ways to escape this atmosphere of uniformity. One was through attending lectures by outside speakers, who were invited with some frequency either by the school or by the students themselves. Over the years speeches and lectures were given by the Hebrew poets Bialik and Tchernichowsky, Zionist intellectuals like Jacob Klatzkin, leaders of the labor union movement, and a great variety of scholars from various American and foreign universities. A program of exchange lectures, begun with the University of Chicago Divinity School in 1927–28, in later years brought to HUC outstanding scholars from Yale, Duke, and Union Theological Seminary. Alumni spoke regularly on important phases of rabbinical life and work.

Though almost no one possessed an automobile, students managed to get out into the Jewish community, directing youth clubs in Price Hill, serving as chaplains at the Jewish hospital, and above all teaching religious school—though the latter ceased to be a requirement of the curriculum. Until the Depression there were numerous bi-weekly

congregations served by the students, giving them the opportunity
not only to get away from the dormitory every other weekend but also
to relish in advance of ordination some of the respect and honor that
would be accorded them as rabbis. During the summers students
usually scattered to their home communities. But occasionally they
took up a special project, as did five of their number who drove west-
ward from Cincinnati in the summer of 1938 dragging a trailer behind
them to bring advice and assistance to isolated Jewish communities
in about twenty-five small towns.

Student activities included the production of plays, which were
either satires on the faculty, written and staged by students, or more
serious efforts, such as the presentation of Stefan Zweig's *Jeremiah*
and Richard Beer-Hoffmann's *Jacob's Dream,* directed by Sheldon
and Amy Blank. College songs and yells reflected the unique character of the rabbinical student's experience.[49]

The most significant activity of the students continued to be the
HUC Monthly. Almost without exception its intellectual level remained high from year to year. For a time a portion of each issue
was published in Hebrew. Faculty, alumni, and occasional outsiders
as well as students wrote for its pages. During the thirties there were
symposia on the major Jewish and non-Jewish issues of the day: Re-
constructionism, the revision of the Pittsburgh Platform, pacifism,
Jewish education, and Zionism. At times the magazine chose to ignore
the internal affairs of the College, at others—especially in its editorials
—it was at least in part devoted to them.[50]

In the *HUC Monthly* criticism was first expressed publicly regarding what had long been a source of anxiety to many students: the
scholarship and loan system. Though tuition remained free, dormitory
and living expenses for the year in Cincinnati were beyond the capacities of most students and their families. In addition, for undergraduates, there was tuition to be paid the University of Cincinnati. Due
mainly to the generosity of various sisterhoods around the country,
scholarships were available for a large portion of the student body,
distributed according to the faculty's evaluation of both academic
performance and general attitude toward the College.[51] The system put
an extraordinary premium on achieving uniformly high marks and

on maintaining proper respect. Discontent with it at length led to its abolition in 1933 in favor of a policy of granting all students, after the first year, a scholarship to cover the cost of residence in the dormitory. In addition, a "Placement Bureau" was established to assist them in finding employment either at the College itself or outside. The additional income would cover their living expenses apart from the dormitory.[52] During the same period a Faculty-Student Relations Committee was created for the first time. Under the chairmanship of Morgenstern himself, it was intended to create a forum for the discussion of such items as curriculum, examinations, and discipline, and above all to produce a healthier and more friendly relationship between the two groups. For a time it seems indeed to have succeeded in its aims.[53]

During the years that Morgenstern was devoting his energies to the expansion of the College in Cincinnati, he also made one significant move to bring an HUC presence to New York City. Not since 1885, when the Preparatory Department at Temple Emanu-El was closed for lack of funds and students, had there been any ongoing activity conducted by the College in the largest center of American Jewish life. Although Stephen S. Wise's Jewish Institute of Religion now filled the need for a liberal rabbinical seminary in the metropolis, there remained another area in which the College could play a role: the training of religious-school teachers.

After much effort, it had proven futile to conduct a significant teacher-training institution for the Reform movement in Cincinnati, a city whose Jewish population had been in decline since reaching a highpoint of 28,000 around 1912.[54] Following World War I, Louis Grossmann, who had been principal of the Cincinnati institute, pleaded with the Board of Governors for the establishment at least of permanent branches outside Cincinnati—especially in New York. The branches would not only train teachers but also sift potential rabbinical students for eventual enrollment in the College. In a lengthy proposal, he included the following:

I should like to call attention to a condition in this country which the Hebrew Union College must recognize. It is the fact that Reform Judaism has its center in New York City, by reason of its numbers, the stress of its life, and the fusion of its elements. One of the functions of the Hebrew Union College is to be a potent factor in the Americanization of the immigrant Jews and that function is the more likely to be effective since the College is expected to furnish educational and spiritual leaders. . . . There was a time when we could conduct a cloisteral, provincial institution. That time has passed. An academic institution must be near the life of the people and a Jewish school must be in constant and intimate touch with it. . . . The time of a strictly "theological" College is over.[55]

As a child of the Midwest, Morgenstern was not a great enthusiast for New York City. Realizing that the College's location in Cincinnati was hardly ideal from the standpoint of financial support, he nonetheless thought that the environment Cincinnati provided "could probably not be improved upon."[56] Yet when members of the New York Association of Reform Rabbis, and especially Samuel Schulman, solicited the College to establish a Hebrew Union College School for Teachers in New York, Morgenstern was not adverse to the proposition. In 1923 the College founded such a school under the direction of Abraham N. Franzblau, a bright young man who succeeded in rapidly building up both quality of instruction and enrollment. By 1925–26, over three hundred students were attending at least one course in its Temple Emanu-El classrooms, though relatively few of them completed the entire curriculum. Up to 1931, the school graduated 146 students, or an average of about eighteen per year. Its part-time faculty included men who would later attain great scholarly distinction: Hebraist Simon Halkin, historian and sociologist Oscar Janowsky, and classicist Moses Hadas.

It was the financial stringencies imposed by the depression that ultimately brought the relatively successful project to its demise. The budget request for the school eventually ran to above $30,000 per year, an amount that became exceedingly difficult for the College to spare in the early thirties. Moreover, there were board members who even earlier believed that it should be financed locally or by the

UAHC—which did in fact agree to take over its budget in 1929. In 1931, Morgenstern decided to bring Franzblau to Cincinnati, as associate professor of Jewish religious education, leaving the school in the hands of Hadas. Its prospects now were dim. With the nearly destitute Union unable to continue support and the College unwilling to reassume it, millionaire Adolph Ochs personally guaranteed $20,000 from the New York community to prevent discontinuance. But when a solicitation for funds in New York produced only the meager result of $267.50, the school's fate was sealed. Ochs refused henceforth to pick up the bill. After the lapse of a year, the Union did make a renewed effort, but its "School for Jewish Studies" was able to maintain itself for only a brief time until it, too, was closed for lack of funds in 1938.[57]

The New York venture, however, seems never to have been a primary concern either of the Board of Governors or of the president. Until the financial squeeze of the depression every effort continued to be focused on expanding the center in Cincinnati.

The faculty continued to grow. After a lapse of some years following the death of David Neumark, Zevi Diesendruck replaced him as professor of Jewish philosophy in 1930. Morgenstern's first choice for the position had been Julius Guttmann of the *Hochschule* in Berlin. But during a semester's teaching at the College in the spring of 1930, Guttmann indicated that he preferred not to remain.[58] The Board of Governors Committee on Vacancies thereupon turned to Diesendruck, a Galician Jew then teaching in Jerusalem.[59] Diesendruck, who was at the College for a decade until his untimely death in 1940, was interested especially in Maimonides and Plato. On the former he wrote scholarly articles; the latter's dialogues he translated into Hebrew. An austere rationalist in his philosophy, demanding and sometimes sarcastic in the classroom, Diesendruck made few disciples, though many students admired his scholarship, and Zionists among them were attracted by this principal proponent of their cause on the faculty.[60]

The year 1930 also witnessed the first major administrative appointment at the school. Ever since Kohler's presidency, the popular

Henry Englander had borne the burden of serving as registrar in addition to his regular teaching duties. Now Morgenstern was finally able to convince the board to appoint a man who would devote himself primarily to such duties as advising students, settling disputes with regard to grades, administering emergency loans, and helping to represent the College before the general public. Morgenstern's choice fell on Shalom B. Maximon, a Hebrew essayist and educator who had taught in the College's School for Teachers in New York. Maximon, who did not possess a doctorate, was also assigned to teach Hebrew conversation in the Preparatory Department, and he seems to have gotten on well with students during his brief tenure at the College.[61]

The final appointment to the faculty before the depression halted all further expansion was that of Abraham Franzblau in 1931. Adept not only as an administrator but also as a teacher of pedagogy, Franzblau was able finally to fill the vacuum left in this area since the resignation of Slonimsky. Over the years, he and his students created numerous syllabi and educational materials for religious-school courses, some of which were later published by the UAHC. Franzblau was generally regarded as a good teacher, his courses ever alive with new ideas. A man of strong will and great energy who stood close to the president, Franzblau successfully undertook and completed psychiatric studies simultaneously with his teaching at the College. Eventually, he was able to utilize this newly gained knowledge by offering the first HUC courses in pastoral psychology.

With the addition of Diesendruck, Maximon, and Franzblau, the faculty reached fifteen regular members in 1931–32, its high-point during the entire Morgenstern period. Of these, only a slight majority were now foreign-born; seven were ordinees of the College. Nearly all possessed an earned doctorate, and all but three were Morgenstern appointments. They earned up to a regularly attained maximum of $8,000 per year, a comfortable salary amounting to two-thirds the compensation of the president.[62] They received tenure after six years;[63] according to a board decision of January 1932, they enjoyed the right to a sabbatical leave with pay every fourteenth year, though worsening economic conditions prevented its exercise by a regular member of the faculty until 1947.[64]

The faculty was divided into a number of committees headed by an Executive Committee presided over by Morgenstern himself. It possessed a close working relationship with the Board of Governors not only through various joint committees but also through combined meetings of the two groups held at least once a year. Until 1928, the average teaching load borne by professors stood at slightly over twelve hours per week, considerably above that of the best seminaries and universities. That year, however, a general reduction was made possible, principally because of the growing size of the faculty. Full professors henceforth taught only eight to ten hours.[65]

The main reason Morgenstern gave the board for reducing the faculty teaching load was that he believed it would allow for greater scholarly productivity. Yet even under the burden of having to spend many hours in the classroom, that productivity had in fact already been considerable. The HUC faculty, individually and collectively, by the late twenties had achieved high standing in the world of scholarship. A number of professors had published important books and articles in their fields; some of them had made major contributions to the *Jewish Encyclopedia* and to the Jewish Publication Society's Bible translation.

On the campus, opportunities for post-rabbinical study had been enhanced through the award of annual fellowships beginning in 1926. Rabbis came during the summers to refresh and advance their learning. Morgenstern himself conducted an ongoing advanced Bible seminar limited to faculty and graduates. The school's status as an institution of advanced studies was officially recognized in 1927 when the College for the first time hosted a major scholarly organization, the American Oriental Society, which that year elected Morgenstern its incoming president.

In 1921, the newly established Hebrew Union College Press published its first volume: a popular work, *Intimate Glimpses of the Rabbi's Career,* given as a series of lectures three years earlier by alumnus Henry Berkowitz. After a considerable interval, there followed Idelsohn's *Divan of Hebrew and Arabic Poetry of the Yemenite Jews,* and in 1931 Mann's monumental *Texts and Studies in Jewish History and Literature.* Following the severest depression years, which allowed few funds to flow into additional publications, the Press was reactivated in the late thirties.

Far more significant a project than these occasional publications, however, was the *Hebrew Union College Annual.* The idea of publishing a yearly collection of scholarly articles under the aegis of the College was first conceived by a student, Ephraim Fisch, in 1904. His volume, entirely a student venture, included learned or popular articles by every member of the faculty as well as by European scholars Wilhelm Bacher and Claude Montefiore. There was also a variety of contributions by students. But Fisch graduated that year and no one carried on his project. It was not until David Neumark began single-handedly to publish his *Journal of Jewish Lore and Philosophy* in January 1919 that there again appeared a local vehicle for the publication of faculty scholarship. Although Neumark's quarterly lasted for only a single year before it collapsed for lack of funds, the editor, using the good offices of David Philipson, was able to persuade the Board of Governors that his journal should become a College publication. After some delay, the first volume of the *HUC Annual* appeared in 1924. Its original editorial board consisted of David Philipson (chairman) and William Rosenau of the Board of Governors, Kaufmann Kohler and Julian Morgenstern, and faculty members Neumark and Lauterbach.

The *Annual* immediately established itself as a first-rate repository of Jewish scholarship, comparable to the *Jewish Quarterly Review* and the German *Monatsschrift.* Scrupulously avoiding partisan tendencies, it attracted to its pages leading Jewish scholars, both in the United States and abroad. Over the years, it became known especially for its articles in Bible, Semitics, rabbinics, and Jewish philosophy. By the time of Morgenstern's retirement, twenty volumes had appeared, and the *Annual,* perhaps more than any other venture, had created an image of the College not alone as a theological seminary, but as a significant force in the advance of Jewish scholarship.

The expansion of the College necessitated a major increase in its budget. From slightly over $100,000 when Morgenstern took office in 1921, yearly expenditures nearly tripled by the end of his first decade. It was clearly not possible to maintain growth of such magnitude from the dues and occasional contributions given by members of the UAHC, especially as the parent body was growing only very slowly, reaching a maximum of 60,270 members in 1929 before beginning to decline. Moreover, since 1924 it had spent more than it had taken in.[66] In 1925, the Union eliminated its Board of Delegates on Civil Rights, choosing to restrict itself to purely religious aims, but it now reserved much of its limited income for aiding congregations and religious schools. Aside from Union dues, the College could draw only on sisterhood scholarships and an insignificant endowment fund of about $500,000, controlled by the UAHC.

The College was in sore need of a large endowment of its own which would grant it a measure of security against the vagaries of yearly campaigns and against competition from other Union projects. Clearly no sizable amount of money could be obtained from the Cincinnati Jewish community. Substantial Jewish wealth lay mainly in the East, especially in New York, or in Chicago. Fortunately for the College, there was one wealthy New York Jew with close ties to the Jewish aristocracy of that city who possessed a special relationship to the College. Adolph S. Ochs, the publisher of the *New York Times*, was also the son-in-law of Isaac Mayer Wise. An anti-Zionist who saw Judaism in exclusively universalistic terms, he was nonetheless devoted to preserving its institutions. Though not on the College's Board of Governors, he was a member of the Executive Board of the Union. In response to a survey circulated to Reform leaders in 1924, Ochs had answered the question of how to educate American Jews following the restriction of immigration by suggesting: "Endow the Hebrew Union College with five million dollars to educate and train men and women to keep the faith and enlighten the world with the spirit and tenets of American Judaism." [67] A year later he proposed in writing to the Union Council meeting in St. Louis that the Union embark on a campaign to raise an endowment for the College.[68] Not surprisingly, he was speedily made chairman of a committee to raise the funds.

At first things went very slowly. An initial $650,000 was secured in large pledges mostly from New York, including $50,000 amounts from Henry Morgenthau, Felix Warburg, members of the Guggenheim family, and Mortimer Schiff. These men could not easily refuse a request coming from so prominent a member of their own circle.[69] Ochs and his wife themselves publicly pledged $200,000. Shortly thereafter, the chairman sent out a letter to prospective contributors which stressed especially that enlightened, liberally educated rabbis would be a force for combating antisemitism: "Public opinion of American Jews depends, in no small measure, on these men." He attached a statement praising the College written by Dr. Frank Gavin, who had been the first Christian student to study at the College (1911–14) and was then a professor of ecclesiastical history at General Theological Seminary. Ochs noted that Gavin had himself contributed $25.[70] Over the next two years, however, the fund grew to only about $1,600,000, far short of the projected goal.

Then one day Ochs noticed that Sears, Roebuck magnate Julius Rosenwald, likewise a member of the Union's Executive Board, in a newspaper interview had expressed concern about the need for improving Jewish education. Ochs wrote a personal letter to Rosenwald and received in reply Rosenwald's promise to give the College half a million dollars. But he posed certain conditions: the total Endowment Fund would have to reach $4 million, including his own contribution, before the gift would become official, and at least $3 million of the principal—in addition to the income—would have to be spent at the rate of between 3 and 5 percent per year. Rosenwald's intention was to challenge the Union leadership to greater campaign efforts and also to make certain that later generations would not simply inherit benefits bestowed on them by their predecessors.[71] He stipulated a deadline of July 1, 1929, by which time a grand total of $4 million (including about $750,000 on hand before the campaign) would have to be raised.

The effect was all that could have been desired. In less than a year—and before the deadline—$2 million in additional pledges were received, bringing the total to over $4 million. The Ochs family had raised its own gift to $500,000 to match Rosenwald, and the Guggenheim and Schiff families had done the same. Far smaller were the gifts coming from Cincinnati, the largest being $10,000 given by Maurice J. Freiberg, a member of the College's board.[72] Though all together more than nine hundred people contributed, 61 percent of the amount raised came from sixteen persons.[73]

With a combined total of about $4,350,000 contained in the Endowment Fund or pledged to it ($3,600,000 of it from the drive), Ochs closed the campaign, hoping that the remaining $650,000 necessary to reach the original goal of $5 million would be forthcoming through unsolicited contributions and bequests.

But of course he was wrong. The completion of the drive preceded the stock market crash of 1929 by only a few months. The Endowment Fund, intended to provide for the College's growth, served another purpose instead: it ensured the school's survival during the dark years of the depression.

Before he took on the responsibility of chairing the Endowment Fund campaign, Ochs insisted on an alteration of the relationship between the Union and the College. Until that time, the College had been strictly an activity of the Union, which wholly controlled its budget; it enjoyed no separate legal existence. When the Union ran deficits, it would encroach on the then very meager College endowment. Ochs therefore demanded that the College be incorporated separately under the laws of the State of Ohio so that its expanded endowment would not be subject to manipulation by the Executive Board of the Union. Moreover, only if it were a separate corporation could bequests properly be left directly to the College, rather than to the Union.

The Union did not oppose this separation. In fact a UAHC committee had made the same proposal as early as 1924. Its leadership felt that the new arrangement would bring in more money for the College, relieving the parent body of some of its responsibility. Rivalry between the two institutions, then both still centered in Cincinnati, was minimal during these years when Morgenstern was president of the College and George Zepin secretary of the UAHC. To make possible a separate incorporation of the College, the Union in 1926 transferred $25,000 to it, and henceforth became its "patronizing body." The College was now able to raise funds on its own and to have sole legal control over them.[74] All land and buildings, however, remained the possession of the Union.[75]

According to a new set of by-laws passed at the time, the Executive Board of the Union retained the right to elect about two-thirds of the Board of Governors, the remainder being chosen by the Alumni Association and from the ranks of the CCAR. Morgenstern for the first time became a board member ex-officio, bringing its total membership to thirty-one. As the board was constituted in 1927, it consisted of twelve Cincinnatians (slightly less than had been the case earlier) with the rest scattered about the country. Instead of meeting monthly as heretofore, the Board of Governors now met only three times a year—in February, May, and November—and on occasion it met outside Cincinnati. However, day-to-day affairs passed into the hands of an Executive Committee of nine, all of whom were from Ohio, seven of them from Cincinnati. The committee held regular monthly meetings and possessed full authority to transact routine business.[76]

The most influential figures on the Board of Governors continued to be the local people. The three chairmen during the Morgenstern years—Alfred M. Cohen, Ralph W. Mack, and Hiram B. Weiss—were all Cincinnatians. The former two were upper-class German Jews; the last, a self-made physician who was the son of poor Lithuanian immigrants, had married into a well-established Cincinnati family. David Philipson remained a regular member of the board until 1947, but his significance gradually waned. Among the laymen who were not chairmen, the most significant seem to have been conservative businessman Simon Lazarus of Columbus and retired whiskey rectifier Carl Pritz of Cincinnati. The former had a decisive say in who became chairman of the board (while refusing to take the office himself),[77] the latter—a cultured liberal—for a lengthy period presided over the College's budget.

The years of expansion in faculty, enrollment, and scholarly projects were also a period of growth for the library. New collections of books and manuscripts were acquired by purchase or donation. Especially noteworthy were a large hoard of Samaritanica and several Yemenite Hebrew and Judeo-Persian manuscripts purchased by librarian Adolph Oko during a trip to the Near East. Sustained by a sizable budget that reached nearly $50,000 in 1930–31 (about 15 percent of the total College budget for that year), the library was able to acquire virtually every newly published item of Judaica and to fill in gaps in its holdings of older volumes. It grew from a mere school library for the immediate use of its students into a major repository of Jewish intellectual achievements for the benefit of the larger world of Jewish scholarship. Although the library building had seemed far more than adequate when it was built in 1912, by 1925 it was already judged too small to house the College's collection of some 80,000 volumes and 2,000 manuscripts. Despite the competition from Ochs's endowment campaign, Oko managed to get together a committee of the Union to raise $250,000 for a new structure. By concentrating on a few large donations,[78] the committee (but mostly Oko himself) was able to secure and even to exceed the projected amount with comparative ease.[79]

The new building, dedicated in 1931, was designed according to a plan submitted by the librarian himself. The completed two-story structure was both modern and lavish. Fireproof throughout, it contained its own up-to-date bindery and an area for the later installation of photostatic equipment. The Manuscript and Rare Book Room was a magnificent creation: allegheny metal and brass, used in conjunction with glass cabinets, made it seem like a "decorative vault" containing the College's most valued treasures. Total shelf capacity was 160,000 volumes, with expansion possible to over a quarter of a million.[80]

The College, which had always been appreciative of Oko's genius and had paid him a salary above that of any faculty member, now presented its librarian with a sabbatical year in Europe and (over some faculty opposition) with an honorary degree as well. Yet his exalted status at the College was short-lived. Only two years after the dedication of the new library, Oko was dismissed from his position as librarian— not for any professional error, but for a "moral offense." The brilliant and charming man who, unlike most members of the faculty, possessed social access to the Cincinnati Jewish aristocracy, had fallen in love with a married woman from the cream of Cincinnati Jewish society. As soon as the lady was able to secure a Reno divorce, they were married—on the eve of the Sabbath and by a Christian minister. The majority of the Board of Governors thereupon felt they had no choice but to request their librarian's resignation. Oko was succeeded during the Morgenstern period by Walter Rothman and Irving M. Levey, but neither man possessed their predecessor's great talents.[81]

The completion of the magnificent new library building was the capstone and climax of the years of expansion that had begun in the early twenties. The following decade, the period of the Great Depression and the beginning of World War II, was marked by severe retrenchment followed almost immediately by the need to respond to the plight of rabbinical students and Jewish professors in Hitler's Germany. It was not a time when the College's growth could continue in planned and orderly fashion.

Even before the Wall Street crisis of 1929, the Reform movement had begun to stagnate. From 1927 until 1929, membership in the Union went up by only 264 souls while the number of congregations decreased by one. Thereafter, the losses were considerable. From 1929 to 1935, UAHC congregations lost 13 percent of their members, and even those who remained in many instances paid only a portion of their dues. Some congregations went out of existence; others merged. UAHC indebtedness climbed rapidly, exceeding $250,000 as early as 1931.[82] To many Reform Jews, belonging to a congregation became a luxury they could no longer afford. With decreased congregational budgets, starting rabbinical salaries went down from about $4,000 per year to $1,200, while men in the field faced reductions from 10 percent up to a total withdrawal of salary. Some congregations would not engage married men because they knew the salaries they could offer would at best sustain a bachelor. There was soon a long list of rabbis looking for any position at all. Some of them, Morgenstern wrote in 1932, "are literally on the verge of starvation and are compelled to accept charity from their colleagues in order to provide food for their families."[83] Not surprisingly, the Alumni Association began to exercise maximum pressure on the College to reduce drastically the number of men it was ordaining every year.[84]

As for the College, thanks to the Ochs Fund it was in a far better state financially than would otherwise have been the case. Its endowment was conservatively invested, largely in railroad bonds and not at all in common stocks. As a result, losses were minimized.[85] In addition, according to Rosenwald's terms, $90,000 to $150,000 had to be removed from the capital for operating expenses every year. During the depression the annual endowment depletion covered from one-third to nearly one-half of the yearly budget. Compared to the Union, the College was fortunate indeed.

Nevertheless, the College's situation during the depression years was not an easy and pleasant one. Many pledges to the Endowment Fund had been made with the arrangement to pay them off over as much as ten years. By 1933, numerous donors were not making their payments or were canceling their pledges. Ultimately, only about $3,200,000 was actually collected.[86] Moreover, no new funds were being pledged to replace those removed by the mandated depletion which yearly reduced the principal and its earnings. It was therefore not possible to maintain the College budget at its previous size, let alone to expand it.

Nor was it possible to provide jobs for all the graduates. In 1927 there were thirty congregations applying for the services of ten newly ordained rabbis; two years later the supply had already met the demand, but almost every graduate was placed by the end of the summer. In 1931 placement became difficult, but not impossible; by 1932 the situation was disastrous. Of eighteen ordinees that year, only two had received positions by the middle of May. After being unable to find any regular pulpit, a few of them were allowed to continue living in the dormitory and were assigned one of the few remaining bi-weekly congregations. With bitter humor they dubbed themselves "rabbis-in-waiting." [87]

In order to cope with the situation, the College began to reduce the number of students it admitted each year. It now had every reason to be more selective than heretofore. In 1931 only fifteen applicants out of forty-five were accepted, in 1932 only eight out of twenty-six.

For the next decade the number of entering students was kept low, with as few as four admitted to the College in 1940. Members of the faculty consoled themselves that the ill fortune of the depression had brought at least one benefit: greater selectivity among applicants.[88] The College also began to thin the ranks of students already admitted. An unpublicized but strict quota of not more than seventy-five regular students in the College was set for 1932–33. Small entering classes and the dismissal of large numbers of students now deemed beneath standards brought total enrollment from 120 in 1928-29 down to fifty-eight—less than half—in 1934–35.[89]

Those students who remained found life in the dormitory somewhat less posh than before. Hired waiters were replaced by students earning a few extra dollars from the Placement Bureau; laundry assistance, too, was rendered by students. During these difficult years for America, when socialism had such broad appeal, students at the College, too, were critical of the fruits of capitalism. They proposed to socialize their earnings so that impecunious classmates might be assured a more equal standard of living. In the *HUC Monthly* one of them expressed the hope that their program would, in turn, "be a challenge to the Board of Governors and men in similar positions to question more firmly the inequitable distribution of earnings in the businesses and occupations in which they find themselves." [90] Recent graduates of the College radicalized the ranks of the CCAR, much to the dismay of the laity. When a straw vote was taken at a dinner of HUC alumni on the Saturday evening preceding the presidential election of 1932, the vast majority voted for the socialist candidate Norman Thomas, while only fifteen favored Roosevelt and a single one voted for Hoover.[91]

Aside from reducing the size of the student body, the main concern was to cut the budget to match steadily declining income. A number of steps were taken: the yearly summer school in Cincinnati, which had been offered for ordained rabbis since 1925, was abandoned, as was the New York School for Teachers and its summertime equivalent in Cincinnati. Publication of the *HUC Annual* was postponed for a year in 1933, and even the published catalogue became a shadow of its former self. The library budget was cut 60 percent. Funds previously available for student activities were diverted to more urgent uses. Faculty salaries—despite a protest to the Board of Governors— were lowered at first by 10 percent and later to an aggregate of 25 percent.[92]

For the faculty the reduction in salaries, which in view of the decline in the cost of living did not make life unbearable, was not the chief worry in the depression years. It was rather the very retention of their jobs. The much smaller student body had created a faculty-student ratio which was exceedingly difficult to justify. In 1933, there were less than five students to each professor. Members of the Board of Governors began to ask whether the faculty was not excessively large. A board committee was created to look into the possibility of reducing its size. Averse to outright dismissal of professors (although not all as yet possessed tenure), the committee recommended instead that mandatory retirement be fixed at age sixty-eight, thus immediately removing Professors Lauterbach and Buttenwieser (the former agreeably, the latter against his will). Idelsohn's illness made his retirement necessary as well. To make up for their loss, teaching loads were raised to an average of twelve to thirteen hours per week.[93] It was likewise decided to eliminate the separate office of registrar, allowing its functions to devolve once again on Henry Englander. This last step, taken over student protests, resulted in the removal of Shalom Maximon—a most unfortunate action followed within a few weeks by the disconsolate and already ill man's untimely death.[94] One additional precaution was taken to provide for possible further dismissals: tenure henceforth was no longer given simply after six years, but only after that period had been spent at the rank of associate professor or above.[95]

Fortunately, not long thereafter, the economic tide began to turn. In 1935–36, both the Union and the College were able to end the year with a surplus. As business began to pick up and prices to rise once again (albeit not consistently), budget cuts were gradually restored, and the opportunities for graduates improved considerably. Responding to the change in economic conditions, the Board of Governors for the first time decided to invest 30 percent of its endowment in common stocks, thereby putting the College in a good position to profit from a long-term rising stock market.[96] The financial upswing came none too soon, however, for the gathering storm clouds in Europe were already imposing a new and heavy burden upon the College.

Hitler's rise to power in the winter of 1933 was followed almost immediately by an initial implementation of his antisemitic ideology: on April 1st of that year Nazi stormtroopers took up positions in front of Jewish businesses bearing placards that warned customers to keep away; Jews were assaulted in the streets and in some instances murdered. Students and faculty at the College could scarcely ignore what was happening to their brethren. They participated in the boycott of German goods; they discussed ways to stimulate American public opinion against Hitler, to advance the cause of German Jewry via diplomatic channels, and to secure relief for the refugees. Five years later, in November 1938, when German synagogues went up in smoke during the infamous *Kristallnacht,* HUC students sent a barrage of telegrams to President Roosevelt and urged their bi-weekly congregations to do likewise. Some of them helped to organize and publicize a giant protest meeting in Cincinnati's Emory Auditorium.[97]

The College had a special relationship to German Jewry. The founders had all come from its ranks, and to a large extent the Board of Governors was still composed of men whose parents or grandparents had immigrated from Germany. Various American-born members of the faculty, beginning with Morgenstern, had received their doctorates there and had made the intimate acquaintance of German Jews. But what, concretely, could the College, as an institution, do?

As it turned out, there was a saving, even unique, kind of action that HUC was able to perform. With the future of German Jewry becoming ever more hopeless, Ismar Elbogen, the head of the *Hochschule* (now degraded by the Nazis to *Lehranstalt*) *für die Wissenschaft des Judentums,* and Julian Morgenstern worked out an arrangement whereby a few students of the German liberal seminary could pursue their rabbinical studies at the College. If conditions permitted, they would return to Germany after ordination; if not, they would seek positions in the United States. Despite the College's

continuing financial difficulties and the ongoing lack of pulpit vacancies, its board agreed to underwrite fully the expenses of the five young
men who arrived from Germany in the fall of 1935. In the next few
years, three more rabbinical students from the Continent came to
study in Cincinnati.[98]

The College might have done still more. Other applicants wanted
to come and were turned down. But by 1938 the refugee students
made up 12 percent of the total enrollment and there was a serious
question of how many foreign-born, and generally quite traditional,
young rabbis the American Reform movement could absorb. Morgenstern had to consider the situation in the United States; obviously he
could not know what the consequences of refusal would ultimately
be.[99] Moreover, compared to other Jewish institutions, the College
was doing better than its share. One of the members of the faculty
summed it up with candor: "It is ironical that the Reform (assimilationist!!) seminary takes in the European semi-orthodox but other
institutions in this country won't give them a break!! We have no
alternative morally, but we are certainly complicating our rabbinical
problems with these men." [100]

The students who came from Europe were not exactly "semi-
orthodox," but they were certainly more favorably inclined to traditional observances than the vast majority of the HUC student body
had ever been previously. For the president, most of the faculty, and
nearly all of the students, ceremonial had remained strictly subordinate
to the theological and moral message of Judaism. Few faculty and almost no students kept the laws of the Sabbath or of *kashrut;* worship
in the HUC chapel was conducted without head covering or prayer
shawl, most students coming regularly on Sabbaths (when attendance
was required), but rarely to the daily services.

However, for the Reform movement as a whole, and so too for
the College, that attitude was beginning to change in the thirties. The
Columbus Platform, adopted by the CCAR in 1937, included a major
section stressing the positive significance of holiday and ritual observances, an area not considered sufficiently significant for inclusion
in the Pittsburgh Platform of 1885. East European Jews in greater
numbers and fresh immigrants from Germany with a more positive

attitude toward tradition were joining Reform congregations. The common threat of Nazism and the need to provide for Jewish refugees in Palestine and elsewhere united American Jewry as never before. When the Jewish Theological Seminary celebrated its fiftieth anniversary in 1937, Morgenstern went so far as to state publicly that the names "Reform" and "Conservative" were only incidental rather than matters of principle and to express the hope that both movements might come together under the banner of "Progressive Judaism." [101]

Given this shifting sentiment, the impact made by the European students on the religious life of the College was considerable. At least for a while they went to services in the chapel with heads covered; [102] they chanted the complete grace after meals and taught others to sing along with them, until the *Birkat ha-Mazon* became an established custom in the dormitory. Even Cronbach, certainly not traditionally inclined himself, was impressed by the extent to which they were influencing at least some of the other students. [103] By their very presence, too, the German refugees served as a continual reminder of the tragedy unfolding for fellow Jews abroad.

Not only rabbinical students desired the opportunity to leave Germany for the sanctuary of the Hebrew Union College. Just as urgent were the needs of Jewish scholars in Europe who sought refuge from Nazi oppression and the chance to continue with their work under conditions of freedom. They, too, hoped for a haven at the Hebrew Union College. And the College—again far more than any other American-Jewish educational institution—recognized its responsibility here as well. Beginning in 1938, and despite major political obstacles, the College succeeded in bringing no less than eight Jewish scholars to the United States and in giving employment to three other refugee professors who had managed to make their way to America by other means. [104] Most of them were not men the College needed for its program of instruction, and the expense of providing for them all was considerable. The majority spoke English only with difficulty. Yet Morgenstern felt the College had no choice but to pluck these brands from the fire. One of the men, Abraham Joshua Heschel, later said that in this regard the HUC president was "the least appreciated man in American Jewry." [105]

Some of those who came to Cincinnati, scholars like Max Wiener and Franz Rosenthal, spent only a short time at the College. Others, such as Eugen Täubler (Bible and Hellenistic literature), Isaiah Sonne (medieval Jewish history), and Franz Landsberger (Jewish art), remained to devote themselves primarily to research. The rest eventually found their way into the ranks of the regular teaching faculty. Of the last group, the one to achieve greatest prominence, Abraham Heschel, chose to leave the College after teaching for five years and attaining the rank of associate professor. During the time he was in Cincinnati, Heschel had drawn to himself a small but devoted group of disciples who appreciated his talents as a teacher of philosophy and a creative Jewish thinker. But his own traditionalism made him feel uncomfortable in the College's Reform atmosphere. In his letter of resignation, Heschel wrote that the College had become very dear to him and that he wanted to be considered "a staunch friend of this illustrious institution," but, he admitted, his own interpretation of Judaism was not in full accord with the teachings of the College.[106] He therefore accepted a position at the Jewish Theological Seminary.

The first of the refugee scholars to come to the College and remain on its faculty was Julius Lewy, appointed as early as 1936. An outstanding Assyriologist, who had taught at the University of Giessen until the Nazis dismissed all Jewish professors, Lewy had been unable to find a permanent position in the United States when the College— at first reluctantly (since Assyriology was not a prime requirement for American rabbis)—gave him a place on the faculty. It proved to be a fortunate decision, for with the expansion of the College in the area of doctoral studies, especially in Bible and Semitics, following the war, Lewy's name as chairman of the Committee on Graduate Study drew talented students to Cincinnati. He remained professor of Semitics and biblical history until shortly before his death in 1963, when he was briefly succeeded by his equally knowledgeable wife, Hildegard, until she too passed away four years later.

Three of the European scholars were still serving on the faculty in 1971. Alexander Guttmann, a former teacher at the *Hochschule,* was born in Budapest where his father, Michael Guttmann, had been head of the rabbinical seminary. A talmudist like his father, he represented the one field in which the College was in genuine need of a new professor following the illness of Finesinger and the death of Mann (who had taught Talmud in addition to history). Guttmann was therefore the first of the refugees after Lewy to receive regular status as a member of the faculty, shortly after his arrival in 1940. Eric Werner had come to HUC a year earlier via New York in order to fill Idelsohn's long vacant post in Jewish music. A Viennese Jew of wide-ranging musical background and accomplishments, Werner taught classes in music and also directed the HUC choir. Later he transferred to the New York campus, there to teach both rabbinical students and future cantors in the School of Sacred Music. The last to arrive was Samuel Atlas, a philosopher and talmudist, who had been able to make his way from Warsaw to London. Born in Lithuania, first a student in local yeshivot and then, in Germany, a disciple of the Jewish neo-Kantian philosopher Hermann Cohen, Atlas combined traditional learning with commitment to philosophical rationalism. Like Werner, he too left Cincinnati eventually to continue teaching at the campus in New York.

The simultaneous absorption of such a large number of immigrant scholars—at one point equivalent to the entire remainder of the faculty—was not an easy process. Some members of the board had qualms about the effect of the influx—this inordinately large importation of men unfamiliar with the American scene; others, however, took a personal interest in their welfare. Among the American members of the faculty, a number went out of their way to be helpful to the new arrivals. A few felt ambivalent about the Europeans, whose backgrounds and Jewish attitudes in many instances differed not a little from their own, and whose skill as teachers of American rabbinical students was in some cases very limited. Most of the refugee scholars were not given regular faculty status until after a trial period, and some were not given it at all. They did not sign the rabbinical diplomas, nor did they participate in the faculty's personnel-selection and policy-making body known as the Faculty Council.[107] For their part, some of the Europeans resented this second-class status and the fact that they were paid relatively much lower salaries than their American colleagues. But every refugee professor felt grateful to Morgenstern for giving him a place at the College. They knew that the alternative, for at least some of them, would have been almost certain death.

The late thirties was also a time when the College finally succumbed to long-standing alumni pressure to liberalize a jealously guarded privilege: the granting of honorary degrees. Until 1939 the faculty was most parsimonious in distributing such honors. The Doctor of Divinity, *honoris causa,* was given only infrequently and was abandoned entirely after Kaufmann Kohler received it upon retirement in 1921. It was replaced by a Doctor of Hebrew Law degree given to both laymen and rabbis. But with the exception of the jubilee in 1925, honorary degrees were never presented to more than three individuals in any single year. Only the most distinguished persons were considered worthy: men like Claude Montefiore, Cyrus Adler, George Foot Moore, Ismar Elbogen, Chaim Weizmann, Leo Baeck, Martin Buber, as well as the pinnacle of Reform's laity and rabbis. Recipients were selected by the faculty, with the consent of the Board of Governors, only for "distinguished service in the cause of Judaism." [108]

However, at least as early as 1929, there was strong sentiment that the College should foster a spirit of greater loyalty among its alumni by granting them honorary doctorates after a given number of years in the field. Pressure was maintained for a decade until at last, in 1938, a joint meeting of the board and faculty decided on a policy of greater liberality. In 1939 the honorary Doctor of Hebrew Law became a Doctor of Hebrew Letters degree and was henceforth given primarily to laymen; the Doctor of Divinity, *honoris causa,* was reinstituted and now presented to as many as seven rabbis in a single year.[109] At the same time the earned Doctor of Divinity was eliminated in favor of an earned Doctor of Hebrew Letters degree, given to ordained rabbis after successful completion of a thesis, and after oral examinations in a major and two minors.

Not long after the increase in the number of honorary degrees, graduation ceremonies began to assume a more academic character. In 1941, the faculty selected black and gold as the official colors of the College's doctoral hoods, and after years of discussion, in 1946 (principally because seniors that year were having difficulty purchasing formal attire) academic dress became standard for faculty and graduates at ordination.[110]

Two projects that would have greatly enhanced the status of the College were seriously discussed during the last Morgenstern decade, but both came to nought. The first was an effort to establish a Hebrew Union College School for Jewish Social Work in Cincinnati. The independent Graduate School for Jewish Social Work in New York City had enjoyed a high reputation for fifteen years when in the late thirties, due to the termination of grants from several foundations, the school began to experience serious financial difficulties. The College was approached to take it over. It was anticipated that income would derive from welfare funds in the various communities which would be sending students to the school. The Board of Governors committee in charge of exploring the matter was at first enthusiastic, while students and faculty looked forward to the opportunity of bridging the gap between social workers and rabbis. But at the last minute negotiations failed as a result of frictions between Maurice J. Karpf, who was to continue as head of the school, and certain members of the Board of Governors. There was also the growing feeling, shared by Morgenstern, that the local Cincinnati Jewish community was entirely too small and its social service problems too simple to offer adequate laboratory facilities for such a school.[111]

The second aborted project concerned the Hebrew Union College Museum. After the new library building was dedicated in 1931, there was talk of remodeling the old Bernheim Library to house and display the art and ritual objects of the museum. Due to the depression, however, funds were never raised and the collection remained packed away in storage. Then, in 1944, Mrs. Felix Warburg presented her lavish home in New York City to the Jewish Theological Seminary to house the Seminary's collection. It was suggested that the College might want to participate with the Seminary in the new museum and that the two collections might be displayed together. Difficult negotiations were carried on for more than a year, with the Seminary's representatives apparently wanting the College merely to be a guest exhibitor in the Seminary's museum, while the College committee insisted on complete equality. The project was dropped, however, not directly on account of these differences, but because the Seminary finally decided it could not at that time afford to undertake the costs for necessary remodeling. Discussion was never resumed and the HUC collection, for the time being, remained in storage.[112]

As the situation of European Jewry became more desperate, the Zionist issue at the College, which had been relatively quiescent during the early thirties, came to the foreground once again. For years, student sentiment had been moving away from Kohler's definition of Judaism in strictly religious terms. Mordecai Kaplan's Reconstructionist ideology, stressing that Judaism was a civilization rather than a religion and the Jews a people rather than a denomination, had found numerous disciples at the College. A 1930 survey of student opinion shows that even then 69 percent were favorable to some form of Zionism, 22 percent were neutral, and only 9 percent were opposed. A generation earlier, only 17 percent had been pro-Zionist.[113] As early as 1932 two Hebrew-speaking societies flourished on the campus; the longer surviving one was named Agudat Neumark in memory of David Neumark, the first devoted Hebraist on the faculty. A decade later, students organized the Mann-Diesendruck Society, a campus branch of the League for Labor Palestine.

A large portion of the students were also favorably inclined to the perpetuation of Yiddish. In 1942 a student organized a small Yiddish *Unterstizungsverein* whose members spoke Yiddish to one another and read Yiddish stories and poems. Students twice petitioned for a regular course in Yiddish, but both times were turned down by the faculty.[114]

Nearly all of the professors were sympathetic to Jewish settlement in Palestine. When Britain was considering closing the Land of Israel to further immigration just before issuing the White Paper of 1939, the faculty as a group sent a letter to President Roosevelt urging him to intercede.[115] Very few of its members (possibly only Diesendruck), however, were actively committed to Political Zionism. Morgenstern's devotion to "American Judaism" left the president with only minimal concern for what was being done by the Jews in Palestine. He increasingly introduced modern Hebrew into the curriculum beginning in the late twenties, but did so only on the lower levels and not for its own sake. He believed in teaching it merely as the most efficient way for students to enter quickly into the spirit of the language and thus learn to read classical texts with greater ease.[116] With regard to Zionism, he wrote in 1930 that he endorsed the colonization of Palestine and would not oppose the development of a strong cultural center there, nor would he be "sorely distressed" if a Jewish state were ultimately established. But he added: "Correspondingly I would not be particularly elated either. . . . I would be somewhat indifferent." [117]

However, as the refugee issue became ever more urgent during the war, indifference to Political Zionism became impossible. In 1942, the Central Conference of American Rabbis passed a resolution supporting the right of the Jews in Palestine to establish their own military force, thereby driving the anti-Zionists in its ranks to form the American Council for Judaism.[118] A year later, the representative American Jewish Conference, in which the UAHC was a participant, included a Palestine plank in its platform, creating a crisis in the Union, which finally determined to remain in the Conference but to take no official position on the plank—lest it tear itself apart.[119] The College Board of Governors, too, was deeply split between members like Hiram Weiss and Carl Pritz who were favorable to Zionism, and an opposing faction, including the chairman, Ralph Mack, which was anti-Zionist.

In this heated atmosphere, Morgenstern, along with Cronbach and Blank, joined his name to those rabbis who had opposed the resolution of the CCAR,[120] and in the fall of 1943, Morgenstern asked rhetorically in his opening-day address: "Is it not sad, is it not tragic for the Jewish people, which has dreamed the dream and voiced the hope and proclaimed the message of world-unity, and of world-salvation in such world-unity, to itself reject its message, its faith and its destiny, and seek for itself a salvation, impossible of realization, in the vain and exploded theory of restored racial statehood?" [121] When the reference in that same address to extreme Revisionist Zionism as being "practically identical with Nazist and Fascist theory" was so excerpted in a press release that it seemed to be referring to Zionism in general (as indeed it did in the original draft), Abba Hillel Silver and Joshua Loth Liebman, both graduates of the College, launched an effort to induce as many alumni as possible to protest publicly against Morgenstern, to repudiate his position, and to deny his authority to speak for Reform Judaism. Not only did forty-five alumni sign the protest, but virtually the entire Jewish press excoriated the HUC president for his speech. It was Morgenstern's saddest hour.[122] About that time his position became more extreme so that, at least in private, he would admit to being "uncompromisingly opposed to the establishment of a Jewish commonwealth in Palestine." [123] Only after the results of the Holocaust were apparent to all, and death-camp survivors were clamoring to enter the Land of Israel, did he change his view, saying in 1947 that the events of the last years "have made Zionists in a certain sense of all of us who are worthy of the name Jew." [124]

The divisive issue of Zionism was not all that burdened Morgenstern during his last years as president. He had to cope with a major faculty-student confrontation over the manner of granting the Master of Hebrew Letters degree; there were severe problems engendered by the need for adjusting to the unusual circumstances created by the war; and there was the necessity for developing and implementing a new vision of the College's role in the postwar Jewish world.

Although the number of graduate years a student was required to spend at the College had increased by stages from none in Isaac Mayer Wise's time to one in Kohler's, and finally, after 1930, to four during the Morgenstern period, the highest academic degree the College offered its graduates had continued to be the Bachelor of Hebrew Letters. Following extended discussion of the matter over a number of years, the faculty finally decided to award all of the graduates a Master of Hebrew Letters degree beginning in 1939. A majority of the faculty, however, believed that the new degree offered an opportunity to reinstitute a comprehensive written and oral examination. Such an exam was in fact given for the first time in 1944.

For three years, there were no problems. Then, in 1947, when the faculty announced its intention to award the M.H.L. selectively only to those ordinees who had shown superior scholarly ability on the test, the senior class (with the exception of one member) sent a petition to the faculty stating that they would not accept the degree and that such a procedure "was in effect placing the M.H.L. on a higher plane than the Rabbinical degree." The petition of the seniors was supported by an endorsement of their views signed by virtually the entire student body. The result was the most severe faculty-student crisis in the history of the College. Despite the pressure—or perhaps because of it—the faculty was unwilling to give in to the student point of view; it decided to award the degree that year only to the one man who had not signed the petition. Nonetheless, perhaps realizing the merit of the students' case after all, the faculty decided shortly thereafter once again to make passing the examination requisite for ordination, no less than for receiving the Master of Hebrew Letters.[125]

Severe as it was, the M.H.L. crisis thus lasted for only a short time. More enduring were the unsettling effects of World War II. Following Pearl Harbor, a large number of rabbis volunteered to serve as chaplains in the armed forces of the United States, often leaving their congregations without rabbinic leadership. The College found itself saddled with the responsibility of somehow providing for these congregations. It could only be done through two measures: allowing students to be ordained early and permitting at least some students to perform regular rabbinical functions before ordination. Both steps meant reducing the amount of study the participating students engaged in at the College. After considerable debate, it was decided to graduate some students in less than the prescribed time, after supplementing their regular year's work with summer courses. Thus two classes were ordained in 1943, one in January and one in July. In addition, by 1944 nine advanced students were "licensed" as rabbis, temporarily replacing chaplains in whose communities they took up residence while carrying on their studies *in absentia;* eight more served sizable congregations on weekends.[126] The effect of this acceleration and licensing was necessarily a lower level of achievement in studies.[127] But students—perhaps in part out of unease at being exempt from the draft in time of war—were most eager to discharge an obligation to the leaderless congregations. And the College, too, could not avoid its responsibilities.[128]

Such wartime burdens, however, seemed very light in comparison with the task that devolved on the College once the war was over. Millions of Jews had lost their lives at the hands of the Nazis; the great institutions of Jewish learning and rabbinical training in Europe were no more. If World War I had brought to an end the mass immigration of Jews to the United States, the Holocaust of World War II cut off the flow of its spiritual leadership. American Jewry, which until now had been able to rely on the outstanding academies abroad, would henceforth have to depend almost entirely on itself. For Hebrew Union College, the extinction of the liberal seminaries in Breslau and Berlin meant that no longer would it be able to draw its faculty from men who had taught or studied at these great German centers of Jewish learning. It would now have to produce its own scholars. As a result of the war, Hebrew Union College had become the oldest institution in the world for the training of liberal rabbis; and it would now have to train scholars as well. American Jewry, together with the small settlement in the Land of Israel, was charged with preserving the Jewish heritage.

Awareness of this new, larger responsibility weighed heavily on Morgenstern even during the war.[129] He urged that the period of retrenchment initiated by the depression now had to end. It was again time for expansion. And he took the first steps to bring it about. Since the Ochs campaign very little money had been raised for the College, although the yearly depletion of the endowment was reducing it ever further. The need for raising new funds became imperative. After some members of the UAHC Executive Board questioned the right of the College to undertake fund-raising efforts on its own, the Union and College together, in 1941, launched a Joint Maintenance Campaign for both institutions. The College was allowed to develop its own "Foundation Fund" for gifts in excess of $1,ooo. For the first time, it now hired a full-time campaign director.[130]

To secure interest and support from alumni and lay contributors, the College had earlier begun to issue a regular *Hebrew Union College Bulletin.* The need for increased publicity was met by a public-relations committee under the chairmanship of local newspaper columnist Alfred Segal. Three convocations for the granting of honorary degrees were held in New York City to draw attention and support to the College in the great metropolis of American Jewry.

Successful exapnsion likewise required a Board of Governors which could spearhead the fund-raising effort. But over the years the board had largely become superannuated. There was a distinct need for younger men with new ideas who would be ready to render active service. Moreover, the Midwest was still greatly overrepresented, and more than a third of the board members were rabbis. Such a group would be unlikely to raise large amounts of money. During his last year in office, therefore, Morgenstern began to expand the Board of Governors while seeking ways to rejuvenate it and make it more representative.[131] He also made a move to expand the administration of the College by engaging Rabbi Alvin I. Fine as director of field work, with his job especially to recruit students for the College at leading universities.

But there was much more to be done. HUC was finally to become a strictly graduate institution; a doctor of philosophy program to include Christians and nonrabbinical Jewish students was under serious discussion; in New York City the College was about to re-establish its School for Teachers.[132] Serious doubt arose as to whether Morgenstern still had the energy to carry the College into what was clearly emerging as a new period in its history.

When HUC celebrated its seventieth anniversary in the fall of 1945 with an impressive national conference on "Judaism and American Democracy," [133] Morgenstern, ill with an attack of pneumonia, was unable to attend. Though he recovered after some weeks, the president felt weaker than before. Shortly thereafter, his personal physician, Hiram Weiss, who was at the time also chairman of the Board of Governors, advised him to retire. In the fall of 1946, Morgenstern read his letter of retirement to the board. It was to take effect at the end of the academic year, when he would be sixty-six. Though he could have continued for another two years, Morgenstern recognized himself that the College "was on the threshold of a new era" and that its challenges could best be met by a younger man. Moreover, he desired to devote his remaining energies more fully to scholarship and teaching.[134]

Not insignificant in Morgenstern's decision must also have been the realization that a very exciting prospect now loomed on the horizon: a merger with Stephen S. Wise's Jewish Institute of Religion in New York. Yet only under a younger man, acceptable to the Zionist supporters of the JIR, could the separate histories of the two institutions flow into a common stream.

Before proceeding with that combined history, we must now first turn our attention to the earlier independent course taken by the Jewish Institute of Religion prior to its merger with HUC.

Kelal Yisrael: THE JEWISH INSTITUTE OF RELIGION

> I felt the time had come for the establishment of a school of Jewish learning without labels, without partisanship. . . .—STEPHEN S. WISE in the *JIR Annual,* 1926

NEARLY HALF A CENtury separates Isaac Mayer Wise's founding of the Hebrew Union College in 1875 from Stephen Samuel Wise's creation of the Jewish Institute of Religion in 1922—a period of radical change for American Jewry. During these years the Jewish population of the United States grew from less than three hundred thousand to well over three million; the Jews of German origin, who had dominated the American scene both in numbers and influence for most of the nineteenth century, were inundated by the great wave of East European immigrants swelling up in the wake of pogroms and economic restrictions. In the last decades of the nineteenth century and thereafter, these Jews, from all areas of the Russian Pale of Settlement, from

Hungary and Roumania, made their presence increasingly felt. Clustering in New York City's Lower East Side, associating themselves in *landsmanshaften* according to their place of origin, they spoke to one another in Yiddish and eked out their meager livings in sweatshops and petty trade. Both economically and culturally they remained separated from their German brethren, who had largely ascended to the middle class and lived an acculturated Jewish life either in uptown Manhattan, in another borough, or in other American cities.

Many of the newcomers clung to the religious orthodoxy in which they had grown up; a few, in reaction to the new environment, broke radically with tradition and became militant atheists. Some espoused socialism, or Zionism, or a combination of the two. But whatever the alternative chosen, one no less than another was bound to scandalize the Jews of German origin, who maintained a capitalist economic outlook and adhered to a classical Reform Judaism composed of firm belief in universalistic theism combined with meager attention to ritual observance. The "Yahudim" feared that the East European newcomers would undermine their efforts at swift integration into American society. For their part, the new immigrants often enough regarded the established German Jews as little different from gentiles—though they were forced to admire their remarkable economic success.

Yet the uptown Jews could not, and did not, entirely ignore their penurious brethren from Russia. In time they established charitable organizations to care for their needs, and eventually they displayed concern for their spiritual well-being as well. Thus leading members of the most prominent Reform synagogue of New York, Temple Emanu-El—Louis Marshall, Jacob Schiff, and Felix Warburg—used their energy and funds to revive the moribund Jewish Theological Seminary of America, intending it to provide an Americanized rabbinical leadership—though one committed to a considerably more traditional practice of Judaism than they themselves espoused.

It was within the milieu of this widely heterogeneous New York Jewry, expressing an abundance of conflicting viewpoints and forms of Jewish identity, that Stephen Wise spent the formative years of his life. Born in Budapest, Hungary, in 1874, he was brought to

America when he was seventeen months old. His father, a rabbi as was his grandfather, had been elected to the pulpit of the traditional Rodeph Sholom Congregation, and he was able to establish the family in a modest home not far away, on East Fifth Street. There the young Wise grew up, combining public school education with private lessons in Jewish subjects. As his family was middle-class, his contacts with the new immigrants fleeing Russian persecution were limited. But while he was still a child, his father would describe to him their sufferings, and he thus developed an early attachment to *kelal yisrael,* to the totality of the Jewish people. That attachment would consistently influence his position on Jewish issues over the years, and it would later be a primary consideration in his decision to establish the Jewish Institute of Religion.[1]

From the first, Wise's vocational goal was to become a link in the rabbinical tradition of his family. Yeshiva training, however, was out of the question, for his advanced secular education (City College and then Columbia) was transforming him slowly into a religious liberal. Hebrew Union College seemed more and more the logical place for him to advance his Jewish learning. Thus, when Stephen Wise graduated from Columbia in 1892, he addressed a letter to the elder, unrelated Wise in Cincinnati inquiring about the program at HUC. But having already decided he wanted to work for a doctorate in Semitics with Professor Richard Gottheil at Columbia, he was not willing to leave New York City; he wanted to pass the required courses in Cincinnati by studying with tutors and then taking examinations. Reluctantly, the president of the College agreed to the proposal and registered the prospective student *in absentia* for the academic year 1892–93.[2]

Yet Stephen Wise soon decided not to follow through even on this program, which he himself had suggested. That summer he set out for Europe where, within a few months, he received personal ordination from Adolf Jellinek, the liberal rabbi of Vienna. By the spring of 1893, Wise was back in New York as assistant rabbi in Congregation B'nai Jeshurun. Simultaneously with his rabbinical duties he worked on his doctorate, which he received from Columbia University in 1901 for his discussion and translation of an Arabic manuscript of the medieval Jewish ethical treatise by Solomon ibn Gabirol, *The Improvement of the Moral Qualities.*

In these early years the tremendous energy and drive that were always to characterize Stephen Wise were already clearly apparent. Even combining graduate studies with the normal functions of a rabbi was insufficient to absorb him fully. He took a stance for labor, asserting the right of workers to organize and to strike, and he became a Zionist, participating in the leadership of the Federation of American Zionists and attending the Second Zionist Congress in Switzerland in 1898.

While winning the sympathy and admiration of the East European Jews, Wise at the same time moved more and more in the social circles of the German-Jewish community in New York, and it was their reform interpretation of Jewish faith and practice to which he was increasingly drawn. Before leaving New York for a new pulpit in Portland, Oregon, he successfully courted Louise Waterman, an artistically talented, socially sensitive young woman from an established and quite wealthy German-Jewish family. His bride, very much under the influence of the Ethical Culture movement, had previously possessed little sympathy for religious particularism, including that of the Jews. Though Wise succeeded in winning her to the causes of the Jewish people, she continued to identify herself easily in Judaism only with the universal message of the Prophets. Gustav Gottheil, rabbi emiritus of reform Temple Emanu-El, was the officiating rabbi at their wedding; Kaufmann Kohler, a friend of the Waterman family, was also in attendance.

After six years in the Northwest, where he championed political reform, Wise returned to New York City—which, indeed, he had never planned permanently to leave. He was seriously considered for the pulpit of prestigious Temple Emanu-El, but negotiations were abruptly terminated when, in a *cause célèbre,* Wise refused to permit the lay leadership to limit his freedom of speech on the pulpit. In protest, he founded a "Free Synagogue," gathering about himself a nucleus of loyal adherents which grew rapidly as Wise's great oratorical talents, combined with a remarkable skill for gaining publicity, brought his Sunday morning services to the attention of large numbers of unaffiliated and alienated Jews. After a short time, only Carnegie Hall was sufficiently spacious to contain the thousands who flocked to hear him discuss the moral and religious issues of the day.

Stephen Wise was a man of indomitable will who combined deep attachments to his fellow Jews and fellow-men with a driving quest for power and influence. Rarely did he willingly subjugate his desires to those of other men. His self-confidence, combined with the gifts of an impressive appearance, a magnetic personality, thunderous, eloquent speech, and a remarkable intelligence, gave him the daring to strike out repeatedly on his own. Dissatisfied with existing institutions, he found that he was able to create new ones in his own image to perform tasks he thought needed to be done. Thus he created the Free Synagogue in dramatic opposition to Temple Emanu-El, later helped to found the American Jewish Congress because of his disagreement with the American Jewish Committee—and so, too, dissatisfied with the Hebrew Union College, he eventually brought into existence a new rabbinical school which would produce disciples devoted to his own broad interpretation of Judaism. They would be rabbis of a different sort from those currently graduated by the older seminary, men fit to deal with the new realities of Jewish life as they appeared to him two decades after the death of Isaac Mayer Wise.

The first reference to Stephen Wise's intention to found a rabbinical school occurs in a letter which he wrote to his wife in 1909:

> A lovely young boy came to me yesterday from Cincinnati,— he is so unhappy at the College. The boy is dejected and almost sullen. Now, Madam, please hold your breath while I tell you something. Why shouldn't I have a school for the training of Jewish ministers? . . . The practical experience, training and discipline, they could get under me! I am just aflame with the idea, and I will do it, and you'll help me and it will be blessed of God.[3]

The decision reached here was not forgotten,[4] though the time was not yet ripe for action. Whenever Wise became perturbed by the anti-

Zionist spirit which then prevailed at Hebrew Union College, he was reminded of his resolve. To his friend and fellow Zionist, Rabbi Max Heller of New Orleans, he wrote candidly in 1914: "Is there nothing to be done to end once and for all that bigotted attitude which stifles every expression of opinion that differs from the gentlemen of the College who are still living in 1840, including Kohler and Phillipson [sic]?" [5] His protracted efforts to influence the policy of the College through the Central Conference of American Rabbis and the Union of American Hebrew Congregations proved to him that he could not hope to bring about changes in rabbinical training through existing institutions. [6] At the same time he became increasingly aware of his power for independent action: his personal prestige was rising in Jewish communities around the country; he was more and more in demand as a speaker, addressing Jewish audiences in as many as fifty to seventy-five cities in a single year. [7] These groups could be expected to contribute funds; and from the university students among them, candidates for the rabbinate might easily be drawn.

It was the Free Synagogue which became the instrumentality for creating Wise's seminary. In 1917, at their rabbi's urging, the Synagogue established training fellowships enabling rabbinical students as well as ordained rabbis to gain experience in the active life of the New York rabbinate. [8] To one of the students, Louis I. Newman, Wise, along with two rabbinical colleagues, even gave a personal ordination in 1918, though Newman, while having acquired considerable Jewish learning, had completed no formal rabbinical curriculum. In 1920, a month-long summer school for rabbis and rabbinical students was inaugurated under the auspices of the Free Synagogue; in addition to other lectures, it featured a series of informal talks by Stephen Wise. By the fall of that year, a special committee of the Free Synagogue was convened "to consider the desirability and the practicability of organizing an institute for the training of Rabbis." [9] It is clear from the minutes of the committee's first meeting that the principal reason for the new project was dissatisfaction with the Hebrew Union College. Those present held that "the Hebrew Union College had outgrown whatever usefulness it may have originally had, that it no longer attracted to it the finest of our American Jewish youth and those that it did attract were but poorly trained to fill the pulpits of forward-looking, progressive American congregations." The new school was to fulfill the Free Synagogue ideal, which, though not spelled out in the minutes, meant commitment to the type of social-activist independent rabbinate represented by Stephen Wise. Its creation at this particular juncture seemed especially appropriate since the synagogue had just succeeded in raising more than a quarter million dollars to construct a house for all its activities except the Sunday morning and High Holy Day services. This new building could easily be shared with a rabbinical seminary.

It is noteworthy that at this stage of the planning the school was thought of entirely as a project of the Synagogue with financial support coming from its budget together with contributions Wise would raise from his friends throughout the country. As yet no consideration was given to providing any role for the Union of American Hebrew Congregations, to which the Free Synagogue belonged. Also, there was still no reference to the school being intended for all three religious denominations in Judaism. The new seminary was to train rabbis for "progressive" congregations, a term which avoided the institutional label "Reform" while making clear the nontraditional character of the proposed school. With this meeting the die was firmly cast. No conceivable new developments, no opposition of any magnitude, would be able to deter Wise from proceeding with his plans.

One might suppose that the change in administration which the Hebrew Union College underwent in 1921 would have convinced Wise to reconsider. He had long objected to Kaufmann Kohler's unwillingness to tolerate the expression of divergent points of view at the College, especially with regard to Zionism. At the time of the Horace Kallen affair in 1915, he had maintained that there was no *Lehrfreiheit,* no academic freedom, at HUC.[10] Now Kohler was finally due to retire, and one of the (less likely) candidates to succeed him was Martin Meyer, a San Francisco rabbi who was both a friend and a fellow Zionist. But in view of his well-advanced plans for the Institute, Wise did not feel free to work for Meyer's election. Moreover, he thought that one man—even at the helm—would not be sufficient to bring about thoroughgoing change. "I have put it crassly, but I have meant it," Wise wrote, "that the only things to be changed at the College are the Faculty, the Board of Governors, the students and the course of studies—to say nothing of the spirit of the place." [11] When Julian Morgenstern was chosen as president, Wise was easily able to banish any qualms. This insider, himself opposed to Political Zionism, would not bring about the "thorough purge" which alone could save the institution. [12]

Meanwhile, however, the Free Synagogue had decided not to proceed alone after all. [13] In the spring of 1921 it sent its president, Abram I. Elkus, to seek approval and cooperation from the Executive Board of the UAHC. The communication which he presented spoke of the Synagogue's intention to establish a "Jewish Institute of Religion for the training of men for the Liberal Jewish Ministry." It enumerated various considerations: the size of the Jewish community of New York, containing close to one-tenth of world Jewry, and offering opportunities of study and "laboratory practice" as could be duplicated nowhere else; the lack of rabbis to fill available pulpits; the intent to enroll only college and university graduates on the model of postgraduate professional schools and modern theological schools of other faiths; the need for a program that would include training in religious education and in social service; and, finally, irrevocable commitment to the principle of academic freedom. [14]

Thereupon, the UAHC Executive Board appointed a special committee to confer with a delegation from the Free Synagogue, the latter headed by Lee K. Frankel, shortly to become the first chairman of the JIR Board of Trustees. Three meetings were held, and at the third the Free Synagogue representatives presented a proposal: a "Basis of Discussion" suggesting that the Institute become an activity of the UAHC coordinate with the HUC and allowing for the interchange of faculty and students. For his part, Wise promised to place his talents at the disposal of the Union to raise funds for the maintenance of both institutions. But in return he insisted that the JIR "shall be an independent and autonomous institution and no arrangement or agreement of any kind shall qualify its independence or limit its autonomy." Although the UAHC would have only 20 percent representation on the Institute's Board of Trustees, it was expected to include the Institute in its budget, providing a minimum of $45,000 per year for the first three years.[15] Despite the belief of Wise and the Free Synagogue committee that they had successfully persuaded the Union representatives,[16] the UAHC leaders—quite apart from their commitment to HUC—were not at all convinced that they should pledge financial support to an institution over which they would not possess control.

Three members of the Union special committee brought this proposal to an informal conference of fifteen representatives of the Executive Board of the Union and the HUC Board of Governors in Cincinnati. Here the major argument against founding a new rabbinical school was clearly set forth: the complete adequacy in every respect—as they saw it—of the Hebrew Union College as presently constituted, and the great financial investment that the Cincinnati institution involved. Thereupon all present at the conference unanimously resolved that "the best interest of American Judaism will be conserved not by founding a new institution, but by strengthening the present support of the Hebrew Union College." Furthermore, should it ever become necessary to create another seminary, it "would necessarily be controlled by the Union of American Hebrew Congregations, composed of more than two hundred congregations representing and speaking for Liberal Judaism in America."[17] When this declaration was printed and circulated by the Union's president, Charles Shohl, it put an immediate end to the question of cooperation.[18] The Institute that Wise was about to create would henceforth have to be his alone.

The controversy generated by Wise's plans echoed far beyond the official documents. A lively discussion of the issues involved was carried on both in the Jewish press[19] and in private correspondence.[20] Here certain officially unstated additional considerations and goals of both sides came to the fore. The Cincinnati opponents of the JIR were apparently more concerned with conceivable financial consequences than they were willing openly to admit. In 1922, HUC had only about eighty students but room in its classes for many more. There was also a commitment to build a dormitory which would accommodate over a hundred students on the campus. The Cincinnati leadership feared that Wise's efforts to obtain funds would result in losses to HUC. To its Board of Governors, Shohl wrote in confidence: "I am of the opinion that Dr. Wise's trip through the West [to raise funds for the JIR], if successful, is apt to be fraught with danger for our institution." [21]

Wise himself encountered similar arguments privately and in the press. He tried to refute them by insisting that there was no fixed sum set apart by the Jews of America for educational purposes; contributions to the JIR would not necessarily diminish the funds potentially available to HUC.[22] But if, as one suspects, the Cincinnatians secretly hoped to nip their rival in the bud, Wise at this stage—and despite later disclaimers—seems likewise to have had a hidden agenda. He meant to reduce Hebrew Union College to a small, provincial seminary in the shadow of what would become the principal school for the training of rabbis in the United States. According to Rabbi Louis Wolsey of Cleveland—admittedly a source hostile to Wise—he is alleged to have said in New York "that in ten years he would have 75% of the rabbinical students in the country." [23] Certainly Wise's mood in 1922 was clearly one of outdoing the older institution, if not in size, then at least in the quality and practical relevance of its rabbinical education.

While the controversy was going on, Wise proceeded rapidly with his plans. By early April he was seriously considering who would compose the faculty. A tentative budget in excess of $40,000 was drawn up and by mid-June it was more than covered. There were already twelve applicants for admission.[24] It had also been decided that the school should be "liberal," by which Wise now meant "liberal enough to welcome and respect men whether reform or orthodox, Zionist or anti-Zionist." [25]

From the beginning Wise was undecided about his own position in the seminary he was calling into being. The "Basis of Discussion" submitted to the Union refers to Wise as the president of the proposed institution, and there can be no question that the role of *rosh yeshiva* appealed to him. But with all of his dynamism and ability to make a lasting impression on people, Wise knew that he lacked two qualifi-cations which other men possessed: he was neither an original Jewish thinker nor a productive Jewish scholar. Very seldom did Wise speak about his concept of God, and at no time did he make an attempt to formulate a theology of his own. Even men who knew him well and were his students cannot recall that Wise devoted very much attention to questions of faith. From what little evidence exists, it appears that Wise's God-concept lay very much in the rationalistic tradition of Reform Judaism.[26] He stressed the God of social impera-tive, not of ritual command.[27]

As he was not a theologian, so Wise was also not basically a Jewish scholar. To be sure, he had published his dissertation on ibn Gabirol and translated the book of Judges for the Jewish Publication Society's English Bible. But later in life, though he claimed to envy men who found time for study,[28] Wise did not muster the patience or interest to devote himself to scholarly discipline; he was too enamored of the active life of the Jewish leader and social reformer. He appreciated Jewish scholarship, and he held Jewish scholars in high regard, but he made no pretense of emulating them.

Wise realized that his Institute would achieve real stature only if a leading theologian or scholar stood at its head, and he therefore remained uncertain of his own fitness for the position. Unlike Kohler or Morgenstern, moreover, he was deeply committed to other tasks and causes. He was not willing to give up his work for Zionism, for the American Jewish Congress, for improving city government—to say nothing of his rabbinical functions at the Free Synagogue—in order to become exclusively the president of a rabbinical school. Thus, from even before the Institute was created and until its last years, Wise repeatedly sought a man who would be willing and able to replace him as president.

Among the elder generation of Jewish religious leaders, the in-dividual for whom Wise had the highest regard was Emil G. Hirsch, the rabbi of Temple Sinai in Chicago. Hirsch was not a Zionist, but he was the outstanding champion of the rabbi's duty to speak out for social justice; his pulpit was a model for Wise's own Free Synagogue. Hirsch was also an intellectual, a Jewish thinker of liberal views who had graduated from the *Hochschule* in Berlin, the only Jewish seminary which at that time, like the Institute Wise was about to create, was dedicated to the principle of free expression of all forms of religious Judaism among faculty and students. But in 1922 Hirsch passed his seventieth birthday and he was not willing to live permanently in New York. He therefore declined the presidency when Wise offered it to him.[29] Hirsch did agree to become honorary president of the Institute and a visiting professor of theology, but his death in January 1923 prevented him from giving even a single lecture. Wise then turned to Israel Abrahams, the senior Anglo-Jewish scholar to whom he presented the first honorary degree of the JIR in 1924, when Abrahams came to New York for a series of lectures at the school. But Abrahams, too, was well along in years and refused to accept even a deanship.[30]

The man Wise made the greatest effort to obtain as president was Mordecai Kaplan, who combined the qualities of thinker and scholar with a commitment to the peoplehood of Israel and the ability to be an inspiring teacher. As Kaplan's divergent theological views put him at odds with the prevailing spirit at his own institution, the Jewish Theological Seminary, he was an obvious candidate to join Wise's school, where academic freedom was guaranteed. On at least two separate occasions he entered into serious negotiations with Wise, only in each instance to back off when he found himself unable to break his ties with the Seminary. Kaplan's relation to the JIR remained limited to a few hours he once taught as a visitor and to occasional lectures.[31]

Grievously disappointed at Kaplan's refusals, Wise kept on looking for someone he could respect to take over his position. Until the faculty unanimously demanded that he assume the title of president in 1927, he persisted in signing his name only as "Acting President." Even later, in 1933, when one of the Institute's professors, Shalom Spiegel, gave a particularly outstanding address at graduation, Wise wrote in confidence to the chairman of his board, Judge Julian Mack:

As I listened to him, I felt he was the one man in sight today who should have my job as soon as it is possible for me to quit—

that is to say, as soon as we decide that the hour has come. I hope that it will soon come and that when it does, we can put a man of his character and quality into the Presidency.[32]

Finally, after World War II, Wise offered the position to Abram L. Sachar, soon to become the first president of Brandeis University—again in vain.

But there was another side to Wise's desires. Not always was he so eager to relinquish his position, especially if it might mean an end to his own influence in the Institute. When Hirsch Chajes, chief rabbi of Vienna, came to New York in the fall of 1924 and gave two lectures at the JIR, Wise was moved to reflect candidly on Chajes in relation to the Institute and on his role as its head:

> As one of the Faculty, I think he [Chajes] would be a very signifi-
> cant acquisition, but he would not be satisfied to be one of the
> Faculty. He would not be satisfied even to be Dean of the in-
> stitution. He is a strong and self-insistent personality, and the
> Institute would not be big enough for both of us. If I felt that
> he could take my place, could do my work, could win men to
> the Institute and win support for the Institute, all of which
> things I do at present, I would be entirely willing to cede my
> place to him. I have no personal feeling, I believe, in the matter.
> I know how much greater is his scholarship than my own, and
> that, if possible, it would be fine to have an outstanding scholar
> as the Institute head, but, strange as it may sound, men will, for
> the present, come to the Institute because I am its head. They
> know of it through me and it is associated with me, and to them
> Chajes's name is and will long remain unknown.[33]

For better or for worse, the Jewish Institute of Religion was indeed associated in the public mind with Stephen S. Wise. Throughout the entire length of its independent existence, from 1922 until 1949, it was Wise who raised the funds for it, Wise who made the major policy decisions, Wise who attracted the students, who served as their rabbinic model, and who obtained positions for many of them when they graduated. His centrality in large measure accounts for both the great strengths and the apparent weaknesses of the Institute. His bold personality was its focal point, his fame brought it glory and renown. But at the same time his enemies became the enemies of the school, and when other activities called for his attention (as they so frequently did), there was no one of equivalent stature to fill the vacuum created by his absence.

The students were Wise's "boys," and they, in turn, loved him like a father even if they sometimes felt their president did not give enough of himself to the school or that he favored some students over others (especially, it seems, those who, like himself, were of Hungarian origin). Yearly, they celebrated his birthday, the Founder's Day of the Institute. Consciously or not, they modeled themselves after Wise. Like him, they conceived the rabbinate as committed to Zion, to the people of Israel, and to social justice; some of them even imitated the gestures and mannerisms that he employed on the pulpit.

Wise was directly involved with the students through a course he gave regularly on problems of the ministry and through his practicum in homiletics. In the former he spoke informally with the students about his activities, his practical problems, his views on Jewish life. And he brought to the sessions as guest speakers prominent figures from the Jewish and non-Jewish worlds. Among them were the Zionists David Ben-Gurion, Chaim Weizmann, and Vladimir Jabotinsky; clergymen such as Reinhold Niebuhr and his good friend and fellow social reformer John Haynes Holmes; and champions of labor such as Norman Thomas and Philip Murray. In the homiletical practicum, he subjected student sermons to careful scrutiny, favoring neither a homily that was removed from present-day reality nor one that quoted contemporary authorities to the exclusion of traditional Jewish sources.

Despite his busy schedule, students generally found Wise accessible to them. They were amazed at how well he remembered personal facts about themselves and their families and at how much genuine interest he seemed to take in each one of them. In the classroom the great man of Jewish affairs could be informal, personal, and witty, even as the very force of his charisma preserved a certain distance between himself and the students. Though in later years they did not always support the school as generously as Wise wished, nearly all of the Institute's graduates harbored a lasting affection for their one-time mentor.

Well before the opening of the Institute, Wise began to select his faculty. He had early determined that it should consist of two kinds of individuals: ". . . three or four outstanding men as heads of departments, giving much of their time and strength to research, and then . . . a staff of men to do the day-by-day teaching, men who will, as it were, fit the young men so that they shall be ready for the great masters who are to be at the head." [34]

Of the early teachers, the most appreciated were Harry S. Lewis and Henry Slonimsky. Lewis, inveterately an Englishman, was chaplain of the Institute and also gave instruction in Hebrew. Little concerned with making a name as a scholar, this genial man gave the students all his available time, studying together with them rather than lecturing, and succeeding remarkably well in transmitting a basic knowledge of Hebrew texts.

Henry Slonimsky was associated with the JIR longer than any other member of the faculty. He began teaching there in 1924 and retired only after the JIR had merged with HUC. His subjects were mainly ethics (especially Midrash) and philosophy of religion. For many years he was also dean of the school, responsible for day-to-day direction of academic matters. Slonimsky had left HUC, where he taught for two years, because he thought they dreaded him there "as a radical, and, above all, as a nationalist." [35] At JIR he felt liberated, free to express himself iconoclastically on every aspect of Jewish belief and practice. And he did—to the shock of more traditional students, but more commonly to the admiration of young men who saw before them a genuine person struggling viscerally to reconcile belief in God with the omnipresence of evil. There can be no question that, aside from Wise himself, Slonimsky had the profoundest influence on JIR graduates. But Slonimsky, though, like Lewis, knowledgeable in Jewish sources, was not a productive scholar—and Wise wanted scholars as well as teachers.

It was not easy for the "acting president" to find first-rate Jewish

scholars in the United States who were willing to come to the projected Institute. Wise therefore decided to seek his men abroad. On
a trip to Europe and Palestine in the summer of 1922, he sought to
engage faculty on a temporary basis for the JIR, hoping that some,
by mutual consent, would remain permanently. For the first semester
he successfully engaged Ismar Elbogen of the Berlin *Hochschule,*
one of the outstanding Jewish historians of this century, as well as
Felix Perles, a leading biblical scholar from Königsberg. Other men
came thereafter: from England, Germany, Austria, and even Palestine. Although a number of them did indeed remain, others, like
Elbogen, resisted Wise's overtures. The Europeans were joined by
American scholars who came on a part-time or visiting basis.

The high reputation of these participants in its program lent
luster to the first years of the JIR, but their presence also made for
some problems. Most of the students lacked the necessary preparation
to profit from what the scholars had to offer. One of them recalled:

> We just weren't ready for what Wise had in store for us. He
> brought us such teachers as Israel Abrahams, Felix Perles, Ismar
> Elbogen, Julius Guttmann, Julian Obermann, Henry Slonimsky,
> Salo Baron, Hirsch Perez Chajes, David Yellin, Harry Wolfson,
> Mordecai Kaplan, George Foot Moore—and what we needed
> was *aleph bes!* [36]

Then, too, the constant shift in faculty militated against any sense of
continuity. Students were never sure what the faculty would look like
the following year.

Of the scholars who came from abroad, none would remain
with the Institute longer than Chaim Tchernowitz, the professor of
Talmud. Tchernowitz was not a critical scholar in the modern sense,
but he was a highly skilled talmudist and was respected by students
for his depth of learning. Religiously, he stood at the opposite end of
the spectrum from Slonimsky. He was traditional in belief and practice, wore a full beard, and conducted class with his head covered.
Speaking several languages, he lectured seemingly in all of them at
once, to the merriment of his classes but, alas, also at the expense of

learning; few students learned much Talmud at JIR. Yet Tcherno-witz's presence was a constant reminder that the Institute was as hospitable to a traditional interpretation of Judaism as to a radical one.

One of the reasons Wise wanted scholars as well as teachers at the Institute was that he hoped to make the JIR not only a semi-nary preparing men for the professional rabbinate, but also a center of scientific Jewish research. Unfortunately, it proved difficult in practice to harmonize these two goals. Few students interested pri-marily in Jewish scholarship came to study at the JIR, and hardly any productive scholars graduated from its classrooms. A program of advanced Jewish studies, later developed for men who had al-ready been ordained, was in general not very successful. Yet some of the more scholarly members of the faculty were less interested in preparing men for the rabbinate than in *Wissenschaft des Judentums,* and a certain tension arose between the professional goals of the school and their own less practical objectives.

Together with considerations of financial security [37] and intel-lectual prestige, the absence of students interested in pure scholarship contributed to the inordinately large number of faculty—among them great scholars—who ultimately left the Institute to teach else-where: the scholar of Jewish philosophy Harry Wolfson to Harvard; historian Salo Baron to Columbia; orientalist Julian Obermann to Yale; Hellenistic scholar Ralph Marcus to the University of Chicago; and Hebraist Shalom Spiegel to the Jewish Theological Seminary. In most cases, Wise was sorry to see these men go and even prided him-self on their scholarly accomplishments of later years. There was only one quality he would not tolerate: institutional disloyalty. When a particular member of the faculty chose repeatedly to hide his affilia-tion with the JIR, Wise decided he would be best off elsewhere and encouraged him to leave. [38]

The faculty's relationship to Wise seems to have been one of almost universal respect. [39] At times they may have badgered him with complaints, finding their salaries inadequate or resenting the fact that he did not always consult them before appointing new men to their ranks.[40] But they acknowledged the role he was playing in the advancement of Jewish causes and they admired him for it.

The early students of the JIR came from mixed backgrounds. About half were born abroad; most came from families of East European origin and of humble means. Nearly all were college graduates—a requirement Wise had stressed in differentiating his school from Hebrew Union College. A few were older men who had already engaged in some occupation, and, in contrast to Cincinnati, a considerable number were married by the time they graduated, or even when they entered. There were also a few women students over the years, the most notable of whom was Irma L. Lindheim, who for two years served as national president of Hadassah. But no woman was ever ordained.[41] Almost all the students came because of Wise, whose broad interpretation of Jewish identity they fully shared. Religiously, their views ran from the moderately traditional to the radicalism of Wise's own son, James. They arrived with varying degrees of preparation in Hebrew. While an entrance examination was required, it was informally administered and a student who had done well in one of the better colleges was not turned away; he was simply asked to make up his deficiencies with a tutor.

The students in the first years of the JIR—and it seems for most of its history—were notably satisfied with the Institute. In one instance, early in 1930, a problem of communication did arise, but it was apparently solved when Wise and the faculty held a series of dinner meetings with the several classes, giving the students an opportunity to voice their criticisms.[42] Complaints were mostly limited to questions of jobs and money. No tuition was charged at the JIR, but students were expected to maintain themselves by working in the Jewish community as student-rabbis or teachers; Wise was opposed in principle to the granting of subsidies, such as were given in Cincinnati. After the school's first year, a number of students were able to live in a dormitory adjacent to the Institute, but the facilities here were most limited, lacking the food and laundry service that existed at HUC. In the late thirties, when few students were still living in the building, it was turned over to the women's division of the American Jewish

Congress and, under the administration of Mrs. Wise, housed refugees from Nazi Germany.

It is very difficult to gauge the intellectual level of the students over the years, but it would seem that some of the best men were graduated in the first years of the Institute's existence. Thereafter, according to one source, it went in cycles: some classes were relatively weak, others strong. At times the dominant mood was one of professionalism, at others—especially in the beginning—broader intellectual interests prevailed.

Because the school was so small, the curriculum had to be quite rigid and uniform. Only after a new program of studies, formulated by the honorary lecturer in education, Samson Benderly, was adopted by the faculty in 1931, was allowance made for individual interests during the entire second half of residency instead of merely in the last year. Among the academic subjects, the emphasis was chiefly on Bible, Midrash, and Hebrew literature. At various times courses were taught in Hebrew, especially by men who had spent some time in Palestine; and from the very beginning the works of the most important figures in the Hebrew national revival were made a required part of the rabbinical curriculum. There was also a program of community service in which students participated under the auspices of the Free Synagogue, and a considerable emphasis was placed on courses in education.

At first it was thought that the rabbinical curriculum should require a minimum of only two years of residency. But that was quickly raised to three, and before the end of the first year, the faculty insisted that it be lengthened to four years,[43] where it remained until the final merger with HUC. In order to graduate from the institute with the titles of Rabbi and Master of Hebrew Literature, a student had to complete 120 (later 130) hours of classroom work. In addition, he had to submit a thesis on an approved subject in the field of Jewish learning, which in nearly every instance involved the use of Hebrew texts. There was also a comprehensive examination immediately preceding graduation and, in the later period, a readiness exam at the end of the second year to eliminate students incapable of proceeding further.[44] As an incentive to greater achievement, a number of prizes

were offered for outstanding work or for a fine essay. The most valuable was the Guggenheimer fellowship for a year's study in Palestine,
awarded annually to an outstanding graduate or sometimes for the
sabbatical of a member of the faculty.

As the Institute had a single president during its entire independent
existence, so too it had a Board of Trustees that changed little over
the years. Three chairmen stood at its head, all of them members of
the Free Synagogue and personal friends of Stephen Wise. The first
was Lee K. Frankel, an insurance executive, who had been the
chairman of the Free Synagogue committee which negotiated with
the Union. He was succeeded in 1927 by Julian W. Mack, a judge
in the U. S. Circuit Court of Appeals and Wise's close associate in
the work of Zionism and the American Jewish Congress. Mack held
the position for sixteen years, until his death in 1943. Though he,
like the other chairmen, generally assented to Wise's suggestions, Mack
did hold certain views of his own. Along with some of the faculty, he
wanted the institution to possess a scholarly rather than a professional
character, and he declared that his chief interest in the Institute
lay "in creating a school of higher Jewish learning, and not in the
establishment of another seminary for the training of rabbis." [45]
Toward the end of his term of office Mack began to retire from
the work of the Institute, giving way to Joseph W. Levine, likewise
a jurist, who served as chairman during the final years of the Institute and together with Wise negotiated the ultimate merger with
HUC.

The board itself was composed mostly of New Yorkers, with the
few out-of-towners rarely present at its meetings. All the members
were Wise's acquaintances and admirers, to whom he turned principally for advice in fiscal and legal matters. In general, the board members had little contact with the teachers or students, though they did
become acquainted with those members of the faculty who later
served as its representatives on the board. They were not required to
do fund-raising, that being left to Wise himself, but the president
did expect his board to contribute generously to the Institute. Of
their number, one man stands out as playing a particularly active

role in the affairs of the JIR: George Alexander. Kohut. From his youth, Kohut had been one of Wise's closest friends, and he became a principal adviser to him at the JIR in all matters relating to faculty and Jewish scholarship. Kohut's financial aid, given to the Institute largely through the Alexander Kohut Foundation established in memory of his father, made it possible for the JIR to publish a number of scholarly volumes over the years. Of the Institute's dozen publications, the one that has remained the most widely known is Gershom Scholem's *Major Trends in Jewish Mysticism,* originally given as a series of lectures at the JIR in 1938.

The physical facilities of the Institute did not change materially during the quarter century of JIR's independent existence. Although for the first academic year classes had to be held at Temple Israel on West Ninety-first Street, by 1923 the new building at 40 West Sixty-eighth Street had been completed and it became the permanent home of the JIR. To be sure, the Institute had to share its facilities with the Free Synagogue until after World War II, but because Wise headed both institutions there seems to have been relatively little friction between the two tenants. The four-story structure was designed in the scholastic Tudor style. The front was made of local traprock with doors and leaded-glass windows trimmed in limestone. On the street level an auditorium, constructed to seat about six hundred people, became the location for most of the graduation ceremonies of the Institute. The second and third stories were shared with the Free Synagogue, while the fourth was devoted entirely to the work of the Institute. Here there were faculty studies, administrative offices, and a chapel accommodating ninety, done in the Gothic style with stone walls and a high vaulted ceiling.

Here, too, was the JIR library, at first totally contained in a small but adequate reading room. The basis of its collection was composed of Stephen Wise's own books, to which were added the library of the Breslau Jewish historian Marcus Brann, and various other donations that were made from time to time. The budget of the library was always very limited, so that only basic items could be purchased; no attempt was ever made to obtain a large collection of manuscripts, incunabula, or other rarities. Wise justified this policy by pointing out that students could easily enough avail themselves of the rich collections in the New York Public Library and the Jewish Theological Seminary. Thus, even as late as 1946, the Institute possessed less than sixty-five thousand volumes.

Nonetheless, the library was able to develop particular areas of strength where its holdings compared favorably with those of other institutions. These were especially biblical studies, modern Hebrew literature, Jewish history and sociology, Zionism and modern Palestine, and Jewish philosophy. Its librarians included Joshua Bloch, who thereafter became head of the Jewish Division of the New York Public Library, Salo W. Baron, Shalom Spiegel, and, from 1943, I. Edward Kiev.[46]

The religious life of the JIR centered around its chapel, where services were held daily before the beginning of classes. Over the years, participation varied, as it did in Cincinnati. Attendance was not officially required, but students were urged—sometimes in no uncertain terms[47] —to appear regularly. One of the most faithful in attending the services was Wise himself, who seldom missed chapel when he was in town. His presence was itself a motive for students to attend often, if only to be seen by him. Harry S. Lewis, the Institute's chaplain, generally conducted the services himself. He usually made use of the *Union Prayer Book,* though for variety he would add psalms, bits of Jewish lore, and occasionally even substitute the orthodox *siddur* or use no prayerbook at all. He did not put on a head covering or prayer shawl, but more traditionally inclined students were free to worship wearing a *kipa.* An additional service was held—for a time on Friday and for a time on Saturday afternoons—where students would read the service themselves and give the sermons. After Lewis retired in 1937, the daily services as well were regularly conducted by the students.

Of all the activities of the JIR, chapel was the one in which it was most difficult to maintain the religiously nonpartisan character of the institution. How could a truly traditional student tolerate a daily service so far removed from the orthodox liturgy? There must have been objections to the unstructured and eclectic character of the service at various times, even as on one occasion there was a member of the faculty who thought the chapel service should be discontinued since "it stamps the Institute as affiliated with the reform group." [48]

But although Wise always claimed his school was one in which any Jew could feel at home, the truth of the matter was that few fully observant Jews chose to study there. Most of its graduates went on to Reform pulpits, a few to Conservative ones, and hardly any to serve Orthodox congregations. The critical scholarship taught in many of the Institute's classrooms, the radical theology and the lack of observance of some of its faculty, and the nontraditional service of its chapel, all made JIR religiously a liberal, if not a Reform institution, whose principal ideological difference from Cincinnati lay less in religious belief or practice than in the common commitment to *kelal yisrael*. [49]

At the end of four years, in 1926, the Institute prepared to graduate its first class. The ceremonies began on May 23rd with a baccalaureate service in which Jonah Bondi Wise, a son of Isaac Mayer Wise and the rabbi of Central Synagogue in New York City, gave the sermon, thereby symbolically linking the work of his father with that of his colleague. The actual exercises were held three days later in the Institute auditorium. Ten men received the degrees of Master of Hebrew Literature and Rabbi. They were not, however, ordained; during most of the history of the school the word "ordination" was not used in the formula spoken by Wise, and graduation from the rabbinical program was simply called "commencement." [50] Only in later years was the term introduced, and the traditional formulation of *semikha,* giving the right to rule in matters of Jewish law, was at no time incorporated into the Hebrew certificate received by JIR's rabbinical graduates. After appropriate hymns and readings, Wise presented a collective charge to these first products of the Institute's labors, and he gave each of them a private word of confidence and his personal benediction.

Two honorary Doctor of Hebrew Literature degrees were conferred at this first ceremony, one of them *in absentia.* Wise's choice had fallen on two men who, for him, represented polar opposites in

Judaism.[51] The first was Claude Montefiore, outstanding Anglo-Jewish scholar and leader of British liberal Judaism, but an outspoken anti-Zionist. Due to illness, he was not able to be present at the ceremony. The second was the outstanding poet of the Hebrew Renaissance, Chaim Nachman Bialik, who was visiting in New York at that time. In accepting Wise's invitation to receive the degree, Bialik replied that he regarded this honor as symbolic of a covenant between Jewish scholarship and Hebrew literature, a covenant which he hoped would bring renewed creative force to the spirit of the Jewish people.[52]

Though they came after only four years, these first graduation exercises were perhaps the highpoint in the entire history of the JIR. Not that the succeeding period of more than twenty years lacked capable candidates for the rabbinate, or that it failed to witness growth in the size of the student body and impressive, moving graduation ceremonies at which leading figures of the Jewish and non-Jewish world were honored. But it seems that the early promise, expressed by Bialik, that the JIR would contribute its share to the spiritual renaissance of the Jewish people, was not realized as fully as some had at first dared to hope. In later years Wise himself, while by no means abandoning the JIR, turned his attention increasingly to other matters. Perhaps—as some believe—he was disappointed that the JIR proved itself unable to hold his own son for the rabbinate, perhaps it was simply the greater urgency of battling Tammany Hall, of raising funds for the United Palestine Appeal, of organizing a World Jewish Congress, or of alerting America to the dangers of Nazism. Whatever the explanation, within ten years after that first graduation, Wise was ranking the JIR last among the five causes which then clamored for his attention.[53] And Wise was the heart of the school. It was necessary for the welfare of the Institute that he maintain his great reputation in Jewish life in order to attract students—and this he did. But it was also necessary that he devote himself almost fully to the problems of the school—and this he found himself unable to do. In particular, there was a tremendous and continuing need to raise funds, for which the JIR, unlike the HUC, could not rely on the Union of American Hebrew Congregations. When depression struck in 1929, it was the financial weakness of the school which proved the most basic of all in preventing the Institute from attaining its early promise.

The early thirties were a period of crisis for the JIR with ramifications for every aspect of its institutional life. Despite the failure of the negotiations with the UAHC, the Institute's financial position until the Great Depression had not been such as to cause concern. The Free Synagogue, federated with the Central Synagogue from 1923 to 1925, covered a large part of the expenses during the first few years; Wise's fund-raising efforts, both in New York and on tours to various parts of the country, proved quite successful. The largest gift, a bequest from the estate of a Mrs. Hannah Heyman, ultimately netted the JIR some $163,000. Thus, although the yearly budget of the JIR climbed from $35,000 the first year to well over $100,000 in 1928–29, income continued to exceed expenditures. The total assets of the school grew steadily until they reached close to half a million dollars.[54] But then the financial situation began to deteriorate: income declined, deficits began to appear and then to grow in size. From the top down, morale was now sagging within all the components of the Institute's community. By the spring of 1932, Wise himself was at the point of despair. To Slonimsky, then on sabbatical leave in Europe and Palestine, he wrote:

> Sometimes I have been amused to think of the ease and delight that have been yours in Palestine while we are literally struggling and slaving here. No one could have greater joy in your delight over Palestine than I. But things have really been in very, very bad shape, and continue to be. I am not easily discouraged, but I confess I do not know what we are going to do next year. It seems all but impossible to carry on. Frankly, I must tell you that if I had known how grave things were to be, I would have asked you to put off the Palestine trip to another year, and spend some months going through the country in the interests of the Institute. . . . No money is coming in at all, and, worst of all, there seems no promise of betterment.[55]

A year and a half later Wise wrote a desperate letter for support to the

Institute's alumni,[56] but he received only the most meager response.

Economic conditions made necessary a reduction of faculty salaries in rough proportion to the lower cost of living. A full professor making $7,000 in 1930–31 received consecutive reductions of 10 percent for three years until in 1933–34 he was earning only $5,103. In 1937–38 his salary went down even further, to $5,000.[57] Necessarily, this progressive decrease in remuneration made for discontent on the part of at least some members of the faculty, and their grievances were exacerbated when salaries did not immediately move upward in the late thirties, once the cost of living began to reverse its direction.

The depression seems also to have affected the spirit and drive of the students. At a faculty meeting held in January of 1931, "all those present mentioned the lack of enthusiasm among the students after a short period of residence and an increasing materialistic attitude." A few months later Wise reported to the faculty his own "disappointment with the quality of the students' work."[58] The student publication, the *Jewish Institute Quarterly,* which was begun in 1924 with high aspirations of leading the way in Jewish life and thought with new, freer interpretations of Judaism,[59] was forced to cease publication with the issue of April 1930. The reason for its demise was lack of funds—and possibly also of enthusiasm. The general mood at the JIR—as at HUC—was made even gloomier by the knowledge that the supply of rabbis in the Reform movement now exceeded the number of pulpits available, a trend aggravated by the current tendency to merge congregations and the inability of smaller congregations in depression times to afford the services of a full-time rabbi.[60]

As the depression dragged on through the thirties, the Institute continued to lead so precarious an existence that as late as 1938 Wise threatened to close it down.[61] Little money was coming in; fewer students of quality were applying for admission;[62] demoralization was everywhere apparent. Finally, Wise called a dinner meeting of faculty and trustees at the Metropolis Club in New York on January 12, 1939. During the discussion, Dean Henry Slonimsky expressed a feeling among the faculty that the Institute had fallen short of its goals. He continued:

It has not lived up to the measure of its founder, nor has it become a great center of Jewish learning commensurate with the size of the Jewish population of New York. It is the charge of American Israel to carry on Judaism. If the Institute is to envisage the task, it must have a better student body—quantitatively and qualitatively—a renewed faculty, a renovated president and an active board of trustees of national eminence, which is convinced of the primary importance of a Jewish school.[63]

But in some respects things began to look up in the last years before World War II. The ledger for 1937–38 showed a slight surplus of income over expenditure, and the budget, at $64,276, had climbed to nearly twice what it was three years earlier (though still considerably less than before the depression). An annual summer institute for rabbis was organized at the JIR by its alumni organization in 1937 and it became a permanent feature. In the late thirties, John Tepfer, a gifted teacher of Jewish history and Talmud who was himself a graduate of the JIR, joined the faculty, as did the distinguished historian Guido Kisch; and in 1940 another graduate, Abram Granison, was appointed full-time national director of rabbinical placement and field activities. Shortly thereafter, new scholars of high potential, Harry Orlinsky (Bible) and Simon Halkin (Hebrew literature), added strength to the Institute's faculty. With the entry of the United States into the war, some forty JIR men served as chaplains in various theaters of combat, bringing renown to their school. Finally, upon his retirement from most of the work he had done at the Free Synagogue, Wise in 1944 could report that he had been able to give "more time and strength to the Institute and its needs than in any year of its history."[64] When the war ended, therefore, the time seemed ripe at last for a major drive to gain the financial security which the JIR needed so badly.

If the Institute was to outlast the aging Stephen S. Wise, a huge endowment had to be raised as soon as possible. In the spring of 1945, a million-dollar campaign was launched to solve the JIR's financial woes once and for all. Albert Einstein, a great admirer of Wise, was declared its honorary chairman; a professional fund-raising company was engaged; and laymen and alumni were called upon for active support.[65] But this last grand effort, though it was maintained for nearly three years, until 1948,[66] proved pitifully ineffective. As of May 1, 1946, the Maintenance and Expansion Fund had received in cash only $60,453.78 and its solicitation had cost more than half that sum.[67] It became increasingly apparent that the enormous goal would not even be approached. Various circumstances may have contributed to this failure: the simultaneous vast campaigns of the United Jewish Appeal; the launching of HUC's $5 million Foundation Fund in 1945; the disinclination of alumni (with exceptions) to support the cause of their alma mater to the extent Wise would have wished; perhaps also the fact that HUC, as a total institution, was ideologically no longer as distant from the JIR as it had been in 1922. Then too, Wise was at last running out of energy. During a meeting of the faculty in those final years, John Tepfer later recalled, Wise threw up his hands despairingly and said: "Gentlemen, what can I do? The congregations are not supporting me. Our graduates are not as loyal to the school as they should be. . . . I've reached the end of my tether."

Wise had come to realize that the only possible future of the JIR lay in conjunction with the Hebrew Union College. His thoughts, therefore, turned increasingly to merger—though in truth, for more than fifteen years, the subject had never been very distant from his mind.

The Institute had made an initial effort at cooperation with HUC as early as 1923. At that time the chairman of the JIR's Board, Lee K. Frankel, proposed to Julian Morgenstern an exchange of professors, students, and credits. But Morgenstern turned him down, arguing that no parity existed between the two institutions.[68] Thereafter, for about five years, contact between HUC and JIR was minimal, limited to words of greeting presented upon ceremonial occasions. In those early days the JIR, with the energy of a youthful, growing institution, seemed perfectly able to function on its own.

Then in 1929, apparently on his own initiative, Walter Hilborn of the JIR board introduced a resolution at the UAHC biennial convention of that year calling for a Union effort to bring about co-operation among the UAHC, the HUC, and the JIR. The resolution passed unanimously, and Wise was pleased by it. It meant to him that "for the first time, we are recognized by them and taken account of by them and dealt with no longer as a negligible institution." [69] Negotiations were soon initiated, but there was disagreement between the JIR on the one side and the College and Union on the other with regard to the purpose of the discussions. Wise wanted to develop areas of cooperation and exchange similar to those proposed by Frankel to Morgenstern in 1923.[70] The UAHC and HUC representatives were more concerned with the increasing difficulty of finding positions for rabbinical graduates and therefore with the necessity of limiting enrollment. Once again Morgenstern proved himself basically un-favorable to tangible arrangements of cooperation.[71] Only two meetings were held, and the matter was dropped.

No further efforts to bring the two institutions together in any respect were made thereafter until 1934, when, under pressure of the general economic crisis, explicit references appear, this time not merely to cooperation, but to a full-scale merger. Two rabbis seem to have initiated the move, Felix Levy of Chicago and William F. Rosenblum of New York.[72] Wise himself was not unfavorable to the proposal, though he immediately stressed a point which recurs with regularity thereafter: "Merging . . . must not mean submerging." [73] Actual negotiations, however, did not get under way until 1938, when Rabbi James G. Heller of Cincinnati, Wise's close friend and a member of the HUC Board of Governors, urged the board to re-open the matter of closer cooperation.[74] It seemed an especially pro-pitious juncture as the HUC board chairman was now Ralph W. Mack, brother of JIR board chairman Julian Mack. Thus there began a series of protracted negotiations commencing in December 1939 and lasting nearly four years. The initial joint proposal called for a merger with two co-presidents, Wise and Morgenstern, and an integrated program divided between the first three years spent in Cincinnati and the last two in New York. JIR's identity would be preserved by the provision that the amalgamated institution would train men for the rabbinate of all groups and bear the name of both its components.[75] The proposal had the support of Cincinnatian Ralph Mack and of Wise. Certain of the JIR alumni were also pushing for its consummation;[76] others, while strongly arguing the importance of retaining the unique features of the JIR, were likewise unopposed in principle.[77] The faculty of the JIR, on the whole, were the least enthusiastic, but they, too, were willing to go along if the teaching staff in New York would be augmented and not reduced.[78]

But then Morgenstern issued a revised text of the proposal which prevented an early consummation of the merger. The HUC president did indeed favor amalgamation, but his revision now included these words: "Inasmuch as the investment of the Hebrew Union College in land, in buildings, in library, is considerably greater, and its facilities measurably better, it shall be understood that the merged institution shall be located in Cincinnati."[79] Naturally, the JIR board would not consider any union that did not preserve a school in New York, and Wise, too, was unalterably opposed to the new text. To alumnus Morton Berman he related what he had said at a Zionist Executive session to James Heller: "While I live, the Institute will not leave New York. It would mean the abandonment of the guidance of more than two million Jews to the care of the [Jewish Theological] Seminary, which is the theological stooge of the assimilationist American Jewish Committee." And he continued to Berman: "We shall probably break there. They don't want merely a merger; they want a submerger. They want to save money. They don't seem to understand that American Jewry would be interested even in the nominal coordination of the two institutions, but, we shall see."[80]

Yet, amazingly, a compromise was reached at a meeting on June 9, 1941, whereby the concentration of instruction in a single city was to become possible only by the decision of the amalgamated board eight years after the conclusion of the agreement. At the same meeting, President Morgenstern also expressed his thought that the merged institution should prepare men for service to the whole community of Israel, without consideration of denomination.[81] The compromise plan was submitted to the respective boards in October and each approved with some relatively minor recommended changes. But progress ceased there—not primarily, it seems, because of any inability to come to terms, but rather because of the course events were then taking within the Reform movement as a whole.

Political Zionism in 1942 split the rabbinate more sharply than ever before. In that year the American Council for Judaism was formed by those rabbis, now a minority, who remained firm opponents of a national conception of Judaism. Ideological antagonism within the movement soon reached a fever pitch, precluding delicate negotiations in an atmosphere of growing acrimony.[82] Wise, the champion of Zionism, and Morgenstern, its opponent, were under these circumstances unable to conclude any final agreement. At the end of 1942 Wise wrote to James Heller:

> It has seemed to me, Jimmy, that the action of Morgenstern in signing that Atlantic City declaration [of "non-Zionist" rabbis meeting on June 1 and 2, 1942] has ended the possibility for me of a union of the College and the Institute. Whatever the Institute may determine after I am out of it is one matter. But you can see the absurdity, the impossibility of my being yoked— though only for a year, until my seventieth birthday—with Morgenstern, seeing that the two of us represent viewpoints diametrically and irreconcilably opposed. He has the same right to what I think his lamentably wrong viewpoint as I have to my unlamentably right viewpoint. But you can see for yourself that as sharers of the leadership of the merged institutions we would be in fundamental conflict with each other. Whether the two schools were merged into one institution, or continued as two in any form of union, what he and I would say would be in clearest contradiction to each other with respect to one of the basic things of Jewish life.[83]

For the next four years Wise concentrated on trying to strengthen the JIR. He spurned approaches aimed at reviving merger plans when made to him by the new director of the UAHC, Maurice Eisendrath, and would consider only cooperation in fund-raising.[84] But then the Biennial Council of the Union, at Eisendrath's urging, in 1946 came out unanimously in favor of exploring the possibilities for greater coordination between the two seminaries. A year earlier, the Hebrew

Union College had decided at long last to confer an honorary degree on the now seventy-one-year-old Wise. As the JIR fund drive proved increasingly to be a disaster, as the UAHC was belatedly recognizing the importance of New York, where it would shortly move its own offices from Cincinnati, as the JIR people came to realize that their negotiating position would only be weakened once Wise had passed from the scene, and most importantly, as it became clear that Morgenstern himself was shortly to retire, the resistance on the JIR side was broken. Then, in 1947, once Nelson Glueck became president-elect of the Hebrew Union College, Wise was assured that, at least with regard to love for the Land of Israel, there was no longer any difference at the top between the two institutions. When the JIR ordination exercises were held in June of 1947, both Glueck and Morgenstern received honorary degrees. By mid-1948, negotiations were again under way and a joint statement had been formulated. It read:

> The Hebrew Union College and the Jewish Institute of Religion resolve to unite for the strengthening and advancement of Judaism in America and throughout the world. The right to serve the Jewish people in its entirety (K'lal Yisroel), with freedom for faculty and students alike, is axiomatic.
>
> This united institution shall continue to maintain schools in Cincinnati and New York, with Nelson Glueck as president and Stephen S. Wise and Julian Morgenstern as presidents emeriti. Upon this union we invoke the blessing of God.[85]

In June the JIR board accepted the resignation of Stephen Wise as its president, elected him president-emeritus, and made Nelson Glueck president of the Jewish Institute of Religion.[86] Earlier that year, Wise had participated in Glueck's inauguration as president of HUC in Cincinnati, and in October he installed him as president of the JIR in New York.[87]

The two institutions now possessed a single head, but they were not yet one. The problems of integrating them smoothly proved formidable; the JIR trustees and faculty jealously protected their freedom of action against what they soon felt was Glueck's "administration by remote control and by directives," while the new president would brook no interference in his administrative prerogatives.[88] It was not until 1950 that the merger finally became complete.

Meanwhile, on April 19, 1949, Stephen S. Wise had died, leaving a memorable legacy of achievement. The Institute he founded was, perhaps, not the best known of his numerous attainments, but it was certainly not of minor significance. From the beginning, he had assembled and presided over a small but talented faculty, whose writings over the years made a considerable contribution to Jewish scholarship. During more than a quarter century, nearly two hundred prospective rabbis had successfully completed their studies at the Institute, and some had become leading figures in American Jewish life. Within his students Wise had successfully nurtured a devotion to the entire people of Israel and to the social ideals of the Hebrew prophets which he prized so highly. In his last days he could look back upon the Institute as a difficult, but gratifying aspect of his career, and as its president emeritus, he could hope that the spirit he had tried to instill in the JIR would not be entirely lost in the newly united institution.

"WITH VISION AND BOLDNESS"

> I have been saying and reiterating
> for years that either we move ahead
> with vision and boldness . . . or we
> must inevitably go backwards.
> There just isn't any standing still.—
> NELSON GLUECK to the Board
> of Governors, October 31, 1968

INSUFFICIENT TIME HAS
elapsed since the death of Nelson Glueck in 1971 to gain a clear
perspective on the nearly twenty-four years that he served as the
school's president. Yet there can be no doubt as to the large role
played by his powerful personality in determining its destiny during
that time. His administration represents a period of immense expansion, from a single campus in Cincinnati to a far-flung institution
with three centers in the United States and one in Israel. The school
grew in every respect: in buildings, numbers of faculty and students,
and in academic prestige. Yet these years were also a period of
protracted controversies and—toward the last—a time of deep uncertainty. Three major disputes loom large: with New York Reform
Jewry over the future status of the JIR, with the Union of American

[171]

Hebrew Congregations over funds and influence in the movement, and with the Central Conference of American Rabbis over the nature of rabbinical training. The Glueck years were at once troubled and exciting; perpetually and inevitably they were controversial. This chapter can present but a first tentative understanding and evaluation of their significance.

In 1947 Julian Morgenstern had been president of the Hebrew Union College for a quarter of a century. He had sustained it during the depression, enlarged its faculty, given it academic freedom and respectability. But the College's situation following World War II demanded new leadership. Without a successful campaign for capital funds, the College could not meet the challenges and responsibilities thrust upon it as American Jewry began to take over hegemony of the Jewish diaspora. The College required a man of youthful vigor, scholarly status, and forceful personality who could rise to meet the new demands. For those in a position to influence the decision, the only candidate obviously meeting all these qualifications was Nelson Glueck.

Glueck's origins were not such as to forecast the eminence he would ultimately attain. His parents were humble Lithuanian immigrants who struggled to raise their nine children in the poor downtown section of Cincinnati. The family was Orthodox, the home kosher, the language spoken initially Yiddish. The elder Glueck, a peddler, could barely make ends meet. Nelson, his third child, born in 1900, had to help support himself by selling newspapers in the neighborhood. As in the case of so many HUC students at that time, the College offered him the only visible opportunity for a higher education as well as financial support and the hope of a more dignified career. He entered the school in 1914 and was ordained in 1923. While at the College, however, he came to the conclusion (probably influenced by Adolph Oko[1]) that he did not want to be a congregational rabbi. Given a traveling fellowship upon ordination, he went immediately to Germany in order to pursue advanced biblical studies with the hope of eventually teaching at the College. After four years, he received his doctorate with a dissertation on the use of the word *ḥesed* in the

Bible. But linguistic and conceptual study of the Bible was not to be a permanent interest. In 1927, he left Germany for Palestine to begin preparing himself for a career in the more exciting and exotic field of biblical archaeology. In a year he managed to learn some modern Hebrew and Arabic and, most importantly, he became the disciple of William Foxwell Albright, the leading Palestinian archaeologist, who at that time was director of the American School of Oriental Research in Jerusalem.

In 1928 Glueck finally returned to Cincinnati, accepting a position as instructor at the College. But the budding archaeologist found little satisfaction in teaching Preparatory Department students the fundamentals of Hebrew grammar. His patience was thin and he angrily threw chalk at those who had difficulty with the subjects he taught. Glueck remained in Cincinnati for only four years, even then spending his summers in Palestine assisting Albright. During that period he met and married Helen Iglauer, a highly intelligent medical student from one of the leading German-Jewish families in Cincinnati. Through Helen and her relatives, he developed social relationships with the aristocracy of Cincinnati Jewry, the very people who served on the Board of Governors and supported the College. They became personally acquainted with the handsome, charming young man who fascinated them with his romantic ambition to reveal the background of the Bible by exploring the terrain of the Holy Land. Later they would easily be convinced that Helen's husband was the only man who could expand the horizons of the school.

But Glueck still did not feel entirely at home in the city of his birth. The challenge for him lay not in the classrooms and library of the Hebrew Union College but in the sands of the Palestinian deserts. Offered the opportunity to spend a year as resident director of the American School in 1932, he grasped it eagerly. He returned to Jerusalem in the spring of 1934 and was there again from 1936 to 1940. Then, after less than two years back in the United States, he received a new and irresistible offer: the government's Office of Strategic Services desired to make use of his background and abilities. Under cover of serving once more as director of the American School in Jerusalem, as well as its field director in Baghdad, he was to act as a clandestine agent. He would gather information of possible military significance and act as an on-the-spot adviser in case either Allied retreat or Allied invasion would require his expert knowledge of the region's topography and its ancient roadways. His super-secret work for the government added a patina of mystique and savoir-faire to a public image already becoming well known beyond the bounds of Cincinnati.

By 1947, Glueck's fame as an archaeologist was considerable. His surface explorations in eastern Palestine had located many hundreds of ancient sites; in the south, he had excavated Tell el-Kheleifeh near the northern shore of the Red Sea, identifying it with King Solomon's fabled seaport of Ezion-Geber. He dated, and in some instances discovered, copper and iron mines that Solomon had established in the Arabah rift, claiming that the copper had been smelted at Ezion-Geber. His findings appeared in scholarly volumes and articles—but not there alone. Glueck possessed a great talent for popularizing his work. *The Other Side of the Jordan,* in 1940, was the first of four major books that he would publish for the lay reader, eliminating scholarly apparatus and presenting his findings in such a way that archaeology seemed as much a colorful adventure as a scholarly enterprise.

From the time of his appointment to the Hebrew Union College faculty in 1928 until his selection as president in 1947, Glueck spent almost twice as much time in Palestine as he did in Cincinnati. Yet the Board of Governors was ever and again willing to grant him another leave of absence, extend his time abroad, advance him in rank, and even supplement the salary he received from the American School.[2] Its members obviously felt that in Glueck the school possessed an unusual asset whose growing fame redounded to its glory.

Throughout all the years that Glueck spent in Palestine, he maintained an active correspondence with Julian Morgenstern.[3] He continually kept the HUC president informed on the progress of his work, parrying repeated pleas for return to Cincinnati by insisting that his work in Palestine was preparing him to be a more useful teacher. Eventually, Morgenstern gave up trying to persuade him that what the College needed was a biblical scholar, not an expert in Palestinian archaeology. He fully appreciated Glueck's talents and potential, and like Glueck himself,[4] he knew the public-relations value of biblical archaeology. At a conference in Glueck's home already during the early forties, the HUC president outlined further plans for his one-time student, which, if they materialized as expected, would eventually make the College Glueck's responsibility.[5]

Morgenstern was eager to have his selected successor's final assent before he tendered his own resignation. He feared that otherwise the presidency might become a "political football" among members of the CCAR. Glueck, however, became increasingly reluctant to accept the position. He was totally at ease in Zion. When Morgenstern began to press him, he responded by recounting all his self-perceived inadequacies: he had never raised a penny in his life and did not think he could; he had always shunned committees, avoided conventions, and eschewed administrative responsibilities. Above all, he was not a philosopher or a public speaker.[6] It was not until August 15, 1946, when he had been joined in Palestine by his wife and young son, that he most reluctantly gave the commitment: "I have made up my mind to accept the offer. . . ."

The conviction did not last. That fall, after Morgenstern had already announced his retirement,[7] Glueck began to have second thoughts. He now wrote that he would prefer not to be president of the College, that he had accepted the post only as an unavoidable moral responsibility, without any real enthusiasm. The result was to give Morgenstern his own second thoughts. Though in recent years he had considered only Glueck to be his successor, the retiring president now felt compelled to look further afield. He wrote to Glueck that there were other worthy candidates, at least one of whom (almost certainly Bernard Bamberger[8]) would in his opinion fill the office with ability and distinction.[9] Morgenstern, however, had not counted on the strong sentiments of the most influential members of his board. On October 7, 1946, he wrote to board member Iphigene Ochs Sulzberger in New York that he no longer believed the unenthusiastic Glueck to be the man for the job and hinted at his preference for Bamberger. In reply, Mrs. Sulzberger told the president that not only was she convinced Glueck was "the ideal man" but that his lack of enthusiasm was merely evidence of his sincerity. Later she pressed for a speedy decision in his favor and stated baldly: "I for one would be unable to 'sell' the College unless I was certain that the new President would continue the present policies and be a true advocate of Reform and American ideals." [10] Faced with insurmountable pressure from the board, Morgenstern beat a hasty retreat. Astonishingly, he wrote to Glueck that he was now reassured the reluctant aspirant really wanted the position, though Glueck himself, while never actually withdrawing his name, wrote back that he had thought the matter was finished and had already turned his thoughts to other plans for the future. [11]

The preponderance of evidence suggests that Glueck was genuinely ambivalent about taking the position. He felt very much at home in Jerusalem, he had a burning desire to continue his archaeological work, and he correctly sensed that if he became president of the College he would lose his position at the forefront of research in the field. He certainly did not look forward to raising money and doing administrative work. But the presidency of the College was unquestionably a great honor and it presented the possibility of making a deep mark on American Judaism. At the same time, his future relationship to the American School was becoming doubtful as severe conflict between Jews and Arabs loomed in Palestine. Finally, his wife wished very much that he anchor his life to Cincinnati.

Early in 1947 Glueck returned to the United States and met with the selection committee—still uncertain in his own mind. Meanwhile, other candidates had been mentioned. Aside from Bamberger, there was Joshua Loth Liebman, who was the choice of some of the student body; Abba Hillel Silver and Solomon Freehof were favored by a portion of the alumni. When it seemed that Glueck would refuse at the last minute, Jacob Rader Marcus was sounded out about accepting the job. What opposition there was to Glueck rested on three grounds: his lack of experience as a congregational rabbi, his "insufficiently Jewish" field of scholarship, and his lack of interest in the position. The arguments in his favor, by contrast, were overwhelming. He was a native son of Cincinnati, an ordinee of the College, and an internationally recognized scholar. His powerful personality, his imposing appearance, and his dignity of manner were qualities that could only be regarded as most desirable in a College president. Moreover, he had gained administrative experience as director of the American School, and it was generally believed that he would be able to raise money easily. His association with Palestine aroused no real opposition as at the time he was not committed to a Jewish state.[12] Finally, on account of his marriage, the child of Lithuanian immigrants had been adopted as a member of the German "crowd," then still in control of the College. There was never any real question that if Glueck wanted the job, it was his. After he was promised administrative assistance and had told the nominating committee he could not contemplate a future which meant absolute separation from Palestine, he accepted the position.

Initially, even after assuming office, his ambivalence remained very strong. At one point he seriously negotiated for the presidency of the Hebrew University in Jerusalem.[13] To Judah L. Magnes, his close friend in Palestine who had urged him to take the College presidency, he complained of the "moods of depression I have been seized with since returning home" and expressed the wish that "someone else had been impressed into this task." But he added: "The die is cast. . . . I have a feeling that if I follow my normal instincts I can establish my way and drive toward a goal which all of us would desire."[14] Although the melancholy moods induced by thoughts of Jerusalem were not easily and never completely banished, Glueck did indeed begin to drive toward goals for the College, though he possessed no clear, encompassing view. His first objective was simply to set the school in motion: raising funds, expanding the student body, and launching new projects.

All during the thirties and the period of the war there had been no capital funds campaign for the College. Economic conditions had not been propitious, and it had always been possible to carry on the regular program of the school with the aid of the $90,000 minimal depletion of endowment capital mandated by Julius Rosenwald. Following World War II, however, the College found itself in a situation where the Ochs-Rosenwald fund was nearly exhausted and the remaining endowment was insufficient to sustain, let alone to expand, the program. Buildings were sorely in need of repair, and pension liabilities, not shown on the balance statements, posed a hidden threat to fiscal stability. Already during the Morgenstern administration the College had responded by launching a Foundation Fund intended to secure the school's finances for the next generation. But the results —by the beginning of 1947 only about $250,000 in pledges—had fallen discouragingly short of the goal of $5 million, and later $8 million.[15] Hope was thus fastened on the new president, and board members were confident that he would provide the impetus necessary for a successful campaign.

With Glueck taking over the presidency and Robert S. Adler of Chicago, a nephew of Rosenwald, assuming the campaign chairmanship, a "Blueprint for the Future" was issued, documenting specific needs and new projects. Though totally inexperienced as a fundraiser, Glueck began to make the circuit of campaign dinners. At the same time the College budget was allowed to increase, though funds were not yet available to cover the higher costs. The resulting deficit in 1948–49 was a bit embarrassing, but could be publicly interpreted as clear evidence of the compelling need for greater income.[16] For the first time in its history the College borrowed money from a bank, about $200,000 to meet its operating needs.[17] In order to raise the amount of individual contributions in relation to the objective, the ultimate campaign goal was tactically elevated to $12 million. Yet even apart from this obviously inflated sum, the final result was far below expectation. By the time it was abandoned in 1951, the campaign had raised less than $1,400,000.[18] Glueck's name and charm had proved less effective than some had believed. But perhaps even more basically, the enormous gifts of Rosenwald, Ochs, the Guggenheims, and others, which had brought the total of the 1920s campaign to over twice what was raised for the Foundation Fund, were simply not available to the College in the late forties.

If nonetheless the HUC budget was able to jump from less than $400,000 in 1946–47 to twice that amount four years later, it was due primarily to Glueck's successful efforts at increasing the College's yield from its principal source of maintenance funds: the congregational dues paid to the Union of American Hebrew Congregations and the yearly contributions made to the Union-College Combined Campaign. Although the Union had succeeded in limiting Foundation Fund donations to gifts above $1,000, during the first years of the Glueck administration it was forced to settle for a progressively decreasing share of the annual revenues accruing from dues and the combined maintenance campaign. While in 1947–48 the Union still received twice as much from these proceeds as did the College, by 1951–52 the net total—which had grown to nearly a million dollars—was by agreement split precisely in half.[19] To further increase College income, dormitory fees were raised, and for the first time in the history of the school, in the fall of 1952, a tuition fee of $350 per year was levied on every student who could afford to pay.

This augmented income was used in the first instance to enlarge the administrative machinery of the school. Glueck had no intention of dealing personally with the minutiae of the school's day-to-day affairs as Morgenstern had done. Instead, he engaged a staff of young rabbis to assist him. Alvin Fine was moved from director of field activities to the newly created post of assistant to the president, while his old job was taken by Robert Katz. Abraham Klausner was given public relations and publicity, while Bertram Korn handled arrangements for Glueck's elaborate inauguration ceremonies before assuming Fine's job as assistant when the latter left to take a pulpit.

Considerable funds and much effort were also now devoted to increasing the size of the student body. Reform Jewry had begun the process of rapid expansion which would bring the number of congregations in the Union from only about three hundred at the end of the war to almost twice that number by 1960, and the total of dues-paying members from less than one hundred thousand in 1947 to about two hundred thousand in 1959. There was an abundance of available pulpits without qualified rabbis to fill them. To attract prospective students, Katz circulated posters publicizing the College, published advertisements in periodicals, and made frequent visits to congregations and university campuses. But in the immediate postwar years, few university students were interested. Some lacked the elementary Hebrew knowledge necessary to pass the entrance examination; others were put off by the long, six-year program; a few failed to pass the newly instituted psychiatric screening process.

To help solve the problem it was decided to encourage men at an earlier stage of their education. Although Morgenstern had prided himself on gradually making the College wholly a postgraduate institution, shortly after his retirement it was decided to embark on a pre-rabbinic program whereby undergraduate students either in Cincinnati or elsewhere in major cities would be encouraged to begin preparing themselves for admission. A few years later, in 1957, such mostly informal prerabbinic training gave way to a more structured "Undergraduate Program" in which the entire first year of the rabbinic curriculum could be completed together with graduation from the University of Cincinnati. The old Preparatory Department thus returned in slightly altered form, not to be abandoned until 1970.[20]

Although the growth of the rabbinical program remained the principal concern during the Glueck administration, in its first years it was the establishment of certain new branches of activity, broadening the scope of the institution, which drew special attention to the school and provided a sense of expansion. Two such early ventures in Cincinnati proved to be both significant and enduring: the American Jewish Archives and the Graduate Department.

The Archives was the brainchild of historian Jacob Rader Marcus, who had been influenced by the Holocaust to shift his scholarly interest from the Jews of Europe to American Jewry. The latter, he was quick to realize, had now taken on new and unprecedented importance. Initially, he proposed simply gathering the records of the older Reform congregations with the intent of making the College the archival center for Reform Jewry.[21] But the scope of the project expanded rapidly until it came to include documentation for all of American Jewish history. The Archives began to receive personal papers and organizational records in such quantities that it was soon necessary to renovate a portion of the old Bernheim Library building to accommodate its growing number of file boxes along with the newly revived HUC Museum. In June 1948, the first issue of *American Jewish Archives* was published, beginning an unbroken chain of

semiannually appearing collections of scholarly articles, brief reviews, and lists of recent acquisitions. Along with the American
Jewish Historical Society in the East, the Archives became one of
the two principal depositories for primary source material in its field.
Over the years, it accumulated an extensive and highly valuable
collection, indispensable for any serious scholar in the field.

No less significant was the new program of graduate studies
established after the war. In part, it represented the College's response
to the need for training Jewish scholars in America now that the
great European centers of learning had been destroyed. At the same
time it was also intended to attract Christian students whose work
at the College would hopefully make them knowledgeable and
sympathetic interpreters of Judaism. Fellowships were obtained for
both Jews and Christians through special donations. At first, Christian
students and Jews who were not rabbis were supposed to receive a
newly created Doctor of Hebrew Studies degree; rabbinical fellows
would continue to be candidates for the Doctor of Hebrew Letters as
heretofore, only they would work for it in residence. However, when
in 1950 the College received authorization to grant a Doctor of Philosophy degree in Hebrew and Cognate Studies, the D.H.S. was discontinued and the D.H.L. returned to its status as basically an *in-absentia*
degree.

The in-residence graduate program grew slowly but steadily in
the following years. In 1947, the enrollment consisted of four Jewish
fellows; a year later of three Jews and five Christians. By the late
sixties there were annually upwards of thirty students. They sat in on
some of the regular rabbinical courses, participated in special graduate
seminars, and wrote dissertations, a number of which were later published wholly or in part. After twenty years, in 1968, the College in
Cincinnati had awarded eighteen Ph.D.'s to Jewish graduate students
and twenty-five to interfaith fellows. A larger number had participated
in the program without gaining the degree. No less than thirteen
of the Jewish students had become members of the faculty on one or
another of the campuses.[22]

A third early innovation was the institution of a Department of
Human Relations. It was established in recognition of the increasing

significance which recent developments in the fields of psychiatry and sociology possessed for the rabbinical profession. Initially the department did not offer required courses but devoted its efforts to arranging symposia participated in by rabbis and psychiatrists. It issued a series of six pamphlets on psychology and religion, two of them posthumous works by Joshua Loth Liebman, the recently deceased HUC alumnus after whom the department was named. The project was intended as evidence to the Jewish community that the College, despite its president's special interest in antiquity, was nonetheless aware of contemporary intellectual concerns and was taking steps to provide its students with the opportunity to confront them. In 1950, upon the retirement of Abraham Cronbach, human-relations offerings, beginning with a course entitled "The Rabbi, the Congregation, and the Community," came to replace Jewish social studies as part of the rabbinical curriculum.

Yet two further projects to extend the scope and outreach of the College were launched at the beginning of the Glueck administration. Neither of these, however, endured. One was a program of studies for "lay students" who were encouraged to take a few Judaica courses at the College in addition to their regular work at the University of Cincinnati. Although it was publicized principally as an attempt to better educate a portion of the Reform Jewish laity, the program was also intended as an additional device for recruitment. For a period of five years younger instructors and fellows of the College offered this group a variety of popular elementary courses in Judaism. Enrollment reached about fifty students at its height, most of them women. The enterprise was abandoned when it was apparent that it had become little more than an adult-education or extension program and seemed no longer to serve the immediate interests of the College.

The other project was known as the Hebrew Union College Reference Department. In response to a regular announcement on the nationwide UAHC "Message of Israel" radio broadcast, questions on any subject related to Judaism were sent to the school. Rabbi A. Stanley Dreyfus, a graduate student at the College, did his best to answer the dozens of queries—most of a serious nature and most from

Jews—which arrived weekly in Cincinnati.[23] Having achieved its public-relations value, this modern responsa project was allowed to die once Dreyfus had completed his studies and left the College.

At the same time that the College was launching these new ventures in Cincinnati, it was also once again, and after the lapse of fifteen years, engaged in reestablishing a school for Jewish teachers in New York City. This School of Education, as it eventually was called, opened in January of 1947, during the last months of the Morgenstern administration. As in the 1920s, it was Abraham Franzblau who initially administered it, creating and supervising its curriculum and engaging its part-time faculty. In addition to teacher certification, the School soon offered bachelor's and master's degrees in Jewish education. Most of its students over the years, however, were always religious-school teachers taking the particular courses required for their positions. Unlike the Rabbinical School, the School of Education imposed only slightly on the College budget, most of its cost being covered by congregationally paid tuitions, a UAHC subvention, and special contributions. After reaching a peak during the mid-sixties, the size of the school declined as teaching positions became more scarce in the wake of decreasing religious-school enrollments.

The School of Education was closely linked with a second, more novel project that the College undertook in New York a year later, in 1948. Reform congregations of the classical variety in America had generally chosen to enhance their liturgy with a choir, but had not employed a cantor. Their members often associated the hazan with East European Jewry and with orthodoxy. By the end of the war, however, rejection was gradually turning into a more favorable attitude. A growing number of Reform congregations were now prepared to employ a cantor if qualified individuals could be found. Responding to this new need and to urging from the nondenominational Society for the Advancement of Jewish Liturgical Music, the College opened a School of Sacred Music in New York.[24] Musicologist Eric Werner, one of the Society's leaders and the originator of the plan, was gradually shifted from teaching responsibilities in Cincin-

nati to working with the new school. On account of the void in
systematic Jewish musical education likewise prevailing in the Conservative and Orthodox movements, the venture was from the start
intended to serve the entirety of the Jewish community.

Initially the school's program was of a three-year duration leading up to cantorial certification, and it also included a certain amount
of training in Jewish education. It was believed that many congregations, which could not afford a full-time cantor, would find
it possible to engage a "cantor-educator." In time, however, the
recognition grew that one man could not be sufficiently trained in
both areas, and the educational part of the program was abandoned.
Concurrently, the cantorial curriculum was lengthened, at first to
four, and then to five years; the academic degrees, Bachelor and
Master of Sacred Music, were introduced. Like the School of Education, the School of Sacred Music operated with a part-time faculty
and was directed at first by Abraham Franzblau and then by Paul
Steinberg. In the sixties it was graduating an average of three or four
cantors per year, with enrollment sometimes running as high as
thirty-five or forty. The vast majority of its graduates went into Reform
congregations, where the demand continued to be high.

Along with cantorial training, the School of Sacred Music also
established and maintained a Sacred Music Press. Beginning with
the reissue of Abraham Baer's *Ba'al Tefila* in 1953, the Press published scores of old and new works in the field of synagogue music
and produced a number of recordings. Another venture was to present Musica Hebraica concerts from time to time, bringing to New
York City audiences some of the finest examples of classical and contemporary Jewish liturgical genius. Most important, however, HUC's
School of Sacred Music gave the cantorate status and dignity in the
Reform movement. Its alumni were organized into the American Conference of Cantors. In later years, Nelson Glueck formally invested
its graduates as cantors at the same ceremony during which he ordained rabbis in New York. The cantor was thus recognized as no
less essential a part of Reform worship than the rabbi.

The Schools of Education and Sacred Music were created concurrently with advancing negotiations to bring about the anticipated merger between the Hebrew Union College and the Jewish Institute of Religion. In January 1950, each board finally approved the consolidation agreement and the two institutions became one. Under its terms,[25] the "principal place of business" of the new corporation would be Cincinnati but at least one board meeting annually would be held in New York. The expanded Board of Governors was to consist of fifty-five members, one-third of them elected by the JIR. The two schools would henceforth be known by the single cumbersome designation: Hebrew Union College–Jewish Institute of Religion (HUC-JIR).[26] A few months later their respective alumni likewise merged into a single organization.

There followed an uneasy but on the whole amicable period of academic adjustment. The JIR rabbinic curriculum was lengthened from four years to five, the HUC curriculum shortened a year from six. An identical 176 credit hours were henceforth required for ordination on each campus and the courses offered became more or less alike. The Cincinnati faculty was of the opinion that it had thereby considerably raised the standards of the New York school. Although the popular Henry Slonimsky remained dean in New York, general administration passed mostly into the hands of Richard Bluestein, a capable young layman who had become assistant to the president in 1950. Bluestein spent much of his time in New York overseeing the affairs of the school; Glueck was there only occassionally.

Despite Stephen Wise's faith in his successor, it soon became apparent that the new president had no intention of expanding the JIR or even of maintaining its existing status. He had taken it over because he realized the value of a single united school for the Reform movement. But beyond the authorization of some necessary repairs, equalization of salary scales, and the appointment to its faculty of Ezra Spicehandler, a young scholar of Hebrew literature, he manifested little evidence of personal concern with its welfare. Aside from Spicehandler, and after Slonimsky's involuntary retirement, the New York faculty in 1952 consisted of only two full-time teachers who were present the entire academic year: John Tepfer in history and

Talmud and Harry Orlinsky in Bible. Both of them were veterans of the JIR. Quite clearly, a full rabbinic program could not be carried out with so small a corps of teachers, however many might be added part-time.

As the Cincinnati School's budget went up, the budget for the New York Rabbinic School went down.[27] With active recruitment limited to Cincinnati, admissions there went from fifteen to twenty-nine in the period 1950 to 1951 while in New York they dropped from fourteen to seven. The figures were an accurate reflection of the new president's purpose. From the first, he was intent on creating a single integrated school with a single rabbinic curriculum in Cincinnati. The New York campus, as he conceived it, might provide rabbinic students with the basics, but advanced studies and ordination would eventually be in Cincinnati alone.[28]

It is not possible to comprehend the course of the ensuing controversy without attempting to understand the president's feelings about New York City. Glueck had a profound disdain for most New York Jews; he regarded them as ungenteel, indeed as vulgar. With the exception of the circle around Temple Emanu-El and the American Jewish Committee, they lacked the refinement and restraint which he valued highly. Glueck did not enjoy being in New York; he felt ill at ease there in an environment which offered neither the polite atmosphere of Cincinnati nor the romantic lure of Jerusalem and the Palestinian desert. The traditionalism of some of the staff and students of the JIR conflicted with his own more classically Reform religious attitude. He could not consider New York a proper place for the training of Reform rabbis. Cincinnati, by contrast, certainly was.[29] Glueck's battle to reduce the New York Rabbinic School from five years to two brought him the only major defeat of his career.

Only a few months after consummation of the merger, Glueck had announced to his board: "Our aim is eventually to have part of the program of studies in New York and part in Cincinnati. Whether that proves to be practical remains to be seen."[30] Three years later, after extensive discussions with the Cincinnati faculty, a specific "Unification Plan" was formulated.[31] It called for students to spend the initial two years of their rabbinic studies, up to the B.H.L. degree, at either school. The following three years, leading up to ordination, would be given in Cincinnati alone. A sixth, intern year, coming after ordination, would then be required in New York before acceptance of a regular congregational position. The special committee charged with the task of formulating the proposal approved it by a vote of fourteen to four and passed it on to the Board of Governors, which, on March 26, 1953, ratified it thirty-five to eight. The plan's opponents on the board, without exception, were either lay members from New York or rabbinical members who had graduated from the JIR.

The Board of Governors was won over to the integration scheme largely by financial considerations. By 1952, expenditure had risen considerably above income. The Ochs-Rosenwald fund was totally depleted, the Foundation Fund had reached scarcely more than a tenth of its final goal, and 3 percent interest was being paid on a bank loan of $150,000.[32] While Glueck was pressing for a still larger percentage of the Combined Campaign, that prospect was by no means certain. The only rational course was thought to be eliminating the luxury of duplicate programs in New York and Cincinnati. Given Glueck's persuasive influence and the greater capital investment in Cincinnati, most board members found they could easily support a program that would save the institution money and preserve a certain role for New York while centering rabbinic training for the entire Reform movement in Cincinnati.

Neither Glueck nor the board was ready for the violent reaction the plan produced as soon as it was made known.[33] Members of the Central Conference of American Rabbis expressed their deep resentment that the organization had not been consulted in advance, and Glueck found himself forced to defend the proposal against two hostile resolutions put forward (and withdrawn) at the CCAR convention that summer.[34] A devastating attack was launched by the Reform Jews of New York. Although the UAHC president, Maurice Eisendrath, had favored the proposal, the local Federation of Reform Synagogues of Greater New York, on May 25, 1953, passed a resolution calling for deferment of the Unification Plan until it could be amply studied. An identical resolution was passed by the New York Association of Reform Rabbis. The New Yorkers called attention to the fact that Reform Judaism in New York was in the midst of a period of rapid expansion. From thirty-five congregations in 1946 with approximately fourteen thousand member families, Union membership in the area had risen in four years to fifty-four congregations with almost twice as many families,[35] and it was continuing to grow apace. The argument was made that this advance would be severely impeded if New York City were divested of a full-scale citadel of learning for Reform Judaism. Most importantly, various newly founded, still fledgling congregations would be deprived of advanced rabbinic students to minister to their needs. Later the General Assembly of the Union added its voice to the protest by passing a resolution calling upon the College to "pay particular heed to the great and growing need for the strongest kind of liberal rabbinic training in New York City." [36]

One man, more than anyone else, took the lead in opposing unification. Louis Newman, rabbi of Rodeph Sholom congregation in New York City, had been closely associated with Stephen Wise over the years, though the two men had had differences in the final period before Wise's death. Newman, who already earlier had publicly decried what he regarded as the "gradual attrition" of the New York School,[37] now marshaled all available forces to prevent its losing the crown of ordination.[38] Initially, he was not successful.

For a time Glueck was able to proceed on the basis that the Board of Governors was sovereign in these matters and that it should not bow to external pressures. In the fall of 1954, the first New York students were shifted to Cincinnati at the end of their second year. In 1955, the next class made the same move, leaving New York with only B.H.L. students and a few seniors. But at that point Newman decided on a drastic, yet ultimately effective course of action. He formally announced the opening of an Academy for Liberal Judaism to be under the auspices of his own congregation.[39] Unlike the HUC-JIR, the Academy would grant ordination at the end of four years instead of five. A few students, not eager to spend time in Cincinnati, immediately left the New York School and joined the new institution;

no less than twenty-two students were quickly recruited for the projected second year of the school, to begin in the fall of 1956. Clearly, if the HUC-JIR proceeded to leave a void in New York City, it would be filled successfully by this fledging rabbinical seminary. That near certainty opened the prospects of a new split in the CCAR between graduates of the rival institutions, of competition among respective alumni for congregational positions, and of funds, otherwise intended for HUC-JIR, being channeled into the coffers of the Academy.[40] It was the creation of this rival school, more than any other factor, which spelled the doom of the Unification Plan.

As early as November 1, 1955, before the Academy had even held its first class, a meeting took place between Glueck and Newman.[41] Although complete agreement was not yet reached, the process of backtracking began at least that early.[42] On February 20, 1956, a newly constituted Committee on Integration of the Merger held an open hearing in New York, listening to speakers on both sides of the issue.[43] Some of those opposed to the integrated merger argued realistically that the vacuum would invariably be filled, if not by the Academy, then by the Jewish Theological Seminary, or that money from congregations with JIR graduates as rabbis would be lost for the Combined Campaign. Others were sentimental: "This room was Dr. Wise's study. . . . I am absolutely certain that what has happened to the Jewish Institute of Religion is not what he expected. . . ." But all the speakers only added impetus to the final determination of what was by then already quite apparent to those in a position to decide: the New York School program would have to be restored to a full five years.

Internal problems, too, had begun to manifest themselves. The New York students were from the beginning unanimously opposed to the plan.[44] Those who finally came to Cincinnati—basically against their will—did not integrate easily into the student body.[45] The fourteen members of the class that was supposed to arrive in 1956 unanimously passed a resolution refusing absolutely to transfer. Cincinnati students, for their part, were equally as opposed to going to New York for the required intern year following ordination.[46]

On June 1, 1956, the Board of Governors decided to reverse its earlier decision.[47] It restored the full rabbinical program in New York and acceded to an agreement worked out between the College-Institute and the Academy whereby, among other provisions, two officers of the latter would join the Board of Governors. After less than a year, the Newman Academy henceforth ceased to exist. Though no ordination exercises were held in New York in 1957, by the following year the school was again complete.

Glueck's attitude toward New York, however, had not changed. If anything, his unhappy defeat had made him more determined to devote his best efforts to building up the Cincinnati School—if need be, at the expense of New York. In succeeding years, occasional lecture series featuring outstanding well-known scholars and public figures were held in the school's auditorium and advanced seminars attracted ordained rabbis from the area. But the faculty in New York was allowed to grow only slightly, the size of the student body was intentionally limited, and capital expenditures were approved for only the utmost necessities. Its dean, Paul Steinberg, its overworked faculty, students, and even some board members otherwise favorable to Glueck all agreed that during his administration New York consistently remained the stepchild, while Cincinnati was always the favored son.

The successful effort to reestablish a full rabbinic program in New York was strong evidence of the degree to which local leadership, rabbinic and lay, could influence the development of the College-Institute. As after the war American Jews underwent a revival of religious identification, affiliating increasingly with local synagogues in areas of suburban settlement, and beginning to seek more intensified Jewish education for their children, sentiment grew among those adhering to the Reform movement that a single central institution of higher Jewish learning in Cincinnati could not adequately serve their needs. The New York community was not alone in this regard; another example was Los Angeles.

Jews had come to Southern California during the mid-nineteenth-century gold-rush days, establishing their first permanent congregation there by 1862.[48] For half a century thereafter they remained a frontier community, which maintained Jewish life only with great difficulty. But once Los Angeles began to grow rapidly, so did its Jewish population. By the end of World War II, there were 150,000 Jews in the city—and the period of most striking growth was yet to come. In the next two decades the Jewish population would rise to about half a million. Most of those who streamed to Southern California lacked the sense of rootedness which characterized their brethren remaining in the East. But as they settled down, they sought to establish links with the Jewish community. The Reform movement in Los Angeles grew from a single congregation (B'nai B'rith, later called the Wilshire Boulevard Temple) at the turn of the century into a sizable council of large and small congregations scattered around the city and its suburbs. As such, it soon felt the need for a local institution of higher Jewish learning.

Shortly after the war, in September 1947, the Union of American Hebrew Congregations established a teacher-training and adult-education school in Los Angeles. It was called the College of Jewish Studies and possessed a part-time faculty composed mostly of local rabbis. A year later, the CJS came under the joint auspices of HUC and the Union, with the former lending its name and academic respectability, while the latter gave it financial support and local direction. The Conservative movement in 1947 also established its own institution in Los Angeles with principal emphasis on training teachers. Known as the University of Judaism, it was publicized as the western branch of the Jewish Theological Seminary. Reform leaders began to feel that their movement could achieve equal status in the community only if the College of Jewish Studies were in similar fashion to become the western branch of the College-Institute. In particular, they thought that there should be a full-time faculty, a regular pre-rabbinic program for university students in the area, and graduate seminars for local rabbis. Unlike other major communities, Los Angeles was so remote geographically from Cincinnati and New York that it required a major local branch of the College-Institute to meet the community's needs. By 1951, there was already pressure for greater College-Institute involvement.[49] Glueck, however, was as reluctant to spend money in California as he was in New York.[50] The first appropriation from the College-Institute budget—$10,000—was not made until three years later, in 1954.

The chief proponent of increased College-Institute involvement in Los Angeles was Jack Skirball, a prominent film-maker and leader of the Reform community who had been ordained at the College. He and some of his friends were eventually able to persuade Glueck and the Board of Governors to authorize the incorporation of an HUC-JIR western branch.[51] Together with a few associates, Skirball then, on May 29, 1954, secured a state charter for a "California School" of the College-Institute. Teacher-training and adult education were to remain under the aegis of the Union, while the new degree-granting programs would be under the direct jurisdiction of the HUC-JIR. Rabbi Isaiah Zeldin, who had taken over direction of the Southern California Council of the Union as well as of the CJS in 1953, became dean of the combined institution.

Initially, sessions of the California School were held in the religious-school building of the Wilshire Boulevard Temple. There formal prerabbinic classes took place for the first time as a regular part of the College-Institute program in the fall of 1954. They consisted essentially of elementary instruction in Hebrew for four students and were conducted by Dov Bin-Nun, a gifted, ebullient teacher of language who was the first full-time appointment to the school. Though not a renowned scholar, the well-liked Bin-Nun was a most effective pedagogue for beginners. That same year witnessed the organization of a Department of Sacred Music headed by William Sharlin, a graduate of the New York School's program and a musician of extraordinary creative talent. Degree programs in Jewish education were launched as well. With the arrival of Samuel S. Cohon in Los Angeles, following his retirement from the Cincinnati faculty in 1956, the California School gained both a veteran professor of academic standing, capable of inaugurating an in-residence D.H.L. program, and the nucleus of a library when Cohon donated his fine collection of some seven thousand volumes to the school.

As yet, however, the school lacked a building of its own. Not only was acquisition of a structure necessary to establish a definite identity, it was also a prerequisite for gaining academic accreditation.

Such status was judged of paramount and pressing significance to the school for it would enable prerabbinic students to receive academic credit for their courses at local universities and CJS teacher-training students to obtain alertness credit from the city Board of Education. Moreover, the University of Judaism already possessed derivative accreditation through the JTS. At first it was thought that the religious-school annex of the Wilshire Boulevard Temple might simply be considered the property of the College for accreditation purposes. But its rabbi, Edgar Magnin, was unwilling to allow such a step. The result was the hasty search for a building which would serve the school at least temporarily and meet the requirement for accreditation.

The four-and-a-half-acre property which was speedily chosen lay on Appian Way, high up in the Hollywood Hills, which separate the western part of Los Angeles from the San Fernando Valley. Once a home for asthmatic Jewish girls, it had lain vacant for a number of years and was now available for only about $30,000. The property contained an elongated stucco structure, partly one-story, partly two-, with a Spanish-style tile roof. There was also a shallow outdoor swimming pool with a cabaña and a parking lot. Distant from the noise of the city, the place was rustic and charming, conducive to undisturbed study either inside the building or out of doors.[52] A short walk along the road led to a promontory where one could look down on the western suburbs of the city and on a clear day even see the Pacific Ocean. The splendid isolation of the site was, however, also its great shortcoming. It was reachable only by driving up the steep and winding roads that ascended from Laurel Canyon. Visitors found it with difficulty if at all, and its remoteness certainly did not further the school's impact on the Jewish community.

Some remodeling was undertaken immediately and classes began on Appian Way in the fall of 1956. Since certain of the neighbors would not allow occupancy of the property by large numbers or permit student cantors to practice there, the CJS courses and the Department of Sacred Music remained in synagogues below. Appian Way became the special preserve of the young men interested in the rabbinate. A full B.H.L. program now enabled them to complete the first two years of graduate rabbinical study in Los Angeles before proceeding to Cincinnati for the final three years before ordination. D.H.L. seminars were held there regularly as well, while weekends would sometimes bring high-school young people up to "the hill" for study and sociability.

In February 1957, the campus was visited by an accrediting team from the Western College Association. The four men, none of them Jews, were favorably impressed. They met with Nelson Glueck, who was present for the occasion, with the dean, with faculty, and with students. After carefully examining the school's records, they recommended accreditation but pointed out the anomalous situation of being asked to accredit the branch of a school whose main campus lay in the jurisdiction of another regional association. The Cincinnati School was not accredited because the North Central Association, at that time, did not accredit seminaries. On account of this jurisdictional problem, the Western Association, despite the favorable report, was not able to act affirmatively, and the California School remained unaccredited. Finally, a change in policy by the North Central Association in 1959 made possible the accreditation of the academic-degree programs in Cincinnati. Only then, after a new—and again positive—evaluation, did the California School finally receive accreditation as well. Even without such official recognition, however, the favorable report of the initial committee led to acceptance of HUC-JIR courses at the University of California, Los Angeles (UCLA) and the University of Southern California (USC), the two most prominent of the local colleges.[53]

Unfortunately, the early history of the California School was beclouded by a complex dispute regarding the respective prerogatives of the Union and the College-Institute. The UAHC regarded Los Angeles as an area where it had taken the first steps in furthering advanced Jewish education by sponsoring the College of Jewish Studies and it was reluctant to lose its primacy. At the same time the College-Institute increasingly came to see Southern California as a fruitful area for rabbinical recruitment and initial training. As the combined institution, CJS and the HUC-JIR California School, began to make considerable progress, there erupted a struggle, locally and nationally, over respective jurisdiction. The issues included the right of appointment to the local Administrative Board and whether the CJS in Los Angeles would come under direct HUC-JIR administration on the model of the School of Education in New York or whether it would remain essentially an activity of the Union. Isaiah Zeldin, as dean of the school, his salary paid in part by the Union and in part by the College-Institute, was caught in the middle. He soon found himself in conflict with Jack Skirball and Nelson Glueck over the selection of members for the local board. While Zeldin wanted the Union to have a decisive say in the appointments, and the board to be composed of a broad spectrum of Los Angeles Jewry, Glueck and Skirball favored a smaller board composed of influential people drawn especially from Skirball's acquaintances, and mostly from two or three of the wealthier congregations.[54] The Union was likewise unhappy with Zeldin, claiming he spent too much time working with the College-Institute. As his position thus became increasingly untenable, he was forced to resign as dean, accepting a local pulpit in 1958.

With Zeldin's departure, the California School of the College-Institute was split off almost completely from the CJS, which for the next decade continued as a separate teacher-training institution with its own Board of Trustees and certification program. Though a cooperative relationship was soon thereafter established, with certain CJS courses counted toward education degrees given by the HUC-JIR and with College-Institute faculty participating in the program, it was not until 1968, when the financial situation of the Union prevented further support, that the Los Angeles College of Jewish Studies was transformed into the School of Education and Jewish Studies of the HUC-JIR.[55]

Meanwhile, the California School had received a new administrator who came in 1957, first to assist Zeldin and then to succeed him as dean. Alfred Gottschalk had been Zeldin's own choice. He had recommended him to Richard Bluestein, who in turn had brought his name before Glueck. Gottschalk, then a senior in the Cincinnati rabbinical school, was eager to pursue graduate study and saw this position as an opportunity both to advance his academic interests and to retain an association with the school. Glueck, for his part, saw the advantage in selecting a younger man, freshly ordained, who would be totally loyal to the HUC-JIR. Skirball, who remained chairman of the local Administrative Board until after Glueck's death, was initially less than pleased with the appointment. Concerned especially with establishing the academic prestige of the California School, he thought it unlikely that so inexperienced a man, and without a doctorate, would be able to gain recognition for the school within the university community. But he soon changed his mind as the California School expanded and enhanced its position in Los Angeles under Gottschalk's leadership.

In succeeding years the full-time faculty grew slowly as some men who had been teaching part-time received regular appointments and new Cincinnati Ph.D.'s were brought to Los Angeles. This core was supplemented by a dozen or so part-time instructors, two of them (Wolf Leslau and Arnold Band) professors at UCLA, most of the others local rabbis. From time to time a member of the Cincinnati or New York faculty would come to the school for a series of lectures or to teach for a semester. The yearly convocations and graduations, held at various synagogues, provided an opportunity to bring the school to the attention of the community and to draw upon the prestige of the well-known individuals to whom it granted honorary degrees.

As long as the school remained on the hill, it was favored with a very pleasant intimacy among faculty and students. Faculty meetings were informal, congenial affairs, and there was a genuine esprit de corps within the small student body. The dean prided himself on knowing every student intimately and in developing personal relationships with potential students whom he would meet at one of the West Coast camps during weekend youth conclaves or summer sessions.

For fourteen years, through continual remodeling and sheer ingenuity, the physical facilities were adjusted and readjusted as satisfactorily as possible to the growing needs of the school. For most of the period there were three small classrooms, a combination chapel and auditorium, a dean's office, a reading room, kitchen, student lounge, and an apartment for the caretaker. Secretaries and faculty were placed wherever there was an available nook, even in corridors and passageways. The greatest problem was the library, which kept on getting larger. In the later years, librarian Harvey Horowitz was ensconced in what had been the garage, while books and periodicals were divided between the main stack room, the cabaña, and a walk-in refrigerator.

As early as 1959, only two years after the move to Appian Way, the first efforts were made to find a suitable permanent site. The original intent was to find a location which could be utilized for the offices of the Union as well as for the HUC-JIR. The plan did not work out, however, as the College-Institute was interested in locating near one of the universities, while the Union at the time preferred to be on a major thoroughfare. The first two sites considered were in West Los Angeles, more or less in proximity to UCLA, the leading university in the area. But in the one case decision was postponed until it was too late and in the other the site was rejected as too remote.[56]

Shortly thereafter, in 1961, the possibility was first raised of purchasing property on the campus of USC in downtown Los Angeles. Although the University of Southern California was not the equivalent of UCLA in academic excellence and was located away from the areas of Jewish settlement, association with it had certain advantages. First, it would be possible to establish a much closer relationship with a private school lacking a department of Judaica than with UCLA, which was a state school unable to associate itself directly with a religious institution and which, moreover, was developing its own Judaica program. Second, being located in the inner city, in a dominantly black neighborhood, would be evidence of the school's commitment to social responsibility. Finally, USC, under its new president, Norman Topping, had ceased to discriminate against minority groups as it had heretofore.[57] Its new administration welcomed the California School's affiliation.

The decision in favor of USC was also influenced by a significant personal factor. Shortly after coming to Los Angeles, Gottschalk had enrolled as a graduate student at USC. He soon developed a close relationship with Dean Geddes MacGregor of the USC Graduate School of Religion with whom he discussed the possibility of an HUC-JIR move to the vicinity of the campus. This led to a meeting between

Topping and Glueck and eventually to inclusion of the California School in the major urban renewal project that was to transform the environs of the USC campus.[58] Though an agreement of academic reciprocity was quickly worked out, actual construction of a building was delayed for a number of years as the entire Hoover Redevelopment Project was held up by political difficulties[59] and came repeatedly under the scrutiny of the Los Angeles City Council. Only in 1970 was work begun on a large modern structure to house the expanded academic program of the school. It was not dedicated until November 5, 1971, almost nine months after Glueck's death, when its dean had already taken over the responsibilities of being Glueck's successor.

It was during the final years before the move to USC that the California School embarked on its most innovative project: the establishment of a School of Jewish Communal Service. Gottschalk projected the idea as early as March 1964, but the plan gained momentum only in 1967, after a feasibility study by Bertram Gold, then director of the Los Angeles Jewish Centers Association, found the prospects favorable. The creation of such a school, it was determined, would not only fill an obvious need for providing Jewish professionals with Jewish knowledge, but it would also enable the California branch of the HUC-JIR to serve a wider spectrum of the Jewish community than the Reform movement alone. Implementation of the plan was begun in 1968 with the appointment of Gerald Bubis, a trained specialist in the field, to be its director and with the first summer session, held a year later. The courses given were both theoretical and practical: Jewish thought and belief on the one hand, Jewish institutions and practices on the other. Beginning with fifteen students at its inception, the school was able rapidly to expand and enrich its program.[60]

With its commitment to the larger Jewish community, expressed through its programs in education and communal service, and with the projected HUC-JIR Museum shortly to be transferred from Cincinnati, the California School was by the late sixties taking on a special character of its own. Gottschalk saw its task as going beyond giving initial preparation to future Reform rabbis. The B.H.L. curriculum, though of primary significance, was steadily becoming only one among the varied branches of the school's activity.

Nelson Glueck's attitude toward the school in Los Angeles was consistently favorable—but only up to a point. He recognized the need for some HUC-JIR presence on the West Coast and recognized also the area's potential for rabbinic recruitment. But he never conceived of it other than as an auxiliary to Cincinnati. Its limited rabbinic curriculum was to make it a "feeder school" of the kind he had initially hoped New York also would become. Just as the New York faculty and local lay leadership felt their needs received something less than an enthusiastic hearing in Cincinnati, so did their counterparts in Los Angeles. Glueck did not have the same horror of Southern California that he did of New York, but he limited his visits to the area as much as possible and insisted that the school's budget reflect its limited role. When it came time to raise funds (ultimately close to $3 million) for the new building, all monies for construction and maintenance had to be raised locally, though a portion was for a time borrowed from the Endowment Fund.

On the whole, Glueck was content to allow Gottschalk to handle the affairs of the school and to take some pride in its growth and achievement. His primary interests lay elsewhere—in Cincinnati and Jerusalem. And his attention was riveted on a prolonged conflict which had already been somewhat reflected in Los Angeles: the extended struggle for funds and influence between the Union and the College-Institute.

The Union of American Hebrew Congregations had fallen upon hard times during the years of the depression. With no Ochs-Rosenwald fund to sustain it, the UAHC had to curtail its program and forgo initiatives. By the end of the thirties, voices were heard calling for more substantial funding and for rejuvenation. At the Union Biennial of 1941 in Detroit, Rabbi Louis Mann of Sinai Temple in Chicago presented a memorable indictment of the Union for its shortcomings entitled: "The Failures of the Union and Where Do We Go From Here?" He pointed to the virtually unanimous feeling within the rabbinate that all was not well with the UAHC. The Reform movement was not growing in proportion to the Jewish population and it had neglected the opportunities and potentialities that lay before it. It had failed to take over the Hillel organization when it had the opportunity, removed itself from antidefamation work, and been unable to develop a medium for communicating Reform Jewish ideas. An attitude of laissez-faire had replaced the zeal of earlier times. He accused the Union's assimilated, "hand-picked" leaders of doing little more than rubber-stamping the rather ineffective work of the office force.[61]

The discontent that received such pointed expression in Mann's speech resulted that same year in a decision to increase Union dues from one dollar per member to three and to retire George Zepin as the Union's secretary. Edward Israel, a highly respected rabbi from Baltimore, was chosen to replace Zepin, but he died suddenly at a board meeting after only a few weeks in office.[62]

With the death of Israel, the Union turned to a Cincinnatian and a member of the HUC faculty to head its staff. On January 15, 1942, its Administrative Committee selected Nelson Glueck to be the Union's executive director. He was to take office on July 1st and would be allowed to continue concurrently on the faculty of the College.[63] It is not difficult to understand why the Union's leadership chose Glueck. Its reasons were much the same as those which led to his election as president of the College five years later. Glueck's acceptance of the offer is more of a conundrum. Why should the archaeologist-scholar who detested fund-raising and shirked petty administrative tasks have taken such a job? The answer seems to lie in his frank desire for the prestige of the position as well as in a dim hope, held at that time, that he would later be able to add the College presidency as well. He would prevent the possibility of friction between the Union and the College by becoming the titular head of all American Reform Jewry.[64]

But Glueck never actually took office. By late spring of 1942 he was already on his way back to the Middle East in the employ of the OSS. At first, the Union simply granted him a leave of absence. But after half a year had passed, it could not let the position remain vacant any longer. The Administrative Committee decided to appoint an "interim director" until Glueck's return. It secured the services of Maurice Eisendrath, the successful and dynamic rabbi of Holy Blossom Temple in Toronto. For about a year, Eisendrath substituted for Glueck. But then he insisted that unless he was given the position on a permanent basis, he would return to his congregation. As a result, in September of 1943, Glueck was prevailed upon to resign his office and Eisendrath became at first executive director and then president of the Union. Though at the time Glueck was not sorry to give up the job, he thereafter harbored some resentment over the requested resignation.

Aided by propitious economic circumstances and a favorable religious climate, Eisendrath meanwhile had begun to expand the size and program of the UAHC. By the time Glueck returned to take over the College presidency in 1947, the Union was no longer the anemic organization it had been during the thirties. It had been thoroughly reorganized, its board increased to one hundred members. Most significantly, it was about to move its offices from Cincinnati to New York City, a step urged by Eisendrath and finally approved by the Biennial Assembly in 1948.

Even before Glueck came into office, there had already been some tension between the two institutions. Once Glueck became president of the College, determined to expand its influence and its physical facilities in Cincinnati, and Eisendrath at the same time determined to expand the Union from New York, the scene was set for a prolonged conflict. Glueck and Eisendrath held contrary views on what the relationship between the two institutions should be. Unlike his predecessors, Glueck did not conceive the College to be a ward of the Union; unlike those who came before him, Eisendrath did not see the principal role of the Union to be support of the College. Each believed his own institution should possess primary influence. Eisendrath was of the opinion that the Union, representing the collective will of Reform Jewry through its biennial assemblies, was the fundamental organization of the movement, and as such should control all its national activities, including its centers for the training of rabbis. As president of the Union, he regarded himself as the principal spokesman for Reform Judaism. Glueck, on the other hand, regarded the College-Institute as an autonomous academic institution with only the loosest ties to the UAHC. For him, HUC-JIR was the more important institution, and he could not help but notice that in Conservative Judaism the Jewish Theological Seminary possessed the greatest influence and its president, Louis Finkelstein, was that movement's most highly respected spokesman.[65] Eisendrath and Glueck, both capable and ambitious men, were each intent on zealously guarding their institution's prerogatives and on seeking to extend its influence— if necessary at the expense of the other.[66] The friction, which began immediately, grew most severe during the decade from 1956 to 1966.

Once the College-Institute gained parity with the Union in Combined Campaign proceeds during the early fifties, relations between the two institutions remained relatively stable until the latter portion of the decade, when the Union embarked on a concerted effort to increase its influence on the HUC-JIR Board of Governors, if not actually to take it over.[67] The UAHC, by constitutional right, was entitled to elect 51 percent of the Board of Governors, the remainder being selected by the alumni and by the board itself. But in practice, the Union had in recent years allowed the Board of Governors to nominate the UAHC quota of candidates as well. It was satisfied merely to approve them.[68] Now, however, the Union sought to place an increasing number of its own people on the HUC-JIR Board.[69] In justifying his resistance to this attempt, Glueck argued that if the Union took control of the College-Institute, independence of inquiry would be endangered, the school would be reduced to a shallow professional institution, and Jewish scholarship would cease to be a primary concern. The Union would favor what Glueck termed a "false Americanization process in which the *yeshiva* is reduced to the role of a *ḥeder* and other aspects are pushed forward at its expense." [70] There is not, however, any direct evidence that the Union's bid for increased influence on the Board of Governors was connected with any real challenge to academic freedom or that it was Eisendrath's intent to reduce the College-Institute to a *ḥeder*. What it apparently was seeking was increased financial leverage.

The leadership of the College was well aware that it possessed a great advantage over the Union. Large donors were in general far more interested in giving to an academic institution, visible through its library and other buildings, and serving a clearly apparent need through its training of rabbis, scholars, and teachers, than to a union of congregations whose program was far more diffuse and whose achievements were far less tangible. Moreover, there was a greater measure of prestige to be gained by association with the College than with the Union. This awareness, shared by the Union's leadership as well, gave the College authorities a powerful weapon with which to cudgel the Union: unless the College had its way, it would wage its own separate maintenance campaign; at the expense of splitting the movement, it would come out financially ahead. Though never actually carried out, such a threat was made as early as 1949 [71] and it always loomed in the background.

In 1959 the policy of conducting joint campaigns was extended from maintenance to a major drive for capital funds. At the Biennial Assembly of the Union that year, the UAHC and the HUC-JIR launched what was called the "Development Fund for American Judaism." The campaign set as its goal $15 million, to be raised over three years. The proceeds were to be split equally between the College-Institute and the Union, each of which set out a detailed list of construction and program projects. But the campaign was not very successful. Although pledges were received for about $5 million, most of that amount came from the national leadership of the two organizations. And the cost of the drive ran to over $450,000. When the campaign agreement expired in 1962, the College-Institute had received only about a million dollars in cash [72] and it was heavily in debt. It therefore refused to go along with the Union's desire to continue the combined effort unless gifts could be earmarked for one or the other institution without equalization from nondesignated donations. [73] In this instance, however, its desire did not prevail. After a stormy meeting of the UAHC Board of Trustees in Washington, the College-Institute was forced to settle initially for a year's extension of the agreement with but a single concession: the exemption of foundation grants from the provision of equal division. Later, in January 1964, a new arrangement was worked out considerably more favorable to the interests of the College-Institute. Henceforth any donor giving $10,000 or more could designate his gift for one of the two institutions. In addition, under a previously adopted provision, funds for the UAHC's expanding camp program and for the HUC-JIR's Jerusalem School were also excluded. At the same time, the Union agreed that it would elect no more than six members of its Board of Trustees to the Board of Governors,[74] while the fifty-fifty arrangement for maintenance funds was continued under a new campaign structure called the "Reform Jewish Appeal."

It was about this time that tensions between the Union and the College-Institute began to ease, though certain issues remained unresolved. The most prominent of these was the title to the property in Cincinnati, still held by the UAHC, and the basis for a certain amount of leverage in its relations with the HUC-JIR. Long discussions were held on this matter and its legal implications carefully researched. Though the property remained officially in the hands of the UAHC, it was generally believed that its title gave the Union no rights of independent action. All real estate occupied by the College-Institute outside Cincinnati was from the start registered in its own name.

The personal relationship between Eisendrath and Glueck was not easily ameliorated. Their intense rivalry continued altogether for some twenty years. Although Union officials had signed HUC diplomas since the first ordination in 1883, Glueck removed all Union signatures, apparently because he did not want that of Eisendrath to appear. Eisendrath and his associates, for their part, minimized the role given to the College-Institute at Biennial Assemblies[75] and gave it little publicity in Union journals such as *American Judaism*. The presidents' competition for primacy occasionally was veiled in a controversy of ideology or even of historical evaluation. In 1963, Glueck chose to offer honorary degrees to two confirmed anti-Zionists, Rabbis Morris Lazaron and William Fineshriber, whereupon Eisendrath and the Union Board protested vigorously.[76] A year later, when Eisendrath at the UAHC Biennial called for a positive reassessment of the role of Jesus as a rabbi within the Jewish tradition, it was Glueck's turn to attack—in part out of concern for how such a view would damage the status of Reform Judaism in Israel.[77] For a long time Eisendrath's social activism was also a point of issue between the two men, Glueck associating himself tacitly with the opposition presented to the Union on such matters by Temple Emanu-El of New York.

Only during the final years of Glueck's life did relations between the two men considerably improve. It is hard to say precisely why the change came about. There was a basis for it in the shared realization that neither one had taken the extreme course of tearing the movement asunder. It was furthered by the more conciliatory lay leadership of the two organizations, especially by the mediating role played by the HUC-JIR board chairman, S. L. Kopald, Jr., who persuaded Glueck, for example, to reduce campaign costs by allowing Union staff members to conduct the Reform Jewish Appeal.[78] But mainly it seems to have been the result of each man in his final years having reason to be satisfied with his own accomplishments. Neither one had been successful in overwhelming the other, but each had enormously expanded the significance of his own institution.

Because the Foundation Fund of the late forties had failed to achieve the hoped-for results and because there had been no choice but to support a full rabbinic program at the New York School, Glueck was unable to launch any major building project during the first decade of his administration. By the end of the fifties, however, the need for at least a modicum of physical expansion had become imperative. In New York and in Cincinnati, library facilities were now woefully inadequate. No new structures had been built in Cincinnati since Oko's library was completed in 1931, the Sisterhood Dormitory was badly in need of renovation, and there was not enough space for faculty offices. A Master Plan,[79] commissioned in 1957, estimated enormous growth for the following twenty-year period. It projected that from 1957 to 1977 the number of rabbinic students in Cincinnati would rise from 108 to two hundred, in New York from forty-five to one hundred, while the faculty in Cincinnati would grow from twenty-four to forty-one and in New York from ten to twenty-five. Such an anticipated increase in numbers, it was argued, demanded proper provision for the future.

Even before the joint Development Fund with the Union was underway, building activity began. The first project undertaken was the addition of a fifth floor in New York to provide a new air-conditioned library reading room and two faculty offices. The New York construction, which cost only about $100,000, was manifestly the most urgent as it made absolutely essential new space available for library stacks where the earlier reading room had been. It was completed in the fall of 1958. Plans for a second building in New York were not implemented for lack of funds.

Construction in Cincinnati did not begin until a year later, but it was on a much more massive scale. After thirty years it was considered again necessary to build a new library structure to house the ever more rapidly expanding collection. A carefully worked out architectural proposal, based on a study of recently built libraries in the United States, resulted in a modern functional building of light-red-colored brick, aluminum, and glass. Contrasting somewhat with the darker brick and Tudor style of the earlier buildings, it was set on twenty-five concrete columns and measured ninety-by-ninety feet square. A special adjoining building was reserved for rare books and manuscripts. The interior of the library was planned for scholars rather than for the general public or for undergraduates. There was no central reading room, but instead some fifty-six carrels for individual concentrated study. Along with the stacks of the Oko library, which continued to be used for the older books, a total capacity of 230,000 volumes was reached, which might easily be increased to 300,000 once the fourth floor, intended only temporarily for administration, would become a stack area like floors two and three.

Along with the building of the new library, work was undertaken to refurbish the Sisterhood Dormitory, expanding its dining room and rebuilding the inside of the structure completely. On the basis of the projected figures of student enrollment it was decided also to build a new dormitory with single rooms, intended primarily for the graduate rabbinical students, while the old dormitory would be occupied by participants in the Undergraduate Program, As no suitable land was available on the same level as the rest of the campus, the new dormitory was built on lower ground at the rear of the campus, its third floor connected by a bridge to the level of a new rear parking lot. Although the second and third floors of the building—the only ones initially completed—were occupied to capacity during the early sixties, the new dormitory soon proved to have been a dreadful, if perhaps unforeseeable, blunder. After a few years, the number of students who were married increased steeply, and even those who remained single much preferred convincing a reluctant administration to let them live in their own apartments. As, furthermore, the gradual demise of the Undergraduate Program vacated an increasing number of rooms in the old dormitory, the new structure became an embarrassing white elephant.[80] In Glueck's last year it ceased entirely to be a dormitory for students, its rooms serving only to house occasional visiting young people and other temporary guests.

Aside from the construction of the library, the renovation of the old dormitory, and the building of the new one, only minor additional improvements were made. Somewhat later, work was done on the Bernheim Library to suit it exclusively to the purposes of the American Jewish Archives; the administration building was adapted to make room for more and larger classrooms; and the reading room of the Oko library was remodeled to become the site of an expanded display of the Museum's rich collection. Later stages of the Master Plan were postponed.

During the week of May 31 to June 4, 1961, the College-Institute celebrated the dedication of its newly expanded Cincinnati campus. There were the usual lectures and speakers, dinners, and religious services, culminating in the dedication of the library. Now consisting of seven major structures, the Cincinnati campus was a far cry indeed from the little building on Sixth Street that had once housed the entire school. But, as board members were well aware, there was still the problem of how to pay for it all.

Faced with the decision of waiting until funds were in hand or beginning construction immediately, the Board of Governors had acquiesced in Glueck's desire to borrow the money and start building at once.[81] Initially, a loan of $70,000 was taken for the fifth floor in New York. Then, once construction began in Cincinnati, indebtedness quickly soared and remained high as the Development Fund failed to produce the desired results. The cost of construction in Cincinnati eventually came to $3,685,116, of which over $2 million went for the library. Bank loans at one time reached a high of $3,300,000, with the College-Institute eventually paying a total interest of about

$400,000. Fortunately, the value of the Endowment Fund's investment portfolio had been steadily rising, so that in 1962 it was worth $7,850,000 on a book value of about $4,500,000. It was thus possible to transfer the bank indebtedness gradually to the Endowment Fund, from which the bank loans were then paid against the increased market value of unrestricted principal.[82]

After 1961 no further new structures were completed on any of the HUC-JIR campuses in the United States during Glueck's lifetime. But a whole new school was coming into being—eight thousand miles away, in Jerusalem.

Even before the establishment of the State of Israel, a few HUC students and alumni had chosen to spend extended periods of time in Jerusalem. They studied at the Hebrew University, involved themselves in the life of the *yishuv* (the Palestinian Jewish community), and in some instances even fought in the Israeli War of Independence. Although some faculty in Cincinnati later expressed doubts about how much students gained academically from the experience, it was Glueck's hope at the very beginning of his presidency that students would regularly spend a year at the Hebrew University in connection with their rabbinic training.[83]

Thought was also early given to the idea of establishing an HUC building in Israel. Already in December of 1947 there is written reference to a suggestion—it is no longer possible to determine its author—"that the Hebrew Union College build a hospice in Jerusalem for students studying there." [84] At the CCAR convention the following spring, Glueck told the assembled rabbis: "It is my avowed purpose to see to it that our program is carried out not only in Cincinnati and in New York, but also eventually, *im yirzeh hashem* [God willing], in Jerusalem." [85] On November 19, 1952, the Board of Governors approved in principle the establishment of an "H.U.C. House" in Jerusalem. As Glueck envisioned it at that time, it was to contain a library, chapel, small lecture hall, office, workroom, and living facilities for perhaps two dozen people. Its purpose would be to serve as hostel and headquarters for students, faculty, and graduates studying or working in Jerusalem. In addition, it would also provide the base for a projected Department of Biblical Archaeology.[86] In 1954 the Israeli government offered Glueck a choice two-acre site on King David Street which looked down over the walled Old City to the east and faced toward the new Jerusalem to the west. The HUC-JIR would receive the property for a mere symbolic rental of one Israeli pound per year provided it erected a building on the site within two to five years.[87] The government also made the important concession of allowing the use of Israel bonds to defray the costs of construction, thus making Glueck's fund-raising for this, his own personal and favorite project, very much easier.[88]

With such a generous arrangement the projected school in Jerusalem should have been completed long before its actual dedication nine years later in 1963. But two obstacles had in turn to be overcome. The first, the opposition of the Orthodox, was to be anticipated, and was speedily, if rather dramatically, set aside. The second, a prolonged quarrel with the contractor, was unexpected and, for Glueck, dreadfully frustrating.

Before leaving for Israel in June of 1956, Glueck received a letter signed jointly by the two chief rabbis, Nissim of the Sephardic community and Herzog of the Ashkenazic, objecting to the inclusion of a synagogue in the plans for the school. The rabbis argued that services in the synagogue, because they would not be according to the orthodox rite, would create religious division within the State at a time when unity was required to resist the Arab enemy. The letter was intended to make the College-Institute amend its request for a building permit that was shortly to come before the Jerusalem Municipal Council. Once Glueck arrived in Israel, he was summoned to a meeting attended by various rabbis and by Zerah Warhaftig, the minister of religions. In the ensuing Hebrew discussion, Glueck refused to promise that the services in the school's synagogue would be orthodox or that they would be open only to members of the College-Institute faculty and student body. He did concede that there would likely be no organ and that the custom would be for the men to wear hats. No question was asked about mixed seating of men and women. Shortly thereafter, the Supreme Rabbinical Council issued a declaration condemning the Reform movement and asserting that it "must not be allowed to strike root in this country and to defile the Holy City." A more vicious statement was published in a letter by the secretary general of the World Mizrahi and Hapoel Hamizrahi, who declared: "There is practically no tenet of historical Judaism left in common between religious Jewry and Reform, especially the obnoxious Cincinnati variety of it." He further accused Glueck of "installing his Reform temple in the heart of Jerusalem by way of the archaeological school's back door." At the same time most of the nonreligious Israeli press came to Glueck's defense, not out of any love for Reform Judaism, but out of support for the principle of freedom of worship.[89]

Shortly thereafter, as Glueck went off to do archaeological work in the Negev, the matter of the building permit came before the Municipal Council. Mayor Gershon Agron favored its approval, as did his Labor colleagues.[90] But the religious parties, who served in his coalition, vowed to fight it to the end. Twice they boycotted the meetings to prevent a vote for lack of a quorum. (In each instance they milled about in the hall outside.) As, according to law, the matter could be passed at the third session even without a quorum, they all finally appeared on August 12th. A day earlier the religious party vice-mayor, Moshe Porush, had declared on Israeli radio that the reform services would be nothing less than a "disaster to Jewry and would bring about the destruction of the State." The meeting was long and tempestuous. When, after three and a half hours of debate, the permit was finally approved by a vote of ten to six, the spokesman for the religious-bloc coalition parties dramatically announced that the Labor-Religious coalition was dead. Two weeks later, however, Agron succeeded in forming a new coalition with the inclusion of but one member of the religious bloc. As a result of the College-Institute request for a building permit, the Jerusalem municipal government, at least for a while, received a religiously freer complexion.[91]

Although thereafter concerted Orthodox opposition ceased, occasional verbal abuse continued[92] and every effort was made to maintain a "low profile." In 1957 it was found prudent to forgo groundbreaking exercises so as to avoid stirring up renewed hostility.[93] In part to prevent arousing an unnecessary furor, the campus received the innocuous title, eventually lettered in gold on the street level: "Hebrew Union College Biblical and Archaeological School," [94] though it was not fully descriptive of the school's purpose.

But far more perturbing than the difficulties encountered with the Orthodox was the prolonged and bitter controversy with the Israeli contractor. When two members of the Board of Governors, Jacob Lichter and Charles Messer, both of whom had competence in the construction business, made trips to Israel to oversee the project, they were aghast to find that the contractor was not proceeding according to specifications. With the intention of saving money for himself, he was cutting corners by using inferior materials and unsound modes of construction. When the decision was finally made to fire him, the contractor did what was his privilege under Israeli law: he seized the property and placed it under guard, erecting barbed wire at the entrances to the unfinished building. The College-Institute thereupon faced the dilemma of whether to fight a protracted battle with the contractor in the courts, thus delaying completion of the structure and possibly hurting the institution's public image in Israel, or to pay him a certain amount to release the property. Despite Lichter and Messer's desire to continue the dispute in the courts, Glueck took the initiative of paying off the contractor. He thereupon immediately took possession and installed guards of his own. With a new contractor taking up the work in 1961, construction thereafter proceeded apace, though the dispute and concurrent inflation pushed the costs up from an earlier estimate of about $500,000 to $864,000 by the time the building was finished in 1963.[95] When it was finally completed, however, the graceful, vaulted structure of white Galilee limestone, designed by the outstanding architect Heinz Rau, became the object of great admiration by nearly all who came to visit it.

On March 27–31, 1963, a highly festive and elaborate convocation was held at the school.[96] Despite continuing controversy about the projected synagogue services, nearly all the leading figures in the Israeli government willingly associated themselves with the event. There were speeches by Prime Minister Ben-Gurion,[97] ex–Prime Minister and Jewish Agency Chairman Moshe Sharett, Minister of Education Abba Eban, Foreign Minister Golda Meir, and Jerusalem Mayor Ish-

Shalom. Only the President of Israel, Yitzhak Ben-Zvi, came to the conclusion that it would be unwise for him to attend, though he agreed to invite the participants to a reception at his official residence instead.[98] It was a notable occasion in other respects as well. For the first time the Board of Governors held a regular meeting in Jerusalem; Julian Morgenstern used the occasion to make his first trip to the State of Israel. And the HUC-JIR gave its initial honorary degrees in Israel: to biblical archaeologist Yigael Yadin of the Hebrew University and to classical archaeologist Carl William Blegen of the University of Cincinnati. Three months later a second ceremony of dedication, to mark the beginning of the academic program, was held in the presence of some 150 members of the CCAR and an audience of leading Israelis.[99] That summer witnessed the first of a series of institutes on Near Eastern civilizations which would annually bring scholars from the United States for an intensive program of lectures and visits to archaeological sites. The institutes were the special project of Paul Steinberg, who, in addition to his duties in New York, became administratively responsible for the Jerusalem School.

In the first years after the school opened, its activities were principally archaeological. Though Glueck knew the implications of establishing an HUC-JIR presence in Israel, and though he fought to retain the inclusion of a synagogue in the building plans, there is no doubt that he was primarily interested in the Jerusalem School as a base for archaeological work. Its relationship to the rabbinic program, while not insignificant to his mind, was clearly secondary.[100] He regarded the school as an equivalent of the American School of Oriental Research, which he had once directed, and which, since it was located in the Arab city, had been inaccessible to Jews since 1948.

The main archaeological project of the school during Glueck's administration was the extensive excavations at Gezer, an important biblical site about twenty-eight miles to the west of Jerusalem. It was G. Ernest Wright of Harvard University, archaeological director of the school in 1964–65, who first launched the project. But, along with Nelson Glueck himself, Wright was soon content to allow younger men—especially William Dever and Joe D. Seger—successively to conduct the actual fieldwork. The award of a series of grants in United States counterpart funds by the Smithsonian Institution in Washington, as well as assistance from the Harvard Semitic Museum, made possible a far more extensive project than the school would have been able to finance with its own resources alone. The "dig" annually drew a core staff of trained field archaeologists and area supervisors who were aided by some one hundred volunteers, Jewish and Christian, from America and Europe. The archaeologists were able to unearth a Solomonic four-entryway gate, fragments of cuneiform writing from the pre-Israelite period, and a tomb containing an unusual, large ceramic sarcophagus from the Late Bronze Period. Using new methods, they succeeded in detecting a total of twenty strata from the surface down to bedrock, making possible a quite accurate reconstruction of Gezer's history of occupation from the Late Chalcolithic Period onward.

With the arrival of Jakob J. Petuchowski of the Cincinnati faculty in the summer of 1963, regular Saturday morning services were inaugurated in the synagogue of the school. Petuchowski developed a special liturgy, based on the reform service but conducted entirely in Hebrew and reincorporating references to Zion and Jerusalem that editors of most liberal prayerbooks had intentionally omitted. He also gave a series of Friday evening lectures on the subject "Judaism for the Twentieth-Century Man." After a year, he was succeeded as rabbi of the synagogue, first by Herbert Brichto and then by Ezra Spicehandler.

Orthodox Jews, whether Israeli or American, rarely attended the services. The sitting together of men and women, the abbreviation of the liturgy, as well as the use of musical instruments (the flute and the cello), kept them away. At the other extreme, American Jews of the older, classical Reform tradition felt equally ill at ease in the Jerusalem chapel. They were unable to understand or accept the wearing of prayer shawls by cantor and rabbi, the use of the traditional cantorial chants, and nearly the entire congregation worshipping with covered heads at what was supposed to be a reform service. Yet the services drew a favorable response from those Israelis who made up the core of worshippers and who attended in very large numbers on the High Holy Days, as well as from most American liberal Jews visiting Israel. They were impressed by the stark simplicity of the synagogue, with its massive but plain marble ark, its wicker benches and unadorned walls, blending in so harmoniously with the serenity of Jerusalem. For American visitors, the College-Institute synagogue increasingly became a place of pilgrimage.

Over the years, however, the synagogue's attraction for visitors created a severe problem. Tourists began to fill its 220 seats nearly every week, driving away some of the Israelis. Nonetheless, services and sermons remained steadfastly in Hebrew lest the synagogue lose its Israeli character and the services become but a slight variation of those held in the United States. Thus an anomalous situation was created where the rabbi's words were fully comprehensible to only a small percentage of the congregation.

During the first seven years of the school's existence, its relationship to the rabbinical program of the College-Institute was only tangential. Students spending a year (usually the third) in Israel studied mainly at the Hebrew University though some classes were conducted for them at the College. The director of Jewish studies, a position at first filled on a rotating basis and then permanently by Ezra Spicehandler, arranged the courses and tried to be of assistance. Occasionally, the president would take the students along on one of his archaeological expeditions. But study in Israel was not a part of the regular rabbinic curriculum until 1970. In that year the Jewish Studies Program radically expanded its scope. As more and more students returned from a year in Israel with notably increased competence in Hebrew, as American Jewry became more Israel-conscious following the Six-Day War, and as Glueck himself came to realize that the significance of the school and support for it would be enhanced by a broadening of its aims, the decision was made to take the bold step of requiring each candidate for the Reform rabbinate to spend his first year at the Jerusalem School.[101]

The basic substance of the first-year-in-Israel program, as it existed initially,[102] consisted of an intensive Hebrew course utilizing the Hebrew-in-Hebrew ulpan method. The teachers, all Israelis trained in language instruction, gave the students a good grounding in modern Hebrew and transmitted the linguistic tools necessary for advanced textual study. In addition to this acquisition of Hebrew knowledge, the program had two other goals as well: encounter with Israel, and confrontation with the problems of modern Judaism, especially its Reform branch. In order to gain acquaintance with various aspects of Israeli life, students listened to lectures by public figures on a variety of social and political topics, and they went on organized tours inspecting both archaeological sites and modern settlements. During vacations some of them worked on kibbutzim, others tutored Israeli pupils in English. To provide intellectual stimulation, to supplement the intensive preoccupation with language study, and to relate the program more directly to their concerns as future Reform rabbis, students were required to take a course (in English) on the development of modern Jewish thought and practice. They were also enrolled in a Jewish liturgy course, and they could further enrich their studies by choosing from a variety of electives taught by visiting faculty of the College-Institute or by guest instructors.

The first-year-in-Israel program necessarily induced a certain degree of inner turmoil in those who participated. Students were confronted with a question most had not previously considered: whether the commitment to Judaism which they sought to express through the rabbinate might not better be fulfilled by settling in Israel. (A small number of them indeed made that decision.) Israel, moreover, presented them with a religious environment consisting of a secularist-Orthodox dichotomy, bridged only by the fledgling Israeli Progressive movement of some seven small congregations. They were forced, therefore, not only to defend Jewish life in America, but also to advocate a locally little understood Reform interpretation of Judaism. And yet, there was hardly a student in the initial years of the program who did not affirm the value of having the first phase of his rabbinical training take place in Israel.

With the completion of the building in Jerusalem in 1963, HUC-JIR had expanded to four campuses, an impressive—if financially problematic—achievement. Concurrently with this external growth, significant internal developments were taking place as well. They included shifts in the composition and character of the Board of Governors, administration, faculty, and student body, along with the introduction of new scholarly projects and curricular reforms.

The Board of Governors, once almost exclusively a Cincinnati preserve, was intentionally [103] transformed into a geographically more representative body during the Glueck years. In 1970 only eight of its more than fifty regular members were residents of the Queen City. Separate administrative boards governed local affairs in New York and Los Angeles. In general, the members of the Board of Governors seem to have been content to follow the lead of their president. Few if any conflicts existed between Glueck and his board. Carefully preparing the way in advance through private conversations, the president was able to gain official approval for every project he brought before it. Lay members generally considered it their primary function to be concerned with the financial situation of the school and its relationship to the outside world. They regarded educational policy as the domain of the president and refrained from raising it as an issue.

Six men served as chairmen of the board during the Glueck administration. The first, Lester A. Jaffe (1947–52), a Cincinnati attorney, had chaired the selection committee which chose Glueck as president. The second, Herbert R. Bloch (1952–57), was a quiet but energetic local stockbroker who enjoyed a very close personal friendship with Glueck. He was succeeded by Frank L. Weil (1957), a prominent, incisive New York attorney who, paradoxically, was more the champion of the Cincinnati School than of New York. (He died shortly after taking office.) From 1958 to 1962, Robert P. Goldman, a Cincinnati attorney whose father, and later he himself, had earlier served the movement as UAHC president, held the position. An early Zionist and an avid student of Jewish history, Goldman took over when the HUC-JIR dispute with the Union was reaching its most bitter stage. Sidney Meyers (1962–66), an affable and devoted Cincinnati businessman, took particular interest in the financial affairs of the College-Institute. He thoroughly enjoyed every battle for funds with the Union leadership, even as he also sought to bring about an improvement in the relationship. Glueck's last chairman, S. L.

Kopald, Jr. (1966–72), a conservative industrialist from Memphis, Tennessee, stood out from his predecessors in the degree to which he took an interest in the internal affairs of the school. He sought to make the personal acquaintance of every member of the faculty and of some of the students. During his administration, board meetings were regularly preceded by a faculty member explaining the nature of his work.

In Cincinnati, the internal administration of the school underwent a number of changes during the Glueck period. After Fine, Klausner, and Korn had all left their positions to take pulpits, Glueck decided to let the chief administrative burden devolve on a layman.[104] Richard Bluestein, a lawyer who had once been president of the National Federation of Temple Youth, was serving as public-relations director of the Jewish Community Council in Cincinnati when Glueck engaged him in 1949. For nine years, until 1958, the genial Bluestein took care of the administrative minutiae of the school, allowing the president to devote more of his time to public appearances and to archaeology. He differed with his boss significantly only on the New York School issue, which, after continued contact with the faculty and students there, he came eventually to see from their point of view. His relations with students were on the whole cordial and pleasant; they did not usually feel ill at ease in his presence. While Bluestein took care of nonacademic administration, such matters as the assignment of teaching responsibilities were handled for most of this period by Sheldon Blank, who served until 1955 as chairman of the faculty.

Shortly after Blank resigned his position, Glueck came to the conclusion that academic and general administration could best be handled by a single individual with the title of provost who would, in addition to acting as dean of the Cincinnati School, also coordinate the activities of all the campuses. Samuel Sandmel, a member of the faculty who had earlier taught at Vanderbilt University, was chosen for the position primarily because of his knowledge of American academic life, his contacts in the scholarly world, and his administrative capacity. One of Sandmel's first major tasks was to prepare a self-survey of the school for the purpose of accreditation, which was successfully gained in 1960. His ongoing responsibilities included recruitment of both faculty and students, formulation and administration of admissions policy, and service as a member of the Provisional Placement Commission of the CCAR. Glueck's relative distance from the day-to-day affairs of the College-Institute and the extent of Sandmel's authority eventually created a situation where the various discontents inherent in the functioning of the institution came to focus on the provost. As, moreover, he came to feel that his heavy administrative responsibilities were threatening his academic career, Sandmel chose eventually to resign as provost in 1966 in favor of devoting himself more exclusively to scholarship and teaching. In the final period of Glueck's life, Cincinnati administration was conducted by a newly ordained rabbi, Kenneth Roseman, who was able to deal flexibly with student discontents in the turbulent late sixties, and eventually achieved the position of dean. The provostship was abolished and a greater degree of academic responsibility came to devolve upon the faculty.

When Glueck assumed the presidency in 1947, the faculty consisted of only twelve regular members. Twenty-three years later the total number of full-time academic staff on all campuses was close to forty. Most of them were rabbis who had been ordained at the College; some had received their doctorates from it. In theology they ran the gamut from traditional to radical, in practice from minimal observance to strict adherence to Jewish law. Some were devoted primarily to scholarship and its ethos of dispassionate, meticulous research, others paid more attention to relating the subjects they taught to current student interests and concerns. Publication was encouraged, but not required for advancement. Faculty salaries were now very high compared to most universities and Christian seminaries, though still considerably less than the remuneration offered in the rabbinate. Since 1960, a regular system of sabbaticals had been in effect and the pension plan was consistently improved.[105] During the Glueck administration, the faculty seldom asserted itself against the president, who presided over the highly formal meetings held in Cincinnati (the deans presiding over more informal faculty gatherings in New York and

California). Glueck insisted on the right to veto any faculty resolution. In practice, however, he seldom contradicted the will of the
majority, and in academic matters of little moment he was content
to let the faculty have the right of decision. At the very end of his
administration, the faculty for the first time sought and gained nonvoting representation on the Board of Governors and its committees.

It is still too soon to attempt an evaluation of the personalities
and effectiveness of current members of the faculty. However, it is
possible at least to indicate the various subject areas represented at the
time of Glueck's death and the men (including only the full-time teaching faculty) who taught them.[106] In Bible and Semitics, Cincinnati
had Sheldon H. Blank, Herbert C. Brichto, Samuel Greengus, Isaac
Jerusalmi, Samuel Sandmel, Matitiahu Tsevat, and David B. Weisberg; in New York there was Harry M. Orlinsky; in Los Angeles,
Alfred Gottschalk. For the rabbinic disciplines (Talmud, Midrash,
liturgy, commentaries, codes) there were Alexander Guttmann, Eugene Mihaly, Jakob J. Petuchowski, and Ben Zion Wacholder in
Cincinnati, Julius Kravetz and Leonard S. Kravitz in New York, and
Lewis M. Barth, Samson H. Levey, and Stephen M. Passamaneck
in Los Angeles. Jewish philosophy and Jewish religious thought were
the domain of Alvin J. Reines in Cincinnati and of Fritz Bamberger
and Eugene B. Borowitz in New York. Jewish history was taught in
Cincinnati by Stanley F. Chyet, Jacob R. Marcus, Michael A. Meyer,
Ellis Rivkin, and Kenneth Roseman, in New York by Martin A.
Cohen, and in Los Angeles by Marc Raphael. Hebrew language and
literature was covered by Warren Bargad, Elias L. Epstein, and
Werner Weinberg in Cincinnati, by Abraham Aaroni and Shaul
Hareli in New York, and by William Cutter and Igal Yannay in
Los Angeles. Finally, subjects in the realm of practical rabbinics
(homiletics, education, human relations, speech) were regularly taught
in Cincinnati by Robert L. Katz, Lowell G. McCoy, Norman B.
Mirsky, and Sylvan D. Schwartzman, in New York by Paul M. Steinberg, and in Los Angeles by a number of part-time instructors.[107]

During the Glueck administration the Cincinnati campus was
host to a series of outstanding visiting scholars who spent a semester
or more in residence on the campus. In the early years, Leo Baeck,

the heroic leader of German Jewry during the Hitler period, lived in the dormitory for extended periods and taught a few elective courses. Later there was a regular succession of Israeli scholars from the Hebrew University: Gershom Scholem and Isaiah Tishby (Kabbalah and Hasidism), Gershon Shaked (modern Hebrew literature), and Uriel Tal (Jewish history). And all along there were congregational rabbis who came for a week or so to deliver lectures on the practical rabbinate. A series of *kallot* (special seminar programs) with invited participants were held in Cincinnati on such subjects as the scientific revolution, theology, mixed marriage, and the nature of seminary education, while individual guest lectures were given with frequency on all campuses by outstanding rabbis, scholars, intellectuals, and artists.

After the death of Board Chairman Frank L. Weil, Fritz Bamberger, who later became assistant to the president in charge of scholarly projects and public relations, conceived the idea of an institute for studies in religion and the humanities to honor Weil's memory. With initial aid from the Rockefeller Foundation and a fund that reached some $200,000, the Weil Institute was able to hold three major scholarly conferences—on "Religion and Scholarship," "The Effects of Urbanization on Religion," and "Mysticism and Society." It also sponsored a number of lecture series in Cincinnati and New York, each one devoted to exploring an aspect of the relation between religion and some secular concept, institution, period of history, or humanistic field of endeavor.

The libraries of the four campuses grew at a phenomenal rate during this period. It was decided that Cincinnati, now one of the two or three largest Jewish libraries in the world, should be the chief depository of materials for scholarly research. The other branches were to draw on its resources through loans while building up their own collections principally for student use. Under the exceptionally capable direction of Herbert Zafren, the Cincinnati library became a model of efficiency and easy utility. With the printing of its catalogue in 1964, the library's treasures became more widely known, resulting in an ever increasing deluge of requests for inter-library loans. The decision to shift from the older Freidus cataloguing system to that of the Library of Congress, and the use of a computerized system, resulted in the ability to absorb new volumes more rapidly than heretofore. While the manuscript collection remained comparatively small, the rare books obtained over the years continued to be the equivalent of the best collections anywhere. Perhaps the most significant acquisition of the recent period was Solomon Freehof's gift of Jewish responsa volumes, which filled some important gaps in the library's holdings.

In 1953, the library began to publish *Studies in Jewish Bibliography and Booklore,* a journal containing specialized articles of extraordinary importance especially for Jewish librarians and historians of Jewish literary creativity. It also undertook a series of book-size bibliographical studies under the title *Bibliographica Judaica.* Of no less significance was a project initiated by Jacob Rader Marcus to microfilm all early American Jewish newspapers and periodicals, making the films available to other libraries. This American Jewish Periodical Center, housed in the Cincinnati library, began its operations in 1956. A Society of Jewish Bibliophiles, which eventually reached a membership of two hundred, met for the first time at the Cincinnati library during its dedication in 1961. It published a number of books and held meetings where members showed one another their most prized volumes.

To advance Jewish scholarship, the HUC-JIR continued to publish regularly the *Hebrew Union College Annual,* which now included a larger proportion of articles dealing with the modern period. The Hebrew Union College Press, through a variety of arrangements, likewise continued its publication activity. And many faculty members, to an even greater extent than before, regularly participated in meetings of scholarly organizations, in various instances serving as their officers. A striking new scholarly venture was launched when a group of faculty and students on the Cincinnati campus undertook an ongoing project to discover and utilize computer applications for rabbinic literature.

In the Glueck period, as in the past, the rabbinic curriculum remained the object of recurrent waves of complaint and of equally recurrent efforts at innovation and change. Perhaps the basic problem was how to enable the student with a meager background in Hebrew to surmount the language barrier rapidly and with a minimum of frustration. A new possibility for alleviating some of the student distress with Hebrew emerged when the school received the gift of an attractive thirty-acre country estate in the Susquehanna River Valley near Towanda, Pennsylvania.[108] Here, beginning in 1954, the College-Institute held intensive eight-week summer sessions for incoming students under the direction of a faculty member assisted by advanced rabbinical students. Other faculty came for visits, lecturing on their specialties and providing some variation from the daily routine of elementary language study. In this tranquil and intimate setting, most students were able to achieve a basic grounding in Hebrew, while those who found it too difficult were asked to discontinue the rabbinic program before they actually began it. Later, after the Sisterhood Dormitory was air-conditioned in 1961, the sessions were moved to the Cincinnati campus and the Towanda property was sold. Summer sessions continued for nearly a decade in Cincinnati (with an equivalent course conducted at the Los Angeles School) until the first-year-in-Israel program finally made them superfluous.

Yet "Towanda" proved no panacea for the Hebrew problem. Other ideas were tried as well. For a time, great hope was placed in the use of a language laboratory on the Cincinnati campus where students could listen to an oral rendition of unvocalized texts and then record their own attempts at a correct reading. Although many thousands of dollars were invested in highly sophisticated equipment, the technique soon proved to be of only the most limited value, and after some debate, it was gradually abandoned.[109] No less controversial was the division of incoming students according to homogeneous sections for the subject-integrated first-year Hebrew I program. While the arrangement had obvious advantages for the more advanced students, those in the lower sections looked forward with intense trepidation to the comprehensive Hebrew Readiness Examination at the end of the first year, fearful that their slower-moving group was insufficiently prepared to pass that obstacle successfully. The same problem existed in the second year, which reached its climax with the

B.H.L. examination. Because the vast majority of students in this period entered the College-Institute with so little preparation in Hebrew,[110] and because some, however much otherwise qualified for the rabbinate, possessed only average linguistic ability, the struggle for competence in reading the traditional texts of Judaism, particularly the rabbinic ones, continued in many instances to be a frustrating one for faculty and students alike.

The final curricular hurdle, aside from the rabbinical dissertation, was the M.H.L. (later M.A.H.L.) examination, held in the senior year. It consisted of a written test in four subject areas: Bible, rabbinics, philosophy and theology, and Jewish history and literature—plus an oral examination in the field of the dissertation. In 1950, the faculty in Cincinnati succeeded in making this degree optional, so that it was possible for a less academically inclined rabbinic student either to forgo taking the examination or to fail it and still receive ordination. Though this measure provoked student opposition once again, as it had when introduced during the last years of the Morgenstern administration, this time there was no reversal, and for a period of nearly twenty years some students were ordained without a master's degree. In 1968, the examination underwent a radical and highly creative transformation. Instead of testing comprehensively a student's knowledge in all major areas, it was limited to a single idea or institution, the evolution of which had been traced through the various eras of the Jewish past in a special course for seniors consisting of assigned reading and faculty symposia for each period. In 1967–68, "The Sabbath in Jewish Tradition and History" was the subject chosen. At the end of that year, however, it became majority sentiment on the faculty that the master's degree should be given to all students for successful course work alone, with no further examinations or special requirements.[111]

At different times plans were put forward to make the curriculum more effective and meaningful. With the thought that students could do better work if they carried fewer subjects simultaneously, the school switched to a quarter system in Cincinnati and New York in 1957 only to abandon it again little more than a decade later because it provided insufficient time for student reading and research.

An honors program, launched in 1964, was intended to allow better or more advanced students to substitute electives or tutorials for required courses, but the program lasted for only a short time. An ambitious though perhaps unrealistic proposal for a goal-oriented, as opposed to the current subject-oriented, curriculum, placed before the faculty a year later, met an impasse when agreement could not be reached as to its feasibility.[112] One change that did come about in response to student insistence during the late sixties was a doubling of the number of electives in Cincinnati from 11 percent to 22 percent and the decision to grade courses above the B.H.L. level only as pass or fail.[113] In the New York School, however, the percentage of electives allowed students continued to be less. In part this was due to the small size of the faculty and the limited hours available to commuting students. In part also it reflected the greater emphasis which the New York professors collectively placed on the mastery of standard Hebrew texts by all who sought to be ordained.

In order to give rabbinical students an opportunity to relate Jewish values to current political questions, a seminar at the UAHC Religious Action Center in Washington was held for the first time in 1965 and repeated thereafter. The participants, from both the Cincinnati and New York schools, were able to meet with government leaders and to discuss such areas of religious concern as poverty problems, civil rights, the morality of foreign policy, and the separation of church and state.[114] A little later a few students participated in a two-week urban affairs program, studying the problems of the urban poor and aiding antipoverty agencies.

A lasting innovation of some significance was the introduction in 1965 of a voluntary internship year for those students who desired a congregational apprenticeship before ordination.[115] For some students this program, though usually postponing ordination for a year, provided a welcome opportunity to interrupt a curriculum concentrating on textual study in order to gain valuable professional experience by assisting in a large congregation.

The size, background, and character of the rabbinical student body changed considerably during the Glueck period.[116] Although enrollment did not increase consistently, declining somewhat in the early sixties, a comparison between 1950, when New York and Cincinnati together had only 120 students, and 1970, when the combined campuses had about double that number, indicates an overall pattern of remarkable growth. This increase in size was made possible by the sustained expansion of the Reform movement during most of this period, which produced the need for ever larger numbers of rabbis to fill newly created pulpits as well as to assist senior men in established ones.[117] Intensive recruitment efforts, and, in the later period, the appeal of a vocation stressing peace at the time of the unpopular Vietnam War, also played a role.

The students who now entered the school were nearly all American-born. Unlike previous generations, the College-Institute no longer served them as the only available ladder to social and financial success. They came mostly from families of sufficient status to assure their children an alternate career of equal prominence should they not have chosen the rabbinate. Unlike their predecessors, they were motivated less by the desire for eminence as great pulpit orators and far more by the wish to help fellow Jews through counsel in time of trouble and to work with Jewish youth. Their religious background, too, had changed. The number of students coming from Orthodox homes decreased steadily following World War II. By 1968, no less than 80 percent of those who entered the College-Institute came from Reform backgrounds; many of them had been active in the National Federation of Temple Youth. Only in New York did there continue to be a sizable number from traditional families.

In the language of the catalogue, students who desired admission to the College-Institute were to "possess academic abilities well above average, the disposition to study earnestly and thoroughly, and qualities of personality and character suitable for the Reform rabbinate." Applicants had to submit undergraduate records and letters of recommendation, undergo psychiatric screening, and in the later period take the Graduate Records Examination. Some were indeed eliminated because of inadequate academic potential or severe psychological problems. Most, however, gained admission with little difficulty, even the rather considerable number who possessed only a B− average or below in their undergraduate work.[118] The result was a student body extremely varied in academic potential, ranging from the exceptionally talented to the very average, with severe pressure placed on weaker students to achieve minimum requirements.

As the students came from ever more affluent homes, a declining percentage required financial assistance. Those who did need aid for tuition and maintenance received funds from the school partly as outright grants and partly as loans repayable in the form of an endowment policy with the HUC-JIR as beneficiary. The many biweekly—in New York often weekly—student congregations were an important source of income for most advanced students, while remuneration for religious-school instruction helped meet the needs of lowerclassmen. Many students were to some degree supported by their working wives. Full scholarships, sponsored by the National Federation of Temple Sisterhoods, were usually available only to foreign students, who during this period came to Cincinnati from such distant places as Israel, India, Turkey, Australia, Hungary, Japan, and South Africa.

During the fifties an active dormitory life continued in Cincinnati, much the same as it had been during the Morgenstern years. But as more and more students married during their five years of study, or were married already when they entered, the percentage living on campus declined steadily. In addition, during the 1960s, many single students in Cincinnati chose the independence of a rented apartment over the comforts and amenities provided by the dormitory. Wives of the married students in Cincinnati early formed a Student Wives' Club with a program that included study with faculty members, planning holiday celebrations on the campus, and other types of participation in the life of the HUC-JIR community. But, on the whole, married students and the single ones living outside the dormitory were more distant from the school than their predecessors of earlier generations, whose involvement had been much more inclusive. In New York, though until the mid-fifties some of the students lived in a building next door to the school, there was never a regular dormitory and students throughout the period tended to be more independent and detached from the institution.

For most of the Glueck era, the chapel of each school continued to serve as its focal point. Though students were no longer required to attend, they came with varying degrees of regularity, especially for the major service of the week, held on Sabbath morning in Cincinnati and on a weekday in New York and Los Angeles. In Cincinnati, a student choir continued to enhance Sabbath worship, while organ music pealed down from the loft at the daily services. In New York, cantorial candidates participated along with rabbinic students, providing a strong musical element, while in California, with only the first two years of the rabbinic program, informality and spontaneity were the rule. For holiday services the Cincinnati chapel was invariably full, especially at Purim and Simhat Torah, when—especially in the late sixties—the high spirit of the occasion usually more closely approximated Hasidic exuberance than the decorous patterns laid down by the originators of reform. To the chapel the College community would also repair at times of American or Jewish catastrophe: the assassinations of John F. Kennedy and Martin Luther King, military threats to the State of Israel, terrorist massacres.

Until 1969 the daily morning and Sabbath services in Cincinnati were conducted in rotation by members of the second-year class and a sermon by a senior was preached on the portion of the week. It was the reader's task to present an original meditation or selected reading before the silent prayer and to read from the Torah. Generally the *Union Prayer Book* was the liturgy used, though creative services were also permitted. The content of sermons was subject to no censorship, even when, as in some instances, the focus was an attack on some aspect of life at the school. Only the structure and delivery of the sermon were subject to regular critique and evaluation at sessions led by the professors of homiletics and speech.

Two matters relating to the worship service in Cincinnati early became subjects of dispute between students, faculty, and administration. The first was the question of whether Hebrew pronunciation in the chapel had to be Ashkenazic or whether, with the establishment of the State of Israel and the increasing adoption of its Hebrew pronunciation by American congregations, it might be Sephardic. For a time a strange dichotomy was allowed to exist whereby Sephardic pronunciation was used in the first-year Hebrew program, but instruction in liturgy, along with worship in the chapel, remained Ashkenazic. An exception was made only for foreign students whose native pronunciation was Sephardic. Finally, in 1967, a gradual transition was allowed to begin that eventually made the chapel's Hebrew exclusively Sephardic.[119]

Of somewhat greater moment was the question of whether the reader might cover his head and/or wear a *tallit*. Glueck and many of the faculty were adamantly opposed to the use of these accouterments of traditional Judaism. But the students, now coming mostly from Reform backgrounds and in some cases seriously desiring more traditional practice, were strongly in favor. As early as 1955, some of them sought to bring about a change in the *minhag* (custom), but to no avail.[120] A decade later the faculty Committee on Religious Activities still confirmed that:

> The services at our Chapel are conducted bareheaded. Foreign students have the option to wear or not to wear a hat, but are to be encouraged to conform to the prevailing custom. An American (United States) student, who has strong feelings in the matter may also wear a hat if he receives special permission. . . .[121]

A radical change in the nature of the chapel service came about in 1969 when the Cincinnati faculty adopted a joint faculty-student committee's proposal separating daily and Sabbath services from the academic aspects of the school and placing them almost exclusively under student control.[122] The motivation for this action was the widespread student feeling that a worshipful atmosphere could not be created as long as reader and preacher were fulfilling academic requirements, in some cases involuntarily, and with the knowledge that their performance was being judged. Thus, at the very end of Glueck's administration, the faculty allowed the students to "liberate" the chapel and henceforth to select participants on a strictly voluntary basis. Though at the time of Glueck's death it was not yet possible to render judgment on this "experiment," one could already conclude that it had resulted in a far greater freedom and variety of religious expression—though clearly at the expense of fixity in custom. In some instances most elevating and well-considered services were presented, and in other instances some that were depressingly shoddy and ignorant. Gradually the need was becoming apparent to regain a greater measure of continuity and careful preparation even while preserving the centrality of the chapel's religious function.

The same quest for more traditional practice which led some students to desire wearing a *kipa* and *tallit* in chapel— and some for a time to conduct their own orthodox services early in the morning— was also responsible for the increasing number of students in the 1960s who wanted to keep the dietary laws. Glueck had very little sympathy for their feelings, and the same may be said for most members of the Board of Governors.[123] Yet in practice the school yielded to student demands in this area. The dining room of the dormitory continued to serve meat that was not ritually slaughtered, but in the late sixties it also provided strictly kosher food for the minority desiring it, and the institution put up with the burden of covering the extra expense. At the same time there were other students who found little value in their fellows' preference for more traditional liturgy and more scrupulous observance. A uniform attitude in such matters was no more characteristic of the student body of HUC-JIR than of the Reform movement as a whole.

After more than a decade of silence, student sentiment and reflection in the sixties once again found a literary outlet through the publication of a student magazine. The *HUC Monthly,* which had died in 1949, remained without replacement until 1961, when Richard Levy, an unusually gifted student in Cincinnati, founded a new journal, *variant,* to take its place. Intended to express diverse opinions in the way that variant readings of a sacred text sometimes reflect differing views, the new magazine was entirely devoted to student creativity. Its editors did not present "news" of the College-Institute, but filled *variant's* pages with philosophical and theological themes, problems of worship, and proposals for curricular reform. Much of its space was given over to student poetry and fiction. For its contributors *variant* mitigated the desensitizing effects of a curriculum that some felt provided little room for individual creativity. For the HUC-JIR community on all campuses (New York[124] and Los Angeles each had a liaison person on the staff), it represented a revival of student self-expression. Sadly, the journal declined in the late sixties and eventually ceased publication altogether. Its demise was due in part to financial problems and in part to the failure of sufficiently talented and devoted students to continue it. But it died also because by that time attention was turning away from literary reflection and poetic musings. HUC-JIR students, no less than their counterparts in universities around the country, were becoming caught up in the anguish of an America beset by racial strife at home and an unconscionable war abroad. Much as the editors tried,[125] they were unable to adapt *variant* to these new concerns.

Though the fifties were generally a period of deep political apathy —at the College-Institute no less than at other schools—at least some HUC-JIR students even in that period chose a measure of social and political involvement. As a border town between North and South, Cincinnati retained a certain amount of segregation in privately owned public facilities. In their desire to change the situation, a group of College-Institute students in the early fifties took a black interfaith fellow with them to a neighborhood restaurant, occupied all the tables, and refused to order until their black comrade was served. A few years later, another group participated in an attempt to integrate the swimming pool of a local amusement park and were arrested in the process. A third group picketed the downtown Woolworth store because the firm's lunch counters in the South remained segregated.

A decade later student moral concern had come to focus on the war in Southeast Asia. Service in the chaplaincy, never very popular, became a major issue as some students declared themselves conscientious objectors to all wars and others selectively to the conflict in Vietnam. Ever since the Korean War each student was considered to have a moral obligation to serve as a chaplain for two years following ordination, and a system of selection according to categories of marital status had been in operation for some time. Later, students were also regularly enrolled in a Seminarian Reserve Program which enabled them to enter the armed services at a higher rank and salary. The moral dilemma of conflicting imperatives—the service of Jewish soldiers versus complete dissociation from the war—was passionately debated in the halls of the College-Institute as it was at the meetings of the CCAR. The issue was finally settled by the Central Conference when in 1968 it accepted selective conscientious objection as grounds for refusal to serve, and when the following year it went still further by making the chaplaincy totally voluntary.[126]

During the last two years of the Glueck presidency, the Vietnam War was the cause for ever more dramatic expressions of condemnation by students and by some faculty.[127] A climactic moment came in December 1968 when a student in Cincinnati stood up on the chapel pulpit and proclaimed that he was sending his selective service cards back to his local draft board and would face the consequences. Glueck, who by this time was himself beginning to have doubts about the war, thereupon ascended the pulpit and said:

> It isn't necessary for me to agree with everything you say but it is necessary for me as president of the Hebrew Union College to practice what we preach: that there is intellectual and spiritual freedom here at the Hebrew Union College and that we in general and I in particular will do everything within our power to nurture and strengthen and, if necessary, to defend it.

Though he said he did not think the student's action would be effective, Glueck added that, if the student qualified, he would surely ordain him.[128]

Although Glueck avoided taking public stands himself,[129] he did indeed consistently protect freedom of expression among faculty and students, and he was willing to endure considerable pressure from members of the Board of Governors and from the public at large on that account. He did not object, for example, when students made news by marching around the Federal Building in Cincinnati while blowing the shofar nor did he prohibit even demagogic opponents of the war from speaking in the chapel.

A major problem arose only where student activism seemed to

threaten the continuity of the academic program. When, in the spring of 1970, the Ohio National Guard shot fifteen Kent State University students, killing four of them, during the bitter student protest against United States military entry into Cambodia, the College-Institute community in Cincinnati immediately gathered in the chapel to mourn the victims and to express its outrage. Some students spoke about the war at Reform congregations the following Sabbath, others arranged a memorial service at the local National Guard armory. The faculty agreed to cancel classes for a few days in favor of symposia presenting Jewish perspectives on war. But many students desired to go yet further: to close the school the following week so that those who wished could attend a rally planned for Washington. Their wishes met the opposition of most faculty, of the administration, and of the chairman of the Board of Governors. In an atmosphere where one university after another found itself forced to close in order to prevent violence, only frenzied night-long negotiations finally prevented a student strike and resulted in a compromise whereby the school would remain open but students would in no way be disadvantaged by choosing to concentrate on what to them seemed the more immediate concern.[130]

It was only natural, in view of the prevalent atmosphere at other educational institutions in the late sixties, that HUC-JIR students should likewise—and at times high-handedly—make certain demands of the administration. In some instances, as in the case of a request by New York School students for full tuition scholarships for all students and an increase in the level of aid for maintenance, the considerations were clearly financial.[131] In others, as when the students successfully gained access to faculty committees and nonvoting representation on the Board of Governors, they reflected a bid for greater power, or at least a greater voice, in the government of the College-Institute.[132]

At the time of Glueck's death the students on all campuses were far more self-assertive and independent than earlier generations. Unlike their predecessors, they resisted sharply any endeavor to shape them into a given mold. But their assertiveness also thinly veiled a degree of uncertainty regarding their own authenticity as Reform Jews, their ability to identify with and to expound the traditional texts of Judaism, and, above all, regarding their own role as future Reform rabbis. In falling prey to this crisis of confidence, they reflected a malaise that was becoming ever more prevalent as well among their elders who had already been ordained as rabbis. Many of the latter were beginning to experience a discontent which came to be focused, at least in part, on the College-Institute.

During the last years of Glueck's administration it was the rabbinical alumni who posed a new challenge to his authority as president. At the very time when relations with the UAHC were beginning to improve, the Central Conference of American Rabbis emerged as Glueck's chief critic, calling into question both the present functioning of the institution and Glueck's plans for the future.

The president's relations with the alumni of the school had never been very good. He preferred not to attend conventions of the CCAR, and when he did make appearances, he would keep aloof from the men, often choosing the privacy of his hotel room rather than mingling among them. He deeply resented any of the younger rabbis calling him by his first name, and he bristled at any criticism of the school. Many members of the CCAR felt that the HUC-JIR president was insufficiently responsive to their concerns. Over the years, Glueck had given the rabbis certain concessions: in the mid-fifties, perpetual Alumni Association agitation had finally resulted in the new policy of granting an honorary Doctor of Divinity degree to nearly every active Reform rabbi after twenty-five years of service;[133] in 1961 Glueck had created an Alumni Board of Overseers with which he met periodically to brief its members on the situation of the College-Institute and to listen to their suggestions. But the D.D. degree—just because it became so universal—was not taken seriously by all who received it, while the Alumni Board lacked power and, some thought, was not fully representative of the American Reform rabbinate.

But CCAR discontent with the College-Institute was founded only in part on resentment of Glueck's distance and autocracy. The Reform rabbinate in the late sixties was undergoing a severe crisis. The period of swift congregational growth had come to an end; the postwar religious revival had given way to faddish claims that God was dead, and then to apathy. The role of the rabbi was less clear than ever in a time when the significance of the synagogue in its existing form was being severely challenged, when Jewish identity was becoming more ethnic and national than religious, and when the Reform movement seemed terribly uncertain about its common denominator. It was only to be expected that what some termed a "crisis of the rabbinate" [134] should result in anxieties, self-doubts, and also in questioning the nature of the institution which, having trained the men to be rabbis, therefore bore responsibility for their situation. Especially—but not only—men who were unhappy in the rabbinate tended to express their frustration as dissatisfaction with what the College-Institute had given them.

A most basic concern of many CCAR members was the number of graduates which the HUC-JIR produced every year. They feared that a surfeit of rabbis would soon make it difficult to place new ordinees and would create more competition for the limited number of larger congregations. Glueck characteristically showed little concern for their fears. He liked to compare the absorptive capacity of the American rabbinate with that of the State of Israel, implying that just as David Ben-Gurion had been right in scoffing at those who claimed Palestine could not absorb millions of immigrants, so too his own boldness in producing ever larger graduating classes would be proven right by experience.[135] In fact, throughout the Glueck period, newly ordained rabbis at least (if not every man already in the field), seldom had difficulty in finding desirable positions.

More idealistically, certain members of the CCAR individually, and then the organization as such, began to ask whether, in view of the ferment in the general and Jewish communities, it was not time to pose some serious questions about rabbinical training now, before any far-reaching decisions were made that might determine the College-Institute's course for decades to come. In 1966, articles critical of the College-Institute and containing suggestions for change began to appear in the *CCAR Journal*. In 1967, Levi Olan, then incoming president of the Conference, proposed that the CCAR sponsor a study of rabbinical education to discover whether the current curriculum of the HUC-JIR prepared men adequately to fill the role of the

contemporary rabbi.[136] A year later, on October 22, 1968, the CCAR
Executive Board accepted the recommendation of its recently established Committee on Rabbinic Training to commission a major professional research project on the character of the American Reform
rabbinate, its probable future needs, and its seminary.[137] Because the
College-Institute was about to embark on a new program of expansion, it also passed a resolution which requested "that the HUC-JIR
Board of Governors defer capital funds efforts until meaningful consultation can be held between the Board of Governors of the HUC-
JIR and the CCAR in regard to the relationship between said capital
funds efforts and the proposed study." [138]

Glueck immediately perceived the CCAR request as a direct
challenge to the autonomy of the College-Institute and to his own
authority as its president. As a decade earlier he had fought the
UAHC's attempt to have a larger say in determining College-Institute
policy, so now he was equally adamant in insisting that the Central
Conference had no right to decide what the school might or might not
do. Since the CCAR's call for a moratorium on further expansion until
completion of its study was accompanied by ever louder demands for
formal CCAR representation on the Board of Governors,[139] Glueck
could brush aside the proposed study, too, as merely an instrument
for undermining his power and subverting plans already laid out for
further construction.

Although the president had told the Board of Governors in 1963
that "with the opening of our Jerusalem School we have come to the
point where we must pause to consolidate our gains and make our
phenomenal advance secure," [140] within four years an updated version
of the 1957 Master Plan had been commissioned. It provided for
nearly $3 million of expenditures in Cincinnati—to build a new
administration building, an auditorium, and a chapel—and for a
slightly higher amount to build a second structure in New York. On
February 7, 1968, the Board of Governors passed a resolution favoring expansion in Cincinnati and New York and committing itself to
raising $6 million to pay for it. A few months later, the CCAR de-
livered its request for deferral of expansion until the completion of
its study. The result was a series of meetings between CCAR and HUC-

JIR representatives which at length produced an uneasy compromise: capital funds might be raised without pause, but for the present there would be no "irrevocable decisions" regarding the construction of new buildings.[141]

Had the financial prospects of the school looked better or the Board of Governors been whole-heartedly in favor of beginning a new building program even without funds as yet in hand, it is likely that Glueck would have ignored the protestations of the CCAR. But by 1969 the College-Institute budget was beginning to show a considerable deficit, casting doubt on the possibility of supporting expanded facilities and programs. Moreover, in view of these circumstances, Board Chairman Kopald was opposed to embarking on any large-scale building program until at least a substantial portion of the funds to pay for it had first been raised. Glueck's reluctant concession in compromising with the CCAR was therefore largely academic. He had no choice. On February 5, 1970, he told the Board of Governors: "I am coming to the opinion that we should not authorize construction of new facilities anywhere on our four campuses from now on, until and unless we are assured not only of the capital funds necessary to build them, but of the monies necessary to defray the increased annual budgets that will automatically be called for once they are built."

Nelson Glueck did not live to witness any further physical expansion of the College-Institute. On February 12, 1971, he died of cancer at the age of seventy, a little more than a year before his projected retirement. His central role in fixing the school's course for nearly a quarter of a century requires a brief evaluative analysis of his personality and his administration, provisional as such an endeavor must be from so short a perspective.

In Nelson Glueck the College-Institute possessed an extraordinary president whose profound effect on the institution was as ambiguous as his own relationship to it. Never before did the school have as its head a man of such widespread eminence. He was the recipient of more than twenty honorary degrees; his name was known among biblical scholars everywhere and among even the schoolchildren in

Israel; his books were read widely by the laity. What some called his charisma, others his personal charm, won him numerous admirers and loyal supporters; his fierce anger cowed nearly all who dared to oppose him. He commanded universal respect. But this external strength shielded an inner complexity: at times he was shy, brooding, withdrawn, at others impetuous and willful. Moods of depression alternated unpredictably with periods of intense activity. Devoted to dispassionate research, he was at the same time a deeply emotional man, who wept freely both in private and when delivering speeches. As president, his drive and stubborn persistence, his ability to persuade, and if necessary to dominate, helped to transform the College-Institute from the small Cincinnati institution it was in 1947 to the complex of four campuses it was at his death. Yet the gains were purchased at the price of frictions within and without that were the necessary concomitant of possessing a president ambitious for the school, but with a lingering ambivalence about his relationship to it.

Perhaps the most significant fact regarding Glueck's presidency is that he never entirely overcame his initial reluctance about holding the position. Until the end, he thought of himself first as a biblical archaeologist and only second as president of a seminary. Every summer was spent in Israel on expeditions to the Negev, every spare moment during the year working on books and articles. When he was frustrated by the pressures of his office, he would retreat to his study, sometimes to repair broken vessels of pottery he had collected. Such activity, he wrote in a letter, gave him "a sense of quiet and a restoration of values." [142] The appearance of Glueck's portrait on the cover of *Time* magazine,[143] showing him clad in Bedouin headdress and set against a desert landscape (à la Lawrence of Arabia), was a proud occasion for the institution no less than for its president. But there was some chagrin at the writer's hyperbolic remark: "H.U.C. is probably the only college in the world that can be governed from the back of a camel 8,000 miles away."

Though he gradually accustomed himself to the presidency, Glueck could not help but be aware that its demands prevented any but a minimum of serious scientific work. Inevitably the office kept him from maintaining his earlier position at the forefront of archaeological research. Though his extraordinary capacity for work enabled Glueck to spend long winter nights at his study table in Cincinnati, and though his remarkable stamina made it possible for him to brave the blistering summer heat of the Israeli desert, he was forced to see younger men develop new techniques in which he had no expertise and late in life to see some of his favorite theories successfully challenged. Even as he adjusted to being president of the College-Institute, he always resented the toll it took in archaeological productivity.

Glueck's ambivalence about his position manifested itself especially in respect to those tasks which he did not enjoy. Though he was successful in obtaining some large gifts for the College-Institute from a few individuals and foundations, he loathed fund-raising dinners, at which he frequently made ill-prepared, ineffective speeches. No less troublesome an area for Glueck was administration, a job he likewise did not enjoy and which most of his associates thought he did poorly. While insisting on the right to make all major decisions, Glueck was bored with administrative details, usually—but not consistently—leaving these to his subordinates. His staff became especially aware of Glueck's perfectionism, his authoritarian manner, his expectation of total loyalty, and his inability or unwillingness to define lines of responsibility clearly. To the students Glueck remained a distant, vaguely respected figure, neither a rabbinical model nor a personal counselor. He gave no courses, showed little interest in students as individuals, and rarely bothered to learn any of their names.

Yet despite his ambivalence, Glueck came to enjoy the status of college president and in later years resisted the idea of retirement.[144] As he increasingly invested his energy in expanding the school, he identified himself with it ever more strongly. In particular, he found much gratification in performing the annual rite of ordination. Often he called the College-Institute "my school," as if it belonged to him personally,[145] or saw himself as the father in what he liked to call the "College family." Though Jerusalem mattered to him most, he was deeply committed to Cincinnati and to maintaining its centrality for Reform rabbinical training. When the capital funds campaign began in the late fifties, he wrote to a prospective contributor: "It is highly desirable that we begin building as soon as possible. . . . I

The first building of the Hebrew Union College in Cincinnati, 1881-1912

The present Cincinnati campus

The first building of the California School in the Hollywood Hills

The College-Institute in New York

The new building of the California School in the urban center of Los Angeles, 1971

Entrance to the Jerusalem School

Hebrew Union College.

בית המדרש הגדול

RABBINICAL DIPLOMA.

The President and Faculty

OF THE

Hebrew Union College,

Acting under the authority, and in conformity with the laws, of

The Union of American Hebrew Congregations,

by these presents, declare and make known to all the House of Israel, wherever dwelling, as follows:

Whereas, Mr. *David Philipson*

has been a student of the Hebrew Union College for *Eight* years, and has progressed from year to year in the prescribed order of studies, and shown his proficiency therein, and has, during his residence in Cincinnati, conducted himself in a religious and moral manner, and has evinced that high character necessary for a Teacher in Israel;

And, having furthermore graduated with honors from the University of

Cincinnati, Ohio,

and in his final examination been found proficient in a knowledge of those branches necessary for the proper discharge of the duties of Rabbi, the aforesaid President and Faculty of the HEBREW UNION COLLEGE do hereby

confer on Mr. *David Philipson* the title of

RABBI,

by virtue of which he is authorized to perform all the functions connected with such vocation.

May the work of the Lord prosper in his hands and, through his labors, may truth, righteousness and peace increase in Israel.

בע״ה

ראש הישיבה והמורים הסומכים

של

בית המדרש הגדול לחנך מורי הוראה בישראל

אשר בצינציננאטי

בפקרת ורשות עקד קהלות ישרון באמעריקא וכפי החקים אשר יסדו על זאת,
מעירים ומודיעים במגלה עדות זאת לכל הקהלות אשר בכל תפוצות ישראל ככל הכתוב
ומפרש כבא:

בהיות שהתלמיד החבר דוד בן יוסף פהיליפפאן

מלידי _____ שקד על דלתות בית מדרשנו, פה

זה שמנה שנים ושנה ולמד בכל שנה ושנה מן הידיעות השונות ערך הקצוב בסדר הלימוד
החקוק לנו, ובהקפת כל שנה עמד על הבחינון והראה למדי כי חלמודו עולה בידו:

ובהיות, שבמשך כל השנים ששמש תלמיד הנוכר את רבותיו בבית מדרשנו פה
לא נמצא בו שמץ דבר אשר יפסלנו בקרוש; אכן החזיק בית ישראל במוסר ובמדות
בכל לב ונפש, כפי אשר יאות לאיש אשר מכין את נפשו להית לאחיו מנחוני בקרש:

ובהיות, שאחר אשר נגמר התלמיד הנוכר כעת את תלמורו בבית מדרשנו פה,
אנחנו העומרונו על כור הבחינה ומצאנוהו מוכן ומושכר כל צרכו לנשת אל עבודת
הקרוש, מצב הרבנות; בקי וחריף בתורה הכתובה והמסורה, בהלכה ואגדה, מבין דבר
מתוך דבר ומוציא חדין הנכון לאמתו, ויריו רב לו גם בשאר חכמות ישראל, וקורות
עמו כתובות על לבו, וגם לשונו לשן למודים, יודע לררוש כמשפט בשפה צחה ולהמשיך
לב שמעיו אל יראת ה׳ ומוסר השכל:

על כל הדברים והאמת האלה נכתירו היום את התלמיד הנכבר הזה בכתר
התורה, ונסמכהו בסמיכת הוראה, מהיום והלאה יכונה בשם הכבוד

רבי דוד בן יוסף פהיל־יפפאן

והרשות בתונה לו להיות רב ומורה בכל עדה ועדה בישראל: יורה יורה, ידין ידין;
משפטי אורים ותמים יהיו על לבו, התומים, ירפא החרום וחזק כל ברק, על דבר אמת
וענוה צדק: צלח ורכב!

לעדות על זאת באנו על החתום

פה צינציננאטי היום יום ד׳ ו׳ תמוז תרמ״ג לפ״ק

In Testimony Whereof, We have appended our names and the seals of the Hebrew Union College and the Union of American Hebrew Congregations.

Done in the City of Cincinnati, State of Ohio, this Sixth day of Tamuz 5643. Eleventh day of July 1883

Isaac M. Wise — President Hebrew Union College.

_____ — Professor of Talmud, H. U. C.

_____ Eppinger, — Professor of Biblical Literature, H. U. C.

B. Bettmann —

President, U. A. H. C. President Board of Governors, H. U. C.

Secretary, U. A. H. C. Secretary Board of Governors, H. U. C.

The rabbinical diploma of David Philipson, a member of the first graduating class, 1883

בעזרת השם

אנחנו החתומים מטה חבר המורים ומועצת הנאמנים של בית המדרש

לחכמת ישראל בניו יארק מאשרים בזה כי תלמידנו

יעקב פרץ בר ליב זוסעל רודין

שקד על דלתי בית מדרשנו וגמר את חק הלמודים הקבועים בו ועמד

למבחן בכתב ובעל פה בהתאם לדרישת המוסד ויצא מוכתר בעטרת

הרבנות והננו חולקים לו בזה את התואר

מורנו הרב

והרשות נתונה לו להיות רב ומורה בקהלות ישראל יהי ה׳ אלהיו

עמו ויעל להפיץ רוח דעת אלהים ותורתו בקהל עדתו אשר יעמד

על משמרתה משמרת הקודש

ובזה אנחנו באים על החתום יום אחד עשר לחדש סיון שנת תבושת

אלפים שש מאות ושמונים ושמנה פה ניו יארק

The rabbinical diploma of Jacob P. Rudin, a member of the Jewish Institute
of Religion class of 1928

Israel Aaron
1859~1912

Henry Berkowitz
1857~1924

Joseph Krauskopf
1858~1923

David Philipson
1862~

The first graduating class, 1883

Isaac M. Wise with the class of 1895 (*left to right*): Morris
Newfield, Seymour Bottigheimer, George Solomon

HUC Faculty and students, 1895; in the second row
(*center*) Isaac M. Wise flanked by David Philipson (*left*) and
Moses Mielziner (*right*)

Professor Sigmund Mannheimer and students, about 1905; front row, Morris
S. Lazaron (*left*) and Isadore Isaacson (*right*)

Class of 1900 (*left to right, seated*): Charles J. Freund, Leon Volmer (class of
1901), Judah Leon Magnes, William H. Fineshriber; (*standing*): Jacob Mielziner, Abraham S. Anspacher, David Lefkowitz, Pizer W. Jacobs, Jacob S.
Raisin, Abram Brill, Emil W. Leipziger, George Zepin

Cincinnati faculty, about 1922 (*left to right*): Harry Slonimsky, Adolph S. Oko, Jacob Z. Lauterbach, Moses Buttenwieser, Henry Englander, Julian Morgenstern (*president*), Abraham Cronbach, Louis Wolfenson, Jacob Mann, Israel Bettan, David Neumark

Cincinnati class of 1920 (*left to right, seated*): Joseph Baron, Bernard Heller, Samuel J. Harris, Jacob R. Marcus, Samuel S. Kaplan; (*standing*): Abraham I. Shinedling, S. Andhil Fineberg, Solomon Landman

Basketball team, Cincinnati, 1921-22

Moses Buttenwieser (1862-1939), *biblical scholar*

Jacob Mann (1888-1940), *historian*

Israel Bettan (1889-1940), *professor of homiletics*

Henry Slonimsky (1884-1970), *philosopher of religion*

FACULTY MEMBERS

Leo Baeck (1873-1956), *leader of German Jewry, arriving in Cincinnati in 1947, two years after his rescue from a concentration camp*

The faculty and class of 1927 of the Jewish Institute of Religion (*left to right, seated*): Nathan Krass, Henry Slonimsky, Stephen S. Wise (*president*), Julian J. Obermann, Chaim Tchernowitz; (*2nd row*): Windsor P. Daggett, Abraham W. Binder, Harry S. Lewis, Nisson Touroff, Sidney E. Goldstein, Zwi Diesendruck, Salo Baron, Joshua L. Goldberg; (*3rd row*): Gershon Tchernowitz, David P. Alpert (class of 1929), Harry Kaplan, Maurice J. Bloom, John J. Tepfer, Mitchell S. Fisher, Samuel Teitelbaum

Stephen S. Wise, JIR president, presents honorary degree scroll to Chaim Weizmann, February 26, 1940

At the opening of the Jerusalem School, March 27, 1963 (*left to right*): Carl William Blegen (*classical archaeologist, Cincinnati*), David Ben-Gurion (*Prime Minister of Israel*), Nelson Glueck (*president, HUC-JIR*), Walworth Barbour (*United States Ambassador to Israel*)

Combined faculty colloquium, Cincinnati, 1974 (*left to right, front row*): Michael Cook, Sheldon H. Blank, Alexander Guttmann, Alfred Gottschalk, Jacob R. Marcus, Paul M. Steinberg, Kenneth D. Roseman, Samuel Greengus, Lewis M. Barth; (*2nd row*): Ellis Rivkin, William Cutter, Judith Bisno, Lowell G. McCoy, Harry M. Orlinsky, Samuel Atlas, Stephen Passamaneck, Eugene B. Borowitz, Eugene Mihaly, Lennard R. Thal; (*3rd row*): Ben Zion Wacholder, Herbert C. Zafren, Matitiahu Tsevat, Sylvan D. Schwartzman, Nathaniel H. Karol, Jakob J. Petuchowski, Lawrence Hoffman, Norman B. Mirsky, Stanley Gewirtz; (*last row*): Uri D. Herscher, Werner Weinberg, Edward A. Goldman, Martin A. Cohen, Samson H. Levey, Samuel Sandmel, I. Edward Kiev, Michael A. Meyer, Herbert C. Brichto, Stanley F. Chyet, Fred Reiner

Isaac Mayer Wise, 1875-1900

PRESIDENTS

Kaufmann Kohler, 1903-1921

Julian Morgenstern, 1921-1947

PRESIDENTS

Stephen S. Wise, 1922-1948 (JIR)

Nelson Glueck, 1947-1971

PRESIDENTS

Alfred Gottschalk, 1971-

want to be sure that the center of our great American Reform Jewish rabbinical tradition remains, for as long as we can humanly provide for, on this campus in Cincinnati." [146]

In his role as president of the College-Institute, Glueck might have been the intellectual spokesman for Reform Judaism. Yet despite his brilliance as a scientist and man of practical affairs, he was not at home in the world of ideas. [147] He formulated no original theological views, no novel conception of Jewish life. Glueck possessed an unsophisticated though not primitive belief in God, never ceasing to wonder at the conceptual breakthrough from paganism to theism which he associated with Abraham. Though not at ease with all forms of Jewish expression or with all Jews, he believed in the genius of an idealized Jewish people. He possessed especially profound regard for Rabbi Leo Baeck, who had preferred to buoy up Jewish spirits in a concentration camp rather than to accept refuge in America, and he could never restrain his emotion when speaking of those Holocaust victims who had indomitably retained their faith even in the hour of death. To potential faculty and to students on the eve of ordination, Glueck frequently stressed the absolute importance of belief in God and the preservation of Judaism.

Like his predecessor, Glueck was not a ritually observant Jew. But at the same time he was insistent that the school display a certain degree of public religiosity. He introduced invocations and benedictions at faculty meetings; he was almost always present in chapel and insisted that faculty be there as well. Though in later years, and to certain people, he would speak proudly of himself as a "Litvak," in religious attitude Glueck, like Morgenstern, was very much the classical Reform Jew. His attitude tended increasingly to remove him from some of the younger rabbis and rabbinical students who were trying to find new meaning in what Reform had earlier left behind.

On the issue of Zionism, Glueck showed great ideological flexibility. Initially a proponent of bi-nationalism like his friend Judah Magnes, after the establishment of the State of Israel he became its ardent champion. Following the Six-Day War he enjoyed explaining to Israeli leaders that there was a biblical basis for the newly expanded boundaries. [148] What remained consistent over the years was Glueck's love of the land, especially of Jerusalem and the Negev desert. When he was in Israel Glueck was a different man. In Cincinnati he felt compelled to represent the dignified, distant, and restrained head of a rabbinical seminary. In Israel he could be Professor Glueck, the archaeologist, the romantic, uninhibited explorer of desert wastelands. In Cincinnati he was always formal in attire and manner, in Jerusalem he dressed casually and mingled easily.

Shortly before his death, Glueck presented an honorary degree to Prime Minister Golda Meir when the College-Institute dedicated a second building in Jerusalem. That stone structure, overlooking the Old City, contained a lavish apartment in which the Gluecks hoped to live following his retirement. For a long time Glueck had wished to spend more time in Israel. With the building's completion he looked forward to the possibility of finally realizing his desire.

Perhaps Glueck's greatest strength—and conversely his most unsettling attribute—was that he tended to act by instinct. He pursued his own ideas—or those of others which he adopted—with little pause for reflection lest their driving force be dissipated. Under his leadership great strides were taken; at the time of his death the consequences were not yet fully apparent.

In the course of almost a century, by 1971, the Hebrew Union College and the Jewish Institute of Religion, separately and then together, had made an immense contribution to Jewish religious life and scholarship in the United States. Over thirteen hundred rabbis had been ordained. The Graduate School had granted about fifty Ph.D.'s and a far larger number of *in-absentia* earned doctoral degrees. Over the years the school had helped to supply the Reform movement with trained religious educators and, more recently, to serve the larger community with cantors and Jewishly trained professionals. Its library in Cincinnati now contained more than two hundred thousand volumes, with about half that number in New York and growing collections in Los Angeles and Jerusalem. The American Jewish Archives was drawing scholars to Cincinnati while the museum, shortly to be located in the new building in Los Angeles, would bring large crowds to the western campus. The faculty's publications and those sponsored by the school, especially the highly regarded *Hebrew Union College Annual,* had established the academic reputation of the school to the point of eminence. As the College-Institute approached its centennial in 1975, there was every reason for pride in achievement and for the hope of an even more significant role in the second hundred years.

Yet there was also some disquiet, some uncertainty, some awareness of problems that needed to be resolved and of certain questions that perhaps would always be with the school. Of most immediate concern was the financial security of the institution. By 1970, its budget had grown to over $3,400,000 and it had begun to experience large deficits. Critics had argued that it was not justifiable to maintain four separate campuses with the degree of duplication which that involved. Yet each campus had much to recommend it and had vocal supporters speaking out on its behalf. Cincinnati, the oldest campus, possessed unrivaled facilities and an atmosphere conducive to serious study. The New York and Los Angeles schools had the advantage of being located in the two largest American Jewish communities with the concomitant potential for direct impact on American Jewry. The Jerusalem School was important not only for its archaeological program, but even more as an increasingly significant spiritual link between the Reform movement and the Jews of Israel; serious thought was being given to ordaining young Israelis there.[149]

There was also the question of the school's very nature. From time to time, and especially in Glueck's last years, some members of the Reform rabbinate had argued that the College-Institute's campuses should be related directly to leading American universities. It was felt that such a relationship—beyond what already existed with local universities—would open the HUC-JIR more to contemporary trends in allied fields of creative thought and scholarship. It would also bring the Cincinnati School, in particular, out of what some regarded as a certain degree of cloistered intellectual isolation. Opponents of the proposal, in turn, held that it was more important to maintain the separate identity of the College-Institute and to avoid submergence into a larger institution.

The issues of geographical location and close university affiliation were linked in turn to the unresolved—and perhaps unresolvable—

question of what constitutes an ideal rabbinical education. In the late sixties new alternative forms of seminary education were beginning to appear in the Christian world. In the Jewish community the Reconstructionists had established a rabbinical school in Philadelphia in conjunction with Temple University, and an informal *ḥavura* program had come into existence in Massachusetts. However small these new institutions, they were a potent factor in making HUC-JIR, the oldest rabbinical school in America, reexamine its own assumptions.

Under Glueck, the College-Institute intensified its commitment to the tradition of *Wissenschaft des Judentums:* analytic, dispassionate textual study focused more on linguistic and historical understanding than on contemporary significance. Though there continued to be courses in subjects of immediate application to the rabbinate, a large portion of the students' time was absorbed in learning disciplines which would be of little direct value after ordination. The issue was ever raised anew: Was it the College-Institute's task to create rabbis who measured up to the scholarly model held by some of the faculty, or to devote itself primarily to developing professional skills, as advocated by other faculty and some rabbis? The question was a source of frequent crises in student morale and consequent faculty discussions on how to deal with them.[150]

And yet certain commitments and objectives remained basic and apparently irrevocable for faculty and students alike. Freedom of inquiry, it was certain, would be maintained regardless of pressures, as would the broadest latitude both in theology and in religious practice. Students would not be indoctrinated into a single narrow conception of Judaism, but would be encouraged to find their own position through exposure to the differing, and often conflicting, views of the faculty. While the various graduate and professional programs would be expanded, the central purpose of the institution would continue to be the education of rabbis. In training them, the school would ever be at pains to shape and reshape its curriculum, continually seeking the right balance between knowledge of sources and professional skills, between preparation for the role of scholar-teacher and training in the specific expertise necessary for practical work. Above all, the College-Institute would endeavor to approach the difficult goal of being both an academic institution committed to standards of achievement and at the same time a religious community recognizing the ultimate worth of each individual.

Shortly before Nelson Glueck died, the Board of Governors selected Alfred Gottschalk, dean of the Los Angeles campus, to be the fifth regular president of the school. Gottschalk's inauguration, early in 1972, came just as the College-Institute stood at the threshold of a long anticipated centennial celebration. It was clearly a time for recalling and reevaluating the past. A new period in the school's history had begun.

Abbreviations

AI	*American Israelite*
AJA	American Jewish Archives, Cincinnati, Ohio
AJA	*American Jewish Archives* (the journal)
BGM	Board of Governors Minutes
BTM	Board of Trustees Minutes, Jewish Institute of Religion
CCARJ	*Central Conference of American Rabbis Journal*
CCARY	*Central Conference of American Rabbis Yearbook*
FM	Faculty Minutes, Cincinnati
FMJIR	Faculty Minutes, Jewish Institute of Religion
HUCA	*Hebrew Union College Annual*
HUCB	*Hebrew Union College Bulletin* (later *HUC-JIR Bulletin*)
HUCM	*Hebrew Union College Monthly*
JSS	*Jewish Social Studies*
LJ	*Liberal Judaism*
UAHCP	*Union of American Hebrew Congregations Proceedings*

Notes

Preface

1. S. Mannheimer, "History of the Hebrew Union College," *The Menorah*, April–Oct., 1892; David Philipson, "The History of the Hebrew Union College," *Hebrew Union College Jubilee Volume* (Cincinnati, 1925), pp. 1–70; Samuel S. Cohon, "The History of the Hebrew Union College," *Publications of the American Jewish Historical Society*, XL (1950–51), 17–55. A collection of documents was published in *AJA*, Nov. 1974. A brief history of the JIR, by I. Edward Kiev and John J. Tepfer, appeared in the *American Jewish Year Book*, 1947–48, pp. 91–100.

2. I have also used recorded interviews conducted by Daniel Syme with Helen Glueck and Maurice Eisendrath; and by Stanley Chyet (joined by students) with Dora Aaronsohn, Maxwell Lyons, and Jacob R. Marcus.

In the Days of Isaac Mayer Wise

1. *AI*, Oct. 8, 1875. (It is of course possible that the reporter was I. M. Wise himself.)

2. For a detailed treatment, see my "Christian Influence on Early German Reform Judaism," *I. Edward Kiev Festschrift*, ed. Charles Berlin (New York, 1971), pp. 289–303.

3. Jacob Mann, "Modern Rabbinical Seminaries and Other Institutions of Jewish Learning," *CCARY*, XXXV (1925), 295–310.

4. Book-length treatments include: Max B. May, *Isaac Mayer Wise, the Founder of American Judaism* (New York, 1916); Israel Knox, *Rabbi in America* (Boston, 1957); and James G. Heller, *Isaac M. Wise: His Life, Work and Thought* (New York, 1965). A striking exception to the rule is the critical treatment by Sefton David Temkin, "Isaac Mayer Wise, 1819-1875" (doctoral diss., HUC-JIR, 1963).

5. May, p. 22.

6. Joseph Gutmann, "Watchman on an American Rhine," *AJA*, X (1958), 135–44.

7. For Wise's years in Europe, see especially Temkin, pp. 1–87.

8. Isaac M. Wise, *Reminiscences*, trans. and ed. David Philipson (Cincinnati, 1901), pp. 14–16. (These recollections first appeared in the *Deborah* in 1874–75.) It is of course possible that Wise composed the dream later as a literary device. But even if that be the case, it would simply indicate that Wise was conscious of the pattern of his life and sought in this manner to dramatize it.

9. See *Reminiscences,* pp. 92, 97–98, 126–27, 141–42, 144, 204–5, 208, 257, 265.

10. Barnett R. Brickner, "The Jewish Community of Cincinnati, Historical and Descriptive, 1817–1933" (doctoral diss., University of Cincinnati, 1933); Temkin, pp. 315, 402–3.

11. *Occident,* VI (1848), 433.

12. Leon A. Jick, "The Efforts of Isaac Mayer Wise to Establish a Jewish College in the United States" (unpublished paper, n.d.), AJA Box 1278.

13. Bertram Wallace Korn, "The First American Jewish Theological Seminary," in his *Eventful Years and Experiences* (Cincinnati, 1954), pp. 151–213.

14. Adler's letter of Feb. 13, 1873 to the president and Board of Trustees of Congregation Bene Yeshurun was followed by a formal contract signed on May 15th of the same year. Both are contained in the American Jewish Archives. The letter was later printed in *UAHCP,* I (1873–79), v–vi. Adler's gift was first announced in *AI,* Dec. 9, 1870. At the dedication of the College building in 1881, Moritz Loth, the president of the Union's Executive Board, said that it was this gift which "gave an impetus of holding a convention of congregations in July 1873" (*AI,* April 29, 1881). It is also possible that Wise's threat to leave Cincinnati and accept an offer he had received from Congregation Anshe Chesed of New York in 1873 may have had the effect not only of increasing his salary but also of spurring the lay leadership to proceed rapidly in establishing the College. On this point see Dena Wilansky, *Sinai to Cincinnati* (New York, 1937), pp. 284–88.

15. *UAHCP,* I, i–xiii, 3–26.
16. Ibid., 37, 82, 97, 118–20, 140, 145.
17. Ibid., 202.
18. In the *AI* for Oct. 22, 1875, he wrote: "No college of this kind has ever opened with a larger class or with better talent. We feel perfectly satisfied with the start, which appears very promising to us, as regards both number and talent, and when among the class feel as happy as a king."
19. Isaac Mayer Wise, "The World of My Books," trans. Albert H. Friedlander, *AJA,* VI (1954), 141. These autobiographical fragments appeared in the *Deborah* in 1896–97.
20. *UAHCP,* II (1879–85), 928, 933–38; David Philipson, *My Life as an American Jew* (Cincinnati, 1941), p. 12. In 1878, the school adopted a seal, proposed by Wise, with two mottos: *ḥatom tora belimudai* ("Seal the instruction among My disciples": Isa. 8:16) and *ha-boker or* ("The morning's light": Gen. 44:3). The stationery was inscribed with *shalom rav le-ohave toratekha* ("Great peace have they that love Thy law": Ps. 119:165).
21. *UAHCP,* I, 148–49. A later, somewhat more modest curriculum is to be found in *Programme of the Hebrew Union College, 1894–1895,* pp. 15–16. This is the first regular catalogue that was issued.
22. Philipson, *My Life,* pp. 10–11; *UAHCP,* I, 369–73.
23. I. M. Wise, *Propositions Respectfully Submitted to the Gentlemen of the Commission Appointed by the Council of the Union of American Hebrew Congregations* (Cincinnati, 1878); "Dissenting Report of Isaac M. Wise to the Union of American Hebrew Congregations," n.d., AJA Documents Files. The Commission report is in *UAHCP,* I, 700–708.
24. In 1876 Wise had been requested by the Board of Governors to submit a plan for the study of German. When it was found that no adequate textbook was available in English for the study of Jewish history, he decided to use a German text by S. Baeck and thus to fulfill the wish of the board. Wise claimed that all of the first group of graduates were able to preach in German. See *UAHCP,* I, 248, 317, 639; II, 1386.
25. Ultimately Wise himself became convinced of the necessity of an additional year and recommended it to the Board of Governors in 1896 (*UAHCP,* IV [1891–97], 3614), but it was not instituted until the administration of Kaufmann Kohler.
26. *Programme,* pp. 17–19.
27. *UAHCP,* I, 342.
28. Ibid., II, 1535–36.
29. *Programme,* p. 20.
30. Ella Mielziner, *Moses Mielziner* (New York, 1931); *UAHCP,* I, 658–59; II, 1558–59. According to Kaufmann Kohler, Mielziner came to Cin-

cinnati at the urging of David Einhorn. This was after the enmity between the two men had somewhat abated (*CCARY*, XXIX [1919],
222).

31. *UAHCP,* I, 640–41.

32. Clifton Harby Levy, "How Well I Remember," *Liberal Judaism,* June
    1950, p. 33; Gotthard Deutsch Diary [in German], Dec. 19, 1893, AJA;
    BGM (preserved in the safe of the HUC-JIR, Cincinnati), July 2, 1889,
    Sept. 9, 1890 (these minutes are cited only for items not included in
    UAHCP); Zirndorf Papers, AJA Box 2288.

33. During 1882–83, Mielziner, the highest paid member of the faculty, re-
    ceived $2,400 per year; Solomon Eppinger earned only $1,200. The first
    ordinees each received $2,000 (Maximilian Heller to his parents, Nov.
    25, 1883, Heller Papers, AJA).

34. *UAHCP,* II, 993; III (1886–91), 1901; BGM, April 1, 1890.

35. *UAHCP,* I, 231–34.

36. The original copy is in the AJA. It appeared in print in 1879.

37. BGM, Sept. 2, 1878.

38. *UAHCP,* II, 1047; V (1898–1903), 3966; Adolph S. Oko, *A History of
    the Hebrew Union College Library and Museum* (Cincinnati, 1944), pp.
    1–2.

39. *UAHCP,* I, 467–69; II, 1526; III, 2561; IV, 2903–4; *AI,* Oct. 8, 1875;
    June 24, 1881; Joseph L. Fink, "Israel Aaron—the First Graduate of the
    H.U.C.," *CCARJ,* Oct. 1960, pp. 34–35; David Philipson, "Personal
    Contacts with the Founder of the Hebrew Union College," *HUCA,* XI
    (1936), 1–4.

40. Deutsch Diary, June 19, 1897.

41. *UAHCP,* I, 339; III, 2208; V, 3900; Reports to the Board of Governors
    of the College by Isaac M. Wise, May 4, 1896–Jan. 30, 1900, AJA Docu-
    ments Files.

42. Levy, March 1951, pp. 14–17.

43. BGM, Nov. 4, 1878; *UAHCP,* III, 2360–62.

44. Richard Hofstadter and C. DeWitt Hardy, *The Development and Scope
    of Higher Education in the United States* (New York, 1952), p. 17.

45. *Telling Tales Out of School,* ed. Stanley R. Brav (*Cincinnati,* 1965), pp.
    5–6, 61, 63.

46. *UAHCP,* II, 1006–7. The reason for this action, however, was to gain
    resident status and hence free tuition at the high school and university
    (ibid., V, 3967).

47. Ibid., III, 2933. Deutsch noted in his diary for April 9, 1892: "Das Ganze
    macht einen sehr peinl.[ichen] Eindruck, bes.[onders] das schulbuben-
    mässige Behandeln der Jungen." For the experience of the *Hochschule*

für die Wissenschaft des Judentums, see its *Festschrift zur Einweihung des eigenen Heims* (Berlin, 1907), pp. 53–55.

48. *UAHCP,* III, 2746–48; *AI,* March 12, 1891.
49. Levy, March 1951, p. 17; *Tales,* p. 7; Heller to his parents, June 19, 1882, Nov. 25, 1883, Heller Papers.
50. *UAHCP,* I, 229; II, 1490. In the nineties both sections of the *Atzile Bene Yisrael* ceased to exist. They were replaced by a variety of other student societies.
51. A hectograph version of the *HUC Journal,* on a much lower level, appeared for three issues from January through March 1896. The printed magazine began to appear in October of the same year. When requested to endorse the journal to the public, the Board of Governors refused to do so and indicated that it "did not wish to be understood as being in any degree responsible, financially or otherwise, for the publication. . . ." (BGM, Executive Session, April 6, 1897).
52. *HUC Journal,* III (1898–99), 36, 72, 208.
53. *UAHCP,* II, 1214, 1490; III, 2548.
54. Ibid., I, 317; III, 2362.
55. Ibid., IV, 3788.
56. *HUC Journal,* III, 185–87.
57. All information on income and allocations is contained in the various volumes of *UAHCP.*
58. *UAHCP,* I, 37, 118; IV, 3664.
59. Ibid., II, 1443. A scrapbook of clippings devoted to this subject is in AJA Box X-2.
60. In 1883 this provision was changed through a constitutional amendment providing that all donations and bequests not otherwise specified would go to the general fund (*UAHCP,* II, 1416).
61. Ibid., 1457, 1567, 1592.
62. In a crossed-out section of the original draft of his report to the Board of Governors for 1897, Wise wrote: "No efforts have been made for the last fifteen years to better the financial status of this institute. We have been placed before the public and before our own employees as seekers of charity" (Reports to the Board of Governors of the College, AJA Documents Files).
63. Some elements in the Union regarded the purchase of the building as a "stretch of authority" (*UAHCP,* II, 1105). No amount even close to the originally stipulated $160,000 had been raised.
64. A table of expenditures for the College for the years 1875 to 1896 is given in ibid., IV, 3563.
65. Philipson, *My Life,* p. 12.
66. *UAHCP,* II, 1066.

67. Ibid., 1229.

68. Deutsch Diary, Feb. 25, 1894. According to the vice-president, Julius Freiberg, students were expected to possess tact and consideration for public opinion; they were to "learn Hebrew and behave like gentlemen" (ibid., Sept. 26, 1893, June 18, 1897).

69. *HUCM,* Nov. 1915, pp. 77–83.

70. David Philipson Diary, Sept. 11, 1890, AJA.

71. Brickner, pp. 66, 255–56.

72. Deutsch Diary, May 1, 1893.

73. Philipson Diary, Sept. 11, 1890.

74. *UAHCP,* I, 481–82; II, 1246–47, 1318; III, 2218; BGM, Nov. 6, 1882.

75. *UAHCP,* II, 1280.

76. Ibid., 1041; BGM, June 30, 1879.

77. Philipson, *My Life,* pp. 21–23; Israel Aaron Scrapbook, AJA Box X-83; *Allgemeine Zeitung des Judentums,* Sept. 11, 1883, p. 607.

78. In 1879 Mendes transmitted a resolution that pupils "who on their enrollment shall express the conscientious desire to study Hebrew with covered heads, in the olden fashion, shall be permitted to do . . . , " but he chose to withdraw the resolution before any action was taken (*UAHCP,* II, 838, 842).

79. Jick, p. 12.

80. *AI,* July 21, 1871. Wise later had the pleasure of having one of his first graduates, David Philipson, take over the pulpit of Einhorn's old congregation, Har Sinai of Baltimore. Noting this irony, one of the HUC students wrote: "So was hätte der sel.[ige] Einhorn wohl nie geträumt, dass ihm so bald nach der ersten Graduation ein Schüler des verpönten Dr. Wise auf seiner Kanzel folgen würde. Der Osten hat sich nunmehr dem Westen unterworfen" (Heller to his parents, Nov. 25, 1883, Heller Papers).

81. *UAHCP,* I, 239–40, 250–51.

82. It is put into perspective by Daniel Jeremy Silver, "The Trefa Banquet Story" (unpublished paper, n.d.), AJA Box 511. See also John J. Appel, "The Trefa Banquet," *Commentary,* Feb. 1966, pp. 75–78. A general treatment of the conflict is provided by Elbert L. Sapinsley, "The Causes of the Split Between the Conservative and Reform Movements in Judaism in the United States" (unpublished paper, 1955), AJA Box 1278.

83. Wise himself, however, later proposed that the College undertake the task of training an Americanized religious leadership for the new immigrants, the very goal which motivated a number of the lay supporters of the Jewish Theological Seminary (*UAHCP,* IV, 2934).

84. *AI,* Aug. 3, 1883, Dec. 28, 1883; May, p. 379.

85. *American Hebrew,* Jan. 8, 1886. (The excerpt is from a letter, signed

"Emeth," written by Jacob Ezekiel, secretary of the HUC Board of Governors.)

86. The degree required a thesis, plus an oral examination on one book of the Bible, one tractate of the Talmud, and one book of Hebraic philosophy or theology.

87. At first Wise was opposed to the granting of honorary degrees (*UAHCP*, II, 1042). Later he relented in order to give an honorary D.D. to Solomon Eppinger on his seventieth birthday in 1883. But the total number of such degrees during Wise's administration was only seven.

88. Andrew F. Key, *The Theology of Isaac Mayer Wise* (Cincinnati, 1962); Lawrence A. Block, "A Significant Controversy in the Life of Isaac M. Wise," *CCARJ*, June 1961, pp. 29–36; Ralph Mecklenburger, "The Theologies of Isaac Mayer Wise and Kaufmann Kohler" (rabbinical diss., HUC-JIR, Cincinnati, 1972).

89. Quoted in Heller, p. 476.

90. "Critical introduction to the history of the text and the old versions of the Bible, with reference to the modern works on textual criticism" appears in the suggested program of the Commission (*UAHCP*, I, 706). It does not appear in Wise's *Propositions*. In 1887 the examiners suggested that students be kept abreast of the latest methods of scientific biblical study (ibid., III, 2118).

91. Philipson, "Personal Contacts," pp. 5–6.

92. Wise, "The World of My Books," p. 37.

93. "Although I can not say that I have entirely succeeded in keeping out of these recitation rooms the latent spirit of agnosticism and materialism in the very atmosphere of the learned and learning world in which we must live and breathe; although furthermore I can not say that the spirit of negation, hypercriticism and habitual repetition of what opponents advance, who have not the duty to educate teachers in Israel and no presumptive critics, is banished entirely from these halls or could be done in the face of the modern literature on the subjects of our studies; yet I must say, I have those excrescences of the age under control, and counteract them to the best of my ability, without forcing the learned and learning into hypocrisy . . . " (Supplement to the Annual Report, 1897–98, Reports to the Board of Governors of the College, AJA Documents Files).

94. For example, when a student submitted as his thesis a critical treatment of "The Attitude of the Prophets to the Cult," Wise at a faculty meeting indicated that he would refuse to sign his diploma. The student, Max Cohen, was, however, ordained (Deutsch Diary, April 4, 1898). An article favorable to biblical criticism was printed in the *HUC Journal*, I (1896–97), 63–66.

95. *CCARY,* VIII (1898), xli; *UAHCP,* V, 4002.
96. *HUC Journal,* IV (1899–1900), 45–47. Cf. Melvin Weinman, "The Attitude of Isaac Mayer Wise toward Zionism and Palestine," *AJA,* III (1951), 3–23.
97. Reports of President I. M. Wise to Board of Governors of HUC, 1899–1900, AJA Documents Files; BGM, Executive Session, Feb. 27, 1900.
98. *CCARY,* IX (1899), 179–91; *HUC Journal,* III, 165–75.
99. Ibid., IV, 114.
100. Ibid., III, 61–62 (reprinted in *CCARJ,* Winter 1974, pp. 17–19).
101. Relations between the University of Cincinnati and the Hebrew Union College had originally been quite close. When a fire damaged the University in 1885, it accepted an offer to conduct classes for a time in the building of the HUC. Max Lilienthal served on the university's Board of Directors until his death in 1882; he was succeeded by Wise, who was a board member until 1898, when he resigned in the midst of the tuition controversy. In part to avoid the demand for payment of university tuition, the College opened a Semitics Department in 1896 with courses offered free of charge to students of the University of Cincinnati. (The department existed mainly in the catalogue and was officially abandoned in 1903.) But a new administration at the University refused to accept the proffered Semitics courses in lieu of tuition, and Wise was finally driven to the point of proposing to the HUC Board that the College undertake its own department of general studies. To Simon Wolf, Wise wrote on November 1, 1898: "We not only have no sinking fund to maintain the institute for two years without income, but stand now as beggars, I am ashamed to say, before the door of the university, which asks about $1200.00 tuition for the year for our non-resident students, and no funds to pay for it. We look like a bankrupt concern" (AJA Box 2333). On the bitter HUC-UC controversy, which resulted in the Board of Governors lending university tuition to HUC students, see various Board of Governors executive sessions beginning Jan. 7, 1896; *UAHCP,* V, 3967, 4000; Correspondence with the University of Cincinnati, AJA Correspondence Files.
102. Philipson Diary, Sept. 11, 1890.
103. The very evening of the day Wise buried his first wife, he met with Lilienthal and S. Wolfenstein to discuss the curriculum for the Preparatory Department of the College. According to Wolfenstein, Wise told his colleagues: "You might be surprised that I am with you after this day of sorrow, busy with our work, but I have disciplined myself during the years of my public activity so as not to permit my personal affairs to interfere with my duties as minister. I have become so objective that, if it could be done, I could take out my heart from its cavity and ana-

lyze its functions" (*Jewish Review and Observer,* Nov. 16, 1915, p. 4). Yet at the same time Wise was a passionate man. He was attached to his farm in the countryside north of Cincinnati, he wrote torrid love letters to Selma Bondi before she became his second wife, and he fathered a total of fourteen children—the last when he was well over sixty years old.

104. See Wise's letters to Rabbi Joseph Stolz in the forthcoming volume of *Michael,* III (Tel-Aviv, 1975).

A Theological School for Reform Judaism

1. *HUC Journal,* IV (1899–1900), 156–57.
2. *Reform Advocate,* XIX (1900), 247–48, 331–33.
3. See my "Differing Views of Modern Rabbinical Education in Germany in the 19th Century" [Hebrew] in the forthcoming *Proceedings of the Sixth World Congress of Jewish Studies.*
4. *Reform Advocate,* XIX, 315, 390, 459, 475.
5. *AI,* May 17 and 24, 1900; cf. Tobias Schanfarber in ibid., Feb. 2, 1905.
6. *American Hebrew,* June 8, 1900.
7. David Philipson, *My Life,* pp. 155–56.
8. BGM, Executive Session, Oct. 28, 1902; Bernhard Bettmann to J. Leonard Levy, Oct. 29, 1902, AJA uncat. According to the Philadelphia *Jewish Exponent,* Feb. 28, 1902, an earlier tentative approach had been made to Rabbi Joseph Krauskopf of Philadelphia.
9. There is still some uncertainty as to why Levy rejected the College's overtures, but correspondence between him and Bernhard Bettmann, recently donated to the American Jewish Archives, suggests his reluctance to attempt breaking a contract only recently made.
10. *UAHCP,* V, 4655.
11. Kohler to Bettmann, Feb. 24, 1903, "Hebrew Union College: Correspondence and Reports of the Board of Governors of the College, regarding the Election of Kaufmann Kohler as President," AJA Documents Files. Cf. Deutsch Diary, March 16, 1903.
12. Schiff's support of the Wise Memorial Fund did not meet expectations ("Hebrew Union College: Corres. of Jacob H. Schiff . . . Concerning Schiff's alleged $100,000 Pledge . . . , " AJA Correspondence Files).
13. In his original proposal to Kohler of February 11, 1903 (file cited in n. 11), Bernhard Bettmann included the following proposition for the candidate to accept: "That . . . in view of the recent liberal endowment of the Jewish Theological Seminary of America, which institution openly proclaims its purpose to perpetuate in this country the old-time rigid,

unyielding orthodoxy, against which, without surrendering one iota of the underlying eternal truths of Judaism, we have successfully waged war during the last half century, the separate and independent existence of the Hebrew Union College has become an absolute necessity, though we also wish to proclaim herewith our desire to maintain with the said institution the most friendly relations which will not involve the sacrifice of principle on either side." Perhaps upon Kohler's insistence, the text was altered to read: "That the independent and separate existence of the Hebrew Union College for the purpose of educating Rabbis and Teachers, who shall expound the principles of American Reform Judaism, is imperative." The latter version appears in *UAHCP*, VI (1903–7), 4924.

14. Kaufmann Kohler, "Personal Reminiscences of My Early Life," *HUCM*, May 1918, p. 229.

15. J. Leonard Levy to Bernhard Bettmann, Dec. 9, 1902, AJA uncat. For the negative evaluation of some alumni, see *JSS*, XXVII (1965), 81.

16. *HUCM*, June 1914, p. 8.

17. *Hebrew Union College and Other Addresses* (Cincinnati, 1916), pp. 323–36.

18. BGM, Nov. 30, 1909.

19. *UAHCP*, VI (1903–7), 4977.

20. BGM, Executive Session, Feb. 28, March 28, and April 26, 1905.

21. *UAHCP*, VI, 5231.

22. Deutsch Diary, Dec. 5, 1903.

23. The first reference to this policy is in ibid., Jan. 9, 1904.

24. Kohler to Isaac Bloom, secretary of the Board of Governors, July 26, 1903, file cited in n. 11.

25. BGM, Dec. 27, 1904.

26.
מרשות האל הגדול הגבור והנורא

משגב לעתות בצרה

מרשות התורה הקדושה

אשר נִתְּנָה לנו מורשה

מרשות הזקנים והחכמים

אשר עמדו לישראל מימות עולמים

מרשות זקן מדרשנו, לו אשתחוה אפים

אשר עוד מעט והיה לנו לעינים

מרשות החברים רבני הארץ

מדריכי עמם העומדים בפרץ

מרשות חברי חכמי הישיבה

הנלוים עלי באהבה וחבה

הנני מעטירכם עטרה

ברכות יעטה מורה
והנני סומך את ידי עליכם
למלא ידכם לאלהיכם
יורה יורה ידין ידין
להורות דת אל לעם מבין

Contained in the Deutsch Diary, June 28, 1903.

27. *UAHCP*, VI, 4977.
28. *Catalog*, May 1906, p. 13, *UAHCP*, VI, 4999.
29. "The Four Ells of the Halakah," *HUCA*, I (1904), 10.
30. The Teachers' Institute was made possible by an endowment of $100,000, given by Jacob H. Schiff and divided between the Jewish Theological Seminary and the College. The HUC Institute in Cincinnati remained very small but expanded its range by conducting summer sessions in Chicago and Cleveland and winter courses in New York. It also sponsored extension lectures in other cities.
31. Somewhat later all students were required to teach for at least three years in a local religious school. The first year was supposed to be without compensation (*Catalog*, 1916–17).
32. Though he was a Zionist (and later became the first president of the Hebrew University), I have found no evidence that Magnes was forced or pressured to leave.
33. Ephraim Feldman to Gotthard Deutsch, June 16, 1904 (AJA Correspondence Files): "Let me incidentally accentuate my great pleasure at seeing you addressed as the Dean of the Faculty, which, in these degenerate days, is one of the few things in our College which are as they ought to be."
34. A board member, Louis S. Levi, purportedly told him: "You were my choice and also of several other members of the Board, but they thought they must have a man of national reputation to get the money . . . " (Deutsch Diary, March 16, 1903).
35. *CCARY*, XIII (1903), 227; XV (1905), 104.
36. "Why I am a Zionist," *Jewish Comment*, Feb. 8, 1907.
37. Feldman saved himself by gathering certificates attesting to the quality of his earlier academic work (Deutsch Diary, Sept. 13, 1905; Joseph Stolz Papers, AJA Box 2119). Levias remained on the payroll until 1906.
38. Deutsch Diary, Oct. 20, 1905.
39. On the dispute see Naomi Wiener Cohen, "The Reaction of Reform Judaism in America to Political Zionism (1897–1922)," *Publications of the American Jewish Historical Society*, XL (1950–51), 372–82.
40. For all the preceding, see Malter's revealing Hebrew letters to David

Neumark (himself later a member of the HUC faculty) in *Ha-Toren,* July 1925, pp. 61–72. In one letter, early in 1902, he wrote: "I have never liked this college, its founder, its instructors, its task and its operation. . . . *I should be most happy* were the College to flounder and even happier were it to collapse completely—even though I should then be destroyed with it. But 'Let me die with the Philistines!' "

41. BGM, Executive Session, May 15 and 31, 1906.

42. Ibid., Regular Session, Jan. 29, 1907.

43. Evyatar Friesel, *Ha-Tenua ha-Tzionit be-Artzot ha-Berit* (Tel-Aviv, 1970), pp. 95–97.

44. Harry M. Hoffheimer at the board meeting of Feb. 26, 1907.

45. Only a few weeks earlier, Levin—remarkably—had been allowed to give a Zionist lecture in Hebrew at the College. When he finished, Kohler arose to "correct" his Zionist statements regarding the Jews of America (BGM, Dec. 27, 1906).

46. BGM, Executive Session, Feb. 26 and March 3, 1907.

47. Already in 1898 Wise had wanted to get Margolis back from the University of California, but Margolis laid down conditions for himself so much more favorable than those granted to the other members of the faculty that the board had no choice but to reject them (ibid., Sept. 20, 1898).

48. Later, however, after Margolis, together with Malter, had joined the faculty of Dropsie College in Philadelphia (founded in 1909), Kohler was able to work with them on scholarly projects. Both men contributed articles to the Kohler *Festschrift,* which the College published in 1913.

49. Julian Morgenstern, as noted by Naomi Wiener Cohen, p. 167.

50. "Why I Am a Zionist," Feb. 8, 1907, and the rejoinder, Feb. 22, 1907.

51. Later printed as "The Message of Moses," *Maccabean,* Feb. 1907.

52. BGM, April 30, 1907. However, in the *American Israelite,* Feb. 28, 1907, Margolis had been very explicit with regard to the Second Isaiah: "The great Babylonian prophet who is made responsible for all the universalism ascribed to the prophets is a Zionist. . . . Modern preachers, in reading from the Second (or Third?) Isaiah are forced to castrate the beautiful sixtieth chapter for instance, lest their congregations be infected with the Zionist heresy."

53. *Jewish Exponent* of Philadelphia, April 5, 1907; *Reform Advocate* of Chicago, April 6, 1907.

54. BGM, Executive Session, April 5, 1898.

55. *American Jewish Chronicle,* I (1916), 612, 637.

56. Jacob H. Kaplan to Board of Governors, Nov. 13, 1919, AJA Box 1205.

57. FM, May 23, 1919.

58. Stanley F. Chyet et al., Interviews with Jacob R. Marcus on the "History of the Hebrew Union College," April–May 1963, AJA Tape 11.

59. FM, April 10, 1913. Later there were clashes between faculty and board regarding their respective prerogatives. See ibid., Jan. 21 and April 20, 1920.

60. See Zane Miller, *Boss Cox's Cincinnati* (New York, 1968).

61. AJA Box 1258.

62. *UAHCP,* VI, 5553; VIII (1911–15), 7030.

63. Ibid., 7202–7.

64. Kohler was one of the speakers at the dedication ceremony of the Seminary in New York. Upon his selection as president, the students of the JTS wrote a letter to their fellows in Cincinnati tendering congratulations. When Schechter died in 1915, the College held a memorial service for him presided over by the president of the Board of Governors, and the students devoted an issue of the *HUC Monthly* (Jan. 1916) to his memory. The relation between the two institutions during this period receives detailed treatment in Howard Allen Berman, "His Majesty's Loyal Opponents" (rabbinical diss., HUC-JIR, Cincinnati, 1974).

65. Deutsch Diary, April 4, 1912.

66. *UAHCP,* VI, 5001.

67. *HUCM,* Feb. 1918, pp. 149–55.

68. BGM, May 31, 1922.

69. Adolph S. Oko, *A History of the Hebrew Union College Library and Museum* (Cincinnati, 1944); *Union Bulletin,* Sept. 1913, pp. 16–23.

70. BGM, Feb. 27, 1912.

71. *HUCM,* Nov. 1920, p. 23.

72. The Hebrew letters yielded the *atbash* equivalents: mem, lamed, alef, the first letters of the biblical verse: *"mi ladonai elai"* (Exod. 32:26). The principal leaders of the fraternity were James G. Heller and Barnett Brickner (Harvey E. Wessel to Edward P. Cohn, July 26, 1973, AJA uncat.).

73. Abraham N. Franzblau, "A Quarter-Century of Rabbinical Training at the Hebrew Union College," mimeographed (Cincinnati, 1933).

74. *Catalog,* 1905, p. 16.

75. BGM, Oct. 29, 1912. As entering students could not receive scholarships or loans during their first year, the percentage of those eligible who received aid was over 90 percent.

76. Board of Governors to Rabbi Henry Cohen, Dec. 4, 1916, AJA Box 1201.

77. BGM, Executive Session, June 29, 1909; AJA Box 1251.

78. Deutsch Diary, Nov. 28, 1904.

79. Stanley F. Chyet et al., Interview with Dora Aaronsohn, May 14, 1963, AJA Tape 13.

80. Kohler to Board of Governors, Dec. 22, 1919, AJA Box 1205.
81. Henry Hurwitz and I. Leo Sharfman, *The Menorah Movement* (Ann Arbor, 1914), pp. 83–84. On another occasion, according to Emil G. Hirsch, Kallen publicly expressed his contempt for religion and for the rabbinate as a profession (*UAHCP,* VIII, 7744).
82. Jan. 6, 1915, AJA Box 1255. The letter was signed by Samuel S. Mayerberg, Simon Cohen, Israel J. Sarasohn, and James G. Heller.
83. FM, Feb. 9 and 10, March 5, 1915. A slightly similar but far more complex incident occurred a few years later on account of the November 1920 issue of the *HUC Monthly.* It contained a rather innocuous piece by Sheldon Blank entitled "The New Ecclesiastes" which counseled fellow students: "Don't wait nine years, you young men, to start living!" Though open to interpretation as hedonistic, it was not so necessarily. The following editorial by Samuel Rosenberg, however, left no doubt of its intent. Written in a cynical tone, it mocked the College and indirectly complained of the fact that "life at H.U.C. must perforce be austere and to a degree ascetic. The urgent realities of the flesh must go unheeded. The restlessness and melancholy which come from an inhibited libido are a typical H.U.C. complex. And such repression has also its morbid and vexing psychic overtones." In a second editorial, Rosenberg heaped scorn on the hyperpatriotism of American rabbis who "bleat in nauseating unison of the high ethical virtue of unquestioning conformity to the State. The gross maniacal [Louis Grossmann] Phillipics [David Philipson] of our prelates during the recent Holy War are still ringing in the ears of many of us." Finally, in the same issue, Ferdinand Isserman, then chairman of the Literary Society, listed the speakers who, subject to the president's approval, would be invited that year. As some of the names were apparently not acceptable to Kohler, it was thought that Isserman was trying to force his agreement by publishing them. While Blank's piece was not considered a serious offense, the faculty, in conjunction with the Board of Governors, launched a protracted inquiry into the conduct of Rosenberg and Isserman. Ultimately Rosenberg resigned while Isserman was placed on probation. It is no doubt significant that earlier that year Rosenberg had been investigated by a Board of Governors committee headed by Philipson for distributing a Bolshevist publication at the College while Isserman was described by one faculty member as a "leftist." (On the case see the relevant minutes of the Board of Governors and the faculty as well as AJA Box 1206). The *Monthly* was at first suspended, then briefly made subject to approval by a committee of the faculty; but already in March 1921 the faculty voted to abolish its censorship.
84. BGM, Feb. 23, 1915. Wise and Heller were able to secure the local assist-

ance of Rabbi Louis Grossmann. Their strategy, in advance of the meeting, was to force concessions from Kohler, not to depose him. They feared that otherwise they might play into the hands of David Philipson, a more formidable adversary (and Grossmann's rival), who was then planning to succeed Kohler. (See the Wise-Heller correspondence in the Stephen S. Wise Papers at the American Jewish Historical Society, Waltham, Mass.)

85. *HUCM,* March 1916, pp. 188–99.
86. Jacob R. Marcus Diary, March 12, 1921, AJA Box 2383. On June 25, 1922, Kohler wrote to Alfred M. Cohen (AJA Box 1261): "Thanks to the hearty cooperation of your honored Board I have been able, though not without opposition at times, to establish the College on the basis of a broader and deeper scholarship joined with true reverence for the God of our fathers and upon the principles of outspoken and positive American Reform Judaism, free from Radicalism and Romanticism and as far as I could, also from Nationalism and Zionism."
87. See G. A. Dobbert, "The Ordeal of Gotthard Deutsch," *AJA,* XX (1968), 129–55.
88. On Deutsch see *HUCM,* May 1916, March 1922.
89. In 1919, following a Hebrew address at the College by M. Scheinkin, a writer for *Ha-Toren,* Deutsch began to give some of his lectures in the Collegiate Department in Hebrew (ibid., March 1919).
90. Deutsch Diary, April 14, 1917.
91. BGM, Nov. 27, 1917.
92. In 1913 the UAHC had requested the Board of Governors to create an Advisory Board composed of its own members together with representatives of the CCAR and the HUC Alumni Association. Though this board did meet annually to exchange ideas, it possessed no significant influence.
93. AJA Scrapbook 136; Marcus Interviews, Tape 11.
94. Marcus Interviews, Tape 9; cf. Marcus Diary, March 13 and Sept. 26, 1921.
95. *UAHCP,* VII (1907–11), 6111, 6687; IX (1916–20), 8582; X (1921–25), 9135.
96. James G. Heller to Max Heller, March 5, 1913, AJA Box 519; Deutsch Diary, Sept. 5, 1912; Marcus Interviews, Tape 11; *Telling Tales Out of School,* ed. Stanley R. Brav (Cincinnati, 1965), pp. 72–75.

American Rabbis for American Israel

1. Jacob R. Marcus Diary, March 12, 1921, AJA Box 2383.
2. BGM, Nov. 1, 1921, as corrected Nov. 29, 1921.

3. Had Philipson succeeded in gaining the presidency, he would doubtless have continued Kohler's policy of enforcing strict ideological conformity. When Morgenstern on one occasion expressed himself against Zionism with unusual force in his opening-day address of 1931, Philipson noted in his diary with obvious satisfaction and probable exaggeration: "He as much as served notice on the Zionist members of the Faculty and on the Zionist students that this is an institution of Reform Judaism and that one of the marks of Reform Judaism is the repudiation of the nationalistic interpretation that Zionism stands for" (Philipson Diaries, Sept. 27, 1931, AJA Box 1323).

4. Louis Finkelstein, ed., *Thirteen Americans: Their Spiritual Autobiographies* (New York, 1953), p. 267. The member of the faculty was probably Jacob Z. Lauterbach.

5. Philipson Diaries, March 19, 1931.

6. Morgenstern to Berkowitz, March 16, 1921, William Rosenau Correspondence, AJA Box 2330. Morgenstern also enjoyed the support of Rabbi Leo M. Franklin of Detroit, the current president of the CCAR (AJA Box 3205, File F) and of influential board member Rabbi Louis Wolsey of Cleveland (AJA Box 3208, File W-Z).

7. BGM, Feb. 28, May 31, and Oct. 31, 1922; *Union Bulletin*, Nov. 1922, p. 16.

8. Finkelstein, pp. 253–62; Morgenstern Autobiographical Questionnaire, AJA Autobiographies; *HUCB*, May 1947.

9. Julian Morgenstern, *The Doctrine of Sin in the Babylonian Religion* (Berlin, 1905); Bernard Bamberger, "The Impact of Julian Morgenstern on American Jewish Life," *CCARJ*, April 1957, pp. 1–4; Morris Lieberman, "Julian Morgenstern—Scholar, Teacher and Leader," *HUCA*, XXXII (1961), 1–9; Joshua L. Liebman, "Kindler of Mental Light," *LJ*, Nov. 1945, pp. 18–23.

10. See especially the essays and addresses gathered in *As a Mighty Stream* (Philadelphia, 1949).

11. See the following chapter.

12. *HUCM*, May 1937, Dec. 1940; *Telling Tales Out of School* (Cincinnati, 1965), pp. 148–59. Perhaps because of his lack of success as a teacher, Mann for a time felt insecure in his position. When Jacob R. Marcus returned from his historical studies abroad in 1926, Mann was concerned that Marcus not "encroach" on any of his teaching prerogatives. Apparently he feared that students would prefer to study with his more attractive, if less erudite, colleague. (See the Morgenstern-Mann correspondence in AJA Box 1559, File M, and the Morgenstern-Marcus correspondence in AJA Box 1560.)

13. See especially the *Israel Bettan Memorial Volume* (New York, 1961).

14. The Pledge is preserved in AJA Box 2397.

15. *HUCM,* Feb. 1935; Cronbach to David Philipson, Dec. 4, 1935, AJA Box 1552, File C.

16. Abraham Cronbach, "Autobiography," *AJA,* XI (1959), 3–81; idem, *Religion and Its Social Setting* (Cincinnati, 1933); Morgenstern to Stanley R. Brav, Nov. 17, 1944, AJA Morgenstern Correspondence; Michael Aaronsohn, *That the Living May Know* (Cincinnati, 1973), pp. 97–101.

17. Philipson, who favored Enelow, believed Morgenstern rejected him because he "cannot endure a great personality on his faculty" (Philipson Diaries, Feb. 23, 1934). See also Morgenstern to Samuel H. Goldenson, May 4, 1922, AJA Box 1260. When Enelow died in 1934, he left his valuable library to the Jewish Theological Seminary although he had graduated from HUC.

18. See my "Samuel S. Cohon: Reformer of Reform Judaism," *Judaism,* XV (1966), 319–28.

19. *CCARY,* XXX (1920), 56–57; *UAHCP,* X (1921–25), 8854; *Catalogue,* 1923–24, p. 76.

20. BGM, June 30, 1925; cf. June 29, 1926, June 27, 1927.

21. See *Catalog,* May, 1906.

22. FM, Feb. 12, 1919.

23. *Catalogue,* 1924–25, pp. 27–29; 1925–26, p. 25; FM, April 22, 1925.

24. E.g., FM, Nov. 30, 1925.

25. The required use of Hebrew sources in theses was first proposed by Neumark at a meeting of the faculty on March 22, 1920. A motion to that effect, initiated by Lauterbach, was passed on Dec. 10, 1930. Yet in 1934 the faculty allowed a thesis on the subject: "The Assembly as an Instrument in Religious Education." On the other hand, in 1939, a thesis topic was rejected because it required no Hebrew sources (FM, April 24, 1939). By 1940 the requirement was dropped from the catalogue.

26. *FM,* May 26, 1921. The faculty reversed its decision a few weeks later after Martha failed to pass one of Morgenstern's courses. At that point only Marcus still favored her cause (ibid., June 15, 1921). Her grades generally were at best mediocre (AJA Microfilm 118).

27. BGM, June 29, 1921.

28. FM, Dec. 21, 1921, Jan. 25 and Jan. 30, 1922; H.U.C. Correspondence and Resolution Regarding Women Rabbis, AJA Miscellaneous Files.

29. *CCARY,* XXXII (1922), 51, 156–77. A joint meeting of the Board of Governors and the Advisory Board, in which rabbis were in the majority over laymen, had already voted on Oct. 31, 1922 to request the board "to amend the rules of the College so as to admit women to ordination as rabbis."

30. BGM, Feb. 27, 1923. There was no woman on the Board of Governors until the appointment of Mrs. Leon L. Watters from New York in 1938.

31. Morgenstern to Jacob R. Marcus, April 8, 1926, AJA Box 1560; Morgenstern to Solomon Foster, July 5, 1934, AJA Box 1554; Philipson Diaries, Sept. 18, 1932, May 29, 1933; AJA Box 3207, Philipson File.

32. Morgenstern to William Rosenau, June 21, 1922, AJA Box 1261.

33. See Mack's "A Report of the Chairman of the Board," BGM, Oct. 20, 1937.

34. *HUCM,* Nov. 1922, p. 23.

35. Probably the extreme instance is that of novelist Lewis Browne, a one-time student at the College, who out of what can only be considered the utmost ill feeling toward Morgenstern created a vile character named Julian of the Morgii for his 1935 historical novel, *All Things Are Possible.*

36. FM, Dec. 9, 1924, Jan. 12, 1925.

37. Morgenstern to Jacob R. Marcus, Feb. 20, 1925, AJA Box 1560; BGM, Feb. 24 and March 31, 1925, Nov. 30, 1926.

38. *HUCM,* May 1915.

39. *Catalog,* 1918–19, 1921–22; *UAHCP,* X, 8854–55; *Union Bulletin,* Feb. 1922.

40. *HUCM,* March 1924; *Catalogue,* 1925–26.

41. *HUCM,* Nov. 1924, Feb. 1925; *Union Tidings,* Nov. 1924.

42. The HUC catalogues give the home cities of the students. A comparison of the backgrounds and attitudes of students in 1900 and 1930, based on a survey, is presented in *HUCM,* June 1930.

43. *HUCM,* Jan. 1925.

44. Morgenstern-Rosenau Correspondence, AJA Box 1561.

45. Morgenstern to I. E. Marcuson, March 18, 1932, AJA Box 1552, File C.C.A.R.

46. *Telling Tales Out of School,* pp. 106–7.

47. FM, Feb. 23, 1925, Jan. 25, 1933; BGM, Sept. 16, 1946; *HUCM,* Purim 1947.

48. Jacob J. Weinstein, diary entries for June 7, 1925 and June 7, 1927, in *HUCM,* June 1929.

49. One of the yells, at least, deserves citation:
    Midrash Rabbah Exodus
    Sam-u-el Leviticus
    Deut Ecclesiasticus
    Aramaic. Pity us.
    H.U.C.
    Songs and Yells of the Hebrew Union College Student Body (Cincinnati, 1923–24), contained in AJA Miscellaneous Files.

50. For the history of the *HUC Monthly*, see especially the Silver Anniversary Issue, Jan. 13, 1938.

51. See, for example, *Catalogue, 1928–29*, p. 37.

52. *HUCM,* June 1927, June 1929; AJA Box 2283; *Catalogue, 1933–34.*

53. FM, Jan. 18, 1932; *Bulletin of Alumni Association,* June 1935.

54. The figures are given in various volumes of the *American Jewish Year Book.*

55. BGM, June 29, 1921.

56. BGM, Nov. 30, 1926.

57. The program of the School for Teachers is given in the HUC catalogues from 1924–25 to 1931–32. For the history of the school, see in addition: BGM, Sept. 25, 1928, Nov. 27, 1928, Oct. 28, 1930, May 29, 1931, Jan. 27, 1932, May 17, 1932; AJA Box 1555, File H; Box 1556; Box 1561, File O.

58. AJA Box 1559, File M; BGM, May 23, 1930.

59. The recommendation had been made as early as Oct. 4, 1927 in a letter from Louis Ginzberg to David Philipson (AJA Box 1561, File P).

60. On Diesendruck see especially Joshua Loth Liebman's article in *HUCM,* Dec. 1940.

61. BGM, Jan. 27, 1930; AJA Box 2381i.

62. BGM, Nov. 25, 1924, Jan. 29, 1926. Leading rabbis, like Louis Mann of Chicago, however, were earning $15,000 per year as early as 1923 (*Union Bulletin,* May–June 1923, p. 9).

63. BGM, May 25, 1926.

64. *UAHCP,* XII (1931–35), 552; BGM, Jan. 15, 1947. The first recipient was Jacob R. Marcus.

65. BGM, Jan. 29, 1926; FM, May 30, 1928. A decade later the overall average was eleven hours per week (BGM, May 25, 1939).

66. *UAHCP,* XI (1926–30), 254.

67. *Union Tidings, Nov. 1924.* It is telling for the attitude of the Reform Jewish leadership at the time that a number of the respondents welcomed the restrictions on immigration.

68. As Ochs was ill and therefore unable to attend in person, the proposal was made in the form of a letter to Rabbi Nathan Krass of Temple Emanu-El, who in turn presented it to the Council (*UAHCP,* X, 9784–85).

69. Morgenstern, by contrast, had little success in raising money for the fund (BGM, May 30, 1929).

70. Letter of Dec. 17, 1926, AJA Box 1484.

71. Ochs to Rosenwald, Aug. 9, 1928, Rosenwald to Ochs, Aug. 31, 1928, Julius Rosenwald Papers, University of Chicago Library, File: Hebrew Union College, 1928/31. In his letter to Rosenwald, Ochs stressed, *inter*

alia, that with sufficient funds the College would be able to attract to its faculty "men not only capable of giving instruction, but of setting an example in the social graces that is consistent with refinement and culture."

72. *UAHCP,* XI, 900–904.

73. BGM, Feb. 27, 1946.

74. *UAHCP,* X, 9595, 9603, XI, 9924–27; *Union Tidings,* Feb. 1925; correspondence and articles of incorporation in the AJA Documents Files.

75. It was felt that stripping the Union of all real property would impair its credit (*UAHCP,* XI, 565). However, in 1929, members of the Board of Governors tried unsuccessfully to effect a transfer (ibid., 959; BGM, June 25, 1929).

76. *UAHCP,* XI, 226–27; *Catalogue,* 1927–28; BGM, May 25, 1926.

77. Lazarus to Morgenstern, Jan. 8, 1937, AJA Box 1559.

78. They included $50,000 from Rosenwald and $25,000 each from Ochs, Ben Selling of Portland, Oregon (who was the first to donate), UAHC Chairman Ludwig Vogelstein, and Isaac W. Bernheim of Louisville, who had been solely responsible for the first building. Only $13,000 came from Cincinnati (*UAHCP,* XII, 53).

79. Ibid., X, 9768, XI; AJA Box 1801.

80. Adolph S. Oko, *A History of the Hebrew Union College Library and Museum* (Cincinnati, 1944); *Hebrew Union College Library . . . Dedication of the New Building: Programme* (Cincinnati, 1931).

81. FM, Jan. 7, 1931; BGM, June 18, 1933; Philipson Diaries, Aug. 2, 1933; AJA Box 2377.

82. Membership figures are given in the various volumes of *UAHCP,* indebtedness in Philipson Diaries, Oct. 1, 1931.

83. *HUCM,* March 1941, p. 3; *Bulletin of the Alumni Association,* April 1934; Morgenstern to Jerome Mark, Sept. 16, 1932 and to Edward Manheim, Nov. 17, 1937, AJA Box 1559.

84. BGM, Sept. 30, 1930; *Bulletin of the Alumni Association,* Jan. 1934.

85. BGM, May 17, 1932.

86. BGM, Jan. 15, 1934, Oct. 20, 1937, Feb. 27, 1946.

87. BGM, May 24, 1927, Sept. 24, 1929, May 29, 1931, May 17, 1932, Oct. 26, 1932; Philipson Diaries, April 22, 1932.

88. BGM, June 30, 1931, June 21, 1932, Sept. 21, 1940; FM, Dec. 6, 1932; *UAHCP,* XII, 235–36.

89. FM, Nov. 13, 1931; BGM, May 17, 1932, *Catalogue,* 1935–36.

90. *HUCM,* May–June, 1933, pp. 3–4. Pro-Communist articles, written by outsiders, appeared in *HUCM* in Jan. 1933 and March 1935.

91. Philipson Diaries, Nov. 17, 1932. Philipson (who was decidedly not a

socialist) added ominously: "We may hear more about this vote and its effects on the capitalistic givers later."

92. BGM, Jan. 24, 1933, March 28, 1933, *UAHCP,* XIII, 366; AJA Box 2381j.
93. BGM, May 17, 1932, Jan. 24, 1933, May 23, 1934, May 20, 1937; AJA Box 1553, File: Eisendrath.
94. AJA Boxes 1559, 2381i.
95. *UAHCP,* XII, 731.
96. Ibid., XIII, 226–27, 471; BGM, Sept. 15, 1936, Feb. 16, 1937.
97. *HUCM,* Oct. 1933, Dec. 1933; *H.U.C.'r,* Nov. 14 and 22, 1938.
98. In expressing his appreciation to the Board of Governors for taking care of his son, Hermann Wolf, who was the father of one of the original five, wrote: "Wir deutsche Juden sind durch das über uns hereingebrochene Unglück für eine derartig grossmütige Unterstützung, wie Sie diese meinem Sohn und dadurch auch mir zuteil werden lassen doppelt empfänglich, zeigt uns diese doch, dass es in der Welt noch Menschen gibt, die mit uns fühlen und ihr Möglichstes tun, um uns dieses Verhängniss leichter tragen zu lassen und uns einen Lichtblick für die Zukunft in unseren Kindern zeigen" (BGM, Jan. 28, 1936).
99. Morgenstern to Samuel Krass, June 13, 1938, AJA Box 1557; idem to Louis Finkelstein, June 15, 1938, AJA Box 1554.
100. Jacob R. Marcus to Morgenstern, June 18, 1938, AJA Box 1560.
101. "Judaism, Conservative and Reform," *Jewish Exponent,* May 14, 1937; Morgenstern to Louis Finkelstein, Jan. 12, 1938, AJA Box 1554.
102. Morgenstern did not prohibit students from wearing a *kipa* or *tallit.* On one occasion, in 1931, when he permitted a student to conduct the Sabbath service wearing a *tallit,* the president so aroused David Philipson's anger that he wrote in his diary: "That youth should have been promptly removed from the pulpit or ordered to remove the praying [sic] shawl, an orthodox symbol that reform repudiated long ago. Strange things are taking place in this supposedly reform! institution" (Philipson Diaries, March 30, 1931). When four of the Berlin students later appeared at his own services wearing hats, Philipson did his best to persuade them they should accept the custom of the congregation in which they worshipped—but to no avail (ibid., Oct. 14, 1935).
103. Cronbach to [Stephen] Wise, Jan. 24, 1937, AJA Box 1552.
104. Samuel Atlas, Alexander Guttmann, Abraham Heschel, Franz Landsberger, Franz Rosenthal, Isaiah Sonne, and Eugen Täubler were brought from Europe to Cincinnati on nonquota visas. Julius Lewy and Eric Werner were already in the United States when the College offered them positions. Max Wiener received his appointment while still in Germany but gained entry to the United States as a congregational rabbi. Ismar

Elbogen was brought to America and maintained as a research professor in New York through a joint effort of HUC, JIR, JTS, and Dropsie College. A detailed discussion of the refugee scholars project is contained in my article for the forthcoming *Festschrift* in honor of Jacob Rader Marcus.

105. Bamberger, p. 4.

106. BGM, May 9, 1945.

107. The Faculty Council, consisting only of tenured professors and associate professors, dealt especially with the appointment of new faculty and with promotions, but it discussed other matters as well. In 1946 it was expanded to include assistant professors and instructors (BGM, May 26, 1938, Jan. 1, 1946; FM, May 5, 1941, April 24, 1945). In 1939 the Council endorsed Morgenstern's nomination of Simon Halkin as instructor of Hebrew, but opposition on the board, led by Murray Seasongood, who saw little value in modern Hebrew, prevented ratification (FM, Dec. 12, 1939; BGM, June 9, 1940). In 1943, with Seasongood no longer on the board, Elias L. Epstein was appointed to the position.

108. *Catalogue,* 1925–26, p. 30.

109. FM, March 30, 1929, Jan. 9, 1939; BGM, April 29, 1929, Oct. 20 and Dec. 21, 1938.

110. FM, Oct. 10, 1941, May 6, 1944, May 27, 1946; *HUCB,* March 1942.

111. Morgenstern to Nelson Glueck, Jan. 12, 1948, AJA Box 1554; correspondence in AJA Box 1234; *HUCM,* Feb. 1940; BGM, May 22, 1940.

112. BGM, May 10, 1944, May 9, 1945, Oct. 10, 1945.

113. *HUCM,* June 1930.

114. *HUCM,* Nov. 1942; FM, May 7, 1935, April 19, 1944. A noncredit course in Yiddish was given by Elias Epstein in 1948 (BGM, May 30, 1948). In the late sixties, students received elective credit for a new Yiddish course taught by Amos Schauss of the library staff.

115. FM, Oct. 11, 1938.

116. Morgenstern to Nelson Glueck, Dec. 26, 1927, AJA Box 1554.

117. *AI,* Oct. 10, 1930.

118. The HUC student body passed a resolution supporting the position of the CCAR majority (*HUCM,* March 1943, p. 3).

119. *UAHCP,* 1943–46, pp. 20, 28–31, 254.

120. Morgenstern did not, however, actually join the American Council for Judaism, which grew out of the opposing faction. Writing to Stanley Brav on August 23, 1944, he stated: "Personally I am in close sympathy with the principles of this organization, but I fear greatly that the organization itself is fraught with potentialities of danger for our Jewish cause. Despite its high protestations, it is nonetheless an organization

with only a negative program. Its effect can only be division in our Jewish ranks. . . . I myself have steadfastly refused to endorse the organization or to affiliate with it" (AJA Morgenstern Correspondence).

121. *Nation, People, Religion—What Are We?* (Cincinnati, 1943). The address was reprinted—but in somewhat altered form—in *As a Mighty Stream,* pp. 349–82.

122. Joshua Loth Liebman to Morgenstern, Jan. 2, 1944, Morgenstern to Liebman, Feb. 28, 1944, Morgenstern to Milton L. Grafman, June 28, 1944, AJA Morgenstern Correspondence.

123. Morgenstern to Philip K. Hitti, March 24, 1944, ibid.

124. *As a Mighty Stream,* p. 437.

125. See especially FM, May 29, 1947. The seniors of 1947 were awarded their M.H.L. degrees one year later.

126. BGM, June 13, 1944.

127. Morgenstern to Nelson Glueck, April 7, 1944: "I am sorry to say that the work being done by the students this year is the poorest and most disappointing in the last twenty-five years" (AJA Morgenstern Correspondence). Almost all applicants for admission were accepted in 1942 and 1943.

128. The College made its extra dormitory rooms available to soldiers. For a time trainees for the Sixth Army occupied the entire fourth floor and part of the third (BGM, Dec. 14, 1943). In December of 1942 the College hosted a CCAR-sponsored "American Institute on Judaism and a Just and Enduring Peace," which formulated a program for the reconstruction of society and international relations following the war. Early in 1945, the American government paid tribute to the College's founder when the navy launched a Liberty ship named the S.S. *Isaac Mayer Wise* (*HUCB,* Feb. 1945).

129. BGM, May 10, 1944.

130. *UAHCP,* XIII, 938; BGM, Jan. 17, 1940, Oct. 23, 1941, May 10, 1944, Feb. 27, 1946.

131. Memorandum from Abraham N. Franzblau to Morgenstern, April 8, 1946, AJA Morgenstern Correspondence.

132. BGM, May 8, 1946.

133. There was also a banquet attended by 725 people and a commemorative volume of essays published by the alumni.

134. Transcript of an Interview with Julian Morgenstern, Jerusalem, March 3, 1963, AJA Miscellaneous Files; *Wisconsin Jewish Chronicle,* Sept. 20, 1946. Morgenstern continued to do limited teaching at the College until 1957.

Kelal Yisrael: The Jewish Institute of Religion

1. *Challenging Years: The Autobiography of Stephen Wise* (New York, 1949), pp. xxiii, 27.
2. Isaac Mayer Wise to Stephen S. Wise, Sept. 4, 1892, AJA Correspondence Files.
3. *The Personal Letters of Stephen S. Wise,* ed. Justine Wise Polier and James Waterman Wise (Boston, 1956), p. 131.
4. *Stephen S. Wise, Servant of the People: Selected Letters,* ed. Carl Hermann Voss (Philadelphia, 1969), p. 40.
5. Wise to Max Heller, Dec. 28, 1914, AJA Box 532.
6. See Floyd L. Herman, "Some Aspects of the Life of Stephen S. Wise to 1925" (rabbinical diss., HUC-JIR, Cincinnati, 1964).
7. Wise to M. Heller, Nov. 15, 1915, AJA Box 532.
8. Edward E. Klein, *A Synagogue of Life and Light* (New York, 1957), p. 13.
9. "Minutes of a meeting of the Special Committee . . . Nov. 2nd [1920]," AJA Box 1509. For the following, in addition to the sources cited, see also Carl Hermann Voss, *Rabbi and Minister: The Friendship of Stephen S. Wise and John Haynes Holmes* (New York, 1964), pp. 209–17; Hyman J. Fliegel, "The Creation of the Jewish Institute of Religion," *American Jewish Historical Quarterly,* LVIII (1968), 260–70.
10. Wise to M. Heller, Feb. 3, 1915, AJA Box 532.
11. Wise to M. Heller, April 3, 1921, ibid.
12. James Heller, the son of Max Heller and rabbi of K. K. B'nai Yeshurun in Cincinnati, was, however, soon of the opinion that Morgenstern was putting some progressive ideas into operation and that "things are beginning to look more hopeful" (J. Heller to Wise, May 3, 1922, AJA Box 1483).
13. The reason may have been because it had not yet raised the over $400,000 necessary to build its new Synagogue House (Wise to M. Heller, March 20, 1922, AJA Box 532).
14. *Open Letter to the President of the Union of American Hebrew Congregations from Committee of Free Synagogue on the Jewish Institute of Religion* (New York, [1922]), pp. 18–21.
15. Ibid., pp. 13–14.
16. *Stephen S. Wise, Servant of the People,* p. 110.
17. *Open Letter,* pp. 14–15. See also Union of American Hebrew Congregations, *Further Correspondence with the Free Synagogue* (Cincinnati, [1922]).
18. Julian Mack of the Free Synagogue did present its case at the regular meeting of the Union Executive Board in June, but to no avail. See *Union Tidings,* July 1922, p. 12.

19. A survey of editorial opinion in some of the American Jewish newspapers reveals a rather even division. Among the papers favoring the establishment of the JIR were the *Hebrew Standard* of New York City, the *Jewish Voice* of St. Louis, the *Reform Advocate* of Chicago, the *Jewish Chronicle* of Columbus, and the *Jewish Chronicle* of Kansas City. Opposed were the *American Israelite* of Cincinnati, the *Jewish Chronicle* of Detroit, the *Scribe* of Portland, Oregon, and the *Sentinel* of Chicago.

20. Among those coming to Wise's defense was Abba Hillel Silver, later his rival for Zionist leadership (A. H. Silver to Charles Shohl, April 21, 1922, AJA Box 1502).

21. Shohl to Louis Wolsey, April 14, 1922, AJA Box 377.

22. Wise to L. M. Franklin, Feb. 28, 1922, AJA Box 1480. Franklin had written an article, "A New Theological Seminary," in the *Jewish Chronicle* of Detroit, which appeared Feb. 24, 1922. The same fear was expressed directly to Wise in a letter to him by Rabbi William Rosenau of April 17, 1922, AJA Box 1500.

23. L. W. [Louis Wolsey] to E. N. Calisch, May 10, 1922. AJA Box 2375JJ.

24. "Minutes: Dinner Meeting of Committee on Jewish Institute of Religion," AJA Box 1509 (no date is given, but internal evidence yields a date in the latter part of March or early in April); Wise to E. G. Hirsch, June 14, 1922, AJA Box 1485.

25. Wise to Julian Mack, n.d., AJA Box 1493.

26. His son, James, who left rabbinical studies at the JIR shortly before graduation, moved even further from traditional views than his father. He could not justify opposition to mixed marriage and objected to what he termed Liberal Judaism's "ultra-positive assertion of the existence of God and the immortality of the soul" (See James W. Wise, *Liberalizing Liberal Judaism* [New York, 1924]). Wise was grieved at his son's withdrawal but respected his view that he was "unable personally to share and therefore to teach the theological conceptions of Judaism" (*New York Times,* April 27, 1926, p. 18).

27. "The 'Jehovah of the Jews' means nothing. The God of Israel is the God of the Prophets" (Wise to M. Heller, Feb. 17, 1897, AJA Box 532). Late in life, however, Wise was more drawn to traditional concepts.

28. *Stephen S. Wise, Servant of the People,* p. 219.

29. Wise's second commencement address, 1927, AJA Box 1465.

30. Ibid.

31. Daniel Polish, "Mordecai Kaplan: His Diaries 1913–1932," AJA Box 2654; Wise to J. Mack, Feb. 24, 1927, AJA Box 1489; Wise to Ismar Elbogen, March 11, 1927, AJA Box 377; FMJIR, June 12, 1927; Kaplan file, AJA Box 1489.

32. Wise to J. Mack, June 7, 1933, AJA Box 1493.

33. "Memorandum for the files re. Dr. Chajes," Dec. 29, 1924, AJA Box 1469. There is also a hint in this document that certain members of his board —Julian Mack, Lee K. Frankel, George Kohut—were urging Wise to find a replacement for himself, or at least an academic dean.

34. Wise to Harry S. Lewis, May 19, 1922, AJA Box 1491.

35. "Memorandum of interview between Dr. Wise and Dr. Harry [sic] M. Slonimsky, Tuesday noon, Jan. 29, 1924," AJA Box 1503.

36. Philip Bernstein in *Telling Tales Out of School* (Cincinnati, 1965), p. 119.

37. Harry A. Wolfson to Julian Mack, Jan. 16, 1925, AJA Box 1493.

38. The man was Julian Obermann, who, it seems, had identified himself publicly with another institution. (On this matter see the correspondence in AJA Box 1497.) Wise also accused Chaim Tchernowitz of never identifying himself with JIR and giving it too little of his interest and devotion ("Memo of SSW's meeting with Dr. Tchernowitz, June 3, 1930," AJA Box 1508). A similar charge was leveled against Harry Wolfson, who defended himself against it and added: "If you really must know the truth, I can tell you that in the eyes of some people I am condemned for being too closely associated with the Institute. But it never occurred to me to offer an apology" (H. A. Wolfson to George A. Kohut, May 16, 1931, AJA Box 1511).

39. The only noteworthy exception seems to have been Cecil Roth, who taught briefly at the Institute. (See Roth to J. J. Obermann, Oct. 23, 1927, AJA Box 1500.)

40. George A. Kohut to Wise, Dec. 11, 1925, AJA Box 1477.

41. Wise, however, favored the ordination of women (Wise to M. Heller, Aug. 8, 1922, AJA Box 532). In 1939, Helen Levinthal Lyons received a Master of Hebrew Literature degree.

42. "Memo of dinner meeting with the first year men, Tuesday, Jan. 14th [1930]," AJA Box 1505; Ralph Marcus to Wise, June 10, 1930, AJA Box 1494.

43. FMJIR, May 24, 1923. (These minutes are kept in the library of the New York School of the HUC-JIR.)

44. For all matters of curriculum and requirements, see the annual catalogues published by the Institute. For a teacher's evaluation of the students' performance in Hebrew, see Nisson Touroff's recollections in *Sefer Touroff* (Boston, 1938), pp. 47–50.

45. Chajes file, AJA Box 1469.

46. *Jewish Institute of Religion Catalogue,* 1946–47, and 1947–48, pp. 41–47.

47. Chapel file, AJA Box 1469; Students file, AJA Box 1505.

48. BTM, Oct. 18, 1937. (These minutes are contained in AJA Boxes 1509–10.)

49. It may not be far-fetched to note in this connection that the seal chosen by

the Jewish Institute of Religion depicts a coin from the period of the national revolt of Bar Kokhba against Rome in 132–35 C.E. (AJA Box 1502).

50. The formula in 1930 was: "By virtue of the authority vested in me by the Board of Trustees of the Jewish Institute of Religion, and with the concurrence of its faculty, I herewith confer upon you the degree of Master of Hebrew Literature and Rabbi and admit you to all the rights and privileges pertaining thereunto."

51. Wise to Ismar Elbogen, May 24, 1926, AJA Box 377.

52. Bialik to Wise (in Hebrew), 20 Iyar 5686, AJA Box 1474.

53. *Stephen S. Wise, Servant of the People*, p. 215.

54. BTM, passim.

55. Wise to Slonimsky, May 2, 1932, AJA Box 1503.

56. Letter of Oct. 11, [1933], Contributions file, AJA Box 1472.

57. Salaries file, AJA Box 1501. But the catalogues of the JIR indicate that whereas a student in 1929 needed $1,000 for maintenance in New York City during the academic year, in 1935 he needed only $700.

58. FMJIR, Jan. 26, 1931 and May 4, 1931.

59. Editorial by J. T. [John Tepfer], *Jewish Institute Quarterly*, May 1925, pp. 116–17.

60. This situation brought about a conference of representatives of the HUC, JIR, JTS, CCAR, and RA held in New York on June 23, 1930. See minutes in AJA Box 1472.

61. Wise to Morton M. Berman, Jan. 20, 1938, *Studies in Jewish Bibliography, History and Literature in Honor of I. Edward Kiev* (New York, 1971), p. 486.

62. Admissions file, AJA Box 1465.

63. "Jewish Institute of Religion Meeting," Jan. 12, 1939, AJA Box 1509.

64. "Jewish Institute of Religion, Annual Meeting of Members—June 4, 1944," AJA Box 1494.

65. *News Bulletin of the Jewish Institute of Religion*, Nov. 1945; BTM, Sept. 27, 1945.

66. See correspondence between Wise and alumnus H. Goren Perelmuter, AJA Microfilm 1033.

67. BTM, May 1, 1946.

68. FMJIR, Nov. 8, 1923; Board of Trustees file, AJA Box 1509.

69. Wise to Walter S. Hilborn, Feb. 15, 1929, AJA Box 1484.

70. Wise's memo of June 21, 1929, in ibid.

71. Wise's circular letter of June 21, 1929; "Report of Committee on Cooperation between the UAHC, HUC, and the JIR," June 4, 1930; Wise to Julian Mack, June 5, 1930—all in ibid. Morgenstern was interested only

in destroying the JIR as an independent institution. See his letter to Ludwig Vogelstein, Dec. 13, 1928, AJA Box 1555.

72. Felix Levy to Wise, Jan. 10, 1934, William F. Rosenblum to Wise, Jan. 26, 1934, AJA Box 1484.

73. Wise to Levy, May 18, 1936, in ibid.

74. Ralph W. Mack to Wise, Sept. 2, 1938, in ibid.

75. BTM, March 21, 1940.

76. Wise to J. Heller, Nov. 28, 1940, AJA Box 1484.

77. Morton M. Berman to Wise, Feb. 5, 1941, Jacob P. Rudin to Wise, Feb. 21, 1941, in ibid.

78. "Memorandum read by Dr. Slonimsky to a Meeting of the Board of Trustees held Feb. 26, 1941," in ibid.

79. Morgenstern to Wise, Feb. 7, 1941, in ibid.

80. Wise to Berman, March 28, 1941, in ibid.

81. "A meeting of the representatives of the Hebrew Union College and the Jewish Institute of Religion regarding the proposed amalgamation of the two institutions . . . ," June 9, 1941, in ibid.

82. J. Heller to Wise, Dec. 31, 1942, in ibid. Rabbi Abraham Shusterman wrote to Ralph J. Mack on behalf of the Atlantic City group that his colleagues thought the JIR, which did not have "the Reform attitude toward our tradition," was "an unacceptable partner with our alma mater and unworthy of fusion with it" (BGM, Oct. 7, 1942).

83. Wise to J. Heller, Dec. 28, 1942, AJA Box 1484. The declaration, with Morgenstern as signatory, is in AJA Box 1704. See also Wise's second, official letter to Heller, breaking off negotiations "for the present" (BGM, Jan. 13, 1943).

84. Wise to Maurice N. Eisendrath, Feb. 8, 1946, AJA Box 1510. Morgenstern thought that Eisendrath's interest in merger was prompted by the lack of support JIR graduates gave to the UAHC (Morgenstern to Glueck, Oct. 27, 1947, AJA "HUC-JIR Papers . . . Merger"). In 1945, JIR graduates served forty-four UAHC congregations (BTM, Sept. 27, 1945).

85. HUC-JIR "Statement of Purpose," Feb. 1, 1948, AJA Box 1509.

86. BTM, June 11, 1948.

87. The speeches are printed in *Opinion,* Dec. 1948, pp. 6–9.

88. BTM, Jan. 25, 1949.

"With Vision and Boldness"

1. When studying in Germany, Glueck had written to Oko with some relish on August 1, 1923: "I am not a *rabbi* here." Later, on September 2, 1941, he told the one-time HUC librarian that he had been one of the prime influences in his life (Adolph Oko Papers, AJA Box 2328a).

2. See especially BGM, Jan. 28, 1936. It is also noteworthy that Felix Warburg had given $50,000 to the American School with the express desire that Glueck receive the post of director. Morgenstern was a member of the governing body of the school.

3. It is contained in AJA Box 1554 and in the uncatalogued AJA Morgenstern Correspondence.

4. To board member Carl Pritz, Glueck wrote on July 19, 1938 that his archaeological work was of value to the College by keeping it in the public eye. A prominent newspaper reporter had once told him: "Together with rape and murder, archaeology is a subject of primary interest to the public" (AJA Box 1353).

5. Morgenstern to Glueck, April 4, 1944, AJA Morgenstern Correspondence.

6. Letter of May 25, 1946.

7. On September 17, 1946, the *Cincinnati Post,* in announcing the retirement, titled its article: "Glueck May Get Seminary Post." The premature suggestion was not allowed to appear anywhere else.

8. Morgenstern to Bamberger, Oct. 23, 1946.

9. Letter of Oct. 23, 1946.

10. Letters of Nov. 14 and 24, 1946.

11. Morgenstern to Glueck, Nov. 20, 1946; Glueck to Morgenstern, Dec. 2, 1946.

12. He was for a time a member of the Executive Committee of the American Jewish Committee and strongly opposed to the American Jewish Conference, which in the name of all American Jews had taken a position in favor of a Jewish political entity (Glueck to Arthur Hays Sulzberger, Dec. 19, 1947, AJA Box 1554).

13. Glueck to Alvin I. Fine, Nov. 11, 1952 in the uncatalogued AJA Glueck Correspondence.

14. Letter of May 19, 1947, ibid.

15. BGM, Jan. 15, 1947.

16. BGM, Nov. 3, 1948.

17. *HUCB,* April 1949.

18. BGM, Oct. 29, 1951.

19. The process can be easily traced in the *UAHCP* for the relevant years.

20. BGM, Oct. 14, 1957, Jan. 21, 1959; FM, April 9, 1957; *HUCB,* June 1957.

21. BGM, Oct. 22, 1947.

22. "Report on the Graduate School," BGM, June 7, 1968.

23. BGM, May 30, 1948.

24. Glueck to Eric Werner, Oct. 17, 1947, AJA Glueck Correspondence. See also *HUCB,* June 1951, Dec. 1955.

25. BGM, Jan. 25, 1950, Appendix A.

26. Efforts were later made to arrive at a new, shorter name, but sensitivities were so acute that the discussions came to nought (BGM, May 16, 1951, May 15, 1957).

27. BGM, May 14, 1952, Appendix D.

28. Glueck's initial thinking was to have only an undergraduate program in New York: "All students who have already earned their B.A. and were accepted for admission to our rabbinic school would be required to study in Cincinnati" (Glueck to Herbert R. Bloch, Sept. 23, 1952, AJA Glueck Correspondence).

29. Ibid.

30. BGM, May 3, 1950.

31. BGM, March 26, 1953, Appendix A. The plan found some support in a letter written on January 16, 1940 by Stephen S. Wise to Ralph W. Mack during an earlier, unsuccessful round of merger negotiations. In this letter (AJA Box 1484), Wise had himself suggested the possibility that rabbinic students might divide their work between Cincinnati and New York.

32. BGM, Jan. 10, 1952.

33. E.g., in *HUCB,* April 1953.

34. *CCARY,* LXIII (1953), 193–94, 310–18.

35. *Hebrew Union School of Education and Sacred Music, Third Anniversary Report, 1947–1950.*

36. *UAHCP,* 77th–80th Annual Reports (Dec. 1955), 587–88.

37. *The Scribe,* Portland, Oregon, April 1952.

38. See his pamphlet, *The Case Against the "Unification Plan"* (New York, 1953), and his article in *Opinion,* March–April 1954.

39. *CCARJ,* Oct. 1955.

40. Jacob R. Marcus to Glueck, Dec. 28, 1955, Feb. 23, 1956, AJA Box 516.

41. *Rodeph Sholom Chronicle,* Mid-Summer 1956.

42. The chairman of the unification committee, Frank L. Weil, wrote to Jack Skirball as early as November 7, 1955: "Unfortunately we are confronted with a condition and not a theory. I am afraid the solution requires the reopening of a complete school in New York" (AJA Glueck Correspondence). Glueck wrote to Weil on February 2, 1956 that in his "heart of hearts" he still favored the plan with elimination of the problematic sixth year, but he realized that such a proposal was unrealistic. Moreover, he added, "I think the Newman Academy will also get good recruits to whom the prospects of being ordained in four years has a powerful appeal" (ibid.).

43. A transcript is contained in AJA Box 2845.

44. Letter of Protest from New York Student Body to Levi Olan, AJA Correspondence Files.

45. Robert Goldman to Frank L. Weil, May 16, 1956, ibid.

46. The petitions are in the Merger file, AJA Glueck Correspondence.

47. The committee report which they approved (BGM, June 1, 1956, Appendix B) stated only three reasons for the reversal: the intern year was inadvisable as it would be followed by an additional two years in the chaplaincy; larger numbers of rabbis were required to meet the priority need; and the financial situation was now improved thanks to better results from the Combined Campaign.

48. On Los Angeles Jewry, see Max Vorspan and Lloyd P. Gartner, *History of the Jews of Los Angeles* (Philadelphia, 1970).

49. See Edward Kozberg's letter to Nelson Glueck in BGM, May 16, 1951.

50. Glueck to Edgar F. Magnin, May 7, 1948, AJA Glueck Correspondence.

51. BGM, Jan. 27 and May 5, 1954.

52. See the feature story on the school in *HUCB,* April 1957; also Alfred Gottschalk, "The California School of the HUC-JIR Today," *CCARJ,* Oct. 1961.

53. *Report on the California School to the Western College Association,* Feb. 1957; *Report of the Committee of Visitation,* Feb. 12 and 13, 1957; *A Supplementary Survey of the California School,* Oct. 1960.

54. The fact that Skirball himself and some of the people he chose for the board were members of the anti-Zionist American Council for Judaism may also have been a factor in the dispute, though Skirball's less than fervent association with the ACJ was certainly known to Zeldin during the earlier, more harmonious stage of their relationship.

55. BGM, June 7, 1968. Over the years, the College of Jewish Studies was kept alive largely through the efforts of its enthusiastic and talented registrar, Samuel Kaminker. His sudden death early in 1964 was a severe blow to the CJS, hastening its absorption by the HUC-JIR.

56. BGM, Oct. 21, 1960.

57. Gottschalk to Glueck, May 4, 1961, AJA Glueck Correspondence.

58. BGM, Jan. 26, 1961.

59. The Urban Renewal Agency of the federal government withheld funds from all urban renewal projects in California due to passage by the voters of Proposition Fourteen, which actually favored segregated housing. The proposition was eventually declared unconstitutional by the California Supreme Court, thus clearing the way for federal support. (See BGM, June 2, 1966, Appendix E.)

60. Gerald B. Bubis, "The Birth of a School," *CCARJ,* Oct. 1971.

61. *UAHCP,* 67th Annual Report (Nov. 1941), 188–202.

62. Ibid., 68th–70th Annual Reports (Dec. 1943), 16–19.

63. Ibid., p. 27.

64. Some outsiders, however, had difficulty in comprehending why the College

allowed Glueck to accept. Ismar Elbogen wrote to William Rosenau on March 21, 1942: "And why did the Board of Governors of the College agree that the one rare bird who is a highly considered specialist in a field terribly neglected by Jews, give up the best of his time and go to work in a field which people with less valuable brains can manage too?" (AJA Box 2330).

65. In the Conservative movement funds for both the United Synagogue and the Rabbinical Assembly were allotted by the Jewish Theological Seminary. (See Charles S. Liebman, "The Training of American Rabbis," *American Jewish Year Book,* 1968, p. 40.)

66. Eisendrath memorandum, April 19, 1955, Glueck to Eisendrath (not sent), Dec. 16, 1955, and draft of Glueck letter to Eisendrath from some time in May, 1961, AJA Glueck Correspondence.

67. See the correspondence between Robert P. Goldman and Earl Morse in BGM, Jan. 30, 1957.

68. BGM, Jan. 22, 1958. Earlier, however, the Executive Board of the Union had made its own nominations without consulting any representative of the College (Morgenstern to Glueck, March 27, 1947, AJA Box 1554).

69. UAHC Executive Board Minutes, Dec. 6, 1960.

70. Speech to the Alumni of HUC-JIR, New York City, April 26, 1961, AJA Tape 132. See also BGM, Jan. 26, 1961.

71. BGM, May 4, 1949; *UAHCP,* 74th–76th Annual Reports (June 1950), 149, 154; Glueck to Maurice Bergman, June 20, 1949, AJA Glueck Correspondence.

72. BGM, Nov. 1, 1962, Appendix E.

73. BGM, Nov. 1, 1962.

74. BGM, Jan. 30, 1964, Appendices G and G-1.

75. Glueck to Eisendrath, April 26, 1961, AJA Glueck Correspondence.

76. Correspondence between Maurice N. Eisendrath and Malcolm H. Stern, AJA Correspondence Files.

77. *Time* magazine, Nov. 29, 1963; Glueck to Hillel Cohn, Jan. 23, 1964, AJA Glueck Correspondence.

78. BGM, June 4, 1970, Appendix D.

79. BGM, May 15, 1957.

80. Yet it was considered necessary to finish and furnish the first and fourth floors as late as 1967 on the basis of a projected increase in student enrollment. At that time no one as yet knew for certain that three years later all students would be spending their first year in Jerusalem and that the Undergraduate Program would at the same time be completely abolished.

81. BGM, Nov. 2–3, 1958.

82. BGM, Feb. 1, 1962, Feb. 7, 1963, Oct. 22, 1964.

83. FM, Nov. 4, 1947. Perhaps influenced by the negative sentiments of some faculty, Glueck later "undertook to inform students that he is no longer impressed with the value of a student's interruption of his course here for study in Israel" (FM, Feb. 13, 1952). Students did not automatically receive credit at HUC-JIR for courses taken at the Hebrew University.

84. Jacob Rader Marcus to Samuel D. Soskin, Dec. 2, 1947, Jerusalem School file, AJA Glueck Correspondence.

85. *CCARY,* LVIII (1948), 339.

86. *HUCB,* Feb. 1953.

87. The gift produced an interpellation in the Knesset, where the prime minister, Moshe Sharett, was asked why such a valuable piece of land should have been given away to a Reform institution (BGM, May 18, 1955). It was helpful that Sharett was an admirer of Glueck's archaeological work, some of which he had read when imprisoned by the British at Latrun in 1946 (AJA Miscellaneous Files: Moshe Sharett).

88. BGM, Oct. 27, 1954.

89. The documents cited and an account of the events are included in Glueck's report to the Board of Governors, BGM, Oct. 23, 1956.

90. The secularist proponents of granting the building permit, however, found it necessary to stress repeatedly that, of course, they personally would not care to attend the services.

91. These events can be easily traced by following the Israeli press for the month of August 1956. There is also a brief account in *HUCB,* Oct. 1956.

92. Glueck loved to quote the castigation: "It is better to be a Christian than a Jew like Nelson Glueck."

93. BGM, Oct. 14, 1957.

94. The original designation, approved by the Board of Governors on October 27, 1954, was to be: HUC-JIR, Jerusalem School.

95. BGM, Oct. 12, 1961, Feb. 1, 1962, March 29, 1963; Glueck to Samuel Sandmel, Aug. 2, 1961, AJA Box 2382; AJA Tape 132.

96. Even before the structure was finished, Israelis seeking a nonorthodox religious expression of Judaism had used the building for seminars and services. They had been invited by Rabbi Herbert Weiner, who served as the school's administrator for a few months before its formal opening (BGM, March 29, 1963, Appendix C).

97. Glueck and Ben-Gurion had a common interest in the Negev. On January 1, 1954, Ben-Gurion wrote to him in Hebrew: "To be sure, I am more interested in the eschatology of the Negev than in its archaeology. But I am certain that for you, too, the antiquities of the Negev are close to your heart, and from the Negev's ancient artifacts we can learn a great

deal about its future—so we share the same concerns" (AJA Rare Documents Files).

98. Ben-Zvi to Glueck, Oct. 28, 1962, AJA Glueck Correspondence.

99. Glueck to Mrs. Alfred R. Bachrach, Aug. 7, 1963, AJA Correspondence Files.

100. See, for example, his dedication speech, printed in *CCARJ*, Oct. 1963.

101. There was some question whether it should be the third year or the first year. But the hope that the Israeli environment would make it easier for students to surmount the initial barrier of learning Hebrew and the consideration that entering students were less likely to be married swayed the decision in favor of the first year. Though some board members and some faculty were initially less than enthusiastic, with the exception of board member Fred Lazarus, Jr. (BGM, June 4, 1970), there was no overt opposition. A considerable portion of the program's cost was offset by a grant from the Jewish Agency, while board members' fears that the Israel program would add the expenses of a sixth year proved eventually to be unwarranted.

102. See: *Hebrew Union College–Jewish Institute of Religion, Jerusalem: The First Year Program 1971/72—5732.*

103. Glueck to Henry Berkowitz, Feb. 11, 1948, AJA Glueck Correspondence.

104. "No one can accuse Bluestein of using his office as a springboard for a magnificent rabbinical position" (Glueck to Sidney E. Unger, July 6, 1950, AJA Glueck Correspondence).

105. The desire for accreditation and the views of the visiting accreditation committees played no small role here. See, e.g., BGM, Jan. 27, 1960; *Report of Review Visit to the HUC-JIR,* Dec. 1965.

106. The listing is taken from the *Catalogue* for 1970—72. Men holding a combined appointment are mentioned only once.

107. Regular full-time faculty appointed during the Glueck period but deceased by 1970 were Moshe Arie Kahana (Talmud) and Leon J. Liebreich (liturgy and Midrash). Those who had taken other positions were Hillel Fine (Bible and Semitic languages), Norman Golb (medieval Jewish studies), Joseph Gutmann (Jewish art and curator of the Hebrew Union College Museum), and William W. Hallo (Bible and Semitic languages).

108. BGM, Nov. 19, 1952; *HUCB,* Feb. 1953.

109. FM, Oct. 25, 1957 and following May 26, 1967; *HUCB,* Jan. 1958; Marcus to Glueck, May 10, 1963, AJA Box 516.

110. In 1956 the school dropped entirely the Hebrew entrance requirements, which until then had always appeared in the *Catalogue* in one form or another.

111. *Catalogue,* 1950–51, pp. 27–28; 1968–70, p. 39; 1970–72, p. 41; BGM,

May 3, 1950; FM, April 6, 1951, Dec. 5, 1967, May 28 and Oct. 25, 1968; Bernard Martin, president of the Student Association, to Nelson Glueck and Sheldon Blank, March 1, 1951, AJA Glueck Correspondence.

112. FM, Oct. 15, 1965, Jan. 28, 1966; *Report of a Visit to the HUC-JIR,* Dec. 1965, pp. 21–22.

113. *Institutional Profile of the HUC-JIR,* Nov. 24, 1970, p. 40; FM, Feb. 17, 1970.

114. BGM, June 3, 1965; FM, May 26, 1967.

115. BGM, June 3, 1965, Appendix C-1.

116. For the following, see especially Norman B. Mirsky, "The Professionalization and Socialization of Hebrew Union College Students" (doctoral diss., Brandeis University, 1971), and Charles Philip Sherman, "Factors Influencing the Selection of the Rabbinate as a Career" (rabbinical diss., HUC-JIR, Cincinnati, 1969).

117. In 1957 there were some sixty congregations without rabbinical leadership (BGM, Jan. 30, 1957).

118. Liebman, p. 17. It is noteworthy that Liebman's admittedly incomplete sample results in the figure of 49 percent B— or below for Cincinnati, but only 15 percent for New York. (The figure for JTS is 30 percent.) Liebman also found the New York students much more satisfied with their instruction (p. 60). For an articulation of the policy, see Samuel Sandmel, "Rabbis and Recruitment of Rabbinical Students," *CCARJ,* April 1960.

119. FM, May 9, 1958, Dec. 5, 1967.

120. Memos Dealing with Herbert Bronstein's Work as Chairman of the Student Body Religious Committee, AJA Correspondence Files. Cf. Open Letter to the College Family by Michael V. Fox, ibid.

121. *Bulletin of the Academic Council,* Dec. 9, 1965. Cf. AJA Tape 231; FM, Oct. 28, 1966.

122. FM, April 29, 1969, May 12, 1970.

123. Kenneth Roseman to Ruth Frenkel, matron of the dormitory, Oct. 20, 1966, AJA Glueck Correspondence; FM, Oct. 28, 1966. On June 4, 1970, when its own Dormitory Committee recommended serving one completely kosher hot meal a day for those students desiring it, the Board of Governors, according to the taped proceedings, voted not to accept the recommendation, ostensibly for financial reasons (AJA Tape 745).

124. During the year of the merger, students of the New York School published three issues of a literary magazine in Hebrew entitled *Reshit* (1949–50). A decade later, they for a time issued a mimeographed *Student Bulletin.*

125. *variant,* Spring 1968, pp. 3–5.

126. See the paragraphs on the chaplaincy in the catalogues for 1966–68 and 1968–70; Mirsky, pp. 276–81.

127. Among senior members of the faculty, the most outspoken was Sheldon
Blank, who had always believed in taking seriously the message of peace
contained in the Prophetic writings. In the winter of 1968, two younger
instructors, along with about twenty students, marched with Martin
Luther King (and Maurice Eisendrath) to the Arlington National Cemetery in silent, prayerful protest of the war.

128. AJA Tape 625.

129. Glueck was a lifelong Democrat and very proud of having been chosen to
deliver the benediction at John F. Kennedy's inauguration. When Jacob
Marcus suggested to him in 1969 (well before Watergate) that since
the president of the Jewish Theological Seminary had preached at services held in the Nixon White House, he, too, should arrange for an
invitation, Glueck replied: "I am sorry to say that I don't want an invitation. I don't want my name . . . connected with the Nixon administration" (July 7, 1969, AJA Glueck Correspondence).

130. FM, May 12, 1970.

131. BGM, June 5, 1969.

132. FM, April 2, 1968.

133. BGM, May 16, 1951, Appendix G; Jacob Marcus to Glueck, April 3, 1956,
AJA Box 516.

134. In 1970 a group of younger rabbis met at the UAHC camp in Warwick,
New York, to reflect upon this crisis.

135. Glueck used the Palestine analogy, off the written record, in at least two
reports to the Board of Governors: Oct. 22, 1964 and June 4, 1970,
AJA Tapes 274 and 745.

136. *CCARJ,* June 1967.

137. The study finally appeared as Theodore I. Lenn et al., *Rabbi and Synagogue in Reform Judaism* (West Hartford, Conn., 1972). It included a
survey of HUC-JIR students, but since the New York school was
omitted and there was only a 30 percent response of rabbinical students
to the questionnaire, the results in this area cannot be regarded as definitive.

138. *CCARY,* LXXIX (1969), 25–26.

139. The request goes back at least to 1954 (*CCARY,* LXIV, 22). It began to
be pressed during the administration of Leon Feuer (1963–65), but resulted only in honorary (nonvoting) membership for the CCAR president and executive vice-president beginning in 1969. On July 3, 1967,
Glueck wrote to Marcus: "The CCAR will never get any appointees on
the HUC-JIR Board as long as I am president of HUC-JIR. . . . Let
the gang try for control after my time. It will be my pleasure to try,
and I believe I shall be able, to stop them before then" (AJA Glueck

Correspondence). Glueck regarded the proposed study as "totally unnecessary."

140. BGM, June 7, 1963.

141. BGM, Oct. 31, 1968, Feb. 6, 1969, Oct. 23, 1969, Appendices J and L, Feb. 5, 1970; AJA Tape 628.

142. To Alvin I. Fine, Aug. 14, 1951, AJA Glueck Correspondence.

143. Dec. 13, 1963.

144. He would even have accepted additionally the presidency of the World Union for Progressive Judaism, had not Maurice Eisendrath vociferously objected (Lily H. Montagu to Glueck, Jan. 7, 1954, AJA Glueck Correspondence).

145. E.g., AJA Tape 132.

146. To Fred F. Florence, Dec. 3, 1957, AJA Glueck Correspondence.

147. However, as a student in Germany he had been interested in biblical concepts, and he continued to regard archaeology basically as a tool for broader historical understanding. See Fritz Bamberger, "The Mind of Nelson Glueck," *Near Eastern Archaeology in the Twentieth Century,* ed. James A. Sanders (New York, 1970), pp. xvii–xxiv; AJA Tape 635.

148. Nelson Glueck, *Dateline: Jerusalem* (Cincinnati, 1968), p. 17.

149. BGM, Oct. 24, 1967; FM, May 20, 1969.

150. FM, Nov. 7, 1950, Feb. 23, 1956. In the fall of 1969, faculty and students of the New York School held a "retreat" to discuss basic questions of common concern; a few months later the Cincinnati faculty took a day to address itself to similar issues.

PART TWO

A Survey of
Scholarly Contributions

SHELDON H. BLANK

Bible

The Bible was the very foundation of the religion of Isaac M. Wise, first president of the Hebrew Union College. He was a staunch defender of the faith of Israel, and for him this meant a defense of the Hebrew Scriptures. The Torah had to be divine, a communication from the mouth of God to the people of Israel. One suspects that it was more than a metaphor when he called one portion of the Bible "a direct revelation from on high . . . a momentary crevice in heaven's impenetrable dome, through which mortals beheld the glory of the Majesty on High." [1] Wise was only secondarily a systematic theologian; [2] he was first of all a *defensor fidei*. These were vital matters. American Judaism was in its formative stage and decisions then were to have lasting impact.

It was in deep earnest: "The authenticity of the Mosaic records is the foundation of all Bible truth"—and on Bible truth all else is built: "the entire canon of divinity and humanity." His conviction fully explains Wise's efforts "to save the records which establish Bible truth." [3] Reporting to the Board of Governors on July 2, 1895, Wise said: "Like you, gentlemen of the Board, we teachers and pupils stand upon our post, courageous and well equipped to march onward into the age of manhood to perform our tasks in the workshops of Providence. Your, our motto is, 'Onward, in the Name of God, Onward!' Your most obedient servant, Isaac M. Wise, President, Hebrew Union College." [4]

The central citadel which all must defend is the "Thorah." "We know of no religion and acknowledge none besides that laid down in Israel's Thorah. . . . Whatever prophets, hagiographists, scribes, rabbis or philosophers wrote and preached . . . is no more than a commentary to the Thorah. . . . There is no Judaism without the Thorah and Revelation." [5] The battle was for "the authenticity of the Mosaic records"; the foe was "the science commonly called Modern Biblical Criticism, actually Negative Criticism." [6]

There is much heat in Wise's struggle with biblical criticism—more heat than reason. The disinclination, or better the aversion, to the historico-critical method comes first, the argument follows. What he attacks in the *Pronaos* is a parody, a caricature of the method. According to Wise, this is what biblical criticism does: it "maintains, on the strength of unscientific methods, that the Pentateuch is not composed of original Mosaic material, no Psalms are Davidian, no Proverbs Solomonic, the historical books are unhistorical, the prophecies were written *post festum,* there was no revelation, inspiration or prophecy"; and so it "must also maintain that the Bible is a compendium of pious or even impious frauds, willful deceptions, unscrupulous misrepresentations." [7] This is not description but invective, and what it says is that the founder of the Hebrew Union College did not like biblical criticism.

With the president taking so firm a stand, the first generation of instructors in Bible at the College would hardly present the Bible after the manner of Wellhausen. In those decades the word *exegesis,* which commonly appears in the titles of the preceptors, instructors, and professors, as well as in the descriptions of their courses, was not a synonym for biblical criticism, and the term *methodic* was to be understood within defined limits. In the *Programme of the Hebrew Union College 1896–1897,* pp. 15–20, "Exegesis" simply means Bible with Targum, Ibn Ezra, Rashi, or Rashbam. A course with the promising title "Methodic Exposition of the History of Biblical Criticism" is pulled up short by the specification: "with special reference to Psalmodic and Solomonic portions of the Bible," and a "Semitic

Department" course (on p. 23) is listed as "Exercises in Methodical Exegesis—Proverbs 10–22.16."

Sigmund Mannheimer, David Philipson, Ephraim Feldman, Max L. Margolis, Casper Levias, and Moses Buttenwieser were among the men who taught Bible or Bible-related subjects under the presidency of Isaac M. Wise (1875–1900).[8] Except for Buttenwieser, of whom more below, these scholars appear to have published little in the area of Bible. They are to be praised not so much for the number of their publications as for the quality of their product—the first generation of HUC alumni.[9] Sigmund Mannheimer was the author of a *Hebrew Reader and Grammar* (1873), which went through several editions; David Philipson delivered *Five Lectures on Cuneiform Discoveries* at the College in 1888, and these were published the following year. Max L Margolis is the author of *The Story of Bible Translations* (1917). Casper Levias was best known for *A Grammar of the Aramaic Idiom Contained in the Babylonian Talmud* (1900). And these are all that I have found in the field of Bible. In a paper on "The Theology of the Old Prayer Book" at the 1897 convention of the Central Conference of American Rabbis, Max Margolis spoke of the Bible in quite the same terms as Wise. To discard the doctrines and hopes which "are rooted in the Bible . . . is to discard so much of the Bible; to discard a part of the Bible means to reject the dogma of the authority of Scripture, to do away with the Canon which signifies a sacred literature with its standard of *norma fidei* within it." [10]

While Wise was still in office, however, cracks began to appear elsewhere in his closed system. Addressing himself to the "Theory of Oral Tradition" at the 1896 convention of the CCAR, Gotthard Deutsch, on the College faculty since 1891, said: "This belief in a tradition [i.e., oral tradition] presupposes the belief that the Pentateuch existed as an entirety at the time of Moses." [11] Considering the evidence produced by "modern criticism," he continued, "we will be hardly willing to accept such a statement." The subject had come up a year earlier in a different context.[12] Wise had said: "This Conference has just adopted a Union Prayer Book, in which are several declarations that we are faithful to the canon of Israel, which means the Bible." Triggered by this reference to the canon, Emil G. Hirsch fired his volley: he regretted to see the subject of the Bible brought up; he did not believe that one single line of the Pentateuch was written by Moses in its present form.

Dr. Wise died on March 26, 1900. He was mourned and eulogized at the CCAR convention in July of that year. Speaking of "Dr. Wise as a Theologian," Dr. L. Mayer properly said: "The theories of the modern school of higher critics met with strong opposition from him. The Sinaitic revelation he regarded as historically unassailable. . . . His defense of his views concerning the authenticity and authority of the Bible, which from first to last, underwent no change made him the subject of many an attack. . . ." [13] Then, at that same convention, confirming these concluding words, Rudolph Grossmann, whom Wise had ordained in 1889, spoke on "The Rabbi as a Scholar" and said in part: [14] "This suggests a study upon which I desire to lay particular emphasis, and that is the *study of the Bible in accordance with the methods of the modern critical school.* [The italics are his.] Whatever our individual opinions may be as to the validity of its conclusions, Biblical criticism has become altogether too well established a science to be ignored by the scholarly rabbi. . . . The evolution of thought is unconquerable." [15]

So, as the College was completing its first twenty-five years, the attitude of the Reform Jewish leadership was in transition. As a matter of fact, such transition was well under way in the world of Bible scholarship without as well as within our ranks. Consider, as an illustration of this thought, the preface in the first volume of the *Jewish Encyclopedia*, just then beginning to appear.[16]

The editors there suggest (on p. xii) what distinguishes the treatment of Bible in a Jewish encyclopedia from the treatment of parallel entries in, for example, a *Hastings Dictionary of the Bible*. They had agreed to treat the "Biblical articles under the three heads of (*a*) Biblical Data, giving, without comment or separation of 'sources,' the statements of the text; (*b*) Rabbinical Literature, giving the interpretation placed upon Biblical facts by the Talmud, Midrash, and later Jewish literature; (*c*) Critical View, stating concisely the opinions held by the so-called Higher Criticism as to the sources and validity of the Biblical statements." The Bible editor was Morris Jastrow, Jr., of the University of Pennsylvania, but Gotthard Deutsch and Kaufmann Kohler (then still rabbi of Temple Beth-El of New York City) were members of the fourteen-man Editorial Board and most certainly had a voice in the shaping of this editorial policy.

The statement suggests the approach to the Bible which at that time one might expect to find in a Jewish institution of higher learning like the College—somewhat noncommittal as regards the "so-called" Higher Criticism but still "stating concisely the opinions held." Dramatic things were happening then of which the editors were well aware. In this same preface (p. xiii), they express their determination "to acquaint the student with the results of modern research in many fields that are altogether new and bristling with interesting discoveries." The fields which they name are "Assyriology, Egyptology, and archeological investigation in Palestine, the inexhaustible treasures of which are constantly casting unexpected light on every branch of Biblical history and archeology." At least two of these "new" fields, Assyriology and Palestinian archaeology, were to be intensively cultivated at the College.

Unlike I. M. Wise, Kaufmann Kohler wholly approved the methods of biblical criticism. Moses Mielziner, and then Gotthard Deutsch, served briefly as acting president between 1900 and 1903, when Kohler succeeded as president. In 1904 the students of the College published an impressive volume for which Kohler wrote the lead article: "The Four Ells of the Halakah, and the Requirements of a Modern Jewish Theological School." He denied that the label "Higher Anti-Semitism" given to Higher Criticism could stand the test of scrutiny, even though "baahizat enayyim—by its seeming truth"— the label might captivate many, and went on to point out the achievements of the science. Once the insights are attained, "the whole Bible presents to the inquirer a gradual evolution of the God idea," and "what geology did for us in laying bare the different strata of the earth telling of the various epochs of creation, Higher Criticism does in disclosing the various stages of growth of the truth of the divine revelation." [17] Darwinism, which seemed to deny the authenticity of the biblical epic of creation, had been anathema to Wise, and with it he had rejected the evolutionary aspects of the documentary hypothesis. Without this inhibiting factor Kohler could readily accept and even utilize the results of source criticism: "The divine revelation in Israel was by no means a single act, but a process of development, and its various stages correspond to the degrees of culture of the people" [18]—a "process of development" in place of the single act, the Sinaitic revelation.[19]

As a teaching member of the faculty Kohler was professor of theology, not Bible, but the Bible was within the range of his broad scholarship. Of Kohler, Cyrus Adler writes in the *Jewish Encyclo-*

pedia[20] that his doctoral thesis at Erlangen in 1868, " 'Der Segen Jacob's,' was one of the earliest Jewish essays in the field of the higher Biblical criticism, and its radical character had the effect of closing to him the Jewish pulpit in Germany."[21] His special interest was the Apocrypha and his entries in the *Jewish Encyclopedia,* signed "K," are largely in the area of Apocryphal and rabbinic literature. *Studies in Jewish Literature (Issued in Honor of Kaufmann Kohler on . . . his Seventieth Birthday)* (1913), contains an exhaustive bibliography by Adolph S. Oko of Kohler's writings to date. His interest in the Bible was deep.

Entertaining such an attitude toward the Bible, Kohler in no wise limited the freedom of his Bible faculty to engage in scientific inquiry. These were the instructors in Bible under Kohler during the first decade of the twentieth century: Casper Levias (1895–1905), Moses Buttenwieser (1897–1934), Judah Leon Magnes (1903–4), Max Schloessinger (1904–7) and again Max L. Margolis (1905–7). With them biblical criticism enters the course of study—though with timid steps. According to the *Catalog* for 1902–3 (p. 31), a course offered by Buttenwieser included "method and principles of Bible criticism" with "a critical examination of the different accounts of Samuel." In the *Prospectus* for January 1905 (p. 18), "Bible" and "Bible Commentators: Rashi, Rashbam or Kimhi," appear as *separate* courses—a radical innovation; and Buttenwieser offers a "Post-Graduate" (adults only?) course with the provocative title "Bible exegesis, modern" (p. 23). In the *Catalog* for May 1906, Kohler presents "the views and principles underlying the plan of studies." "One of the fundamental rules of academic instruction," he writes, "certainly is that freedom of thought and independence of research be granted to all the teachers. . . . Indeed, scientific research (Wissenschaft) should be as the light of heaven—colorless. Truth alone is its aim and object" (p. 10). And he goes on to draw from the views of Bible critics (theoretical) conclusions affecting the structure of the curriculum: Since the "ethical theism held forth by the prophets . . . helped in the shaping of the books of Moses," the course of study would take up "the great prophetical books" *before* "the Book of Moses" (p. 12).[22] Apparently this shift in the order of courses was more readily proposed than executed. The only innovation in the Bible curriculum for 1906–7 is the course on "The Apocryphal and Hellenistic Literature" offered by Kohler. In the *Catalog* May 1908

(p. 54), in the "Report of Work Done during the School Year 1907–1908," the following entry appears: "First Collegiate Class. *Introduction to the Bible: Canon and Text.* Method and Principles of Biblical Criticism. Composition and origin of the Hexateuch. One hour weekly (Buttenwieser)." For some reason or other it does not appear in the "Course of Studies" for 1908–9 (p. 58). An "Introduction by President Kohler" on p. 11 of the May 1908 *Catalog* speaks of "scientific methods": *"Bible Exegesis* which, while following the purely scientific methods of our age, is to maintain its historical continuity with the past by the consultation of the medieval commentators and the ancient interpretations." Did scientific methods seem to threaten the Bible? Was the Bible in danger?

When, or just before, Kohler wrote this introduction, Stephen Samuel Wise gave a "series of addresses . . . at the Hudson Theatre, January to March 1907, preliminary to the founding of the Free Synagogue." [23] The sixth address in the series asked, "Is the Bible in Danger?" By profession Stephen Wise was neither a theologian like Kohler nor a Bible scholar like Buttenwieser or Morgenstern, and I have in fact found little besides this one address in his published works to suggest a more than ordinary interest in the Bible or to indicate further his attitude towards the scientific method as applied to the Bible. [24] But the one address "Is the Bible in Danger?" is wholly unambiguous. In his characteristically outspoken manner Stephen Wise answers his own question: "Yes, the Bible is in danger, not by reason of the searching of the critics but at the hands of its friends. . . . For my part I believe the higher criticism was not only timely but saving" (pp. 163 f.). It has brought men now to "focus their attention on the authority of the content of the Bible"; not "to be diverted by theorizing as to its external sanctions" (p. 163). "The Bible of the twentieth of Exodus or the nineteenth of Leviticus or the sixth of Micah or the fifth of Amos, or the twenty-third and fifty-first Psalms can never be lost nor endangered" (p. 175). The same Stephen Wise who said this in the spring of 1907 was fifteen years later to establish the Jewish Institute of Religion in New York, subsequently merged with the Hebrew Union College. [25]

From Kohler to the present, the "scientific" study of the Bible has never been seriously challenged. Most recently, at the Inaugural Service on February 24, 1972, the chairman of the board, Mr. S. L. Kopald, Jr., charged the new president of the College, Alfred Gottschalk, "with preserving unlimited academic freedom, resting on the belief that the affirmatively critical study of Judaism insures its survival and enhances its sanctity." In that same sense, Dr. Gottschalk himself has referred to "our total School with its long time commitment to the liberal temper and free scholarly inquiry." [26]

Still under the presidency of Isaac M. Wise, in 1897, when Max Margolis resigned to accept a position at the University of California, Moses Buttenwieser joined the faculty of the College as assistant professor of exegesis.[27] His approach to the Bible was scientific, but, since his interests centered on the Prophets and the Writings rather than the Pentateuch, he did not come into collision with I. M. Wise. His major writings were to be *The Prophets of Israel* (1914), *The Book of Job* (1922), and *The Psalms* (1938).

Buttenwieser was by no means conservative in his treatment of the text, permitting himself to reshape it, with a free shifting of the order of clauses and verses, to conform to his understanding of the intended sense. The results are unquestionably attractive in thought and form; the confessions of the prophet Jeremiah, the Psalms, the speeches of Job and of his orthodox friends, all take on a new beauty and clarity in his sensitive translations. But even though he constantly invoked the witness of the versions, a broad knowledge of classical antiquity, and the fine points of Hebrew syntax in support of his innovations, we must admit that a fair amount of subjectivity attaches to his method.

He was not, after the manner of I. M. Wise or Kohler, theologically oriented: it was his aim to let values shine forth from the ancient text for the enlightenment of our age. His admiration for the prophetic message was boundless, and his influence on the generations of students who passed through his classes was vast.

The prophets speak for themselves, and no one on our faculty will claim to have done more than to help interpret and point up their message, hoping to make it live in our day. No one of us has done more than Moses Buttenwieser to implant the social teaching of the prophets in the lives of generations of American rabbis. Among his disciples were Samuel H. Goldenson, who eloquently voiced the message, and Abraham Cronbach, who translated it into action—these along with countless others.

When Moses Buttenwieser was completing his first twenty-five years on the College faculty, the students dedicated to him an issue of the *Hebrew Union College Monthly* (May 1922). Among the appreciative contributors were Goldenson, Cronbach, and Adolph S. Oko. Oko allows himself a rare enthusiasm: "Searching investigation, infinite detail, firsthand authority, as well as broad scope are the distinguishing characteristics of [Buttenwieser's] solid learning" (p. 207). Cronbach writes: "We do not overlook the charms and the sublimities of the Midrash, but are simply stating an urgent need if we parody Ecclesiastes to the extent of saying that there is a time for *Derush* and a time for *Peshat*. In Dr. Buttenwieser's classes one could be certain of the clear cold air and the solid ground of the 'plain meaning' " (p. 194). Goldenson (HUC, 1904) was and remained for life a friend of Buttenwieser, and it was appropriate that in later years Congregation Emanu-El of the city of New York, naming a lectureship at the College in honor of Goldenson,[28] should specify that "this Lecture each year should be on some aspect of Prophetic Judaism." In a letter to me about Moses Buttenwieser, Goldenson wrote: "No man on the Faculty meant more to me. . . ."

Destined to become the first American-born president of the College, Julian Morgenstern[29] attended the University of Cincinnati and the College until his ordination, in 1902, and then the Universities of Berlin and Heidelberg. He wrote a doctoral dissertation on "The Doctrine of Sin in the Babylonian Religion," with Assyriology as his area of concentration, and he received a Ph.D. degree in 1904. After a three-year interval as rabbi in Lafayette, Indiana, he accepted the position of instructor in biblical and Semitic languages, as one of the men who joined the faculty after the resignation of Professors Malter, Schloessinger, and Margolis in 1907.

If it is just to assign scholars to this or that "school," we may say that Morgenstern is essentially a cultural historian. His aim is to set forth values mined from ancient literatures.

Already in his first year as instructor Morgenstern offered a course which many of his students (among them a number of drop-outs) remember with awe, his "Deuteronomy, complete, only unvocalized text used"; but he waited five years to offer the other courses long associated with his name: "Introduction to the Hexateuch," "Biblical Aramaic," and "The Book of Amos." As concerns Pentateuchal criticism, his position is quite as liberal as that of Stephen Wise. In a paper read before the Central Conference of American Rabbis at its annual convention in Charlevoix, Michigan, in 1915 and printed in vol. XXV of the *Yearbook,* he presented his views: [30] Reform Judaism should early on have faced "clearly and bravely the very difficult and delicate question of the historic truth of the tradition of the divine origin and Mosaic authorship of the Torah"; it should first have denied this "tradition"[31] and only then have adopted a selective attitude towards the laws.[32] Morgenstern's mind was very clear about progressive revelation. "Each prophet, convinced of his divine call in the most literal sense, felt himself to be, *and actually was,*[33] a link in the great chain of God's self-revelation to His people." I suspect that Morgenstern was speaking firmly to himself when, in the expanded form of the paper, he observes that, alas! "Modern Jewish scholars have done almost nothing for the development of the new science, and scarcely has the problem of its actual significance for Judaism been boldly faced and definitely solved by Jewish scholars at large!" [34] This was his inaugural vision.

A magnificently organized and disciplined craftsman, Morgenstern managed to write voluminously even while teaching a full load (and later serving as a one-man administration of the College). His first book, *The Book of Genesis: A Jewish Interpretation,* appeared in 1919 (2d ed., 1965). His impressive card file, the garner of broad reading, shaped itself year by year into monographs for the *Hebrew Union College Annual* (a solid essay in every one of the *Annuals* from the first in 1924 to vol. XL–XLI in 1969–70!), contributions to periodicals, entries in encyclopedias, papers, addresses, and in 1963 a book: *The Fire upon the Altar,* and in 1966, *Rites of Birth, Marriage, Death and Kindred Occasions among the Semites.* He has mingled records of Semitic, especially Arabic, customs and traditions with classical and rabbinic lore and an intimate overview of Scripture, again and again to challenge current Bible scholarship. His more notable contributions have been in the areas of calendar studies, Pentateuchal law, the ark, Amos, and Deutero-Isaiah, with (perhaps the most controversial of his proposals) a hypothetical sack of Jerusalem in 485 B.C.[35]

Original ideas are hard to come by in the field of Bible. In search of thesis projects or publications to "publish or perish," or for the pure joy of research and the delight of discovery, so many generations of students, scholars, and devout Christians and Jews over so many centuries have scouted the territory that few corners remain unexplored. Among Morgenstern's predecessors there are mere hints at a certain idea which he has developed with a persuasive force. As in detective fiction, where the avid sleuth carefully considers all the bits and pieces that seem discordant in an otherwise rational scene, then assembles and arrays these pieces until they take the shape of an unanticipated, enlightening resolution, so Morgenstern teases out, assembles, and arrays the materials for his hypothesis. Vituperations directed against Edom, Ammon, Moab, and others, but especially Edom, are not consistent with the report in Jeremiah 40 of these peoples' apparent friendly reception of fugitives from Jerusalem at the time of the Babylonian conquest. Nehemiah's apparent amazement and shock when he learns, in Nehemiah 1, that the walls and gates of Jerusalem lie in ruins and the remnant of its inhabitants are desolate is incomprehensible if we assume that the ruins and the desolation are the aftermath of the Babylonian conquest. Why the amazement a century and a half subsequent to the event? Assembling from all parts of Scripture a troop of similar incongruities, Morgenstern fits them all together and proposes a hypothesis: With Edom as ring-leader, the nations neighboring on Judea attacked and sacked Jerusalem in the year 485 B.C., when the Persian king Xerxes, engaged with affairs in his own capital and in Egypt, authorized those nations to deal with a rebellious province. No matter that the attack is nowhere recorded; assume it as a fact and you solve a host of problems.

Morgenstern has never hesitated to follow a hunch way out on a limb, but the array of pieces which he gathers at the end of the limb always fall into a persuasive pattern. His writings are not infrequently controversial, but they are consistently stimulating and evocative.

Of the men on our Bible faculty, Morgenstern is the one who has paid the highest homage to the documentary hypothesis. He has not simply accepted the rubrics J, E, D, and P but has added K (for Kenite) and distinguished within the major sources a goodly number of strata and substrata, one for example in J that he dates at least as late as the Second Isaiah (cf. Gen. 12:2). Others among us, while endorsing the method, apply it not so much in the Pentateuch, where source criticism has the greater relevance, as in the Writings and the Prophets. I, for example, would distinguish a number of "later Isaiahs." For his archaeological explorations Nelson Glueck could use the biblical data unconcerned as to their source or date. Samuel

Sandmel concludes his essay on "The Haggada within Scripture," in *Two Living Traditions,* with the observation: "For the Graf-Wellhausen hypothesis to merit the high accolade of being the point of departure implies the need to depart from it." [36] This "departing from" is perhaps the direction that most of us are taking today—that is to say: we clearly recognize the presence of diverse parallel literary units, but we draw other than the traditional conclusions.

The method of form criticism also figures in our approach. I have used it in a study of "The Curse, Blasphemy, the Spell and the Oath" and in my treatment of Jeremiah's "Confessions" (I would call them "prayers") in *Jeremiah: Man and Prophet.* Morgenstern uses the method most effectively in "The Oldest Document of the Hexateuch" and in parts II and III of "The Book of the Covenant," where he deals with types of biblical law.

Carrying these historico-critical methods to their ultimate conclusion, Morgenstern shows that the textual history of the Pentateuch is far more complex than many have been aware of—which means, incidentally, that the Torah is truly the product of a people and not of a select few, and that it was of such central importance in the lives of that people that, by revising, re-editing, and supplementing it, they kept it alive.

In 1921, Kohler retired as president and Julian Morgenstern became acting president, and in the following year—the year that Stephen Wise opened the Jewish Institute of Religion in New York—president of the College, which post he held until 1947. He did not, however, give up teaching. Indeed, he rounded out fifty years of fruitful instruction, even as *emeritus,* until 1957.

In addition to Buttenwieser he had as colleague on the Bible faculty Henry Englander, a most friendly man. Englander's special interest was medieval commentaries. His scholarly studies, in the areas of biblical Hebrew grammar and the Jewish exegetes, among them Rashi in particular, appeared in the *Hebrew Union College Annual.*[37]

Encouraged by Morgenstern, Nelson Glueck and I undertook a program of graduate study to follow our ordination in 1923. Morgenstern found funds to help us finance our years in Germany, England, and Palestine. As president then, he had a place for me on the faculty when I returned in 1926 with a Ph.D. from Germany, and for Glueck when he too returned in 1928. Sometime in the spring of my senior year I had spoken also with Kaufmann Kohler about my intentions. I remember now something of that conversation. He seemed to sense that I might be seduced by *Wissenschaft* at a German university and not return to occupy an American pulpit. Kohler may just then have been preparing to write for the *Jubilee Volume,* which was to appear in 1925, his article "The Hebrew Union College of Yesterday and a Great Desideratum in Its Curriculum Today." There he wrote (pp. 77 f.): "Too often does greater intellectuality in our faith lessen the spiritual view of things, engendering irreverence and doubt, and the future leaders . . . have often nothing but cold reason to offer. . . ." "Prophets we need, men of the spirit, men of vision, not of mere mentality. . . ." Kohler was making a point in this article, and he may have spoken more negatively of intellectuality than he meant—though he did alert me to the possible effects of an exposure to *Wissenschaft.* But Morgenstern, apparently satisfied with the effects upon himself of such experience, encouraged the project.

I came to the faculty as instructor in Hebrew in 1926. The title was changed to instructor in Hebrew and Bible in 1928, when Nelson Glueck returned for the same title. I have cultivated a limited field—first teaching Bible text to beginners, then adding Pentateuchal criticism, and eventually, courses in prophetic literature, with seminars on sundry topics. My doctoral dissertation (Jena, 1925, unpublished) was on "Das Wort *torah* im Alten Testament." My published books are on the prophets: *Prophetic Faith in Isaiah* (1958, 1967), *Jeremiah: Man and Prophet* (1961), and *Understanding the Prophets* (1969). I have widened the area at times to write entries for the *Universal Jewish Encyclopedia* and for the *Interpreter's Dictionary of the Bible* (1962).[38] I will accept some responsibility for the development of such themes as "irony by way of attribution," "the oath as a literary device," the motif of "self-pity," "the Promethean element in biblical prayer," "prophetic agony." And in the direction of Kohler's "desideratum," I have tried to give the prophets their due. After my manner and according to my capacities I have gone with Buttenwieser some of the way, attempting to clothe with reality the persons of some of the prophets and to disseminate, in the classroom and for a larger public, their teachings. Morgenstern too has largely influenced my thinking. Even after I had become a colleague I participated in his Bible seminars and learned to look closely at a text. But over the years (along with a majority of scholars) I have grown less prodigal in the matter of emendations. Also I have given more attention to religion in the prophets than to problems in the Pentateuch.

An alumnus reading this account will remember the questions and challenges current in his generation at the College, broad questions of method, narrow questions of interpretation (I have been grateful for these fruitful challenges). "Why do we need to know Hebrew?" This question started to fade at about the time Israel was born. "Is this emendation necessary?" On mature consideration perhaps *this* one is not; perhaps the language is less rule-bound than one has supposed. "Were the prophets saying that God rejects the sacrificial cult absolutely? Weren't they really just rebuking the people for their hypocrisy?" Why do you want to think so?

Nelson Glueck served the College in two capacities, first as a member of its Bible faculty, 1928–47, then as president of the College, 1947–70. During the earlier period he divided his time and interest between teaching in Cincinnati, including courses formerly taught by Buttenwieser, who became *emeritus* in 1934, and involvement in Palestinian archaeology as well as other realities in the Middle East. By 1936 his title was professor of Bible and biblical archaeology, and during the years 1936–37 and 1937–38 he was on leave of absence as director of the American School of Oriental Research in Jerusalem. On the Cincinnati campus, in 1940–41 and subsequently, he offered an elective course: "The Archaeology of Palestine." He was on leave again in 1942–43 on war-related duty—with the Office of Strategic Services.

Glueck's title suggests the two cognate areas of his academic interest, Bible and archaeology. As a matter of fact, however, his publications in the field of archaeology far outnumber and outweigh those in Bible. His Jena dissertation was a word study: *Das Wort ḥesed im alttestamentlichen Sprachgebrauche als menschliche und göttliche gemeinschaftgemässe Verhaltungsweise.* It was published in 1927 as a *Beiheft* to the *Zeitschrift für die alttestamentliche Wissenschaft* and in 1967 in English translation as *Hesed in the Bible*— translated by Alfred Gottschalk. His authoritative statement is widely quoted. He contributed several similar studies to the *Universal Jewish Encyclopedia* ("Abomination," "Chosen People," "Egypt"—1939–41). Otherwise—to twist a metaphor—he "used the Bible as a spade to dig with," a Baedeker to his explorations, an aid to archaeology. He says as much in "The Bible as Divining Rod: By following clues in the scriptures, archaeologists are lighting up the ancient history of the Holy Land." [39]

His major works in archaeology are his four-volume *Explorations in Eastern Palestine, The Other Side of the Jordan, The River Jordan, Rivers in the Desert: A History of the Negev, Deities and Dolphins: The Story of the Nabataeans.* These are only the larger works; a full "Bibliography of Nelson Glueck" by Eleanor K. Vogel concludes the volume *Near Eastern Archaeology in the Twentieth Century,* edited by James A. Sanders and published in 1970 in celebration of Nelson Glueck's seventieth birthday—less than a year before his death in February 1971. [40]

Fritz Bamberger, professor of intellectual history at the New York School, contributed to that volume a preface, "The Mind of Nelson Glueck." In a perceptive analysis there he suggests how in the mind of Nelson Glueck the Bible and biblical archaeology were related. "Throughout his career," he says, "Glueck has distinctly separated the historical data furnished by archaeological research from religious truth, which is unaffected by it. He frowns on using archaeology as an instrument to prove the Bible" (p. xix). Glueck was fully aware of the limits of archaeology. He clearly said so in his contribution to the volume *In the Time of Harvest* (ed. Daniel J. Silver, 1963, p. 195): "The truths of the Bible . . . can neither be buttressed nor invalidated archaeologically." But it should not be supposed that the scientific judgment on the intellectual plane, involved in this distinction, was without its affective accompaniment. "The awareness that his research carried him to the 'background' of a great biblical idea provides Glueck with a great deal of personal and emotional satisfaction" (p. xx). This awareness could bring tears to one's throat.

Perhaps this is why Nelson Glueck became a "founder" and opened the Hebrew Union College Biblical and Archaeological School in Jerusalem. But several other things happened before that. One of these was the program of graduate studies on the Cincinnati campus. During the presidencies of Morgenstern and Glueck, from 1923 to 1970, three developments relate to the study of Bible, in its broader sense, at the College: the emergence of a department of Semitic languages, the addition of courses in Hellenistic studies and New Testament, and the expansion of the program of graduate studies.

Our Department of Semitic Languages got off to a start with the arrival of Julius Lewy. His name first appears on the faculty list in 1935–36 as lecturer in the history of the Ancient Near East—later as professor of Bible and Semitic languages.[41] In 1963, with a doctorate from the Sorbonne, Isaac Jerusalmi (HUC, 1956), became instructor, later professor, of Bible and Semitic languages. Samuel Greengus joined the Semitic languages faculty in that same year. When Julius Lewy died in 1963 his widow, Dr. Hildegard Lewy, offered courses in Assyriology, as visiting professor. David B. Weisberg was appointed to the department in 1967. Even this long list does not tell the full story of the expanding program in Semitic languages, because two men officially on the Bible faculty, Matitiahu Tsevat and Herbert C. Brichto, are qualified Semitists as well.

I needed to survey the *Reports, Programmes, Catalogs,* and *Catalogues* of the Hebrew Union College starting in 1875 to discover that this Semitics program was not, in 1935, an innovation. The department opened, nominally, on October 1, 1896.[42] Caspar Levias, S. Mannheimer, Max Margolis, and David Philipson were prepared to offer courses in Syriac, Arabic, Assyrian, and Ethiopic as well as Hebrew and Aramaic.[43] Students at the University of Cincinnati might enroll in these courses without payment of tuition. By 1897 the faculty, with the addition of Buttenwieser, was "prepared to teach also Coptic, Egyptian, Persian, Avestan and Sanscrit, Hebrew, Phoenician and Sabean Inscriptions." A note in the *Catalog* and *Program,* 1900–1901, p. 15, announces that the Semitic course "has not been opened this year." And, indeed, the word *nominally* earlier in our paragraph was (unfortunately) proper because, in a "History of the Hebrew Union College" (1906) [44] we experience the following deflation: "A Semitic department, planned as part of the University, and consisting of courses given by the instructors of the College, was announced in 1897. Its object was to overcome the difficulty created by the demand of a tuition fee by the University from the students of the College, who had formerly been admitted free. The department, however, was not activated." This historical note[45] sets the record straight: our Semitics department did have its origin with the arrival of Julius Lewy in 1935—but we look back with respect to the faculty assembled in our first quarter-century and their linguistic capacities.

Matitiahu Tsevat was educated in Germany, Israel, and the College-Institute, with Bible consistently as his major subject. His doctoral dissertation (HUC, 1953) was *A Study of the Language of the Bibli-*

cal Psalms. It was published as volume IX in the Monograph Series of the *Journal of Biblical Literature* in 1955. The title properly suggests his interest in linguistics and his meticulous scholarship. But he does not lose himself in a forest of detail; he has an eye for the open spaces. His paper on "The Meaning of the Book of Job" (*HUC Annual* 1966) suggests the broad range of his spirit.

Quite convinced that the books of the Bible have a literary prehistory, yet at the same time skeptical of our ability now to retrace the course of that prehistory, he prefers to approach these books as they are. Also, he keeps in separate compartments the Bible and the rabbinic commentaries. Within the Bible he is partial to the prophets and their social concern. His own warm concern as teacher is for the needs of the future rabbis.

Herbert Brichto, ordained in 1950 at our New York School, did graduate work in Semitic languages and literature in the Department of Oriental Studies of the University of Pennsylvania, where he received the Ph.D. degree in 1962. His doctoral dissertation, *The Problem of "Curse" in the Hebrew Bible,* was also published in the *JBL* Monograph Series (vol. XIII, 1963). He was a member of the Bible faculty of the New York School from 1955 to 1964. He has twice been annual professor at the Hebrew Union College Biblical and Archaeological School in Jerusalem. He has a broad acquaintance with rabbinics and general Judaica as well as Semitics.

As concerns method, he does not find disturbing the thought that the Bible text has suffered corruptions and even dislocations in the course of its transmission. He assigns no more authority to rabbinic commentaries than to any others. He feels the absolute need to assume "sources" (J, E, D, P) in the Pentateuch, but he would not date them according to any principle of evolution, rejecting the idea of "progressive revelation" in favor of what he calls "continuous" revelation. His interest is in "the thought world of the Bible." He sees the Bible as the wellspring of Western culture, and he holds knowledge of the Bible and acceptance of its cultural values to be the essential ingredients in the education of Western man in general, all the more so in the education of an American rabbi.

David Weisberg, with a Ph.D. from Yale University and experience as a research associate of the Oriental Institute of the University of Chicago, came to us as assistant professor of Bible and Semitic languages in 1967. Moved by a deeply religious spirit and a passionate sympathy for the struggle of biblical man to find his God, he wants to share with his students this spirit and this sympathy. These in no way collide with his wholly objective approach to the Bible text. He recognizes a faulty text when he sees it and looks for a remedy. He regards the Pentateuch, as well as other books, as composite but sees fragments rather than continuous documents, and he doubts our ability now to recover the original order of composition. He sees the Bible growing by accretion, revelation following on revelation. The Masorah is a special interest. And his knowledge of the history and literature of the ancient Near East puts his studies in a broad perspective.

Our program had not been totally neglecting the Hellenistic period—both Kaufmann Kohler and Moses Buttenwieser offered occasional courses in the noncanonical writings—but in 1952, with the appointment of Samuel Sandmel (HUC, 1937; Ph.D., Yale) as professor of Bible and Hellenistic literature, Hellenistic studies became a solid segment of the Department of Bible. With an encyclopedic range of thought and knowledge and a dedicated pen, Sandmel teaches and writes widely on many aspects of the broader subjects: introduction, Hellenistic literature, New Testament, Christianity and Judaism.[46]

Sandmel has felt the need, as many do, to go beyond the method of source criticism and sees in the literary history of the Hebrew Bible organic growth, a demythologized version of "progressive revelation." [47] He will assume corruption in the Hebrew text rather than attempt strained exegesis. He assigns the medieval commentaries to the rabbinics department. His favorite books among the Hebrew Scriptures are Amos, Jeremiah, the Second Isaiah, and Job, and he would hope that an appreciation of these products of the Jewish spirit might add to a student's social sense and understanding of himself.

Sandmel's name will appear frequently in the references below to projects furthered by our Bible faculty.

Add to the Bible fare offered by Blank, Brichto, Tsevat, and Weisberg the varied offerings in Semitic languages and Near Eastern history on the one hand and those of the one-man faculty of Hellenistic literature on the other, with, until his recent, much too early death, Nelson Glueck's authoritative interpretation of biblical archaeology, and incentive enough appears for the growth of a respectable department of graduate studies.

In 1949 "the Department of Education of the State of Ohio authorized the Hebrew Union College to award the degree of Doctor of Philosophy in Hebraic and Cognate Studies."[48] This degree was made available to our rabbinical alumni and other qualified Jewish students with a B.A. degree, as well as to graduates of other Jewish or Christian theological seminaries. Since 1951 we have awarded this earned doctoral degree to numerous Jewish and Christian students. Jewish candidates have tended to specialize in Jewish history, rabbinics, or philosophy-theology. Most non-Jewish candidates, however, chose Bible as their major subject, or Bible-related fields (Semitic languages, tannaitic and Hellenistic literature). Considering the fact that in large numbers these men accept teaching positions in their denominational seminaries or other institutions of higher learning, this contribution of the College to Bible scholarship in America is substantial. The impact can be observed, for example, in the programs of the annual meetings of the Society of Biblical Literature and in the pages of the *Journal of Biblical Literature*. Published doctoral dissertations in the field of Bible include *Suffering as Divine Discipline in the Old Testament and Post Biblical Judaism* (1955) by James A. Sanders, *The Hebrew Conception of the World* by Luis I. J. Stadelmann (Analecta Biblica 39, 1970), and *The Language of Biblical Psalms* by Matitiahu Tsevat, mentioned above.[49]

Contributions in the field of Bible by our rabbinic alumni cover a wide range; they include scholarly books and essays along with high-level popularizations, textbooks for religious schools and study groups along with homiletical expositions, all well designed to bring from the academies to the people the values resident in Holy Writ.[50]

The merger of the Hebrew Union College in Cincinnati and the Jewish Institute of Religion in New York was effected soon after Nelson Glueck became president. The Institute opened in the fall of 1922 and went its separate course for twenty-eight years. Then, in 1950, along with the College, it assumed a hyphenated existence— as the right-side half of the designation "College-Institute."

As the creation of Stephen Wise the Institute has quite naturally manifested his liberal spirit and devotion to "truth." The literature, history, and religious experience "are studied scientifically in the classroom." Everyone, teacher and student alike, "is free to seek and to state the truth as he sees it."[51]

Julian Obermann, Ralph Marcus, Harry S. Lewis, and Shalom

Spiegel taught Bible for a sizable number of years at the New York school prior to the merger.[52] Harry M. Orlinsky (Ph.D., Dropsie) came to the faculty of the Institute in 1943; he was on the faculty when the merger took place, and he has carried the major burden of Bible instruction there through the later years. This has by no means kept him from other scholarly pursuits. A special interest early and late has been the Septuagint. In 1949 he published his work: *The Septuagint, the Oldest Translation of the Bible.* If they were assembled under one cover, the series of "Studies in the Septuagint of the Book of Job," which he contributed to the *Hebrew Union College Annual* from 1957 to 1965, would themselves form a respectable volume. He is the founder and currently the president of the International Organization for Septuagint and Cognate Studies. He is a co-translator of a five-volume English edition of Rashi's commentary to the Torah (1949–50) and author of *The So-Called "Servant of the Lord" and "Suffering Servant" in Second Isaiah* (1967). His most used work may be his *Ancient Israel,* which has gone through several printings.[53] He has been associated with a number of significant scholarly undertakings. In some of them he is one among several members of our Bible faculties to be involved, in others he has played a leading role. His name, too, will reappear in the section concerning certain Bible projects.

The California and Jerusalem schools of the College-Institute also came into being during the administration of Nelson Glueck. "In September 1954, a Rabbinic Department was inaugurated [in Los Angeles] to include Pre-Rabbinic studies, the first two years of the regular Rabbinic course, and a graduate course of studies leading to the Doctor of Hebrew Letters Degree." [54] Bible courses were taught by Dov Bin-Nun and Samson H. Levey, and beginning in 1959 also by Alfred Gottschalk. Ben Zion Wacholder and later Stephen M. Passamaneck taught Commentaries. Gerald A. Larue and Wolf Leslau were visiting professors in the area. Stanley Gevirtz joined the faculty as professor of Bible in 1972. Judging by the quality of the product— the students who, after completing the two-year rabbinic program in Los Angeles, come to Cincinnati for the remaining years—the level of Bible instruction there is high.

Dr. Gottschalk, who first attended the College-Institute in New York, was ordained at the Cincinnati school in 1957. President Glueck sent him to Los Angeles immediately after his graduation, first as director, later as dean, of the school there. He received the Ph.D. degree in 1965 from the University of Southern California with a dissertation on *Aḥad Ha-ʿAm, the Bible and the Bible Tradition*. In 1965 he held the title Professor of Bible and Jewish religious thought. Among his published works is his translation of Nelson Glueck's *Ḥesed in the Bible* (1967). In 1971 he became president of the College-Institute.

Alfred Gottschalk's inclination toward the study of Bible is unmistakable. He combines this inclination with an awareness of the Jewish realities of our times—a healthy combination. The State of Israel is among these realities, and he is not likely to neglect our Jerusalem School of Bible and Archaeology.

The Hebrew Union College Biblical and Archaeological School in Jerusalem is the creation of Nelson Glueck, born of his attachment to the old-new land. It is "a post-doctoral research center serving American and other universities, seminaries and museums as a base for advanced Biblical and related studies and archaeological investigation in Israel." [55] The school buildings, with lecture rooms, library, and chapel, dedicated in 1963, and including the Nelson Glueck School of Biblical Archaeology, named in 1973, are on King David Street in Jerusalem; the aggregate of archaeological sites in the land of Israel and, in particular, the excavations at Gezer, begun in 1965 jointly with Harvard University and continuing season after season, have served as laboratory.

The school in Jerusalem draws on the other three schools for faculty. From the Cincinnati Bible faculty Herbert Brichto and Matitiahu Tsevat have each spent a year or more at the Jerusalem School. Shemaryahu Talmon of the Hebrew University has been attached to the school as visiting professor of Bible. [56]

Starting with the class that entered the three schools (Cincinnati, New York, and California) in the fall of 1970, each incoming class spends the first year in Israel, enjoying the facilities of the HUCBAS, learning basic Hebrew, making contact with the land and people, and filling in the background against which future Bible study will have richer meaning.

Certain projects remain to be mentioned: *The Hebrew Union College Annual*, Bible translations and commentaries, the Goldenson Lectures, editorial activities, association with learned societies.

The *Hebrew Union College Annual* was projected in 1922: it was to be "a journal devoted to the promotion of Jewish Science." In the forty-three volumes of the *HUCA* which have appeared since its actual inception in 1924, articles by members of our Bible faculties figure prominently.[57]

Still within the nineteenth century, the Jewish Publication Society of America undertook a new translation of the Bible, but the completed work, *The Holy Scriptures according to the Masoretic Text, A New Translation,* first appeared in 1917. Over that period alumni of the College and men associated at one time or another with our faculties participated in the project. Max L. Margolis served as editor-in-chief; Kaufmann Kohler and David Philipson were on the nine-man Board of Editors; Rudolph Grossmann, Kaufmann Kohler, Joseph Krauskopf, Moses Mielziner, David Philipson, William Rosenau, and Stephen S. Wise were among the translators.[58]

When, in 1955, the JPS undertook a still newer translation of the Hebrew Bible, "the Society appointed a committee of seven scholars" for the task—with H. M. Orlinsky as editor-in-chief, and, as a member, Bernard J. Bamberger, later also Martin S. Rozenberg. First to be published (in 1962) was *The Torah . . . A New Translation . . . According to the Masoretic Text.* On his way to the editorship of this translation Orlinsky had served for some years (1945–52) as a member of the Revision Committee for the *Revised Standard Version* of 1952.[59] In 1970 the Jewish Publication Society published *Notes on the New Translation of the Torah* by Orlinsky.

At the time of this writing (March 1973), an annotated edition of the *New English Bible,* to be published by the Oxford University Press, is in preparation. Samuel Sandmel is the general editor of the Old Testament section. The annotators include S. H. Blank (Jeremiah), David Weisberg (Ezra, Nehemiah, 1 Esdras), as well as three of our doctoral alumni: Lloyd R. Bailey, Richard A. Henshaw, and Clyde M. Woods.

The Union of American Hebrew Congregations has in preparation a Commentary on the Pentateuch from a liberal Jewish point of view, with Bernard Bamberger and Gunther Plaut among the commentators.

The four-volume *Interpreter's Dictionary of the Bible,* which appeared in 1962, contains important contributions in the field written by members of our faculties.[60]

In a paragraph on Moses Buttenwieser above,[61] mention was made of the Goldenson Lectures. From 1955 to 1966, twelve of these lectures "on some aspect of Prophetic Judaism" were presented, eight of these by members of our faculties or our alumni.[62]

Orlinsky has served as general editor of the Library of Biblical Studies, and members of our faculties have contributed a number of the prolegomena for the series. Morgenstern, Blank, Sandmel, and Orlinsky have had their turns as national president of the Society of Biblical Literature.

These are among the Bible-area projects in which the College-Institute has been actively engaged.[63]

There are three ways to approach a Bible text—all legitimate—all represented in the study of Bible at the College: (1) we may ask what the words have meant; (2) we may ask what the words meant; (3) we may ask what the words can mean.

1. When we ask *what the words have meant,* we are reviewing the history of the exegesis, noting what the generations of interpreters have found in, or have read into, the Bible text. This first way is the way of "tradition." In a rabbinical school the resources for such a study are the *targumim* and the *Mefarshim* (Rashi, Rashbam, Ibn Ezra, the Kimhis, and the rest). It has its attractions, this method: it is unquestionably "Jewish"; it is in itself cultural history; it yields matter that is significant for the second way—and for the third.

2. When we ask *what the words meant,* we focus on the Bible text in its own time and circumstance; we employ the "scientific," or historico-critical, method. We attempt to see things simply, as we find them, as they are—to get at the "truth," to interpret the Bible on its own terms. The resources for such a study are archaeological materials, the languages and literatures of the ancient Near East, and the like—but they are also, and preeminently, the Bible text itself. This is the way which Abraham Cronbach invoked in his tribute to Moses Buttenwieser,[64] "the solid ground of the plain meaning."

3. When, finally, we ask *what the words can mean,* we are in search of the inherent values. We do not revert to the first of the ways, the *derush* or homily (at least we do not intend to do so); we go on beyond the second way. Having learned what the words meant (so far as possible), we ask: Well, what then? What profit was there in the search?

An inventory of the matter reviewed in these pages will suggest that over the decades this College has used all three methods in its exploration of the Bible. Though the expositors have not employed one method to the exclusion of the others, in the writing and teaching of this professor or of that, this or that method was dominant. With Isaac M. Wise the emphasis was without doubt on the "tradition"; with Morgenstern, and possibly Glueck, it was heavily on the "historico-critical"; with Buttenwieser, and possibly Blank, apparently, too, with Sandmel, Brichto, Weisberg, and Tsevat, it has also been a historico-critical approach, but with a warm concern for the "meaning-for-us" aspect as well. These names as examples. All would have claimed, and with justice, that their loyalties embraced all three kinds of meaning. But the trend in the shifting scene has been toward the study of Bible as a search for roots and nurture, requisite for growth and stability.

Those who taught and teach in this home of American Reform Judaism, those of us who teach Bible at the College-Institute, have approached our assignment in various ways and, selective, have shown a predilection for one or another segment of the whole. We have done "basic research"; scholarship, yes, it is there, solid and plenteous; but also, indeed first and foremost, "applied science." It is fair to say that the Bible faculty have always thought their prime goal and function to be the adequate preparation of rabbinic students for rabbinic service. We have seen the Bible as an unrivaled instrument for such preparation, a rich respository of social values, of what Isaac M. Wise called "Bible truth." Today, through a drift of ceremony and of *halakha,* a current of the "prophetic" still makes its certain way.

Notes

1. From *Judaism and Christianity* (Cincinnati, 1883), p. 10, cited in *Isaac M. Wise, His Life, Work and Thought* by James G. Heller (New York, 1965), p. 634. In his address at the Chicago World's Congress of Religions in 1893 on the "Theology of Judaism," he speaks of "direct transcendental revelation," *The World's Congress of Religions, the Addresses and Papers* (Chicago, 1894), p. 159.
2. In his work, *The Theology of Isaac Mayer Wise,* Monographs of the American Jewish Archives, no. V (1962), p. 58, Andrew F. Key observes that Wise "does not . . . , while using a 'philosophical' style, ever delve deeply enough into his material to achieve a carefully worked out philosophical presentation of the whole of his thought."
3. From the Preface, pp. 5 f., of Wise's *Pronaos to Holy Writ, Establishing, on Documentary Evidence, the Authorship, Date, Form, and Contents of Each of Its Books and the Authenticity of the Pentateuch* (1891).—For a number of years the *Pronaos* served as textbook for its author's course with juniors and seniors: "Introduction to Holy Writ and Authenticity of the Pentateuch according to Wise's Pronaos, the Entire Argument," *Proceedings of the Union of American Hebrew Congregations,* vol. IV, "Report of the President of the Hebrew Union College," October 1892, p. 2995.
4. *Proceedings of the UAHC,* IV, p. 3544.
5. *Ibid.,* IV, p. 3208.
6. *Pronaos,* p. 4.
7. *Ibid.,* p. 4; cf. p. 157. "Therefore we are bound to admit," he begins on p. 182—but his admissions do not go very far.

8. A fuller listing with years of incumbency: Solomon Eppinger (1875–86), Max Lilienthal (1876–82), Louis Aufrecht (1878–82), Sigmund Mannheimer (1884–1900 and beyond), Henry Zirndorf (1884–90), David Davidson (1886–92), David Philipson (1889–1900 and beyond), Charles S. Levi (1889–98), Ephraim Feldman (1892–1900 and beyond), Max L. Margolis (1892–97), Caspar Levias (1895–1900 and beyond), Moses Buttenwieser (1897–1900 and beyond).

9. In his "Autobiography" in *American Jewish Archives,* April 1959, p. 22, Abraham Cronbach says of Ephraim Feldman: "Despite his extraordinary gifts Feldman published almost nothing," but consider the shining context of this remark there.

10. *CCAR Yearbook,* 1897, pp. 9–10.

11. *Ibid.,* 1896, p. 145.

12. *Ibid.,* 1895, p. 60.

13. *Ibid.,* 1900, p. 88.

14. *Ibid.,* 1900, p. 144.

15. *Wissenschaft* was the subject of a sharp exchange between Emil G. Hirsch and S. H. Sonnenschein at the turn of the century. Sonnenschein found it necessary to say: "The Pentateuch was not produced by Judaism . . . it produced Judaism." This was his response to Hirsch, who, discussing a Conference paper on "The Synod in the Past and Its Feasibility in the Present," had insisted that "laws are collected not made. They come from the people not from the synods." "The laws which we call fundamental wrote themselves" (*CCAR Yearbook,* 1900, p. 60).

16. The twelve volumes were completed from 1901 to 1906.

17. *Hebrew Union College Annual 1904,* ed. Ephraim Frisch, pp. 10–13.

18. Kaufmann Kohler, *Jewish Theology Systematically and Historically Considered* (New York, 1918), p. 36.

19. In an as yet unpublished rabbinical thesis, "The Theologies of Isaac Mayer Wise and Kaufmann Kohler" (HUC Cincinnati, 1972)—a very lucid exposition—Ralph D. Mecklenburger calls this thought by its popular name, "progressive revelation" (p. 88).

20. Vol. VII, p. 533.

21. When I was working at the Prolegomenon to the recent reisssue of C. D. Ginsburg's *The Song of Songs and Coheleth* (1970), I came across a little-known work of Kohler's: *Das Hohe Lied übersetzt und kritisch neu bearbeitet* (Chicago, 1878) with the descriptive subtitle: *Ein Jerusalemisches Singspiel.* Kohler had arranged it as an operetta and he dedicated it to his father-in-law, David Einhorn of New York, and Samuel Hirsch in Philadelphia on the occasion of the marriage of their children, Mathilda Einhorn and Emil Hirsch, in Louisville, Ky.

22. In his work *The Hebrew Scriptures* (1963, pp. 21 f.), a full half-century later, Samuel Sandmel, sharing Kohler's view, treats the Prophets (and the Writings) before the Pentateuch.

23. *Free Synagogue Pulpit, Sermons and Addresses* by Stephen S. Wise, vol. 1 (New York, 1908), p. 147 n.

24. The third address in that same series (pp. 75–102), "The Religion of the Hebrew Prophets," is more in line with his ongoing interests and life-style: "For my part, I am free to confess that I go back to the Hebrew prophets for a definition of the principles of the religion of Israel" (p. 77)—a statement that deserves more than a footnote.

25. See below, p. 305. ◦

26. In *A Jubilee of the Spirit*, address on the occasion of the fiftieth anniversary of the founding of the Jewish Institute of Religion, May 31, 1972, p. 9.

27. *UAHC Proceedings*, 1897, p. 3832.

28. See below, pp. 308–9.

29. Born in St. Francisville, Ill., March 18, 1881. For this and other biographical notes, see Morris Lieberman, "Julian Morgenstern—Scholar, Teacher and Leader," *HUC Annual*, XXXII (1961), pp. 1–9.

30. The quotations here are from the somewhat enlarged version of the CCAR paper as published in a volume of his essays and addresses entitled *As a Mighty Stream: The Progress of Judaism through History* (Philadelphia, 1949). The paper is called "The Foundations of Israel's History."

31. "That the Torah, *i.e.*, the Pentateuch, had been divinely revealed to Moses, and constituted, therefore, the eternal, unchangeable, all-sufficient law for all Israel" was no more than a "tradition" which found general acceptance only after the completion of the Pentateuch (*As a Mighty Stream*, p. 15).

32. *As a Mighty Stream*, p. 25.

33. *Ibid.*, p. 12. These italics are mine.

34. *Ibid.*, p. 22.

35. The calendar studies: "The Three Calendars of Ancient Israel" and supplements (*HUC Annual*, 1924, 1926, 1935, 1947, 1948, 1952–53, 1968); the area of Pentateuchal law: "The Oldest Document of the Hexateuch," "The Book of the Covenant," etc. (*HUC Annual*, 1927, 1928, 1930, 1931–32, 1955, 1962); on Amos: "Amos Studies" (*HUC Annual*, 1936, 1937–38, 1940, 1961—the first three Amos Studies assembled in book form in 1941; on certain Psalms (*HUC Annual*, 1939, 1941, 1945–46, 1964); on the ark of the covenant: "The Ark, the Ephod, and the 'Tent of Meeting' " (*HUC Annual*, 1942–43, 1944, also in book form, 1945); on the hypothetical sack of Jerusalem in 485 B. C. (*HUC Annual*, 1950–51, 1956, 1957, 1960, 1966); on Deutero-Isaiah (*HUC Annual*, 1949, 1958, 1959, 1965). These are a selection out of the contributions which he has made year after year to the pages of the *Hebrew Union College Annual*. As an authority in such areas he was invited to supply entries on these subjects in, for example, the *Universal Jewish Encyclopedia* ("Decalogue"), the *Encyclopedia Judaica*, and the *Interpreter's Dictionary of the Bible*.

36. A thought which he develops more fully in *The Hebrew Scriptures*, pp. 332 ff.

37. Others, with appointments in other disciplines, offered occasional Bible courses: Solomon B. Freehof, Jacob R. Marcus, Abraham Cronbach, Israel Bettan, and Elias L. Epstein. Cronbach contributed to the study of Bible outside of the classroom as well as within. A book, *The Bible and Our Social*

Outlook, appeared in 1941. Among his last publications was an attractive article on "Unmeant Meanings of Scripture" (*HUC Annual,* 1965, pp. 99–123), an expansion of an article with the same title which he wrote for the student publication, the *Hebrew Union College Monthly* (October 1931). An earlier article on "The Social Ideas of the Apocrypha and Pseudepigrapha" appeared in the *Hebrew Union College Annual* for 1944. Israel Bettan is the author of *The Five Scrolls: A Commentary* (1950). Among Freehof's biblical writings are *The Book of Psalms: A Commentary* (1938), *Preface to Scripture* (1950), *The Book of Job: A Commentary* (1958), and *The Book of Isaiah: A Commentary* (1972). David Neumark (professor of Jewish philosophy, 1907–24) published *The Philosophy of the Bible* in 1918. The first volume of Jacob Mann's work, *The Bible as Read and Preached in the Old Synagogue: A Study in the Cycles of the Readings from Torah and Prophets, as well as from the Psalms, and in the Structure of the Midrashic Homilies,* appeared in 1944, vol. II (posthumously) in 1966. Mann was professor of Jewish history at the Cincinnati School from 1922 to 1940. Isaiah Sonne, lecturer in medieval Jewish history, prepared the second volume for publication, but he too died, in 1960, before it appeared. Victor E. Reichert was then largely responsible for its completion.

38. See n. 60, below.
39. *Horizon, A Magazine of the Arts,* November 1959, pp. 4–10, 118–19.
40. His voluminous *Explorations in Eastern Palestine,* I–IV, appeared in the *Annual of the American Schools of Oriental Research* (1933–34, 1934–35, 1937–39, 1951). *The Other Side of the Jordan* appeared in 1940, revised 1970; *The River Jordan* in 1946, revised 1968; *Rivers in the Desert: A History of the Negev* in 1959, revised 1968; *Deities and Dolphins: The Story of the Nabataeans* in 1965. He wrote much in his favorite field, in English and Hebrew, in the *Biblical Archaeologist,* the *Bulletin of the American Schools of Oriental Research,* the *Hebrew Union College Annual,* the *Journal of the American Oriental Society,* the *Journal of the Palestine Oriental Society,* the *American Journal of Archaeology, Ba-Machaneh, Davar, Hadoar, La-Merchav,* and more.
41. Franz Rosenthal joined him in 1940–41, first as fellow—later, and until 1948, as professor of Bible and Semitic languages. Hillel A. Fine, who had been a graduate fellow (his doctoral thesis—Ph.D., Cincinnati, 1950: *Studies in Middle-Assyrian Chronology and Religion,* HUC Press, 1955), held the position of assistant professor in Bible and Semitic languages from 1951 to 1956. William W. Hallo came in 1956 as instructor and remained as professor of Bible and Semitic languages until 1962.
42. "Programme of the Hebrew Union College, 1896–1897" in *Proceedings,* IV, pp. 3631, 3636.
43. *Proceedings,* IV, p. 3832.
44. *Catalog,* May 1906, p. 29.
45. Which, however, is at variance with a statement on the prefatory page of Philipson's *Five Lectures* (see above, p. 289): The lectures "were in-

tended as an introduction to the formation of a class for Assyrian study. Such a class has been formed and is now in regular pursuit of the work."

46. These are his major works: *The Hebrew Scriptures: An Introduction to Their Literature and Religious Ideas* (1963 and 1968), *The Enjoyment of Scripture* (1972), *Herod: Profile of a Tyrant* (1967), *Philo's Place in Judaism* (1956 and 1971), *A Jewish Understanding of the New Testament* (1956 and 1968), *We Jews and Jesus* (1965), *The Genius of Paul* (1959 and 1970), *We Jews and You Christians* (1967), *The First Christian Century in Judaism and Christianity* (1969), *The Two Living Traditions* (1972), *The Several Israels and an Essay: Religion and Modern Man* (1971), and a novel about Moses and the Exodus: *Alone Atop the Mountain* (1973).

47. See the reference above, p. 298, to his essay "The Haggada within Scripture," and see also "The Ancient Hebrew Mind and Ours" in *Understanding the Sacred Text* (1972).

48. *Catalogue*, 1949–50, p. 45.

49. Sanders is the author also of *The Old Testament in the Cross* (1961), *The Dead Sea Psalms Scroll* (1967), and *Torah and Canon* (1972).

50. A full listing—which should include scholarly papers, entries in encyclopedias, etc., as well as books—is not possible; a partial listing would be unfair.

51. According to the statement of "Scope and Purpose" in the *Annual Catalogue* (1925–26, p. 9).

52. Other eminent Bible scholars came, for briefer periods, as visiting professors, and in several instances the Institute sponsored the publication of their lectures. These include: Reuben Levy (*Deutero-Isaiah: A Commentary*, 1925), Hugo Gressmann (*Israel and the Tower of Babel*, 1928), Charles Cutler Torrey (*The Jewish Foundations of Islam*, 1933), also William Foxwell Albright and Harry Torczyner (1929).

53. Published 1954 and 1960; in Japanese translation in 1961; with additions and revisions under the new title *Understanding the Bible through History and Archaeology* in 1972.

54. Quoted from HUC-JIR *Catalogue*, 1956–57, p. 223.

55. Quoted from HUC-JIR *Catalogue*, 1964/5–1965/6, p. 115.

56. Scholars of repute in the field of Bible or biblical archaeology from other institutions have also served as annual professor or resident director: Frank Moore Cross, William G. Dever, John S. Holladay, Marvin H. Pope, Saul J. Weinberg, G. Ernest Wright.

57. Faculty men whose names appear with less or greater frequency among contributors of articles on the Bible and related matter include Blank, Brichto, Buttenwieser, Martin A. Cohen, Englander, Hildegard Lewy, Julius Lewy, Leon J. Liebreich, Morgenstern, Orlinsky, Sandmel, Sylvan Schwartzman, and Tsevat.

58. See *The Holy Scriptures,* Preface, pp. v–vi.

59. See *An Introduction to the Revised Standard Version of the Old Testament* by Members of the Revision Committee, Luther A. Weigle, chairman (New York, 1952), p. 89.

60. Blank ("Ecclesiastes," "Proverb," "Proverbs, Book of," "Wisdom"), Cronbach ("Ethics," "Righteousness," "Worship"), Hildegard Lewy ("Mari"), Morgenstern ("Israel, Social and Economic Development of," "Jubilee, Year of," "New Year," "Sabbath," "Sabbatical Year"), Orlinsky ("Maccabees"), Sandmel ("Herod"), Isaiah Sonne ("Synagogue"), Eric Werner ("Masoretic Accents," "Music," "Musical Instruments"), to mention only the longer entries in the Bible field.

61. P. 295.

62. Blank, Cronbach, and Orlinsky; Bernard Bamberger, Leon I. Feuer, Levi A. Olan, Edgar F. Magnin, and Lou H. Silberman, Jr. In 1969 the Hebrew Union College Press published the twelve lectures in one volume: *Interpreting the Prophetic Tradition,* one of the Library of Biblical Studies series.

63. This article was already completed in typescript when I came upon the competent, bibliographically rich, review by Harry Orlinsky: "Jewish Biblical Scholarship in America" (in the *Jewish Quarterly Review,* April 1955 and April 1957). He limited himself to scholars no longer living, but these then included Isaac M. Wise, Kaufmann Kohler, David Neumark, Max Margolis, Caspar Levias, William Rosenau, Henry Englander, Moses Buttenwieser, and Eugen Taeubler. Our emphases are different, but he and I cover a lot of common ground, and if I had found his article sooner my way would have been shorter. A notable feature of Orlinsky's review is his enthusiastic appraisal (*JQR,* 1957, pp. 392–98) of the work of Margolis, whose few years of association with the Hebrew Union College were only a segment of his long scholarly career (see above, p. 289 and p. 292).

64. Quoted above, p. 295.

LEWIS M. BARTH

Rabbinics

Preface

In the course of a century, the scholars and teachers of the Hebrew Union College–Jewish Institute of Religion have published well over 350 items, including books, scholarly articles, and popular pieces, relating to the study of rabbinic Judaism. No area of this religious phenomenon or its literary manifestation has escaped searching examination for its own sake or for the bearing it might have on contemporary practice and belief. This combination of pure scholarship with a constant concern for the Reform context and modern Jewish life explains the unique tension in the totality of the writings of the Hebrew Union College faculty in the field of rabbinics.

What follows here is a survey of this vast scholarly and popular literature. My purpose is to highlight the major areas of concern, to point out significant contributions within these areas, and to provide, through the attached bibliography, a glimpse of the enormous contribution of the Hebrew Union College to the study and understanding of rabbinic Judaism and its literature. The material is divided into subject categories and treated within each category on a chronological basis.

Literary Studies

The task of training American-born students in the various disciplines of rabbinics stimulated the production of an extensive auxiliary literature at the Hebrew Union College. Already in the early 1880s, Moses Mielziner (1823–1903) published articles on the talmudic syllogism (*qal ve-homer*) and the talmudic analogy (*gezera shava*) which later became chapters in his book, *Introduction to the Talmud.* The *Introduction,* of which four editions have been printed (1894, 1903, 1925, 1968), was to be "the first comprehensive work of its kind in the English language." It contains four parts: (1) a historical and literary introduction, (2) the legal hermeneutics of the Talmud, (3) talmudic terminology and methodology, and (4) outlines of talmudic ethics, plus additional notes, indexes, special biblical, midrashic, and talmudic references, and abbreviations used in the Talmud and commentaries. Mielziner's *Introduction* remains the standard work for beginning students, "indispensable to a proper understanding of talmudical discussions." [1]

In relatively recent years additional study aids have been developed at the College, generally in the form of mimeographed pamphlets. These include bibliographical works,[2] collections of selected passages of rabbinic literature,[3] and textbooks for the study of rabbinic Hebrew and Babylonian Aramaic.

Of the linguistic aids, *A Grammar of the Aramaic Idiom Contained in the Babylonian Talmud* (1901) by Caspar Levias (1860–1934) is almost a companion to Mielziner's *Introduction.* This volume, still recognized as a pioneering study, presents Babylonian Aramaic grammar in a thorough and systematic way, lacking only a section on syntax. More recently, Isaac Jerusalmi has compiled excellent aids for rabbinic Hebrew and Babylonian Aramaic. In *The Talmud Is in Aramaic* (1966), Jerusalmi gives selected Aramaic aggadic passages with vocabulary lists and grammatical explanations. His *Basic Pirqe Avoth* (1968) is a philological commentary to this tractate and provides a word-by-word linguistic analysis of the text.[4]

We turn now from works designed for students to serious researches in Hebrew grammar, philology, and manuscripts. Henry Englander (1877–1951), in a series of articles, deals with "Grammatical Elements and Terminology in Rashi's Biblical Commentaries" (1936–39). He lists and describes the meaning or function of various terms used by Rashi and gives a detailed discussion of Rashi's views on the Hebrew verb, vowel terminology, and the grammatical elements in his commentary. In later articles Englander elaborates on his analysis of Rashi's grammatical comments and offers a commentary to Rashi's commentary on the *Tanakh*.

Several excellent philological studies have been produced at the College in recent years. Franz Rosenthal, who taught at the Cincinnati campus for a brief period in the 1940s, devotes an article to the term *yom tov* (1944). He traces a transition in meaning from "day of plenty" to "holiday," and argues that this occurred during the Maccabean period, a time of celebration of festivals of national rather than of strictly "religious" importance. In "Studies in Talmudic Philology" (*HUC Annual,* 1950–51), Harry Orlinsky deals with the allegedly Greek word *'afilon* in Pal. *Berakhot,* IX, 3 and related passages. He cites and criticizes all previous attempts to explain the word particularly from a Greek origin and argues that it is merely a corruption of *'afilu*. With a slightly different focus, David Weisberg examines cross-cultural influences in late Babylonian and rabbinic texts (*HUC Annual,* 1968). He demonstrates a reciprocal influence by showing that a noticeable number of Aramaic words can be found in late Babylonian texts and numerous late Babylonian terms occur in rabbinic texts. In a further article written in collaboration with Israel Lehman (1970), Weisburg emends an Aramaic phrase found in Bavli *Berakhot* 4lb. The usual translation, "feet of iron," is inappropriate to the context, which requires an image of speed and agility. The suggested emendation from "iron" (*farzela'*) to "fleet-footed gazelle" (*'arzela'*) requires a change of only one letter, and the substitution is well attested in classical Hebrew, Akkadian, Aramaic, and Arabic.

In the area of manuscript study, Jacob Z. Lauterbach's (1873–1942) work on the *Mekhilta,* to be discussed later, provided the basis for articles on scribal activity and techniques. In "Abbreviations and Their Solution" (1929), Lauterbach describes the tendency of over-ambitious copyists to remove abbreviations in the course of their work and classifies the types of mistakes which resulted. Lauterbach continues this research in "Substitutes for the Tetragrammaton" (1931), which traces the development of the written abbreviations of *YHWH* in medieval manuscripts to their origin in rabbinic times. He presents a list of eighty-four separate abbreviations found in manuscripts and early printed books, arranged not chronologically but according to size and simplicity of form. All these, he argues, can be accounted for by graphic developments from the old original *yod he* abbreviation, and they have no special theological or mystical significance. Isaiah Sonne (1887–1960) focuses on a different kind of problem in a series of articles on the history of the publication of Hebrew books, one of which deals with the published editions of Rashi's commentary to the Torah (1940). Sonne gives a history of the publication of the commentary and, after criticizing the effort by A. Berliner, suggests that the manuscripts and printed editions of Rashi should be grouped according to the geographical centers in which Rashi was studied. My own area of interest has been in manuscript studies, and in *An Analysis of Vatican 30* (1973), I treat the scribal characteristics, paleography, and linguistic peculiarities of this manuscript of *Bereshit Rabba* in an attempt to reevaluate the manuscript's position in the tradition of this text.

With regard to the publishing of manuscripts themselves, Lauterbach's excellent edition of the *Mekilta* (1933–35) is the first and only scientific publication of an entire major volume of rabbinic literature by an HUC faculty member. Its introduction describes the background of this Midrash, the sources for the edition, the methods followed in deciding on the text ("the text . . . is eclectic"), and the apparatus. A translation, scriptural references, rabbinic parallels, and significant variant readings are provided. Other midrashic manuscript publications of Lauterbach include *Midrash WaYis'u* (1933) and unpublished parts of *Yalkut ha-Makhiri* on Hosea and Micah (1936). Jacob Mann (1888–1940), whose volumes and articles on the Gaonic period contain numerous texts and fragments covering all aspects of Jewish life, also published a significant amount of midrashic manuscript material. "Some Midrashic Genizah Fragments" (1939) includes new versions of *Midrash Tehillim,* a leaf from a new Midrash to Canticles, fragments of the Midrash on contradictory biblical verses, and a Gaonic-period epistle in Midrashic style. Mann's two volumes on the history of the Jewish homily, *The Bible as Read* and *Preached in the Old Synagogue* (1940 and 1966), contain extensive new manuscript material from midrashic literature. The arrangement is according to the Palestinian cycle of Torah readings as Mann conceived it; each section opens with a brief introduction describing the content of the fragment, its place in the literature, and its importance for Mann's hypothesis on the development of the sermon.

A major focus in the area of text publication has been in halakhic material, mostly from the medieval period. The only earlier piece is Mann's contribution, *Sefer Ha-ma'asim Li-vene 'erez Yisra'el* (1930), a work probably from Palestine before the Arab conquest, which reveals customs and practices of Palestinian Jews under Byzantine rule. Isaiah Sonne published the text of a *Taqanah* of R. Meshulam Feibish, suggesting that its origin is Krakow at the end of the sixteenth-century (1935). The decree concerned a detail about Sabbath observance issued by R. Meshulam and agreed to by the rabbinic council of the Council of Four Lands. Over the years numerous manuscripts were published by Samuel Atlas, including *A Section from the Yad Ha-Hazakah of Maimonides* (1940), *Novellae on Tractate Baba Kamma by Abraham ben David (Rabad of Posquieres)* (1941), and a three-part study on criticisms by R. Moses Ha-Cohen of Lunel, a thirteenth-century French rabbi, of the Code of Maimonides (1956, 1963, 1966). Each text has an excellent introduction and is annotated with extensive and detailed comments by Atlas covering philological and halakhic problems. Similarly, Ben Zion Wacholder has published Hebrew Union College Library Manuscript #80, containing *Tosafot Yeshanim* and Novellae of the Rabad on chapters I and II of tractate *Kiddushin* and chapter I of *Yevamot* (*HUC Annual,* 1966, 1969, 1970). In his introductions, Wacholder describes differences between this material and the *Tosafot* printed in the standard editions of the Talmud since the sixteenth-century and the relation of this material to the Rambam, Rashba, and Ha-Me'iri.

Nearly all the books and articles of Jacob Mann covering the Gaonic period contain manuscript material published for the first time by the author. The major portion, though by no means all, is from the Cairo Geniza and serves as the basis of Mann's historical essays. Prior to his coming to the College, Mann had already published Gaonic responsa (1916–21), book lists from the Geniza (1921), and a wealth of diverse materials, especially in Vol. II of *The Jews in Egypt and in Palestine under the Fatimid Caliphs* (Oxford, 1920–22). He continued to work extensively in this area after his appointment at the College and published additional material as a basis for Gaonic Studies in *HUC Annual, Tarbiz,* and the major two-volume work, *Texts and Studies in Jewish History and Literature* (1931 and 1935).

In the area of translations, apart from Lauterbach's *Mekilta,* no major works have appeared.[5]

Studies in the history of the literature form the last category in this section. These works treat the origin, structure, dating, and literary problems connected with specific rabbinic compositions.[6] In terms of literary treatment, it is fair to say that only one rabbinic collection has attracted sustained attention at the College: the *Mekhilta.* As a result of his labors preparing the edition of this text, Lauterbach devoted a series of articles to its origin, history, and organization. In "The Name of the Mekilta" (1920), Lauterbach notes that the first to designate our Midrash as *Mekhilta* were R. Nissim of Kairwan and R. Samuel Ha-Nagid, that the word *mekhilta* means the same as *masekhta,* "tractate," and that the distinguishing feature of this midrash to Exodus is that it is organized by *masekhtot* or tractates, unlike the other tannaitic Midrashim. This last point provides the background for Lauterbach's next article, "The Arrangement and the Division of the Mekilta" (1924), which traces the organization of the work from its original division into tractates, chapters, and *halakhot,* through a rearrangement in the Middle Ages when the more conventional division by weekly *sedra* was imposed on it. In a further article, "The Two Mekiltas" (1933), Lauterbach elaborates on the fact that since the name *mekhilta* means tractate, it was applied freely to numerous other works by the authorities of the Middle Ages.[7]

Many of the assumptions of a generation of rabbinic scholars, culminating in Lauterbach, on the origin, composition, and dating of the *Mekhilta* have been challenged in a provocative article by Ben Zion Wacholder, "The Date of the *Mekilta* de-Rabbi Ishmael" (1968). Wacholder rejects two basic statements which had the assent or endorsement of most scholars: that the *Mekhilta* is a genuine tannaitic Midrash, and that it reflects second-century tannaitic *halakha* of the School of Ishmael. Rather, he suggests that it is a "post-Talmudic compilation, or indeed concoction, deliberately using the names of Tannaim for authority or even inventing names."

Observations about authorities cited, exegesis, Hebrew style, and technical terminology of this Midrash lead Wacholder to the view that the *Mekhilta* was written by an author who used as sources the Mishna, the Palestinian and Babylonian Talmuds, minor talmudic tractates, and *Bereshit Rabba;* in addition, the *Mekhilta* seems to make reference to Arabs and Byzantine Christians. The work, he argues, would therefore fit into the cultural context of numerous pseudepigraphical compositions and the revival of the Hebrew language during the sixth to eighth century.

The other rabbinic text which has drawn some attention at the College is the Mishna of R. Judah Ha-Nasi. Literary questions relating to the Mishna were already the subject of Alexander Guttmann's interest before he joined the Hebrew Union College faculty. In two major monographs published in German in 1928, Guttmann deals with problems of the redaction of the Mishna and its relationship to the Tosephta. On the basis of a comparison with the Tosephta, Guttmann demonstrates Judah's conscious redactional intention, the purpose of which was "to create a basic but not too detailed code" for the governing of life. He has outlined the steps in this redactional process which explain the differences between the Mishna and Tosephta and the particular style and composition of the Mishna itself.[8] Finally, Guttmann treats the literary problems of tractate *Avot* in an article in which he examines its place in rabbinic literature (1950). After noting that the Tosephta does not include this tractate, tracing the reference to *Avot* through the Talmud, and comparing its location in the Talmud to that in the Mishna, he concludes that *Avot* is not an original part of the Mishna and that it was added about A.D. 300, probably for apologetic reasons relating to the rise of Christianity.

Studies in Halakha

We turn now from the area of literary studies to subject-related discussions of the *halakha*, its history, development, major categories and concepts, and related modern questions of Reform Judaism and the *halakha,* and contemporary applications of Jewish law. The works to be mentioned first are intended as broad histories of Jewish law; they contain large sections, however, which could be classified equally as well under the history of rabbinic literature or of the rabbinic period. Lauterbach's article, "Midrash and Mishna" (1916), sets the stage for the later major volumes of Chaim Tchernowitz and Alexander Guttmann in the history of the *halakha*. Lauterbach argues that the *halakha* was originally taught in the Midrash form, in which the traditional law is given with its scriptural basis. The latest the Mishna form could have been introduced was the time of Jose ben Joezer (d. 165 B.C.), mentioned in Mishna *Eduyot* 8:4. Lauterbach sees the use of the two forms as part of the conflict between Pharisees and Sadducees and suggests that the Midrash, preserved by the Sadducees, contained older *halakha*, while the Mishna form of the Pharisees reflected younger *halakha*. The Talmud was silent about this process because the Pharisees did not want to mention it for fear of strengthening the Sadducees, and later the Gaonim followed their example because of the Karaites.

For Tchernowitz, the issue of Midrash-Mishna form is only one of the numerous problems treated in his massive four-volume *Toledoth Ha-Halakah: History of Hebrew Law* (1934–50). Tchernowitz attempts to show the connection between the halakhic material, its time of origin, and the historical forces which brought it into being. However, the organization of the work is peculiar, being neither strictly chronological in approach nor systematic in subject categories.[9] Although this work met with severe criticism, it is clear that Tchernowitz treated every major scholarly issue in the early history of the *halakha*. His summaries of the views of other scholars and the questions he raises are good; his analysis, hypotheses, and conclusions are often highly speculative or groundless and must be rejected.

To be compared with Tchernowitz on this period is Alexander Guttmann's *Rabbinic Judaism in the Making: A Chapter in the History of the Halakhah from Ezra to Judah I*. Although published in 1970, it is in fact a summation of Guttmann's previous studies in this area, many of which are reprinted here. The work covers the same broad period as Tchernowitz's, but is organized on a more or less chronological basis.[10] Guttmann states briefly scholarly problems in the various subjects, with occasional references to the opinions of other scholars and with extensive citation of original material from the Mishna and other rabbinic sources. Specific hypotheses in the book will be treated below; suffice it to say here that this work represents a balanced, though conservative, handling of numerous scholarly problems in the history of the early *halakha* and the period from 400 B.C. to A.D. 200.

The third work to be mentioned here is again from the pen of Chaim Tchernowitz, *Toledoth Ha-Poskim: History of Jewish Codes* (1946–47). The title page contains the following description: "The History of Hebrew Law in the Period of its Codification; the Codifiers and the Codes, their Principles and Methods, from the Geonim to the Shulhan Aruk and its Commentators." This is an adequate description of a highly praised pioneering contribution to the later history of Jewish law. Again it must be said that clear organizational principles seem to be lacking.[11]

Quite distinct from these works of Tchernowitz and Guttmann is Samuel Atlas's unique contribution to the history of the *halakha* found in a series of articles on the development of the *suggya* (1935–64). Atlas introduces these acute and extremely technical investigations with an outline of his conception of talmudic studies and methodology. The purpose of talmudic research is to remove the veil thrown over the Talmud by its peculiar nature as a literary creation which developed over hundreds of years. In this examination of particular *suggyot*, he finds that when talmudic sages from later periods encountered difficulties in the expressions of earlier sages, they inserted into the text new meanings which sometimes confuse the issue. The task of the scholar is to recover original expressions and statements of earlier sages and to discover how later teachers understood these statements. The development of the *suggya* reflects the unfolding of the *halakha* itself, for its earliest parts are related to the earliest laws and the additions were brought into the *suggya* to suit it to later law. These additions can be discovered only by combining a kind of talmudic higher criticism with an understanding of talmudic logic. Such an effort requires the minute analysis of the *suggya*, but reveals what we may term the real internal legal-literary development of the *halakha*.

A different emphasis is found in a group of separate studies by Alexander Guttmann. In "The Problem of the Anonymous Mishna" (1941), and a series of articles (1938–47) on the relations of custom (*minhag*) to law, he examines specific aspects of the judicial process of determining the *halakha*. He notes that the Talmud's purpose in investigating the authorship of an anonymous Mishna reflects a method by which the legislation of Judah Ha-Nasi was revised or criticized. Citing numerous cases, he shows that it was the practice of Judah Ha-Nasi to designate a statement as being anonymous or by the *hakhamim,* even though the author was known to him, in order to give the statement the status of recognized law. Thus, in rediscovering the original author, the Talmud could easily dismiss or affirm the *halakha* under discussion. Regarding the relationship of custom to law in the Talmud, Guttmann notes that (1) *halakha* is in principle higher than *minhag,* (2) custom precedes law when it is stricter than the law (a *seyyag*), (3) the phrase "custom annuls the law" was not operative in talmudic times, (4) in both Talmuds the importance of *minhag* is emphasized in that it serves to establish a law, or as a reminder of a law forgotten in the academy, or to firm up a law which was shaky in the courts.[12]

About the time these studies were being produced, Samuel Atlas published his article on legal fictions in the Talmud, which deals with quite another aspect of determining the *halakha* (1946). Atlas is not concerned here with practical legal fictions whose purpose is to circumvent a particular law, but with a situation in which the legal process falsifies and says that one judicial phenomenon is to be considered like another so that existing legal forms could cover both of them. The *halakha,* he argues, has a strong "idealistic" bent in that it wanted to spread its rule over life situations which were not easily forced into previous legal modes. To accomplish this, the halakhic process cut itself off from the concrete world to shape a new legal reality under which all phenomena would be subsumed.[13]

These studies of Atlas and Guttmann covered mainly the judicial process. We now turn to works on various aspects of the law itself: civil-criminal law, the status of special persons, and miscellaneous studies. The earliest effort in this area is a useful little pamphlet by Moses Mielziner, *Legal Maxims and Fundamental Laws of the Civil and Criminal Code of the Talmud* (1898), in which the author collects, arranges, and explains his material under four headings: man's responsibility, property, donation, and testament. A similarly useful study was produced by Tchernowitz before he came to the JIR, in his published Talmud lectures dealing in a systematic way with the laws of damages, theft, and robbery and their various definitions, categories, and punishments (1913). A general paper by Atlas delivered to the CCAR in 1944 concerns "Rights of Private Property and Private

Profit" and is based on a broad comparison of basic attitudes of Roman, English, and Jewish law on the subject.

In the past decade, Stephen Passamaneck has published a number of articles on various aspects of Jewish civil-commercial law, including questions of compensation, property rights, and surety-insurance. "The Talmudic Concept of Defamation" (1965) is an attempt to discover whether Jewish law has a concept of defamation comparable to that found in Roman and modern legal systems.[14] Passamaneck's researches into maritime and caravan law and custom appear to be unique in the literature of the College. In the first of these studies (1966), he discusses all Mishna terms dealing with ships, their implements and crews, and concentrates on the problem of valuation suggested in *Baba Qama* 116b: when a ship in a storm needs to jettison its cargo, how the "general average contribution" is assessed of what was required to save the ship. It appears from the phrase "custom of sailors" that Rhodian sea law was adopted by Jewish sailors and perhaps by the rabbis of the Talmud since they did not develop their own maritime law. In "Caravan Customs in Early Rabbinic Sources" (1968), Passamaneck applies a similar type of analysis, discussing the organization of the caravan and concentrating on the problems of apportioning the loss among the traders in case of attack and robbery.

Moving from talmudic to medieval rabbinic law, Passamaneck analyzes *Shulhan Arukh, Hoshen Mishpat* 156:1–5 in "Aspects of Land Use and Commercial Regulation in Medieval Rabbinic Sources" (1969). His method is to translate each rule in the passage, identify and date its constituent elements and sources, note the legal principles involved and the apparent social and economic context, to discover how later authorities used basic talmudic strata to draft specific statements of law, and to trace how these statements fared over the centuries. Using the same technique of translation and analysis of sources and arguments, Passamaneck treats a responsum of R. Moses Alshech (1508–1600) concerning "A Case of Piracy" (1970), which took place in 1583. The responsum reflects a difficulty in sixteenth-century commercial life and the rabbinic approach to the commercial practices of Jewish merchants in the Ottoman empire.[15]

A number of scholars at the College have been attracted to problems of various classes of persons under Jewish law. Prior to his coming to the United States, and during the heat of the slavery controversy, Moses Mielziner published in German his doctoral dissertation (1859), which was later translated and distributed widely in the United States under the title, *The Institution of Slavery among the Ancient Hebrews, According to the Bible and Talmud.* While the approach is apologetic in its defense of biblical and rabbinic law, the essay does treat in a very systematic manner the condition of Hebrew and non-Hebrew slaves, their status, rights, obligations, duration of bondage, and opportunities for freedom. In an interesting study on "The Inheritance of Illegitimate Children According to Jewish Law" (1927), Chaim Tchernowitz discusses the definition of *mamzer* in Jewish law, his ability to inherit, and problems in the Gaonic period relating to the inheritance of an apostate. Ben Zion Wacholder's early excellent article, "Attitudes towards Proselytizing in the Classical Halakah" (1958), treats the post-talmudic *halakha* of the tenth to thirteenth centuries and concentrates on the differing approaches of the Tosephists and the scholars of Spain–North Africa. Wacholder argues that "differences in their concept of the meaning of Judaism and its relation to the outside world" explain the stricter, more negative attitude toward the proselyte among the Spanish school and the openness and flexibility of the Franco-German Tosephists. In "The Mumar—A Study in Rabbinic Psychology" (1959), Jakob Petuchowski endeavors to shed light on the rabbis' psychological understanding of various types of sinners. He concludes that the *mumar* is not an apostate, *min, or apiqoros,* but "represents a type of sinner living completely within the structure of the Jewish community life and, on the whole, abiding by the provisions of the Torah." Stephen Passamaneck picks up Tchernowitz's interest in illegitimate children in "Some Medieval Problems in Mamzeruth" (1966). Passamaneck begins with the definition of *mamzer* in the Talmud, sketches the outlines of the *halakha* on the category, and assesses the rabbinic attitude toward *mamzerut* as a factor in Jewish social structure. Finally, in an essay on the legal status of kings (1968), Samuel Atlas analyzes Mishna *Sanhedrin* 2:2 and its *gemarah* to trace the principles behind the statement, "A king does not judge nor does one judge him." [16] He also analyzes the question of kings acting as witnesses and reviews problems of kingship in Maimonides' Code. [17]

It is, of course, natural that rabbinic scholars teaching at the Hebrew Union College should be concerned with problems of Reform Judaism and the *halakha.* Israel Bettan's "Early Reform in Con-

temporaneous Responsa" (1925) describes the opposition to Reform
in the responsa of leading exponents of Orthodoxy of the nineteenth
century. The first section treats the need expressed by the various Orthodox authorities to uphold the law and tradition at all costs; the
second section examines responses to Reform innovations in the
liturgy begun mainly in the Hamburg Temple in 1818. Eugene
Mihaly's "Reform Judaism and Halacha . . ." (1954) explores "the
contemporary relevance of the *Mishneh Torah* of Maimonides" and
urges the modern Reform rabbi "to apply the divine imperatives
of historic Halacha to our life situation." Mihaly sees the *halakha* as
constantly developing, reflecting a continuous revelation which is an
expression of change. The *Mishneh Torah* is viewed from this perspective, and Maimonides' creativity is revealed "in a number of radical
innovations in his legal code." In "Problems of Reform Halakhah"
(1955), Jakob Petuchowski sets out to lay a philosophical and theological groundwork for the observance of *mizvot* in Reform Judaism.
He argues against the concepts of "primitive origins," *Wissenschaft*,
and higher criticism of the Bible as a basis for rejecting the Law and
then moves to problems of Reform *halakha* as it relates to Reform
concepts of revelation. A good practical essay in this area is Stephen
Passamaneck's "Reform and Halakhah: The State of the Art" (1967),
in which he gives (1) a brief sketch of the historical significance of
the Juristic frame of reference for Judaism, (2) a discussion of Jewish
legal theory and psychology, (3) a characterization of *halakha* as
found in Reform Judaism historically, and (4) suggestions about the
future of the halakhic enterprise. Finally, Jakob Petuchowski's "Some
Criteria for Modern Jewish Observance" (1970), deals with the history
of the 613 commandments and urges criteria for selecting which commandments one might observe; these include "the main thrust of . . .
Jewish tradition" as well as "the voice of my own conscience."

In addition to these articles on Reform and the *halakha*, attention
has been given to the practical application of *halakha* in the modern
setting. Beginning with Moses Mielziner's *The Jewish Law of Marriage
and Divorce in Ancient and Modern Times and Its Relation to the
Law of the State* (1884), the areas of marriage and divorce attracted
the interest of every generation of Hebrew Union College faculty. Mielziner's booklet is an excellent semipopular presentation of the development of Jewish marriage laws through the ages. The essay also
treats late-nineteenth-century concerns of liberalism and intermar-

riage, as well as problems of Jewish divorce law in relation to the laws of various states. In 1915, Kaufmann Kohler (1843–1926) picked up one aspect of these concerns in "The Harmonization of Jewish and Civil Laws of Marriage and Divorce." Kohler gives a serious discussion of various categories of Jewish law dealing with marriage and divorce and their relationship to contemporary American law. He sees in Reform Judaism the only possibility of revising Jewish law to bring it into harmony with civil law; he also deals with the status of women in Judaism and urges changes based on modern life. Samuel S. Cohon treated a particular halakhic problem in "Marrying a Deceased Brother's Wife" (1925). After tracing historically the whole question of levirate marriage and indicating that this issue had agitated Reform Judaism since the time of Isaac Mayer Wise, Cohon urges a prohibition against marrying a deceased brother's wife. In a popular article, "The Jewish View of Marriage" (1954), Eugene Mihaly summarizes the traditional material on various aspects of married life and gives a very positive view of the Jewish attitudes toward partnership and sex in marriage. Jakob Petuchowski's articles in the area of marriage and divorce urge the reinstitution of the *get* in Reform Judaism (1964) and offer contemporary and traditional arguments against rabbis' officiating at mixed marriages (1966).

In other areas, Lauterbach, writing for himself and for the Committee on Responsa of the CCAR, treated such subjects as the attitudes of Jews toward non-Jews (1921), the ordination of women (1922), the question of whether a non-Jewish contractor building a synagogue can work on the Sabbath (1927), the Jewish attitude toward autopsy (1925), birth control (1927), and many more topics. Such discussions always include a thorough presentation of traditional sources in addition to the author's own opinion. Chaim Tchernowitz writes a very interesting responsum to the question: can fund-raisers for a synagogue collect only for the synagogue and not for the Talmud Torah which adjoins it? His answer, based on classical sources, is that the Talmud Torah is the prime responsibility and more important than the synagogue itself (1941). In "Who Is a Jew?" (1959), Jakob Petuchowski traces the historical background of this problem, rejects David Ben-Gurion's nationalistic interpretation, and sides squarely with the Chief Rabbinate in his opinion that a Jew is one born of a Jewish mother or properly converted.

This section cannot be concluded without mentioning the massive contribution of Solomon Freehof to the responsa literature of Reform Judaism. His works (*Reform Jewish Practice* and the series of *Reform Responsa,* published by the Hebrew Union College), though written long after Dr. Freehof had left the faculty for congregational life, clearly overshadow in their scope all other efforts in this area.[18]

Targum, Aggadah, and Homiletics

Some scholarship at the College, though not as much as might be imagined, has been devoted to the exegetical-eisegetical literature of the rabbis and their successors. This includes targumic studies, aggadic studies, and homiletics—classical, medieval, and modern. References to particular *targum* passages are to be found throughout the writings of the faculty; and in the case of both Kaufmann Kohler and the late Leon Liebreich (1899–1966), a few articles were produced in this area before these men came to the College-Institute. However, the only complete studies devoted to the *Targumim* at the Hebrew Union College are those of Samson Levey: *The Messianic Exegesis of the Targum* (1955) [19] and "The Date of Targum Jonathan to the Prophets" (1971). The former is a systematic analysis of individual passages in the *Targumim* which explores targumic messianic exegesis of the *Tanakh* and its relation to rabbinic and Christian messianic thought. Levey takes each section of the Bible in order, examines passages, and compares the results with rabbinic literature, with the versions, and with the Church Fathers, to discover relationships and dependence. A careful sifting of the material leads to the conclusion that "Targumic Messianism . . . is a reflection of Rabbinic Messianism . . . but in Messianic exegesis the Targum displays a remarkable independence, at times offering Messianic interpretations which have no parallel whatsoever in other rabbinic sources." In his study of *Targum Jonathan* to the Prophets, Levey is concerned primarily with the date of the final redaction of this work. From the statement in Tar. 2 Sam. 22:32, "There is no God but Yahweh," and parallels in Saadia's Arabic translation of the Bible, which contain early references to Armilus, he concludes that *Targum Jonathan* to the Prophets was redacted after the advent of Islam and probably in the time of Saadia (A.D. 892–942).

The few aggadic studies to be mentioned here trace the image of a biblical character through rabbinic literature. In "The Death of Zachariah in Rabbinic Literature" (1938), Sheldon Blank explores the background of the New Testament and *Targum* traditions that Zachariah was killed in the Temple on Yom Kippur day.[20] Jakob Petuchowski's "The Controversial Figure of Melchizedek" (1957) is an attempt to refute the view that the rabbinic interpretation of this figure was "a polemic against the role played by Melchizedek in Hebrews." He suggests that R. Ishmael's identification of Melchizedek with Shem (*Nedarim* 32b) was indeed polemical, but could have been aimed against the Jewish universalists of Alexandria, who propagandized for conversion without circumcision, or R. Ishmael might be repeating a tradition of opposition to the Hasmonean dynasty begun by the early Hasidim and transmitted by the Pharisees.[21]

Serious scholarship in homiletics can be divided into work on the homiletic *midrashim* and on the medieval sermon. The first chapter of Israel Bettan's *Studies in Jewish Preaching* (1939) is an attempt to outline the components of the rabbinic sermon. Bettan describes the synagogal context and the relationship of the Torah reading to the development of the sermon. He concentrates on the techniques used by the preacher to show harmony between the biblical text and their message by first categorizing the type of texts which the preacher had at his disposal. Bettan then lists and explains the literary devices and illustrative material found in the *midrashim*. He concludes with a brief survey of the central themes around which the wisdom, poetry, and admonition of the early preachers revolve: the majesty of God, the grandeur of the Torah, and the unique destiny of Israel.

A much more technical study is the massive work of Jacob Mann, *The Bible as Read and Preached in the Old Synagogue* (1940 and 1966), which concentrates specifically on the relationship of the *midrashim*, especially in the internal structure of the homilies, not only to the *sedarim* of the triennial cycle, "but also on [to] the respective Haftarot to the latter." Mann suggests the hypothesis that the midrashic homilies are actually based on the triennial cycle and its *haftarot;* however, the *haftarot* verses are not used explicitly because they are tacitly employed throughout the sermon. What follows in Vol. I is an analysis of seventy-three *sedarim* and fifty-three subsections in 126 little essays dealing with sermons based on Genesis and Exodus in which Mann endeavors to show how a verse chosen for the proem tallied linguistically with a verse found within the compass of the *haftarah* and how the structure of the sermons reveals both formal and conceptual connections with the *haftarah*. Vol. II, published posthumously, covers sermons on Leviticus and Numbers and represents a continuation of Mann's work, revised by Isaiah Sonne. In his two prefaces to this volume, Sonne indicates weaknesses in Mann's hypothesis as well as an acceptance of its basic direction. His own tendency is to link the sermon much more closely with the *Seder* verses than with the *haftarah*.

An analysis of Mann's contribution and a superior discussion of problems regarding the triennial cycle, its origin, development, and relationship to the liturgy and *midrashim* is found in Ben Zion Wacholder's prolegomenon to the reissue of Vol. I of *The Bible as Read and Preached* . . . (1971). Although he concentrates primarily on problems relating to the *sedarim*, Wacholder points out that "an awareness of the liturgical use of Scripture may shed considerable light on the structure and contents of the halakic midrashim," and that the Palestinian cycle of scriptural readings had a powerful, perhaps decisive influence on the development of the *aggadah*.[22]

Liturgical Studies

While the roots of Jewish liturgy are in the Bible, the major liturgical development was a product of the rabbinic period and therefore falls within the context of this essay. Works on Jewish liturgy by Hebrew Union College faculty members fall into three classes: introductions and general surveys, studies of special liturgical compositions, and prayerbook reform and Reform liturgy. Before coming to the College, Kaufmann Kohler foreshadowed his later views on specific aspects of the liturgy in "Ueber die Ursprünge und Grundformen der Synagogalen Liturgie" (1893), in which he traces to the Essenes-Hasideans the origin of most of the religious innovations of the synagogue. A. Z. Idelsohn's standard work, *Jewish Liturgy and Its Development* (1932), is still the best-known general introduction to the field. The book "attempts to give a comprehensive presentation of Jewish liturgy in all of its phases." Each liturgical composition is described briefly, biblical and rabbinic sources given, differences in rites noted with some scholarly discussion of these differences, and a brief summary of arguments on the historical background of the prayers. While this work is not in a class with that of Elbogen or Heinemann, it is still the best overall introduction to liturgy in English.

Jakob Petuchowski served as author and editor of two quite different volumes: *Contributions to the Scientific Study of Jewish Liturgy* (1970) and *Understanding Jewish Prayer* (1972). The former contains an introductory essay by Petuchowski on the problems, methodologies, and text materials in this field plus bibliographies of recent works.[23] The latter is a two-part volume in which the broader thematic aspects of Jewish prayer are treated in a popular style. Part I contains Petuchowski's views, all of which were published elsewhere in separate articles, on such themes as *qeva'* and *kavvanah, tefilat reshut* and *tefilat hova,* and *hidur mizvah.*[24]

In surveying studies of individual liturgical compositions, we begin with Kaufmann Kohler's views on the historical background of the *Shema* (1919) and the Eighteen Benedictions (1924). Kohler's hypothesis about the Essene-Hasidean origin of the liturgy in general is applied to these compositions. In both cases, Kohler rejects the view that they were instituted by the Men of the Great Assembly. He sees the *Shema* in its liturgical usage as the product of the Essenes, who went out into the open fields before dawn, lifted their heads in prayer, and recited the *Shema* just as the sun came up. The origin of the use of this biblical verse in the liturgy was opposition to Persian Mazdean worshippers, who similarly greeted the sun god Mithras at dawn. It stands as a symbol of the unity and uniqueness of Israel's God in contrast to Zoroastrian dualism. Similarly, Kohler traces the Eighteen Benedictions primarily to the *Hasidim Ha-rishonim,* a class of wonder-workers going back to Maccabean times, of which Honi the Circle-Drawer was a prime example. He analyzes each benediction, suggesting its source, composition, possible historical origin, and place in the development of Jewish religious ideas.

Much less speculative than Kohler and much more closely based on supporting textual materials were the liturgical studies of Jacob Mann. Before coming to the College, Mann had already published "Anan's Liturgy and His Half-Yearly Cycle of the Reading of the Law" (1919), in which he reconstructs from Genizah fragments Anan's liturgy for daily, Sabbath, and festival services, and compares these with talmudic liturgy. Later, Mann's excellent "Genizah Fragments of the Palestinian Order of Service" (1925) represents a reconstruction of the Palestinian ritual from Genizah fragments found in the Palestinian synagogue in Fustat. Mann describes the unique peculiarities of the Palestinian rite, giving the fragments with explanatory notes and comparing with the order of service of Saadia, Rav Amram Gaon, and the Babylonian ritual. In a fascinating study combining his historical acumen and knowledge of liturgy, Mann deals with "Changes in the Divine Service Due to Religious Persecutions" (1927). He points out that in general the dominant Christian authorities in Palestine and the Zoroastrian religious leaders in Babylonia often forced changes in Jewish liturgy to overcome passages they considered objectionable or a challenge to their own religious point of view. Specifically, he treats changes based on opposition to the *Shema, Kedusha,* daily *Amidah,* and the reading of the Torah and Prophets, in each showing the impact of historical events on the position in the service, wording, and development of these compositions.

Mann's method in *The Bible as Read and Preached* . . . in dealing with the relationship of the midrashic homily to the biblical readings is a primary influence on Isaiah Sonne's "An Unknown Keroba of Yannai" (*HUC Annual,* XVIII). Sonne indicates the close relationship of the fragment he is publishing here to material previously published by Israel Davidson and Menahem Zulay. However, he raises new questions for scholarly concern: the connection between Yannai's compositions and the biblical verses of the *Seder* and the nature of Yannai's use of *midrashim,* especially the *Yelammedenu.* Sonne's footnotes to the text are unique in that he endeavors "to penetrate the central process of Yannai's compositions and to establish their inner structure."

Beginning in the 1940s, long before he joined the faculty of the New York School, Leon Liebreich began a series of analyses of liturgical formulae, treating linguistic, literary, and intellectual structure. One senses in these excellent and tightly written essays a certain debt to Jacob Mann in the manner in which Liebreich uncovers the "plan of composition" of such diverse pieces as *Atah Behartanu* (1943), the benedictory formula in the *Targum* to Canticles 1:2 (1944); *U'-ba' Le-Ziyyon* (1948), the *Barekhu* (1948 and 1949), and the *Pesuke de-Zimra* benedictions (1950). The same pattern of analysis is found in Liebreich's last three studies, "The Impact of Nehemiah 9:5–37 on the Liturgy of the Synagogue" (1961), and two articles on aspects of the High Holiday liturgy (1963 and 1964).

In the former, Liebreich traces the beginning of the post-Ezra liturgy to Nehemiah 9:5–37, which "determined to a large extent the structural and ideological pattern of Jewish worship." After examining specifically the history of the *Barekhu* and *Shema* and their relationship to the Nehemiah text, he shows how the various themes found in this biblical passage emerge throughout the liturgy. The second of the two studies on the High Holiday liturgy treats, "The Insertions in the Third Benediction of the Holy Day Amidoth" (1964). It concludes with an examination of the *U-vekhen* paragraphs which reveals verbal, ideological, and historical affinities with benedictions XI and XIV of the weekday *amidah*. Liebreich suggests that they are all liturgical products of the Roman domination in Palestine, "not later than the 1st century C.E." [25]

It is perhaps peculiar that the Passover Haggadah has not been dealt with to any extent in the writings of the faculty, except for studies in illuminated Haggadot which fall outside the scope of this paper. Apart from a brief note written by Kaufmann Kohler before he came to Cincinnati (1891), there is only Eugene Mihaly's "The Passover Haggadah as PaRaDiSe" (1966). This imaginative essay treats the Haggadah under the four exegetical categories: *Peshat, Remez, Drush,* and *Sod.* Mihaly concludes that the Passover Haggadah combines both the rational and the poetic and illustrates various deeper images— blood and bread—eschatological symbols leading up to God's redemption of the Israelites.

The material on Reform and the prayerbook is quite diverse. Eugene Mihaly's "A Guide for Writers of Reform Liturgy" (1965) urges an understanding of the synagogue and fixed prayer as the basis for writing liturgy and notes that the purpose of corporate worship is to teach as well as to evoke prayer, and requires discipline and maturity. Mihaly also stresses the influences of the earth's daily cycle on man's worship, and indicates that the lack of acceptance of the obligatory character of the evening service was the result of the essentially private nature of night.

A central part of Jakob Petuchowski's scholarly interest has been specifically in the area of Reform liturgy. In "Karaite Tendencies in an Early Reform Haggadah—A Study in Comparative Liturgy" (1960), he analyzes the Passover Haggadah of the West London Synagogue, listing all passages from the traditional Haggadah which are omitted, then describing the Karaite Haggadah and comparing it to that of the West London Synagogue.[26] The article "Reform Benedictions for Rabbinic Ordinances" (1966) traces the history of the Hallel and Hanukkah and Purim benedictions within the context of Reform prayerbooks of the nineteenth and twentieth centuries in Germany, France, England, and the United States to determine the approach of prayerbook editors to rabbinic Judaism and rabbinic ordinances.[27] Finally, his major work, *Prayerbook Reform in Europe* (1968), is a history of changes and developments within European Liberal and Reform congregations and prayerbooks of traditional formulae. The book contains excellent bibliographies and lists of changes in various liturgical compositions. For example, in "The Problems of 'Particularism' in the *Alenu* Prayer" (chap. 12), Petuchowski deals with changes in wording, the prayerbooks in which these changes occurred, and the broader context of historical, socioeconomic, and ideational forces which encouraged the variations. A similar pattern of treatment is found in discussions of the Eighteen Benedictions, the *musaf* service, and other major parts of the liturgy.

Folklore and Customs

The Hebrew Union College faculty has produced a wealth of material drawn from rabbinic literature which can be classed, in one sense, as belonging to the scientific study of religion. It includes matters of folklore, articles on specific holidays and festivals, and discussions of the observance of traditional practices in modern times. The major contribution to the study of Jewish customs and ceremonies is that of J. Z. Lauterbach. Lauterbach prefaces his study "The Ceremony of Breaking a Glass at Weddings" (1925) with an apology on the value of the study of Jewish ceremonies. He outlines the typical history of a ceremony, including rabbinic opposition and subsequent spiritualization through which the objectionable or primitive basis of foreign custom is removed. The breaking of the glass is chosen as illustrative of this process. Its origin was in heathen superstition belonging to a group of wedding ceremonies based on the common belief "that the evil spirits or demons are jealous of human happiness and therefore seek to spoil it or harm the happy individual." The pattern of protection against demons, which is the aim of breaking the glass at weddings, is also exemplified in Lauterbach's "The Naming of Children in Jewish Folklore, Ritual, and Practice" (1932). Here he shows how the concept of fooling destructive angels and the general lack of trust in angels caused changes in names.

Similar concerns inform the studies about customs associated with the Sabbath and particular festivals. In "The Custom of Looking at the Fingernails at the Outgoing of the Sabbath" (1937–38), Sol Finesinger, who taught at the College from 1925 through the late 1930s, argues that this custom, discussed widely in the Gaonic period, represents a form of light divination opposed by the more enlightened teachers. Lauterbach's "The Origin and Development of Two Sabbath Ceremonies" (1940) traces the use of fragrant herbs or aromatic plants on Friday evening and in the Havdalah service, and especially the use of myrtle in these ceremonies. He notes that ideas and practices associated with the myrtle were ignored in normative rabbinic literature but preserved through mystic channels and given fullest expression in Lurianic circles. The elaboration of the use of spices on Saturday night and the decline in their use on Friday night is put into the context of a general theory of the coming into being, survival, adaptation, and decline of ceremonies. In a posthumously published essay, "The Sabbath in Jewish Ritual and Folklore" (*Rabbinic Essays,* 1951), Lauterbach deals with a limited number of customs preceding the Sabbath. He suggests that the lighting of the candles, perhaps anti-Sadducean in origin, had as its primary purpose the keeping away of demons. He also notes that the blessing of the lights was not introduced until Gaonic times, possibly as an anti-Karaite move.[28]

Studies treating the New Year period[29] and Passover customs[30] also concentrate on folkloristic elements. Finally, Jakob Petuchowski's "The Magnification of Chanukah" (1960) deals with the rise of Hanukkah from a minor festival to a major celebration in the nineteenth and twentieth centuries. He discusses the talmudic question as to the source of the command to kindle and bless the Hanukkah lights and suggests that while the Maccabean war was a struggle against Hellenism, the celebration of victory in battle with lights was typically Hellenistic.

First among the articles dealing with modern problems of ritual and observance one should mention Lauterbach's excellent essay, "Should One Cover the Head When Participating in Divine Worship?" (1928), in which he offers ample evidence that the practice of covering the head began in Babylonia, while Palestinian custom was to go bareheaded. Jakob Petuchowski has a series of popular articles dealing with such diverse themes as the holiness of Sabbath candles (1960), the joy of the commandment (1961), the growing of *etrogim* (1965), and the second day of Rosh Ha-shanah (1970).[31]

The History of Rabbinic Judaism

The contributions of the Hebrew Union College faculty to the study of Jewish history are dealt with elsewhere in this volume. This section treats those internal aspects of Jewish history which reflect the emergence of rabbinic Judaism, its major movements, personalities, and institution.

In 1919 Henry Englander published an article, "Problems of Chronology in the Persian Period of Jewish History," in which he argues for a new chronological scheme of the period of the early Second Temple, placing the careers of Haggai, Zachariah, and the complection of the Second Temple in 419 B.C., and the work of Ezra and Nehemiah nearly half a century later.[32] In "Misunderstood Chronological Statements in Talmudic Literature" (1934), Lauterbach also discusses contradictory talmudic statements about the chronology of the Second Temple period. He finds tannaitic statements historically correct although misunderstood by the later Amoraim.

A major concern in discussions of early Judaism has been the development of the synagogue and its relationship to the Pharisees. In *The Origins of the Synagogue and the Church* (1929), Kohler offers a two-pronged hypothesis that the lay assemblies in Babylonia and the rejection of the Zadokite-Saducean priesthood by the Hasidim eventually led to the beginnings of this institution early in Maccabean times. Sheldon Blank's "The Dissident Laity in Early Judaism" (1946) offers evidence for the existence of dissident groups in the demand for local autonomy, dissatisfaction with the modes of worship, and criticism of Temple personnel, all of which help set the stage for the later emergence of Pharisaism and the synagogue. Julian Morgenstern, in "The Origin of the Synagogue" (1956), finds the establishment of the synagogue to be a reaction to the Deuteronomic Reformation, in 618 B.C., and an attempt to continue local worship, perhaps led by disenfranchised priests.

Probably one of the best overall presentations is Isaiah Sonne's article "Synagogue" in the *Interpreter's Dictionary of the Bible* (1962). The section on the origin of the synagogue contains an excellent review of all hypotheses on the subject from Carolus Sigonius in the sixteenth century to Morgenstern's view. In "Ben Sira and the Nonexistence of the Synagogue: A Study in Historical Method" (1963), Ellis Rivkin examines the Wisdom of Ben Sira as a historical source for third-century B.C. Judaism. He argues that the Temple is the center of Jewish religious life and that Ben Sira, who gives every indication of broad knowledge of his period, would have mentioned the synagogue had it existed. Rivkin's view is disputed by Samuel Sandmel in *The First Christian Century in Judaism and Christianity* (1969). Sandmel states "that the synagogue *as an edifice* may not have existed in Ben Sira's time, but the synagogue as a place of study of Scripture, and thereby removed only by a step from prayer, must surely have existed."

The history of rabbinic Judaism itself has been of tremendous interest to the HUC faculty. The many works in this area represent their accumulated effort to deal with the origin, history, and development of Pharisaic Judaism as the foundation of all subsequent manifestations of Judaism until the emergence of Reform in the nineteenth century. In this regard, it is fair to suggest that a deep apologetic motif on behalf of Reform, as well as "a defensive reaction to Gospel slurs," as Samuel Sandmel argues, provide the double stimulus for the exploration of this seminal period in the history of Judaism.

Lauterbach's series of studies begins with "The Sadducees and Pharisees" (1913), in which he suggests the fruitful hypothesis that both groups had "Tradition," but the Sadducees never gave their traditions a status equal to the Torah.[33] In "A Significant Controversy between the Sadducees and the Pharisees" (1927), Lauterbach examines the controversy of whether the incense offered by the High Priest on the Day of Atonement is to be placed on the fire pan outside the Holy of Holies, according to the Sadducees, or inside it, as was the Pharisaic view.[34] Lauterbach reveals his bias in the summary statement, "the Pharisees with their purer God conception were opposed to superstitious notions and primitive beliefs fostered by the conservative priests." Finally, in "The Pharisees and Their Teachings" (1929), Lauterbach summarizes his views on the Pharisees, their attitude toward law and tradition, and their idea of God and Israel. He emphasizes the contribution of Pharisaic Judaism to religious liberalism, "for, directly and indirectly, within Judaism and outside of it, it has helped much to bring about a finer appreciation of religious ideas, a higher spiritual conception of God, a better understanding of men as the Children of God, and of their relation to one another."

Against this laudation of Pharisaic Judaism only the voice of Isaiah Sonne has been raised, in "The Schools of Shammai and Hillel Seen from Within" (1945). Sonne is interested in the thinking process in each school and notes that the Hillelites disregard the "context for the sake of the particular word," leading to a process of disintegration regarding both the biblical text and reality in general. The Shammaites, on the other hand, were concerned with "context" and the discovery of unity in diversity. He concludes that "we have gone too far, especially in the last four decades, in our glorification and exaltation of the Pharisees in general, and the Hillelites in particular."

Alexander Guttmann's studies in the history of rabbinic Judaism deal with the foundations of Pharisaism, and the transition from Pharisaic to tannaitic Judaism. He is concerned particularly with the Pharisees' source of authority among the people, and what happened to the Pharisees, to the schools of Hillel and Shammai, and to the sacrificial cult after the destruction of the Temple in A.D. 70. In "Foundations of Rabbinic Judaism" (1951), Guttmann argues that after Gabinius abolished the Pharisaic Sanhedrin, the authority of the Pharisaic teachers was based on voluntary rather than governmental control. Indirect legislation through interpretation was the major characteristic of rabbinic Judaism, and it is Hillel's distinction that he emphasized interpretation as the major method for the development of new law.

Changes in Pharisaic Judaism, the relationship between the rabbis and the Pharisees, the inconsistent attitudes of the Talmud toward the Pharisees, and their eventual decline, are Guttmann's major concerns in "Pharisaism in Transition" (1964). From a close analysis of numerous Mishna and Tosefta passages, Guttmann suggests that the Talmud distinguishes between Pharisees who lived before the destruction of the Temple and those who lived after it. He stresses that classical Pharisaism and rabbinic Judaism were not identical but congenial and that, in his view, the primary concern of the former is theology, while law is the main emphasis in rabbinic Judaism.[35]

Finally, in "The End of the Sacrificial Cult" (1967), Guttmann seeks to discover whether the destruction of the Temple was the only, or even the main, reason for the termination of the sacrificial cult in A.D. 70. He focuses on historical considerations which made the restoration of the sacrificial cult unlikely: the Romans did not want it, and Yohanan ben Zakkai was anti-Sadducee and anti-Priest and had no cause to revive his adversaries. Yohanan considered *gemilut hasodim* as replacement for the sacrifices, and the end of the Temple and the cult a lasting state of affairs.

Ellis Rivkin's conception of the Pharisees has minor points in common with Lauterbach's and is quite at odds with that of Guttmann. It is based on a structural analysis of the differences in Jewish society during the periods prior to and following the Maccabean revolution. Utilizing Josephus, the New Testament, and tannaitic literature, Rivkin seeks to define the term *perushim,* to discover when the Pharisees emerged into the historical continuum, and to explain their contribution to Judaism and world religious culture. His general articles in this area, "Pharisaism and the Crises of the Individual in the Greco-Roman World" (1970–71) and "The Internal City" (1966), put the emergence of the Pharisees into the context of change from an agricultural society religiously ordered by Aaronide Pentateuchalism through the ultimate impact of urbanization and polisification leading to the need for revolutionary shifts in the religious and political structure of society.[36] In "The Pharisaic Revolution" (1966), Rivkin spells out the changes he attributes to the Pharisees which are not found in prior Judaism: the concept of the oral law, authority in a scholar class with new titles, the creation of the *Bet Din Ha-gadol* to promulgate the oral law, new names for God, new doctrines of the world-to-come and resurrection, new literary forms to handle the oral law, and new legal terminology and methods of deriving law. His "Defining the Pharisees: The Tannaitic Sources" (1970) is a close analysis of all the tannaitic material in which the name *perushim* appears. On the basis of his analysis Rivkin rejects any suggestion that the Pharisees are to be characterized by their adherence to the laws of ritual purity and concludes "that the Pharisees were the scholar class of the two-fold law, nothing more, nothing less."

Samuel Sandmel examines the whole field of modern scholarly inquiry about Pharisaic Judaism in Lecture II, "Palestinian Judaisms," of his *The First Christian Century.* He expresses serious doubts about our knowledge of the relationship between Pharisaism and Rabbinic Judaism, and goes on to ask, "Was it a thoroughly organized movement with its brotherhoods, or instead, or else in addition, an impulse, rather than essentially an organized movement? . . . We do not know" (p. 71).

Working in the tannaitic period, Alexander Guttmann deals with major personalities and their place in Jewish history. "Akiba, 'Rescuer of the Torah' " (1942–43) is an attempt to discover the sense in which Akiba kept the Torah from being forgotten.[37] In "The Patriarch Judah I—His Birth and Death" (1954), Guttmann deals specifically with dating and suggests that Judah was probably born about A.D. 130–37 and died about A.D. 200–207. Finally, in "Hillelites and Shammaites—A Clarification" (1957), Guttmann explores the general problem of Tannaim who were considered Hillelites or Shammaites after the destruction of the Temple when these schools no longer existed.[38]

Two articles by Hebrew Union College faculty members have been devoted to institutions mentioned in the Babylonian Talmud. In "The Names of the Rabbinical Schools and Assemblies in Babylon" (1925), Lauterbach examines the term *kallah* used to designate schools and regular assemblies held during three-month periods to study Torah. He argues that the term is not taken from Arabic *kallah,* meaning "university" or "assembly," but is an abbreviation of the name of smaller groups organized for Torah study, *kenesset lomde 'orayyta,* or *kalla.* Ezra Spicehandler's *"Bey Do'ar* and *Dina' dimegista',* Notes on Gentile Courts in Talmudic Babylonia" (1955), traces the occurrence of these terms in the Talmud and Gaonic literature, in variant readings, and in the subsequent modern scholarly literature. Spicehandler concludes that the first refers to "an Iranian court . . . presided over by a judge," while the second sugests procedures in violation of what Jewish law considers to be correct legal practice and may derive from a talmudic term meaning an ignorant or boorish person.[39]

Hellenistic Judaism, Sectarianism, and Christianity

If we accept the term *normative Judaism* as adequate for describing what goes under the names Pharisaic and rabbinic Judaism, then the studies treated in this section can be categorized as dealing with various forms of non-normative Judaism. These include Hellenistic Judaism, sectarianism, and Christianity, and their relationships to rabbinic Judaism. The most important scholarship at the College on the relationship between Hellenistic and rabbinic Judaism has been taking place in relatively recent years.[40] The two-part study by Samuel Sandmel, "Philo's Place in Judaism: A Study of Conceptions of Abraham in Jewish Literature" (1954–55), raises all possible aspects of the problem of Philo's relations to rabbinic Judaism. To discover essential differences between Philo and the rabbis, Sandmel traces the different use of a common item, in this case the biblical Abraham material, by Philo and in the Apocrypha, Pseudepigrapha, Josephus, the Greco-Jewish writers, and especially rabbinic literature. Sandmel's summary of the differences between Philo and the rabbis on Abraham is a model of literary-conceptual analysis. He concludes that Philo either has little knowledge of or else rejects the characteristic content of rabbinic exegesis, that Philonic Judaism is the result of a hellenization which transcends language, and that in contrast to normative rabbinic Judaism, Philo reflects a marginal version of Judaism.

Jakob Petuchowski has two popular articles touching upon the broader issue of Hellenistic Judaism. In *"Ha-megillah she-'eynena"* (1959), he discusses the relationship between Jews of Palestine and Alexandria, or more generally the Hellenistic world, through an analysis of Tos. *Megillah* 2:5.[41] The ongoing debate on the relationship between contemporary diaspora Jewry and the State of Israel motivated a historical survey of past relationships in "Diaspora Judaism—an Abnormality? The Testimony of History" (1960). Petuchowski gives a good summary of the conflict over Onias' Temple, the history of diaspora and Palestinian Jewry in the talmudic period, and halakhic issues such as "commandments dependent on the Land.[42]

Ben Zion Wacholder's work in the area of Jewish Hellenistic history and literature often touches on rabbinic parallels and contrasts. His doctoral dissertation, *Nicolaus of Damascus* (1962), contains an excellent section comparing the *Autobiography* of this Hellenistic historian and servant of Herod with the material preserved in rabbinic literature on the life of Hillel. Wacholder's "Pseudo-Epolemus' Two Greek Fragments on the Life of Abraham" (1963) is primarily a study in Hellenistic legendary history, although there is brief comparison between the views of Pseudo-Eupolemus, writing sometime between 293/2 and 63 B.C., and normative rabbinic literature on the Abraham legends. More to our concern is the article "How long Did Abraham Stay in Egypt?" (1964), which has the subtitle: "A Study in Hellenistic, Qumran and Rabbinic Chronography." Wacholder points out that the event of Sarai's seizure by Pharaoh, Gen. 12:11–20, became crucial in the mind of Hellenistic Jewish writers, who made Abram's meeting with Pharaoh significant for the Jewish people and for mankind. For Josephus and the Greco-Jewish writers the period had to be long enough for Abram to introduce the sciences into Egypt. The period of seven years in Jubilees and the Genesis Apocryphon becomes important because of an apparently conscious conflict with the chronology of rabbinic literature as represented in *Seder Olam*. In comparing the approach of all three "schools," Wacholder notes that rabbinic literature was "interested in exegesis rather than history, the reconciliation of contradictory verses became an end in itself, no matter how improable these reconciliations were."

A few studies treat the sects and the Dead Sea Scrolls and have to do in a tangential way with the history of the rabbinic period. In "Wer Waren die Zeloten oder Kannaim? Eine Studie" (1908), Kaufmann Kohler, following Hippolyt's *Refutatio omnium Haeresium*, finds the Zealots to be a special class of Essenes. They oppose putting images on coins, going through gates on which there were statues, and permitting non-Jews to study Torah. Thus, the character of the group was essentially religious, in contrast to Josephus' picture of them as robbers and murderers. Kohler continues his interest in sectarian issues in "Dositheus, the Samaritan Heresiarch, and His Relations to Jewish and Christian Doctrines and Sects" (1911). His article examines *Fragments of a Zadokite Work* published by Solomon Schechter, and traces the document to a Samaritan origin. He identifies the *moreh zedek* as Dositheus, the founder of a new Samaritan sect, whom he pictures as a messianic-type figure emerging out of Sadducean circles and opposing the Pharisees. Broadening the perspective, Kohler traces apocalyptic ideas from early times through the Samaritans to their later flowering in post-Pharisaic rabbinic Judaism. Kohler's concern with apocalyptic literature and its sectarian origin is further treated in "The Essenes and Apocalyptic Literature" (1920). He suggests that the Essenes began this literature, carrying forth the prophetic spirit in a new and esoteric form which only reentered rabbinic Judaism with Akiba much later.[43]

Thirty years after Kohler's studies, Isaiah Sonne devoted a series of articles to the Dead Sea Scrolls, which had recently come to light. Though Sonne's work is directed primarily against the views of Solomon Zeitlin, it stands out more as a plea for care and thoroughness in the treatment of the Scrolls. In "A Hymn against Heretics in the Newly Discovered Scrolls" (1951), Sonne gives his own reconstruction and commentary on the text of a hymn previously published in facsimile edition by Sukenik. Sonne deciphers the text and suggests that its historical background reflects a critical moment of persecution in the life of the sect, when rival prophets and heretical teachers were provoking schism in the ranks.[44] A shorter article, "Final Verdict on the Scrolls?" (1951), is devoted to refuting Zeitlin's late dating of the Isaiah Scroll by showing that the Scroll is similar to the *vorlage* of the text used in the LXX and centuries later by the Massoretes. Again, in "The Newly Discovered Bar Kokeba Letters" (1954), he argues against Zeitlin's contention that the letters are medieval by referring to parallel formulae in *Genesis* and *Leviticus Rabba*.[45]

Serious studies in Christianity, the Gospels, and the life of Jesus have been a continuing interest at the Hebrew Union College. Just prior to his coming to Cincinnati, Kaufmann Kohler published the article, "Abba, Father. Title of Spiritual Leader and Saint" (1901), in which he traces the term *abba* in the Bible and rabbinic literature in order to understand its use by Jesus in Matt. 23:1–10. He discusses in detail the sages who bore this title and comments that with one exception they belonged to the age of the Tannaim and lived in Palestine. He concludes that *abba* denotes an Essene or Hasidean saint, often a wonder-worker or else a proponent of Essene ideas and ideals. Much later Kohler was to sum up all of his views on Jesus and early Christianity in *The Origins of the Synagogue and the Church*. Applying his Essene hypothesis again, he contrasts the differing religious approaches of Jesus and John the Baptist, both of whom, he states, were members of the Essene party. Kohler discusses the problem of the Jesus of the Gospels and the historical Jesus, traces the contradictory legends about his birth and life and the historical data derived from the Gospels, and provides rabbinic parallels to most of his sayings. Kohler shows Jesus to be not unique in his message but nevertheless one of the great champions of the oppressed, the poor, and women.[46]

Jacob Mann's work on the New Testament commenced before his appointment to the faculty with the articles: "Jesus and the Sadducean Priests: Luke 10:25–37" (1916), and "Oaths and Vows in the Synoptic Gospels" (1917). He continued his interest in early Christianity in the first article he published after coming to the College: "Rabbinic Studies in the Synoptic Gospels" (1924). Mann uses rabbinic sources for a fuller understanding of the Gospels, while pointing out the dangers of reading later talmudic notions back into the first century and of reading Babylonian Jewish ideas as if they were accepted by Palestinian rabbis. The article is a collection of miscellaneous essays on the rite of circumcision and the naming of children, the redemption of a first-born son, and the pilgrimages to Jerusalem, marriage and table customs, the "Last Supper" as a Pascal meal, and funerals and tombs.

Samuel Cohon's "The Place of Jesus in the Religious Life of His Day" (1929) discusses the messianic portraiture of Jesus. While the Gospels cast Jesus into a messianic mold which combined various elements from the biblical apocryphal, and apocalyptic literatures, Jesus in Galilee actually represented a position quite divergent from the militant revolutionary and religious nationalism of Judah the Galilean or John of Gischala. Cohon, in opposition to Kohler, points out the differences between Jesus and the Essenes in that Jesus had no particular concern with ritual purity or desire to overthrow the sacrificial cult. Finally, Jesus is identified as an *'am ha-arez hasid* because of his rejection of many Pharisaic teachings, such as eating untithed food with unclean commoners, while he exhibited the qualities of a *hasid:* piety, love, and an emphasis on faith and prayer.

In "Jesus in the Talmud," a posthumously published essay (*Rabbinic Essays,* 1951), Lauterbach is concerned with discovering whether there is any knowledge of the historical Jesus in talmudic literature or if references to him represent merely a later legendary Jewish view. Lauterbach concludes that the latter is true, but only after giving a close analysis of (1) passages where Jesus is supposedly mentioned by name, (2) passages in which Jesus is supposedly alluded to by other names, such as Balaam, Ben Satada, Ben Pandera, Ploni, or Adam Ha-rishon, (3) passages in which Jesus is actually or supposedly alluded to as one who claims, or is considered by his followers, to be

of unique or divine character or possessing special authority, and
(4) passages in which an express reference or a veiled allusion may
be found to the disciples of Jesus or to Christians in general. Especially
useful here is the full quotation of original sources and complete notes
on the secondary literature. In general, it emerges that the Tannaim
did not mention Jesus, but the Amoraim and particularly those of
Babylonia did elaborate stories about him which were common in
the culture and identify him with various characters who originally
have no connection with Jesus.

Sylvan Schwartzman's "How Well Did the Synoptic Evangelists
Know the Synagogue?" (1952–53) is a careful examination of the
material on the synagogue in Matthew, Mark, and Luke, and a
comparison with contemporary rabbinic sources. After setting out
what the Gospels do say of the synagogue, Schwartzman concludes
that "key synagogue information as well as adequate detail are missing
from the Synoptic Gospels." The insignificance of the role of the
synagogue in the Gospels is noted, as well as the special purposes for
which the meager synagogue information was introduced, to supply
Jewish color and to illustrate the background of hostility to Jews
and Judaism.

Samuel Sandmel has devoted a major portion of his scholarly
career to the study of early Christianity and its relationships to the
Judaisms of the first centuries B.C. and A.D. It is those aspects of his
work which deal with the Jewish context of early Christianity rather
than his researches into Christianity itself which have a place in our
study. In "Judaism, Jesus and Paul: Some Problems in Scholarly
Research" (1951), Sandmel sketches problems and concerns which
are later fully developed in *The First Christian Century in Judaism
and Christianity: Certainties and Uncertainties* (1969). He indicates
the difficulties facing the scholar of this period by showing the practically unachievable mastery one must have of historic setting, specific
and general literatures, and requisite languages. In discussing rabbinic literature and its relation to the New Testament, he emphasizes
the comparatively late redaction of the Mishna and Talmud yet the
fact that "the oldest strata of Rabbinics are contemporaneous with the
intertestamental literature." Noting the time span covered by this
literature, the various historical groups involved, and the problems
attendant to the phrase of G. F. Moore, "normative Judaism," Sandmel concludes that "the precise status of Judaism in the first Christian

century before 70 is well nigh not to be recovered." The question is
then, can obscure or laconic passages in the Synoptics be elucidated
or amplified by a knowledge of rabbinic literature? And the answer
is a qualified yes, depending on the methods employed. Sandmel concludes with a plea that the scholar be in touch with all the fields
involved so that Greek influences on Hillel can be understood as well
as the broader influences of the first century on the New Testament.

Sandmel has also made a significant contribution to the popular understanding of early Christianity in three works directed toward "the
intelligent layman" and "thoughtful Jewish people" concerned with
achieving a balanced view of the issue. Of interest to us are the
chapters dealing with the Jewish background of early Christianity
in *A Jewish Understanding of the New Testament* (1956) and *We
Jews and Jesus* (1965), and the first two chapters of *The Genius of
Paul: A Study in History* (1958). To provide a general background
for an understanding of the New Testament as a whole and of Jesus
in particular, Sandmel gives a broad statement of his views on the
environment and times. He reviews political history and the yearning
for the messiah under Roman domination, and gives a brief sketch
of the Pharisees, Sadducees, and Essenes, as well as of the question
of the historical reliability of the Gospels. With respect to Paul, he provides an insight into Paul as a Hellenistic Jew and suggests problems
in Paul's relationship to the Law. Paul represents a unique combination—a concern with the universal predicament of man, the apocalyptic motif, and a Hellenistic orientation leading to a highly
metaphysical intuition and purpose. Regarding Paul the Jew, the
basic issue is Paul's relation to the Law and the crucial event is the
Letter to the Galatians, in which "the manner of Paul's defense
amounts to a virtual obrogation of the Law." Sandmel deals with the
Law of Moses as a general problem for Hellenistic Jews and contrasts
Paul's position with that of Philo, for whom the "Law of Moses is
the very best imitation of the law of nature, and fully consistent with
it." He also shows the antithetical positions of Paul and the rabbis
with respect to the Law and to the concepts of sin and repentance,
revelation, and the nature of religious experience. Sandmel concludes
that rabbinic Judaism and Pauline Christianity share little but a
common point of departure—the Bible.

Jakob Petuchowski has devoted three articles to quite diverse
aspects of the New Testament and Christianity and their relation to

Rabbinic Judaism. The first, "Do This in Remembrance of Me (I Cor. 11:24)" (1957), discusses the concept of *zekher* found in this verse. Petuchowski agrees with Dalman and Davis "that the *zekher* which Jesus instituted was, according to Paul, a *zekher* by which the disciples were to remember him and his redemptive act rather than a prayer that God may remember him." [47] "Halakhah in the Church Fathers" (1964) is devoted to the discovery of similarities between rabbinic *halakha* and legal passages in the Church Fathers. To demonstrate halakhic material in the Church Fathers and to encourage further studies in this area, Petuchowski gives parallels in works by Tertullian and in the Apostolic Constitutions with passages from rabbinic literature, showing a common source for both. Finally, in a study entitled "The Theological Significance of the Parable in Rabbinic Literature and the New Testament" (1972), Petuchowski criticizes the views of Christian scholars who argue that Jesus' use of the parable form as a weapon against the Pharisees was a prime reason for his crucifixtion.[48]

Eugene Mihaly and Samson Levey each have studies the prime focus of which is rabbinic literature and history, with, however, a direct bearing on Christian-Jewish relations. The stated purpose of Mihaly's "A Rabbinic Defense of the Election of Israel" (1964) is "to demonstrate a variety of methods in the analysis and interpretation of midrashic texts," using as an example *Sifre* Deuteronomy 32:9, *Pisga* 312. This *Sifre* passage is seen as a point-by-point response to Christian arguments found in Romans, Galatians, the Epistle of Barnabas, and in the writings of Justin Martyr against the doctrine of the election of Israel. The analysis concentrates on biblical proof-texts, the understanding of special technical terminology, the form of the rabbinic syllogism and of the rabbinic sermon as a whole with its messianic conclusion.[49] Samson Levey's recent and controversial "The Best Kept Secret of the Rabbinic Tradition" (1972) is a study of Ben Zoma and his position with respect to normative Judaism. Levey discusses the history of interpretation of the story in which Ben Zoma contemplates the *ma'aseh bereshit* in all its versions and rejects views which find in Ben Zoma various forms of heretical Gnosticism, Neoplatonism, or speculative cosmology. The most potent heresy of the time was, of course, Christianity, and Levey puts forth the hypothesis that Ben Zoma converted and became a professing Christian.[50]

Rabbinic Theology

Elsewhere in this volume the broad area of Jewish religious thought is presented. My purpose in this section is to treat those works which can be classed as dealing specifically with the rabbinic period, including rabbinic theology and philosophy, the question of authority in Judaism, and studies of such subjects as God, messianism, the afterlife, sin and repentance, and ethics and charity in rabbinic literature. Since Kaufmann Kohler and Samuel Cohon's major volumes (1918 and 1971) on Jewish theology cover the entire span of Jewish religious history, they treat rabbinic concepts as part of a much broader intellectual-religious development. Cohon, of course, authored numerous special theological studies, some of which will be discussed later in this section. Henry Slonimsky's "The Philosophy Implicit in the Midrash" (1956) is a far-ranging philosophic-poetic portrait of major religious, philosophical, and theological themes in midrashic literature. Slonimsky deals with the Platonic and Neoplatonic overtones of the opening passages in *Genesis Rabbah,* and with suffering and its implications for various aspects of Jewish theology and philosophy. He spells out in philosophical terms the theory of tragedy in rabbinic literature, as well as its profound humor, and concludes with a discussion of the rabbinic concept of the messiah. This deeply moving essay, in a sense, represents the philosophy of Slonimsky as much as that of rabbinic literature and must be read with caution as well as appreciation.

A special theological-practical concern within Reform has been the question of authority in Judaism. Gotthard Deutsch's almost Karaite approach to rabbinic tradition is found in an excellent critique, "The Theory of Oral Tradition" (1897). Deutsch examines the concept of the binding character of the oral tradition from within the tradition itself. He indicates that the authority of tradition is refuted on the basis that the tradition is not genuine, that there is ample evidence of a continuous struggle against "ecclesiastical authority," and that there is conscious circumvention of law and inconsistent application. He has a superb section on tradition and pseudo-tradition, challenging views which traced laws to Moses at Sinai by showing at what historical point such laws were really introduced, and also emphasizing the tendency of rabbinic teachers to ascribe their works to older authorities, "if they thought they might meet with opposition." Deutsch concludes that "tradition as authentic interpretation of the Mosaic law is illusion. . . ." [51]

Quite a different approach is taken by Samuel Cohon in "Authority in Judaism" (1936), where a historical analysis is given of the development of authority through revelation and tradition. Cohon notes that "authority inheres in the very nature of religion" and that "progress" in religion is the history of replacing lower forms of authority with higher forms. The section on tradition deals specifically with the rabbinic period, in which the authority of the rabbis was based on their claim of the prerogative, to expound divinely revealed Scripture through exegesis, and the power to make decrees, ordinances, new rites, and customs.

Specific theological studies produced by the faculty include those dealing with God in rabbinic literature. Samuel Cohon's early essay, "Love, Human and Divine, in Post-Biblical Literature" (1917), has as its purpose "to indicate the right of Judaism to the doctrine of Love." The sources, rabbinic, Hellenistic, apocryphal, and pseudepigraph, philosophic and mystic, are examined in a systematic way to delineate God as a God of love, mercy, concern, and support for man. Much later Cohon produced two articles, "The Name of God: A Study in Rabbinic Theology" (1950–51) and "The Unity of God: A Study in Rabbinic and Hellenistic Theology" (1955). In the former, Cohon notes that the names of the deity "constitute milestones in the progress of religion," and "the use which the rabbis made of the divine name and its related expressions reveals the intensity of their efforts to reach out for a fuller and firmer comprehension of the divine." Cohon discusses the Tetragrammaton, liturgic use of the Name, theurgic use of the Name, and God's attributes. Much earlier, Kohler had devoted an article to this same subject, "The Tetragrammation (*shem ham-m'forash*) and Its Uses" (1919), but Cohon's treatment is both broader and in specific areas fuller. Cohon concludes by categorizing the various names into groups expressing various aspects of God's being and His relation to space, the world, Israel, and man. The study, "The Unity of God . . . ," sees monotheism as the central dogma of Judaism and the supreme challenge to heathenism. The rabbinic sages emphasized this view because of persistent attacks from anti-Jewish philosophies and cults which Cohon details. He traces this emphasis on monotheism through the *Shema* as a liturgic creed, the rabbinic passages which are opposed to polytheism and idolatry, in the rabbinic response to Gnosticism and Christian trinitarianism, and in the internal Jewish treatment of angelology.

Finally, an essay with quite a different emphasis, "Qol Adonai; a Study in Rabbinic Theology" (1972) by Jakob Petuchowski, is a theological and conceptual discussion of *Mekhilta, Bahodesh,* chap. V. Petuchowski reconstructs this passage as a sermon by R. Eleazer Ha-Moda'i (d. ca. A.D. 135) on Psalm 29 in which the *qol 'adonai,* a thunderclap, is identified typologically with the thunder of the revelation at Sinai. Other occurrences of this phrase suggest God's *dibbur* is operative in creation, leading to the conclusion that "the inter-relationship between the cosmic and the revelatory aspects of the word is the main burden of R. Eleazer's sermon."

Under the broad rubric of eschatology are those studies which discuss the world-to-come, heaven and hell, and the messiah. "Eschatology of the Jews until the Close of the Talmud" (1895) is an excellent presentation by Gotthard Deutsch. He traces the concepts of God's justice, the afterlife, immortality, and resurrection from the late biblical period through Maccabean times. Deutsch indicates the difficulty in distinguishing in rabbinic literature betwen *'olam ha-ba'* and *gan 'eden;* in general, the former is the messianic kingdom and the latter is the place where the dead dwell until judgment day, although both are often equated in the Talmud. Kaufmann Kohler discusses the afterlife in a German study, "Die Nachstenliebe im Judentum. Eine historische Studie" (1912), and in a delightful book, *Heaven and Hell in Comparative Religion* (1923). The latter was written on the occasion of the six hundreth anniversary of Dante's death and presents descriptions of heaven and hell, eschatological hopes and messianic visions in a variety of cultures—Babylonian, Egyptian, Hindu, Persian, Greek, Roman, Jewish, Moslem, and Christian. He treats the various sources, including those drawn from rabbinic literature, by describing their contents, tracing cultural connections, and indicating their impact or lack of it on the *Divine Comedy.*

The concept of the messiah and its later Reform substitute, the messianic age, is presented at length by both Kohler and Cohon. However, the few specific studies in the area deal with very special aspects of historical evaluations of the concept. Jakob Petuchowski has a popular article, "Man's Part in Bringing about the Messianic Age," which appeared in *Ideas,* a journal of politically conservative Jewish thought (1970). He describes the two basic Jewish positions on redemption—through man's actions or through God's intervention, and shows how the rabbis tried to reconcile these views and the fact that both were held, even though only one may have been emphasized at any particular historical period.[52] Ellis Rivkin's "The Meaning of Messiah in Jewish Thought" (1971) is a historical inquiry into the gestation period of the "messiah" concept and tries to explain the powerful appeal of the concept in the time of Jesus. For our inquiry, Rivkin's idea that messianic movements were a problem for Pharisaic Judaism deserves mentioning. In his view, Pharisaic thought had to establish criteria for the messiah which could never be fulfilled since "the Scribes-Pharisees never emphasize the messianic concept prior to the destruction of the Temple in the year 70."

Sin and repentance form the subject of studies by Samuel Cohon and Jakob Petuchowski. In "Original Sin" (1948), Cohon has a section on the rabbinic ideas of the fall and original sin in which he discusses the *dramatis personae,* the nature of sin, the effect of the fall, the imputation of guilt and merit, and the way of justification. He notes that during the first century A.D., within Judaism three ideas existed: (1) the corruption of the race was hereditary, (2) there was a vague connection between Adam's sin and posterity's liability to punishment, and (3) all sin is a result of man's own fault and action—a view which was generally held in rabbinic Judaism. Repentance, circumcision, the study of Torah, the Day of Atonement, all help to cleanse from sin and overcome spiritual death. Two popular articles by Petuchowski deal with the theme of repentance in Judaism: "Repentance Means Return" (1960), and "The Concept of *Teshuvah* in the Bible and the Talmud" (1968). The latter contains a discussion of the presuppositions of *teshuvah,* its phenomenology, and the roles of man and God in effecting it. Basic to the Jewish understanding are views already adumbrated by Cohon—that man can right the wrongs he has committed, that God wants repentance, that *teshuvah* means going back to God. After outlining the steps one must take to "return," Petuchowski notes that the burden of the Bible and the Talmud is "to get man to the stage where he *wants* to do *teshuvah,* where he becomes aware of his need for God's assistance. . . ."

In the area of rabbinic ethics, apart from Mielziner's sketchy "Outlines of Talmudical Ethics" in his *Introduction,* the only major discussion is that of Lauterbach, "The Ethics of the Halakhah" (1914). The article reflects a strong anti-Christian bias and contains the underlying conception that unlike other religious and ethical systems, the theoretical basis of Judaism has remained the same, although practical applications have changed. The view that the rabbis are the true successors of the Prophets leads Lauterbach to a description of halakhic regulations in social ethics as a concretization of prophetic ideals. These include the conservation of human life based on the halakhic principle that the purpose of the law is the furtherance of the cause of humanity and that every person can help realize God's plan. Lauterbach concludes with the thought that the practice of Reform Judaism is really a continuation of earlier trends in which the separateness of the Jews was essential to the fulfillment of their special mission in perfecting the world.[53]

Finally, Robert Katz's "Empathy in Modern Psychology and in the Aggadah" (1959) has a special section in which the purpose of empathy in modern psychology, to heal the patient, is contrasted with Judaism's source of ethical behavior, *imitatio Dei*. In addition, Katz notes that "empathy may be seen (in Judaism) as a moral and practical quality which is demanded of the individual in his human relationships by an omnipotent God." The article contains a collection of source material in various categories paralleling the modern areas of psychological and psychoanalytic concern.

It was my original intention to conclude this survey with suggestions about future directions the study of rabbinic Judaism and its literature might take at the College. As I now see it, however, such speculation would reflect only my own interests and be inimical to the entire spirit with which rabbinics has been studied at our institution. The scholars and teachers who have explored this crucial area in the development of Judaism are not members of a single school of thought, religiously or intellectually. Their varied interests are a legitimate expression of an open and free scholarly environment which has rejoiced in an unbridled exploration of the past and encouraged the broadest expression of views on the relationship of this past to the present. It is that tradition alone which should spark the future of rabbinic studies at the Hebrew Union College.

Notes

1. Caspar Levias, *A Grammar of the Aramaic Idiom Contained in the Baby-lonian Talmud* (Cincinnati, 1900), p. 2.
2. Alexander Guttmann revised a work compiled by B. S. Jacobson, *Some Rabbinical Authorities and Codifiers* (1957), which lists medieval authors, books, dates, and locations as well as the usual abbreviations of their names. A similar type of guide is Stephen Passamaneck's *A Handbook of Post Tal-mudic Halakhic Literature* (1965), containing a brief description of the place of *halakha* in Jewish life and introducing the areas of responsa, com-pendia, and commentaries. From the vast material he had collected for the bibliography to the fourth edition of Mielziner's *Introduction,* Dr. Guttmann compiled *Talmud and Rabbinics: A Selected Bibliography for the Student's Library* (1970). It contains lists of basic texts in the various areas of rab-binics and a good sampling of secondary literature. Further bibliographical aids are found in the syllabi of numerous courses. To cite but two examples: those of Eugene Mihaly in the expositional and homiletic Midrashim and of Jakob Petuchowski in rabbinic theology. Petuchowski has also provided the student with a word-by-word systematic introduction to the beginning of tractate *Berakhot, The First Steps in the Study of the Talmud* (1962).
3. Israel Bettan's (1889–1957) readers include selections of *aggadah* from the *Eyn Ya'aqov,* medieval sermons, and two pamphlets of midrashic material from Tannaitic and other midrashic compilations and from the Rabbot. The material is organized according to the order of its appearance in the original source and generally reflects the compiler's interests in homiletics. A thematic arrangement is found in Samuel Cohon's (1888–1959) source book on the

[356]

doctrine of God in rabbinic literature and in Jakob Petuchowski's *Rabbinic Texts as Apologetic and Polemic Source Material* (1956). Alexander Guttmann's *Hebrew and Aramaic Documents: A Selection of Significant Documents Used in Jewish Life* (1941; 2d ed., 1971) provides legal forms for engagement, marriage, divorce, *Haliza,* and excommunication plus a copy of the Hebrew Union College *semikhah.* Guttmann has also selected responsa texts of great authorities from the medieval period to modern times (1968).

4. In addition, Werner Weinberg's pamphlet, *Rabbinic Usage: Examples for Sentence Structure in Rabbinic Hebrew* (1966), presents various syntactical forms and rabbinic idioms chosen from Mishna *Berakhot, Avot, Sefer Haaggadah,* and other sources.

5. One should mention, however, the popular translations by Jakob Petuchowski of portions of David Nieto's *Matteh Dan* and *Esh Dath,* as well as selections from Maimonides and Malbim which appeared in *Commentary* from 1954 to 1957. An alumni contribution of note is William G. Braude's translations, *The Midrash to Psalms* and *Pesikta Rabbati,* both published by the Yale Judaica Series. In a review of *The Midrash to Psalms,* Eugene Mihaly has described some of the hazards of translating rabbinic and especially midrashic texts (1959).

6. The earliest contributions seem to be a brief newspaper notice containing a passing discussion of the *Midrash Ha-gadol* (1898) by Gotthard Deutsch (1859–1921) and the full text of the excellent *Outline of Neo-Hebraic Apocalyptic Literature* (1904) by Moses Buttenwieser (1862–1939). The latter traces the growth of the Hebrew apocalypses of talmudic times from the older apocalyptic literature. Buttenwieser argues that the apocalyptic tradition remains essentially the same from the Maccabean period to the close of the Middle Ages and is characterized by harsh particularism, narrow nationalism, wild imagination, supernatural revelations through the medium of angels, and hoped-for realization of Torah in the world-to-come.

7. In the appendix he lists "passages quoted by rabbinic authorities as being from the Mekilta but not found in our *Mekilta deRabbi Ishmael*" and tries to determine the sources from which the passages were taken. Finally, in an article in *Sefer Klausner* (1937), Lauterbach analyzes specific passages from this Midrash, arguing that they reflected original readings misunderstood by the editors of the *Tosephta* and *Bereshit Rabba,* or garbled by later copyists and interpreters.

8. The specific order of traditions in the Mishna was treated by Chaim Tchernowitz (1871–1949) in a brief article entitled "Mishna 'aharonah" (1944), in which the author suggests that R. Judah often placed the opinion of a disciple before that of his teacher, of Bet Shammai before Bet Hillel, because in this way R. Judah indicated the general rule that the *halakha* is according to the latest or most recent Mishna, a view which Guttmann would, of course, reject.

9. Vol. I deals with basic concepts of *halakha,* technical definitions, the concept of the oral law, and its legal foundation in the written Torah; vol. II begins with the biblical period and ends with a section on sects, including the

Pharisees and Sadducees; vol. III returns to the period of the Second Temple and describes the restoration after 586 B. C., Ezra and the *Midrashe Halakhah,* the foundations of ancient *halakha,* points of contact with Babylonian law, and then a discussion of categories of Jewish law including the family, marriage, divorce, inheritance, and slavery; vol. IV contains historical-legal studies from the time of the *Soferim* to Hillel, a section on the historical development of such legal institutions as the Sanhedrin and the *Nesi'ut,* a discussion of Bet Hillel and Bet Shammai, and finally a description of the *halakha* in the Apocrypha and Pseudepigrapha.

10. I. Soferic Period, II. Pharisaic–Early Tannaitic Period, III. Tannaitic Period. Each of these is subdivided into sections reviewing contributions to the development of the *halakha* by significant individuals, groups, and legislative bodies: the Sanhedrin, Hillel and Shammai and their Houses, Pharisees-Sadducees-Essenes, Akiba, and Judah I, to name but a few.

11. Neither history nor literary form explains completely the arrangement of the material. Vol. I gives a general review of Hebrew law followed by a discussion of the Geonim, their efforts to establish the sovereignty of the Babylonian Talmud, various forms of their literature and specific works, Alfasi and his school, and a major section on the legal works of Maimonides, including sources, organization and purpose, relation to the *aggadah,* and halakhic style. Vol. II treats Rashi and his school, discusses the Tosephists and their work as well as those works organized according to lists of *mizvot,* and reviews the contributions of numerous individuals and groups: Nahmanides, Solomon ibn Adret, Asher ben Yehiel, the *Mesaderim,* the *Tur* and its commentaries, and the *Ba'ale 'asufot,* among others. Vol. III is completely devoted to the *Shulhan Arukh* and represents a revision and elaboration of an early effort by Tchernowitz; it treats this code in detail, gives a sketch of Joseph Karo, his period and contemporaries, and traces the impact of the *Shulhan Arukh* on the works of later commentators, listing the whole literature descended from it.

12. Guttmann's other conclusions are: (5) custom in general had the character of practical law since the sages commanded it to be observed, (6) in contrast to the attempt of the sages to reconcile conflicting laws and impose legal uniformity, they encouraged each geographic region or province to observe its own customs, (7) the sources of custom were individual, group, and congregational practices, past events, superstitions, and even the influence of Christianity, and (8) the place of *minhag* was probably more important in Palestinian than in Babylonian Jewry.

13. Atlas finds in the Talmud four types of legal fictions and offers examples of each: (1) historical fictions in which new phenomena are forced into the existing though unrelated categories, (2) limiting fictions which restrict the private individual's power of acquisition, (3) dogmatic fictions whose purpose is to create a new legal reality by a leap into an ideal world, and (4) fictive activities such as forcing a man to say *rozeh 'ani,* which is not a true statement but is accepted at face value.

14. After a close analysis of specific cases, he concludes that (1) in Jewish law

there is no general concept under which defamation becomes an actionable offense, (2) the concepts of "slander" and *inuria* are not reflected in rabbinic literature, (3) the *mozi' shem ra'* is a special case, not of defamation but related to monetary claims involving the bride suspected of prior unchastity (Deut. 22:13–20), (4) the closest to a concept of degration in Jewish law is *bi'ush bi-devarim,* (5) although words alone are not a sufficient basis for a fine, some physical contact and injury is required, and (6) the Talmud is generally free of cases in which insult or defamation are concerned.

15. Too late to be included in this survey is Passamaneck's latest volume, *Insurance in Rabbinic Law* (Edinburgh: Edinburgh University Press, 1974), which was just published.

16. Atlas elaborates on the differences in Jewish law behind the "ideal" concepts: "Kings of Judah"—who recognize the sovereignty of law and the judicial system as being above them and therefore judge and are judged— and "Kings of Israel"—authoritarian monarchs who make their private will the sovereign source of law in the state and cannot judge or be judged because they are considered robbers.

17. Miscellaneous studies in various areas of halakhic concern includes a discussion by Gotthard Deutsch on the historical background of the controversy as to whether the printed Bible could be used in place of the Torah scroll in worship services (1896), studies of the halakhic significance of miracles in talmudic Judaism (1947) and the place of Jerusalem in tannaitic law (1970) by Alexander Guttmann, and Jakob Petuchowski's discussions of the category *hukkot ha-goyim* to define what is and is not Jewish in Judaism ("A Fence with Loopholes," 1962), and societal commandments as a foundation of Judaism (1970).

18. These include *Reform Jewish Practice and Its Rabbinic Background,* I and II (combined edition), (New York, 1963); *Recent Reform Responsa* (Cincinnati, 1963); *Current Reform Responsa* (HUC Press, 1969); *Modern Reform Responsa* (HUC Press, 1971). For the full bibliography see *Essays in Honor of Solomon B. Freehof,* ed. Walter Jacob and others (Pittsburgh, 1964), pp. 53–93.

19. In a thoroughly revised and updated form this work is just being published as *The Messiah: An Aramaic Interpretation,* Hebrew Union College Monograph Series, vol. 2 (New York, 1974).

20. Blank notes that there were three men in the Bible named Zachariah whose identities were probably consciously confused in rabbinic literature and that this confusion is responsible for the supposed martyrdom of Zachariah. In explaining the legend in Jer. *Ta'anit* 69ab that Nebuzaradan found Zachariah's blood boiling in the Temple crying for vengeance, and that the king slaughtered thousands until God finally had compassion, Blank suggests a historical origin, during the Hadrianic persecutions, and shows how tradition embellished the supposed crime of killing the prophet to make the subsequent punishment commensurate with it.

21. In a more popular format, Petuchowski has translated and summarized the

views of Rashi, Ibn Ezra, and Nachmanides on the *Akedah,* showing possible Christian influence on rabbinic thought which is reflected in Rashi's commentary. The need for a willing sacrifice and intercessor causes Rashi to make Isaac—thirty-seven years old and actually sacrificed—the hero of the story; for Ibn Ezra and Nachmanides, on the other hand, Abraham is central (1960).

22. While outside the main scope of our study, a word is in order about those works which deal with the medieval and modern sermon. The major portion of Bettan's volume, *Studies in Jewish Preaching,* is composed of essays which had appeared in the *HUC Annual* on a number of significant preachers from the thirteenth to eighteenth century. Although extremely florid in style, Bettan does give an insight into the historical context of these preachers, their sermonic style, sources, methods, and message. Similarly, Ellis Rivkin has a study "The Sermons of Leon de Modena" (*HUC Annual,* 1950–51). On the modern sermon, the College has published a mimeographed series, *Aspects of Jewish Homiletics* (6 vols., 1957–61), which contains lectures on homiletics by alumni: Robert Kahn, Abraham Feldman, Ely Pilchik, Joseph Narot, and Roland Gittelsohn. Early in the 1960s Jakob Petuchowski published suggested sermons based on classical sources in the *American Rabbi.*

23. The major portion of the volume is composed of well-selected articles by noted scholars, reprinted from the *Jewish Quarterly Review* and *HUC Annual,* which illustrate significant scholarly issues.

24. Part II includes essays on various aspects of Jewish prayer by Abraham Heschel, Steven Schwarzschild, Dudley Weinberg, and Milton Himmelfarb, among others.

25. Another aspect of the High Holiday liturgy is taken up by Jakob Petuchowski in a popular article, "The 'Malkhuyoth,' 'Zikhronoth,' and 'Shofaroth' Verses" (1972). He describes these three insertions, their composition and form, explains their thematic development, and traces their source and place in the liturgy.

26. He concludes that the West London Haggadah represents an attempt to "reform" the Rabbinite one, whereas the Karaite Haggadah tries to develop "a liturgy *de novo.*"

27. Petuchowski sees trends, for both historical reasons and theological purposes, of including or excluding traditional benedictions, and the body of the article catalogues the various changes made. He concludes that, "the earliest generation of Reformers . . . did not yet make any distinction between biblical commandments and rabbinic ordinances when it came to the recitation of benedictions."

28. In addition, he explores why this *mizvah* is performed by women, the number of candles and material from which they are made, and the reason women cover their eyes—in order not to see angels in the flames and also to enjoy the *mizvah* after the blessing.

29. Sol Finesinger's "The Shofar" (1932) is an attempt to trace the use of the shofar from its primitive origins through the "higher conceptions" of the

rabbis. The essay is divided into two sections, the first covering the use of the shofar in the Bible and the second in the talmudic period. In the latter it is argued that the rabbis hide the more primitive notions associated wtih the shofar through the interweaving of verses for the *malkhuyot, zikhronot,* and *shofarot* selections. Nevertheless, the Talmud (*Rosh Hashanah* 16a) still records the view that the sounding of the shofar is to confound Satan, and thus the history of the shofar represents "the struggle between the more advanced ideas of the Rabbis and the more primitive ideas of the people." In "The Ritual for the Kapparot-Ceremony" (1935), Lauterbach deals with this ritual and its accompanying recitations. He suggests that the Kapparot-ceremony as performed in early Gaonic times, with horned animals, was a revival of the ancient ritual of sending the goat to Azazel, and as such was a sacrifice to Satan to persuade him not to accuse the people. One year later, in 1936, the article "Tashlik, a Study in Jewish Ceremonies" appeared, in which Lauterbach offers abundant evidence from the Bible, Philo, and rabbinic literature of the belief that God was to be found near water. He suggests that a cluster of ideas emerged in the Gaonic period which explain the function of *Tashlik* at the High Holiday season: (1) spirits, fallen angels, and Satan have their abode in the depths of the waters, (2) the mediation and aid of angels and spirits was sought, (3) Satan could be made favorably disposed through gifts and sacrifices. Lauterbach outlines the modifications of this ceremony along rationalistic-rabbinic or mystic-rabbinic lines through the late medieval period.

30. On the subject of Passover customs, Julian Morgenstern and Lauterbach each devoted an article to the prohibition in Exod. 12:46 against breaking the bones of the Pascal sacrifice. Developing Kohler's suggestion "that the prohibition of breaking the bones of the Pascal lamb points to a belief in its subsequent resurrection and reincarnation," Morgenstern traces this idea through the New Testament, the Testament of Abraham, the Koran, and the Midrash (1916). While his essay is basically a comparative study, he does point out that "in the imprecation frequently applied in Rabbinic literature to such arch-enemies of Israel as Nebuchadnezzar, Titus and Hadrian, *sehiq tamya*, 'may his bones be crushed,'" is the suggestion that the enemy may be "denied all possibility of resurrection." Lauterbach's Hebrew article on this subject (1925) approaches the problem from an entirely different perspective, that of the specific and contradictory halakhic provisions regarding the bones of the pascal lamb. Neither the Bible nor the sages give any reason for the *mizvah*. In contrast to Morgenstern's suggestion, Lauterbach argues that the law reflects a concept of sympathetic magic: as long as the bones of the *pesah* are whole, the Israelites will be whole and have peace. This may explain why the rabbis, who opposed such superstitious practices, changed the law, restricting the ruling regarding the breaking of the bone until it practically had no effect. On quite another aspect of Passover observance, Lauterbach, in "The Date of the Slaughter of the Pascal Lamb" (1942), deals with the questions of which day of the month was fixed for the slaughter of the *pesah*. Pointing out the many divergent

views in the literature, he argues that there were groups which did slaughter the sacrifice on any day during the period from the tenth through the fourteenth of Nisan.

31. On the matter of the second day, which is a problem for Conservative Judaism, he traces the history of the argument and discusses in detail the value of *minhag* and the question of authority in traditional Judaism.

32. Some support for this dating is offered from the Targum, *Seder Olam,* and other rabbinic sources, although Englander cautions that rabbinic literature is not concerned with chronological accuracy. Englander also offered another interesting hypothesis about "The Men of the Great Assesmbly" (1925), in which he suggests that the title of this group should be translated to "Leaders of the Community of Greatness." He rejects the notion that the *anshe keneset ha-gedolah* constituted a legislative body and sees them as leaders of a community from the Persian period to about 270 B.C. that was later idealized by Pharisaic Judaism.

33. The Pharisees did, however, and they argued that both written and oral law were revealed to Moses at Sinai, and that they alone possessed hermeneutical and exegetical rules by which law was to be developed.

34. No real explanation emerges from the halakhic discussion as to the source of this controversy, yet Lauterbach finds in it basic theological differences between the two parties. The Sadducees, he suggests, preserved earlier primitive notions about the visible presence of the Deity in the Holy of Holies, from which they tried to protect the priest. The Pharisees, on the other hand, imbued with the lofty and "true" conception that God is everywhere, reject the primitive notion and offer the incense within.

35. In a parallel study, "The End of the Houses" (1968), Guttmann discusses the story in *Erubin* 13b of the *bat qol* which decided that the *halakha* is according to the School of Hillel. In relation to the question of whether both "Houses" continued to exist after this verdict, Guttmann concludes that the two schools actually ceased to exist after the destruction of the Temple. The distinguishing names were retained only when past discussions were recalled, as we find constantly in the Mishna. Once the bitterness of the rivalry was forgotten, objectivity prevailed and some of the laws or views of Bet Shammai were then accepted in theory or practice.

36. In this context, Rivkin traces to the Pharisees three central ideas which ultimately made for the spread of monotheism and Christianity: (1) the concept of an omniscient, omnipotent, yet personal Creator; (2) the value of the individual in God's sight and the hope of eternal reward; and (3) the stress on achieving this reward through the internalization of God's will.

37. Guttman analyzes the difficult problems connected with the phrase *setam mishna* and concludes that there is no basis to the view that Akiba created an outstanding Mishna. Nevertheless, Akiba did organize the whole of tradition, arranging *halakhot* by subject matter and evaluative classification. This work, completed by Judah Ha-Nasi, meant that the Mishna was a code of carefully collected *halakhot* to be used in actually governing the life of the Jewish people.

38. He specifically treats the case of Eliezer ben Hyrcanus, who is called Ha-Shammuti. Guttman argues that "ha-Shammuti" comes from the root *shmt*, "to ban," which was used commonly in Babylonia. Because this word was not part of the Palestinian vocabulary, the Palestinian Talmud, in accepting the title, mistakenly thought it meant Shammaite.

39. Reference should also be made here to chap. IV of Ellis Rivkin's *The Shaping of Jewish History* (1971). Rivkin stresses the achievement of Judah ha-Nasi in compiling the Mishna as a code of law, but notes that because it contains contradictory traditions it needed to be elaborated and interpreted even as the Bible itself. The central effort of interpretation took place in Babylonia by a powerful non-ordained scholar class, which shaped the teaching of the Mishna to a Sassanian-Zoroastrian environment. In Palestine, however, as a response to Christian exegesis and propaganda, there emerged instead a rich homiletical literature whose purpose was to sustain faith and provide a defense against Christianity.

40. See, however, Lauterbach's essay on "The Ancient Jewish Allegorists in Talmud and Midrash" (1911), which discusses the background and methods of the earliest Jewish interpreters of Scripture: the *Dorshe Reshumot* and the *Dorshe Hamurot*. The former, he argues, were Palestinian and were not influenced by Philo; the *Dorshe Hamurot,* however, employed a method which was Alexandrian and not Palestinian. They were not concerned with observance, but with the idea or real meaning of a law to be derived through Greek allegorical interpretation. Lauterbach suggests that there was a strong reaction in Palestine against the *Dorshe Hamurot* because their method caused neglect of observance and was used by Jewish-Christians to bolster their views.

41. This passage describes the story of R. Meir's visit to a synagogue in *Asia* and how he dictated there a Scroll of Esther. Petuchowski argues that the town and congregation were sufficiently important to have a Scroll, but only in a Greek version, and therefore what R. Meir dictated was the Hebrew text.

42. He concludes that "out of the Tannaitic period ... there evolved a Judaism viable in any locality, and ultimately independent of any central authority in the Land of Israel or anywhere else."

43. Kohler states here that the Hasideans of Maccabean times were not precursors of the Pharisees but of the Essenes who lived in the Dead Sea region, whose calendar was reflected in Jubilees and Enoch, who were anti-Pharisaic, and who developed an eschtological and cosmological system with angelology and demonology influenced by Persian lore.

44. He further examines the use of Scripture in the hymn and the type of exegesis involved and suggests that the author used a kind of *Dorshe Reshumot* allegorical approach.

45. Rejecting the historical reconstructions of Fathers de Vaux and Milik, Sonne puts the material into the context of the first to second centuries A.D. and suggests that the letters might refer to the few years of the Bar Kokeba administration, A.D. 133–35, or might come from a later member of the

same family named Simeon who was a deputy of Judah Ha-Nasi at the end of the second century.

46. Turning to Church history, Kohler sees an early split between the Galilean and Jerusalem groups, with the communistic and communal character of the latter being formed primarily by the Essenes who joined it. He finds in the *Didache* and *Apostolic Constitutions* an Essene Jewish basis of values, prayers, ecclesiastical organization, and charitable institutions. Kohler discusses Paul at length, rejecting the view that he was a disciple of Gamaliel and arguing rather that he was influenced by Greek Judaism and was an agent of the Sadducees. He also deals briefly with Gnosticism as a springboard for numerous anti-Jewish views which found their way into Pauline Christianity.

47. He goes on to show that one could have a remembrance of an individual, as is indicated in the Passover Haggadah by the phrase *zekher le-miqdash ke-Hillel,* in which the custom of Hillel is recalled. Thus, "within Judaism itself, the symbolic Passover foods, whatever their original significance, lent themselves to association with the memory of persons, so that, when they are eaten, it is done in remembrance of," as the phrase is found in the New Testament.

48. He rightly points out the nonsense of this position and shows rabbinic parallels to the parables of the Laborers and the Vineyard (Matt. 20:1–16) and the Prodigal Son (Luke 15:11–32). He makes the point that Jesus used parables skillfully to draw his listeners, but that this took place within the framework of "the Pharisaic-Rabbinic world of thought and within the broad limits of the realm of Aggadah," even though Jesus has his own emphasis.

49. The article concludes with an appendix on *Midrash Tannaim* to Deut. 14:2. This passage might lead to a rejection of the analysis found in the article. However, Mihaly shows it to be late and composite. Most useful here is the summary of the literary history of the *Midrash Tannaim* and the description of sources upon which the compilor drew—especially the *Midrash Ha-gadol.*

50. The article concludes that Ben Zoma's "words, even when they are Christological, were preserved in the Talmudic tradition, although at times in esoteric fashion"; moreover, the sage was never excommunicated or embarrassed but always treated with sensitive consideration. For the scholarly debate which this article engendered see: "Communications," *Judaism,* XXII, no. 3 (Summer 1973), 354–359.

51. In a popular article, "The Supposed Dogma of the Mosaic Authorship of the Pentateuch" (1959), Jakob Petuchowski challenges one of the implied criticisms leveled by Deutsch and others against the authority of tradition, that it is based on the erroneous view of the Mosaic authorship of the Torah. Petuchowski points out the difference between the literary question and the theological one, quoting rabbinic sources which speak of *Torah min ha-shamayim,* but not its Mosaic authorship. Indeed, the whole problem of the impact of the Higher Criticism on Jewish practice and belief becomes a crucial issue in Petuchowski's *Ever Since Sinai: A Modern View of Torah*

(1961), in which the meaning of covenant and other rabbinic concepts is reinterpreted in modern terms.

52. The political thrust of the article is evident in the notion that good deeds are important, but not if they impose on personal freedoms, the right of property or of expression.

53. Within the broad category of ethics, the popular pamphlet *Philanthropy in Rabbinical Literature* (1927) by Abraham Cronbach should be mentioned. Cronbach examines rewards, ulterior motives, sensibilities, imposters, and organizations; he notes that "disbursers of charity seem to have been as much subject to the criticism and execrations of their clients as their moderns successors. The Jewish law code goes out of its way to assure charity workers that the more invectives they endure, the greater will be their heavenly reward."

BIBLIOGRAPHY

This bibliography is not intended to be exhaustive. It represents the bulk of works by HUC-JIR faculty members on rabbinic Judaism and rabbinic literature listed in the catalogue of the Klau Library. In many cases, for the benefit of the reader, I have included published bibliographies of the individuals mentioned. Jakob Petuchowski was kind enough to share with me a complete bibliography of his publications from which I have selected a number of items.

Thanks go to so many teachers and friends on the HUC-JIR faculty who have been helpful in making suggestions about this project, and to Amos Funkenstein of UCLA, to Herbert Zafren and his staff for making the resources of the Klau Library available by mail, to Harvey Horowitz and the staff of the Frances-Henry Library at the California School for numerous hours of effort in uncovering local resources and expediting interlibrary loan, and to my wife, Nancy, whose encouragement and aid have seen me through this project.

Atlas, Samuel H. "Leheqer Ha-talmud" in *Sefer Ha-yovel Likhvod Moshe Shorr*, pp. 19–35. Warsaw, 1935.

———. *A Section from the Yad Ha-Hazakah of Maimonides: From a Holograph Ms. in the Bodleian Library*. Edited and annotated by S. H. Atlas, London, 1940.

———. *Novellae on Tractate Baba Kamma by Abraham ben David* (RaBaD of Posquieres). Edited with introduction and notes by S. H. Atlas, London, 1940.

———. "Letoledot Ha-sugya'." In *Studies in Memory of Moses Schorr*, pp. Hebrew Section, 1–12.

———. "Letoledot Ha-sugya'." In *Studies in Memory of Moses Schorr*, pp. 1–11. New York, 1944.

———. "Rights of Private Property and Private Profit." *CCAR Yearbook*, LIV (1944), 212–41.

———. "Ha-'aramah Mishpatit Ba-Talmud." In *Sefer Ha-yovel Likhvod Levi Ginzberg,* Hebrew Section, 1–24. New York, 1946.

———. "Lishe'elat Hilkhat 'idit." *Horev,* XI (April 1946), 59–78.

———. "Der Derekh Ha-havanah in die Litvvishe Yeshivot," in *Lite,* I, edited by Mendel Sudarski, Uriah Katzenelenbogen, Y. Kisin, pp. 605–14. New York, 1951.

———. "Letoledot Ha-sugya'." *HUCA,* XXIV (1952–53), Hebrew Section, 1–21.

———. "Some Notes on Claude Montefiore's Conception of Rabbinic Judaism." *Synagogue Review* (March 1954), no pagination.

———. "Ha-ratzon Ha-tziburi Ba-tehugah Ha-talmudit." *HUCA,* XXVI (1955), Hebrew Section, 1–38.

———. "Hasagot She-hesig Ha-Rav Moshe Ha-Cohen Me-Lunel 'al Sifre Rabennu Moshe Z"L." *HUCA,* XXVII (1956), Hebrew Section, 1–98; XXXIV (1963), Hebrew Section, 1–40.

———. "A Critical Investigation of the Sugya *Heylach.*" In *Abraham Weiss Jubilee Volume,* Hebrew Section, pp. 73–90. New York, 1964. (Hebrew title: "Ha-'ad'at 'edim Ve-heylakh")

———. "Hasagot Ha-Rama"kh 'al Hilkhot Shevitat 'asor Mi-sefer Yad Ha-Hazaqah Le-RaMBaM." In *M. Waxman Jubilee Volume,* Hebrew Section, pp. 33–44. New York, 1966.

———. "Ha-melekh Lo' Dan Ve-Lo' Danin 'oto." *Sinai,* LXII (June–July 1968), 99–126.

Barth, Lewis M. *An Analysis of Vatican 30.* Monographs of the Hebrew Union College, No. 1. Cincinnati, 1973.

Bettan, Israel

Bibliography: Theodore Weiner, in *Israel Bettan Memorial Volume,* (New York, 1961), pp. 52–62.

Works:

Bettan, Israel. "Early Reform in Contemporaneous Responsa." *HUC Jubilee Volume,* pp. 425–43. Cincinnati, 1925.

———. *Post-Biblical Judaism, Its Biblical Foundation—The Midrash.* Cincinnati, 1927. (Pamphlet No. 7, Commission on Judaism of the UAHC and CCAR).

———. "Israel and the Synagogue." *CCAR Yearbook,* XLIII (1933), 294–316.

———. "Mivhar Midrashim." Mimeographed. Cincinnati, 1935 and 1957.

———. "Lequte 'agadot." Mimeographed. Cincinnati, 1935.

———. "Derashot Nivharot Me-ha-darshanim She-bimey Ha-benayim." Mimeographed. Cincinnati, 1939.

———. *Studies in Jewish Preaching.* Cincinnati, 1939.

———. "Lequte Midrashim." Mimeographed. Cincinnati, 1953.

———. "The Relation of Progressive Judaism to Rabbinic Judaism." In *Aspects of Progressive Jewish Thought.* London, 1954.

Blank, Sheldon H. "The Death of Zachariah in Rabbinic Literature." *HUCA,* XII–XIII (1937–38), 327–46.

———. "The Dissident Laity in Early Judaism." *HUCA,* XIX (1945–46), 1–42.

Buttenwieser, Moses

Bibliography: Adolph Sigmund Oko, "List of Writings of Moses Buttenwieser," *HUC Monthly,* VIII (1922), 207–8.

Works:

Buttenwieser, Moses. *Die hebräische Elias-Apocalypse.* Leipzig, 1897.

———. *Outline of Neo-Hebraic Apocalyptic Literature.* Cincinnati, 1901.

Cohon, Samuel S.

Bibliography: Theodore Weiner, "The Writings of Samuel Cohon, a Bibliography," *Studies in Bibliography and Booklore,* II (1956), 160–78.

Works:

Cohon, Samuel S. "Love, Human and Divine, in Post-Biblical Literature." *CCAR Yearbook,* XXVII (1917), 244–300.

———. "Palestine in Jewish Theology." *HUC Jubilee Volume,* pp. 171–209. Cincinnati, 1925.

———. "Marrying a Deceased Brother's Wife." *CCAR Yearbook,* XXXV (1925), 364–79.

———. "The Place of Jesus in the Religious Life of His Day." *JBL,* XLVIII (1929), 82–108.

———. Review of *Josephus: The Man and The Historian,* by H. S. J. Thackeray, *Am. Oriental Society Journal,* LIII (1933), 176–78.

———. "Theology Lectures." 4 Vols. Mimeographed. Cincinnati, 1933–40.

———. "Authority in Judaism." *HUCA,* XI (1936), 593–646.

———. "Original Sin." *HUCA,* XXI (1948), 275–330.

———. "Ancient Jewish Philosophy." In *A History of Philosophical Systems,* edited by Vergilius Fern, pp. 57–68. New York, 1950.

———. "Meqorot Ha-Yahadut: Ha-ʿelohut Be-Torat Rabotenu." Mimeographed. Cincinnati, 1950.

———. "The Name of God: A Study in Rabbinic Theology." *HUCA,* XXIII (p. I, 1950–51), 579–604.

———. Review of *The Rabbinic Mind,* by Max Kadushin. *JQR,* XLIV (1954), 244–51.

———. "The Unity of God: A Study in Hellenistic and Rabbinic Theology." *HUCA,* XXVI (1955), 425–79.

———. *Jewish Theology.* Assen, 1971.

Cronbach, Abraham. *Philanthropy in Rabbinical Literature.* Cincinnati, 1927. (Pamphlet, tract commission, UAHC and CCAR no. 9)

Deutsch, Gotthard. "Zur Sprachlichen Erklarung von ʾayyre." *Jüdisches Litteratur-Blatt,* XVII, no. 42 (1888), 163.

———. "Zur Geschichte des Neujahres-Festes." *Allgemeine Zeitung des Judentums,* LIV (1890), 455–57.

———. "Eschatology of the Jews until the Close of the Talmud." *CCAR Yearbook,* IV (1895), 100–111.

———. "The Scroll of the Law." *CCAR Yearbook,* V (1896), 68–78.

———. "The Theory of Oral Tradition." *CCAR Yearbook,* VI (1897), 129–71.

————. "The Ramsgate College and the Sources of the Midrash Haggadol." *Reform Advocate,* XIV (1897–98), 582–83, 673–74.

Englander, Henry. "Problems of Chronology in the Persian Period of Jewish History." *Journal of Jewish Lore and Philosophy,* I (1919), 83–103.

————. "The Men of The Great Synagogue." *HUC Jubilee Volume,* pp. 145–69. Cincinnati, 1925.

————. "Grammatical Elements and Terminology in Rashi's Biblical Commentaries." *HUCA,* XI (1936), 367–89; XII–XIII (1937–38), 505–21; XIV (1939), 387–429.

————. "Rashi as Bible Exegete and Grammarian." *CCAR Yearbook,* L (1940), 342–59.

————. "Rabbenue Jacob ben Meir Tam as Grammarian." *HUCA,* XV (1940), 485–95.

————. "Joseph Karo's Commentary on Micah in Relation to Rashi's Commentary." *HUCA,* XVI (1941), 157–62.

————. "A Commentary on Rashi's Grammatical Comments." *HUCA,* XVII (1943), 427–98.

Finesinger, Sol Baruch. "The Shofar." *HUCA,* VIII–IX (1931–32), 193–228.

————. "The Custom of Looking at the Fingernails at the Outgoing of the Sabbath." *HUCA,* XII–XIII (1937–38), 347–65.

Guttmann, Alexander. *Das redaktionelle und sachliche Verhältnis zwischen Mishna und Tosephta.* Breslau, 1928.

————. "Das Problem der Misna redaktion aus den Sätzen Rabbis in Misna und Tosephta synoptisch beleuchtet." In *Festschrift zum 75 Jahrigen Bestehen des Jüdisch-theologischen Seminars Fraenckelscher Stiftung,* II, 95–130. Breslau, 1928.

————. *Enthüllte Talmudzitate.* Berlin, 1930.

————. "Der Minhag der Bibel in Spiegelbild des Talmuds; ein Beitrag zur Geschichte der mündlichen Lehre." In *Festschrift für Leo Baeck,* pp. 55–65. Berlin, 1938.

————. *Dizisionsmotive in Talmud* . . . Berlin, 1938.

————. "Mivhar Shetarot." Cincinnati, 1941. 2d edition with English title: "Hebrew and Aramaic Documents: A Selection of Significant Documents used in Jewish Life." Mimeographed. Cincinnati, 1971.

————. "The Problems of the Anonymous Mishna." *HUCA,* XVI (1941), 137–55.

————. "Akiba, 'Rescuer of the Torah.' " *HUCA,* XVII (1942–43), 395–421.

————. "Der Talmud Bavli vi a Literarishe Einheit." *Yivo Bletter,* XXIV (1944), 103–108.

————. "Li-she'elat Ha-yahas: Minhag-Halakhah Bi-tequfat Ha-talmud." *Bitzaron,* XIV (1946), 95–103, 192–98.

————. "Das Verhältnis Praxis-Gesetz in der Mischna." In *Jewish Studies in Memory of M. Guttman,"* I, 115–28. Budapest, 1946.

————. "The Significance of Miracles for Talmudic Judaism." *HUCA,* XX (1947), 363–406.

———. "Tractate Abot—Its Place in Rabbinic Literature." *JQR*, XLI (1950), 181–92.

———. "Foundations of Rabbinic Judaism." *HUCA*. XXIII (1950–51), I, 453–73.

———. *The Mood of the Talmud and the Great Talmudic Dictionary.* New York, 1951.

———. "The Patriarch Judah I—His Birth and Death." *HUCA*, XXV (1954), 239–61.

———. "Some Rabbinical Authorities and Codifiers." Compiled by B. S. Jacobson, revised by A. Guttman. Mimeographed. Cincinnati, 1957.

———. "Hillelites and Shammaites—a Clarification." *HUCA* (1957) 115–26.

———. "Eliezer ben Hyrcanus—a Shammaite?" In *Ignace Goldziher Memorial Volume*, II, 100–110. Budapest and Jerusalem, 1948–49.

———. "Pharisaism in Transition." In *Essays in Honor of Solomon B. Freehof*, pp. 202–19. Pittsburgh, 1964.

———. "The End of the 'House'." In *Abraham Weiss Jubilee Volume*," English Section, pp. 89–105. New York, 1964.

———. "Pharisees and Sadducees." *London Jewish Chronicle*, March 5, 1965, no pagination.

———. "The End of the Jewish Sacrificial Cult." *HUCA*, XXXVIII (1967), 137–48.

———. "She'elot u-Teshuvot." Mimeographed selections. Cincinnati, 1968. (*Mafeteah le-Sefer She'elot u-teshuvot*, arranged according to 1955 edition by M. Noyman(?). Mimeographed. Cincinnati, 1955.

———. Preface and Bibliography of 4th edition of Moses Mielziner, *Introduction to the Talmud* (New York, 1969).

———. "Ein Revolutionaire Wandlung in Jeudische-Religioesen Leben." *Tradition und Erneuerung*, XXVII (May 1969), 477–82.

———. "Jerusalem in Tannaitic Law." *HUCA*, XL–XLI (1969–70), 251–75.

———. "Spätphariäertum." *Forschung am Judentum, Festschrift zum sechzigsten geburtstag von Rabbiner Dr. Lothar Rothschild*, pp. 53–59. Bern, 1970.

———. "Talmud and Rabbinics: A selected Bibliography for the Student's Library." Mimeographed. Cincinnati, 1970.

———. *Rabbinic Judaism in the Making.* Detroit, 1970.

Idelsohn, Abraham Zevi

Bibliography: Moses Weiler, and T. S. Ross, in *HUC Monthly*, XX (1933), 9–11 (authorized list, about 100 articles not listed).

Works:

Idelsohn, Abraham Zevi. *Jewish Liturgy and Its Development.* New York, 1932.

Jerusalmi, Isaac. *The Talmud Is in Aramaic.* Cincinnati, 1966.

———. *Basic Pirqe Avoth.* Cincinnati, 1968.

Katz, Robert. "Empathy in Modern Psychotherapy and in the Aggadah." *HUCA*, XXX (1959), 191–215.

Kohler, Kaufmann

Bibliography: *Studies in Jewish Literature, Issued in Honor of K. Kohler*

(Berlin, 1913), 266–301; *Studies, Addresses, and Personal Papers* (New York, 1931), 563–77.

Works:

Kohler, Kaufmann. *Der Segen Jacob's.* Berlin, 1867.

———, and Rosenberg, M. "Das Targum zur Chronik." *Juedische Zeitschrift für Wissenschaft und Leben,* VIII (1870), 72–80, 135–63, 263–78.

———. "Wie alt ist die Pesach-Hagadah? Ein Studie zum 'Buch der Weisheit'." *Algemeine Zeitung des Judenthums,* LV (1891), 321–22.

———. "The Kaddish: Its Origin and Significance." New York, 1892 (a lecture).

———. "Ueber die Ursprünge und Grundformen der synagogalen Liturgie, Eine Studie." *MGWJ,* XXXVII (1893), 441–51, 489–97.

———. "The pre-Talmudic Haggada." *JQR,* o.s. V (1893), 399–419; VII (1895), 581–606.

———. "The Testament of Job. An Essene Midrash . . . " In *Semitic Studies in Memory of Alexander Kohut,* pp. 264–338. Berlin, 1897.

———. "Abba, Father. Title of Spiritual Leader and Saint." *JQR,* o.s. XIII (1901), 567–80.

———. "Zur Beleuchtung Jüdischer Sagen und Bräuche." *Mitterlungen der Gesellschaft für Jüdische Volkskunde,* V (1902), 9–12.

———. "Zum Kapital der Jüdischen Wohlthätig-keitspflege." In *Festschrift zum siebzigsten Geburtstage Abraham Berliner's . . . ,* pp. 195–203. Frankfurt a. Main, 1903.

———. "The Four Ells of the Halakah, and the Requirements of a Modern Jewish Theological School." *HUCA* (1904), 8–25.

———. "The Origin and Function of Ceremonies in Judaism." *CCAR Yearbook,* XVII (1907), 205–29.

———. "Wer Waren die Zeloten oder Kannaim? Eine Studie." In *Festschrift zum 70. Geburtstage A. Harkavy's,* pp. 6–18. St. Petersburg, 1908.

———. *Grundriss einer systematischen theologie des Judenturs auf geschichtler Grundlage. Leipzig,* 1909–10.

———. "Seltsame Vorstellungen und Bräuche in der biblischen und rabbinischen Literatur." *Archiv fur Religionswissenschaft,* XIII (1910), 75–84.

———. "Die Nachstenliebe in Judentum. Eine historische Studie." In *Judaica: Festschrift . . . Herman Cohen,* pp. 469–80. Berlin, 1912.

———. "The Harmonization of Jewish and Civil Laws of Marriage and Divorce." *CCAR Yearbook,* XXV (1915), 335–78.

———. "Hellenism and Judaism." *HUC Monthly,* IV (1917), 51–63.

———. "The Halakik Portions in Josephus's Antiquities" (*HUC Monthly,* February 1917), reprinted in *Studies, Addresses, and Personal Papers,* pp. 69–85. New York, 1931.

———. *Jewish Theology.* New York, 1958.

———. "The Tetragrammaton (shem ham-m'forash) and Its Uses." *Journal of Jewish Lore and Philosophy,* I (1919) 19–32.

———. "Shma Yisroel; Origin and Purpose of Its Daily Recital." *Journal of Jewish Lore and Philosophy,* I (1919), 255–64.

————. "The Essenes and the Apocalyptic Literature." *JQR,* n.s. XI (1920), 145–68.

————. *Heaven and Hell in Comparative Religion.* New York, 1923.

————. "The Origin and Composition of the 18 Benedictions, with a translation of corresponding Essene Prayers in the Apostolic Constitutions." *HUCA,* I (1924), 387–425.

————. *The Origins of the Synagogue and the Church.* New York, 1929.

————. "Dositheus, The Samaritan Heresiarch, and His Relations to Jewish and Christian Doctrines and Sects." In *Studies, Addresses, and Papers,* pp. 37–68. New York, 1931. (Reprinted from *American Journal of Theology,* XV, 403–35)

Lauterbach, Jacob Z.

Bibliography: Jacob Z. Lauterbach, *Rabbinic Esssays* (Cincinnati, 1951), 1–20.

Works:

Lauterbach, Jacob Z. "The Ancient Jewish Allegorists in Talmud and Midrash." *JQR,* n.s. I (1911), 291–333, 503–31.

————. "The Sadducees and Pharisees." In *Studies in Jewish Literature, issued in Honor of K. Kohler,* pp. 176–98. Berlin, 1913.

————. "The Ethics of the Halakah." *CCAR Yearbook,* XXIII (1914), 249–87.

————. "Midrash and Mishna." *JQR,* n.s. V (1915) 503–27; VI (1916), 23–95, 303–23.

————. Review of Bacher's *Tradition and Traditionalists in the Schools of Palestine and Babylonia. JQR,* n.s. VIII (1918), 101–12.

————. "Three Books Found in the Temple at Jerusalem." *JQR,* VIII (1918), 385–423.

————. Review of *The Origin of the Shulchan-Aruch." JQR,* IX (1919), 489–96.

————. "The Name of the Mekilta." *JQR,* XI (1920), 169–96.

————. "The Attitude of the Jew towards the Non-Jew." *CCAR Yearbook,* XXXI (1921), 186–233.

————. "Report of the Committee on Responsa." *CCAR Yearbook,* XXXII (1922), 41–42, 156–62; XXXIV (1924) 71–74, XXXVII (1927), 202–206; XLII (1932), 81–86.

————. "The Arrangement and the Division of the Mekilta." *HUCA,* I (1924), 427–66.

————. "Shevirat 'ezem Be-pesah." *Hazofeh,* IX (1925), 235–41.

————. "An Introduction to the Talmud." Cincinnati, 1925. (First chapter of a work never completed; printed but not published.)

————. "The Names of the Rabbinical Schools and Assemblies in Babylon." *HUCA Jubilee Volume,* Special/1925, 211–22.

————. "The Ceremony of Breaking a Glass at Weddings." *HUCA,* II (1925), 351–80.

————. "The Jewish Attitude toward Autopsy." *CCAR Yearbook,* XXXV (1925), 130–34.

————. "A Significant Controversy between the Sadducees and the Pharisees." *HUCA,* IV (1927), 173–205.

———. "Talmudic-Rabbinic View on Birth Control." *CCAR Yearbook,* XXXVII (1927), 369–84.

———. "Should One Cover the Head When Participating in Divine Worship?" *CCAR Yearbook,* XXXVIII (1928), 589–603.

———. "Hats on or off? The Synagogue Question . . . Historically Considered . . . " *American Hebrew,* CXXIII (1928), 307, 310, 329, 332.

———. "Abbreviations and Their Solutions." In *A. S. Freidus Memorial Volume,* pp. 141–49. New York, 1929.

———. "The Pharisees and Their Teachings." *HUCA,* VI (1929), 69–139.

———. "Substitutes for the Tetragrammaton." *Proceedings of the American Academy for Jewish Research,* II (1931), 39–67.

———. "The Naming of Children in Jewish Folklore, Ritual, and Practice." *CCAR Yearbook,* XLII (1932), 316–60.

———. "The Two Mekiltas." *Proceedings of the American Academy for Jewish Research,* IV (1933), 113–29.

———. "Midrash Wayis'u, 'o Sefer Milhamot Bene Ya'aqov." In *Abhandlungen zur Erinnerung an H. P. Chajes,* pp. 205–22. Vienna, 1933.

———. *Mekilta.* 3 Vols. Philadelphia, 1933–35.

———. "Misunderstood Chronological Statements in the Talmudic Literature." *Proceedings of the American Academy for Jewish Research,* V (1934), 77–84.

———. "The Ritual for the Kapparot-ceremony." In *Jewish Studies in Memory of G. A. Kohut,* pp. 413–22. New York, 1935.

———. "Unpublished Parts of the Yalkut ha-Makiri on Hosea and Micah." In *Occident and Orient: Gaster Anniversary Volume,* pp. 365–73. London, 1936.

———. "Tashlik: A Study in Jewish Ceremonies." *HUCA,* XI (1936), 207–340.

———. "Mi-Be'ure Ha-Mekhilta." In *Sefer Klausner,* pp. 181–88. Tel Aviv, 1937.

———. "The Belief in the Power of The Word." *HUCA,* XIV (1939), 287–302.

———. "Rashi the Talmud Commentator," *CCAR Yearbook,* L (1940), 360–73.

———. "The Origin and Development of Two Sabbath Ceremonies." *HUCA,* XV (1940), 367–424.

———. "Zeman Shehitat Ha-pesah." *Proceedings of the American Academy for Jewish Research,* XII (1942), Hebrew Section, 1–5. (English summary: "The date of the Slaughter of the Pascal Lamb," same volume, English section, 49–50)

———. "Jesus in the Talmud." In *Rabbinic Essays,* pp. 473–570. Cincinnati, 1951.

———. "The Sabbath in Jewish Ritual and Folklore." In *Rabbinic Essays,* pp. 437–70. Cincinnati, 1951.

Lehman, Israel O., and Weisberg, David B. " 'Feet of Iron' in the Babylonian Talmud?" *Zeitschrift der Deutschen Morgenländischen Gesellschaft,* CXX, i (1970), 30–31.

Levey, Samson H. *The Messianic Exegesis of the Targum.* Los Angeles, 1955 (USC Microfilm 520). [In revised form soon to be published by HUC Monograph Series.]

———. "The Date of Targum Jonathan to the Prophets." *Vetus Testamentum,*

XXI, 2 (1971), 186–96.

———. "The Best Kept Secret of the Rabbinic Tradition." *Judaism,* XXI, 4 (1972), 454–69.

Levias, Caspar. "The Palestinian Vocalization." *American Journal of Semitic Languages and Literatures,* XV (1898–99), 157–64.

———. *A Grammar of the Aramaic Idiom Contained in the Babylonian Talmud.* Cincinnati, 1900.

———. *A Grammar of Babylonian Aramaic.* New York, 1930.

Liebrich, Leon J. "Silverstone's *Aquila and Onkelos.*" *JQR,* XXVII (1937), 287–91.

———. "The Expression 'God drew us near (unto)' in Various Liturgical Contexts." *JQR,* XXXIII (1942–43), 461–69.

———. "Benedictory Formula in the Targum to the Song of Songs." *HUCA,* XVIII (1944), 177–97.

———. "An Analysis of *U'ba' Le-Ziyyon* in the Liturgy." *HUCA,* XXI (1948), 175–209.

———. "The Invocation to Prayer at the Beginning of the Yozer Service." *JQR,* XXXIX (1948–49), 285–90, 407–412.

———. "The Pesuke de-Zimra Benedictions." *JQR,* XLI (1950–51), 195–206.

———. "The Impact of Nehemiah 9:5–37 on the Liturgy of the Synagogue." *HUCA,* XXXII (1961), 227–37.

———. "Aspects of the New Year Liturgy." *HUCA,* XXXIV (1963), 125–76.

———. "The Insertions in the Third Benediction of the Holy Day 'Amidoth." *HUCA,* XXXV (1964), 79–101.

Mann, Jacob

Bibliography: Simon Federbush, *Hokhmat Yisrael Be-ma'arav 'eropah* (Jerusalem, 1958–63), I, 499–500; R. Mahler, "Y'aqov Mann un sein Lebenswerk," *Yivo Bletter,* XVI (1940), 178, 181; XVII (1941), 92; J. R. Marcus, *CCAR Yearbook,* LI (1941), 247–49.

Works:

Mann, Jacob. "The Observance of the Sabbath and the Festivals . . . According to Philo, Josephus, the New Testament and the Rabbinic Sources." *Jewish Review,* IV (1914), 433–56.

———. "Jesus and the Sadducean Priests: Luke 10, 25–37." *JQR,* VI (1916), 415–22.

———. "Oaths and Vows in the Synoptic Gospels." *American Journal of Theology,* XXI (1917), 260–74.

———. "The Responsa of the Babylonian Geonim as a Source of Jewish History." *JQR,* VII (1916–17), 457–90; VIII (1917–18), 339–66; IX (1918–19), 139–79; X (1919–20), 121–51, 309–65; Addenda, XI (1921), 433–71.

———. "Note on Solomon b. Judah and Some of His Contemporaries." *JQR,* IX (1918–19), 409–21.

———. "Anan's Liturgy and His Half-yearly Cycle of the Reading of the Law." *Journal of Jewish Lore and Phylosophy,* I (1919), 329–53.

——. *The Jews in Egypt and in Palestine under the Fatimid Caliphate.* 2 vols. Oxford, 1920–22.

——. "Early Karaite Bible Commentaries." *JQR,* XII (1921), 435–526; XV (1925), 361–88.

——. "The Last Geonim of Sura . . . " *JQR,* XI (1921), 409–432.

——. "A Polemic Work against Karaites and other Sectaries." *JQR,* XII (1921), 123–50.

——. "Listes de Livres Provenant de la Gueniza." *REJ,* LXXII, no. 144 (1921), 163–83.

——. "Teshuvah Me'et R. Shemu'el ben 'ali Gaon Be-Bagdad Mi-Shenat 1166 Le-SFH"N." *Ha-ZoFeh Le-Hokhmat Yisra'el,* VI (1922), pages unknown.

——. "A Tract by an Early Karaite Settler in Jerusalem." *JQR,* XII (1922), 257–98.

——. "Glanures de la Gueniza." *REJ,* LXXIV, no. 148 (1922), 148–59.

——. "Rabbinic Studies in the Synoptic Gospels." *HUCA,* I (1924), 323–55.

——. "Genizah Fragments of the Palestinian Order of Service." *HUCA,* II (1925), 269–338.

——. "Ha-tenu'oth Ha-meshihiot Bime Masa'e Ha-zelav Ha-ri'shonim." *Ha-tequfa,* XXIII (1925), 243–61, XXIV (1928), 335–58.

——. "Gaonic Studies." *HUCA Jubilee Volume,* Special, 1925, 223–62; Additional Note, *HUCA,* III (1926), 309–10.

——. "A Second Supplement to *The Jews in Egypt and in Palestine under the Fatimid Caliphs.*" *HUCA,* III (1926), 257–308.

——. "On the Terminology of the Early Massoretes and Grammarians." In *Paul Haupt Festschrift,* pp. 437–45. Leipzig, 1926.

——. "Shirtutim Hadashim Le-toledot Rav Sherira Gaon." *Hazofeh,* XI (1927), 147–52.

——. "Changes in the Divine Service in the Synagogue due to Religious Persecutions." *HUCA,* IV (1927), 241–310.

——. "Mesharet Ro'sh-Ha-golah Be-vavel Ve-hista'afutah Be-sof Tequfat Hage'onim." In *Lievre d'hommage à la memoire du Dr. S. Poznanski,* pp. 18–32. Warsaw, 1927.

——. "Geniza Studies," *American Journal of Semitic Languages and Literatures,* XLVI (1930), 263–83.

——. "Sefer Ha-ma'asim Li-vene 'erez-Yisra'el." *Tarbiz,* I, no. 3 (April 1930), 1–14.

——. "New Studies in Karaism." *CCAR Yearbook,* XLIV (1934), 220–41.

——. *Text and Studies in Jewish History and Literature.* 2 vols. Cincinnati, 1931–35.

——. " 'inyanim shonim Le-heqer Tequfat Ha-ge'onim." *Tarbiz,* V, no. 1 (October 1933), 148–79; V, no. 2 (January 1934), 274–304; VI, no. 1 (October 1934), 66–88; VI, no. 2 (January 1935), 238–42.

——. "An Early Theologico-Polemical Works." *HUCA,* XII–XIII (1937–38), 411–59.

——. "Some Midrashic Genizah Fragments." *HUCA,* XIV (1939), 303–58.

———. "A Commentary to the Pentateuch à la Rashi's." *HUCA,* XV (1940), 497–527.

———. *The Bible as Preached in the Old Synagogue.* 2 vols. Cincinnati, 1940 and 1960. (Vol. II was edited by Victor E. Reichert and is by both Jacob Mann and Isaiah Sonne. Vol. I was reprinted by KTAV Publishing House, New York, 1971, with a prologomenon by Ben Zion Wacholder.)

Mielziner, Moses

Bibliography: Ella McKenna Friend Mielziner, *Moses Mielziner 1828–1903* (New York, 1931).

Works:

Mielziner, Moses. "The Talmudic Syllogism; or, The Inference of Kal vechomer, Explained and Illustrated." *Hebrew Review,* I (1880), 43–53.

———. "On Translations of the Talmud." *Hebrew Review,* I (1880), 280–85.

———. "The Talmudic Analogy; or, The Rules of Gezera Shawa and Heckesh." *Hebrew Review,* II (1881–82), 79–84.

———. *The Jewish Law of Marriage and Divorce in Ancient and Modern Times, and Its Relation to the Law of the State.* Cincinnati, 1884.

———. "The Marriage Agenda," *CCAR Yearbook,* I (1891), 32–42.

———. *The Institution of Slavery among the Ancient Hebrews, According to the Bible and Talmud.* Cincinnati, 1894. (Translation of article in German. First printed in Copenhagen and Leipzig, 1859; translated by H. I. Schmidt, in *Gettysburg Evangelical Review,* XIII, no. 1 (no date); appeared in *American Jews' Annual,* 1885–86.)

———. *Introduction to the Talmud.* Cincinnati, 1894 (4th edition, New York, 1968, with a new bibliography, 1925–67 by Alexander Guttmann).

———. *Legal Maxims and Fundamental Laws of the Civil and Criminal Code of the Talmud.* Cincinnati, 1898.

Mihaly, Eugene. "Reform Judaism and Halacha: The Contemporary Relevance of the Mishna Torah of Maimonides . . . " *CCAR Yearbook,* LXIV (1954), 214–26.

———. "The Jewish View of Marriage." *CCAR Journal,* II, no. 7 (October 1954), 32–38.

———. "Moses Maimonides, Author and Teacher for the Ages." *CCAR Journal,* III, no. 2 (October 1955), 19–27.

———. *Religious Experience in Judaism.* London, 1957.

———. "Jewish Prayer and Synagogue Architecture." *Judaism,* VII (1958), 309–19.

———. "On Translating the Oral Law." *CCAR Journal,* VII, no. 27 (October 1959), 50–55.

———. "A Rabbinic Defense of the Election of Israel." *HUCA,* XXXV (1964), 103–43.

———. "A Guide for Writers of Reform Liturgy." *CCAR Journal,* XIII, no. 49 (April 1965), 5–20.

———. "The Passover Haggadah as Paradise." *CCAR Journal,* XIII, no. 53 (April 1966), 3–27.

————. Prologomenon to reprint of *Robbinical Literature and Gospel Teaching,* by Claude G. Montefiore. New York, 1970.

Morgenstern, Julian. "The Bones of the Pascal Lamb." *Journal of the American Oriental Society,* XXXVI (1916), 146–53.

————. "Three Calendars of Ancient Israel." *HUCA,* I (1924), 13–78.

————. "The Chanukkah Festival and the Calendar of Israel." *HUCA,* XX (1947), 1–136; XXI (1948), 365–496.

————. "The Origin of the Synagogue." *Studia Orientalistici . . . Levi Della Vida,* pp. 192–201. 2 vols. Rome, 1956.

————. "Lag be'omer—Its Origin and Import." *HUCA,* XXXIX (1968), 81–90.

Orlinsky, Harry M. "Studies in Talmudic Philology." *HUCA,* XXII, Pt. 1 (1950–51), 499–514.

Passamaneck, Stephen M. "A Handbook of Post-Talmudic Halakhic Literature." Mimeographed. Los Angeles, 1965.

————. "The Talmudic Concept of Defamation." *Revue Internationale des Droits de l'Antiquité,* 3rd series, XII (1965), 21–54.

————. "Traces of Rabbinical Martime Law and Custom." *Tijdschrift voor Rechtsgeschiedenis,* XXXIV (1966), 525–51.

————. "Some Medieval Problems in Mamzeruth." *HUCA,* XXXVII (1966), 121–45.

————. *Reform and Halakah: The State of the Art.* Los Angeles, 1967.

————. "Caravan Custom in Early Rabbinic Sources." *Tijdschrift voor Rechtsgesehiedenis,* XXXVI (1968), 73–88.

————. "Aspects of Land Use and Commercial Regulation in Medieval Rabbinic Sources." *Revue Internationale des Droits de l'Antiquité,* 3rd series, XVI (1969), 31–71.

————. "A Case of Piracy." *HUCA* XL–XLI (1969–70), 277–98.

————. "A Note on Dignity." *CCAR Journal,* XVIII (1971), 76–78.

————. *Insurance on Rabbinic Law.* Edinburgh, 1974.

Petuchowski, Jakob J. *The Theology of Haham David Nieto.* Welch, W. Va., 1954.

————. "An Eighteenth Century Defender of the Faith (translations from David Nieto's *Matteh Dan* and *Esh Dath*)." *Commentary,* July 1954, 64–66.

————. "Halakhah in an Age of Transition." *Reconstructionist,* XXI, no. 7 (May 13, 1955), 17–21.

————. "Problems of Reform Halakhah." *Judaism,* IV (1955), 339–51.

————. "Rabbinic Texts as Apologetic and Polemic Source Material." Mimeographed, with Bibliography. Cincinnati, 1956.

————. Review of *Understanding the Talmud,* by Ernest R. Tratner. *Jewish Social Studies,* XVIII, no. 4 (October 1956), 288–91.

————. "The Pharisaic Tradition Today." *Commentary,* February 1956, 112–17.

————. Review of *Maccabees, Zealots and Josephus,* by William Reuben Farmer. *Commentary,* March 1957, 287–90.

————. "A Note on W. Kessler's *Problematik des Dekalogs.*" *Vetus Testamentum,* VII, no. 4 (October 1957), 397–98.

———. "Do This in Remembrance of Me (I Cor. 11:24)." *JBL,* LXXVI (1957), 293–98.

———. "The Controversial Figure of Melchizedek." *HUCA,* XXVIII (1957), 127–36.

———. "Love to Thy Neighbor (translation of Malbin's commentary on Lev. 19:18)." *Commentary,* September 1958, 250–51.

———. "Early Science and Jewish Belief (translation from David Nieto's *Matteh Dan*)." *Commentary,* February 1958, 149–50.

———. "Who Is a Jew?" *Jewish Frontier.* June 1959, 6–10.

———. "A Feminist Before Her Time (translation of a Responsum by Maimonides)." *Commentary,* November 1959, 429–30.

———. "The Bible of The Synagogue; the Continuing Revelation." *Commentary,* XXVII (1959), 142–50.

———. "Paul and Jewish Theology: A New View of the Christian Apostle." *Commentary,* XXVIII (1959), 231–36.

———. "The Supposed Dogma of the Mosaic Authorship of the Pentateuch." *Hibbert Journal,* LVII (1959), 356–60.

———. "Ha-megillah She-'eynena." *Hadoar,* June 19, 1959, 549.

———. "The Mumar—A Study in Rabbinic Psychology." *HUCA,* XXX (1959), 179–90.

———. "Karaite Tendencies in an Early Reform Haggadah—A Study in Comparative Liturgy." *HUCA,* XXXI (1960), 223–49.

———. "Nochmals Zur Anfertigung des Godenen Kalbes." *Vetus Testamentum,* X, no. 1 (June 1960), 74.

———. "Diaspora Judaism—An Abnormality? The Testimony of History." *Judaism,* XI, no. 1 (Winter 1960), 17–28.

———. "The Hero of the Isaac Story." *Jewish Frontier,* (April 1960), 11–14.

———. "The Magnification of Channukah." *Commentary,* January 1960, 38–43.

———. "Qedushah She-benerot." *Hadoar,* December 9, 1960, 91.

———. "Major Themes of Jewish Liturgy." *Jewish Spectator,* October 1960, 14–15.

———. "Repentance Means Return." *Jewish Information,* I, no. 1 (1960), 15–20.

———. Review of *Jewish Gnosticism, Merkabah Mysticism, and the Talmudic Tradition,* by Gershom G. Scholem. *Commentary,* February 1961, 177–79.

———. "Review of *The Second Crucifixtion,* by Maurice Samuel. *Congress Bi-Weekly,* January 16, 1961, 37–38.

———. "Midrash and Homiletics." *American Rabbi,* I, October 1961, 21–24.

———. "Rejoicing in the Commandment," *Jewish Spectator,* October 1961, 10–12.

———. *Ever Since Sinai.* New York, 1961.

———. "Preaching on a Rashi Text," *American Rabbi,* I, no. 4 (1961), 17–20.

———. "The Wayfarer's Prayer—A Yom Kippur Sermon," *American Rabbi,* April 1962, 16–20.

———. "The First Steps in the Study of the Talmud." Mimeographed. Cincinnati, 1962.

———. "A Fence with Loopholes." *Menorah Journal,* XLIX (1962), 77–88.

———. "The Christian-Jewish Dialogue: A Jewish View." *Lutheran World,* X, no. 4, October 1963, 373–84.

———. "Some Reflections on the Reform Attitude toward Divorce." *CCAR Journal,* April, 1964, 11–13.

———. "Halakhah in the Church Fathers. In *Essays in Honor of Solomon B. Freehof,* pp. 257–74. Pittsburgh.

———. "Qebha' Wekhawwanah Be-toledoth Ha-tephillah Beyisrael." *Prozdor,* nos. 9–10 (Adar 5725; 1965) 27–32.

———. "The Fruit of a Goodly Tree." *Jewish Spectator,* September 1965, 21–23.

———. "The Dialectics of Reason and Revelation." In *Rediscovering Judaism,* edited by Arnold J. Wolf, pp. 29–50, 271–78. Chicago, 1965. (Hebrew version of same article: "Hitgalut U-tevunah." *Prozdor,* nos. 11–12 [Tishre 5728; 1967], 16–27)

———. Review of *Prayer in the Period of the Tannaim and the Amoraim,* by Joseph Heinemann. *Judaism,* XV. no. 1 (Winter 1966), 114–20.

———. "Realism about Mixed Marriage." *CCAR Journal,* October 1966, 34–38, 41.

———. "The Bible of the Synagogue." In *Jewish-Christian Relations,* edited by Thomas Lay. Kansas, 1966, 11–22.

———. "Reform Benedictions for Rabbinic Ordinances." *HUCA,* XXXVII (1966), 175–89.

———. Review of *The Talmud,* translated into English with a commentary by Dr. A. Ehrman. *Conservative Judaism,* XX, no. 3 (1966), 79–84.

———. *Prayerbook Reform in Europe.* New York, 1968.

———. "The Concept of 'Teshuvah' in the Bible and the Talmud." *Judaism,* XVII, no. 2 (Spring 1968), 175–85.

———. ed. *Contributions to the Scientific Study of Jewish Liturgy.* New York, 1970.

———. *Heirs of the Pharisees.* New York and London, 1970.

———. "Ha-mizwot Ha-hevratiot Ka-yesod Ha-Yahadut," *Shedemoth,* no. 39 (Fall 1970), 50–53.

———. *Cult, Entertainment, and Worship.* New York, 1970.

———. "Some Criteria for Modern Jewish Observance." In *Tradition and Contemporary Experience,* edited by Alfred Jospe, pp. 239–48, 366–67. New York, 1970.

———. "Qol Adonai; A Study in Rabbinic Theology." *Zeitschrift für Religions- und Geistesgeschichte,* XXIV, Heft. 1 (1972), 13–24.

———. "Second Thoughts About the Second Day." *Conservative Judaism,* XXIV, no. 2 (Winter 1970), 48–59.

———. "Man's Part in Bringing about the Messianic Age." *Ideas,* II, nos. 2–3 (Winter–Spring 1970), 69–73.

———. "Plural Models within the Halakhah." *Judaism,* XIX, no. 1 (Winter 1970), 77–89.

———. "The Rabbi and the Tree." *CCAR Journal,* January 1970, 52–56.

―――. "Review of *New Light from the Prophets,* by Louis Finkelstein. *Conservative Judaism,* XXV, no. 2 (Winter 1971), 81–83.

―――. "A Closed Book?" *London Jewish Chronicle,* March 26, 1971, 16.

―――. *Understanding Jewish Progress.* New York, 1972.

―――. "The 'Malkhuyoth', 'Zikhronoth', and 'Shofaroth' Verses," *Pointer,* Autumn, 1972, 4–6.

―――. "The Theological Significances of the Parable in Rabbinic Literature and the New Testament." *Christian News From Israel,* XXIII, no. 2 [10] (1972), 76–86.

Rivkin, Ellis. "The Sermons of Leon da Modena." *HUCA,* XXIII, Pt. II (1950–51), 295–317.

―――. *Leon Da Modena and the Kol Sakhal.* Cincinnati, 1952.

―――. "Who Crucified Jesus?" *Jewish Heritage.* Fall 1958, 11–16.

―――. "Paul and the Parting of the Ways." *Jewish Heritage,* Winter 1959, 23–28.

―――. "The Saadia–David Ben Zakkai Controversy." In *Studies and Essays in Honor of Abraham A. Neuman,* pp. 388–423. Leiden, 1962.

―――. "Ben Sira and the Non-existence of the Synagogue: A Study in Historical Method." In *In The Time of Harvest,* edited by Daniel Jeremy Silver, pp. 321–54. New York, 1963.

―――. "Solomon Zeitlin's Contribution to the Historiography of the Intertestamental Period." *Judaism,* XIV, no. 3, (Summer 1965), 354–67.

―――. "The Pharisaic Revolution." *Perspectives in Jewish Learning* (1966), 26–51.

―――. "The Internal City: Judaism and Urbanization." *Journal for the Scientific Study of Religion,* V, no. 2 (Spring 1966), 225–40.

―――. Wacholder, Ben Zion, and others. "A Symposium on the Pharisees." *CCAR Journal,* June 1967, 32–47.

―――. Prolegomenon to reprint of *Judaism and Christianity,* edited by W. O. E. Oesterley, pp. vii–lxx. New York, 1969.

―――. "Defining the Pharisees: The Tannaitic Sources." *HUCA,* XL–XLI (1969–70), 205–49.

―――. "Pharisaism and the Crises of the Individual in the Greco-Roman World." *JQR,* LXI (1970–71), 27–53.

―――. "The Meaning of Messiah in Jewish Thought." *Union Seminary Quarterly Review,* XXVI, no. 4, Summer, 1971, 383–406.

Rosenthal, Franz. "Yom Tob." *HUCA,* XVIII (1944), 157–76.

Sandmel, Samuel. "Judaism, Jesus and Paul: Some Problems of Method in Scholarly Research." *Vanderbilt Studies in the Humanities,* I (1951), 220–50.

―――. "Philo's Place in Judaism: A Study of Conceptions of Abraham in Jewish Literature, Part I." *HUCA,* XXV (1954), 209–37; "Part II." *HUCA,* XXVI (1955), 151–332.

―――. "Myths, Genealogies, and Jewish Myths and the Writing of Gospels." *HUCA,* XXVII (1956), 201–11.

―――. *A Jewish Understanding of the New Testament.* New York, 1960 [first paperbound edition; first printing, 1956].

————. *The Genius of Paul: A Study in History*. New York, 1958.

————. "Genesis 4:26b." *HUCA*, XXXII (1961), 19–29.

————. *We Jews and Jesus*. New York, 1965.

————. *The First Christian Century in Judaism and Christianity*. New York, 1969.

Schwartzman, Sylvan D. "How Well Did the Synoptic Evangelists Know the Synagogue?" *HUCA*, XXIV, (1952–53), 115–32.

Slonimsky, Henry. "The Philosophy Implicit in the Midrash." *HUCA*, XXVII (1956), 235–90.

Sonne, Isaiah. "Le-reshito shel Ha-defus Ha'ivri Bi-Sefarad." *Kirath Sefer*, XIV (1937), 368–78.

————. "Leo da Modena uber die Schrift 'kol Sachal'." *MGWJ*, LXXVII (1933), 384–85.

————. "Taqanat shel 'isur Shabbat ve-yom tov She-tiqen R. Meshullam Wayybesh Me-Cracow." *Horeb*, II (1935), 237–46.

————. "Le-biqoret Ha-text shel Perush Rashi 'al Ha-torah." *HUCA*, XV (1940), Hebrew Section, 37–51.

————. *Expurgation of Hebrew Books: The Work of Jewish Scholars*. New York, 1943.

————. "An Unknown Keroba of Yannai." *HUCA*, XVII (1944), 199–220.

————. "The Schools of Shammai and Hillel Seen from Within." *American Academy of Jewish Research; Louis Ginzberg Jubillee Volume*, pp. 275–91. New York, 1945.

————. "The Use of Rabbinic Literature as Historical Sources." *JQR*, XXXVI (1945–46), 147–69.

————. "Saadia-literature." *JQR*, XXXVI (1945–46), 427–34.

————. "The Paintings of the Dura Synagogue." *HUCA*, XX (1947), 255–362.

————. "Leon Modena and the DaCosta Circle in Amsterdam." *HUCA*, XXI (1948), 1–28.

————. "A Hymn Against Heretics in the Newly Discovered Scrolls." *HUCA*, XXIII, Pt. 1 (1950–51), 275–313.

————. "Traces of Hellenistic Thought in Talmudic Literature." In "Proceedings of the Summer Institute of HUC-JIR. Mimeographed. Cincinnati, 1948.

————. "Final Verdict on the Scrolls?" *JBL*, LXX (1951), 37–44.

————. "Biblical Criticism in the Middle Ages." In *Freedom and Reason: Studies . . . in Memory of M. R. Cohen*, pp. 438–46. Glencoe, 1951.

————. "The X-sign in the Isaiah Scroll." *Vetus Testamentum*, IV (1954), 90–94.

————. "The Newly Discovered Bar Kokeba Letters." *Proceedings of the American Academy for Jewish Research*, XXIII (1954), 75–108.

————. "Khinuyye Bet-Ha-kheneset." *Tarbiz*, XXVII (1958), 557–59.

————. "Synagogue." In *Interpreter, Dictionary of the Bible*, III, 476–91. New York, 1962.

Spicehandler, Ezra. "*Bey Do'ar* and *Dina' Di-Megista'*, Notes on Gentile Courts in Talmudic Babylonia." *HUCA*, XXVI (1955), 333–54.

Tchernowitz, Chaim

Bibliography: Eliezer Raphael Malachi, *Peri 'ez Hayyim*. (New York, 1946).

Works:

Tchernowitz, Chaim. "Hakhra'ah Be-mahloqet Yahid Ve-rabim." In *Festschrift zu Israel Lewy's Siebzigstem Geburtstag*, Hebrew Section, pp. 1–9. Breslau, 1911.

——. *Ha-Talmud*. Warsaw, 1912.

——. *Shi'urim Ba-Talmud*. 2 Vols. bound in one, Warsaw, 1913.

——. *Qizur Ha-Talmud*. 3 Vols. Lausanne, 1919–23.

——. *Die Entstchung des Schulchan Aruch, Beitrag zur Festlegund der Halacha*. Bern, 1915.

——. *Toledoth Ha-Halakah: History of Hebrew Law*. 4 Vols. New York, 1934–50.

——. "Demai." In *Jewish Studies in Memory of G. A. Kohut*, Hebrew Section, pp. 46–58. New York, 1935. (Appeared later as part of *Toledoth Ha-Halakah*.)

——. "Maimonides as Codifier." Translated from Hebrew by H. S. Lewis. New York, 1935. Hebrew original in *Mihlat*, V (1920), 348–85.

——. "Rashi, Parshan Ha-Talmud." *Bitzaron*, II (1940), 358–71.

——. "She'elah U-Teshuvah." *Bitzaron*, V (1941–42), 147–49.

——. "Ha-Bavli Ve-ha-yerushalmi: Darkhe Limudehem Viysede Ha-hevdelim She-benehem." *Bitzaron*, VI (1942), 560–72, 686–69.

——. "Mishnah 'aharonah." In *Studies in Memory of Moses Schorr*, pp. 259–63. New York, 1944.

——. *Toledoth Ha-Poskim: History of the Jewish Codes*. New York, 1946–47.

Wacholder, Ben Zion. "Attitude towards Proselytizing in the Classical Halakah." *Historica Judaica*, XX (1958), 77–96.

——. Review of the *She'iltot*, edited by S. K. Mirsky. *JQR*, LIII, no. 3 (1962–63), 257–61.

——. *Nicolaus of Damascus. Berkeley*, 1962.

——. "Pseudo-Eupolemus' Two Greek Fragments on the Life of Abraham." *HUCA*, XXXIV (1963), 83–113.

——. "How Long Did Abraham Stay in Egypt?" *HUCA*, XXXV (1964), 43–56.

——. "Tosafot Yeshanim We-hidushe HaRaBaD 'al Pereq Ri'shon U-pereq Sheni Shel Masekhet Qidushin." *HUCA* XXXVII (1966), Hebrew Section, 65–90.

——. "The Date of the Mekilta de-Rabbi Ishmael." *HUCA*, XXXIX (1968), 117–44.

——. "Supplements to the Printed Edition of the Tesafot Yesanim, Yevamot, Chapter I." *HUCA*, XL–XLI (1969–70), Hebrew Section, 1–30.

——. Prolegomenon to reprint of *The Bible as Read and Preached in the Old Synagogue*. Vol. I, New York, 1971.

————, and Weisberg, David B. "Visibility of the New Moon in Cuneiform and Rabbinic Sources." *HUCA,* XLII (1971), 227–42.

Weinberg, Werner. *Rabbinic Usage.* Cincinnati, 1966.

Weisberg, David B. "Some Observations on Late Babylonian Texts and Rabbinic Literature." *HUCA,* XXXIX (1968), 71–80.

LOU H. SILBERMAN

Theology and Philosophy:

Some Tentative Remarks

I. An Introduction by Way of an Apology

It can be argued that many, perhaps most, although certainly not all of the members of the faculty of the Hebrew Union College have been theologians, in the broad sense that they have reflected critically and imaginatively on the faith of Israel. Whatever particular academic field was their concern, in one way or another, sometimes as a second order of interest, at others as peripheral or tangential, many have had something to say, in a variety of ways, about how Judaism was and is to be grasped hold of and understood. On occasion, the ideas of a faculty member as a second-order or tangential theologian have had wide influence, although, on reflection, the claim that the thinking of first-order theologians has commanded less attention does not appear to have been sustained. Given then the scope of the faculty's involvement in theologizing, one needs some limitation if he is not to find himself dealing with that "many, perhaps most." Fairly or unfairly—and the latter seems more certainly to be the case—we shall deal only with those who quite self-consciously saw themselves doing theology—that is, concerned as scholars to examine with scholarly care the tradition, to make judgments, to draw conclusions, and to suggest and argue contemporary normative positions.

It cannot be argued that many, perhaps most, of the members of the faculty were philosophers, or more accurately, religious philosophers, unless—of course—we unwrite the previous paragraph, discard the term *theology* in all its parts, and insist that Judaism does not have theology, only religious philosophy. Since this is not the place to carry on the debate, let those who take this position substitute *religious philosopher or religious philosophy* for each and every occurrence of *theologian* and *theology*. Nonetheless, there were members of the faculty who consciously saw themselves concerned with a limited and technical part of the tradition designated as philosophy, either as historian of the same, as critic, or as innovator. Claim for such activities can be made for far fewer than those in the previous category.

If any attention has been paid thus far to the tenses of the verbs, it will have been noted that the past perfect is regnant. The reason for this is quite simple: the present is not yet perfected. Thus any attempt to indicate more than present presence is bound to be partial, perhaps in both senses. Furthermore we are enjoined not to say more than half a man's praise in his presence, but that certainly means not an iota less than half, otherwise one may be guilty of *halbanat panim*.

Finally, there were those whose tenure at the College was of such comparatively short duration that whatever luster they previously or subsequently shed, is, for the College, reflected glory that it may claim *in petto* alone.

Having thus laid out the circumference of this exploration, one more confession is required. Controversy—*kin'at soferim tarbeh hokhmah*—is part of the story. It has been faced, not glossed over. The problems and puzzles it has engendered have been wrestled with, and occasionally an attempt has been made to explain what seems to have been going on beneath the surface. There have been and are other ways of reading the material. No finality is here claimed.

II. Some Reflections on the Thought of Isaac M. Wise

Although it may appear that a discussion of Wise, however brief, contravenes immediately the restrictions noted above, it must be recognized that he did in some way or other claim to be both religious philosopher and theologian. Given the very newness of modern Jewish thought in his days, he, like many others, was and had to be a *kol bo'*, dealing with areas in which he was only at most an informed amateur.

James G. Heller, in Part Three of his volume, *Isaac M. Wise: His Life, Work and Thought*,[1] tried to sort out the thought of Wise, giving due heed both to development and to change. ". . . it should be obvious," he wrote, "that the systematization of his thought . . . will make them more schematic than in fact they were, more logical and consecutive in their order and expression."[2] Heller had set out to combat what was to him the "misconception and even misrepresentation of Wise's opinions," and he hoped that with a "complete outline of his opinions . . . these distortions or fantasies will be exposed."[3] As part of that task, Heller epitomized Wise's religious philosophy, *The Cosmic God*, while disclaiming any ability "to help [the reader] with the terminology, history, or adequate exposition of many of the points made." Nonetheless, on several occasions, Heller did comment, sometimes within square brackets, on others, without, not unfavorably on "some rare remarkable aperçu," while calling attention as well to "some naive and thoroughly dated ideas."[4] There is no need to provide another resume; Heller carried out his with diligence. What is evident is that Wise, writing—as Heller noted—*mi-maamakim,* brought together ideas gathered from wide and perhaps indiscriminate reading into a statement that served him in his own need and provided him with a foundation on which to rebuild the shaken structure of his intellectual and spiritual life. In this work he proposed, in Heller's phrase, "to go over all essential problems concerning the religion, philosophy and science of the 19th century and to search out what may be thought by intelligent men."[5] That was, indeed, a formidable task, one that could well occupy the entire attention of a first-rate philosophical mind. In Wise, the answer is personal, reflecting in largest measure the varieties of nineteenth-century German idealism to which he responded, with no overarching synthesis to hold them in place. This was not uncharacteristic of Wise's approach to such questions; an approach that often placed him at an intellectual disadvantage when a more single-minded thinker challenged him.

Kaufmann Kohler, several years earlier, in a slashing attack in the *Jewish Times* (1871), wrote, "He takes his arguments, wherever he finds them . . .," and continues several paragraphs later: "He is now studying Spinoza and therefore writes of nothing but substance and accidence. . . . If in time he will have reached Kant's logic, Herbart's psychology and Schleiermacher's *Glauben,* he might give us a better definition of religion, than the one with which he begins his 'essence of religion' where he says: 'Religion is to know God and to worship him'; equally as logical as if one would say: 'Geography is to describe the surface of the earth and to know its inhabitants.' " [6] The occasion for this outburst was a statement made by "Mayer of Cleveland" at a rabbinical conference in June, 1871, held in Cincinnati, that he did not believe in a personal God. Philipson mentions the conference without discussing the episode.[7] Heller provides a brief account of it and writes of "much abuse of Wise, who was entirely innocent in relation to this incident." Now there had been a protest on the part of the eastern rabbis that enlarged the matter beyond its real importance and centered its attack on Wise. What Heller did not follow up, or at least did not enlarge upon, was Wise's responses in the *American Israelite* and the *Deborah.* Rather than let the matter die, he proceeded to argue Mayer's case from Jewish sources, suggesting that "the idea of a personal God is not Jewish. God is only the substance and the essence of all that is, was, or will be. This cause and this all comprising love, justice, holiness can not be thought as personal."

What is at stake in discussing this episode is not the substance of the controversy but the typically off-handed way in which Wise launched himself into theological debates and—observing the details— the uncautious fashion in which he used material from traditional literature, even though he was often tripped up by his opponents.[8] Yet Israel Abrahams was constrained to write of him later on: "A careful study of his writings on religion will convince any unprejudiced reader that Wise was . . . a theologian of no mean order." More than that, Abrahams attends with care to Wise's *Pronaos to Holy Writ establishing, on documentary evidence, the authorship, date, form, and content of each of its books, and the Authenticity of the Pentateuch.* This is, he writes, "among the earliest of the reasoned replies to the *Higher Criticism.*" What particularly commended Wise to Abrahams was "the argument of *continuity.*" Summarizing the position he writes that Wise argued, "There is an uninterrupted tradition, the whole is a logical organism, every part in its right place, fulfilling its due function. . . . There are variations in the points of view of various inspired writers, but the whole tendency is one, there is consistency of purpose." [9]

Heller, in epitomizing this and several other smaller works as "the chief source for a study of Wise's theology," points to "a common strand running through all these. . . . Wise was quite consistent in his general attitudes toward the problems of authority, of the Bible as a revealed book, of the rabbinic law, and of other associated questions." The unwavering center of Wise's thought was that "Judaism is a revealed religion, and that the revelation was that on Mt. Sinai." [10] In his understanding of religion, "beyond reason lies revelation, and in Judaism this revelation is 'The Torah of Moses.' " Yet while the entire Torah is Mosaic, Wise seems on occasion to have limited revelation to the Ten Commandments. Moses had "enlarged upon them in accordance with the needs of his age and country; the prophets expounded and the sages applied them to meet emergencies. . . . The decalogue contains the unchangeable principles of law, but all other biblical laws are subject to modification by proper authority."[11] Heller sees this as central to Wise's entire philosophy of Reform, which "adhered to Judaism as a revealed religion, resting upon immutable theological and ethical doctrines, but permitting and even necessitating change and development." Abrahams comments that "the most orthodox book on the Pentateuch was written by the leader of American reform." He, however, does not refer to the certainly unorthodox relationship between this Mosaic Torah and revelation. Perhaps he did not recognize it.

Wise has had to be set at the beginning of this discussion, despite a doubt as to his place in it, because he brought the College into being and continued to dominate it until his death. Indeed, it remained his stronghold after the Central Conference of American Rabbis began to slip out of his control. If one takes Wise's thought seriously, it is difficult to deny that from 1885, the year of the Pittsburgh Platform, onward, Wise's real influence began to wane as his opponents took over.[12] One is hard put to harmonize the *Pronaos* of 1891 with principles one and two of the platform. Indeed, at the first meeting of the Central Conference in 1890, although Wise was thwarted in his hope that *Minhag America* would be accepted as the Conference's prayerbook, the attempt to have "the Declaration of Principles adopted by the Pittsburgh Conference . . . reasserted and inclosed in the Year Book"—although the majority report of the committee appointed to consider the matter—was defeated. In its place the Conference merely printed the resolutions, or précis of such resolutions, of West European conferences, beginning with the Napoleonic Sanhedrin.[13] One wonders if Wise's words at Pittsburgh, following the reading of the platform, were not tinged with irony: "Gentlemen, what are you going to do with this Declaration of Independence?" It is equally fascinating to read the discussion concerning Kohler's attempt to have the words "of Divine Revelation" inserted in the platform. The old foes were in agreement, although Wise did not speak to the point and Kohler lamely withdrew his suggestion because "all agree as regards the acceptance of the idea of revelation, and . . . only the use of the word is disliked in the platform . . ."[14] Again, was the *Pronaos* Wise's reply to the platform?

III. Max Leopold Margolis and *The Theological Aspect of Reformed Judaism*

In 1892, the year following the publication of the *Pronaos*, Wise appointed Max Margolis, who held the Ph.D. in Semitic languages from Columbia University (1891), as instructor and subsequently assistant professor of Semitic languages and biblical exegesis. Apparently his views on biblical criticism caused Wise no concern, nor did the fact that Margolis had been secretary to Felix Adler, the founder of the Ethical Culture movement. His acceptability to Wise is noteworthy, for when he left in 1897 to accept an academic appointment at the University of California, Berkeley, in 1897, Wise rejected the suggestion that Louis Ginzberg be appointed, on the ground that his attitude toward biblical criticism was unsatisfactory. Instead he appointed Moses Buttenwieser, who—according to an oral tradition—assured him that his attitude was constructive.

In October of 1902, the Executive Committee of the CCAR invited Margolis, who had maintained his membership in the body, to read a paper dealing with the subject noted in the heading of this section. It was read at the Detroit meeting of the Conference in 1903, printed in the *Yearbook* (vol. XIII), and published by the Conference as a separate monograph to "be circulated among the clergy and laity."[15] The paper, running from page 185 to page 308, was commented on by Sigmund Hecht in a statement of ten pages, and by M. Friedlander in one of twenty pages. At the following meeting of the Conference (1904), apparently in response to a series of motions offered by Margolis at the end of his paper, a standing committee "On Advisability of Formulating a Creed" was appointed, with Kaufmann Kohler, who had become president of the College in February 1903, as chairman. At the meeting of the Conference in 1905, Kohler presented the report of the committee, signed by him as chairman. Appended thereto were letters from Margolis, Max Heller, M. Friedlander, and B. Felsenthal, all members of the committee, commenting on Kohler's reply. Two other members of the committee, Joseph Silverman and Gotthard Deutsch, did not, apparently, comment. Margolis's paper and Kohler's response will be considered shortly. Here what needs to be noted is Kohler's conclusion: the call ought to be a formulation, not of the principles of Reform Judaism, but *"of Judaism."* [16] The upshot was that on the motion of David Philipson, it was voted that "a committee be appointed to place itself in correspondence with other bodies with the object of considering a creed."

What makes this historical background germane is the fact that the following autumn—that is, of 1905—Margolis rejoined the faculty of the College, undoubtedly at the behest of Kohler. However, he remained there for but two years, leaving in 1907 as the result of the controversy that saw H. Malter and Max Schloessinger also depart. The matters at issue were complex. Certainly the question of Zionism was involved, for Margolis, who in his paper had been an outspoken opponent of Political Zionism, had made an apparent *volte face* and considered himself then to be a Zionist. [17] But there is evidence that there were other factors at work, so any attempt to limit the situation to a single cause cannot be sustained. What is here called for is not a reexamination of this debate, but a consideration of Margolis's paper.

As a sort of motto for the essay, Margolis set two quotations at its head. One was from Maimonides' Commentary on Berakhot, "I had rather teach one of the fundamental doctrines of our religion than anything else in the world"; the other, from I. M. Wise, "Let the world know clearly and distinctly what is the substance of Judaism." The essay itself is divided into three sections, preceded by a very brief introduction and, in its separate edition, by a brief preface. The introduction surveys the several ways in which Reformed Judaism had previously been presented: its cultural aspect—that is, as "The Judaism of the Citizen"; the aesthetic aspect—that is, "remodeled on the ground of offensiveness to the aesthetic sense; the geographical aspect—that is, when it emerged; the national aspect—that is, as a "somewhat regrettable, but . . . necessary chapter in Jewish history which is to usher in the new synthesis." These, for Margolis, do not exhaust the possibilities: "But is not the Jewish reformation a religious movement? Has it not a theological aspect? . . . To emphasize this theological aspect and to place it in the forefront of our movement is the aim of the present paper." [18] In the preface he indicates that "the proportionately large space given to the biblical sources in the elaboration of the articles of the creed is probably due to my better knowledge of that branch of Jewish literature, but is at the same time justified by the importance which necessarily attaches to the beginnings of spiritual thought . . . . my paper has shown how our religious thought is rooted in the Bible and . . . remains largely Scriptural." [19]

Part I seeks briefly to justify, as against its frequent omission or rejection, the use of the term *theology* and to indicate its value for religion. Margolis examines the struggles within nineteenth-century Protestantism over not just the term but the whole concept, and, without any direct reference to contemporary Jewish thinkers, makes it evident that any attempt to exclude the speculative element is bound to fail. Religion cannot help but sooner or later express itself in theological terms. Neither "history of religion" nor "science of religion" is capable of taking the place of theology as the reflective stage through which religion "makes its own content clear to itself and so sure for itself." Nor is philosophy of religion a substitute for it. Margolis suggests that theology's task is that of "giving systematic thought to the thoughts imbedded in sacred documents, or underlying religious institutions, or rooted in the consciousness of a religious community." It is the theologian's task, "by dint of philosophical insight and of a particular tact which knows how to seize upon the constant and essential and living, [to seek] to sum up in a definite number of leading principles, called dogmas, which in their totality make up the creed of the church." [20]

Part II, the greater part of the paper, is, in Margolis's words, "[an] account of the history of Jewish dogmas in its general aspects." [21] He holds that "in Judaism . . . the life of dogma runs in three clearly distinct stages: that of origination, or creation, or, in theological language, revelation, that of formulation and that of re-formulation." He explains what he means by these several terms and then moves forward to examine the justification for his insistence that Judaism does indeed possess dogmas, beginning with the literature of the tenth through eighteenth centuries and proceeding backward through time to "Midrash, Talmud, Mishna, Targum, Prayer Book," to the "summaries of the beliefs held by Pharisees, Sadducees and Essenes found in the works of Josephus." This, he states, "links us to the theological and apologetic works of the Jews writing in Greek." He concludes by pointing to "the Jewish canon," which is "quite an important source." Although it offers no "systematic exposition of doctrine, the Bible . . . contains the theological data" whose collection and systematization is part of the task. More than that, "we shall find there certain fundamental beliefs, dogmas, if you please, which we may recognize by their frequent repetition, the emphasis which is placed upon them and the solemnity with which they are enunciated, and sometimes by their selection as a mark for the questioning of doubt." These dogmas, he argued, are found in Maimonides' Thirteen Articles, reorganized under five general headings borrowed from Christian systematic theology.[22]

However problematic this whole program may have turned out to be, it represented a constructive attempt to establish a mode of organizing and discussing the dogmas or principles of Judaism. If the organization is systematic, the content is itself, in general, historically arranged. Thus under each of the subheadings, Margolis provides a succinct discussion in which, as he himself indicated, the biblical material is central but by no means exclusive. At the end of this second section he examines Mendelssohn's claim that "Judaism is primarily a system of laws to be obeyed, not of articles of faith to be believed," and argues that this position indicates Mendelssohn's failure to comprehend historical development, while at the same time it is itself the reflection of Mendelssohn's own time and place. But he grants Mendelssohn the merit of having made it possible to distinguish between "the imperishable, eternal, religious part of Judaism [and] the perishable, national."[23] It had now, Margolis argued, become imperative to set down those "dogmas, principles, doctrines, precepts,"[24] for a very obvious reason: "—as Reformed Jews we are determined that we do not mean to be a community distinct and separate and holding aloof from our neighbors in any but religious matters . . ." [25] Judaism had become "a religious body in which the true intent of the founders of Judaism, realized in the past imperfectly and less adequately, expresses itself now (I am referring to the Church-idea) most perfectly and most adequately." This being so, Margolis proceeded to offer what he, on the basis of his previous analysis, understood to be the "CREED OF REFORMED JUDAISM." [26] In order to transform this creed into an effective reality or to construct another creed, Margolis called for the establishment of "a SYNOD as the key-stone of our CHURCH." [27]

This bare recital does not begin to capture the passion of the document, or its ecclesiasticism—"Whatever is inimical or even indifferent to the synagogue must be wiped out of existence. . . . we are not ready for an episcopate . . ."—or its breadth of learning. Yet it is not possible to examine these and other aspects of the paper. Rather must our attention center on the fact that its author had been a member of the faculty of the Hebrew Union College for five years, chosen by I. M. Wise, and that two years after he delivered the paper he once again rejoined the faculty, this time chosen—apparently —by Kohler. Yet Kohler in his response—and it is clear that the response is Kohler's alone—takes his newly appointed colleague to task on several scores. It is this response, more than anything else, that seems to represent the real impact of Margolis on the Hebrew Union College, for two years later he had resigned or been dismissed, and he seems never again to have ventured into the thorny ground of theology or even of "Reformed Judaism."

IV. Kaufmann Kohler and His *Jewish Theology Systematically and Historically Considered*

Before turning to Kohler's contribution, it is important to observe Margolis's response to a stricture of Friedlander and its disregard by Kohler. Friedlander had accused Margolis—in a not entirely accurate citation—of insisting upon "the finality of reform, and, with it the finality of Judaism." The citation is the one quoted above about the "true intent of the founders of Judaism" now being expressed most perfectly and most adequately. Margolis recognized that he had been misunderstood and so he added—in brackets—in the separately printed version, the words "I am referring to the Church-idea." [28] What he seems to be saying is that the ideas of Judaism are most perfectly and adequately expressed in the Jewish Church divested of "those politico-national" ideas that had been entangled with the religious. [29] Kohler's response was based—apparently—on the text in the *Yearbook,* not in the separate volume, so he returned to the theme: "your Committee observes in the paper a certain tendency to lend to Reform Judaism the character of finality." [30] As evidence he brings forward Margolis's use of the word *Reformed.* The latter, in his reply, simply pointed to the fact that the attributive use of *Reform*—a commonplace in German compound words—was a "Germanism with which we of the younger generation prefer not to burden our speech." [31] Far more important was Kohler's straightforward warning: "any attempt at formulating a Creed for one section of Judaism, with the exclusion of the rest, is a dangerous proceeding which should by all means be discouraged, as it tends to create a schism in antagonism to the spirit and tradition of Judaism." Thus he called for the appointment of a committee that would "report on the feasibility of a plan of presenting for the English-speaking world a systematic exposition of the Jewish tenets of faith from an historical as well as a dogmatic point of view." [32]

The fulfillment of that undertaking was Kohler's own *Jewish Theology.* [33] He had, he notes in the preface, been approached by Gustav Karpeles and asked to prepare "a compendium (*Grundriss*) of Systematic Jewish Theology." He had undertaken the same "only with the understanding that it should be written from the view-point of historical research, instead of a mere dogmatic or doctrinal system." This reflected, he continued, his understanding of Judaism as a "dynamic process of growth and development." This concept of "revelation as a continuous force in shaping and reshaping the Jewish faith" did not prevent him, he claimed, from being "just and fair to conservative Judaism, which will ever claim the reverence we owe to our cherished past, the mother that raised us and nurtured us." [34]

Within this paragraph there occurs a sentence that, when confronted by Margolis's paper and his own reply thereto, cannot but be a puzzle: "I had no work before me that might serve me as a pattern or guide." It is a puzzle, for allowing for the considerably enlarged content, the structure of Kohler's *Theology* reflects Margolis's paper. He had, as noted above, quite correctly pointed to the influence of Christian theology on that paper, particularly in the headings. Nevertheless, if one discards those headings and substitutes Kohler's own tripartite division: "God," "Man," "Israel and the Kingdom of God," the ordering of the contents under these is basically that of Margolis. It seems, given the evidence, that Margolis, although he soon removed himself totally from the scene of theological discussion, actually provided the framework and methodology that influenced the way in which systematic-historical theology was done at the Hebrew Union College for the next fifty years.

What is of greatest interest, however, is the way in which Kohler's reply to Margolis most clearly adumbrates his own basic theological attitude and position. In the article attacking Wise, referred to above, Kohler, who had been on the American scene but two years, made his initial claim. Condemning the blind party allegiances he found so prevalent on the scene, he wrote there of, "the firm-minded theologians [who] have but one parole which is: God and truth!" These were they who "in the aggregate represent amongst the Jews in America the German Theology." Yet over the years the theological position he claimed to represent did not find concrete and systematic expression in his writings. There are 801 items listed in Oko's bibliography [35] and another 166 in the supplement of Max T. Kohler.[36] Of these, a number are scholarly items of very high quality dealing with Kohler's academic speciality, Midrash, and, most particularly, apocryphal and pseudepigraphic literature. The greatest number, however, are addresses, sermons, and reviews appearing in the popular Jewish press. This is not to suggest that these were mere ephemera; Kohler's scholarship was too broad and deep for that and made itself felt everywhere. What is suggested is that among all of these there are few if any extended systematic statements of a theological position. The twenty closely printed pages of the report represent, therefore, a movement toward a formulation, albeit negatively as a critique of the Maimonidean Creed and that proposed by Margolis. It is Kohler's attitude toward Maimonides that is central to his thought.[37]

Picking up a comment of Margolis concerning the faulty exegesis of *da'at Elohim* as "philosophical speculation," Kohler continues, "Maimonides' whole conception of Judaism as a religion is inadequate, one-sided, and incorrect. His theology is bad. His God is divested of all those attributes which remain forever the postulates of faith. . . . we need a Divine Personality [38] to whom we feel akin and to whom we are drawn by bonds of affinity; we need an all-loving and all-providing

Father to trust in and to commune with in prayer. . . . Intellectualism is a failure. We must learn 'to know God' as the power of the soul; He must become a matter of inner experience." This is followed by a praise of a more mystical approach to religion, culminating in a somewhat perplexing definition: "Judaism is throughout all its steps of development preeminently ethical Theism." It is perplexing for the appearance of the term *ethical* is not prepared for. What is at stake here, as is immediately evident, is the meaning of *kadosh*,[39] the term used by Margolis in his exposition of the creed. Margolis understands the word to mean "transcendent," while Kohler—apparently taking his cue from Friedlander, who had referred to the Mekilta's rendering of the term as *parush*—argues that it denotes "ethical." This is crucial for Kohler, since as a modern man he found himself required to pay heed to biblical criticism with its evolutionary thesis, hence to the suggestion that monotheism is the result of a "slow growth." It is, therefore, not the adjectival prefix *mono-* that is central to the wide sweep of Jewish religious development, but the adjective *ethical*. The ethical nature of God is, for Kohler, crucial. ". . . as a moral power . . . He appears from the very beginning. The God of Abraham, of Moses, and of Isaiah is a moral personality. . . ." It was "the purely ethical character of Judaism's God [that] led"—he here is referring to Hermann Cohen's *Ethik des reinen Willens*—"to absolute monotheism."

Without pursuing the matter any further, it seems clear that Kohler found himself at this juncture challenged—although not directly—to formulate a statement that would do justice to what he understood a correct exposition of Judaism to be. Although at the end of his report he wrote: "Let the theology of Judaism be written not in an apologetic nor in a partisan subjective, but in an objective spirit in the light of modern research. Let it be written both in an historical and systematic form, not by one man—no single individual can undertake this heroic task—but by a body of men, each master in his special sphere, upon a plan large enough to do justice to each view, conservative as well as progressive . . . ,"[40] it was he alone who faced and responded to the challenge, bringing his enormous learning to bear.

It is, therefore, important, considering the role that Kohler played as president of the College and as systematic theologian, to understand the underlying philosophical position that informed his thought.

Samuel Cohon, his successor as professor of theology at the College, quoted Kohler, in the concluding chapter of his own theology lectures,[41] concerning the influence of German philosophy on the thought of Reform Judaism: "The men unfamiliar with German philosophy and philology and uninfluenced by a Lessing, by Mendelssohn and Schiller, by Kant and Hegel, can to this very day have no real understanding of the development of the leading principles of Reform Judaism. They lack the deeper insight into the historic forces that ever create new currents of thought and cause the changes affecting religious views, in common with the general world-view."

Thus, to ask about the formative factors in Kohler's thought is to follow his own lead. One clue is the adjective *ethical;* another is the phrase "inner experience." When these are joined to his references, in the 1871 paper,[42] to "Kant's logic, Herbart's psychology and Schleiermacher's *Glauben,*" and his citation of Cohen's *Ethik des reinen Willens* in the report, the essential structure of Kohler's thought becomes evident. He was deeply influenced by the line of European thinkers in the post-Kantian period who sought to join Kant's claim to have established religion on the foundation of the moral conscience to the romantic view, particularly of Schleiermacher, that saw religion rooted in emotion or feeling. Thus he wrote: "God-consciousness, or 'knowledge of God,' signifies an inner experience which impels man to practice the right and to shun evil, the recognition of God as the moral power of life."[43] If this provided the general philosophical framework of Kohler's thought, determining what he understood religion to be, his understanding of Judaism in its particularity was deeply influenced by the *Völkerpsychologie* of Moritz Lazarus and H. Steinthal: "The religious genius of the Jew falls within the domain of ethnic psychology concerning which science still gropes in the dark, but which progressive Judaism is bound to recognize in its effect throughout the ages." In his chapter "What Is Judaism?" he found no difficulty in asserting that "religion and race form an inseparable whole in Judaism. The Jewish people stand in the same relation to Judaism as the *body* to the *soul.*" Further, it is this people who among all the nations have "perceived God as the moral power of life."[44] It is interesting to note how pervasive this attitude was and how deeply it influenced Reform. Samuel Schulman, reviewing the earlier German edition of the work, agreed wholeheartedly with Kohler's insistence upon the indissoluble union of the people and the faith, "which is the expression of the genius of the people." [45] Indeed, tireless as Kohler and most of his colleagues were in denouncing Zionism, they had no hesitancy in writing about the genius of the Jewish race.[46] Yet this is but a detail. What is disclosed is, once again, the real intellectual sources of Kohler's thought.

Albert Lewkowitz, in his work *Das Judentum und die geistigen Strömmungen des 19. Jahrhunderts*,[47] attempted to trace the various strands of European, most particularly German, thought upon the Jewish community of Western Europe emerging from its medieval exclusion and exclusiveness. In a volume of 570 pages, 284 are devoted to a discussion of the relationship between the world-views of pantheism and Judaism. In it he examines the variety of ways in which thinkers of the nineteenth century sought to repair the breach Kant had introduced between scientific and ethical religious knowledge. It was romantic philosophy in its several forms that offered Jewish thinkers the possibility of constructing an understanding and view of Judaism and of the Jewish people that would respond to the new situation in which faith and people found themselves. The influence of the romantic understanding is everywhere apparent in Kohler's thought and explains the apparent contradiction between his unwavering insistence upon the inseparable unity of religion and nationality and his equally unwavering rejection of Zionism. For him the latter was simply an inadequate expression of nationality that could only be harmful to its true expression as a religious community, but certainly not, as Margolis would have it, a church. Most particularly, however, as noted above, is the influence of Moritz Lazarus to be seen. Kohler's understanding of *kadosh* as an ethical term, indeed his exposition of holiness, is derived, as his citation indicated, from Lazarus.[48]

Much as one is awed by Kohler's encompassing grasp of the material, one is left at the end with a sense of dissappointment. Basically Kohler was an erudite collector and organizer of material, but he was not a systematic thinker. His contribution is primarily a homiletic intensity that for the moment made it seem as though the garnered references held together in a constructive whole. But, in fact, they often lie side by side, their relationship imputed and indeed believed, but not made clear, not brought into focus. The title *Jewish Theology* claims too much. Kohler's own translation of the first word of the

German title, *Grundriss,* as "compendium" promised less and thus delivered more.

V. David Neumark and the Tasks of Jewish Philosophy

When David Neumark came to the Hebrew Union College late in 1907 as professor of Jewish philosophy, he had not only determined in his mind what he understood his tasks to be, but had long since begun to transform his vision into reality. The first footnote on page 1 of volume one of his *opus magnum, Geschichte der jüdischen Philosophie des Mittelalters,* whose preface is dated October 13, 1907, lists a whole series of preliminary studies that were preparatory for the work at hand.[49] His inaugural address, January 29, 1908, "The Philosophy of Judaism and How It Should Be Taught," refers, in its first sentence, to the formulation, in the work noted, of his understanding of "the functions of Jewish philosophy as a branch of systematic knowledge." He saw his task as the continuation of that endeavor: "to foster and keep alive the realization that the true principles of Judaism are not antiquated, but that they are in full accord with the most positive findings of modern science and philosophy." The "new element of my task consists," he continued, "of constant clarification and enlargement of the doctrines of Judaism in the sense of our modern conception of the world." He had introduced, he claimed, "new methods and points of view" into the discussion, and was now ready, briefly to indicate how he expected to "develop his program." [50]

For Neumark, behind and beneath Judaism as "a practical *system of life,"* there lay a definite conception of the world, "a definite philosophic system of thought." "Judaism is *the* religion because its theoretical fundaments . . . actually represent philosophic doctrines that are as far removed from all mythology and superstition as from any unhealthy degeneration into agnosticism." These philosophic doctrines were first embodied and expressed—not, as was generally and usually stated, in the medieval period—but by the prophets. Yet it was not until the later and the latest periods that "conscious, logical intellectual effort" gave and continued to give those ideas "a universally comprehensible form." It was the union of the Jewish and Greek spirits in Jewish philosophy "that led to the clarification and expansion of the prophetic doctrines." But again, this coming together was early rather than late. For Neumark the Hellenistic period was on one side only a struggle between "the Hellenists and their opponents, the Hassideans." Actually, he argued, "the Hassideans were full of appreciation of Greek philosophy and . . . their writings are full of philosophic thoughts and motifs taken from or formulated under the influence of Platonic philosophy." Indeed, not only were their noncanonical writings shot through with Platonic ideas, but Scriptural books too, Koheleth, and elements in Psalms, Proverbs, Chronicles, Daniel all "mirror" the influence of Plato.[51]

Given this development: the promulgation of the fundamental philosophic ideas of Judaism by the prophets and a "fermentation . . . caused by the first contact with Greek philosophy," called by Neumark a "psychological" union, and whose effect was "purifying"—the first task of Jewish philosophy is "the presentation of the history of Jewish dogma from the philosophic point of view."[52] This had been undertaken by Neumark first in an article in *Ozar ha-Yahdut* bearing the title "Ikkarim" and subsequently in a book already in manuscript at the time of the publication of the *Geschichte*.[53] The second task was an examination of what he designated "the second union of Jewish prophecy with Greek philosophy . . . the logical union." This had already resulted in the *Geschichte* and was to be followed by the third task: *"the exposition of the philosophic system that supports the theoretical doctrine of Judaism."* This exposition in the inaugural lecture was based, as Neumark indicated, upon a more elaborate statement in the introduction to the *Geschichte*. There he laid down the position from which he never swerved throughout his entire career: philosophical thought was coeval with Judaism itself and its task was liberation from myth. The Bible itself was a philosophic work whose theoretical principles in their development could be traced. For him, the prophets of Israel were speculative philosophers whose abstract ideas are visible in their writings to the trained mind.[54]

Lewkowitz, reviewing the first volume of the *Geschichte*, commented: "Neumark begins his History of Jewish Religious Philosophy of the Middle Ages—with the Bible. This is not loquacity, but is the consequence of his basic conviction. Jewish spiritual life of all centuries is for him an absolute continuous unity, so that no single occurrence is to be understood in itself but only from the vantage of the whole." [55] It was this conviction that led Neumark to divide the whole of Jewish thought into two schools that emerged and reemerged again and again: that of Jeremiah and that of Ezekiel. The entire development of Judaism from the period of the Deuteronomic reform is periodicized and systematized by the interaction of the basic ideas found in each. "Jeremiah and Ezekiel, the two great opponents in world-conception, historical view and outlook into the future, became the two great central figures on which the following ages oriented themselves." [56] Not only rational but mystical philosophy as well is caught up in this net. In the first, the two views are represented by the Saadia group combining the Jeremianic position with that based upon the *Physics* of Aristotle, "which is free of all mysticism," [57] and the Gabirol group, which combines the Ezekielian position with that rooted in Aristotle's *Metaphysics,* "which is much nearer to Platonic mysticism." [58] The position of Maimonides in this development is that of uniting "the authoritatively acceptable elements of both groups." At the same time, "Philosophy and Qabbalah represent, respectively, the schools of Jeremiah and Ezekiel of biblical times." Indeed, "[*Ma'aseh*] *Merkabah* and [*Ma'aseh*] *Bereshit* go back to the schools of Ezekiel and Jeremiah, respectively." [59]

Neumark used these distinctions through all of his writings. They provided the structure of his *Toledot ha-Ikkarim,* of his *Geschichte,* of his *Philosophy of the Bible* and his monographs in Hebrew, German, and English. The two critics who discussed the first volume of the *Geschichte* soon after its appearance, Lewkowitz[60] and Vexler,[61] found this totally untenable, requiring him—as he does—to force the entire development of both rational philosophy and mysticism into a straitjacket.[62] Yet it was not to their trenchant critique of his entire position that he replied but to the challenge to one technical but crucial point in his exposition of the development of medieval philosophy. He saw, as noted above, the two indigenous schools of Jewish thought, the Jeremianic and Ezekielian, supporting themselves by reference to Greek philosophy, or more specifically to Aristotle. Both schools, he insisted, were Aristotelian, so that the distinction between them had to be sought in Aristotle himself. Thus, crucial to his entire interpretation of medieval Jewish philosophy was his claim that there was an unbridgeable gap between Aristotle's understanding of the relationship between matter and form in the *Physics* and in the *Metaphysics*. Both Lewkowitz and Vexler rejected this distinction, but Neumark does not seem to have replied to them. Rather, he trained his heaviest guns upon Isaac Husik and involved himself in a discussion that—whatever the merits of his position—was not worthy of an eminent scholar.

General attention to this sad and too long continued episode has revolved around Neumark's review of Husik's *A History of Medieval Jewish Philosophy* and Adolph Oko's pamphlet attacking the review.[63] However, the real encounter occurred earlier, when Husik published a critique of Neumark's discussion of matter and form in Aristotle.[64] Neumark's reply, both in *Archiv für Philosophie*[65] and in the supplement to volume one of the *Geschichte,* makes his review pale in comparison.[66] Without enlarging the discussion, one must confess sadly that Neumark's language was—whatever he understood to be the provocation—inexcusably rude.[67]

What is most disconcerting in viewing Neumark's writings is the fact that what could and should have been his very real and constructive contribution to the development of Jewish philosophy in his own time—the third task of his system—was never carried out, although it is present in the introduction to the *Geschichte* and in a truncated and half-hearted but nonetheless stimulating way in a paper read before the CCAR.[68] It is quite evident that an important influence on Neumark's thought was the writings of the distinguished philosopher Hermann Cohen. Vexler noted this in his critique, and Neumark himself discussed it in what is the most interesting portion of the *Geschichte*. In the third chapter of the introduction, entitled "Orientierung und Disposition," he sought to relate prophetic Judaism to transcendental (i.e., Kantian or neo-Kantian) philosophy. This, of course, is what Cohen had done in his *Ethik des reinen Willens* and *Der Begriff der Religion im System der Philosophie*. The prophets had intuitively and imaginatively envisioned the future, the one humanity that is the infinite goal of ethics. Thus prophetic religion provided ethics with its challenge; offered the ideal toward which ethics could point as the direction of the process but could itself not articulate. Religion, for Cohen, says what the concept of mankind—ethics' goal—is.

Neumark took hold of Cohen's ideas and, radically transforming them, used them as the hidden blueprint for his formulation of what he insisted was the history of Jewish philosophy—coextensive with Judaism itself.[69] There is little doubt that Neumark's insistence that the central task of Judaism is *die Befreiung vom Mythos* ("liberation from the myth") was taken over from Cohen. The crucial difference between Neumark and his intellectual mentor was the absolute way in which he used Cohen's thought to provide a unified structure for the entire theological development of Judaism. But even more than that, he argued that the critical philosophy of Kant was beholden to this historical development, so that—unlike Cohen—the prophets were not intuitive projectors of the ideal toward which ethics strove, they were themselves the creators of the very speculative ideas that were ultimately expressed in the transcendental philosophy of Kant and his followers.

That other thinkers influenced Neumark seems evident from three papers published between 1915 and 1924, but these influences cannot, given the nature of Neumark's writings, be documented. These papers suggest to me that Neumark may have been influenced by William James, but it may well be that it was Fechner—whose writing influenced James—who was the source of Neumark's position "that the individual human spirit is a manifestation of the world-spirit, of God . . ."[70]

Under any circumstances, however, it is sad to recognize that Neumark's obtuse approach to Jewish philosophy—there seems to have been a sort of desire for *hidushim*[71]—prevented him from being the link between the philosophic tradition that found its most notable expression in Hermann Cohen and American Jewish intellectual life. Cohen's thought, which gave rise in German Jewry—both as positive and negative response—to such commanding figures as Leo Baeck, Martin Buber, and Franz Rosenzweig, never touched the intellectual center of American Jewish life. The Hebrew Union College, which could well have found in Cohen's superb system a dynamic stimulation for the emergence and development of a notable Jewish philosophy, seems to have been little influenced in that direction either by Neumark or by another pupil of Cohen—Henry Slonimsky, who had a brief tenure in its chair of philosophy.[72] There were, of course, other reasons why transcendental philosophy found no foothold at the College, but that failure had, in my opinion, fateful consequences for the intellectual development of the American Jewish community.

VI. Samuel S. Cohon: Holiness as Feeling

The problem in dealing with one's teachers in the immediate or personal sense of the word is not only that of objectivity but of subjectivity. It is possible and even probable that, haunted by the fear of unreflective filio-piety, one endeavors to "let the facts speak for themselves": or, recognizing one's "infidelity," one writes a disguised *apologia pro sua fide* that fails in its acknowledgement of influence, obligation, and gratitude. On the occasion of his retirement from the Hebrew Union College as professor of Jewish theology, I wrote to Samuel Cohon confessing the latter and the former. Perhaps the recollection of that confession will make possible on this occasion a subjective objectivity that is inversely an objective subjectivity, for both are required and both are present, hopefully, in all that has been written to this point.

An appraisal of Samuel Cohon from this stance requires us at once to acknowledge that unfortunately, yes even sadly, his intention never found the means of adequate expression. This is not meant as a literary judgment; his writings are, as exposition, straightforward and clear, unpretentious and uncluttered. No, the matter is quite other. He chose, or perhaps was forced by his intellectual environment, to view himself most generally as expositor, occasionally as apologist or critic, all too rarely as unabashed, and almost never as passionate advocate. His vast erudition was a bulwark behind which he took up a defensive position; it was never a weapon to press the battle or, eschewing that metaphor, never a cutting tool to open the pathway he so evidently saw and wanted others to see and follow.

It is certainly no mere coincidence that the center of Cohon's thought is the term that played such an important role in Margolis's creed and Kohler's theology, *kadosh*. Indeed, in a very particular way, he provided—although on the evidence not intentionally—a synthesis of the two interpretations: transcendent, ethical.

In his *Theology Lectures: Theology and Religion*,[73] Cohon undertook in chapter six, "Religion in the Modern World," a survey of what had happened in European thought from the Protestant Reformation onward. It represents his expository mode, moving rapidly through the reformers to "Religious Views of the Enlightenment" and beyond. When one examines the way in which the material is marshaled and observes the varying emphases, certain basic but all too frequently obscured directions of Cohon's own position become clear. The section in chapter six entitled "Romanticism," dealing with Schleiermacher and, to a lesser degree, with Schelling, concludes with a paragraph that notes "the validity of intuition as a ground of faith." The following section contains both an appreciation and critique of Hegel and most particularly of the left-wing Hegelians. This is followed by an extended critique of Comte's "Positive Religion" and then an examination of Ritschl and his conception of religion as the realm of independent value judgments. In the latter's approach to theology Cohon seems to have found, in large measure, his own theological method: "The object of theology . . . is not speculation but the ordered exhibition of the faith of the community as a whole and in particular, its view of the world and of human life, and the inter-relations of its component elements." [74] This had been the goal of his *What We Jews Believe*[75] and was, as noted above, the ongoing method in his *Theology Lectures*.

What has been too little noticed is Cohon's use of the scientific, that is, the anthropological, study of religion and the theories of the origin and essence of religion that were developed in the various schools. It is evident that he was deeply influenced by Marett, whose discussion of *mana* provided him with a means of grounding Schleiermacher's "feeling" in a widespread, observable phenomenon. The concluding sentence of section 32 of chapter six puts this into focus: "The attitude toward mana reveals *the two indispensable aspects or polarity of religion: the consciousness of inner personal power or spirit, and of power outside oneself, with which one can stand in close relation.*"[76] It is "sacredness" as interpreted by Marett that pointed the way, outside the field of anthropology, to the root notion of Cohon's position. He found Marett's scientific interpretation confirming Rudolph Otto's "idea of the Holy," and it is this latter that is the foundation of his own structure.[77] The last nine pages of his exposition are devoted to Otto's position and are followed by a chapter bearing the heading "Retrospect," which examines the way the exposition has moved and suggests the inadequacy—although the importance—of conceiving religion as deriving from man's social situation, his search for the true, his quest for the good or the beautiful.

It is only when attention is paid to emotion that the origin of religion is disclosed: "Religion, though intricately connected with the true, the good and the beautiful, is *sui generis* and must be regarded as growing out of a different psychological root." [78] That root is, following Otto, "the consciousness of the holy or the sacred." Thus for Cohon, "religion is essentially man's consciousness of the sacred or his response to the Divine as apprehended outside of himself and within his own mind, heart, and conscience." The task of religion thus apprehended is "to witness to the Divine unto the individual and unto society." [79] And again: "To the three dimensions of man's higher life: the true, the good, and the beautiful—corresponding to science, ethics, and aesthetics—religion adds a fourth: the *holy*.[80] For Cohon this sense of the holy—the numinous of Otto—"developed into the idea of the *Holy One*," as man anthropomorphizes and personalizes the "sense of awe and of dependence upon the powers outside of himself . . ." Man then seeks to bridge "the gulf between himself and the object of his worship," "to establish intimate and harmonious relations between himself and his God." [81] Out of the bond of union "the characteristic feature of religion" emerges: "*sanctification,* the sense of the holy affects all life." [82] For religion, the holy is an end in itself. "The holy is not the expedient but the ultimate in the scale of values," and it is believed to endure, resisting the ravages of time. The "unique object of religious experience, *i.e.,* God," as it is "brought out of vague obscurity into the realm of conscious reason . . . becomes the *central force* in human feeling, thought and conduct." [83] "The emotional responses embody themselves in art and in ritual, in prayer and in song, in festive occasions and in drama. The operation of reflection produces mythologies, cosmogonies, philosophies and theologies. The personal and social behavior occasioned by the consciousness of the Holy One incorporate themselves in the mores of a certain type, in tabus, restrictions, laws, ethical codes and ideals." Thus it is for Cohon that "religion constitutes the *unification of the diverse activities and aspirations of man in the single aim of the sanctification of life.*" [84]

In his posthumous volume, *Jewish Theology: A Historical and Systematic Interpretation of Judaism and Its Foundations,*[85] Cohon returned to this theme: "In a sense all religion is revelation and inspiration. The root of this spiritual phenomenon is the awareness of the holy and the transcendent. Man has ever found himself confronted by the unknown and overwhelmed by the mysterious. Overawed and humbled by the uncanny power that surrounds him and baffled and at the same time fascinated by the strange and invisible

forces that are manifested in all things, man grows aware of a power
distinct from all physical force with which his own life and destiny
are bound up. He feels himself 'absolutely dependent' upon 'numinous
presence' and stands before it as a creature before his Creator." [86] It is
interesting to note that despite the quotation marks in the last
sentence there are no citations. Schleiermacher and Otto are completely absorbed in Cohon's thought. For Cohon, here is the source
of Judaism: "The consciousness of the holy discloses new levels of
value to man." It is this awareness "in minds gifted with prophetic
power that produces an inner illumination . . ." Yet Cohon argued
that what must be stressed is "the human element," the "receptivity
to the divine message." [87]

Earlier in this chapter, Cohon began his interpretation of "the
Ways to God in Judaism" by reference to Halevi's emphasis on the
historical experience of the Jewish people as the basis of the faith of
Israel. This he joined to his own fundamental position—as yet not
laid out: "Judaism is not a theistic philosophy, derived by speculative reflection, but the millennial response of the Jewish people to
the holy." [88] From this stance it was possible for Cohon to accept
apocalypticism as a continuation of prophecy, although his comments
are primarily expository. He clearly did not want to reject this aspect
of the Jewish past, but beyond exposition he was unable to fit it into
his scheme. Again, in dealing with mysticism, his attraction to the subject is evident: "Mysticism appears where religion transcends the
conventional, traditional and dogmatic forms, as a state of personal
experience, of direct and intuitive awareness of the Divine, a consciousness acquired not through the perceptive processes of sensation and
ideation but through immediate feeling and identification." This is
quite clearly what he meant by the experience of the holy, yet he
backed away. The mystic is not interested in history; the mystic
loses sight of moral obligation; the mystic "tends to dissociate himself
from the community."[89] Since "mysticism tends to exaggerate truth
to the point of distortion, and conduces to credulity," what is required
is "the application of the critical function of reason." [90] Thus, having
rejected the notion that Judaism is "theistic philosophy, derived by
speculative reflection," he found it necessary to discover a new role
for reason, but in doing so he tended to contradict himself: "the
sage also employs his own reason as an independent source of knowledge relying upon observable phenomena and upon the accredited

canons of knowledge." Indeed, it is difficult to follow the chain of thought at this point, but one senses Cohon's struggle. Writing in a situation where emphasis had presumably been placed on the primacy of reason and confronted by claims of "scientific thinking," he was constrained and rightly so to attend to the rationalistic side of the tradition. But at most, although this is not entirely clear—his rhetoric failed him at this point—he wanted reason to be "a function of religion." Yet after traversing the highways and byways of rationalistic philosophy he concluded: "The rationalist and the mystic, for all their divergences, are alike in that they derive their conclusions not at second hand, but directly, one through reflective reason, the other through his intuition." [91] What he never did was relate his understanding of reason to the source of religion as he understood it, the Holy.[91]

Although section three of *Jewish Theology* begins: "the three pillars of Judaism which we have examined, vis., Israel, Torah and God, find their completion in the doctrine of man and his destiny," [92] the first and second subjects are not treated in the volume nor are there any *Theology Lectures* devoted to them. The system both as exposition and interpretation is incomplete.[93] But it is, as has been suggested, incomplete in a deeper sense. It seems evident that either Cohon was not able to make his theoretical understanding of religion work when he applied it to an understanding of Judaism or, for whatever reason, he failed or eschewed applying it to Judaism. Indeed, it was this failure or refusal that left a void into which the thought of his self-chosen *bête noir*, Mordecai Kaplan, flowed. He had in the grasp of his thought the means of restructuring a modern understanding of Judaism in the face of the dissolution of the mid-nineteenth-century eclectic idealism propounded by Kohler. His *Theology Lectures: Theology and Religion* move with critical insight in that direction, but one waits in vain beyond that point. His understanding of the Holy One in philosophical terms as transcendent, in ethical terms as the power making for righteousness, and in religious terms as the numinous, never came together in a compelling and commanding unity. The word awaited seemed always behind his lips, never on them.[94]

If this is a negative note on which to close, it is—as indicated at the beginning—sadly so. What makes the sadness even more profound is the knowledge that this learned and sensitive man was embittered by the lack of response he felt his devoted efforts had elicited. We were—his pupils and he—unable to meet.

VII. Zevi Diesendruck: Philosophical Fragments

There is a particular difficulty in writing about Zevi Diesendruck because in a peculiar way only a part of the man was engaged in the Hebrew Union College, and of the unengaged part most of his students knew little or nothing.

In the notice of his death printed in the *Proceedings of the American Academy for Jewish Research,* of which he was vice-president at the time of his untimely death, the authors wrote of him as "a distinguished figure in modern Hebrew literature." [95] His closest pupil, Joshua L. Liebman, in his memorial address at the meeting of the Central Conference of American Rabbis, just two weeks after his death, wrote, "his Hebrew style was remarkable, considered by some to be the equal of the prose of Achad Ha-Am and of Agnon." [96] A. J. Heschel, in his tribute in the *American Jewish Year Book,* described him as "an eminent figure in modern Hebrew literature." [97] Indeed, the tributes paid to him in Hebrew periodicals were those of literary persons. [98] His Hebrew essays, combining, in Heschel's words, "a command of the vast stores of the language and an exceptional imagination in coining new expressions . . . with a sharp, analytical insight into psychological and esthetic phenomena," [99] were quite beyond our ken.

This talent had come to focus in what his memorialists noted as his "second contribution," his Hebrew translation of Plato (*Phaidros, Crito, Gorgias,* and the *Republic*). "Here again," they wrote, "painstaking quest of adequate expression went hand in hand with searching analysis of philosophic thought." [100] Heschel noted that "Diesendruck was one of the first Plato translators in the history of Hebrew literature," and "in these translations, he displayed his mastery of the Hebrew language, combining accuracy with inventiveness in finding proper Hebrew equivalents for the disparate Greek phrases, and pouring the softness of the Greek into the solemn Hebrew words." [101] Liebman wrote: "His translation of Plato's 'Dialogues' from the Greek into the Hebrew will live as long as the Hebrew language itself survives." [102] All commented on the introductions and notes, suggesting that they in themselves were "invaluable contributions to the appreciation of Greek thought." [103]

Again, what did most of his students know of this side of Diesendruck's work? I can recall faintly a single, typical student put-down, referring to a negative judgment of these translations.

His third field of endeavor was Jewish philosophy and most particularly the philosophy of Maimonides. This was the center of his work during the decade he taught at the College, although he was already engaged in it before he arrived in Cincinnati. Two of his essays had appeared in the late twenties and brought him into conflict with I. Heinemann, whose review of *Maimonides' Lehre von der Prophetie*[104] and *Die Teleologie bei Maimonides*[105] ended with a disdainful: "In the meantime Diesendruck has been chosen as Neumark's successor. It is to be hoped that he inherits only his virtues." [106] Unfortunately there are hardly two handfuls of essays dealing with Jewish philosophy. His *magnum opus,* a comprehensive study on "The Concept of God in the Philosophy of Maimonides," said by Heschel to be nearing completion at his death, has never appeared, although Baron and Spiegel too referred to it as "nearing completion," and wrote that "undoubtedly it will open new vistas on the position of the leading Jewish medieval philosopher in the history of human thought." [107]

There is one brief paper that may be said to summarize Diesendruck's approach to and understanding of Maimonides, for it carries the note, "this address is based mainly on the results I arrived at in my detailed studies on Maimonides, some of which have already been published in various places . . ." What is most evident from this paper is that his interest in Maimonides was not antiquarian. "Celebrating the past can be of meaning and value only if it leads to the arousing of the present," he wrote, and because philosophy is primarily interested in interpretation, in method and approach . . . it can . . . extract the method from the so-called contents; it can save the *form* and leave the *matter.* This is the specific device of philosophy by which it makes past ideas productive in the present." He was convinced that "a certain return to Maimonides seems to be necessary; . . . a revaluation of his teaching for our present needs." In this essay Diesendruck undertook what he called *"historical translation."* This was not to be understood as modernization, viz., "identifying older terms or sets of terms with modern ones." Rather was this understood to be the "discovery of guiding principles, of a methodological attitude *within* the old terms or *among* them . . ."

To accomplish this, he undertook first a critical examination of the several approaches to Maimonides then—and still—current: that he was an "exponent of extreme intellectualism . . . a compromiser between Aristotle and Judaism; his concept of Judaism is usually regarded as abstract and pale and lacking the desirable vitality." In response to such characterizations he wrote: "A closer examination will show that the 'intellect' has a much deeper and much more inclusive cosmic meaning than that which we commonly call human rationality; it will show that Aristotle was merely a point of departure which had to be overcome. . . . The seemingly abstract Judaism was primarily intended for a deeper reformulation of the Jewish essence." His demonstration of this reappraisal moves with deliberate pace. He pointed first to the all-inclusiveness of Maimonides' concept of Judaism, disclosed in his Code, which focused upon the "entire historical life of the people," not merely its present mode, using "the Bible as a direct source—even if the subject was not treated in the Talmud—and including the latest customs in various lands. Jewish life and law were looked upon as a unified historical phenomenon developing its various expressions from the earliest beginnings up to the latest generation." The second "innovation" was "the inclusion of philosophy as a *part* of Judaism. . . . To present philosophical cosmology and general ethics as *Halacha* . . . was a revolutionary step toward the widening of the concept of Judaism to comprise all that which is universally human. . . . " It was this point that seems crucial for Diesendruck, for at the end of the paper he returned to it in summarizing what we may learn from Maimonides: ". . . we Jews may learn to fill the framework of our traditional teaching with wider wisdom of the world, to devise productive *methods* for the *motifs* of Judaism, and so to give our earthly racial existence a higher meaning."

Diesendruck understood Maimonides as a constructive philosopher confronted by three elements: "Judaism, Aristotle, in his later Neoplatonic interpretation, and the Islamic speculation, 'the so-called Kalam.' " They are not, wrote Diesendruck, "combined in an eclectic manner but are used as starts and stimulants for a new way of looking at the problems, a way which leads to different results than those contained in the original components."

Diesendruck saw Maimonides opposing Aristotle in order to save that which is "above Nature, the transcendent." He understood him to oppose Islamic speculation to save "the natural order." He viewed him as enlarging traditional Judaism and filling its frame with new contents. The central part of the paper is devoted to an examination of the three main realms of Maimonides' thinking, the realms of God, of the World, and of man, from this perspective. He concludes by pointing to "a certain duality of aspects" disclosed in the examination of these realms. "In God the aspect of the moral attributes, near to man's cognition, demanding imitation; and behind them the unknowable, first principle of lawfulness and intent. In the world—the multitude of concrete perceptible objects, subordinated one to another; and behind them the idea of an organic unity with the universal purposiveness. In man, his concrete, material existence—a thing among things—and in it the possibility to rise to immortal significance and to safeguard the unity of the world."

The conclusion of the paper suggests what we may learn from the examination of Maimonides' thought, but unfortunately its rhetoric falters. What he seems to be saying is that the dualism we observe in each of the three realms makes us aware of and leads us "to the supremacy of the one idea as the foundation for the many phenomena of reality." Further, he seems to suggest that as Maimonides' "classical philosophical endeavor" arose from "the low plane of a shallow enlightenment," so too "we may learn to follow" it out of the "agonies of the decline of a stretch of shallow enlightenment in human history." Again, he points to "the crisis in the sciences of nature and the perplexing consequences coming from it" and suggests that "we may learn to preserve nature and its lawfulness—without abandoning that which is beyond and above the visible nature." Finally, he indicates—as cited above—the way in which Maimonides may teach us "to fill the framework of our traditional teaching with wider wisdom of the world...." [108]

But to do this required a clear and careful understanding of what Maimonides had done, and it was to that difficult and demanding task that Diesendruck had so conscientiously devoted himself in the technical essays he so diligently produced. Without recognizing this, we can see him only as a technical scholar lost in a bygone age and that is—sadly—how he was seen.

It is important, however, not to do him less than full justice as a "technical" scholar. To do this I am obliged to recall his role as a teacher in two of the three courses I was enrolled in. Of the course in medieval philosophical texts little should be said. He did not have the temperament to endure the boredom—for him and thus for us —of attempting to teach unprepared students how to read texts whose content and structure was quite beyond them. But as it has turned out, his course entitled "Philosophy of Religion," which was devoted to a minute exposition of the thought of Hermann Cohen, has been pivotal in my own understanding of modern and contemporary Jewish thought. The notes taken have been read and reread for more than twenty years and have provided me with the key to open the door into a realm I knew nothing of as I laboriously, perhaps even mechanically, set down his definitive words. The same must be said of the last course he taught during the academic year 1939–40, "Medieval Philosophy." Even then, we in his last class recognized that something important had happened; he had, with care, consideration, and enormous penetration, laid before us the whole problem of medieval philosophical thought so that we were being prepared to make up for the failure of our text studies. We began to catch a glimpse of what those impenetrable texts could have disclosed.

Diesendruck's own ideas as a constructive thinker are found in the volume *Min ha-safah velifnim*[109] and in two essays in English.[110] Heschel has summarized the central thought of the Hebrew volume in the following paragraph: "The central motive which actuated Diesendruck's own thinking was the problem of human expression. In the process of expression, emotion, the inner shock, is to him primary. Language as an external addition effaces what is elementary and primeval. While gesture originates in inwardness, language, in its conventional use, is borrowed from the environment. It does not reveal the inner concern and is rather a failure, a deviation from inwardness, from the subjective, and abandonment of naturalness to the concrete, to the purpose. Surrendered to and humbled before the object, language tries to adjust itself to the object, abandoning the inner elements of the soul, the subjective values of experience. Diesendruck's approach is related to the expressionist movement in general literature, which was a rebellion against the objectivization of life, an attempt to save the personality in a civilization which levels and destroys the unique, a plea for the survival of the individual who refuses to be lost in an ocean of uniformity." [111]

The two English essays disclose other aspects of Diesendruck's thought. One, a posthumous essay, "Antisemitism and Ourselves," [112]

argues the ultimately irrational nature of antisemitism, and while
calling for a modification of the ways in which it is to be dealt with,
focuses far more on the irrational response on the part of the Jews
to this irrationality. That irrational response expresses itself on the
one side in the interpretation of "our fate as our guilt" and on the
other into a hypostatization of "our history of suffering into a destined
role imposed upon us, as the servant of the Lord, for the sanctification
of His Name." Recognition of the irrationality of antisemitism will,
he suggested, free the Jew of his irrational response. Yet he concludes
the essay with a rueful Latin tag: *Utinam interpres falsus sim!*

The other, more extensive and detailed, appeared in the *CCAR
Yearbook.*[113] It is entitled "The Ideal Social Order in Judaism." This
paper is concerned to discover within the Jewish past the operative
ideas that can provide "some conception of an *ideal social order*" that
did and can animate "the sheer mechanics of state, law and society."
Diesendruck meant by "ideal social order" a "postulate of what, according to some conception of justice, ought to be" when one views
the actualities of the "several institutions regulating the gradations and
inequalities of human wealth and privilege . . ." Thus one is required to look at "1) the facts as they are, 2) a unifying concept, 3)
a postulate based upon a specific conception of justice."

His analysis turned first to an examination of "the Jewish conception of justice" with its "peculiar complexity." It is not only—
as in other conceptions—"a principle of distribution and co-ordination"
but "includes . . . something positive and material, namely, love." It is
important to recognize that for Diesendruck "love . . . is not something outside of justice but contained within justice." It is this
recognition that leads us to the discovery that the essentials of Jewish
social ethics show forth similar antinomies: in the relation of the
individual to the community; in the religiously collectivistic conception of Israel and the crucial role of and demand upon the individual,
this expressed in "the promise of national immortality" and the concept of "individual immortality"; in the concept of all property belonging to God while at the same time providing through "the Sabbatic
and Jubilee institutions" "the protect[ion] and restor[ation of] . . .
private possessions both of individuals and families"; in the "this-
worldiness so pronounced in Judaism and contrasted therewith the
faith in the ideal Messianic future."

Recognizing these antinomies, Diesendruck was concerned to dis-

cover their resolution "at some higher level of thought." The clue
was, of course, the unique conception of justice. It suggested that
the antinomies seen in the social order are resolved when it is recognized that Judaism does not function as a society or a social order but
as a community, "an organic integration." "Judaism is a community
not merely because it represents a blood and spirit kinship but rather
because it manifests an inevasible bond which antedates individuals
and classes and into which the individual is born as into his parental
home. . . . Primary and ultimate is that oneness which affords through
the covenant, the *Berith,* the basis of the common life. The *Edah,*
later the *Keneset Yisrael,* is a community in the real sense of that term.
That community is the *Berith* function and that function includes
blood and doctrine as well as fate."

From this consideration Diesendruck drew what he understood to
be "the ideas operative in the Jewish system—*totality* of the person
and the community, *equality* as a continuing endeavor, *returning* as a
renewal and all of this viewed as *history* realized." These were rooted
in and bound together by "the *idea of unity,* the dynamic unity in
God and in His covenant. . . ." Thus, for Diesendruck there was in
Judaism "an implicit metaphysics" disclosed in its "ethical fundamentals."

It was only in antiquity that the social problem was "viewed in its
entirety." Subsequently the "community" was concerned with "self-
preservation amid alien surroundings," or with "interpreting the
social institutions of an earlier day." But for Diesendruck, writing
in 1932, the possibility of "a revival of social activity" was again
present. It would, he predicted, be carried out in two directions. "One
is the heroic attempt to revive in Palestine a truly Jewish commonwealth. The other is our notable participation in the moves at recon-
structing and improving the social order in those lands in which, as
full-fledged citizens, we share civic responsibility. To both of these
endeavors our principles are relevant. A Jewish society which does no
more than import into Palestine the rusty junk of European institutions would be a society of a sort. . . . But it would not be a Jewish
community. Regarding the other enterprise we will say that the struggle for improved social conditions is certainly Jewish and by all means
praiseworthy; yet that is a false *equation* which would identify Judaism
with such social palliatives as collective bargaining, old age pensions,
etc., claiming that this is all there is to Judaism." "Judaism," he

concluded, "is a system of fundamental principles, formulate them as we may. One may accept them as a basis for the upbuilding of our life here and there, or one may reject them. *Tertium non datur.*"

The discussion of this paper, read, apparently, on late Friday afternoon, was participated in—reports the *Yearbook*—"by Rabbis Thurman and Lauterbach." [114] "The Conference adjourned," and Diesendruck's call for "a system of principles . . . as a basis for the upbuilding of our life here and there" was entombed in the pages of the *Yearbook*. His students never sat with him to discover the possibilities an examination of the past offered the present; we did not even know he was interested in the problem. Heschel wrote in the obituary: "In his yearnings he remained lonely and unhappy. He did not achieve renown, nor did his writings ever become popular. The essays he published were read by but few." [115]

He died a young man. His major work has never been published. . . . *Tēku.*

VIII. Abraham Joshua Heschel: Not Yet at Home

A strict reading of the caveat at the beginning of this paper concerning those to be included and those to be excluded from consideration may well be understood to make reference to Abraham Joshua Heschel out of place. The College was not the seat of his major accomplishments, nor can it be written that he was at home or happy during his incumbency of five years. Yet as he himself recognized and acknowledged, his relationship with the College was real and in a particular and peculiar sense on-going even after he had left to become a member of the faculty of the Jewish Theological Seminary.

On the very last occasion I was with him, he spoke of his years at the College and most particularly of his relation to President Morgenstern. It was not one of gratitude; that would have been too pallid a word to reflect his sense of reverent obligation. Although the gap between their modes of thought was wide and the obstacles between their understandings of Judaism many, there seems to have been a sense of mutual respect and responsibility that touched Heschel's life deeply. The College had, in a desperate moment, provided him with —if not a home—a haven, and he never forgot it but affirmed it with affection.

These comments are, in these circumstances, far less than an assessment of Heschel as theologian and philosopher.[116] They have as their focus a survey of his intellectual activites during the five years he served on the faculty of the College and are concerned to point out that whatever the *Angst* of those years, they were constructive in a very high degree.

Heschel's contributions during this period may be divided into three parts. He continued his technical studies in the field of medieval Jewish philosophy; he began his Kaddish for the Eastern Jewish communities done to death by the Nazi murderers; he laid the foundation for his major theological works.

Under the first heading we find his two papers on Saadia Gaon, "The Quest for Certainty in Saadia's Philosophy," and its continuation, "Realm and Revelation in Saadia's Philosophy." [117] Since the Hebrew essay "Hahe'emin ha-Rambam she-zakah li-nevu'ah?" appeared in the *Louis Ginzberg Jubilee Volume,* published in the fall of 1945, it may be assumed that it too was written during Heschel's stay in Cincinnati. In addition to these technical writings, Heschel published for the students of the College a pamphlet entitled *A Concise Dictionary of Hebrew Philosophical Terms* that is a helpful glossary for those wetting their feet in these texts.

Heschel's eulogy for the Jews of Eastern Europe, *The Earth Is the Lord's,* was prepared for by his address to YIVO, "Di mizrakh-europeishe tekufah in der yiddishe geschichte," and by *Der mizrakh-europeisher yid,*[118] stemming from this period.

Most importantly, these years found him already at work on generative parts of his theological system. "The Pious Man," the concluding chapter of *Man Is Not Alone,* which is the keystone of his thought, was first published in 1942, bearing the title "An Analysis of Piety." [119] In a conversation at the time, I asked Heschel if the concluding paragraph of the essay, with its dialectic construction, was not its nucleus; indeed, was it not the first paragraph written? His answer was: Yes. Part of chapter twenty-two of the same work, entitled "What Is Religion?" appeared in 1943 under the title "The Holy Dimension," [120] and part of chapter seventeen, "Beyond Faith," appeared in 1944.[121]

The brief essay "The Meaning of This Hour," which concludes and in a sense summarizes *Man's Quest for God: Studies in Prayer and Symbolism,* was published in 1943,[122] while chapter one of this work was first published under the title "Prayer" in January of 1945.[123] There are in addition two Hebrew papers, " 'Al mahut ha-tefillah" and "Perush 'al ha-tefillot," [124] stemming from this period that most certainly contributed to Heschel's developing thought.

When Heschel left the Hebrew Union College in 1945 to join the faculty of the Jewish Theological Seminary, several students, deeply influenced by his thought, followed him. Others, touched perhaps less radically, nonetheless had received a new perspective from him. Still others, who did not know him in the context of the College, responded to his thought as it was expressed in the volumes that appeared over the subsequent years, or if not to it, to his manifest social conscience in the civil-rights and anti-war movements of the sixties. It is for these reasons, it seems to me, that the Hebrew Union College may rightfully and justly place his name on its roster of theologians and philosophers.

IX. Samuel Atlas: Jewish Kantianism At Last Arrives

David Neumark, as noted above, had not only been deeply in-fluenced by Herman Cohen but considered himself to be the con-tinuator of Cohen's neo-Kantian thought; however, as suggested, he never carried out the constructive task he set for himself. Although Kohler and Cohon make reference to Cohen's philosophical position, the former did not have the particular technical philosophical train-ing that would have made Cohen's thought available to him, and the latter, as noted, responded more affirmatively to other directions of thought. Diesendruck certainly had paid careful attention to Cohen, but it is not at all certain what influence his thought had had, although there are traces of it in the paper on "The Ideal Social Order . . ." All of this is strange indeed, for there is no doubt what-soever that Kantian or neo-Kantian thought played a significant role in the development of Jewish theology and philosophy in Western Europe.[125]

It was, then, not until the arrival of Samuel Atlas at the Hebrew Union College that Kantian thought found an expositor and expon-ent. Again, in terms of the original promise of this paper, one could—because he is still active—refrain from dealing with Professor Atlas's philosophical contributions. In actual fact, as the better part of valor, no attempt will be made to deal with the technical exposition of the thought of Solomon Maimon, the contemporary of Kant, which forms —it seems to me—the foundation upon which Professor Atlas has built the imposing intellectual structure culminating in *From Critical to Speculative Idealism: The Philosophy of Solomon Maimon.*[126] All that will be attempted is a suggestion as to what is going on in, through, and behind this meticulous exposition, for it is evident that there is something more present than the technical virtuosity of the philosophical scholar. There is, I venture to suggest, a philosopher with a position.

Basically, what Atlas has set out to do is to demonstrate that the true heir of Maimonidean intellectualism in modern thought was the eighteenth-century critical idealist Solomon Maimon,[127] and that the recovery of Maimon's thought and its development, together with that of Hermann Cohen, will provide a firm basis, indeed the only firm basis, for Jewish philosophical speculation today.

Hugo Bergmann has pointed out in his essay "Maimon und Cohen" the affinity, although not always the relationship, between these two thinkers. More important for our consideration is his emphasis upon Przywara's insight that the agreement between their thought derives from the relationship between each and the thought of Maimonides.[128] It is exactly this point that Atlas has seized upon and developed. In his paper "The Philosophy of Maimonides and Its Systematic Place in the History of Philosophy," [129] he refers to the "profound influence" Maimonides' work exerted on Spinoza, Mendelssohn, Solomon Maimon, and H. Cohen, noting, "Maimonides' works were the source of inspiration for their independent philosophic thought although subsequently they went different ways." It is, most particularly, to the continuing influence of Maimonides on Maimon and on Cohen that he directs his attention. "Many points can be traced in Solomon Maimon's thought which show his close connection with Maimonides"; and, "Hermann Cohen, the founder of the 'Marburg School' of neo-Kantianism loved to emphasize the relation between his own thought and that of Maimonides." When this essay is taken together with the much larger and detailed paper "The Contemporary Relevance of the Philosophy of Maimonides," [130] one sees what Atlas is striving for.

Maimon's idealist system lies, in its own interests and concerns, outside the circumference of Judaism, for Maimon, like his contemporary Mendelssohn, viewed philosophy from a universal perspective; there was nothing "Jewish" about philosophy nor could there be. With Cohen this point of view, while certainly dominant in the major development of his thought, loses its sharp focus in his later writings, first, as he attempts to find a role for religion in his system, and subsequently as he seeks to relate religion *par excellence,* Judaism, to his philosophic structure. Thus the naturalization of Maimon's and Cohen's critical philosophies into Judaism—that is, the availability of a particular form of philosophy deriving from Kant as the basis for a contemporary interpretation of Judaism—is, on its face, an arduous undertaking.[131] Indeed, in Maimon's case it cannot be done directly; in Cohen's case, too, mediation is necessary. That mediation is, as noted above, available through the claimed relationship of both to the thought of Maimonides. But even that relationship may not suffice. What is required is a demonstration that there is a congruency between the critical idealism of Maimon and Cohen and the thought of Maimonides that authorizes and justifies it as a constructive basis for a contemporary philosophical statement of Judaism. It is in the essay previously noted that Atlas undertook to make this demonstration.[132]

The demonstration is carried out by proposing the following portrait of Maimonides' thought: ". . . it is particularly proper to call to mind the sound and sober rationalism of Maimonides which implies a belief in the human capacity of reason, making belief in the idea of progress possible. The feasibility of progress is dependent on the belief in man's capacity to master the problems with which he has to cope.

"The specific characteristic of man consists, according to Maimonides, in his rational capacity. Man is capable of attaining an intellectual comprehension of the logical forms of thought and the forms of being, and by developing, i.e., bringing forth from a potential state into an actual state, his rational faculty, man is capable of achieving a clear idea of God and the world."[133]

That this is a reading of Maimonides cannot be gainsaid, but it seems to be a reading of only a part of Maimonides, for it revolves primarily around the philosophical problems deriving from Maimonides' struggle with the doctrine of creation and all but ignores the extended analysis of prophecy and the suggestions about the nature of man that are to be drawn from it. It is, I suggest, a reading of Maimonides that is formed by a concern to show that "[his] conception of the unity of truth, of the identity of philosophy and revelation, and of his view of Judaism, prophetic as well as rabbinic, as containing a philosophy which is in complete harmony with rational thought, opens up new vistas for the possibility of a development of Jewish thought in the light of further growth of philosophic thought in general. Maimonides laid the basis for the possibility of the development of Jewish religious thought beyond the stage he had attained . . ." Maimonides is not transformed into a critical idealist, but critical idealism is evidently the means by which "with Maimonides we can supercede Maimonides." [134]

Thus, in the concluding chapter of *From Critical to Speculative Idealism* we read of the Marburg School of Neo-Kantianism: "According to this school of thought, the ordered world of our scientific experience conforms to *a priori* concepts because the phenomena acquire objectivity only through these concepts. It is through the methodological thinking of science that the objective world is generated. The process of objectification is however never completed; it is an endless process. The human mind, through the development of scientific thought, is constantly striving for more adequate objectification. The ultimate correspondence of objects of reality with *a priori* principles of thought is an ideal goal; it is an endless task." [135]

Granted the difference in terminology, it seems clear that a congruence with the thought of Maimonides is assumed.[136] Nor indeed does Professor Atlas shy away from such a suggestion. In his discussion of the ethical task of man, which "follows the attainment of the metaphysical cognition of God and his attributes," he writes: "The formulation of the ultimate value for man, with which Maimonides concludes his treatise, is bound up with a concept of man as a being having the capacity to transcend himself and to transform the world. This is possible only under the assumption that man is endowed with a creative faculty and that this world provides the material for man's ethical creativity. Hence the world itself must be thought of as having its origin in an act of creation, for a world which exists of necessity and from eternity is a static world and everything in it is the same as it has always been. But ethical life can have a place only in a world of non-necessity." The following paragraph begins: "The similarity of Maimonides' position to that of critical philosophy can conclusively be demonstrated," [137] and Atlas continues with that demonstration.

My concern is not to deny Atlas's reading of Maimonides. Such an attempt is beyond my ability, although I readily admit a discomfort at points with the analysis. The question to be put is simply, does the introduction of a critical idealist interpretation of Judaism require the "approval" of Maimonides? What if Maimonides' rationalism was of a different order? What if he were far more contaminated with "unreason" than Atlas would like? Would any of this really interfere with or negate critical idealism as a basis for a contemporary philosophy of Judaism? But Atlas's paper, with all its magisterial command of the material, conceals that issue. Quite frankly, I would prefer to read it not as "The Contemporary Relevance of the Philosophy of Maimonides" but as a statement of a critical idealist interpretation of Judaism, for that is what it is, and that is what has been needed for some time in order to avoid the "obscurantism," "dogmatism," and "the elevation of all sorts of personal, imaginary, subjective experiences to the level of a divine oracle" which Atlas decries. I do not suggest that such an idealist position can win the day.[138] What it will do is demand from those who reject it a quality of thought that will be responsible in its responsivity. From that point of view, Atlas's writings must be attended to as demands upon our thinking that it be both consequent and tough. But in all events we can be grateful that the philosophical position so closely related to the rise of liberal Judaism in the nineteenth century has received the thoughtful attention at the Hebrew Union College it always deserved.

X. Concluding Remarks Not Entirely Conclusive

The introductory apology suggested that I do not consider my own contemporaries to be yet ready for—not unworthy of—the sort of assessment here undertaken. Eugene Borowitz, Jakob Petuchowski, and Alvin Reines [139] are so clearly still on the way that to focus on their positions, taken at a particular time entirely unrelated to their own intellectual development—the one hundredth anniversary of the Hebrew Union College—seems quite unsatisfactory. This is not to suggest that a center has not emerged for the thought of each, only that it would be wiser to allow judgments to be made *'ahare me'ah shanah.* Thus I leave it to my esteemed colleagues yet unborn to display, *'im yirtzeh ha-Shem,* the ample virtues of these three as well as others yet to come.

What then is the sum of the tale that has been told? One can say affirmatively that no dogmatism, theologic or philosophic, has held sway in the Hebrew Union College. No test clauses have been imposed, no party line inexorably required. A variety of virtues has been manifest. Individual insight has been given due regard. For all this, thanks must be given. Intellectual freedom is—we have learned—no small matter in this world. Yet for all this, self-congratulations are not in order. Philosophical and theological studies that were, with history, the particular mark of a nontraditional, liberal approach to the vast body of thought bearing the name Judaism, have not made the impact hoped for. Somehow the intellectual instrumentalities with which to struggle with an increasingly obdurate and unfriendly world of thought have not been fashioned. The tradition has not been faced in the mutual enterprise of transforming and being transformed. No compelling wisdom for the day has at any point emerged so forcibly as to capture minds and hearts. Decent, honest craftsmanship everywhere abounds, but no vision of a structure—not eternal but for each generation—has been seen.

We see this and say this, not because we are wiser than the good men here written of, but because at the end of that hundred years, we find ourselves in a different world from that in which most of them lived. It may be that we live in one of those end-of-an-age periods when against need and desire we ourselves are not able to say what must be said and thus can find in that which they wrote, in a more secure—so it must have seemed to them—world, little to support us or to cast light upon the obscurity of our way. Perhaps for us the testimony remains bound up, the instruction is still sealed.

Notes

1. James G. Heller, *Isaac M. Wise: His Life, Work and Thought* (New York: UAHC, 1965).
2. Ibid., p. 503.
3. Ibid., p. 504.
4. Ibid., p. 508.
5. Ibid.
6. "Für oder wider den persönlichen Gott? Zum Schultz und Trutz," *Jewish Times,* III, 190, 25–26; "For or Against the Personal God? To Defend and Defy" (translation), *Jewish Times,* III, nos. 27–28.
7. D. Philipson, *The Reform Movement in Judaism,* new and revised ed. (New York: Macmillan, 1931), p. 355.
8. See, in the Margolis monograph to be discussed below, the reference to Wise's "Introduction to the Theology of Judaism" and the comment "though open to grave objections on its philological and historical sides . . ." (p. 3, n. 20).
9. I. Abrahams, *By-Paths in Hebraic Bookland,* (Philadelphia: Jewish Publication Society), pp. 347–52. I have omitted internal quotation marks.
10. Heller, op. cit., p. 521.
11. Ibid., p. 524.
12. L. H. Silberman, "The Union Prayer Book: A Study in Liturgical Development," in *Retrospect and Prospect* (New York, CCAR), pp. 60–61.
13. *CCAR Yearbook, I,* pp. 31, 80–125. One must use the précis with great care for they are not always accurate.
14. It is interesting to note that Kohler had, in the 1871 article noted above, rejected this excuse that it was only the phrase "personal God" and not the idea that was being called into question.

15. The title page of the separate publication has at the top, "Published by the Central Conference of American Rabbis," and directly beneath, in parentheses, the sentence at the head of the Yearbook version, "The writer alone is responsible for views expressed in this publication." It bears the date 1904 and was printed in Baltimore by the Friedenwald Company. The monograph is 147 pages, including 27 pages of indexes. The preface of the monograph says that the invitation was extended on Oct. 20, 1903; that is clearly a misprint.

16. The emphasis is Kohler's. The remark by Margolis cited in n. 8 above concludes with this interesting phrase, "It [the "Introduction"] is significant both because of the omission of the qualification 'reformed' in the title and for its insistence upon the necessity of a formulated creed" (p. 3, n. 20).

17. See *Theological Aspect* . . . , p. 110, n. 13 (*Yearbook*, XIII, 344). But too his article in *JQR* (o.s. XVII, 531–44), "The Mendelssohnian Programme." Margolis was an incipient Ahad ha-Am-ist even at this point and was willing to concede that spiritual Zionism would require "the political independence of Palestinian Jewry as an ultimate goal."

18. N. 20, previously referred to, remarks that the term *theological* has been shunned and promises to explain why this is so.

19. Op. cit., pp. v–vi.

20. Ibid., pp. 5–6.

21. On p. 112 Margolis writes that he prefers the Greek word *dogma* to the Latin *principles*. The first quotation is from p. 8, n. 1; the second, from the text, p. 8.

22. See Kohler's strictures at this point in *CCAR Yearbook*, XV, 84.

23. Op. cit., p. 109, the reference to Holdheim (*Yearbook*, p. 293).

24. Ibid., p. 110, quoting I. M. Wise (*Yearbook*, p. 294).

25. Ibid., p. 111 (*Yearbook*, p. 295).

26. Ibid., pp. 111–12 (*Yearbook*, p. 296) The capital letters are Margolis's.

27. Ibid., p. 123. The capital letters are Margolis's.

28. See his response to Kohler in the *Yearbook*, XV, 103.

29. *Theological Aspect* . . . ., p. 110.

30. *Yearbook, XV*, 83.

31. Ibid., p. 102. Kohler himself, in his 1871 article cited in n. 6 above, had translated *Reform Judenthum* as Reformed Judaism.

32. Ibid., p. 83. *Pace* the Pittsburgh Platform.

33. K. Kohler, *Jewish Theology* (New York: Macmillan, 1928). The German volume was entitled *Grundriss einer systematischen Theologie des Judentums auf geschichtlicher Grundlage,* and was published in 1910.

34. Ibid., pp. viii–ix. Notice the odd—at this point—usage, "conservative Judaism."

35. In *Studies in Jewish Literature Issued in Honor of Professor Kaufman Kohler, Ph.D.* (Berlin: Georg Reimer, 1913).

36. In *Studies, Addresses and Personal Papers* (Alumni Association—Bloch Publishing Co., 1931), pp. 561–77.

37. In 1906 Kohler published in serial form in the *Allgemeine Zeitung des Judenthums* an article entitled "Die dreizehn Artikel des Maimonides und das moderne Judenthum." Although it was not available to me, I would conjecture that it is an elaboration of Kohler's critical analysis that occupies pp. 84–93 of the report (*Yearbook*, XV).

38. Kohler's emphasis on Divine Personality was the basis of his earlier attack on Wise (see n. 6), the title of which was "For or Against the Personal God."

39. See *Theology*, pp. 102–3, where Kohler clearly discloses the influence of Margolis's thinking. But see below for other sources.

40. *CCAR Yearbook*, XV, 101.

41. The first edition of these was published by the HUC Co-operative Store in 1933. Vol. I is entitled *Theology and Religion*. The quotation, on p. 143, was omitted in the revised edition, 1940. It comes from Kohler's "Biographical Essay on David Einhorn" in *CCAR Yearbook*, XIX, 252.

42. See n. 6 above.

43. *Theology*, p. 29; but see the whole of chap. V.

44. Ibid., p. 35. The influence of M. Lazarus on Kohler must not be underestimated.

45. *Jewish Exponent*, (Philadelphia and Baltimore) vol. 50, no. 24, March 25, 1910.

46. The "racial" component of some Reform thought of the period deserves investigation. Schulman, in the article cited above, chides Kohler for crediting the Church for the development of the plastic arts and music in Western culture. Kohler, wrote Schulman, "does not sufficiently allow for the native genius of the western races in this." However, Margolis, the incipient Zionist, making reference to H. S. Chamberlain's *Grundlagen des neunzehnten Jahrhunderts*, wrote of his opponents: "You are fond of appealing to the Jewish heart. If you mean by it an organ of 50 per cent Hittite, 5 per cent Semite, 10 per cent Amorite and 35 per cent bastard origin [this is Chamberlain's formulation] you are crypto-Zionists but not Reformed Jews."

47. Breslau: M. H. Marcus Verlag, 1935.

48. See the references to chaps. IV–V of Lazarus' *Ethik des Judentums* in *Jewish Theology*, p. 101. These chapters are not found in the English translation, which is not complete.

49. *Geschichte der jüdischen Philosophie des Mittelalters, 1* (Berlin: Reimer, 1907); II, 1 (1910); *Anhang zum ersten Band,* 1913; II, 2 (Berlin: de Gruyter, 1928).

50. In *Essays in Jewish Philosophy* (1929), p. 2.

51. Ibid., "The Beauty of Japhet in the Tents of Shem," p. 13.

52. Ibid., "The Philosophy of Judaism," p. 5.

53. This work bears the title *Toledot ha-Ikkarim beYisrael*. Vol. I appeared in 1912; vol. II, in 1919. Both were published by Moriah in Odessa.

54. Op cit. I, pp. 15–20.

55. *MGWJ*, 55 (N. F. 19), 100–11. At the very heart of Lewkowitz's critique

is the claim: " . . . N. geht von einem falschen Begriff der Religion aus . . . " p. 102.

56. *The Philosophy of the Bible* (Cincinnati: Ark Publishing Co., 1918), p. 137.
57. Ibid., p. 299.
58. Ibid., p. 300.
59. Ibid., pp. 300, 295.
60. Op. cit.
61. *REJ* 50 (1908), 291–307.
62. Cf. Gershom Scholem, *Ursprung und Anfang der Kabbala* (Berlin: de Gruyter, 1962), pp. 6–7: "In the Hebrew edition of his work Neumark more than doubled the chapter 'The Kabbala' so that it is one of the most extensive monographs dealing with the early Kabbala up to the Zohar but at the same time it is one of the most erroneous."
63. "Jewish Philosophy" in *Hebrew Union College Monthly*, November 1916, pp. 8–13; see too, "Medieval Jewish Philosophy" in *American Jewish Chronicle* (New York,) Jan. 5, 1917), pp. 265–66. The response by Adolph Oko, then librarian of the Hebrew Union College, appeared— signed with Oko's *nom de plume* S. Baruch—as a pamphlet with the title "Professor David Neumark, Ph.D., and 'Mr.' Husik."
64. "A Recent View of Matter and Form in Aristotle," *Archiv für Geschichte der Philosophie* (N. F.), XXIII, 4, pp. 447–71. There is a reply to Neumark's paper, "Matter and Form in Aristotle." It is a sad comment on the impact of Jewish scholarship that I can find no subsequent scholar of classical Greek philosophy who refers to, let alone agrees with, Neumark's position.
65. Ibid., XXIV, 3 and 4, pp. 271–322, 391–432; and the final retort in the same XXVI, pp. 195–96.
66. See above, n. 1.
67. Cf. the concluding "Anmerkung" on p. 432 of the article cited in n. 65: "Dem Ansuchen der Redaktion entsprechend habe ich im zweiten Teile meiner Erwiderung einige Ausdrücke gemildert. . . . Ich wollte damit nur dem Gedanken Ausdruck geben, dass ich H. nicht als einen wissenschaft-lichen Gegner, sondern als einen zur Kritik meines Buches Unberufenen betrachte."
68. "Historical Systematic Relations of Judaism to Kant." This was first pub-lished in the *CCAR Yearbook* and reprinted in *Essays in Jewish Philosophy*, cited in n. 50. It is, strangely, not recorded in the bibliography appended to that volume.
69. *Geschichte,* I, 1: "Das Nachdenken über die theoretischen Grundprinzipien der jüdischen Religion ist so alt wie diese selbst."
70. See Neumark's paper "Spirit" in the volume cited in n. 50.
71. Cf. Joshua Bloch, *Sefer Ha-Shanah, V,* ed. M. Ribalow, (New York, 5701/ 1940), p. 259.
72. It may seem thoughtless and discourteous to reduce Slonimsky to such a brief reference. I can only claim that his small literary productivity makes any extended discussion impossible. His pupils at the Jewish Institute of

Religion speak glowingly of him as a teacher, but I have never learned much from them about the direction of his thought.

73. Revised edition, mimeographed, Hebrew Union College, 1940.
74. Op. cit., p. 191.
75. Published by Department of Synagogue and School Extension of the Union of American Hebrew Congregations (Cincinnati, 1931).
76. Cf. secs. 31 and 32 of the work cited in n. 73.
77. Ibid., sec. 33.
78. Ibid., p. 233.
79. Ibid., 234.
80. Ibid., p. 235.
81. Ibid., p. 236.
82. Ibid. This sentence has been recast without distorting its meaning. In a note Cohon wrote, "hence the covenant figured as the supreme symbol of the religion of Israel. It betokened both the union of the individual and tribe with God and the social bond which linked the individuals and the community . . . "
83. Ibid., p. 238.
84. Ibid., p. 239.
85. Assen: Royal Vangoreum Ltd. 1971.
86. Op. cit., p. 138.
87. Ibid., pp. 123–28.
88. Ibid., pp. 123–28.
89. Ibid., pp. 146–51.
90. Ibid., p. 151.
91. Ibid., pp. 151–59.
92. Ibid., p. 283.
93. The *Theology Lectures* appeared in three parts: *Theology and Religion; Man and His Destiny; Judaism as a Way of Living.* Of these, the last was published under the title *Judaism: A Way of Life* by the UAHC in 1948. Sec. 3 of *Jewish Theology* reproduces *Man and His Destiny.* The introduction to this volume reproduces chaps. 1, 2, and 3 of *Theology and Religion.* Secs. 1 and 2, "Definition of Judaism and of its Creedal Content" and "The Doctrine of God in Judaism," have no parallel in the *Theology Lectures.* "Israel" and "Torah" are dealt with in *What We Jews Believe* in a popular fashion.
94. It is clear from occasional references that he was acquainted with the writings of Hermann Cohen, but there is no engagement with his thought. Neither Buber nor Rosenzweig is dealt with in his major writings, although they are touched upon briefly but with appreciation in the paper on existentialism read before the CCAR (*Yearbook,* LXIII, 348–85). That paper is, unfortunately, devoted largely to exposition of existentialist tendencies in Christian theology and to a sharp, but not unjustifiably so, assessment of Will Herberg's thought. Leo Baeck's *Essence of Judaism* is noted in the bibliography of *Judaism: A Way of Life* but not in *Jewish Theology.* In addition to the works cited above there are a number of valuable ex-

positary essays that appeared in the *HUC Annual*: "Palestine in Jewish Theology" (Jubilee Special, 1925); "Authority in Judaism," (XI, 1936); "Original Sin," (XXI, 1948); "The Name of God, a Study in Rabbinic Theology" (XXIII, P. 1, 1950–51); "The Unity of God, a Study in Hellenistic and Rabbinic Theology" (XXVI, 1955). See *Studies in Bibliography and Booklore,* II, 4 (1956), "The Writings of Samuel S. Cohon," for a complete bibliography.

95. *Proceedings of the American Academy for Jewish Research,* X (1940), 3–4.
96. *CCAR Yearbook,* L (1940), 248–51.
97. *American Jewish Year Book,* vol. 42 (5702/1941), pp. 391–98.
98. *Encyclopedia Judaica* (1973), s.v., Diesendruck.
99. Op. cit.
100. *PAAJR,* loc. cit.
101. Op. cit.
102. Op. cit.
103. See the review of the translation of *Gorgias* in *Kirjath Sefer* 7, 568–69 by I. Sonne, and the review of *Republic,* op. cit. 13, 419–24 by E. Simon.
104. *Jewish Studies in memory of Israel Abrahams* (New York, 1927), pp. 74–134.
105. *HUCA,* V (1928), 415–534.
106. *MGWJ* LXXVI, 476–18; see Diesendruck's reply, LXXVII 141–44 and Heinemann's response, 144–45.
107. Heschel, op. cit. in n. 97; Baron and Spiegel, op. cit. in n. 95.
108. *CCAR Yearbook,* XLV (1935), 335–67.
109. Published in Tel Aviv, 1934, by Dvir.
110. See below n. 112 and 113.
111. Op. cit.
112. In *Essays on Anti-Semitism,* edited by Koppel S. Pinson (1st ed., New York, 1942; 2nd ed., 1946).
113. *CCAR Yearbook,* XLII (1932), 238 et seq. The title given in the text is that printed at the head of the paper. The title in the Contents, p. 8, is "The Ideal Social Order as Expressed or Implied in Jewish Ethical Thinking."
114. Op. cit., p. 135.
115. Op. cit.
116. For a wider assessment see my two papers, "The Thought of Abraham Joshua Heschel," *Jewish Heritage,* Spring 1969, and "Rebbe for our Day," ibid., Fall 1971.
117. *JQR* (ns) XXXIII (1924–43), 265–313; ibid., XXXIV (1943–44), 391–408.
118. *YIVO Bletter,* XXV, 2 (March–April 1945), 163–83; Schocken Books, 1946.
119. *Review of Religion,* VI, 3 (March 1942), 293–307.
120. *Journal of Religion,* XXIII, 1 (January 1943), 117–24.
121. *Reconstructionist,* X, 13–14 (1944).
122. *Hebrew Union College Bulletin,* II, 3 (1943). In a note appended to the

text in *Man's Quest,* Heschel indicates that a first version was read to a conference of Quakers meeting in Frankfurt a.M. in March 1938.

123. *Review of Religion,* IX, 2 (January 1945), 153–68; see too his paper "Das Gebet als Aeusserung und Einfühlung" in *MGWJ,* LXXXIII, (1939).

124. *Bitzaron,* II (1940–41), 346–53; *Kovetz mad'ai lezekher M. Schorr.* (New York: 1944), pp. 113–26; see too "Yirat Shamayim" in *Sefer ha-Shanah lihude Amerika,* VI.

125. See Nathan Rotenstreich, *Jewish Philosophy in Modern Times: From Mendelssohn to Rosenzweig* (New York: Holt, Rinehart and Winston, 1968); Albert Lewkowitz, *Das Judentum und die geistigen Strömungen des 19. Jahrhunderts* (Breslau: M. & H. Marcus, 1935), pp. 6–166; Emil Fackenheim, "Judaism and the Idea of Progress," in *Quest for Past and Future* (Bloomington: Indiana University Press, 1968), pp. 83–95.

126. The Hague: Martinus Nijhoff, 1964. In addition to the two chapters of this volume, VII and X, that are "substantial revisions in form and content" of articles appearing in *HUC Annual,* "Maimon and Maimonides" (XXIII, P. 1 [not XXII]), and "Solomon Maimon's Treatment of the Problem of Antinomies and Its Relation to Maimonides" (XXI), three other studies appear in that annual: "Moses in the Philosophy of Maimonides, Spinoza and Solomon Maimon" (XXV), "Solomon Maimon's Philosophy of Language" (XXVIII), and "Solomon Maimon and Spinoza" (XXX).

127. See particularly op. cit., chap. VII.

128. *MGWJ,* LXXXIII (1939), 548 et seq.

129. *Philosophy (The Journal of the British Institute of Philosophy),* XI (1936), 60–75.

130. *CCAR Yearbook,* LXIV (1954), 196–213.

131. See Emil Fackenheim, *Encounters Between Judaism and Modern Philosophy* (New York: Basic Books, 1973), "Abraham and the Kantians," pp. 33–77.

132. Actually the two papers—that cited in n. 129 and "Maimon and Maimonides" cited in n. 126—must be taken together. The second suggests the basis of important parts of Maimon's thought in that of Maimonides. The first supports the claims of critical idealism by reference to Maimonides.

133. *Yearbook,* p. 187.

134. Ibid., p. 213.

135. Op. cit., p. 329.

136. Note the phrase on p. 133 of this work, "Translating Maimonides' thought into Kantian language . . . " The assumption seems to be that since Maimon was influenced by Maimonides, a Kantian reading of Maimonides is the preferred or, perhaps, the correct reading.

137. *Yearbook,* p. 207.

138. See Fackenheim's essay cited in n. 131.

139. Although at the outset I eschewed discussing "present presences" and here— a few lines below—leave them to the future, decent respect and personal regard require that a brief suggestion as to the variety of their thought be

offered. Petuchowski and Borowitz clearly represent the "existentialist" position so ably adumbrated by Arnold J. Wolf in his introduction to *Rediscovering Judaism* (Chicago: Quadrangle Books, 1965). There he wrote: "We have all been moved and instructed by the rebirth of Jewish thinking during this century under Rosenzweig and Buber. In a sense we are only their American continuators" (p. 10). Both men acknowledge with reverent gratitude that spiritual debt; the impact of the thought of Buber and Rosenzweig is everywhere felt in their writings. They have, each in his own way, lifted up the concept of "covenant" as central to Jewish thought and have developed it into inclusive interpretations of Jewish existence.

Wolf further wrote: "We are also under the tutelage of American philosophy, liberal religion, and existentialism." The impact of the first two is far more evident and effective in Borowitz's thought than in Petuchowski's. Indeed, the latter does not, at least on the surface, grapple with the "outside" world in the way the former does. Yet to both, granting important differences, the words of Wolf apply: "For us, Judaism is not so much a heritage as an achievement. Or, perhaps, more accurately, to make it our heritage has become our decisive task" (p. 8).

Of Reines, I find my characterization written in 1969 still cogent: " . . . an idiosyncratic application of logical positivism, one not of the most recent variety, to the history of Judaism. It seems evident that this method was undertaken not for its own sake, but to provide an apologia for a process-philosophy interpretation of Judaism. Had Reines devoted himself to the latter rather than the former he could have produced, as he may yet produce, a valuable statement of a possible contemporary position" (*American Jewish Year Book,* 1969, p. 55).

MARTIN A. COHEN

History

REFORM JUDAISM has always been historically rather than halakhically oriented. In theory at least, it has sought its identity not in conformity of practice but in allegiance to the timeless elements of a tradition of experience. In the definition of these elements it has assayed to blend scholarly probity and religious devotion with "the confidence," as one of its recent towering leaders said, "that the accurate and affirmatively critical and free study of our tradition will ensure its survival and enhance its sanctity." That leader was the late president of the College-Institute, Nelson Glueck. These words, as well as his dictum that "nothing in the Jewish past or present is alien to our interest," voiced the historical orientation of the institution. They also expressed the hope of informing the graduates of the College-Institute with a solid knowledge of Judaism's historical roots and a pride in its millennial achievements.

The lofty goal of imparting a sense of the eternal through a study of the temporal may yet be far from fulfillment at the College-Institute. No attempt to coordinate the various disciplines taught at the College-Institute under a historical or, for that matter, any other umbrella, has met with success. Its curriculum has traditionally been fragmented, at least in part because of laudable insistence by the College authorities on academic freeedom. Each discipline, and, in most cases, each professor, has been free to determine the fulfillment of the needs of Reform Judaism as has seemed fit. Besides, rarely have professors of history at the College-Institute agreed on a comprehensive program of historical instruction. As a result, the history of historical studies at the College-Institute is largely the history of its historians, the impact of their personalities, and the cumulative thrust of their contributions.

In the century of its existence, the College-Institute has attracted or bred some of the outstanding figures in the field of Jewish history. These professors have come from a wide variety of backgrounds— native and foreign, German and East European, traditional and liberal. Some have been excellent scholars but only fair teachers, others good teachers as well as outstanding scholars. Some have stressed the philosophy of history over detail, others detail over philosophy. Each, however, in his own way has approached Jewish history with the curiosity of a scientist, a disciplined academic mind, and, in most cases, an understanding of contemporary developments in the broader fields of the social sciences. The essential similarity of their visions of Jewish history at the College-Institute has overcome many of the problems inherent in its curricular fragmentation, and in a broad sense has provided continuity and development.

The Cincinnati School

Like many other disciplines, historical studies at the College got off to a slow start. In 1876, shortly after the creation of the College, the faculty consisted of Isaac Mayer Wise and David Lilienthal, both unsalaried, and Solomon Eppinger, the first salaried instructor. Learned as it was, this triumvirate could hardly provide for specialization in all areas of Judaic studies.

Wise himself taught Jewish history as well as Bible and theology. In 1884 he appointed as professor of history,Heinrich Zirndorff (1829– 1893) a German rabbi and poet who since 1876 had been serving as rabbi of Congregation Beth-El in Detroit. Zirndorff brought with him a wide range of interests. He had studied German and English classics, published a five-act tragedy, *Kassandra*, in German in 1856, and wrote German poetry. He was not really a trained historian. His major contributions to the field of history consist of a book of reminiscences of Isaac Marcus Jost (*Isaak Markus Jost und Seine Freunde,* 1886) and articles on Jewish women published in German in the *Deborah,* and later collected and translated into English for the Jewish Publication Society in 1892. Neither of these works reveals a structured or analytic approach to history.

It was not until 1891, when the student body numbered more than thirty, that the College appointed a man who may more appropriately be called its first historian. He was the forty-two-year-old Gotthard Deutsch, who also served as professor of philosophy. Deutsch had been born in Moravia, had received a doctorate in philosophy at the University of Breslau, and rabbinic ordination from Isaac Hirsch Weiss. He had studied history under Heinrich Graetz at the Breslau Theological Seminary.

During most of his thirty-year career at the College, Deutsch was typically characterized by students as "the most colorful person on the campus." Tall and stately, with white beard and shaggy brows, he seemed like the archetype of the traditional European rabbi. This impression was strengthened by his appreciation of European Orthodox Judaism. He hankered after the populous communities of East European Jewish immigrants and reveled in his visits to the Atlantic seaboard, where he could mingle freely with them.

Deutsch was a hospitable man. The students enjoyed their visits to his home. His hearty laugh, sharp wit, and engaging causerie provided topics for discussion reminiscent of the postprandial wisdom of a Hasidic *tsaddik.* No less colorful, if at times embarrassing, was Deutsch's notorious Germanophilia. It went so far as to express itself in a daring way during the years of World War I. Deutsch would open the windows to his living room and loudly play German anthems on his phonograph so that the entire neighborhood might hear. This commitment—or eccentricity—nearly cost Deutsch his job on the eve of American entrance into World War I.

Under Deutsch Jewish history was chronologically divided into four courses, and in each Deutsch presented a general survey of a major period.

At first, the freshman collegiate class at the College began its studies with Yohanan b. Zakkai, but later it surveyed Jewish history from biblical times to the year 70. The second class then continued to the death of Judah Ha-Nasi, "with the object in view to make

the class acquainted with the methods of historical investigation."
The third studied medieval history, concentrating on the Gaonic
period and surveying the rest of the Middle Ages from 1040 to 1492
"in a cursory manner." The seniors selected various problems, beginning with the Crusades but concentrating on the nineteenth century and American Judaism. No specialized courses were offered in
history, and amazingly for a person like Deutsch, none in the philosophy of Jewish history. A graduate curriculum beginning in 1899 did
not include history.

Deutsch was gifted with a prodigious memory. His classroom frequently became an arena for the display of its virtuosity. His mind
was a magnet for countless details, and he possessed knowledge of some
of the most recondite facts of Jewish history. His mnemonic feats
spiced his classroom lectures, which students found otherwise "tedious
and repetitious." Actually they were not really lectures, but rambling
discussions that not infrequently touched on points of interest other
than the topic of the day.

Fortunately for posterity, Deutsch had the habit of carefully recording many stray facts on cards. In this way he developed a substantial catalogue of rare details of Jewish history. The catalogue
is now housed in the College-Institute in Cincinnati.

Deutsch's talents lay more in writing than in teaching. From his
typewriter poured forth articles for journals and periodicals, including the *American Israelite* and the *Deborah,* whose editorship he assumed after the death of Isaac Mayer Wise in 1900. His interests
covered a broad range—the passing scene of Jewish life (collected
in two volumes called *Scrolls* and his *Andere Zeiten* [1898]; the
drama *Israel Bruna: An Historical Tragedy in Five Acts* (1908),
and, of course, above all, Jewish history. He wrote a small but, for
the time, respectable textbook, *The History of the Jews* (1921). He
also edited the section on modern Jewish history in the *Jewish Encyclopedia.* Perhaps his most profound effort was a lengthy essay
entitled "Philosophy of Jewish History." "History is more a scientific
method than a science, just as time is not a concept but a motive
conception," he said in this essay. In it he emphasized that Jewish
history is comprehensible only in the light of world history. "We will
understand every single fact of Jewish history in connection with
the whole, and the whole of Jewish history in its drift toward the
goal of humanity."

For all its breadth, Deutsch's productivity, even in the area of Jewish history, lacked the dimension of depth. This flaw is evident in most of his works. His *Memorable Dates of Jewish History* (New York, 1904) indiscriminately juxtaposes the trivial and obscure with the essential and enduring. Many of his other works also reveal both the impressive breadth of his learning and his difficulty in the area of synthesis. Deutsch's influence was slight. He left two outstanding contributions: one his card catalogue; the other, a student named Jacob Rader Marcus.

After the death of Gotthard Deutsch in 1921, the College invited Jacob Mann, a native of Galicia and a 1914 graduate of Jews' College in London, to succeed him as professor of Jewish history. Then thirty-three years old, Mann's researches in the responsa of the Babylonian Geonim and his extensive Genizah studies had already earned him a wide reputation as a Judaica scholar. Besides, the first volume of his masterly work, *The Jews in Egypt and Palestine under the Fatimid Caliphs,* had recently (1920) been published and its sequel was on the way. Mann was in the United States lecturing at the Baltimore Hebrew College when he was invited to the College. He accepted and spent the next eighteen years there, until his untimely death in 1940, indefatigably investigating the documentary legacy of medieval Judaism and becoming one of the world's leading scholars of Geonica and Karaitica. His two volumes, *Texts and Studies in Jewish History and Literature* (1931–35; reprint ed., KTAV, 1970, with an introduction by Gerson D. Cohen), and *The Bible as Read and Preached in the Old Synagogue* (vol. 1, 1940; vol. 2, completed by Isaiah Sonne and Victor Reichert, 1966; reprint ed., KTAV, 1971, with a prologomenon by B. Z. Wacholder), are epochal contributions to Jewish scholarship.

Mann's basic building block for historical research was always the text. He continually searched for the telling literary remains of daily Jewish life—the contracts, deeds, rent receipts, booklists, business agreements, and writs of marriage and divorce. Yet he was never content with the mere recording and analyzing of this raw material, though in these activities he was at his best. His interest lay in weaving these details into broad historical patterns; and he succeeded in demonstrating the institutional interpenetration and the essential cultural unity of the Jews in the Moslem world. This achievement was not equaled in scope or magnitude until Goitein's *A Mediter-*

ranean Society (1967–). Mann's contribution remains an indispensable starting point for many aspects of medieval studies in Judaica.

Mann was not exciting as a teacher. A short, pudgy man whose feet barely touched the floor when he sat in his professorial chair, he delivered his lectures in seeming oblivion to his students, as he read endlessly and, many said, monotonously, from his notes. He rarely opened his classroom to questions and discussions. Yet when he did indulge in extempore expositions, the class was overwhelmed by his vast erudition. Everyone acknowledged that Mann was a giant in Jewish learning. He was thoroughly at home in the Talmud, Midrash, Commentaries, Codes, liturgy, and the philosophy of Judaism as well as its history. He was not only professor of history but also of Talmud at the College. One student, embellishing a sentiment commonly held among his classmates, even went so far as to declare "that Dr. Mann . . . knew enough to teach every course listed in the College catalogue except Cora Kahn's elocution classes." The last part of the statement was a humorous jab at Mann's distinctive accent, a Yiddish overlaid with a British tang, and an exaggerated broad *a* acquired in his London days.

Indelible though Mann's impression on historical studies at the College was, a far greater impact was exerted by his younger colleague, Jacob Rader Marcus. More than anyone else Marcus deserves credit for establishing history as a structured discipline and encouraging historical scholarship at the College. Marcus extended the areas of history taught at the College to cover nearly the entire gamut of Jewish experience. He was its first professor to emphasize the importance of the utilization of the latest techniques and methods for the teaching of history. He laid the foundation for the scientific study of Jewish history at the College through seminars in the methodology and theory of history and through a study of the relationship of history to other fields in the social sciences. He raised up numerous disciples and set the example of scholarly achievement by becoming the most prolific historian in the history of the College and one of the most prolific on the scene of American Jewry. Marcus was the first alumnus to become a professor of history at the College.

He was born in 1896 in Connellsville, Pennsylvania, and came to Cincinnati in 1911 to attend high school and simultaneously, as was then the custom, the Preparatory Department of the Hebrew Union College. Immediately upon his ordination in 1920 he was appointed an instructor in Bible and rabbinics. His initial teaching in history was limited to the biblical field. But when Gotthard Deutsch died in 1921, Marcus assumed responsibility for the entire history curriculum. Even during Mann's tenure, it was Marcus who set the guidelines for the history program.

At the time Marcus was interested primarily in the social and economic history of the Jews of the Middle Ages. In order to deepen his knowledge of the field he took a leave of absence in 1922 to pursue his studies in Europe. He received his Ph.D. degree in 1925, after defending a dissertation on "The Mercantile Relations between England and the Hanseatic League in the Years 1576–1585."

On his return, Marcus shared the teaching of the basic courses in history with Mann and developed a wide variety of elective offerings, outstanding among them his seminars on the bibliography and methodology of modern and contemporary Jewish history.

Even more impressive than his array of course offerings was the content that Marcus poured into them. Marcus was—and in his late seventies still is—a dynamic teacher. His preparation has always been flawless, his delivery exciting, his sense of humor refreshing. He has always been one of the most popular teachers on the campus. This popularity won him election to the presidency of the Central Conference of American Rabbis in 1949. What has always magnetized his students even more than his learning and his charm has been his deep interest in them as individuals and his desire to help each develop his potential.

In his teaching as in his scholarship, Marcus has been a stickler for precision. He believes that "knowledge, meticulous, painfully accurate, all embracing knowledge, leaves with it the power to create, to mold, to survive" (*The Quintessential American Jew*). Yet he has always viewed the details of history not as ends in themselves but instrumentally, and has always striven to transmute them into the living tissue of his students' lives.

During his early years at the College, Marcus was interested in medieval Jewish history and the history of German Jewry and Central European Jewry from the sixteenth to the nineteenth century. His first major work was a study on Israel Jacobson, the founder of Reform Judaism in Germany. Originally published in the *CCAR Yearbook* of 1928 and recently republished in book form, it is still the standard work on the subject. The year 1938 saw the appearance of

The Jew in the Medieval World, a collection of documents covering every facet of the life of medieval Jewry, judiciously organized in faithful and artistic translation. The same meticulous recourse to source material is evident in *The Rise and Destiny of the German Jew* (1934) and *Communal Sick-Care in the German Ghetto* (1947), the latter an enlightening study on the *hevra kaddisha,* the Jewish hospital, and other basal organizations of Jewish life.

No less reflective of Marcus's concern for a thorough knowledge of sources and bibliography are *A Brief Introduction to the Bibliography of American Jewish History* (1935), *The Index to Jewish Festschriften* (1937), and *An Index to Scientific Articles on American Jewish History* (1971).

As late as the dawn of the Nazi regime, Marcus had hoped for the survival of the German Jewish community. When its fate was sealed, he recognized that the center of world Jewry had shifted to the United States, and he turned his energies wholeheartedly to the history of American Jewry. His interest in American Jewish history had been growing progressively for a number of years and had revealed itself unmistakably in his Founder's Day address at the College in 1931. Entitled "The Americanization of Isaac Mayer Wise," it was a brief study of the passions and prejudices of Isaac Mayer Wise, and his love for the democratic principles of his adopted land.

This essay marked the inception of a tireless search for materials on American Jewish history and eventually, in 1947, the creation of the American Jewish Archives. The concept of the Archives was enthusiastically received by the American Jewish community, eager now more than ever to demonstrate its rootedness in America and contribution to its development.

As late as 1951, in the preface to the first volume of his *Early American Jewry,* Marcus still found it necessary to say,

> It is no more difficult today to write American Jewish history than it is to make bricks without clay. The clay, the sources, are still to be dug up. In this field there are no biographical or historical dictionaries, no atlases, no auxiliary works, few collected sources, no satisfactory union list of Jewish serials, no genealogical tables, not a single complete history of the American Jew that

satisfies the canons of modern methodology and criticism. The basic tools with which every historian works are still missing.

The American Jewish Archives has gone far toward the alleviation of this condition. Today the American Jewish Archives is one of the major centers for the study of American Jewish history. Its comprehensive collections, its judicious acquisitions, its superb cataloguing, and its competent staff have made possible the researches of numerous scholars. Today they are available for a new breed of American Jews, less concerned with the apologetic establishment of their American roots than with the study of Jewish identity and Judaic devotion.

One of the most important contributories in this regard has been the journal, the *American Jewish Archives.* Marcus founded the publication and has been its editor ever since.

From his newly found literary wealth Marcus began to publish some of the most important of the primary sources for American Jewish history. Part of the fruit of these labors is seen in his two-volume pioneering study, *Early American Jewry* (1951–55), and the impressive *American Jewry: Documents: Eighteenth Century* (1959). In these collections, Marcus focuses on the role played by individual Jews in American life without losing sight of broader social, political, and intellectual currents.

These and other studies by Marcus have filled a number of gaping lacunae. His research has led him to the publication of countless monographs, additional memoirs, and, most recently, a monumental and definitive three-volume work, *The Colonial American Jew* (1970). Through his own life and experience, Marcus exemplifies the development of Jewish consciousness and institutions in America in the late nineteenth and twentieth centuries. His own living contact with this history and his broad grasp of the currents of contemporary Jewish life have strengthened Marcus's faith in the vitality and potentialities of American Jewry. He believes that in America the Jew can develop a distinctive Jewish life consonant with his needs and aspirations. Above all, he recognizes the historical necessity and the importance of an autonomous Jewish culture in America, covalent and complementary with that of Israel.

With the growth of the American Jewish Archives and the extension of its activities, Dr. Marcus began to search for an associate to assume the responsibility for the instructional program in history.

His quest led him to a young scholar from Baltimore named Ellis Rivkin.

Rivkin had studied and later taught at the Baltimore Hebrew College, where he came under the influence of Louis Kaplan, Cyrus Gordon, and Harry M. Orlinsky. He also completed his doctorate in medieval and Renaissance history at Johns Hopkins University and mastered the rigorous techniques of historical methodology under Frederick C. Lane. At the time Marcus met him, Rivkin was teaching at Gratz College in Philadelphia and pursuing postdoctoral studies under Solomon Zeitlin at Dropsie College.

Rivkin began teaching at the College in 1949 and immediately became a favorite of the students. From the moment of his arrival he fired their imagination by his irrepressible enthusiasm and scintillating lectures, which displayed not only broad historical knowledge but penetrating insights into human nature. The students sensed in Rivkin the rare combination of academic discipline and Jewish devotion that had already endeared Marcus to two generations of their predecessors. There was another element in Rivkin that magnetized the students. Rivkin was a product of orthodox upbringing and was at the time rethinking his theology and practice, struggling for a new synthesis with academic integrity and religious commitment.

Rivkin's fields of concentration and his doctoral dissertation, later developed in his book *Leon Da Modena and the Kol Sakhal,* brought him into contact with the multifaceted world, Jewish and general, of sixteenth-century Europe. His researches in this field have led to the publication of various monographs on the Renaissance, including one on the sermons of Leon Da Modena and a pioneering contribution to Inquisition studies, entitled "The Utilization of Non-Jewish Sources for the Reconstruction of Jewish History" (*JQR,* XLVIII [1957–58], 183–203).

On arriving at the College, Rivkin immediately assumed responsibility for the entire gamut of its history courses and seminars, from the biblical to the modern period, except for those in American Jewish history. These Marcus retained and enriched with source material from the Archives. Rivkin also began offering seminars in Jewish history from the Renaissance to modern times, Jewish historiography, and, gradually, the period of the Second Commonwealth, where he focused increasingly on the knotty problem of the identity of the Pharisees. Applying rigorous canons of historical research, he strove for a coherent reconstruction of the sparse and scattered data, free from the theological or apologetic bias that informs most of the secondary sources on the subject. The fruit of this labor has been a spate of studies, including the recent methodical exposition of the entire problem, entitled "Defining the Pharisees: The Tannaitic Sources" (*HUCA,* XL–XLI [1969–70], 205–49). Even more important, Rivkin has been preparing a monumental study of the Pharisees, to be called *The Hidden Revolution,* which bids fair to become the definitive resolution of the problems in this area.

No less important has been Rivkin's impact as a theorist, or more correctly, a philosopher of Jewish history. While never neglecting the specifics of the Jewish experience, Rivkin has focused particularly on its changing contours and configurations. Like his predecessors at the College, he has recognized the inextricability of Jewish history from the pattern of world experience, and has painstakingly plotted not only the interplay of the Jewish and non-Jewish worlds, but also its philosophical and even theological significance. The broader canvas of Jewish experience is discernible in all of Rivkin's works, but a number are devoted specifically to this question. This strand of Rivkin's activity has culminated in a heralded major book entitled *The Shaping of Jewish History: A Radical New Interpretation* (1971). This work contains a sweeping panorama of the highlights of Jewish history, identifying its root principles, and relating them in a crescendo of increasing breadth to the complex structures of the modern world. Central to all of these is what Rivkin calls the unity concept or unity principle.

"The problems of Jewish history," he says, "can be understood by means of the unity concept. . . . Each successive form of Jewish history represents a solution to problems posed to the idea of unity by changing historical circumstances. The unity concept became the source and justification for variation and even radical transmutation of Jewish life. Commitment to unity did not breed repetitive conformity, but creative diversity."

Rivkin had already presented the major contours of this unity principle in his book *The Dynamics of Jewish History* (1970). He clearly expressed its implications in a paper entitled "Judaism and History," first given at the international colloquium on religion and published in *Civilizations* (1957, vol. 4). Here he says,

History is a process which appears to move towards a larger and larger unity, a greater and greater complexity, a higher and higher differentiation. . . . In the midst of disunity these processes in their very ebb and flow are driving towards a world unity that generates diversity and yet comprehends it; that daringly innovates, yet selectively preserves; that demands equality, yet rejects conformity; that, above all, evaluates all that is on the basis of dedication to life and its optimal expression in creativity and love. To the extent that we understand the processes and their direction, to that extent do we participate in the achievement of that Unity.

Like Marcus, Rivkin has been instrumental in the preparation of valuable materials for the teaching of Jewish history. He conceived of an entire library containing in English translation classics of Jewish history in languages other than Hebrew. To date, this collection includes such material as Uriel da Costa's *Example of a Human Life,* Bruno Bauer's *On the Jewish Question,* and *The Transactions of the Napoleonic Sanhedrin.*

It is no small tribute to the combined inspiration of Marcus and Rivkin that at present three professors of history at the College-Institute chose to do the bulk of their doctoral work in their department.

One of these, Stanley F. Chyet, at the Cincinnati School, now serves as professor of American Jewish history and associate director of the American Jewish Archives. A native of Boston and a product of the Boston Latin School and Brandeis University, Chyet displayed unusual writing skills and archival patience while yet a student at the College. These qualities were strikingly blended in his master's and rabbinic dissertation entitled "Ludwig Lewisohn: The Years of Becoming." In 1957 an essay based on this study took first prize in a competition sponsored by the New Haven, Connecticut, Jewish Community Center Library. It was published by the *American Jewish Archives* in 1959.

From the time of his ordination in 1957, Chyet has been officially associated with the Archives, where he has helped Dr. Marcus in its multifaceted program of expansion and service, and in the editorship of its publications. Yet at the same time he has neglected neither his own research nor his devotion to his teaching. In 1970 he published a definitive biography of Aaron Lopez entitled *Lopez of Newport*. In addition, he has contributed essays on American Jewish history, including a number on Lewisohn, to numerous learned journals. He has also edited such works as Lewisohn's *The Island Within* and, most recently, a fine collection of nine memoirs of American Jews of the nineteenth and twentieth centuries entitled *Lives and Voices*. He has taught seminars on research problems and methodology of American Jewish history at the College, some together with Professor Marcus, and for several years offered the course on medieval Jewish history at the College. In 1971 he helped inaugurate an area of specialization on the Cincinnati campus known as contemporary studies. In recent years Chyet's interests have turned increasingly to history-in-progress and to a study of contemporary American Jewish and Israeli literature as vital factors in this history. An important study entitled "Three Generations: An Account of American Jewish Fiction (1896–1969)" appeared in the January 1972 issue of the *Jewish Social Studies*.

The second is Michael A. Meyer. Born in Germany under the Nazi regime, Meyer came to the United States as a child and was educated at the University of California at Los Angeles and at the Hebrew Union College–Jewish Institute of Religion in Cincinnati. Meyer's interests have understandably dwelled upon the heritage of German Jewry, and he has devoted himself to its elucidation. Among his many monographs of note are his analysis of the "Great Debate on Anti-Semitism: Jewish Reaction to New Hostility in Germany 1879–1881," published in *Year Book XI* of the Leo Baeck Institute (1966), pp. 137–70, and his study of "Christian Influence on Early Reform Judaism," in *Studies in Jewish Bibliography, History and Literature in Honor of I. Edward Kiev*, edited by Charles Berlin (X, 1971), pp. 289–303. Most noteworthy is his first book, entitled *The Origins of the Modern Jew: Jewish Identity and European Culture in Germany, 1749–1824* (1967), which won the prize for Jewish thought of the National Jewish Welfare Board in 1969. Meyer's work contains a delineation of personalities like Moses Mendelssohn, David Friedlander, and Leopold Zunz, as well as a depiction of the intellectual impact of the Enlightenment on Jewish thought. Meyer has recently produced an outstanding anthology, entitled *Ideas of Jewish History* (New York, 1974), with a substantial introduction and useful notes.

The third of these doctorates, Martin A. Cohen, has been teaching as professor of Jewish history at the New York School of the College-Institute.

During the course of the years other courses in history at the Cincinnati school have been given by professors of Bible or Talmud or by part-time professors who have also served as administrators or librarians.

Outstanding within this group was Professor Isaiah Sonne (1887–1960), born in Galicia and educated in Switzerland, Italy, and the Collegio Rabbinico at Florence. He came to the College in 1940 as a librarian, and was soon asked to offer courses in history.

Like Professor Mann before him, Sonne was a specialist in both rabbinic literature and Jewish history, and a man of encyclopedic interests. His writings include studies on Spinoza, Uriel da Costa, Immanuel of Rome, Judah Abravanel, Leon da Modena, and Shabbetai Zevi; on the Dead Sea Scrolls, Jewish music, the *piyyutim,* and the paintings of the Dura Synagogue. He composed a work in Hebrew entitled *Avnei Binyan leToledot ha-Yehudim beItalyah* (Sources for the History of the Jews in Italy) (1938–40). Like Professor Mann, Sonne could also assemble and trace the most recondite details. In class he would frequently spend several weeks on one paragraph of text, discussing the parallels and ramifications of every statement.

Sonne had great difficulty expressing himself in English and much preferred to speak Hebrew or Italian, but he always managed to overcome linguistic barriers in his incandescent controversies with other leading scholars on the fine points of Jewish history.

The New York School

Like the Hebrew Union College in its beginnings a half-century earlier, the Jewish Institute of Religion opened in 1922 with a modest program in history. This program was announced for the first time in the catalogue for the academic year 1924–25. It showed only two courses, each meeting two hours per semester. One course covered Jewish history to the destruction of the Second Temple; the other brought it down to modern times. Only one year of history was required of the students. The redeeming feature of the program lay in the fact that the course in Jewish history after the destruction of the Temple in Jerusalem was taught by a thirty-seven-year-old scholar of exceptional promise named Harry Austryn Wolfson, who enthralled the students with his problem-oriented approach to history. Wolfson was always interested in the why of historical phenomena. With his penetrating philosophical mind he sought to fathom the logic of historical causation, to the great delight and edification of his listeners. From 1923 to 1926 the course in biblical history was taught by a shy and retiring young English scholar named Ruben Levy, who was to make his mark on the scholarly world after leaving the school with his works on the sociology of Islam and the Persian language and literature.

This modest, if excellent, program was somewhat enriched by Stephen S. Wise's policy of inviting renowned scholars to give special lecture series in their respective disciplines at the Institute. A number of these series dealt with Jewish history, though they tended to concentrate on the rabbinic period and the relationship of Judaism to Christianity. In the early years of the Institute these presentations included R. Travers Herford's stimulating lectures on *Pirke Aboth* in 1925, the series entitled "The Evolution of Christianity in the First Three Centuries," by Kirsopp Lake, then professor of ecclesiastical history at Harvard, during the academic year of 1923–24, and seven lectures on "Judaism and Primitive Christianity," offered the following November by J. F. Foakes Jackson, the Briggs Graduate Professor of Christian Institutions at the Union Theological Seminary. Only one series of lectures touched in any way on the Jewish experience in modern times. That was Israel Abrahams' on "The Jewish Worthies of the Nineteenth Century," offered in the year 1923–24.

Yet for all the luster that such extraordinary lectures shed upon the Institute, Stephen Wise could not have helped but discern the limitations of a program dependent on change and insusceptible to systematization. By 1924 he was clearly planning to create a permanent chair in Jewish history. He had already narrowed his consideration to two young European scholars of unusual promise. Though both had a comprehensive interest in Jewish history, their specialities at the time lay in medieval and early modern Jewish history. One of these was an Englishman, Cecil Roth. He was only twenty-four when Wise considered him, but he had already published a number of significant studies in Judaica, and the first of his many books was about to go to press.

The other, Salo W. Baron, only slightly older, already possessed a distinguished record. He held a rabbinical degree and doctorates in philosophy, jurisprudence, and political science, and was teaching at the Pedagogium in Vienna. Roth's forte lay in the Romanic languages. Baron knew the Germanic tongues. He also had a thorough command of Hebrew and could lecture in that language.

Wise decided to extend an invitation to each to be a visiting lecturer during the academic year 1925–26. He invited Roth for the fall semester and Baron for the spring, without apparently making it clear to them that they were competing with one another. Roth offered courses in Jewish historiography, the settlement of the Jews in Europe, and the history of the Jews in Italy. Baron's program included courses on the Jews in medieval Europe from the ninth to the thirteenth century, the economic history of the Jews in the Middle Ages, and the Jews in the sixteenth and seventeenth centuries.

Both men brought welcome currents of fresh air into the Institute. Trained in Europe in secular history and historical methodology, they were able to analyze the Jewish experience not only in its literary and religious manifestations but from the sociological, economic, and political perspectives as well. In addition to being stunningly erudite and disciplined scholars, they were dynamic lecturers, capable of communicating their passion for their work and igniting interest in the students.

Stephen Wise opted for Baron. Rumor has it that Roth's eccentricities influenced Wise against him. But it also appears that Roth antagonized some of the influential people connected with the Institute. Roth apparently did not think so. He felt throughout the rest of his life that his visiting lectureship should have led to a permanent appointment. As a result, Roth always harbored a smoldering dislike for Stephen Wise.

No sooner was Salo Baron appointed, first as lecturer and subsequently as professor, than he began to develop a systematic program of offerings for the history department. He initiated students into Jewish history with a year-long survey of the entire field, and then, in succeeding years, led them to such areas as the Jewish historiography of the sixteenth century, the history of the Jews in the period of revolution and reaction from 1789 to 1848, and contemporary Jewish history. Baron also offered seminars on historical methodology. His course on the Book of Kings represented the first attempt at the Institute to deal with political, economic, social, and intellectual history during the biblical period.

Combined with his broad knowledge, Baron's organizational ability made him a natural choice in 1928 to be chairman of a newly developed Department of Advanced Studies at the Institute. Baron was able to inspire large numbers of students to write their dissertations in history. After completing their work at the College-Institute many of these, including Irving Levitats and Herbert I. Bloom, proceeded to postgraduate work and Ph.D. degrees at other universities.

The arrival of Chaim Tchernowitz to offer courses in the development of the Talmud and *halakha,* Ralph Marcus to teach Hellenistic Judaism, and Julian J. Obermann to offer systematic analyses of biblical history, enhanced the field of history and gave it a position of dominance at the Institute. Marcus' offerings were eventually incorporated formally into the history department, and Baron himself added a course on "The Talmud as a Source of History." Baron also served as acting director of the library.

In 1930 Baron accepted a professorship in Jewish history at Columbia University, the first such chair at an American university. He remained on at the Institute through the fall term of 1936 as visiting professor of history and director of the Department of Advanced Studies.

When Baron left the Institute, the responsibility for the entire department fell on the shoulders of a young and gifted teacher named John J. Tepfer. Tepfer was born in London, England, into a famous Hasidic family. His great-grandfather was the Belzer Rebbe, and young Tepfer was nurtured on Hasidic lore and practice. He took his intermediate B.A. degree at London University, studied Talmud privately with the renowned Rabbi Abraham Abba Werner of *Mahzike Ha-Das,* and then at Jews' College. Arriving in the United States in 1922, he studied at Temple University, then at the University of Pennsylvania, receiving a master's degree in economics in 1924. He then taught economics for a year at the University of Pennsylvania before Professor Isaac Husik recommended him to Stephen S. Wise. Tepfer then came to the Jewish Institute of Religion, where he was ordained in the class of 1927. He returned to the Institute as a graduate fellow, but studied primarily in the Department of Semitics at Columbia University under Richard Gottheil. As his dissertation, he began the study of the known manuscripts of Sambari's Chronicle.

At the Institute, Tepfer was Baron's associate in the history department for several years. He taught a course entitled "Readings, His-

torical Sources and Historiographical Material" as a supplement to
Dr. Baron's course in "Method and Historiography." He was gradually entrusted with other courses, including the general survey of
Jewish history and the history of the Jews during the Second Commonwealth. He soon also offered a seminar in methodology and a
survey of the history of the Jews in Poland, an area to which he was
attracted by his own background and interests.

In the academic year 1937–38 he was joined by Dr. Guido Kisch,
a renowned and much published professor of law who had taught at
several leading universities in Germany before the advent of the
Nazis. Kisch was invited by Wise to the Jewish Institute of Religion
as a visiting professor.

Kisch's lengthy paper on "The Jewry-Law of the Medieval German Law Books," read before the American Academy of Jewish
Research in 1935 (published in the *PAJR,* VII [1935–36], 61–145),
formed the foundation for a massive work entitled *The Jews in
Medieval Germany: A Study of Their Legal and Social Status,* first
published in 1949 (reprint ed., New York, KTAV, 1970). It also
marked the inception of Kisch's prolific productivity in America. His
interests were far-ranging. His works include "Studies in the History
of Jew-Hatred in the Middle Ages," "The Jews' Function in the
Medieval Evolution of Economic Life," "Relations between Jewish
and Christian Courts in the Middle Ages," "A Fourteenth Century
Jewry Oath of South Germany," "The Yellow Badge in History,"
and numerous others. Many of Kisch's studies appeared in *Historia
Judaica,* a journal of high quality founded by him in 1938 and edited
by him until its merger with the *Revue des Études Juives* in 1962.
Kisch has remained on the editorial board of the merged journal as
co-editor. Interestingly, Kisch was also editor-in-chief of a Chinese-
Jewish encyclopedia in the late forties. The encyclopedia, however,
never saw the light of day. In addition, Kisch's wide range of interest
can be seen in the fact that he has collected and written on numerous
other subjects, from Czechoslovakian Jewry to medallic art.

On arriving at the College Kisch announced two year-long courses,
one an advanced seminar on the legal status of the Jews of Germany
during the Middle Ages, the other a survey of the legal, social, and
economic history of the Jews from the late Middle Ages to the beginning of the nineteenth century.

Kisch retained the rank of visiting professor until after the Jewish

Institute of Religion merged with the Hebrew Union College, at which time he was given a regular professorial appointment.

Kisch shared the responsibilities of teaching history with Tepfer. He continued his concentration on medieval and modern central European Jewish history. He offered seminars on Jewry-law and Zionism and taught the research course for all students preparing dissertations in the history department. He also taught a course on the sociology of the Jews beginning with the Emancipation.

Kisch and Tepfer complemented each other in many ways and together formed a strong department. Both are methodical scholars, scrupulous with details and scientific in their presentation. Each had a myriad of facts at his fingertips, and each was sensitive to the modern ramifications of the discipline of history. But there the comparison ends. Kisch was primarily a writing scholar. His effectiveness in class was always hampered by his slow and measured delivery, doubtless due somewhat to the fact that English is not his native tongue. He has written continually and almost compulsively and, as witnessed by his recent works on the Jews of Czechoslovakia, his productivity has not decreased since his retirement in 1958.

Tepfer, on the other hand, has been the teacher par excellence, one of the most eloquent, provocative, and challenging in the history of the College-Institute. He has written comparatively little. But he has spent his life mastering the widest variety of disciplines—Bible, Talmud and Hasidism, history, economics, and philosophy, and English and foreign literature—and has acquired an almost encyclopedic knowledge.

Tepfer never taught merely the courses he announced. Even during the years preceding his retirement as dean of the New York School of the College-Institute, he would always conduct additional sessions of assigned classes. He even created special classes to discuss problems of history and Talmud that could not be covered fully in the prescribed curriculum. For years he has been giving noncredit courses during the summers. In these courses he has always managed to bring students back to his lectures week after week and to elicit serious work from them. He has even given seminars to junior members of the faculty. Despite his official retirement in 1962, Tepfer continues to teach several courses and to meet privately with students and occasionally with faculty for special seminars.

Tepfer is a congenital iconoclast, yet his iconoclasm is constructive rather than wanton. Across the years his students have come to see in his critiques of Hasidism and Reform Judaism or the structures and patterns of Jewish contemporary life a combination of objective scientific method on the one hand, and on the other a passionate commitment to the creation of a learned American Judaism. His interest is to build a Judaism weaned from superstition and hero-worship and superior to internal divisiveness.

After Kisch's retirement, the New York School had no full-time professor in history for four years. Occasionally students humorously referred to this period as "The Great Hiatus" or even "The Great Interregnum." The gaps left by Kisch were filled by various visiting professors, including Samuel Kurland of Dropsie College, a specialist in medieval history and philosophy, and various instructors from other departments of the College, such as Rabbi Jack Bemporad, then teaching philosophy, and Dr. Arie Kahana, a specialist in rabbinics.

In 1962 Martin A. Cohen, then on the Cincinnati faculty, transferred to New York to assume responsibility for the history courses.

Cohen is a native of Philadelphia and a graduate of the University of Pennsylvania, where he came under the influence of the late John L. LaMonte, the Henry C. Lea professor of medieval history. This influence, combined with work in Romance languages, made him gravitate toward West European studies at the College-Institute. There, inspired by Professors Marcus and Rivkin, he concentrated on Renaissance and Inquisition studies. These have resulted in such works as his edition and translation of *Samuel Usque's Consolation for the Tribulations of Israel* (1965) and most recently *The Martyr* (1973) and his two-volume anthology, *The Jewish Experience in Latin America*, as well as other studies in Sephardica.

Cohen has equally been interested in political history and the relationship of ideas to institutions. His studies in biblical history on "The Shilonite Priesthood" and "The Rebellions during the Reign of David," applying social-scientific methodology to biblical research, are increasingly referred to. He has applied similar structural approaches to such subjects as "The Hasmonean Revolution Politically Reconsidered," "The Text and Context of the Disputation of Barcelona," and "Four Notes on Anan ben David."

At the New York School Cohen has offered various seminars in Second Commonwealth, medieval and Renaissance Jewish history, and Jewish historiography. He has also taught the required courses, except for American Jewish history.

The courses in this area have been taught by Bertram W. Korn. Dr. Korn was a full-time member of the College faculty as a professor of history and assistant to the president. In the years since he left full-time teaching at the College for the congregational rabbinate, Korn has achieved a wide reputation as a scholar, producing books such as *American Jewry and the Civil War* (1951), *Eventful Years and Experiences: Studies in American Jewish History* (1954), *The American Reaction to the Mortara Case* 1858–1859 (1957), and *The Early Jews of New Orleans* (1969). Most recently he has published an important pamphlet entitled *German-Jewish Intellectual Influences on American Jewish Life (1824–1972)*.

In these works, and in a host of other studies, he continues to manifest the theoretical and practical training of his mentor, as well as his own original gifts in shaping available facts into compelling narratives. Like Marcus, Korn is an original thinker and an indefatigable researcher who believes in giving his students the practical experience that comes from working with primary documentary evidence, such as journals, minute books, and private correspondence. Despite the limited time he can devote to the College, he has inspired a number of commendable dissertations. One of them, Reeve Brenner's thesis on the response of American Jewish organizations to the rise of the Third Reich, recently won first prize in a competition sponsored by YIVO.

Despite the focus of his interest on American Jewry, Korn has never failed to conceive of American Judaism as an integral part of a greater, indissoluble unity. He sees the history of the American Jews as an integral part of the mainstream of Jewish history and optimistically regards the will to survival of the Jewish people as capable of overcoming the loss of Jewish identity on the part of its assimilated numbers.

That the College-Institute has a history of outstanding historians and excellent programs in the field of history is a proposition that requires no defense. But as the historians of the College-Institute have always believed, past history is merely a prologue to the future. It may well be that the future will be even brighter than the past.

History, and more broadly, the social sciences in general, have been gaining status on the academic scene. Increasingly the world and its productivity of both matter and thought are being scanned by the light provided by these disciplines. The problems of the contemporary world have not only thrust social scientists, historians, sociologists, political scientists, and economists to the fore, but they have also catapulted the philosophers in these areas to unprecedented productivity.

It may be that the time has come for the College-Institute to provide, through the history department, the long-needed umbrella under which to structure its entire curriculum, in this way creating a point of reference for the proper study of the complexity of the Jewish experience.

EZRA SPICEHANDLER

Hebrew and Hebrew Literature

THE ROLE WHICH MODERN HEBREW PLAYED AND PLAYS IN BOTH THE
curriculum of the Hebrew Union College and the scholarly concern of
its faculty is a function of the changing attitudes toward Hebrew within
the Jewish world in general and the Reform movement in particular.

Modern Hebrew literature first served as the literary vehicle of
the *Haskalah* (the Jewish Enlightenment movement), which began
at the end of the eighteenth century and reached its zenith during
the nineteenth century. The *Haskalah* advocated the reformation of
Jewish social, cultural, and religious life so that Jews might be integrated into the modern era. Historically, the German Reform movement was also a product of the *Haskalah*. Although some of its leaders
and scholars rejected the more blatant Hebraism of many East
European *maskilim*, others retained a deep affection for the Hebrew
language.

In its so-called classical phase, American Reform Judaism's attitude
toward the Hebrew language was ambivalent. On the one hand, it
considered Hebrew as the cultural language of the "obscurantist"
Jewish *ancien regime*, rejected it as the main language of Jewish
prayer, and replaced it, to a great extent, with the English vernacular.

[*453*]

However, even those who favored anglicization of the prayerbook never viewed the Hebrew language with the uneasy disdain which they had for Yiddish. Hebrew was, after all, the language of the Bible and Jewish learning. Even the non-Jewish world considered Hebrew to be a classical language, and the opinion of non-Jews affected the attitudes of Reform Jews. Many Reform rabbis and scholars also evinced a deep feeling of veneration for both the language of Jewish tradition and the *Haskalah*. This feeling was usually not extended to embrace the rising nationalism of either the *Hibbat Zion* movement or Herzlian Zionism.

Isaac Mayer Wise's views reflect this ambivalence. Although he favored the settlement of Jews in Palestine in pre-Zionist days, he consistently opposed political Zionism. Yet at the same time, he expressed a deep and sympathetic interest in modern Hebrew letters. He not only subscribed to several Hebrew periodicals, but supported their publication in both Europe and America. He also applauded the revival of modern Hebrew in Palestine.[1]

On several significant occasions rabbis and professors penned paeans and broadsides in Hebrew in honor of Wise.[2] S. B. Schwarzburg, the editor of *Ner Ma'aravi*, the sole Hebrew periodical then published in America, lauded Wise for his moral and financial support.

> Dr. Wise, whose greatest enemies would not dare accuse him of dishonesty or love of flattery . . . eagerly supports the *Ner Ma'aravi*. Four times he wrote in his magazine, *The American Israelite*, ardent words . . . urging our people in the United States to support our project. . . . We shall never forget our debt to him. . . . The sublime words which he uttered on behalf of *Ner Ma'aravi* testify that Dr. Wise loves our tongue. . . .[3]

Wise praised A. M. Luncz, the blind Jerusalem geographer, and Eliezer Ben Yehudah, who had begun working on his later famous dictionary.[4]

I. The Early Years

Despite Wise's attitude, no courses in modern Hebrew were offered at the College until the year prior to his death in 1900. The introduction of modern Hebrew to the curriculum can probably be attributed to the growing influence in the faculty of Gotthard Deutsch, who assisted Moses Mielziener when the latter served as interim president of the College between 1901 and 1903, and who was appointed acting president during the academic year 1902–3. Deutsch, as we shall see, was a warm supporter of the new Hebrew literature.

Caspar Levias, one of the more active Hebraists on the faculty, taught the new subject. Levias selected *Ha-Zofeh Leveth Yisra'el*, Isaac Erter's collection of *Haskalah* satires, as his text for the first two grades of the Preparatory Department.[5] Erter's barbs were aimed against the *Hasidim* and *Mithnagdim* of his day, and called for radical social and religious reforms in Eastern Europe. The following year, he also offered readings from Taviov's *Sifruth Yisra'el* to "B" grade and selections from 'Ahad Ha-'Am's *Al Parashat Derakhim* to the "A" grade.[6] These texts contained Cultural Zionist views which still appeal to Reform Jews in our times.

The initiation of instruction in modern Hebrew was hailed by A. B. Rhine in an editorial in the *HUC Journal*.

The course of readings in neo-Hebraic literature in Hebrew Union College promises the most gratifying results. The study of Modern Hebrew is essential to an American Jewish theological student. By means of it he can enter into intellectual association with his coreligionists, can appreciate their ideals and aspirations, study their ways of life, their weltanschauung and their attitudes toward Jewish questions. . . . students of the HUC, let us study Modern Hebrew![7]

The introduction of modern Hebrew was also undoubtedly influenced by the increasing number of *hovevei sefat 'ever* on the College faculty. These included not only such "Germans" as Gotthard Deutsch and S. M. Mannheimer, but a growing number of East European scholars.

Gotthard Deutsch, who taught Jewish history at the College from 1891 until his death in 1921, was fervent in his advocacy of modern Hebrew literature. Deutsch's attitude toward Zionism altered during the course of years, shifting from initial hostility to guarded support.[8] However, his love for the Hebrew language was constant. During the long period in which he served as chairman of the Central Conference's committee on contemporaneous history, he stressed the significance of modern Hebrew literature and advocated financial assistance to several Hebrew writers. He hailed the achievements of Abraham Mapu, Micah Josef Lebensohn, and Kalman Schulman,[9] noted the death of Judah Steinberg, Joshua Bershadsky,[10] Gershon Rosenzweig,[11] Peretz,[12] Sholom Aleichem,[13] Mendele,[14] Ben Avigdor, and Berdichevski,[15] and recommended stipends for scholarly projects undertaken by A. M. Luncz[16] and Judah David Eisenstein.[17] He also urged the Conference to underwrite the publication of one of the volumes of Ben Yehudah's dictionary.[18] It was probably Deutsch who extended the invitation to Reuben Brainin to address the Conference in Hebrew shortly after the latter arrived in the United States in 1921. Brainin in turn expressed warm admiration for Deutsch.[19] Deutsch published several articles in modern Hebrew, both in American as well as European periodicals, and contributed articles to *'Oẓar Yisra'el,* the Hebrew encyclopedia published by J. D. Eisenstein. During the First World War he discontinued writing his diary in German and shifted to Hebrew instead.[20]

S. M. Mannheimer, who taught at the College from 1884 to 1904, praised 'Aḥad Ha-'Am's *Ha-Shiloah* in an early number of the *HUC Journal.* "We must admire," he wrote, "the enthusiasm of these writers who with such zeal and perseverance cultivate the field of Hebrew literature and secure the tongue a permanent place among the living languages. . . . a periodical like *Ha-Shiloaḥ* should find hundreds, yea thousands of subscribers in our country. Even those of our wealthy coreligionists who are not able to read Hebrew books and periodicals should feel the obligation of joining the ranks of subscribers. . . ." He then added a plea for the support of *Ner Ma'aravi.*[21]

Caspar Levias was one of the more active Hebraists on the Cincinnati faculty. Born in Lithuania, he received his doctorate in Semitics at Columbia and was appointed to the faculty in 1895. At Bialik's behest, he published his major work, *Diqduq 'Aramith Bavlith,* in Hebrew.[22] Levias contributed many articles in the field of Hebrew philology to several Hebrew periodicals, and he conceived the idea of editing a linguistic dictionary of the Hebrew language, of which, unfortunately, only one volume appeared. For many years, Bialik tried to publish the remainder, but was unable to raise the funds to finance the project. Bialik also accepted the manuscript of Levias's Hebrew medical dictionary, but never succeeded in financing its publication. He referred to both works in a letter to J. L. Magnes as being "two marvelous lexicons. One of them has been in my hands for several years and includes a large and marvelous thesaurus of medical terms found in our literature from Biblical times . . . until our own." [23] Levias was also a pioneer in the developing of modern grammatical terminology in Hebrew, although most of his innovations are no longer in use.[24]

Another Hebraist and Zionist in those early years was Henry Malter, who came to Cincinnati in 1900. A native Galician, he studied at the *Hochschule* in Berlin and soon joined the literary circle associated with 'Aḥad Ha-'Am and the *Aḥi 'asaf* publishing house. Later, he also was a member of the "young writers" group led by Micah Joseph Berdichevski. Throughout his career, Malter published many articles in modern Hebrew. Like Deutsch, he was a contributor to Eisenstein's *'Oẓar Yisra'el*. While still in Europe, he published articles on medieval Jewish philosophy in the major Hebrew periodicals.[25] He translated Steinschneider's *Jüdische Literatur* into Hebrew, thoroughly updating the notes,[26] and edited a Hebrew translation of a work by Alghazali, adding a Hebrew commentary.[27]

The eminent biblical scholar Max Margolis, who taught at the College from 1892 to 1897, and 1905 to 1907, was a committed Hebraist and Zionist who published many articles in the Hebrew press.[28] In the wake of the famous controversy over Zionism, he resigned from the College in 1907, together with Malter and several other colleagues, and moved to Dropsie College. Later he was appointed visiting professor of Bible at the Hebrew University.

The most prominent among the Hebraists at the college during the first quarter of this century was David Neumark, who served as professor of Jewish philosophy from 1908 to 1922. He was another of the many *ḥakhmai Galiẓiyah* who were prominent at the Cincinnati School.[29] Long before his appointment in 1907, he had won great esteem in Hebrew literary circles. While in Berlin, he too became a close associate of 'Aḥad Ha-'Am, who had selected him to serve as divisional editor for Jewish philosophy of *'Oẓar Ha-Yahaduth*, the projected Hebrew encyclopedia.[30] 'Aḥad Ha-'Am and Neumark would later differ on the role of religion in modern Jewish life.[31] Neumark contributed articles on Jewish philosophy and on social literary problems to almost all the leading Hebrew journals of the period. His major work, *Toledoth ha-Filosofiah be-Yisra'el,* was written in modern Hebrew.[32]

Both 'Aḥad Ha-'Am and Bialik credited Neumark with introducing "the new national spirit" at the Hebrew Union College.[33] For many years, Zionists and Hebraists in the student body looked to him as their mentor. In Cincinnati he founded the *Ivriah*, the local Hebrew-speaking society, which has survived to this date. The Hebrew Club at the Cincinnati campus was named in his honor.[34]

Mention should also be made of Judah L. Magnes's role as a Zionist and Hebraist member of the faculty. After obtaining his doctorate in Germany, Magnes was appointed as both librarian and instructor in rabbinic exegesis in 1903. His personal magnetism and his romantic Zionist views had a marked effect upon a large number of students.[35]

The Zionist-Hebraist ferment at the College in the early years of this century finds expression in the comparatively large space devoted to articles on modern Hebrew subjects in the old *Hebrew Union College Annual* (1904). Meyer Lovitch wrote on "Isaac Erter, His Life and Works," [36] Nathan Gordin on "Joseph Perl's *Megalleh Tmirin*,"[37] and Judah Magnes on "Some Poems of H. N. Bialik."[38] This was the first article on Bialik's work to appear in English. The two men became close friends.

Magnes's romantic enthusiasm over Hebrew is typical of the attitude of many of his contemporaries.

In every Jewish cultural revival the Hebrew language has played an important part and today, when the Jewish nation is again witness of the marvel of its own renaissance, when like the old tree in the spring time, it is shooting forth new cultural blossoms, the Hebrew language is again fulfilling its mission as the national vehicle through which young Judah expresses his fears and hopes.[39]

With the increase in the number of East European rabbinical students at the College, frequent articles on modern Hebrew literature began to appear in the *HUC Journal*.[40] Abraham Rhine wrote about M. H. Mane [41] and about the *Ma'asef*.[42] Rhine would later publish a first-rate work on J. L. Gordon, an expansion of his rabbinical thesis.[43]

Rhine's introduction to his book on Gordon is indicative of the growing desire of American Jews of "Russian" origin to receive recognition as cultural equals of the "Germans" and to claim for themselves a place in the history of the struggle for emancipation:

The study of this period . . . will come in the nature of a revelation to the reader to whom the Hebrew language is a *terra incognita*. It will unfold . . . a tale of the struggle between the old order of things and the new, between medievalism and modernity. . . . He will meet with men of power and of genius . . . whose life was a constant battle in behalf of enlightenment and civilization. Incidentally, a study of nineteenth century Hebrew literature cannot but tend to raise the Russian Jew in the estimation of his American brother, and bring about a clearer understanding between them, which will inevitably result in closer fellowship and a firmer tie of sympathy.[44]

Max Raisin began editing a special section of the *Journal* entitled "Hebraica" in December 1900, and gave his own rationale for the revived interest in modern Hebrew literature.

No other Jewish periodical conducts a department of this kind. . . . the intention is to acquaint my fellow students with one of the most interesting phenomena in the Jewish world, the revival of the old Hebrew language and the rise of a new Hebrew literature based on the ruins [sic] of the Biblical, Talmudical and Rabbinical literature. . . . this literature is nowadays the great link which connects hundreds of thousands of our coreligionists in Russia, Galicia, Palestine, and even America, and is the great factor which moulds and shapes their spiritual life and inspires them with that great and lofty ideal of a revival of Judaism through the regeneration of the Jewish nation. In its present form, this literature is a combination of occidental and oriental ideas, of many of the old orthodox Jewish sentiments with those of modern progressive Judaism. . . . Zionistic as it is in its general tendency, it is by no means an expression of one-sidedness and narrow mindedness, but rather strives to reconcile old thoughts with new ideas.

Raisin went on to advocate the reading of this new literature since it contained many important articles and works in the field of Judaic studies.[45]

Raisin's "Hebraica" included reviews of Bernfeld's biography of Rapaport,[46] an appreciation of 'Aḥad Ha-'Am,[47] and a review of Brainin's book on Mapu.[48] Before he came to the College, Raisin had been a regular contributor to *Ha-Shiloah*, and he continued to write books and articles in modern Hebrew throughout his long rabbinical career, including *Dapim MiPinqaso Shel Rabbi* ("Memoirs of a Reform Rabbi").[49] He was permitted to submit a reworking of his Hebrew book, *Toledoth ha-Yehudim ba'Ameriqah*, as his rabbinical thesis. According to S. Kressel, the well-known bibliographer of modern Hebrew literature, Raisin's was the first academic thesis ever written in modern Hebrew.[50]

This growing pro-Hebraism was opposed by Kaufmann N. Kohler, who as president of the College from 1903 to 1921 took a militant anti-Zionist position and eliminated modern Hebrew from the curriculum.[51] Yet, when the *HUC Monthly* began to appear in 1914, student interest in modern Hebrew literature continued unabated. S. Felix Mendelsohn wrote about Mendele Mocher Sefarim,[52] Sholom Aleichem,[53] 'Ahad Ha-'Am,[54] and Moses Leib Lilienblum.[55] Jacob Marcus reviewed Abraham S. Waldstein's "The Evolution of Modern Hebrew Literature."[56] Gotthard Deutsch dealt with "America in Haskalah Literature."[57] J. Sales wrote an article on Bialik which included an excerpt of *Ha-Mathmid* translated by Edward Israel.[58] Other Hebrew or Yiddish writers discussed in the early issues of the *Monthly* were S. S. Frug,[59] Abraham Mapu,[60] J. L. Novechowich,[61] and Jacob Gordin.[62] A translation of Meir Letteris's *Galei Mayim* was done by Sheldon Blank.[63]

Of more than parochial significance were two books on the *Haskalah*, both reworkings of rabbinical theses, which were published by alumni of the College during the early years of this century. Jacob Raisin's *Haskalah Movement among Russian Jews*,[64] although somewhat dated, is still the best work in English on the subject. A. B. Rhine's *Leon Gordon*,[65] the earliest biography of Gordon, is a standard work on the life and achievement of this key figure of the Russian *Haskalah*.

II. The Second Fifty Years

A. Curriculum

The beginning of the second fifty years of the College postdates by four years the election of Julian Morgenstern to its presidency. Although a non-Zionist, Dr. Morgenstern was far more sensitive than

Kohler to the new currents in Jewish life. The restoring of modern Hebrew to the curriculum of the College in 1923–24 was one of several changes made by the new administration. Jacob Mann, who joined the faculty as professor of Jewish history in 1922–23, was also charged with the teaching of Hebrew literature, and offered "Selections from Modern Hebrew Writers." The text he used was Rabinson's *Sifruthenu Ha-Hadashah*.[66] At the same time, David Neumark introduced a one-hour course in spoken modern Hebrew, which was dropped following his death in 1924.[67]

A decided impetus to the teaching of modern Hebrew was given by Nelson Glueck, who in 1928 returned to Cincinnati from Jerusalem, where he had acquired a love for spoken Hebrew. In the Preparatory Department, Hebrew conversation and composition were again introduced as part of a ten-hour course in "D" grade, and modern Hebrew short stories and essays were read in "C" and "B" grades.[68] Jacob Mann continued to offer courses in modern Hebrew in the Collegiate Department.[69]

Shalom Maximon, the Hebrew educator and writer, was appointed to the faculty in 1930–31 and immediately took over the instruction of Hebrew.[70] Following Maximon's death in 1933, Nelson Glueck was put in charge of most of the modern Hebrew instruction. Zvi Diesendruck, who came to Cincinnati as professor of Jewish philosophy that year, taught "A" grade, concentrating on Bialik, Berkowitz, and Sholom Aleichem.[71] At least according to the 1935–36 catalogue, Abraham Cronbach was assigned to teach modern Hebrew in "B" grade, using the *Ivrit b'Ivrit* method![72] It was only in 1943 that a full-time instructor in modern Hebrew, Dr. Elias Epstein, was finally named. In 1955–56, Ezra Spicehandler was transferred from the New York School to Cincinnati, and in 1963–64, Werner Weinberg was added to the department. Warren Bargad joined the Cincinnati department (1970) after Spicehandler settled in Jerusalem.

B. Faculty

In the 1920s and 1930s, Zvi Diesendruck was a recognized figure in Hebrew letters. A native of Galicia, he had taught at the Pedagogium in Vienna, the Jewish Institute of Religion in New York, and the Hebrew University in Jerusalem. He translated several of Plato's works, including the *Republic*, into modern Hebrew, thus enriching its philosophical terminology. While he was still in Vienna, he joined Gershon Schofmann in editing the periodical *Gevuloth* (1919). His most important work in Hebrew, *Min Ha-Safah Ve-Lifnim,* is a collection of philosophical essays on the problems of language and expression (Tel Aviv: Dvir, 1934) and was praised by Bialik. Several of these essays had previously appeared in Hebrew periodicals. Bialik's famous *Galuy Ve-Khasuy Ba-Lashon* may have been influenced by Diesendruck's work. Bialik was responsible for recommending Diesendruck's appointment as lecturer at the Hebrew University, and, upon learning of his impending departure for Hebrew Union College, strove to keep him in Jerusalem.[73]

Shalom Maximon had been a member of 'Aḥad Ha-'Am's circle in London and for a while served as his Hebrew secretary. He was also a close associate of Brenner's during the latter's period. He published in *Ha-Me'orer, Ha-Toren, Ha-Shiloaḥ, Ha-Po'el Ha-Za'ir.* A selection of his essays appeared in New York (1925).[74]

Half of Abraham Idelsohn's major work, *Neginoth Yisra'el,* was published in Hebrew. He was also the author of a Hebrew opera, *Yiftaḥ* (1922), and *Toledoth Ha-Neginah Ha-'Ivrith* (Berlin, 1925, and Cincinnati, 1931). His authorized bibliography lists ten books and twenty-seven pieces in Hebrew, including several short stories.[75]

S. S. Cohon published his Hebrew articles in American periodicals such as *Sefer Ha-Shanah* and *Ha-Do'ar.* Although not a Zionist, he had a deep and genuine love for both the Hebrew language and its literature. Cohon drew about him a small circle of Hebraist students, held informal classes in modern Hebrew literature in his home, and acted as mentor to the Neumark Club on the campus.[76]

A decided contribution to the study of medieval Hebrew grammarians was made by Michael Wilensky, who was curator of Hebrew manuscripts at the Cincinnati library (1936–55). Wilensky, who began in Hebrew journalism, soon confined his writing to Judaic studies. He published a critical edition of Jonah Ibn Janah's *Sefer Ha-Riqmah* (Berlin, 1939–41), studies on the style of Ibn Ezra, *Mo'oznayim* (Berlin, 1923–26), and the incompleted *Sefer Safah Berurah* (Berlin, 1924).[77]

Ezra Spicehandler's contributions have been mainly as an anthologist and as a biographer of Joshua Heschel (Oaias) Schorr, a radical Galician *Maskil* of the nineteenth century. In his Schorr studies, Spicehandler stresses the interconnection between the second generation of Galician *Maskilim* and Reform Judaism in Germany. Besides *Peraqim Beyahaduth,* which he co-edited with Jakob Petuchowski, he joined Stanley Burnshaw and T. Carmi in editing an anthology, with commentary, of modern Hebrew poetry (*The Modern Hebrew Poem Itself*) and published a dual-language anthology entitled *Modern Hebrew Short Stories.* The principle of selection followed in both anthologies was current literary taste rather than the status of particular authors in the past. He published several articles on Schorr, including his letters to Bernhard Felsenthal, his bibliography, and a Hebrew anthology of Schorr's major articles (*Sifriyath Doroth,* Mosad Bialik, 1972).[78] He also served as divisional editor for modern Hebrew of the *Encyclopedia Judaica,* for which he also wrote several articles, including the comprehensive one on "Modern Hebrew Literature." Now dean of the College's Jerusalem School, he is also a visiting professor of modern Hebrew literature at the Hebrew University.

Werner Weinberg's doctoral dissertation dealt with the novels of A. A. Kabak. Since his appointment to the College, his major area of concentration has been in the problems of modern Hebrew orthography and transcription, and the emerging new grammar of spoken Hebrew. His recent work was published by Magnes Press of the Hebrew University.[79]

Warren Bargad's doctoral dissertation dealt with the literary career of Hayyim Hazaz—one excerpt of which was published in the Israeli periodical *Molad* and another in the prestigious *Ha-Sifruth.*[80]

Alfred Gottschalk, the president of the College-Institute, wrote his doctoral dissertation on "'Aḥad Ha-'Am's Conception of Jewish History," chapters of which also appeared in *Molad* and *Haguth 'Ivrith ba' Ameriqa.*[81]

William Cutter of our California School has been studying the development of the post-*Haskalah* Hebrew novel. A long article on the various manuscript versions of Brenner's *Shekol Ve-Kishalon,* which he co-authored with Dr. Josef Even of the Hebrew University, is full of insights into the painstaking literary experiments which that novelist undertook before arriving at the final version of his greatest novel.[82]

III. HUC Scholarly Publications

Modern Hebrew literature received scant attention in the *HUC Annual.* In all it contains only seven articles in the field: Prof. Simon

Rawidowicz published an important essay, "War Nachman Krochmal Hegelianer?",[83] which was later incorporated in his monumental work in Hebrew on Krochmal. Rawidowicz suggests that Krochmal was not a Hegelian and believes that Vico had the greater influence upon him. Joseph Reider[84] and Jacob Agus[85] discussed some of the "anti-Judaic" views of modern Hebrew literature, Ezra Spicehandler wrote three articles on Joshua Heschel Schorr,[86] and William Cutter wrote on Bershadski's novel *Be'en Matarah*.[87] Medieval Hebrew literature fares much better.[88] The *Annual* contains thirty-six articles in Hebrew and one in Yiddish. The first article in modern Hebrew appeared in 1927.[89]

Studies in Bibliography and Booklore contains four articles in the field of modern Hebrew literature: Simchah Berkowitz's treatment of the traveler and book-dealer Ephraim Dinard,[90] Ezra Spicehandler's bibliography of Osais Heschel Schorr,[91] and Sonne and Tsevat's report on the Moshe Hayyim Luzzato manuscripts at the College.[92] Werner Weinberg also published a "Bibliography of Proposals for the Reform Hebrew Script." [93] Medieval Hebrew literature again fares somewhat better with three articles.[94]

JEWISH INSTITUTE OF RELIGION
(THE NEW YORK SCHOOL)

I. Curriculum

Because of its Zionist orientation, the Jewish Institute of Religion placed greater emphasis on modern Hebrew than did the Cincinnati School. This was reflected in the number of instructional hours assigned to modern Hebrew, in the caliber of the instructors in modern Hebrew, and, in the early years, in the size and quality of the modern Hebrew literature collection in its library.

Yet in its salad years, the New York School had some difficulty in making an appointment in modern Hebrew. In 1924–25 it had invited David Yellin of Jerusalem, the noted grammarian and scholar of medieval Hebrew poetry, to serve as guest professor.[95] He was followed by Shalom Maximon, who doubled the number of courses, which now included a seminar on the so-called period of national revival (Smolenskin to Brenner).[96] Maximon, too, taught only for a single year, and was replaced by Nissan Touroff, a Hebrew essayist, educator, and psychologist, who served as professor of modern Hebrew for six years (1926–32). Under Touroff, the list of offerings soon expanded. By 1928–29, six courses were taught and a clear-cut distinction was made between elementary courses, required in the first two years, and designated merely as Hebrew, and advanced courses, which were labeled modern Hebrew literature.[97] In 1926–27 Zvi Diesendruck came to New York as a visiting professor and taught "A History of Hebrew Literature—Haskalah to Smolenskin" and gave a seminar on the "Social Problem in Contemporary Hebrew Literature." [98]

Shalom Spiegel joined the faculty in 1929–30 and was charged with teaching the elementary course in modern Hebrew. Spiegel also introduced a survey course in medieval Hebrew literature.[99] When Nissan Touroff left the JIR for Jerusalem in 1932–33, Shalom Spiegel and Ralph Marcus, the Hellenistic scholar who joined the faculty in 1930–31, shared the courses in modern Hebrew.[100] This emphasis on modern Hebrew continued under subsequent professors and instructors in the field. These included Simon Halkin (1944–48), Ezra Spicehandler (1950–55), Shaul Hareli (1957–71), and Abraham Aaroni since 1971.

II. Faculty Publications

Simon Halkin, a leading contemporary Hebrew poet and professor emeritus of modern Hebrew literature at the Hebrew University, is the faculty member who made the greatest contribution in Hebrew letters. Although born in White Russia, he was educated in the United States and his literary work (poetry, fiction, and criticism) was influenced by American and British views and trends. The subject matter and the landscape he describes in his poetry and prose frequently reflect his American experience. Halkin spent only four years of his very fruitful career at the JIR, but these were significant years. There, he earned his doctorate in Hebrew literature for his dissertation, "The Emergence of the Jew in Modern Hebrew Literature" (1947), which served as the basis for his popular work, *Modern Hebrew Literature . . . Trends and Values* (New York, 1950). Although Halkin's English book was primarily influenced by the then prevailing sociological school of Hebrew criticism and by Zionist apologetics, it remains the best survey in English on the subject. Of particular import is his essay on the "Religious Motifs in Modern Hebrew Poetry." After his return to Israel to succeed Joseph Klausner as professor of modern Hebrew literature at the Hebrew University, he became one of the first Israeli academicians to apply more aesthetically oriented critical theories to the study of Hebrew literature. During his stay at the College, Halkin published a collection of essays in literary criticism in which he treated prominent American writers.[101] His second and yet unfinished novel, *'Ad Mashber,* although mainly written in Tel Aviv, also appeared while he was at the New York School.[102]

The main character of the novel, Dr.Fuller, is a prominent American Conservative rabbi with Reconstructionist leanings. Halkin brilliantly portrays the world of an American "professional Jew" and the conflicts between his ideals and the reality of his family and environment. He records faithfully the physical and intellectual world of "Jewish" New York during the Great Depression. His description of Jewish student life at New York's City College is one of the best in any language.

Shortly before he left New York, Halkin published *Al Ha-'Iy,* his collected poems to that date.[103] His verse reflected the modernist trends of the period and had a decidedly "American texture," combining an intellectual precision with a mystical-romantic view of life. They confirmed that Halkin was the most important of the so-called American School of Hebrew poets. During this fruitful period he also published several poems in the United States and Palestine, among them, "On the Sand Dunes in Michigan."[104] Halkin wrote a pamphlet on the problems of American Judaism in which he took a dim view of the possibility that it could survive the onslaught of assimilatory trends and concluded that Jewish life and culture could only survive in Israel.[105] In 1947 Halkin was appointed professor of Hebrew literature at the Hebrew University in Jerusalem, where he served until his retirement.

Although a leading talmudic scholar, Chaim Tchernowitz (Rav Ẓa 'ir) was also a popular publicist and editor. He had begun his career as a modern Orthodox rabbi in Russia, where he was closely associated with Bialik and 'Aḥad Ha-'Am and the Odessa circle of Hebrew writers and scholars, which dominated Hebrew letters at the turn of the century, and frequently published in *Ha-Shiloah*. He arrived in New York in 1923 and taught at the College until his death in 1949.

In 1939 Tchernowitz founded and edited *Bitzaron,* a Hebrew monthly devoted to Jewish scholarship, Hebrew literature, and current Jewish problems, and which still appears in New York. During his editorship, *Bitzaron* published articles by Israeli and American scholars and writers, several of whom were faculty members of the College. Simon Halkin served on the editorial board for a number of years. From time to time academic events at the JIR were reported in its pages.[106] Tchernowitz also wrote many lead articles dealing with Jewish problems in *Bitzaron* and published his memoirs,[107] which were later issued in two volumes. Of particular interest to the College-Institute community is Tchernowitz's attack on Julian Morgenstern's strongly non-Zionist presidential address, "Nation, People or Religion." [108]

Shalom Spiegel began his academic career at the Jewish Institute of Religion. His major work in the field of modern Hebrew literature is *Hebrew Reborn* (New York, 1930), which surveys the development of modern Hebrew literature until the close of the age of Bialik. Spiegel's most significant accomplishments have been in the field of medieval literature and Bible. His *Me-'Agadoth Ha-'Aqedah,* an examination of the *Akedah* theme in medieval Hebrew poetry, is a masterpiece combining profound erudition with a keen literary sensitivity.[109]

Another important Hebraist at the JIR was Nissan Touroff, who came to the JIR in 1926 after a successful career as student and educator in Russia, Poland, Germany, Switzerland, and Eretz Israel. He had been headmaster of a teachers college for women in Jaffa and Tel Aviv, and for a short time served as the editor of *Ha'aretz,* the important Tel Aviv newspaper. In 1940 he was called to teach education at the Hebrew University but soon resigned and returned to New York. Touroff wrote mainly on psychological and educational subjects but also dealt from time to time with literary and aesthetic problems. He translated Knut Hamsen's *Earth* into Hebrew.[110]

Shaul Hareli, who taught modern Hebrew between 1955 and 1972, wrote many articles in Hebrew on Middle Eastern problems and Zionist subjects, and a book on modern Turkey.[111] Before coming to the College he served as editor of publications of the Educational Department of the Jewish Agency in New York. He was succeeded by

Abraham Aaroni, a prominent educator and teacher, whose textbook on modern Hebrew grammar is widely used in the United States.[112] During the academic year 1973–74, Gideon Telpaz, the Israeli novelist, taught at the New York School.

Modern Hebrew has a preeminent place in the curriculum of our Los Angeles School. Professor Arnold Band of the University of California, Los Angeles School, and one of the leading modern Hebrew scholars in the United States, serves as visiting professor at the School. Band's *Nostalgia and Nightmare* is a classic work in the field of Agnon criticism. Working with him, William Cutter wrote his dissertation on the *Talush,* the uprooted Eastern European intellectual. His work on the Ur-texts of Yosef Chaim Brenner, *Shekhol VeKishalon,* has shed new light on the composition of Brenner's last and best novel.

This review of a century of the modern Hebrew scholarly activity of the College indicates that modern Hebrew did indeed form an important part of our College curriculum. Key figures in Hebrew Literature—Neumark, Diesendruck, Halkin, and Tchernowitz—spent a good part of their careers on its faculty. Two presidents of the College, Nelson Glueck and Alfred Gottschalk, taught modern Hebrew. Alfred Gottschalk, now president of the College, earned both his graduate degrees with dissertations dealing with 'Aḥad Ha-'Am. Two faculty members of our California School, Dean Lewis Barth and Dean William Cutter, earned their M.A.'s in modern Hebrew, and the latter his Ph.D. as well. The dean of the Jerusalem School also serves as a visiting professor of modern Hebrew literature at the Hebrew University.

A major contribution by several of our faculty and alumni has been their works in English on the history and development of modern Hebrew. Halkin's *Modern Literature,* Spiegel's *Hebrew Reborn,* and Raisin's *The Haskalah Movement* are still the best of their kind. To this list should be added Spicehandler's comprehensive article on modern Hebrew literature in the new *Encyclopedia Judaica* and his anthologies of English translations of Hebrew poems and short stories, which are widely used as textbooks for college Hebrew. Another area of research has been the exploration of the interrelationship between the Haskalah and the Reform movements. Evidence of the continuing participation of our faculty in Hebrew letters can be found in a recently published series of three Hebrew volumes entitled *Haguth Ivrit Ba- 'Ameriqah,* issued by the World Jewish Congress, in which seven members of our faculty participated.[113] Finally, the Hebrew Union College Press, in cooperation with Western Reserve University, has published Bernard Martin's English translation of Zinberg's excellent *History of Jewish Literature.*[114]

Looking ahead into the future, one might venture to predict that the increased interest in modern Hebrew, reflected in the expansion of modern Hebrew programs at all branches of the College and the Year-in-Israel Program, should result in even greater scholarly activity in the field during the next century of the College's existence.

Notes

1. *American Israelite,* XXXIV (1888), p. 4. See his remarks in a paper he read before the World Parliament of Religions, "An Introduction to a Bibliography of the Jewish Periodical Press," as quoted by James Heller in *Isaac M. Wise . . .* (UAHC, 1965).
2. *CCAR Yearbook,* IX (1898), pp. 61–62; *HUC Journal,* V (1901), p. 171.
3. S. B. Schwarzberg: *Tikathev Zo'th Le-Dor Aharon* (New York, 1898), pp. 20–21.
4. See Heller, op. cit., p. 592.
5. *HUC Catalogue,* 1901, p. 32.
6. Ibid., 1901–2, p. 30. Erter's work is merely listed as Haçofeh and 'Ahad Ha-'Am is simply called Ginzberg.
7. *HUC Journal,* IV (1902), p. 84.
8. S. S. Cohon, *HUC Monthly,* VIII (1924–25), pp. 145–48.
9. *CCAR Yearbook,* XI (1901), pp. 142–44.
10. Ibid., XVIII, (1908), p. 53.
11. Ibid., XIV, (1914), p. 114.
12. Ibid., XXV (1915), p. 65.
13. Ibid., XXVI (1916), p. 74.
14. Ibid., XXVIII (1918), p. 74.
15. Ibid., XXXII (1922), pp. 274–75.
16. Ibid., XIX (1909), p. 70; XXII (1912), p. 288.
17. Ibid., XIX (1909), p. 70; XX (1910), p. 83.
18. Ibid., XX (1910), p. 83; XXII (1912), pp. 287–88.

19. *Ha-Toren,* IX, no. 1 (1922–23), pp. 78–80. Brainin was also a close friend of Neumark's, his son having married Neumark's daughter.
20. Joshua Bloch, "Dr. Gotthard Deutsch," *Sefer Ha-Shanah Liyhudey Ameriqah,* VI (1942), p. 460, n. 1. Max Raisin, *Dapim Mi-Pinqaso Shel Rabbi,* pp. 220–28, and *Mi-Sefer Ḥayay,* pp. 48, 53–54. Adolph Oko, "Selected List of the Writings of Gotthard Deutsch," *HUC Monthly,* II, no. 8.
21. *HUC Journal,* II (1898), p. 214.
22. New York, 1930.
23. *'Igroth Ḥ. N. Bialik,* V, p. 114, letter dated November 24, 1930. Neither project was completed. See also IV, p. 272, and Bialik's letter to Levias dated April 2, 1933, V, p. 211.
24. G. Kressel, *Lexiqon Shel Ha-Sifruth Ha-'Ivrith,* II, p. 191; Joshua Bloch, *Universal Jewish Encyclopedia,* VI, p. 628.
25. He published in *Hi-Shiloaḥ, Ha-Meliẓ, Ha-Magid,* and *Ha-Ẓefirah.* See *'Igroth 'Aḥad Ha-'Am,* II, pp. 76–77, 148–49, and also in the American *Ha-Toren* and *Hadoar.*
26. *Sifruth Yisra'el* (Warsaw, 1897–1900).
27. Berlin, 1894; See Kressel, op. cit., II, pp. 370–71, and Alexander Marx, *Essays in Jewish Bibliography* (1947), pp. 255–64. A most interesting literary "curiosity" is 'Aḥad Ha-'Am's suggestion to Berdichevski that he have Malter correct Berdichevski's grammar! *'Igrot,* II, p. 68.
28. Robert Gordis, *Max Leopold Margolis, Scholar and Teacher* (Philadelphia, 1952). Professor Reider lists Margolis's Hebrew articles in his bibliography, but, as Kressel indicates, several were omitted; op. cit., II, p. 421.
29. Among the Galicians were Henry Malter, Jacob Z. Lauterbach, Jacob Mann, Zvi Diesendruck, and Isaiah Sonne. On the fifteenth anniversary banquet which the student body tendered in Neumark's honor, Neumark remarked, "What would the Hebrew Union College be today, if not for Galicia." *HUC Monthly,* X, no. 2 (1923–24), p. 3.
30. On Neumark's important role in modern Hebrew letters, see Fischel Lachower, *Toledoth Ha-Sifruth Ha-'Ivrith Ha-Ḥadashah,* vol. III, pp. 177–89. According to Joseph Klausner, Neumark was appointed as manager of the Berlin office of *'Oẓar Ha-Yahaduth;* see *"Bialik Ha-'Orekh"* in *Kneseth,* I (1936), p. 105; see also *'Igroth 'Aḥad Ha-'Am,* V, p. 28 (letter to Joshua Bloch dated March 24, 1917). "I have known, respected and loved Neumark ever since he was a student at the *Hochschule* in Berlin sixteen years ago. We have been faithful friends from then on. . . . He was one of my main assistants at *Ha-Shiloaḥ* from its inception." See also *'Igroth 'Aḥad Ha-'Am,* II, p. 164; III, pp. 141, 180–82; VI, pp. 25–28.
31. Ibid., p. 178. See Neumark's article *"Ha-Yehudim Ve-ha-Riformim"* and *"Yahadutho shel 'Aḥad Ha-'Am"* in his book *Mi-Qeren Zavith.* An alleged response by 'Aḥad Ha-'Am appeared in the *American Jewish Chronicle,* Passover 1917. However, 'Aḥad Ha-'Am indicated that the article was concocted from an interview and does not accurately reflect his views. *'Igroth 'Aḥad Ha-'Am,* V, no. 312, letter to Neumark, dated August 24, 1917.

32. Other works in Hebrew were *Toledoth ha-'Iqarim be-Yisra'el* (Odessa, 1913–19); and *Mi-Qeren Zavith* (New York, 1917).

33. Prof. Henry Englander attributes to Neumark the introduction of the '*Ivrith be-'Ivrith* method in Hebrew instruction, HUC Monthly, XVI, no. 3 (1928–29). See also '*Igrot 'Ahad Ha-'Am* as cited above.

34. *'Agudath Neumark* founded in 1924–25 or at least named then. See "'*Agudath Neumark Umgamothehah*," *HUC Monthly,* XVI, no. 3 (1928–29), p. 15. See Peiser and Taxay's article "The Life of Dr. Neumark" in the *HUC Monthly* dedicated to him, X, no. 3 (1923–24), pp. 7–15; the bibliography by H. Goldberg and Martha Neumark, ibid., pp. 15–19; and S. S. Cohon's list appended to Neumark's *Essays in Jewish Philosophy* (1929).

35. Magnes's Hebrew works are *Kemo Kol Ha-Goyim* (1930), *Ne'umey Ha-Qanzler Shel Ha-'Universitah Ha-'Ivrith* (1936), *Sheney Mikhtavim El Ghandi* (with Martin Buber) (1939), *Leqet Ra'ayonoth Ve-'Imroth* (1949), *Bimvukhath Ha-Zeman* (1946).

36. *HUC Annual* (1904), pp. 225–34.

37. Ibid., pp. 235–42.

38. Ibid., pp. 177–86.

39. Ibid., p. 178.

40. According to Max Eichhorn, by 1900, 48 percent of the students admitted to having parents of East European origin. One would have to check if those stemming from Galicia reported their parentage as Austrian, not as East European. *HUC Monthly,* XVII, no. 6 (June 1930), p. 9.

41. "The Painter Poet," *HUC Journal,* V (1900–1901), pp. 81–82, 167–70.

42. *HUC Journal* VI (1901–2), pp. 74–77.

43. *Leon Gordon* (Philadelphia, 1910).

44. Ibid., p. 7.

45. *HUC Journal,* V (1900–01), pp. 88–89.

46. "*Toledoth Shir*," ibid., pp. 89–90.

47. Ibid., pp. 175–78.

48. Ibid., pp. 224–29.

49. Brooklyn, 1941.

50. The revised book was published a year before Raisin's graduation: *Toledoth Ha-Yehudim Ba-'Ameriqah* (Warsaw, 1902). Compare: M. Raisin *Toledoth Hayay*, p. 53, and Kressel, II, pp. 861–62. When Moses Mielziener died, several memorial poems appeared in the *Journal;* among them were epitaphs by Henry Malter and Ephraim Feldman, members of the faculty. *HUC Journal,* VII (1902–3), pp. 97–102, 133–35.

51. See Michael Meyer's essay in this volume, p. 59.

52. *HUC Monthly,* II (1915–16), pp. 164–68.

53. Ibid., pp. 285–87.

54. Ibid., III (1916–17), pp. 36–45.

55. Ibid., IV (1917–18), pp. 70–78.

56. Ibid., II, pp. 304–5.

57. Ibid., III, pp. 210–11.

58. Ibid., pp. 81–90.
59. Abraham J. Feldman, ibid., pp. 13–20.
60. Joseph L. Baron, ibid., IV, pp. 178–82.
61. Jerome Rosen, ibid., pp. 18–26.
62. Abraham Fried, ibid., VIII (1921–22), pp. 76–81.
63. Ibid., p. 45.
64. Philadelphia: Jewish Publication Society, 1910.
65. Philadelphia: Jewish Publication Society, 1913.
66. Mordechai Rabinson (1877–1953).
67. *HUC Catalogue,* 1923–24, p. 50.
68. The text used in "C" grade was Fichman's *Peraqim Ri'shonim* and in "D" grade, Krinski's *Ha-Signon Ha-'Ivri.*
69. *HUC Catalogue,* 1928–29, p. 53.
70. Ibid., 1930–31, p. 57. The following year Maximon added a course in conversational Hebrew ("A" grade), which also included readings from Bialik, Feierberg, and Berdichevski. He also replaced Krinski's text with Fichman's *Perakim Ri'shonim,* vol. III: ibid., 1931–32, pp. 62–63.
71. Ibid., 1933–34, pp. 45–46.
72. Ibid., 1935–36, p. 45.
73. See G. Kressel, *Lexiqon Ha-Sifruth Ha-'Ivrith,* I, p. 548 and the bibliography he lists. Bialik was fond of Diesendruck. See *'Igroth Bialik,* II, p. 146; IV, pp. 12–13, 87, 130; V, pp. 60, 161–62, 294–95, particularly the last two letters. See also M. Ungerfeld, *Bialik Ve-Soferey Doro,* (Tel Aviv, 1974), pp. 104–8. Prof. Ruth Kartun-Blum suggests this possibility in "Diesendruck uVialik," *Mo'znayim* XLI, 2 (June 1975, pp. 90 ff.).
74. *Sefer Maximon* (1935) contains much biographical and autobiographical material. On his relationship with Brenner, see *'Igroth Y. H. Brenner,* I, p. 276; II, p. 35. See also Kressel, op. cit., II, 414–15.
75. Moses Weiler and Theodore Ross, "Abraham Zevi Idelsohn," *HUC Monthly,* XXII, 2 (December 1932), pp. 9–11. See bibliography on p. 11. See also Bialik's letter to Idelsohn, *'Igroth,* III, pp. 139–40 (Nov. 17, 1926) and p. 172 (Jan. 16, 1927). Bialik asks Idelsohn to send him all the publications of the College, in particular the first three volumes of the *HUC Annual.* These were sent to him and acknowledged in his letter of Feb. 17, 1927, *'Igroth,* III, p. 199. See also S. Cohon, "Abraham Zevi Idelsohn," *CCAR Yearbook,* XLIX (1939), pp. 287–91.
76. Theodore Wiener, in "The Writings of Samuel S. Cohon," *Studies in Bibliography and Booklore,* II (1955–56), pp. 160–79, lists eleven Hebrew articles by Cohon.
77. Kressel, I, p. 652. See also Samuel Atlas, "Michael Wilensky, 1877–1955," *Studies in Bibliography and Booklore,* II (1955–56), pp. 51–52.
78. *Perakim Ba-Yahaduth* (Tel Aviv, 1961). *The Modern Hebrew Poem Itself* (New York, 1965). *Modern Hebrew Short Stories* (New York, 1971). *Yehoshua Heshel Shor: Ma' Amarim* (Jerusalem, 1972).
79. *Tiqun Ha-Kethiv Ha-'Ivri* (Jerusalem, 1972). Weinberg has written several

articles in Hebrew on the subject: (a) "Al To'mar . . . 'Emor," *Haguth 'Ivrith Ba-Ameriqah,* I (Yavneh, Tel Aviv, 1972). (b) "Be-Shulei Ha-Pirsum He-Hadash Shel Klalei Ha-Kethiv Hasar Ha-Niqud," *Leshonenu,* XXXVI (Jerusalem, 1972), pp. 203–11. (c) "Kevi'at Klalei Ha-Kethiv Hasar Ha-Niqud," *Hadoar,* LI (New York, 1972), pp. 432–34. He also published "Kabak's Connection with America," *American Jewish Archives,* XXII (Cincinnati, 1970), pp. 166–73.

80. "Ha-Sipor Haraayoni Shel Hayyim Hazaz," *Molad,* IV (1972), pp. 660–65, "Hebet Hadash Bi-Yzirothav Ha-Temaniyoth shel Hayyim Hazaz" *Ha-Sifruth* IV (1973), p. 232–25. Bargad also contributed articles to *Shde-moth,* no. 49 (1973), pp. 64–80, and to *Hadoar* dealing with the Israeli novelists Amalia Kahna-Carmon (Sept. 1, 1972), pp. 616–17; Aharon Meged (December 1972), p. 103; and Aharon Applefeld, p. 124. He also translated some poems of Jerome Rothberg into Hebrew, *Siman Kri'ah,* I, no. 3 (June 1973), and of Stanley Chyet of our Cincinnati faculty *Mo'znayim,* XXXVI, nos. 4–5 (March–April 1973), p. 326.

81. "Ha-Morashah Lefi 'Ahad Ha-'Am," *Molad,* V (1972), pp. 106–13, and " 'Or Ha-Tevonah Ve 'Or Ha-Ruah Shpinoza Va'Ahad Ha-'Am," *Haguth Ivrith Ba-Ameriqah,* II (Tel Aviv, 1975), pp. 198–209.

82. W. Cutter, *The Uprooted: A Study of the Protagonist in Three Novels* (University Microfilms, Ann Arbor, Mich., 1972). "Bershadski's Be'en Ma-tarah: A Study in Late Nineteenth Century Characterization," *HUC Annual* XLIV (1973), pp. 227–57. "Be-'Iqvoth Brener Ba-Derekh el Shekhol Ve-Kishalon", *Ha-Sifruth,* no. 17 (September 1974), pp. 127–41.

83. *HUC Annual,* V (1928), pp. 535–82.

84. *HUC Jubilee Volume* (1925), pp. 445–82.

85. *The Prophet in Modern Hebrew Literature,* XXVIII (1957), pp. 289–324.

86. *HUC Annual,* XXXI (1960), pp. 181–222; XLXVI (1969–70), pp. 503–28; XXVIII (1957), pp. 1–21 (Hebrew).

87. See n. 82.

88. The *Annual* contains several articles dealing with a theological text written in verse. Alexander Scheiber, "Unknown Leaves from the *She'eloth 'Atiqoth,*" XXVII (1956), pp. 291–303; XXXVI (1965), pp. 227–60; Ezra Fleischer, "Le-Zivyon Ha-She'eloth Ha-'Atiqot, etc.," XXXVIII (1967) (Hebrew), pp. 1–23; Israel Davidson contributed three articles—the most significant being his "New Supplement to the Thesaurus of Medieval Hebrew Poetry," XII–XIII (1937–38), pp. 715–823. There are contributions from Ismar Elbogen, III (1926), pp. 215–24, IV (1927), pp. 405–31; and Alexander Scheiber in Kalir studies, XXIII, p. 2 (1950–51), pp. 353–68; Moses Poznanski and Israel Davidson on Moses Ibn Chiquitilla as poet, I (1924), pp. 599–601; Isaiah Sonne on "An Unknown Keroba of Yannai," XVIII (1944), pp. 199–220; Eric Werner on "Hebrew and Oriental Christian Metrical Hymns," XXIII, pt. 2 (1950–51), pp. 387–432; Alex-ander Marx on Gabirol's authorship of "Choice of Pearls," IV (1927), pp. 433–48; Richard Gottheil on "An Unknown Version of the Sayings of

Aesop," V (1928), pp. 315–52; VI (1928), pp. 349–50; Louis Ginzberg, "14 Philological Notes on Italian and Spanish Poetry," XV (1940), (Hebrew), pp. 1–36; Simon Bernstein on Solomon Da Piera, XIX (1945–46) (Hebrew), pp. 1–74; and Caleb Ben Eliahu Afendopolo, XXIV (1952–53), pp. 1–83; see also XVI (1941), pp. 99–159; and Leon J. Weinberger on Yehosef Ha-Ezovi and Byzantine Hebrew poets, XXXVII (1966) (Hebrew), pp. 1–11; XXXIX (1968) (Hebrew), pp. 1–62.

89. Jacob Moses Toledano: *"Te'udoth Mi-Kitvey Yad,"* IX (1927), pp. 449–67.
90. *SBB,* IX (1971), pp. 137–52.
91. Ibid., II (1955–56), pp. 20–36.
92. Ibid., II (1955–56), pp. 156–59.
93. Ibid., X (1971–72), pp. 3–18.
94. Peninah Naveh's monograph on the poet Joseph Ben Tanḥum of Jerusalem, *SBB,* X (1971–72), pp. 57–75; Dov Yarden's text of a poem by Samuel Hanagid, *SBB,* VI (1962–63), pp. 43–50; and S. M. Stein's report on a manuscript of Alharizi's poetry in Leningrad, ibid., pp. 94–98. There are twelve Hebrew articles in the *SBB* to date, of which five were written by the late Isaac Rivkind. Others are by Solomon Freehof, Jacob Dienstag, Judah Rosenthal, Nehemia Aloni, and Naftali Ben Menahem.
95. Yellin taught a single two-hour course, using Fichman's *Lashon Va-Sefer,* vol. 4, as his textbook, *JIR Catalogue,* 1924–25, p. 23.
96. Ibid., under Hebrew & Cognate Languages.
97. Under the latter, Dr. Touroff offered "a systematic survey . . . from Frishmann to the present as well as a seminar in Modern Hebrew Literature." Ibid., 1928–29, pp. 28–29.
98. *JIR Catalogue,* 1926–27, pp. 26–27.
99. This course was now four hours weekly throughout the year. His text was Fichman's *Lashon Va-Sefer,* vols. 1 and 2, and "Easy Selections from Modern Hebrew Literature and Palestinian Journals." Ibid., 1929–30, p. 29. Touroff continued to teach the intermediate (four hours weekly throughout the year) as well as a history of modern Hebrew literature "from Luzzato to the present day" and a seminar in modern Hebrew literature; p. 30. After 1930 a great variety of courses were offered in the field. In 1930–31, for example, Touroff introduced Bialik and Ravnitski's *Dor Dor Ve-Sofrav* in the advanced class and ran a joint seminar with Spiegel. The latter taught Hasidic and anti-Hasidic literature and Hebrew letters in Italy (ninth–eighteenth century), 1930–31, pp. 31–32.
100. Ibid., 1932–33, p. 27; The catalogue of the 1939–40 provides a good illustration of the range of offerings in the late 1930s. First-year students received a three-hour course in Hebrew fiction "with emphasis on grammar, vocabulary and Hebrew conversation" (Marcus), intermediate students studied "Selections from Modern Hebrew Essayists" for two hours (Marcus) and Hebrew poetry—selections from medieval and modern authors—for two hours (Spiegel). Advanced students took a course in "Modern Hebrew Letters from Aḥad Ha-'Am to the Present Era" for two hours

(Spiegel), 1939–40, pp. 28–29. All courses ran the length of the academic year.

101. *Ara'i Va-Keva': 'Iyunim Ba-Sifruth* (New York, 1942).

102. *'Ad Mashber* (Tel Aviv, 1945). The second part of this novel is in manuscript form, awaiting revision by the author. For a biography of S. Halkin, see Boaz Shekhovitz in *Sefer Ha-Yovel Le-Shim'on Halkin,* Jerusalem, 1975. For his role at the College see pp. 76–77, 84, 89.

103. *Al Ha-'Iy* (Jerusalem, 1946).

104. In *Kneset,* IX (1945), pp. 134–40.

105. *Yehudim Vi-Yhaduth Ba-'Ameriqah* (Jerusalem, 1946).

106. Vol. I (1939–40), pp. 428–31; the awarding of a DHL to Chaim Weizmann; XVI (1946–47), p. 145; XVII (1947–48), p. 68.

107. *Masekheth Zikhronoth* (New York, 1945), and *Pirkey Hayim* (New York, 1954).

108. *Bitzaron,* V (1944), pp. 1–11, 81–89.

109. *Sefer Ha-Yovel Likhvod Alexander Marx* (New York, 1950). English translation: *The Last Trial* (New York, 1967).

110. For biographical and bibliographical data see *Sefer Turov* (New York, 1938), and *Sheviley Ha-Hinukh,* December 1948, and Winter 1954. Kressel, II, pp. 17–18.

111. *Turkiah* (Tel Aviv, 1941).

112. Abraham Aaroni, and Reuben Wallenrod, *Modern Hebrew Reader and Grammar* (New York, 1942).

113. *Haguth 'Ivrith Ba'Ameriqah,* vol. I (1972), vol. II (1973), vol. III (1974). Faculty members who participated are Werner Weinberg, Harry Orlinsky, Alfred Gottschalk, Samuel Atlas, Eugene Borowitz, Nelson Glueck, and Stanley Chyet.

114. Seven volumes have appeared thus far.

ALFRED GOTTSCHALK

Into the Second Century

THIS BOOK DESCRIBES IN ITS FIRST PART THE HISTORY OF THE College-Institute from its inception one hundred years ago until the death of Nelson Glueck, my predecessor, and details in its second the contributions which the College-Institute, through its professors, has made to Jewish scholarship. There are many ways to read it.

One way is to read it as the unfolding story of an amazing academic achievement: a one-room college growing from absurdly modest beginnings into an imposing educational complex ranking among the finest institutions of higher learning; a collegium of two or three teachers without the normal academic qualifications developing into faculties equipped to cover wide and diverse areas of scholarship and making rich contributions to many disciplines of learning; a motley group of students, mostly high school boys, being superseded by a carefully selected student body of considerable academic potential.

Another way is to read the book as a record of how the vision of one man, against all odds, reached beyond the restrictions and the limited means of his contemporary fellow-Jews to become a center of American Jewish learning from which a great Jewish community would benefit.

Again, a different way to read the record of the past one hundred years is with the focus on this Jewish community, which carried the College-Institute as a cherished possession from generation to generation, even in times of austerity, when maintaining it was no simple task.

Others may read the book as a source book providing insights into the development of American Reform Judaism, its changes of philosophy and its controversies and theological quarrels. The ideology of college teachers often shaped Reform, and usually, when ideological discussion arose in the community, the leaders and teachers of the College-Institute did not stand aloof. Often, it seems, finding dissension on a personal level, they transformed it into a higher objective niveau and saved the unity of American Reform.

There are still other ways to read the book, but whatever the reader will take from it one fact stands out. Taking the overview of one hundred years, the reader, whatever his interest or approach, will find that the history of Hebrew Union College is not characterized by one quality which shows in the chronicles of many learned institutions—namely, academic isolation. There were, certainly, periods of relatively self-contained academic existence. But they did not last long. From the beginning, Hebrew Union College reached into life and life invaded the halls of this Jewish academe. I am careful not to exaggerate. Still, one may safely state that from its very early origins the College-Institute never lost sight of the realities of Jewish life. There were temptations to do so. And there were periods when the College-Institute, looking at Jewish life outside, acted myopic and neglected to see all of current Jewish thought and action, or did not manage to see them as clearly as they deserved. But even then, as this book shows, the isolation was never complete and the ferment always active. One need only think of early Zionist thought, which certainly did not make itself generally felt, yet there were always professors who did not participate in the dominant neglect.

In Hegel's famous words, Minerva's owl starts to fly only at nightfall. By this he meant that scholars deal with the present only after it has sunk into the darkness of the past. From my reading of this history, I venture to say that such was not the climate of opinion in which scholarship at the College-Institute prospered. True enough, there were many remote areas of Jewish life and thought that were considered worthy of exploration, there was and probably still is, a good deal of learned antiquarianism. Yet altogether, the guiding philosophy of the College-Institute was that Jewish scholarship served living Jewish religion, was a fount of ideas for the shaping of a viable Judaism, and that the critical application of the scholarly process would not destroy but rather vitalize the current validity of Jewish thought and norm.

This conviction, of course, did not originate at Hebrew Union College. The founders of modern Jewish scholarship (*Wissenschaft des Judentums*) had assigned to Jewish learning very practical tasks. Leopold Zunz and his friends related Jewish knowledge to Jewish life, and maintained that the insights gained from scholarship shape and direct life. When in 1822 the journal of the "Culturverein" published the concept of a science of Judaism, it made Jewish scholarship the medium through which the principles of Judaism would assume a shape in harmony with the spirit of the time and a vitality responding to the needs of the Jew.

This practical aspect of Jewish learning remains with us to this day. It is specifically Jewish. It is hard to imagine that a Christian would require scholarship for the fortification of his faith and his religious affiliation the way a Jew does, the Jew being told that to be a full Jew is to be, if not a learned Jew, then certainly a well-instructed Jew.

As Jewish education is for life, learning for the Jew progresses along an unending continuum. Pragmatically its task is constantly a reciprocal one of forcing the Jew to confront his people's past by immersing himself in the classic texts of its genius and then facing the world in an attempt to relate Jewish knowledge to reality. The instrument making the relationship possible is the Jew himself. The interlocking of past and present is accomplished through his person. As Franz Rosenzweig observed, "Foremost, the purpose of Jewish learning is to create a Jewish human being." A Jewish human being is no less Jewish because he is part of the universal family of man, nor less a member of the family of man because he is Jewish. This notion is important because it goes to the core of Jewish learning. Or, as Karl Jaspers pointed out in his work, *The Idea of the University,* academe proves its value wherever there are people who have merged their personal with their intellectual existence.

Yet there were instances, too many of them, and stretching over periods too long, when among those who devoted themselves to Jewish studies personal commitment had fallen entirely away from the intellectual. Franz Rosenzweig has assailed this trend of splitting learning from life. In his essay written in 1917, entitled "It's Time," he took to task scholarship that is isolated from actual Jewish life. The purpose of Jewish learning, then, is to create the human being who is a Jew, passionately attached to the knowledge and values of the past, deeply involved in the burning present and in the life of his people. He recognizes the need to build new bridges of learning and understanding to a whole body of knowledge which is being constantly created in other disciplines. The need for Jewish learning of this type is not reserved only for a learned class of rabbis, teachers, cantors, and educators, but is the domain of every Jew worthy of the name.

It is this indispensability of Jewish learning for Jewish life which will have to be to the fore when we consider the role of the College-Institute in the future.

At this time of its one-hundredth anniversary, the College-Institute is obligated to test its convictions on Jewish learning against the academic constellation as well as the community needs of today. Isaac Mayer Wise's dream of a college was rooted in his understanding that learning can never be solely unto itself if Jewish society is to bear the imprint of the Jewish spirit. Wise, who had an intuitively pragmatic outlook, wanted to create a theological and organizational union to weld American Judaism together. He sought a *minhag* America—a common guide for the religious practices of American Jewry. To accomplish this, he created a college which was to serve liberal religion as it was then conceived. A Jewish college in America, he felt, must appeal to all American Jews and, therefore, Wise designed it as a "Union College," open to all regardless of their shades of religious belief.

This college had as its historic mission the task of becoming a center of Jewish creative scholarship, and not merely a research institute. Wise designed the college to be a *general* college to educate the Jewish youth of America. While the chief function of the college was to house a religious seminary, to train graduates who wanted to serve Judaism as rabbis, his vision for the school was broader. Wise did not succeed in his plans for *one* Jewish college to serve *all* of American Jewry. Yet, to a large extent, what the Hebrew Union College has become today, a complex of schools—graduate and undergraduate, rabbinic, cantorial, educational and communal service—conforms in general terms to his scheme.

The examination of the validity of this concept and its underlying philosophy, and of the means of translating them into current use, takes by necessity a number of directions. The first concerns a new slant in the relationship of the College to American Jewry. American Jews today want to *know* why they are Jews. Multitudes of Jews are potential learners. To an extent unimagined decades ago, the Jewish laymen who form the Jewish community show a desire for Jewish information and for systematic Jewish knowledge. Our College should meet this demand with all of its intellectual resources. Toward that end it will train rabbis, cantors, educators, and others, who in their positions can serve as teachers. In addition, it will have to create new channels in cooperation with other institutions and organizations to stimulate and direct a flow of Jewish ideas and Jewish information to the Jewish community. Obviously, the College cannot be an active center of Jewish learning operating in direct contact with Jewish communities in large numbers of cities. But if it were to operate as a laboratory for Jewish creativity in the field of Jewish mass education, it would truly fulfill the dream of its founder and the hopes of educationists like Franz Rosenzweig and Martin Buber, who struggled with schemes to make one institution the center for a widespread system of continuing education.

I do not know to what extent economic conditions will allow the organization of such a network of educational facilities emanating from the schools and departments which the College already maintains. There is no desire on the part of the College to monopolize any aspect of the educational task. The College and its patron body, the Union of American Hebrew Congregations, should link efforts to intensify the educational services they render to the congregations and their members in order to meet needs that reach considerably beyond the present scope of educational activities. I foresee a systematic participation of the College-Institute in a comprehensive endeavor of Jewish adult education on a college level. We must realize that for all practical purposes the membership of our congregations soon will consist almost entirely of college graduates. We must further acknowledge that the vast majority of nonaffiliated Jews, whose absence from congregational life is a grievous loss, are college graduates. We do not belittle—in fact we applaud—the many efforts that are being made by nonreligious Jewish organizations to attract these men and women by various educational means, such as first-rate journals and magazines. However, we do feel that these endeavors do not absolve Liberal Judaism from the obligation of serving the Jewish intellectual needs of Liberal Jewry.

At the same time, the College-Institute will have to develop its graduate school, which trains scholars and professors. There was a time when Jewish scholars were mostly the graduates of European schools. These schools are either gone or no longer maintained with the standards that would attract young American graduates. After the war the Jewish theological schools of America were aware that it was now their task to replace the Jewish academic scholar who no longer could be imported from Europe. Today, graduate education at Jewish theological schools is being criticized as parochial because it occurs at a theologically committed school, and as incomplete because a theological school, such as ours, does not have the wide general humanistic underpinning that a university provides. Academic teachers have contemplated the possible conflict between Jewish commitment and the universalist character of "true scholarship," and the specific Jewish community needs that potentially impinge on general professional obligations and norms. This is, indeed, a problem, but one, as I see it, which need not develop into a conflict in the academic independence and excellence of a scholar's work.

While Hebrew Union College developed its graduate programs leading to advanced proficiency in Jewish scholarship, it has been extremely careful and successful in keeping the training entirely free from the encumbering or destructive influences of sectarian bias. More than one hundred Christian fellows have attended our graduate school and gone through their various study programs without meeting religious prejudice. Throughout its first century, the College-Institute has insisted on the inviolate freedom of academic teaching. It did so convinced that the free application of critical scholarship would enhance rather than curtail religious expression.

Indeed, the great variety of "religious talent" which appeared during the first one hundred years at Hebrew Union College—professors, students, and alumni who derived their inspirational cues as well as their theological beliefs from scholarly insights—is evidence that Jewish learning does not bar religious creativity. Quite to the contrary. This is true whether one considers Jewish learning in its strictly scholarly, creative sense or as the popular, adaptive kind in which Jews have always engaged. In producing the first kind and in fructifying the second, Hebrew Union College will find much of its mission as it enters its second century.

In an essential way, then, the College-Institute is engaged in a demanding enterprise. Reform Judaism, after one hundred years of organized existence in this country, stands at the threshold of new opportunities. Perhaps at no other time in the recent history of the Jewish people was there a greater need for keeping fresh the intellectual stimulation which flows from our tradition and the classic tenets of our faith. At no other time in our recent history, also, did there exist the means to tie that tradition to the living history of the Jewish people as presented by the fact of Israel Reborn. Therein lies the deepest meaning of our Jerusalem School. A center of learning of many facets, it serves various purposes. Yet in every aspect of its work it is expressive of one notion: the closeness of American and Israeli Jewry and the conviction that each will benefit from contact with the other and from the mutual exchange of ideas.

Our people today want to *learn* about Judaism in order to find a way to *live* as Jews, consciously and conscientiously. They want to continue their Jewish learning because it guarantees their Jewish living. Jewish learning today, as always in our postbiblical tradition, represents, as well as creates, a facet of Jewish existence. To enable that existence, structure is required as well as spontaneity. The structure will be provided by the continuity of learning and the tradition of scholarship. The spontaneity will become truly creative as it becomes the delicate synthesis of idea and religious emotion. The blend of structure and spontaneity will satisfy the intellectual and spiritual hunger that is the symptom of our time. It is for this task that Reform Judaism has to gear itself.

When, in 1920, Franz Rosenzweig opened his *Lehrhaus* in Frankfurt, he asked for a *new* Jewish learning which would lead the modern Jew to embrace his heritage and make it his own instead of merely take him back into a remote past. The needs of today's Jew have made this demand acutely urgent. The means to bring this new learning to the Jewish community and its method and scope may differ from those expounded by its proponent more than fifty years ago, but the task as such remains valid.

Hebrew Union College–Jewish Institute of Religion must be an academic institution of highest rank. Yet it has to make its influence felt beyond its academic ground. The College-Institute has a mission stemming from its founding days but strongly enlarged since. As a fount of creative Jewish ideas, as one of the main sources of Jewish thought, it is charged with keeping strong and unbroken, through an influx of great ideas, the continuity of Reform Judaism. This task requires intensification of its present endeavors on almost all its fronts.

From its inception, Hebrew Union College and the community it serves have formed a partnership in which the ideals and expectations were shared and the practical measures to make them come true promoted together. My hope is for this partnership to be forged even stronger during our School's new century.

INDEXES

INDEX OF PERSONS

A

Aaroni, Abraham, 219, 465, 468
Abraham, 239, 344, 345, 395
Abrahams, Israel, 148, 152, 386, 387, 445
Abravanel, Judah, 444
Ach, Samuel, 81
Achad Ha-'Am, see Aḥad Ha-'Am
Adelstein, Gertrude, 5
Adler, Cyrus, 128, 291
Adler, Felix, 74, 93, 388
Adler, Henry, 17, 18
Adler, Robert S., 5, 178
Adler, Samuel, 25, 39
Agnon, Samuel Joseph, 408
Agron, Gershon, 210
Agus, Jacob, 464
Aḥad Ha-'Am, 63, 307, 408, 455, 456, 457, 459, 460, 462, 466
Akiba, 343, 346
Albo, Joseph, 22
Albright, William Foxwell, 173
Alex, Rissa, 5
Alshech, R. Moses, 327
Aristotle, 400, 410
Atlas, Samuel, 127, 321, 325, 326, 328, 417-421
Avigdor, Ben, 456

B

Bacher, Wilhelm, 113
Bachrach, Alice, 5
Baeck, Leo, 128, 219, 239
Baer, Abraham, 184
Bailey, Lloyd R., 308
Bamberger, Bernard J., 5, 175, 176, 308
Bamberger, Fritz, ix-x, 5, 219, 220, 301

Band, Arnold, 196, 468
Bargad, Warren, 219, 461, 463
Baron, Salo W., 152, 153, 158, 409, 445-448 *passim*
Barth, Lewis M., *x*, 219, 468
    Chapter on Rabbinics by, 317-355
Bauer, Bruno, 442
Beer-Hoffmann, Richard, 107
Beerman, Leonard, 5
Bellah, Robert, *xvi*
Ben-Gurion, David, 150, 211, 234, 330
Ben Sira, 340
Ben Yehudah, Eliezer, 454, 456
Ben Zoma, Simeon, 350
Ben-Zvi, Yitzhak, 212
Benderly, Samson, 155
Bemporad, Jack, 450
Berdichevski, Micah Joseph, 456, 457
Bergmann, Hugo, 418
Berkowitz, Henry, 87, 112
Berkowitz, Simchah, 461, 464
Berlin, Charles, 443
Berliner, A., 320
Berman, Morton, 166
Berman, Oscar, 81, 98
Bernfeld, Simon, 459
Bernheim, Isaac W., 72
Bernstein, Marsha, 5
Bershadsky, Joshua, 456, 464
Bettan, Israel, 91-92, 93, 328, 332
Bettmann, Bernhard, 35, 81
Bialik, Chaim Nahman, 106, 160, 456, 457, 458, 460, 461, **462**, 466, 467
Bin-Nun, Dov, 192, 306
Blank, Amy, 107
Blank, Sheldon H., *x,-xiv,* 5, 96, 107, 131, 217, 219, 287, 304, 308, 309, 310, 332, 339, 460
    Chapter on Bible by, 287-310

[485

S

T

INDEX OF SUBJECTS